Ordinary Life and Holiness in the Teaching of St. Josemaría

A Study in Spiritual Theology

VOLUME II

Ordinary Life and Holiness in the Teaching of St. Josemaría

A Study in Spiritual Theology

VOLUME II

Ernst Burkhart and Javier López

Scepter

Published by Scepter Publishers, Inc.
info@scepterpublishers.org
www.scepterpublishers.org
800-322-8773
New York

Translated by Javier del Castillo
Text and cover design by Rose Design

Library of Congress Control Number: 2020934267

ISBN: 9781594173691 (pbk.)
ISBN: 9781594173707 (eBook)

Printed in the United States of America

CONTENTS

VOLUME II

CHAPTER FIVE

The Freedom of the Children of God / 137

CHAPTER SIX

The Love of the Children of God: The Christian Virtues / 247

PRINCIPAL ABBREVIATIONS

AAS: *Acta Apostolicae Sedis*

ASS: *Acta Sanctae Sedis*

AGP: General Archive of the Prelature of Opus Dei

CCC: *Catechism of the Catholic Church*

CIC: *Codex Iuris Canonici* (Code of Canon Law)

DS: H. Denzinger—A. Schönmetzer (eds.), *Enchiridion symbolorum definitionum et declarationum de rebus fidei et morum*, Herder 1976

PG: J.P. Migne (ed.), *Patrologiae Cursus completus. Series Graeca*, Paris 1857–1886

PL: J.P. Migne (ed.), *Patrologiae Cursus completus. Series Latina*, Paris 1844–1890

P01, P02, etc.: Collection of printed documents from sections of AGP

VOLUME II

PART II

The Subject of the Christian Life

The Christian: "Another Christ—Christ Himself"

"Be perfect as your heavenly
Father is perfect" (Matthew 5:48)

GENERAL OVERVIEW TO PART TWO

The ultimate end of Christian life includes two inseparable aspects: the glory of God and the perfection of man. Whoever strives to give glory to God (with all that this entails, namely seeking the kingdom of Christ, building up the Church) reaches his own perfection and happiness because the ultimate end includes "the perfect and complete good of oneself."[1]

Since the glory of God entails man living a supernatural life according to the well-known words of St. Irenaeus,[2] that is, that he be holy and an instrument to sanctify others, the text of Sacred Scripture that best applies to Part I is, "Be holy for I am holy" (see Lev. 19:2; see 1 Pet. 1:16). Now, we have to consider that this participation in the intimate life of the most Blessed Trinity in communion with all the saints (as sanctity and apostolate) transforms the Christian: it elevates him and perfects him. In other words, union with God "enables man to achieve the fullness of his perfection."[3] Sanctity and perfection are, in any case, inseparable concepts; hence the epigraph we chose for Part II is "Be perfect, as your heavenly Father is perfect" (Matt. 5:48). This text completes the message conveyed in Part I. There, we studied the first aspect of the ultimate end: that sanctity consists in giving glory to God, seeking the kingdom of Christ, and building up the Church. Now, we will speak about the second aspect: that sanctity implies the perfection and happiness of the Christian.

But in what does this perfection consist? "If you would be perfect, go, sell what you possess and give to the poor, and you will have treasure in heaven; and come, follow me" (Matt. 19:21). According to this, perfection consists in following Christ, preferring him to any other good. As we

1. "*Cum unumquodque appetat suam perfectionem, illud appetit aliquis ut ultimum finem, quod appetit ut bonum perfectum et completivum sui ipsius*" (St. Thomas Aquinas, *S. Th.*, I-II, q. 1, a. 5, c). The perfection of the subject is the purpose of the last end: "*Omnes appetunt suam perfectionem adimpleri, quae est ratio ultimi finis*" (ibid., a. 7, c).

2. "*Gloria enim Dei vivens homo; vita autem hominis visio Dei*" (St. Irenaeus, *Adversus Haereses*, IV, 20, 7). We have commented on this text in chapter one, section 1.1.1.

3. José Luis Illanes, *Mundo y santidad* (Madrid: Rialp, 1984), p. 38.

will see, this means ordering everything to following him. And following him implies dealing with him, entering into friendship with him, sharing one's life with him, and not merely imitating him externally. St. Josemaría describes this in a very expressive way: "identification." *To follow Christ: that is the secret. We must accompany him so closely that we come to live with him, like the first Twelve did; so closely, that we become identified with him.*[4] He defines perfection as *identification with Christ.*[5] At other times, he comments that the Christian has to be *alter Christus, ipse Christus*: *another Christ, Christ himself.*[6]

"Identifying oneself with Christ," being *ipse Christus*, are certainly daring words, but not surprisingly so if we consider the numerous references in the theological tradition of both the East and the West, as we will have occasion to see. In St. Josemaría, they reveal a lively perception of the "mystery" of the Christian's union with Christ, so prevalent in Pauline texts. Let us quote just one: "God chose to make known how great among the Gentiles are the riches of the glory of *this mystery*, which is *Christ in you*, the hope of glory" (Col. 1:27, emphasis added). To speak of "identification" is nothing more than a way of designating this mystery of the supernatural interpenetration of a Christian with Christ that the Holy Spirit brings about if he finds a person who cooperates with his grace.

How can we describe this identification with Christ? For now, we are not referring to the process of identification (i.e., how one attains it and by what means); these are topics that we will study in Part III. At this point, we wish to consider the very reality of this identification. We will ask in what it consists and what changes occur in the one who seeks it. The answer can be condensed in three points which will be the object of the chapters of Part II. We will now describe them succinctly.

In the first place, a Christian is transformed into an adopted child of God in the great moment of baptism: a son (or daughter) of the Father, in the Son, through the Holy Spirit. We will see that this supernatural filiation brings with it a presence of Christ in the Christian, thanks to which he can be said to be "Christ himself." But this is not a static reality. This identification that had its beginning in baptism ought to grow throughout one's lifetime. And here we find a characteristic teaching of St. Josemaría: that of

4. *Friends of God*, no. 299.

5. *Christ Is Passing By*, no. 58; see *Friends of God*, no. 110.

6. *Christ Is Passing By*, no. 96.

putting the *sense of divine filiation*,[7] or that is, the vivid awareness of being a child of God in Christ, as the foundation of this growth. It is not a matter of a theoretical knowledge of the truth of our adoptive divine filiation nor, much less, a mood. The "sense of divine filiation" is a simple wisdom of the heart about one's deepest supernatural identity. It is undoubtedly a divine gift, but only if one opens oneself to it without placing obstacles, is one able to receive it. Hence, it is a gift and a task; and not just one more task, but the one that is the foundation for the entire edifice of sanctity; for, should not a person aware of being a son of God in Christ and of sharing in his life feel urged to make it his own by putting aside everything that proves to be an obstacle to it, by dying to the *old man* (see Rom. 6:6) in order to be able to say with St. Paul: "I have been crucified with Christ; it is no longer I who live, but Christ who lives in me" (Gal. 2:20)? To ask the Holy Spirit to impress this sense of divine filiation in our souls and to cultivate it is, for St. Josemaría, the foundation of the spiritual life. As such, it will be the first topic of Part II: "The Sense of Divine Filiation" (chapter four).

Second, we will consider that a Christian has received a new freedom: the freedom of the children of God, the freedom that Christ has won for us (see Gal. 5:1). An immediate consequence of the sense of our divine filiation is the awareness of this freedom. *We have to know ourselves to be children of God and live with the desire to fulfill the will of our Father, to carry out our tasks according to God's wishes because* we feel like it [porque se nos da la gana], *which is the most supernatural of reasons.*[8] God *does not want the forced service of slaves; he prefers to have children who are free*,[9] writes St. Josemaría. Throughout his teaching, the term "free" frequently follows that of "children," because freedom belongs to the condition of being children of God. This is the gift that enables us to love by corresponding to the grace of the Holy Spirit. Christian life demands that it be actively exercised; there is no room for inertia. In order to identify oneself with Christ, one has to employ all the energies of his freedom in order to love God and men, with works of service, seconding the action of the Spirit that moves him to use his freedom. St. Josemaría insists on the importance of respecting and fostering the freedom of the ordinary faithful in order to seek sanctity and carry out an apostolate in keeping with their vocation, with personal initiative and

7. *The Forge*, no. 987.

8. *Christ Is Passing By*, no. 17.

9. *Friends of God*, no. 33.

responsibility. The role that he assigns to freedom shows that in the process of identifying oneself with Christ, there is no alienation of the *I*. It is, on the contrary, the realization of one's personal vocation (see Eph. 1:4), and it entails the authentic development of freedom, which is at the very core of the person. These are some of the elements of the second topic we will examine: "The Freedom of the Children of God" (chapter five).

Third, we will see that the sense of divine filiation, with an awareness of freedom, is the basis for growing in the virtues that configure the Christian to Christ. St. Josemaría teaches us to practice them with the spirit of the children of God called to sanctity in the middle of the world. When he mentions a particular virtue, he often adds the words "of a son of God," or "of the children of God," (e.g., the justice of the children of God; the joy, the loyalty, the obedience "of a child of God," etc.). It is natural that the first virtue in this filial spirit should be charity and that charity inform all the other virtues, because adoptive divine filiation (participation in the Son), and charity (participation in the infinite Charity that is the Holy Spirit) are inseparable in an analogous way to how the Son and the Holy Spirit are inseparable within the Trinity. A Christian who "feels" his divine filiation will necessarily strive to make his life one of love. St. Josemaría emphasizes the preeminence of charity and, at the same time, gives great importance to the human virtues that are indispensable if one is to become identified with Christ, "*perfectus Deus, perfectus homo*."[10] These virtues are especially needed by the faithful who are to sanctify themselves in temporal activities, since the perfect realization of this would be impossible without them. St. Josemaría's preaching in this area is very broad. We will see this in the third topic of Part II: "Love of the Children of God: The Christian Virtues" (chapter six).

In conclusion, the figure of a Christian that emerges from these three chapters will be that of a person profoundly aware of his divine filiation who commits his freedom to love God and others with works of service, practicing all the virtues with the desire to identify himself with Jesus Christ in the affairs of ordinary life.

We point out that the various levels of the ontological constitution of the human being are contained in these three topics: his *person*, his *nature*, and his *faculties*. In effect, adoptive divine filiation is a personal property:

10. Athanasian Creed *Quicumque* (DS 76).

(i.e., the new relation to God which the human *person* acquires on being raised to the supernatural order that also brings with it a new relation to others; the fraternity of the children of God), and a new relation to temporal realities (the inheritance of the children of God). In its own right, Christian freedom characterizes human *nature* elevated by grace:[11] the Christian enjoys a newfound freedom with respect to one who had been enslaved by sin. Finally, charity and the other virtues informed by charity elevate the person's *faculties* so he or she will be able to act as a child of God. As we can see, all the themes of Christian anthropology are contained in the three chapters of Part II.

We might ask whether it is necessary for the Christian to adopt his own perfection as his explicit end, or whether it would suffice for him to hope for it as an effect from the union with God that he will attain if he exclusively strives to give him glory. In other words, since the end of Christian life is at once giving glory to God and one's own perfection, wouldn't it suffice to seek the first in order to obtain the second without needing to formally strive for it? Isn't this what St. John implies when he writes that in glory "we shall be like him, for we shall see him as he is" (1 John 3:2)? If the beatific vision makes the saints fully Christ-like, wouldn't contemplation in this life lead to Christian perfection, without needing to seek it deliberately?

And yet, the Lord says, "You, therefore, must be perfect, as your heavenly Father is perfect" (Matt. 5:48). He thus exhorts us to tend to perfection. In reality, there is no difference between seeking the glory of God and setting out for perfection or identification with Christ, for this lies essentially in charity, supernatural love for God, which is precisely what it means to give him glory, as we saw in chapter one. Consequently, to seek one's own perfection is not something different from union with God nor an effect of it. It is, rather, its source in the same way that the virtue of charity (as a "*habitus*") is the source of acts of love. The Christian must seek his own perfection that is found in charity because only thus will he give glory to God with his being and his acts. Only does a good tree bear good fruit (see Matt. 7:17). In order to bear good fruit (i.e., acts of love with which a Christian glorifies God), the Christian has to strive to be a "good tree"; in other words, he has to seek his own perfection.

---

11. As part of the conceptual basis used to explain the teaching of St. Josemaría, in chapter five we will refer to the distinction between person, nature, and faculties, as well as to the relation between freedom and the spiritual dimension of the human person.

Proposing the quest for human and supernatural perfection as an end could seem as if we are framing the spiritual life in an anthropocentric way. Nevertheless, this anthropocentrism is not opposed to a radical Christian theocentrism. Actually, the latter demands the former. St. John Paul II identifies this idea as the core message of Vatican II: "While the various currents of human thought both in the past and at the present have tended and still tend to separate theocentrism and anthropocentrism, and even to set them in opposition to each other, the Church, following Christ, seeks to link them up in human history, in a deep and organic way. And this is also one of the basic principles, perhaps the most important one, of the teaching of the last Council."[12] It seems to us that St. Josemaría points to the root of this question when he teaches to place the sense of divine filiation in Christ as the basis of the love of God and consequently of the desire to identify oneself with him.

Finally, let us allude to the relation between the topics of Part II (on the subject of the Christian life) and those of Part III (on the path of the Christian life). While in Part II, we will study *what* identification with Christ consists in, in Part III, we will see *how* a Christian tends to it in the course of his earthly life. For an ordinary person, the way is none other than the sanctification of professional work, family, and social relations (chapter seven); a way that requires effort, and interior struggle against sin and its consequences (chapter eight), but one which he can count on with the means of sanctification and apostolate that the Church offers (chapter nine).

---

12. St. John Paul II, Encyclical *Dives in misericordia* (November 30, 1980), no. 1; see Encyclical *Veritatis Splendor* (August 6, 1993), no. 40.

CHAPTER FOUR

The Sense of Divine Filiation

The Foundation of The Spiritual Life

The foundation of [one's] spiritual life is the sense of divine filiation.
(*The Forge*, no. 987)

In this chapter, we will now take up a theme that for Álvaro del Portillo is the "core" or "nerve center"[1] of St. Josemaría's preaching. This is the nerve

1. "[The] core is a sense of divine filiation" Álvaro del Portillo, Foreword to *Christ Is Passing By*, p. 11 of the second edition (New York: Scepter, 1982). See Javier Echevarría, *Paths to God* (New York: Scepter, 2010), p. 3.

that transmits to the whole body of his teaching a special characteristic feature. As Fernando Ocáriz puts it, "Divine filiation is what entirely informs [St. Josemaría's] spirit and his word [. . .]. If he speaks or writes on faith, he deals with the faith of the children of God; if he preaches on fortitude, he speaks about the fortitude of the children of God; if he contemplates the reality of conversion and penance, his word is about the conversion of the children of God. . . . Every virtue, every aspect of Christian life—and even of human life in general—is characterized from within—in his life, in his voice, or in his pen—as being that *of the children of God*."[2]

Since the Son of God became man and dwelt among us so that we might become his brothers (see John 1:12–14; Rom. 8:29), a Christian's life objectively unfolds in a filial environment. But not everyone is aware of this reality, and not everyone appreciates the air he breathes. St. Josemaría says to those who follow the way of sanctity he proposed, *The foundation of our spiritual life is the sense of our divine filiation*.[3] He does not simply remind them of *the fact* that supernatural divine filiation is at the basis of the Christian life; he advises them to make the *sense*—the *living awareness*—of this adoptive filiation the foundation of their quest for sanctity. He teaches everyone to *be aware of being oneself a beloved child of God*,[4] to draw all the consequences from this awareness, to feel oneself as "another Christ," and to desire to identify oneself more and more with Christ.

This "sense of divine filiation" is something more than the theoretical knowledge of a truth. It is a divine gift, an immense grace of God aimed at guiding all our thoughts and desires, our feelings, and our actions. A gift that, in persons with use of reason, accompanies in some way the very fact of their filial adoption, because in making us his children, God wants us to possess the awareness of that fact so that we might call him Father (see Matt. 6:9). But it is a gift that, like fire, needs to be stoked so that the Christian's behavior is enlightened and warmed up by it.

In St. Josemaría's life, there was a moment in 1931 when God chose to intensify this gift in an extraordinary way, so that he could see it (and teach others to see it) as the foundation of the spiritual life, and specifically as

---

2. Fernando Ocáriz, "La filiación divina, realidad central en la vida y en la enseñanza de Mons. Escrivá de Balaguer," in idem, *Naturaleza, Gracia y Gloria* (Pamplona: Rialp, 2001), p. 179. For various points we are inspired by this substantial article, originally published in *Scripta Theologica*, 13 (1981): 513–552.

3. *Letter, January 25, 1961*, no. 54. See *Christ Is Passing By*, nos. 64 and 126; *The Way*, no. 265; *The Forge*, no. 987; *Conversations*, no. 102.

4. *Christ Is Passing By*, no. 126.

the foundation of the spirit of sanctification in the middle of the world he had been called to live since 1928. The notion of this being "foundational" is present from the very moment in which he discovered this aspect of his spiritual message. When we look at a building, it is normal for our gaze to settle on the form, the dimensions, and the materials employed. We do not ordinarily think about the foundation that supports the whole building. Something similar occurred to St. Josemaría on October 2, 1928, when he saw for the first time the spirit that he was to incarnate and spread. He understood that God was calling everyone to holiness and that the great majority of men and women were to seek holiness in their ordinary affairs: in their families, at work, and in social relationships, etc. One of these affairs, professional work, appeared to him as the "axis" of the building. This was a central element of his message on that morning of 1928. But it was not the only one. There were other less visible but no less important ones. Concretely, the building and its axis were supported on a rock that guaranteed the building's stability. The rock was the fact and awareness of adoptive divine filiation. That foundation was there from the beginning, but it was hidden. St. Josemaría would discover it clearly three years later, in the final months of 1931, thanks to a new interior light he received. Reflecting later on the succession of events, he would say that *this defining feature of our spirit was born with the Work* [*in 1928*], *and took form in 1931.*[5] From then on he would always teach people to make the sense of divine filiation the foundation of their spiritual life.

We might ask how it was possible for an essential feature of his message to be born in 1928, and yet not take a fully developed form until 1931. We do not know for certain whether St. Josemaría explained this, even though perhaps studies on his handwritten documents will cast light on this point in the future. In any case, it was not a problem for him to affirm that in 1928 he saw the complete message that he was to preach, and that in 1931 he perceived with greater clarity one of its essential aspects. In 1928, he understood that all the faithful are called to Christian perfection *by the simple fact of their Baptism*,[6] and that precisely in baptism they are born to the supernatural life of adopted children of God. In his preaching about the universal call to sanctity from 1928 onward, he was already inviting people to become aware of their dignity as sons and daughters of God. In fact, there

5. *Letter, January 9, 1959*, no. 60.

6. *Conversations*, no. 47.

is no lack of testimonials alluding to the forcefulness and ardor with which he spoke about divine filiation to those who came to him for spiritual direction in this period. We have, for example, what a student from the Central University of Madrid confided to him as he wrote in *The Way*: *I was thinking of what you told me—that I'm a son of God!—and I found myself walking along the street, head up, chin out, and a proud feeling inside . . . a son of God!*[7] St. Josemaría remembers his own response: *With sure conscience I advised him to encourage that "pride"*:[8] the holy pride of being a son of God. The author of the critical-historical edition of *The Way* situates this conversation in 1929 or shortly thereafter, and this testifies to the intensity with which St. Josemaría transmitted the sense of divine filiation between 1928 and 1931. Starting from this latter date, the invitation to place the foundation of one's spiritual life on the sense of divine filiation will become more urgent and it will emerge with well-defined features. By means of this chapter we will identify and study these features more deeply.

The sequence of events also seems to offer us a way to understand the path to sanctity that St. Josemaría teaches from a theological point of view. The years that transpire from the birth of this feature until it takes on its full form lead us to intuit that the sense of divine filiation can take time to develop. In effect, it is not unusual for someone who tries to follow the way of sanctity St. Josemaría teaches to need time to learn (under the action of grace) that our dealings with God have to be based on this awareness of being his children. Doesn't something similar happen to a child who, even though he gets to know his parents very quickly, realizes only when he grows up that he owes them his life, food, education, etc.? It is only then that this reality begins to influence his conduct in a practical way, leading him to act in keeping with his role as a child. St. Josemaría channels the spiritual life toward this discovery. He teaches us to strive to attain this by seconding the action of the Holy Spirit. He advises those who are beginning the search for sanctity in a serious way to consider their divine filiation frequently every day[9] even though perhaps they may not fully understand what it means.

The historical sequence of events to which we have referred, however, should not determine the order of the theological explanation. Nothing obliges us first to explain what St. Josemaría saw in 1928, and then what

7. *The Way*, no. 274.

8. Ibid.

9. See *Christ Is Passing By*, no. 10.

he understood in 1931. It is not necessary to speak about the house before speaking about the foundation, to deal first with sanctification of work, and then with the sense of divine filiation. On the one hand, we have already seen that adoptive filiation was present from the beginning; and on the other hand, it would be difficult to understand the scope of sanctification of work without keeping in mind that the one who works has to know that he is a son of God, "another Christ." That is why we have chosen to study the sense of divine filiation first, and only later, in chapter seven, sanctification of work. The first will help us to understand the second better.

We will now analyze (section 1) the origin of this doctrine (the experience of divine filiation in 1931), and afterward, study the theological notion of divine filiation, which lies beneath this experience (section 2). Thus, we will prepare the pathway to the main object of this chapter: the "sense" or "awareness" of our divine filiation as the foundation of the Christian life (section 3).

1. The Experience of Divine Filiation in 1931

St. Josemaría's teaching on the sense of divine filiation in the spiritual life is not the result of theological speculation. It was formed in his soul on the occasion of an intense interior experience that came at different moments in September and October of 1931 as he struggled to carry out the supernatural enterprise God had entrusted to him and that which completely surpassed his strength to accomplish.[10]

According to Vázquez de Prada, various annotations in his *Apuntes íntimos* (personal notes) show that in those months "his whole being was taken over by the joyful clarity of knowing himself to be a son of God."[11] Thus, on September 22, 1931, St. Josemaría writes,

> *I was considering God's good favors* [bondades] *to me and, filled with an interior joy, I would have shouted out in the street, so that everyone would know of my filial gratitude: Father! Father! And—if not shouting—at least in a low voice, I walked along calling him thus* (*Father!*) *many times, certain that I was pleasing him.*[12]

10. See Vázquez de Prada, *The Founder of Opus Dei: The Life of Josemaría Escrivá* (New York: Scepter, 2001–2005), vol. I, pp. 293–297.

11. Ibid., pp. 293–294.

12. *Apuntes íntimos*, no. 296, as cited in Vázquez de Prada, *The Founder of Opus Dei*, vol. I, p. 293.

That light in his soul came to illuminate a mystery he already knew and believed in. Up to then, he certainly knew that he was a son of God. But only at that moment did he begin to "feel" it and to perceive it in a new way with all its consequences. In the weeks that followed, those interior sentiments were prolonged. The sense of divine filiation would settle deep in his soul as a result of a shower of graces that surprised him in the most diverse circumstances. What he then experienced on October 16 of that same year would remain fixed in his soul as one of the most intense moments of prayer in his life. At the end of that day, he jots down what happened in these words:

> *Feast of St. Hedwig, 1931: I wanted to pray, after Mass, in the quiet of my church. I didn't succeed at it. In Atocha, I bought a newspaper (the A.B.C.) and got on the streetcar. Up to this moment, when I'm writing this, I haven't been able to read more than a single paragraph of the paper. I felt flowing within me the copious and ardent prayer of affection. That's the way it was in the streetcar and all the way home.*[13]

The content of his prayer that day was the mystery of his adoptive divine filiation, as he would later explain:

> *The most elevated prayer I've experienced* [. . .] *was traveling on a streetcar and then wandering through the streets of Madrid, contemplating that marvelous reality: God is my Father. I know that, without being able to stop, I kept repeating:* Abba, Pater![14]

The fact of finding himself on the street and on a streetcar also held special meaning for him: *the street doesn't impede our contemplative dialogue; the bustle of the world is, for us, a place of prayer.*[15] It was a practical manifestation that the sense of divine filiation, as a hidden foundation, forms an essential part of the contemplative spirit lived out in the middle of the world as God had shown him. It was then that God made him clearly realize his condition as a son of God. The purpose of this new *divine*[16] intervention was to lead him to understand that the foundation for contemplation in ordinary life, the basis for the transformation of

13. Ibid., no. 334, as cited in Vázquez de Prada, *The Founder of Opus Dei*, vol. I, p. 294.

14. *Instruction, May 1935/September 1950*, note 28.

15. *Letter, January 9, 1959*, no. 60.

16. He had no doubt that it was the Lord who was acting, and later on we will explore how he expresses this.

work and of all secular affairs into prayer, has to be the sense of divine filiation. But we will leave the analysis of this teaching for later and continue with the details and account of 1931.

Spiritual theology employs the concept of "experience"[17] to embrace phenomena such as this in the life of the saints. Even though St. Josemaría does not use this term when he refers to those moments (nor does he define them in any other way, as he limits himself to describing what happened), the details he offers lead us to think that this is the most adequate term to describe them. "Experience" is, in general, the knowledge of a certain happening through immediate contact without needing to make use of the discursive process of reason. It may be a sensible experience, if it proceeds from the corporeal senses, or it may be spiritual. When the spiritual experience refers to the mystery of a Christian sharing supernaturally in the life of the most Blessed Trinity (through Christ, with him and in him), it can be termed a "mystical experience." St. Bonaventure refers to a certain "experiential knowledge of God"[18] that is not speculative and has no need for rational discourse or images. St. Thomas calls it "affective or experimental":[19] "affective" not only because it arouses love, but because it takes place within the context of love (i.e., by means of love, it places a person in immediate contact with God). For this reason it is also called "experimental."

In our case, St. Josemaría's experience is very similar to the "contemplation of God" of which we have already spoken in chapter one, even though it cannot be reduced to that. It includes infused contemplation (*I was contemplating with light that was not mine that astonishing truth* [. . .]),[20] but leaves behind an indelible memory (*which remained enkindled like a burning ember in my soul, never to be extinguished*),[21] akin to something that goes with the notion of experience. It is also proper to experience that the reality known (or experienced) be a singular and concrete truth, not something

---

17. See André Léonard, "Expérience spirituelle," in Marcel, Viller, et al., *Dictionnaire de spiritualité ascétique et mystique*, vol. 4 (Paris: Beauchesne, 1960), cols. 2004–2005. The bibliography on the notion of "experience" in the spiritual life is very extensive in the twentieth century, especially after the work of Jean Mouroux, *L'expérience chrétienne: introduction à une théologie* (Paris: Aubier, 1952).

18. ". . . *cognitio Dei experimentalis*" St. Bonaventure, *In III Sent.*, d. 35, q. 2, c.

19. "*Alia autem est cognitio divinae bonitatis seu voluntatis affectiva seu experimentalis, dum quis experitur in seipso gustum divinae dulcedinis et complacentiam divinae voluntatis, sicut de Hierotheo dicit Dionysius, II cap. De div. Nom.*" St. Thomas Aquinas, *S. Th.*, II-II, q. 97, a. 2, ad 2.

20. *Letter, December 8, 1949*, no. 41. The full text is cited in the following paragraphs.

21. Ibid.

abstract and universal. As we can see in the texts of St. Josemaría, what he saw and what remained fixed in his soul was above all "his" adoptive divine filiation, not a general doctrine. Later, what he experienced in those moments would lead him to describe the richness of divine filiation as it is presented to us in Sacred Scripture and in the Tradition of the Church,[22] and it will be the awareness of this truth that he will propose, in general, as the foundation of the Christian life.

Another element in the notion of a spiritual experience that we discover in the different accounts of St. Josemaría is that the whole of the person is involved, including the sensible sphere. This can be seen, for example, in a text (of which we have already quoted a few lines) referring to the events of October 16, 1931:

> *I was probably praying out loud. And I walked along the streets of Madrid, perhaps for an hour, perhaps two, I can't say; the time passed without my realizing it. People must have thought I was crazy. I was contemplating with light that was not mine that astonishing truth, which remained enkindled like a burning ember in my soul, never to be extinguished.*[23]

One could inquire as to the meaning of these sensible manifestations (e.g., of his not knowing whether he was speaking out loud, or of his losing track of time). One might think that they are nothing more than the effect of the state of soul that translates an intense interior experience to the body. If that were the case, the sensible element would be like a sounding box resonating with the vibrations of the spirit. But this explanation would be insufficient to explain the facts because St. Josemaría speaks expressly about a "feeling": *I felt the action of the Lord, who with the power of something overwhelmingly necessary, sowed in my heart and on my lips this tender invocation:* Abba! Pater![24]

How are we to understand this "feeling"? When St. John of the Cross speaks about this type of "particular perceptions"[25] of divine things that the Holy Spirit grants at times, he mentions among other things "spiritual sentiments"[26] that occasionally accompany the "visions, revelations and

---

22. See José Luis Illanes, "Experiencia cristiana y sentido de la filiación divina," in *PATH* 7/2 (2008): 474. Later we will cite some texts in which we will be able to see St. Josemaría's reflection on the teaching of St. Paul.

23. *Letter, December 8, 1949*, no. 41.

24. *Letter, January 9, 1959*, no. 60.

25. St. John of the Cross, *The Ascent of Mount Carmel*, II, 10, 4.

26. Ibid.

locutions."[27] For the Mystical Doctor all these perceptions, including the spiritual sentiments, take place "without the intervention of a corporeal sense"[28] because of the absolute disproportion between the subject and the object. Consequently, we need to understand St. Josemaría's "feeling" in a spiritual way. In effect, an ancient tradition that goes from Origen and St. Gregory of Nyssa to St. Bernard and St. Bonaventure, speaks of certain "spiritual senses" in a Christian who is docile to the action of the Holy Spirit by which he is enabled to "see," or "hear," or "sense" supernatural realities (if God grants them) in a way analogous to how one can see, hear, or feel with one's external and internal corporeal senses.[29] What they call "spiritual senses" would not be anything other than the operations of the intellect and the will that assume a likeness to the corporeal senses. They are called "senses" only by mental association through an allegorical use of language.

Nonetheless, this interpretation does not satisfy some authors. They hold that it does not sufficiently explain the way of speaking used by saints who refer to the experience of supernatural realities as if they experienced them also in some way by means of the corporeal senses. In this line, Anselm Stolz holds that the notion of 'spiritual senses' "implies a spiritualization of the [bodily] senses directed by the Holy Spirit, and not the existence of senses in the spirit."[30] It is a hypothesis that is not without difficulties, but perhaps it should not be set aside completely if we keep in mind that the deifying action of grace entails a certain spiritualization of the whole person, including the bodily dimension.[31] The topic is familiar to St. Josemaría, who writes (without any reference to Stolz's hypothesis) that *We are men and women, not angels. We are flesh and blood, people with sentiments and passions, with sorrows and joys. But divinization creates in the whole of man a kind of foretaste of the glorious resurrection.*[32] St. Thomas observes that after the resurrection of the dead, the saints will be able to perceive with their glorified bodies, not God in his essence, but yes, "in his bodily effects

27. Ibid.

28. Ibid. According to St. John of the Cross, the sensitive sphere and its powers "cannot essentially and properly taste spiritual goods, because they do not have the proportioned capacity, neither in this life nor in the future" *Spiritual Canticle*, 40, 5.

29. See Marriette Canévet, "Sens spirituel," in *Dictionnaire de spiritualité ascétique et mystique*, vol. 14 (Paris: Beauchesne, 1989), cols. 598–617; Jean Mouroux, *L'expérience chrétienne*, ch. 10 ("Le sentir spirituel"), pp. 281–323.

30. Anselm Stolz, *Teologia della mistica* (Brescia: Morcelliana, 1947), p. 192.

31. See Canévet, "Sens spirituel," 604–611.

32. *Christ Is Passing By*, no. 103.

[. . .], principally Christ's flesh."[33] Since grace is a beginning of glory, one could think that there can be a certain anticipation of this experience. It would not be what is classically called an "extraordinary phenomenon" (as for example, apparitions of the Lord or the Blessed Virgin Mary, which at times have been recognized by the Church), but an ordinary phenomenon of grace vested with extraordinary intensity.

St. Josemaría's testimony does not allow us to deduce whether that "feeling of God's action" should be understood in a metaphorical way, as if alluding to an exclusively spiritual operation (with repercussions in the body), or whether it can be interpreted as a certain participation on the part of the bodily senses elevated by grace in the awareness of his divine filiation. Perhaps a more detailed study of the texts and the doctrines we have referred to will clarify this point in the future. But there can be no doubt that St. Josemaría considered himself powerfully engaged with the whole of his being in that experience. Not only did he know it, but he also "felt" himself to be a son of God, "another Christ, Christ himself" (an expression we will later explore) in his body and soul.

"People must have thought I was crazy," he notes in one of the texts we have seen. By temperament and upbringing, he was not prone to calling attention to the extraordinary, and all the more so in light of his message about sanctifying *ordinary* life. But on those occasions in 1931, a force came upon him that gave rise to manifestations foreign to his natural way of being. It is clear that that clarity came from above. "I was contemplating with light that was not mine that astonishing truth," he writes. He realized that the step from "knowing" to "sensing" his adoptive filiation was a divine gift, and he understood that the Lord wanted to make use of him to grant this "sense" to other souls.

How can the content of what he understood and felt in those weeks of 1931 be described? And how does St. Josemaría explain the essence of divine filiation? In order to answer these questions, let us examine the foundation of the building (in the following section) so as to be able to study how the edifice of the Christian life is built on it (in the last section of this chapter).

---

33. "The eye of the flesh cannot attain the vision of the essence [of God]; therefore, for one to be granted a congruent rest in the beatific vision, one will see the Divinity in its corporal effects, in which there will appear openly the indications of God's majesty: principally, in the flesh of Christ; and afterward in the bodies of the saints; and later in all of the other bodies. Therefore, it is necessary that other bodies also receive a greater influx of the divine goodness: but not changing their nature, but adding to it the perfection of a certain glory. And this will be the renewal of the world; from whence at the same time the world will be renewed and man will be glorified." St. Thomas Aquinas, *In IV Sent.*, d. 48, q. 2, a. 1, c.

1.1. The Awareness of Being a Child of God the Father in Union with Jesus Christ through the Holy Spirit

In the points from his *Apuntes íntimos* that we cited earlier and in other passages where St. Josemaría reflects on the light received on that occasion, we have seen that the sense of divine filiation entails a triple aspect: it is an experience of (1) divine paternity or fatherhood, (2) the action of the Holy Spirit who makes us children of God, and (3) union with Christ, in whom we are made children of God.

1.1.1. The Perception of Divine Fatherhood

First, what stands out in these accounts is an intimate awakening to the vital discovery of God's fatherhood. He felt divine filiation springing up in his heart and it brought to his lips the *tender invocation: Abba! Pater!*[34]

"*Abba! Pater!*"[35] It is the cry that Jesus addressed to the Father in the Garden of Olives: "Abba, Father, All things are possible to thee [. . .]" (Mark 14:36).[36] St. Josemaría feels the impulse to cry out as Jesus did, addressing his Father. He does not simply address God as Father, but rather invokes the first Person of the Holy Trinity. Indeed, this kind of experience of filiation lies far above the one by which everyone can call his or her Creator "Father." It is a supernatural filiation akin to Christ's, "the first-born among many brethren" (Rom. 8:29), and at the same time, also different and of an infinitely inferior order to that of the "only begotten Son" (see John 1:14; 3:16; 1 John 4:9) since our filiation is not natural but "adoptive" (see Rom. 8:15, 23; Gal. 4:5; Eph. 1:5).

> According to Joachim Jeremias, "Abba" was the term Jesus habitually used to refer to God. It was truly an unusual term in the Old Testament since "abba" was a familiar term (like "daddy"), revealing the unique relationship Jesus had with his Father God, a new relationship, unknown until that moment in the Bible.[37] As we know, its newness consists in that Christ

34. *Letter, January 9, 1959*, no. 60.

35. He wrote "*Abba!*" without an accent (*Abbá*) as does the Vulgate in Mark 14:36, Rom. 8:15, and Gal. 4:6 in transcribing the Aramaic term which the Greek text shows as Αββα. However, when he cited Spanish translations he usually wrote *Abbá!* with an accent, as is usual in many Spanish versions.

36. An interesting Biblical study can be seen in Miguel Ángel Tabet "La oración de Jesús: 'Abbá, Padre' (Mc 14:36)," in José Luis Illanes (ed.), *El Dios y Padre de Nuestro Señor Jesucristo: XX Simposio Internacional de Teología de la Universidad de Navarra* (Pamplona: Eunsa, 2000), pp. 63–71.

37. Joachim Jeremias, "Kennzeichen der 'ipsissima vox Jesu,'" in Alfred Wikenhauser (dir.), *Synoptische Studien* (Munich: Zink, 1953), pp. 86–89. See idem, *Neutestamentliche Theologie. I. Die Verkündigung Jesu* (Gütersloh: Gerd Mohn, 1971). The thesis of Jeremias has been accepted by numerous exegetes. See Jacques Schlosser, *Le Dieu de Jésus: étude exégétique* (Paris: Cerf, 1987).

> openly reveals the mystery of the most Holy Trinity. He speaks of the Father, the Son and the Holy Spirit as three Persons in the unity of the one God, and he reveals himself as the only begotten Son made man so that we might become children of God (see John 1:13), and also be able to say "Abba, Father!" This *supernatural* filiation that derives from that of Jesus and gives us "access to the Father" (Eph. 2:18) is what St. Josemaría experienced in 1931.

St. Josemaría pronounces the words "Abba! Father!" as a "tender invocation," with the confidence of a small child who throws himself into the arms of his father. This confidence will be engraved forever in his soul "like a burning ember" that spreads warmth to everything in his life: the warmth of a filial spirit that lets us feel that we are "members of the household of God" (Eph. 2:19) because *by loving us as his children, he has taken us into his house, in the middle of this world, to be members of his family, so that what is his is ours, and what is ours is his, and to develop that familiarity and confidence which prompts us to ask him, like small children, for the moon!*[38]

The experience of divine fatherhood is thus translated into a filial and confident dealing with God, similar to how a small child deals with his father from whom he expects everything: *What confidence, what rest, and what optimism it will give you, in the midst of difficulties, to realize that you are children of a Father who knows all things and can do all things.*[39]

In a text from *Friends of God*, St. Josemaría illustrates this attitude from his personal experience. After quoting the words of St. John, "Beloved, we are God's children now" (1 John 3:2), he comments:

> *Over the years, I have sought to rely unfalteringly for my support on this joyous reality. No matter what the situation, my prayer, while varying in tone, has always been the same. I have said to him: Lord, you put me here. You entrusted me with this or that, and I put my trust in you. I know you are my Father, and I have seen that tiny children are always absolutely sure of their parents.*[40]

God is a merciful father who opens his arms wide to the weak and needy child; and even to the "prodigal" son who returns repentant (see Luke 15:1–24). Sin is not the last word in the life of a Christian:

---

38. *Christ Is Passing By*, no. 64.
39. *Letter, January 9, 1959*, no. 60.
40. *Friends of God*, no. 43.

> *It is God who has the last word—and it is the word of his saving and merciful love—and therefore, it is the word of our divine filiation. Therefore, I repeat to you today, with St. John:* See what love the Father has given us, that we should be called children of God; and so we are." (1 John 3:1)[41]

The "sense" of divine filiation is a joyful perception of God's paternity that accords completely with the teaching of St. Paul: "You did not receive the spirit of slavery [. . .] but you have received the spirit of sonship [in which] we cry, 'Abba! Father!'" (Rom. 8:15). Commenting on this text, Heinrich Schlier shows that the "state of being children of God" is manifested precisely in the "confident invocation" (Abba! Father!), the antithesis of servile fear and of the anguish produced by slavery to sin and death.[42] It is a basic attitude that St. Josemaría transmits in all his preaching. *A child of God treats the Lord as his Father. His relationship is not a servile offering, nor formal observance out of mere courtesy, but rather one that is fully characterized by sincerity and trust.*[43] A son of God can rest serenely in the mercy of his Father who, in addition to forgiving the faults of his children when they go to him with confidence, does not allow them to be tempted beyond their strength. Instead, he gives them his grace so that they might overcome any test (see 1 Cor. 10:13). Along with the Psalmist, St. Josemaría asks himself, "The Lord is my light and my salvation; whom shall I fear?" (Ps. 27:1), and he immediately responds: *No one. If we approach our heavenly Father in this way, we will have no grounds for fearing anyone or anything.*[44]

Here, we find ourselves with one of the keys to St. Josemaría's whole existence that explains the joy and certainty with which he struggled for sanctity and carried out his apostolic endeavors. Even in the most difficult situations (as narrated by an eyewitness of his life), "he always maintained his good humor. Those of us who were at his side in those moments, never saw him sad. On the contrary, he was always cheerful and optimistic. The source of that serenity was the deep sentiment of the divine filiation that God wanted to place as the foundation of the spirit of Opus Dei."[45]

---

41. *Christ Is Passing By*, no. 66.

42. See Heinrich Schlier, *La Lettera ai Romani* (Brescia: Paideia, 1982), pp. 417ff.

43. *Christ Is Passing By*, no. 64.

44. *Friends of God*, no. 95.

45. Álvaro del Portillo, "Mons. Escrivá de Balaguer, instrumento de Dios" (Address at the University of Navarra, June 12, 1976), in idem, *Una vida para Dios* (Madrid: Rialp, 1992), p. 39.

1.1.2. Awareness of the Action of the Holy Spirit

Let us look once again at the beginning of one of the texts that we have already seen: "I felt the action of the Lord [. . .]." Normally when St. Josemaría writes "the Lord," he is referring to Jesus Christ. That can also be understood here because Jesus is the one who has won adoptive filiation for us and teaches us to address God the Father (see Luke 11:1–2). But we can also understand that "action of the Lord" which leads him to cry out "Abba! Father!" as the action of the Holy Spirit. St. Josemaría explicitly points that out a number of times, above all when he quotes the Letter to the Galatians: "Because you are sons, God has sent the Spirit of his Son into our hearts, crying out: Abba, Father!" (Gal. 4:6). We find a parallel text in the Letter to the Romans: "You have received the spirit of sonship. When we cry, 'Abba! Father!' it is the Spirit himself bearing witness with our spirit that we are children of God" (Rom. 8:15–16). *The action of the Paraclete within us confirms what Christ had announced to us: that we are children of God, that we* have not received a spirit of bondage so as to be again in fear, but a spirit of adoption as sons, by virtue of which we cry: Abba! Father! (Rom. 8:15).[46]

On the basis of these texts and in order to parse them better, we must distinguish two effects of the action of the Paraclete: the communication of the very gift of adoptive filiation itself in baptism, and the experience of this gift on the part of the Christian. St. Josemaría refers directly to this experience, but obviously he presupposes the gift on which it depends. Let us proceed in an orderly fashion.

In regard to the first effect (divine filiation itself), we need to consider that, since supernatural adoption is a work of God in creatures (a work *ad extra*), the cause is the three divine Persons and not just the Holy Spirit.[47] Nevertheless, we can say that adoption is granted us "by the Holy Spirit." We will pause to consider this point in the second part of this chapter as we delve more deeply into supernatural adoption considered theologically. For now, it suffices to recall that this aspect of the action of the Paraclete is found explicitly in Galatians 4:6: "Because you are sons, God has sent the Spirit of his Son into our hearts, crying, 'Abba! Father!'" The modern exegesis on this verse confirms the reading of the Greek Fathers. The words "because you are sons" do not signify that a Christian is "first" a son

46. *Christ Is Passing By*, no. 118; see no. 131.

47. See *Catechism of the Catholic Church* (hereafter cited as *CCC*), no. 292.

of God in order to "later" receive the Holy Spirit. But it is the Holy Spirit who makes him an adopted son such that the clamor, "Abba! Father!" is a "proof" of the presence of the Spirit in the heart of a son of God.[48]

The Christian receives this gift of participation in the divine nature through the grace infused by the Holy Spirit: we have been *made children of God by grace*,[49] St. Josemaría would say, using the traditional terminology to indicate that the formal cause of the supernatural elevation is created grace (sanctifying grace) given to the Christian by the sending of the Holy Spirit (uncreated grace).[50]

The sending of the Paraclete not only makes a person a son of God; it makes him aware of his condition so that he can cry out, "Abba, Father!" This is the second effect of his action and the one most directly implied in St. Josemaría's experience. For example, he writes that *this pouring out of the Holy Spirit, in "christifying" us, makes us acknowledge ourselves as children of God.*[51] We will soon return to the expression "to christify." For now, we take note of the last words. Analogous to how the Gospel relates that Jesus "rejoiced in the Holy Spirit and said 'I thank you, Father, Lord of heaven and earth [. . .]'" (Luke 10:21), so also the same Holy Spirit, present in a Christian, "makes us acknowledge ourselves as children of God" (i.e., gives us an awareness of our divine filiation).

This aspect of the Paraclete's action can be described in the already mentioned words of the apostle: "It is the Spirit himself bearing witness with our spirit that we are children of God" (Rom. 8:16). Exegesis and theology have given greater emphasis to this in recent times. As Schlier writes, the Holy Spirit "reveals to man his adoption as son [. . .]. He does not leave us in ignorance or uncertainty about the filial adoption to which he himself has given us access in Baptism. A sign of this is the inspired cry

48. See Nello Casalini, *I misteri della fede. Teologia del Nuovo Testamento* (Jerusalem: Franciscan Printing Press, 1991), pp. 212–213. Along the same line, Albert Vanhoye, "Lettera ai Galati. Nuova versione, introduzione e commento," in *I Libri Biblici. Nuovo Testamento*, vol. 8 (Milano: Edizioni Paoline, 2000), p. 109.

49. *Christ Is Passing By*, no. 133.

50. We have already seen in the Preliminary Part, section II.2 a), how St. Josemaría distinguishes between habitual created grace (sanctifying grace) and uncreated grace (the Holy Spirit), and how he uses the texts of St. Cyril of Alexandria, excluding a formal or "quasi-formal" causality of the Paraclete in the supernatural elevation. It appears to us that what is most in conformity with his spiritual doctrine is to consider the supernatural elevation as a whole as filial adoption. The infusion of created grace that grants participation in the divine nature gives the new creature its (accidental) "formal being." The Holy Spirit makes possible this new supernatural way of being by his inhabitation in the soul (i.e., by his presence as the one sent by the Father and the Son, who also abide in the Christian who is living a supernatural life).

51. *Christ Is Passing By*, no. 87.

'Abba, Father!' which makes present our condition of being children, a condition actualized as a baptismal gift insofar as we allow ourselves to be guided by the Spirit. In Baptism, he makes us be 'children of God.' If we abandon ourselves in him, we adopt in our existence this mode of being in the Spirit, that of 'being children.'"[52] In this line, Jean Galot observes that divine filiation "is not only an object of faith; it is a reality that is felt and lived in the cry 'Abba' which comes from the Holy Spirit."[53] According to another author, when St. Paul says that the Paraclete makes us cry out "Abba! Father!," he is bearing witness to the vividness with which he himself and his immediate readers, the first Christians, experienced this reality as truly "popular" among them.[54] This theme is very much present in the Fathers of the Church.[55] We could mention here some words of St. John Chrysostom (which St. Josemaría in fact quotes): "If the Holy Spirit did not exist we could not call God Father. How do we know this? Because the Apostle teaches us that 'since you are children, God sent the Spirit of his Son into our hearts, crying, Abba, Father.' When you invoke God the Father, then, remember that it was the Spirit who moved your soul and gave you that prayer."[56]

Let us return to the account of 1931: *I felt the action of the Lord, who with the power of something overwhelmingly necessary, sowed in my heart and on my lips this tender invocation:* Abba! Pater![57] After what we have seen, it should be clear that in these words St. Josemaría recognizes the action of the Holy Spirit. St. Josemaría's awareness of divine filiation is not only his being aware of God's paternity, but also of the action of the "Spirit of the Son" in his soul, which becomes a spur to learn to "hear" the Paraclete and follow his inspirations. In fact, the annotations in his *Apuntes íntimos* where he

52. Schlier, *La Lettera ai Romani*, p. 419.

53. Jean Galot, "Adozione divina," in Luigi Borriello (dir.), *Dizionario di mistica* (Vatican City: Libreria Editrice Vaticana, 2000), p. 55.

54. We refer to Julien Bellamy according to whom, in the first centuries, "the dogma of divine filiation was so well known and, so to speak, so popular among the faithful that the Fathers made use of it as the basis of argumentation to show other dogmas, on the occasion of the heresies of Arius and of Macedonius. See above all St. Cyril of Alexandria (PG 75, cols. 610, 1086, 1087, 1098, 1122, etc.). In addition, they were enthusiastic in emphasizing the excellence and sublimity of supernatural adoption. For them, it was a topic that led them both to lofty and practical considerations at the same time" as quoted from "Adoption surnaturelle," in *Dictionnaire de Théologie Catholique*, vol. 1 (Paris: Letouzey et Ané, 1909), col. 426.

55. See ibid. The author includes an extensive series of patristic references on this point.

56. St. John Chrysostom, *Sermones panegyrici in solemnitates D. N. Iesu Christi*, hom. 1, *De Sancta Pentecoste*, nos. 3–4, cited in *Christ Is Passing By*, no. 131.

57. *Letter, January 9, 1959*, no. 60.

narrates this filial sense are followed by others on the need to intensify his dealings with the Paraclete. Here, we transcribe only one passage as it would later appear in *The Forge*, where he records in the third person something he experienced in his own interior life. Regarding a piece of advice he received in spiritual direction, he writes:

> *Don't confine yourself to speaking to the Paraclete. Listen to him! In your prayer, consider that the life of infancy, in enabling you to discover more deeply that you are a son of God, filled you with filial love toward the Father; think how, before that, you have gone through Mary to Jesus, whom you adore as his friend, as his brother, as his lover that you are . . . Afterward, in receiving this advice, you realized that until now you had known that the Holy Spirit was dwelling in your soul, to sanctify it . . . , but you hadn't "comprehended" this truth of his presence. That suggestion was timely: now you feel Love within you, and you want to talk to him, to be his friend, to confide in him . . . , to facilitate the work of polishing, uprooting, and enkindling . . . 'I wouldn't know how to set about it!' you thought. Listen to him, I insist. He will give you strength. He will do everything, if you so want . . . And you do want!—Pray to him: Divine Guest, Master, Light, Guide, Love: may I make you truly welcome inside me and listen to the lessons you teach me; make me burn with eagerness for you, make me follow you, and love you.*[58]

This text is an entire program for the "spiritual" life inasmuch as it is the life of the children of God guided by the Spirit. We will not go into a detailed commentary of this passage now because that would lead us into themes that we will cover later. For now, we would like to emphasize that the awareness of divine filiation in St. Josemaría includes an awareness of the presence and action of the Holy Spirit in the soul.

1.1.3. "Knowing Oneself to be Christ"

In order to describe the content of this experience in 1931, we have to consider another significant text that presupposes and includes the previous ones. We introduce this by recalling that St. Josemaría (as he himself says) was then going through "humanly difficult moments," different trials that

58. *The Forge*, no. 430. The handwritten annotation of what precedes this point of *The Forge* is found in *Apuntes íntimos*, no. 864, of November 8, 1932 (AGP, P01 1991, pp. 507 ff.).

are narrated in some detail by his biographers.[59] These circumstances were the occasion for him to understand that being a son of God means "being Christ," since he is the only begotten Son; and "being Christ" implies suffering with him, that is, sharing in his Cross, because he became man in order to redeem us, becoming "obedient unto death, even death on a Cross" (Phil. 2:8).

With this in mind, let us look at the following text:

> *When God sent me those blows back in 1931, I didn't understand. Then all at once, in the midst of such great bitterness, came the words:* You are my son (Ps. 2:7), *you are Christ. And I could only stammer:* Abba, Pater! Abba, Pater! Abba! Abba! Abba! [. . .]. *You've led me, Lord, to understand that to find the Cross is to find happiness, joy. And I see the reason with greater clarity than ever: to find the Cross is to identify oneself with Christ, to be Christ, and for that reason, to be a son of God.*[60]

"You are my son . . . you are Christ." We can understand the interior anguish of the young priest when he was faced with these words. The verse from Psalm 2 ("You are my son, today I have begotten you") takes on an unsuspected vividness. One could almost say that these words burst with meaning when they are transformed into "You are Christ" and they appear not only as a messianic prophecy, but as a call from God the Father to his adopted children: to St. Josemaría at that precise moment. He felt himself to be in soul and body "another Christ," or in a certain sense "Christ himself;" and the meaning of "those blows," of the great difficulties that he was going through and "did not understand" because it seemed that God himself was placing obstacles to the mission that he had entrusted to him, was thus unveiled. Now he understood that those setbacks were nothing other than the cross that he had to carry in following Christ. Until that moment he had found himself truly beside Christ's Cross. But he was in darkness, not knowing how to interpret those sufferings. It was a painful situation that called for the obedience of faith. "All at

---

59. See Vázquez de Prada, *The Founder of Opus Dei*, vol. I, ch. 6, especially pp. 253–254 for more on the difficulties related to his situation as a priest from a diocese (that of Saragossa) other than the one in which he was residing (that of Madrid), and all the permissions required by Church authorities to remain there. See pp. 265–276 for more on the bitter religious persecution in Spain involving the burning of churches and numerous martyrs. See pp. 299–308 for more on the difficult economic situation in which his mother and his brother and sister found themselves.

60. Notes taken from preaching, April 28, 1963 (AGP, P01 XII-1963, pp. 12–13).

once," however, God wanted to enlighten him with an extraordinary light that penetrated into the depths of his soul, enkindling it once and for all. He saw and felt that to be a son of God was "to be Christ" and that that was why God the Father treated him as he treated Christ in entrusting to him those physical and moral sufferings: the Cross. It was the clear proof of his filiation, for just as the Father had willed the Passion and Death of his incarnate Son for the redemption of men, so too those contradictions of his were the way to fulfill the mission that he had been entrusted with as a participation in the redemptive work of Christ. God the Father not only treated him "as Christ," but in inviting him to take up the cross, he was also saying to him: "You are Christ," and "you are my son." Years later, contemplating Christ's prayer in Gethsemane, St. Josemaría would explicitly say what was already in his heart in 1931:

> *Jesus prays in the garden.* Pater mi (Matt. 26:39), Abba, Pater! (Mark 14:36). *God is my Father, even though he may send me suffering. He loves me tenderly, even while wounding me. Jesus suffers to fulfill the Will of the Father . . . And I, who also wish to fulfill the most holy Will of God, following in the footsteps of the Master, can I complain if I too meet suffering as my travelling companion? It will be a sure sign of my sonship, because God is treating me as he treated his own Divine Son. And then* [. . .] *there will rise up to the Lord a cry from the depths of my soul:* Pater mi, Abba, Pater . . . fiat![61]

Because of the presence of suffering in his life, St. Josemaría had access to a lofty contemplation of the Christian mystery in its entirety, that is, the mystery of the intimate union of the Christian with Christ. For this is what it means "to be a Christian." That experience of divine filiation in 1931 led him to understand in some way that a Christian is "another Christ" and in a certain manner "Christ himself," not only when he suffers and offers his sufferings in union with those of the Lord on the Cross, but at every moment. When he works and when he rests, in family and social life, the Christian "is Christ" and he is called to live Christ's life because divine adoption is effected "in Christ" by means of his most holy humanity in whose fullness of grace a Christian shares. And the Son of God made man lives the supernatural life and fulfills his mission carrying out perfectly the will of the Father in

61. *The Way of the Cross*, First Station, no. 1.

all the circumstances of his stay on earth: not just on Calvary, even though there, his obedience is revealed in the highest way when he surrenders his earthly life, but also in Bethlehem, in Nazareth, and in his public preaching. That is why the divine filiation perceived by St. Josemaría in 1931 is not exhausted in the teaching (which is certainly deep, but perhaps somewhat abstract) of being "sons in the Son"; rather, it is a divine filiation "in Christ," a divine filiation "incarnated" and "redeeming." The consequences of this are decisive for sanctification lived in the middle of the world, as we will have occasion to study in the next section.

Before moving on to other themes, let us turn to the last phrase of the principal text under discussion: *to find the Cross is to identify oneself with Christ, to be Christ, and for that reason, to be a son of God.*[62] It is worthwhile pausing to note the wording. St. Josemaría speaks about "identification with Christ"; "being another Christ"; and also (as on many other occasions) about a Christian being "*ipse Christus*—Christ himself." These expressions are not unknown in Tradition. We will document this later in some detail. But if they are not more frequent, it could very well be because they could lead to misunderstandings in confusing Christ and a Christian. Hence, it seems opportune to state clearly now that in St. Josemaría there is no room for such confusion. It suffices to leaf through any of his works to see this. "Identification with Christ" does not imply losing one's own identity. It is merely a way of expressing the intimate union between a Christian and Christ, a compenetration that has no comparison on earth given that no matter how deep the union might be between two human beings, the comparison would fall short. The only adequate reference by analogy is to the union between the Father and the Son at the heart of the Blessed Trinity, according to the Lord's own words in his Eucharistic discourse and in his words of farewell: "As the living Father sent me, and I live because of the Father, so he who eats me will live because of me" (John 6:57). "I in them and thou in me [. . .]." (John 17:23). This is well expressed by Tillard when he writes that "on 'living in Christ' the disciple does not lose his personal identity. Just as the Son is not fused in the Father but remains a free subject of action and life with respect to him, so too the disciples are not fused with the Son but remain free subjects."[63]

62. Notes taken from preaching, April 28, 1963 (AGP, P01 XII–1963, pp. 12–13).

63. Jean-Marie Roger Tillard, "Comunione," in Jean-Yves Lacoste (dir.), *Dizionario critico di Teologia* (Rome: Borla-Città Nuova, 2005), p. 320.

Certainly the expressions "identification with Christ" or "a Christian is *ipse Christus*" are daring, but St. Josemaría cannot fail to use them after having received those lights on divine filiation. They are expressions that reveal a singular penetration into the mystery of union with Christ and it can be said that he needs them in order to transmit his message. The real danger is not so much in possibly leading to confusion as we have said, but rather in seeing them merely as hyperboles or "mystical exaggerations" that lack precise theological content.

These formulas are merely a way of expressing the nucleus of the Pauline doctrine on the incorporation of the Christian into Christ. In St. Josemaría's works we can, in effect, appreciate the same basic thread that we find in the words of St. Paul to the Galatians: "I have been crucified with Christ; it is no longer I who live, but Christ who lives in me" (Gal. 2:19–20). The context is justification through faith in Jesus Christ and not through the works of the old Law. Nevertheless, writings on the spiritual life usually interpret the apostle here declaring his awareness of living the same life of the risen Christ ("Christ lives in me"), since he has given over his life to co-redeem with Christ, dying to the selfishness of his own ego ("I am crucified with Christ"). St. Josemaría belongs to this same school of thought. Contemplating the crucifixion in *Via Crucis,* he addresses the Lord with vibrant words of love: *I am yours and I give my whole self to you; gladly do I nail myself to your Cross, ready to be in the crossroads of this world a soul dedicated to you, to your glory, to the work of Redemption, the coredemption of the whole human race.*[64] And this "nailing myself to your Cross" signifies dying to oneself in order to live the life of Christ. This can also be seen in a later writing of his: *We must bring into our life, to make them our own, the life and death of Christ. We must die through mortification and penance, so that Christ may live in us through Love.*[65] We can thus see that in order "to live the life of Christ" it is necessary "to be crucified with Christ," dying to oneself through mortification and penance, that is, dying to sin and to all that impedes or makes it difficult to live the life of Christ. All this is not a consideration foreign to the literal meaning of Gal. 2:19–20, nor to its context, as several exegetes have

---

64. *The Way of the Cross*, Eleventh Station. The reference to Gal. 2:20 is implicit when St. Josemaría states, "I nail myself to your Cross," which corresponds to the "I have been crucified with Christ."

65. Ibid., Fourteenth Station. Here, too, the reference to Gal. 2:20 is implicit when he states, "die [. . .] so that Christ may live in us," which corresponds to the "it is no longer I who live, but Christ who lives in me."

shown.[66] St. Josemaría, like St. Paul, realizes that when Jesus invites us to follow him in taking up the cross of each day (see Luke 9:23), he is teaching us that "to follow him" in embracing the cross is much more than imitating his example. It is to live his very life. He speaks about "identification with Christ" because, in embracing the cross with love and generosity (dying to oneself and giving one's life for others), he has the certainty that Christ's life is present in him, the certainty St. Paul has when he dares to affirm that he makes up in his flesh what is lacking in the sufferings of Christ for his body, the Church (see Col. 1:24).

St. Josemaría delights to find that Scripture has left us a clear testimony to the mysticism of St. Paul in which he finds the authentic guarantee of what he himself feels. When he evokes the figure of the apostle in the same meditation that recalls the lights received in 1931, his words reveal that enthusiasm:

> *With those invisible wounds, he considered himself to be* alter Christus, ipse Christus. *Yes, Paul, the great Paul! Thank you for this doctrine that you have left to us, because the Holy Spirit inspired it in you! You are Christ! Paul, rejoice that we Christians love you, that we thank you for this treasure of doctrine!*[67]

As we have said, in St. Josemaría's experience we find the same thread that in St. Paul unites "being with Christ on the Cross" and "living Christ's life." For a Christian, he writes, *there is only one way of living on earth: to die with Christ so as to rise again with him, to the point that we can say with the Apostle:* It is no longer I who live, but Christ who lives in me (Gal. 2:20).[68] This awareness of the presence of Christ's life in a Christian is the basis and the heart of the "sense of divine filiation" that he says must be the foundation of the spiritual life.

---

66. According to Albert Vanhoye, the phrase "I live, but it is no longer I who live, but Christ who lives in me . . ." (see Gal. 2:20) "completes the perspective [of the preceding verse]. Paul, who affirmed that he had suffered death (Gal. 2:19), specifies now that he is alive, but alive as one raised from the dead: dead to himself, he now lives for Christ. *Death to himself is now added to death to the law* and demonstrates that the rupture with the law should not be understood in the sense of an emancipation that opens the way to egoism and debauchery. On the contrary, *it is a matter of renouncing one's own self in order to leave space for the life of Christ which is a life of generous love*" in *Lettera ai Galati: Nuova versione, introduzione e commento* (Milano: Edizioni Paoline, 1999), p. 71; emphasis added. In the same way, for Juan Leal "the application to ascetical mortification is not a departure from the text [of Gal. 2:19] [. . .]. In Baptism all that is sin dies, but the passions and concupiscence that lead to sin and are derived from it only die as one progresses in the Christian life" *Carta a los Gálatas. Traducción y comentario por Juan Leal*, in *La Sagrada Escritura: Texto y comentario por profesores de la Compañía de Jesús. Nuevo Testamento*, vol. II (Madrid: Biblioteca de Autores Cristianos, 1962), pp. 614–615.

67. Notes taken from preaching, April 28, 1963 (AGP, P01 XII-1963, pp. 13–14).

68. *The Way of the Cross*, Fourteenth Station, no. 2.

> St. Josemaría understands that Galatians 2:20 speaks about a presence of the life of Christ in a Christian not only in the intentional sense (as the known is present in the knower, and the beloved in the one who loves), but ontologically. Some light can be shed on this by considering that the context, as we have previously seen, is the justification through faith in Christ, and not through the works of the old Law (see Gal. 2:15ff). In effect, after affirming that "Christ lives in me," the Apostle adds, "And the life that I now live in the flesh *I live by faith in the Son of God*, who loved me and gave himself for me" (Gal. 2:20). The words in italics could lead us to think that he is speaking about a union with Christ that is merely intentional if we take a "forensic" or extrinsic view of grace and justification. But, as Albert Vanhoye observes, the "life by faith" "is the life of Christ in him (Paul) and of him in Christ, with a marvelous reciprocal interiority. The faith is not presented here as the seat in the mind of certain truths, but as adherence of one's whole being to the person of Christ."[69] This same author comments that the affirmation "Christ lives in me" is a wonderful novelty and allows for no analogies, as for example, the presence of the prophetic spirit in a man. "Here we are dealing with a man, Christ, who lives in another man, the believer, in a way that is so real that the life of the believer is attributed to Christ more than to the believer himself."[70] One can find similar biblical commentaries (classical and more recent) that fall in this same line.[71]

In the forge of sorrow, God granted St. Josemaría the awareness that "being a son of God" means "being Christ": to live the same Life of Christ who in some way is present in the Christian. From then on, this conviction would never leave him. It sustained him in all the moments of his life as the unmovable foundation when faced with the violent assault of setback, and as the vital root that gave his earthly passage a continual sparkle. The awareness of "being Christ" would be revealed in a spirit of freedom and of filial, priestly love, full of fortitude in the face of difficulties, filled with joy

69. Albert Vanhoye, *Lettera ai Galati, Nuova versione, introduzione e commento* (Milan: Figlie di San Paolo, 2000), p. 72.

70. Ibid.

71. Among the classic commentaries contemporaneous to St. Josemaría, we mention, for example, J. Leal, "*Cartas a los Gálatas. Traducción y comentario*," pp. 614–616. Among more recent works, see Richard N. Longenecker, *Galatians*, in David Allan Hubbard and Glenn W. Barker (eds.), *Word Biblical Commentary*, vol. 41 (Dallas: Word Books Publishers, 1990), pp. 92–93.

and peace, fruits of the Holy Spirit (see Gal. 5:22): the same Spirit through whom we are children of God. He in fact refers to these fruits when he describes the "tone" of the life of a child of God:

> *I understood that divine filiation has to be a fundamental characteristic of our spirituality:* Abba, Pater! *And that, in living divine filiation, my children would find themselves filled with joy and peace, protected by an impregnable wall; that they would know how to be apostles of this joy, and how to communicate their peace, even amid their own or others' suffering. Precisely for this reason: because we are convinced that God is our Father.*[72]

One can understand that he sums up the apostolate of a son of God as *giving witness to Christ and bringing to all those who surround us the joy of knowing themselves to be children of God.*[73] That is, in transmitting to everyone *the happy news that he is a Father who loves without measure.*[74]

To conclude this section, we can recall that St. Josemaría experienced divine filiation as a Trinitarian reality: it is about knowing oneself as immersed in the life of the Holy Trinity, being an adopted son of the Father, united to Christ through the Holy Spirit. This implies a particular relationship with each of the three divine Persons, present in the Christian through grace, which leads us to distinguish each of them through a knowing and loving relationship that constitutes the essence of the contemplative life.

> *Since divine filiation—as I just reminded you—is the sure foundation of our spiritual life, try to meditate frequently on these words of St. Paul:* For all who are led by the Spirit of God are sons of God. For you did not receive the spirit of slavery to fall back into fear, but you have received the spirit of sonship by which we cry, "Abba! Father!" For it is the Spirit himself bearing witness with our spirit that we are children of God, and if children, then heirs, heirs of God and fellow heirs with Christ, provided we suffer with him in order that we may also be glorified with him (Rom. 8:14–17). *These words sum up how we should approach God the Father, in union with his Son and with the Sanctifying Spirit.*[75]

---

72. *Letter, December 8, 1949*, no. 41.
73. *Christ Is Passing By*, no. 30.
74. Ibid., no. 100.
75. *Letter, March 11, 1940*, no. 8.

1.2. Divine Filiation: Incarnate and Redeeming

St. Josemaría's experience is not new in history. In all ages, many Christians who sought sanctity were illuminated by God to contemplate this mystery and delve deeper into its inexhaustible content. St. Augustine exults with the goodness of the Father experienced in the forgiveness of sins;[76] St. Francis of Assisi, on receiving the stigmata of the Passion, felt himself to be another Christ, and that same perception of divine paternity brought him to practice mercy without limits toward others;[77] St. John of the Cross fell into ecstasy before the fatherly and motherly tenderness of God;[78] St. Thérèse of Lisieux knew that she was a little daughter of God, and that conviction became a fruitful fountain in her spiritual life.[79] The examples are too numerous to sum up here.[80]

Our purpose is only to show that the doctrine on divine filiation has special characteristics in St. Josemaría related to sanctification in the middle of the world. He experienced adoptive filiation as "incarnate," that is, as a condition that prepares a person to take on earthly realities (the inheritance of the children of God), and as a "redeeming" mission that brings to the forefront a person's relation to the priesthood of Christ.

1.2.1. Incarnate Filiation

Abba! Pater! *I was in the street, on a tram: the street doesn't hinder our contemplative dialogue.*[81] These words are essential in describing St. Josemaría's account of the experience. They show that he perceived divine filiation as connected with the sanctification of ordinary life: as the foundation of the sanctification sought in the middle of the world. The spirit of Christian life that he preached is a spirit of adoptive filiation "incarnate" in ordinary life, in the "hubbub of the world," "in the street," that is, in the exercise of all honest secular and civic activities.

As a paradigm of this spirit, he pointed to the daily life lived by the Son of God in Nazareth. There, he was always in filial dialogue with the Father

76. See St. Augustine, *Confessions*, 10, 37–40 ff.

77. See St. Francis of Assisi, *Paraphrase of the Our Father*, 7–8.

78. See St. John of the Cross, *Spiritual Canticle*, 27, 1.

79. See St. Thérèse of Lisieux, *The Story of a Soul*, 1, 14; 9, 56; 10, 26; etc.

80. For various testimonies of saints, see D. de Pablo Maroto, "Experiencia mística de la paternidad de Dios," in J.L. Illanes (ed.), *El Dios y Padre de Nuestro Señor Jesucristo* (Pamplona: Eunsa, 2000), pp. 547–558. See also Javier Sesé, "La conciencia de la filiación divina, fuente de vida espiritual," ibid., pp. 495–517.

81. *Letter, January 9, 1959*, no. 60.

in the midst of the tasks proper to his work, and his family and social life. None of these ordinary tasks disrupted that dialogue in the slightest. On the contrary, they were the "theme" of his conversation and the "matter" that he shaped as he fulfilled the will of the Father. If precisely the things of this world (the object of temporal activities) have been created "in him," "through him," and "for him," or "in view of him" (see Col. 1:16), that is, if Jesus Christ is the "heir of all things" (Heb. 1:2), how would they not be the means and the occasion for his dialogue with his Father? And how would they not also be for his adopted children? For St. Josemaría, the awareness of being a son of God implies a vision of earthly realities that brings with it the sureness that the world does not impede the trusting intimacy of adopted children with their Father. In fact, this is the place, the setting, and matter for this intimate relationship.

There is a link between the adoptive filiation of a Christian and the Incarnation of the Son. The tie is clear: "God sent forth his Son, born of woman [. . .], so that we might receive adoption as sons" (Gal. 4:4–5). "But to all who received him, who believed in his name, he gave power to become children of God; who were born, not of blood nor of the will of man, but of God" (John 1:12–14). The Fathers of the Church, both in the East and in the West, understood that the Son became incarnate not only so that man could become a son of God, but also so that man could precisely do so in the likeness of the Son made flesh, and be united to him through the Holy Spirit.

> Let us recall some words of St. Irenaeus: "The Word of God became man and the Son of God became the son of man so that man, united to the Word, might receive adoption and become a son of God."[82] In an even more developed way, St. Cyril of Alexandria writes, "Since the Word of God dwells in us through the Spirit, we are raised to the dignity of filial adoption, having the Son himself within us. This makes us like unto Christ through sharing in his Spirit, and rising up to a higher level of freedom, we dare to say: 'Abba, Father!'"[83] St. Augustine expresses himself in similar terms.[84] These are some testimonies of a common teaching present in the Christian tradition.

82. St. Irenaeus, *Adversus Haereses*, III, 19, 1.

83. St. Cyril of Alexandria, *Thesaurus de sancta et consubstantiali Trinitate*, 33.

84. See St. Augustine, *Sermo* 185, 3.

Let us leave aside the theological polemics concerning the formal cause of adoption and the action of the Holy Spirit who dwells in the soul (the positions of Lessius y de Petau, Scheeben and Granderath, etc.).[85] We are only interested in the indisputable fact that adoptive filiation is "similar" to Christ's filiation and is in some way united to it, which we will study in more detail in the second part of this chapter.

Hence, the concept that a Christian will have of divine filiation depends in large measure on how he understands the Incarnation. If one thinks that the Son of God assumed only the "appearance" of man, his "life in the world" and his "temporal activities" will lack practically any meaning for our adoptive filiation. But the faith of the Church is other than that; it is diverse. We believe that the Son of God is truly "Son of man" and that he did assume a complete human nature. Precisely because of this we know that a man can really become a son of God in body and soul, and that the temporal activities God has entrusted to man in order to perfect creation (such as work, the formation of a family and society, etc.) are something proper to his life as an adopted child of God.

A stance like the one criticized could reasonably be called "Docetist." As is well known, Docetism was one of the first heresies that arose in the Church and even St. John had already warned his readers that "many deceivers have gone out into the world, men who will not acknowledge the coming of Jesus Christ in the flesh" (2 John 7; see John 1:14; 1 John 1:1).[86] Some, in effect, in order to exclude from Christ what they consider to be unworthy of the Son of God, denied that the Logos had assumed true flesh.[87] Today, it would be hard to find anyone who would defend this idea but, as Studer observes, the temptation to minimize the salvific value of the Incarnation, including the weaknesses of the man Jesus who assumed a human nature subject to the consequences of sin (which range from hunger and thirst to pain and death) "will never be absent from Christian theology."[88]

---

85. For a summary of this, see Antonio Aranda, *Identità cristiana: i fondamenti* (Rome: Edusc, 2007), pp. 220–227.

86. See also St. Ignatius of Antioch, *Ep. ad Smyrnaeos*, 1–3; *Ep. ad Trallianos*, 9.

87. See Alois Grillmeier, *Jesus der Christus im Glauben der Kirche*, vol. I, Freiburg 1979, pp. 187 ff.; Antonio Orbe, *Cristología gnóstica. Introducción a la soteriología de los siglos II y III*, vol. I (Madrid: Editorial Católica, 1976), pp. 380–412.

88. Basil Studer, "Docetismo," in *Dizionario patristico e di antichità cristiane*, vol. I (Casale Monferrato: Marietti, 1983), p. 1001.

> Without falling properly into Docetism, the danger of a "spiritualistic" view of the Incarnation that would imply a "weak" understanding of the role of human values in the divine filiation of the Christian is always present. St. Josemaría seems to refer to this tendency when he speaks about certain "spiritualistic" and "pietistic" notions that are not compatible with the truth of the Incarnation.[89]

One of the documents for the cause of canonization of St. Josemaría, the decree on heroic virtues, states that his "vivid perception of the mystery of the Incarnation made him see how supernatural life penetrates all human realities in the heart of a person reborn in Christ. These realities thus become the setting for holiness and the means to that goal."[90] Contemplating the Incarnation is thus key to his understanding our adoptive filiation lived out among temporal activities.

There are two fundamental aspects to this understanding of adoptive filiation that derives from the "vivid perception of the Word Incarnate":

(1) Above all, St. Josemaría is well aware that the Son of God *hasn't clothed himself as a man: he has become incarnate.*[91] Christ's human nature is not a disguise nor a mere appearance; it is the humanity of the Son of God. When St. Josemaría writes at times that Jesus *vested himself with our flesh,*[92] he is making a different point; namely, that the Divinity of Christ has become visible in his humanity: *All this human behavior is the behavior of God.* For in him dwells all the fullness of the godhead bodily (Col. 2:9). *Christ is God become man: a perfect man, a complete man. And in human matters, he makes his divinity known to us.*[93] In no way does he mean that the humanity is united to the Divinity in a merely external way, as the garment a person might be wearing. He writes of Jesus: *I contemplate you who are* perfectus Deus, perfectus homo, *truly God, yet truly man: with flesh like mine.* [94] This emphasis on the true humanity of Christ that is not a "vesting" of the Divinity stands out in the writings of various authors whom St. Josemaría recommended, as for instance, Karl Adam.[95]

---

89. See *Conversations*, nos. 113 and 121; *Friends of God*, no. 74.

90. Congregation for the Causes of the Saints, *Decree on the heroic virtues of the Servant of God Josemaría Escrivá de Balaguer, Founder Opus Dei*, April 9, 1990, §3: AAS 82 (1990): 1451.

91. Notes taken from preaching, December 25, 1972 (AGP, P09, p. 188).

92. *Christ Is Passing By*, no. 12.

93. Ibid, no. 109.

94. *Friends of God*, no. 201 (refers to the Symbol *Quicumque*).

95. Karl Adam, *Jesus Christus* (Augsburg: Haas & Grabheer, 1934), ch. I.

"The Word became flesh" (John 1:14). The One who existed before the beginning and "was with God, . . . and was God" (John 1:1), did not take on a human nature in order to later take it off after consummating the Redemption. When Marcelus of Ancyra, in the fourth century, claimed that after the final Judgment, Jesus Christ will leave behind his human nature, "The first Council of Constantinople opposed him and added to the Symbol of faith the words: 'and his kingdom will have no end.'"[96] The Church has always professed that the hypostatic union will never end; and to St. Josemaría, this was a joyous certainty:

> *Christ is alive; he lives as a man, with the same body he took when he became man, when he rose after his death, the glorified body which subsists in the person of the Word together with his human heart.* [97]
>
> *The divine Word assumed a human nature: a rational soul and a body, which was formed in the most pure womb of Mary. The divine nature and the human were united in a single Person: Jesus Christ, true God and, thenceforth, true Man* [. . .], *the second Person of the Blessed Trinity who has united our human nature to himself for ever, without any confusion of the two natures.*[98]

With these words St. Josemaría proclaims—as on other occasions—the faith of the Church formulated in the first ecumenical councils, particularly due to the Nestorian and Monophysite heresies.[99]

Thus we come to the culminating point. We have just seen how St. Josemaría professes the doctrine of faith on the Son of God truly made man. How, then, does he understand the "emptying" (see Phil. 2:7) of the Second Divine Person, who assumes a human nature? If this "emptying" were a "degrading," we would have to admire our divine adoption, but earthly realities and activities would be presented to us as a dead weight or as an obstacle to living in accord with the dignity received.

Let us first recall the words of St. Paul:

---

96. German Bishops' Conference, *Katholischer Erwachsenenkatechismus. Das Glaubensbekenntnis der Kirche* (Kevelaer: Butzon und Bercker, 1985), p. 216. See also DS 355, 358, 414.

97. *Christ Is Passing By*, no. 180.

98. *Friends of God*, no. 274.

99. An exposition of dogmatic theology with an approach that facilitates reflection on spiritual theology can be found in Fernando Ocáriz, Lucas Francisco Mateo-Seco, and José Antonio Riestra, *El misterio de Jesucristo* (Pamplona: Eunsa, 1991), ch. III (pp. 136 ff.).

> "Have this mind among yourselves, which was in Christ Jesus, who, though he was in the form of God, did not count equality with God a thing to be grasped, but emptied himself, taking the nature of a servant, being born in the likeness of men. And being found in human form he humbled himself and became obedient unto death, even death on a cross. Therefore God has highly exalted him and bestowed on him the name which is above every name, that at the name of Jesus every knee should bow, in heaven and on earth and under the earth, and every tongue confess that Jesus Christ is Lord, to the glory of God the Father." (Phil. 2:5–11)
>
> Now, let us look at a text of St. Josemaría, who contemplates,
>
> *that indescribable marvel where God humbles himself to the point of becoming man, and in doing so does not feel degraded for having taken on flesh like ours, with all its limitations and weaknesses, sin alone excepted. He does all this because he loves us to distraction!* [*¡porque nos ama con locura!*] *He does not in fact debase himself* [*rebajarse*] *when he empties himself. On the contrary, he raises us up and deifies us in body and soul.*[100]

Following St. Paul, he describes the assumption of a human nature on the part of the only begotten Son as an "emptying" of the divine person. Besides, the Son assumes our nature not as it was in the beginning, but "with all its limitations and weaknesses, except sin." In effect, any stain due to sin would be incompatible with the Divinity (see Heb. 4:15). But the "limitations and weaknesses" are not incompatible with it, as would be experiencing hunger and thirst, or pain and death, which come from the loss of the preternatural gifts after sin. These essentially imply a "humbling" of oneself. Up to this point, St. Josemaría repeats almost verbatim the Pauline teaching. Then, he clarifies his understanding of this doctrine: by "humbling" himself, he does not "degrade" himself. And in "emptying" himself, he is not "debasing" himself.[101]

Even though we should not take these terms in a rigid way, as he is not proposing academic definitions, it is unquestionable that they contain certain nuances: the Son of God "does not in fact debase himself when he empties himself," nor does he "degrade himself" by humbling himself. In one

100. *Friends of God*, no. 178.

101. Some words of St. Peter Chrysologus suggest the same idea: "*Ergo quod Creator in creatura sua, quod Deus invenitur in carne, creaturae honor est, non est Creatoris iniuria*" (*Sermo* 148: PL 52, 596).

sense, he does certainly "empty himself," given that the ontological distance between God and creatures is such that to become man while being God is akin to "emptying" oneself completely and reducing oneself to "nothing," for creatures without God simply are nothing. Nevertheless, on emptying himself he does not debase himself in the sense that, in assuming our nature, Christ does not do something unworthy of the divine nature: in fact, human beings have been made in the image and likeness of God in view of Christ (see Col. 1:16) with the most perfect spiritual and corporeal nature in the visible world, and have been willed by God to rule over all other creatures (also created in Christ, through Christ, and for Christ). All creatures indeed are calling upon man and woman to be their conscious and free interpreters of their hymn of glory to the Creator. Thus, far from debasing himself on becoming man, Christ infinitely dignifies our nature: "he raises us up, he deifies us in our body and soul," to the point that we become a "new creation."

(2) The second aspect of St. Josemaría's understanding of adoptive divine filiation that derives from his contemplation of the mystery of the Incarnation refers not to human nature but to human activities. And it means that all these noble activities can be activities of a son of God, given that the Son has assumed them:

> *We cannot say that there are things—good, noble or indifferent—which are exclusively worldly. This cannot be after the Word of God has lived among the children of men, felt hunger and thirst, worked with his hands, experienced friendship and obedience.*[102]

The following text returns to the same idea, but from a point of view that complements the previous one, allowing us to observe the question with greater clarity. Here, he begins with the native vocation of man to possess this world, perfecting it by means of his work. He then affirms that the Son of God made man fully carried out this vocation of assuming a human task (that of a craftsman: Mark 6:3) which, in his hands, was converted into a "divine task." The implicit conclusion is that this work and any other honest work is an activity proper to an adopted child of God. It can be a "divine task," a means for growth as children of God and for the betterment of the world.

> *God created man to work. We have come to call attention once again to the example of Jesus, who spent thirty years in Nazareth, working as a carpenter.*

102. *Christ Is Passing By*, no. 112.

> *In his hands, a professional occupation, similar to that carried out by millions of people all over the world, was turned into a divine task.*[103]

On being adopted as a child of God in baptism, a Christian is made an heir, according to the words of St. Paul: "and if children, then heirs, heirs of God and fellow heirs with Christ" (Rom. 8:17; see Gal. 4:7). An heir is a person who has the right to possess a good received in inheritance; a good, and in this case, the highest good: the glory of heaven (see ibid., Tit. 3:7; etc.), which essentially is the beatific vision of God. But it also includes possessing all the goods created by God for man (see Ps. 2:8; Heb. 1:2; etc.) once they have been purified of the consequences of sin and transformed in the eschatological consummation of history and the cosmos. Thus, the children of God already possess in the present life not only the promise, but the foretaste of these goods that form the content of their inheritance, given that sanctifying grace is "a certain beginning of glory."[104] Furthermore, for them, created realities are the matter of sanctification that is "eagerly longing for the revealing of the sons of God" (Rom. 8:19), given that a Christian begins to "possess" them when he sanctifies the activities whose object are those very temporal realities, all the while himself growing in sanctity and working for the sanctification of others.[105]

All in all, the core of St. Josemaría's teaching on divine filiation involves the mystery of the Incarnate Word enlightening the human person and temporal activities as these take on value and meaning after the Son of God made man assumed them.[106] St. Josemaría harmonizes the "emptying" of Christ with the affirmation of the dignity of the assumed human nature and as a result, also with the value of the activities proper to man. Understanding this harmony is key in order to grasp the notion that divine filiation can be unfurled in ordinary life; and even more so: it offers a radically positive vision of Christian life in the midst of the world that derives from the truth of the Incarnation. *Christ is* perfectus Deus, perfectus homo. *He is perfect God, the Second Person of the Blessed Trinity, and perfect man. He comes to save, not to destroy nature.*[107]

---

103. *Conversations*, no. 55.

104. St. Thomas Aquinas, *S. Th.*, II-II, q. 24, a. 3, ad 2.

105. In chapter seven we will study the sanctification of work and of other temporal activities.

106. María Jesús Soto Bruna, "Elegidos antes de la creación del mundo. Verbo e imagen en la doctrina del Beato Josemaría Escrivá de Balaguer sobre la persona humana," in Antonio Malo (ed.), *La grandezza della vita quotidiana*, vol. III (Roma: Edusc, 2003), p. 30.

107. *Friends of God*, no. 73.

1.2.2. Redeeming Filiation

These last words open up a new consideration which is central here. We have seen that the Son of God "emptied" himself on assuming a human nature, but he did not "degrade" himself because it was created for him and in view of him. Nevertheless, one could think that he "degraded" himself by assuming a nature that, as a consequence of sin, had lost the (preternatural) gifts that had kept it free from suffering and death. But that is not the case; in fact, it is rather the opposite. He has transformed these consequences into a means to atone for sin and to redeem us.

Certainly the Lord "humbled" himself in taking on the reality of a nature with its "limitations and weaknesses," as the Evangelist expressly states when narrating the moment in which Jesus came to the well at Sichar "wearied as he was with his journey" (John 4:6), hungry and tired. St. Josemaría is moved, contemplating *how generous our Lord is in humbling himself and fully accepting his human condition!*[108] But precisely because he freely accepts these limits that go against the human will, making himself "obedient unto death, even death on a cross" (Phil. 2:8; see Rom. 5:12–19; Heb. 9:27), he offered the Father reparation for the sin of disobedience that had caused them. And he obtained the gift of the Holy Spirit, who infuses the life of the children of God and frees them from the slavery of suffering and death. From then onward, the children of God should not fear these evils as something definitive. In fact, the Christian can convert them into an occasion to co-redeem with Christ (see Col. 1:24).

Hence, Jesus' death on the cross does not signify the condemnation and destruction of human nature. Instead it signifies redemption and salvation. Nor does it signify "degradation" since all of this has been done *because he loves us to distraction*, as St. Josemaría writes in the text we are commenting on. There is no degradation in this humiliation offered out of love. On the contrary; this is the highest revelation of the glory of God who is love (see John 3:16; 1 John 4:8, 16), *the glory of the cross*, to the Jews a stumbling block, and to the Gentiles foolishness (1 Cor. 1:23).[109]

108. *Christ Is Passing By*, no. 61. Elsewhere, while contemplating Jesus who suffered hunger and sought something to eat on a fig tree (see Matt. 21:18), St. Josemaría comments, *He was hungry. The Maker of the universe, the Lord of all creation, experiences hunger! Thank you, Lord, for inspiring the sacred author to include this small touch here, a detail that makes me love you more and which encourages me to desire ardently to contemplate your most sacred humanity!* Perfectus Deus, perfectus homo (*Athanasian Creed*), *perfect God and perfect Man, of flesh and bone, just like you and I. Friends of God*, no. 50.

109. *Christ Is Passing By*, no. 121.

St. Josemaría always contemplates the Incarnation of the Son of God as a redeeming Incarnation. *The Word willed to incarnate himself in order to save men; in order to make them one thing with him. This is the reason for his coming into the world:* for our sins and for our salvation, he came down from heaven, *we pray in the Creed.*[110] He affirms that, *you cannot separate the fact that Christ is God from his role as redeemer. The Word became flesh and came into the world* ut omnes homines salvi fiant (see 1 Tim. 2:4), *to save all men.*[111] The Son of God made man is the Redeemer of man and he redeems us with his priestly mediation.

Therefore, since Jesus Christ is the Son of God and Priest forever (see Heb. 5:5–6), a Christian participating in his divine filiation is also made sharer in his priesthood so that he might be truly *alter Christus, ipse Christus*. A Christian's divine filiation has a priestly meaning; it implies the calling to co-redeem with Christ: *With all our personal defects and limitations, we are other Christs, Christ himself, and we too are called to save all men,*[112] St. Josemaría writes, continuing the words above. He considers how the Son becomes mediator between God and men, by assuming not only the human realities created by God but also the "limitations and weaknesses" that are the consequence of sin in order to make up for sin by means of them. By this he understands that the adoptive divine filiation of a Christian implies sharing in this priestly mediation, exercising it in all temporal activities in order to save men and to free the world from the consequences of sin.

These consequences do not eclipse divine filiation, but instead exalt it, because they are an occasion to show that the children of God have the power to overcome evil with good (see Rom. 12:21), and that "whatever is born of God overcomes the world" (1 John 5:4).[113] Even in the most tragic moments of history in which the powers of evil seem to be unleashed, as in some decades of the twentieth century that St. Josemaría lived through,[114] a

110. Ibid., no. 122. See 1 Tim. 2:4; Tit. 2:13; 2 Pet. 1:1.

111. *Christ Is Passing By*, no. 106. See ibid., no. 122; *Friends of God*, no. 256.

112. *Christ Is Passing By*, no. 106.

113. The term "world" here has the negative meaning of "sin in the world" (see Rom. 5:12). We have already noted that in St. John, as in other books of Sacred Scripture, there is also a positive meaning of "world" as the creation of God (see John 3:16).

114. "At the end of the second millennium, *the Church has once again become a Church of martyrs*" (St. John Paul II, Apostolic Letter *Tertio millennio adveniente*, November 10, 1994, no. 37). In the Letter *Novo millennio ineunte* (January 6, 2001), he recalls again the great number of Christian martyrs in the twentieth century and states, "For the Church, the martyrs have always been a seed of life. *Sanguis martyrum, semen christianorum.* Tertullianus, *Apol.*, 50,13: PL 1, 534. This famous 'law' formulated by Tertullian has proved true in all the trials of history. Will this not also be the case of the century and millennium now beginning?" (n. 41).

son of God knows that this world is his inheritance and that if he is united to Christ he can order it to the glory of God the Father with the grace of the Holy Spirit.

> *Therefore don't be alarmed by the situation today, or think that it has no solution. Don't let yourselves by frightened by the fury of the waves stirred up on the sea of this world. Don't seek to flee, because the world is ours: it is God's handiwork and he has given it to us as an inheritance. Each week we recite and meditate on the psalm of Jesus Christ's royalty:* Filius meus es tu, ego hodie genui te. Postula a me, et dabo tibi gentes hereditatem tuam, et possessionem tuam terminos terrae (Ps. 2:7–8). *We, who are children of God, brethren of Jesus Christ, share in his inheritance, which is the whole world:* si autem filii, et heredes: heredes quidem Dei, coheredes autem Christi (Rom. 8:17): *if children, then heirs, heirs of God and fellow heirs with Christ.*[115]

The light of divine filiation received in 1931 was in continuity with that other light from August 7 that same year when, in elevating the sacred host at Mass, he understood in a new way the words of Jesus, "*et ego si exaltatus fuero a terra, omnia traham ad meipsum*" [and I, when I am lifted up from the earth, I will draw all things to myself] (John 12:32). We already expressed this in chapter two: if Christians strive to place Christ at the summit of all human activities, sanctifying their professional work and all their other ordinary tasks, he will draw all things to himself and his Kingdom will become a reality. This new discovery clearly showed that to reach this ideal, a Christian should base himself on the awareness of being a son of God, "another Christ, Christ himself." This ought to be the firm foundation for his sanctification and for the transformation of the world.

1.2.3. Divine Filiation and the Awareness of Divine Filiation

We return once again to the text of St. Paul to the Philippians to point out a final aspect of the experience of divine filiation that was granted to St. Josemaría. In speaking about the emptying of the Son of God, of his humbling himself and his obedience, the apostle does not want the knowledge of this truth to be simply theoretical. He has a practical purpose as he declares in his first words: "Have this mind among yourselves, which was in Christ Jesus" (Phil. 2:5).

115. *Letter, April 30, 1946,* no. 46.

The exegete Nello Casalini rightly emphasizes the importance of this practical purpose of St. Paul to properly understand the meaning of this passage.[116] According to him, all that the Apostle says about Jesus' emptying, his humbling himself, and his obedience, have a pedagogical purpose: to teach the faithful to have his same sentiments. In this he agrees with Hawthorne in the Word Biblical Commentary.[117] On the other hand, he feels that Gnilka's interpretation is insufficient, for he refers the expressions "he emptied himself" and "he humbled himself" to the objective fact of the redeeming Incarnation without connecting them to the opening words: "Have the same sentiments of Christ Jesus."[118] For us, Casalini's observation is interesting because it shows an exegetical basis for a similar reading to St. Josemaría's.

For St. Josemaría, the practical interpretation of this Pauline text is connatural. He does not stay in the speculative realm. He teaches us to place the foundation of Christian life in an "awareness of divine filiation," knowing and feeling ourselves to be united to Christ as children of God. This is nothing else than saying, "have the same sentiments as Christ Jesus," if we understand "sentiment" to be the act that arises from the "heart" in the biblical sense (i.e., as the source of thoughts, intentions and affections, or as the interiority of the person, not reducible to a state of mind or a thoughtless inclination).[119]

What are these sentiments? St. Paul directs us to Jesus Christ "who, though he was in the form of God, did not count equality with God a thing to be grasped, but emptied himself" (Phil. 2:6–7). He speaks about self-emptying, humiliation, obedience, and glorification. Clearly he is not dealing here with the sentiments of Christ, but with the manifestations of these sentiments. What Christ "feels," what he is aware of, is his "divine status" and, inseparably, his love for the Father and for all men loved by the Father. And this is what leads him to empty himself, to humble himself, to obey, and to receive the glorification of his most sacred humanity. He does this so we too might be glorified with him and contribute in

116. See Nello Casalini, *I misteri della fede. Teologia del Nuovo Testamento* (Jerusalem: Franciscan Printing Press, 1991), pp. 363–364.

117. See Gerald F. Hawthorne, "Philippians," in *Word Biblical Commentary*, vol. 43 (Dallas: Word Books Publishers, 1983), pp. 85–86 and 89.

118. See Joachim Gnilka, "La lettera ai Filippesi," in *Commento teologico al Nuovo Testamento*, vol. X/3 (Brescia: Paideia, 1972), pp. 210 and 217–219.

119. In chapter five, section 2.2, we will speak at greater length about this subject.

recapitulating all things under his dominion for the glory of the Father (see Rom. 8:17; Eph. 1:10).

A Christian should have these same sentiments that are summed up in knowing himself to be a son of God, and giving himself out of love to co-redeem with Christ. The Christian should not consider the dignity of adoptive filiation as a treasure for himself or as a good that affirms his ego. It is a supernatural gift that gives a new capacity to love; it is about the possibility of giving oneself in a much broader way than would otherwise be possible by means of human effort alone. St. Josemaría uses the term *endiosamento* ["becoming God-like," or "deification"] when referring to the awareness of being a son of God through sanctifying grace. He notes that this is *a deification* [endiosamento] *which, by bringing you nearer to your Father, will make you more a brother of your fellow-men.*[120] This filial awareness leads a person to empty himself out of love for God and men, as Christ emptied himself. A son of God must be able to say with St. Paul: "I have become all things to all men, that I might by all means save some" (1 Cor. 9:22). He humbles himself, accepting the limitations of his present condition, and obeys the divine will to the point of giving up his life to atone for the disobedience of sin by serving others. He cooperates in the Redemption by carrying out his human activities for the glory of the Father. He loves the world as the Son of God loves the world, with a saving love that leads him to surrender his life to purify it from sin and offer it to God the Father. He loves his fellow men with Christ's love: a love that is both fraternal, like "the first-born among many brethren" (Rom. 8:29), and also "paternal," as when Jesus calls his disciples "children" or "little children" (see John 13:33), because he is in the Father and the Father is in him (see John 14:10–11). Analogously, in a Christian there is "a mysterious participation in the *circumincessio* of the divine Persons,"[121] thanks to which he can have paternal sentiments toward his brothers and sisters, as we see in St. Paul when he says, "My little children, with whom I am again in travail until Christ be formed in you" (Gal. 4:19).

> *Having in our souls the same sentiments as Christ on the Cross, we will turn our entire life into incessant reparation, assiduous petition and permanent sacrifice for all mankind. For God will grant you a supernatural instinct to*

---

120. *The Way*, no. 283.

121. Leo Scheffczyk, "Die Heilsverwirklichung in der Gnade," in Leo Scheffczyk/Anton Ziegenaus, *Katholische Dogmatik*, vol. VI (Aachen: Michael Müller Verlag, 1998), p. 309.

> *purify all your actions, elevating them to the order of grace and converting them into instruments of apostolate. Only thus will we be contemplative souls in the middle of the world, as our vocation demands, and become truly priestly souls, making everything that is ours a continuous praise to God.*[122]

In the expression "priestly soul" in the above text, St. Josemaría condenses the sentiments that a Christian should have in order to reflect those of Jesus Christ. At other times, as we will later see, he also refers to a "lay mentality" that expresses the Christian's love for the world in its relative autonomy with respect to sacred things, an autonomy that demands love for freedom. In the preceding text, this lay mentality is implicit in reference to all human activities (civil and secular) that have to be raised up to the glory of God. In general, the two concepts "priestly soul" and "lay mentality" appear together in St. Josemaría's preaching and writings. But we will study this in the last part of this chapter. Here we merely want to say that he makes use of these terms in order to sum up the interiority of a child of God who has the "sense of divine filiation," and who harbors in his or her heart "the same sentiments as Christ Jesus" (Phil. 2:5).

To conclude this section, we could point out that the contemplation of the redeeming Incarnation of the Son of God leads St. Josemaría to adopt a vision of adoptive divine filiation as "incarnate" and "redeeming." At the same time it brings him to place the "sense" of this filiation as the foundation of the quest for holiness. In 1931, God disposed that he would find this treasure in the field of ordinary work so that it would no longer remain hidden (see Matt. 13:44).

2. St. Josemaría and the Notion of Adoptive Divine Filiation

The experience of 1931 afforded St. Josemaría no mere theoretical "learning" of the truth of adoptive divine filiation (as the doctrine was not unfamiliar to him), but rather the "comprehension" or "vital grasping" of it, so that it could serve as the foundation of the spiritual life. It was not about discovering a "new truth," but rather about attaining a "new understanding" of a truth already present in Tradition and of its place in the edifice of the Christian life.

---

122. *Letter, February 2, 1945*, no. 11. The words "as our vocation demands" refer to the specific call to Opus Dei, but they can be applied in general to the vocation to holiness in the middle of the world.

This new understanding refers to two questions that are intimately related: (1) What does it mean to be a son of God in Christ, and how are we to understand Christ's presence in a Christian; and (2) what role does the awareness of divine filiation have in the life of the faithful?

Regarding the first, it would be pointless to look for a systematic exposition in the teaching of St. Josemaría. He received the insights on divine filiation in order to guide the Christian life in practice, and thus, he transmitted them. He did not attempt to write a treatise on dogmatic theology, but rather transmit a spiritual teaching. Nevertheless, such spiritual teaching presupposes the notion of adoptive filiation as "participation in Christ's divine filiation." And we need to explain this in order to grasp what he means when he refers to a Christian being "another Christ, Christ himself." This is what we are going to see in this section.

With regard to the second point, there are numerous texts where St. Josemaría constantly insists on basing the Christian life on the sense of divine filiation. We will deal with this in parts three and four of this chapter.

2.1. Theological Sources and Context

The spiritual experience of St. Josemaría that we described above is the origin of his understanding of divine filiation as the foundation of the spiritual life. But it is not the source of the notion of divine filiation he uses. The notion is to be found both in the New Testament passages that deal directly with God's fatherhood, Christ's filiation, and the adoption of a Christian,[123] as well as in many others and, in a certain way, in the whole of the New Testament, because all of the revealed Word speaks about the Son of God made man.

Together with Scripture, the Fathers of the Church have left a deep impression on St. Josemaría. They contemplate the elevation to the supernatural order (the "divinization" or "deification" of man) as filial adoption carried out by being united to the incarnate Word.[124] As we know,

123. We point out some texts, marking in boldface those which St. Josemaría cited most frequently: (a) In the synoptics, see Matt. 5:45; 6:9, 26; 10:29; 16:17; 18:10, 14, 19; 23:9; Mark 8:38; 11:25; 13:32; 14:36; Luke 2:49; 6:36; 10:21–22; 11:2, 13; 12:30, 32; 15:11ff; 22:29, 41; 23:34, 36; 24:49; etc.; (b) For St. John: see John 1:12–13; 3:3–5, 14–15; 8:28; 11:52; 12:32, 36; 14:7, 23; 1 John 2:29; 3:1–3; 4:7, 8, 16; 5:1–5; etc.; (c) In St. Paul the passages are quite numerous; in addition to those which speak of the being or the life of the Christian "in Christ," see, mainly, Rom. 8:14–30; Gal. 2:20; 3:26–27; 4:4–7; Eph. 1:4–5.

124. See Jean-Hervé Nicolas *Les profondeurs de la grâce*, Paris 1969, p. 59; Irénée-Henri Dalmais, "Divinisation (II. Patristique grecque)," in *Dictionnaire de spiritualité ascétique et mystique*, 3 (1957): col. 1387.

this idea is of fundamental importance to the Greek Fathers,[125] but it too is greatly emphasized by St. Augustine.[126] After him, theological speculation on divinization tended to be centered on curing man from the wounds of sin, and became less focused on adoption.[127] Nevertheless, in St. Thomas Aquinas this theme comes to the fore once again.[128] We owe him the explanation of adoptive filiation as a participation (*participata similitudo*) in Subsistent Filiation with all the richness that the term "participation" brings with it. We will see later that St. Josemaría employs this same term and there are very good reasons to suggest that he does so thinking about the teachings of St. Thomas. Scott Hahn stated that St. Josemaría's teaching

> is not a novelty, strictly speaking, but a recovery—a *ressourcement*—a return to the Christian sources. Inspired by God, Bl. Josemaría retrieved a particular idea at the heart of Christianity, an idea that had been obscured by the controversies of recent centuries. It is an idea that encompasses grace and conversion, salvation, justification, and sanctification. [. . .] Bl. Josemaría's recovery of "divine filiation" represented a reintegration of Christian experience, a recovery of the Patristic and Thomistic unity that had somehow gotten lost amid the shouting. [. . .] In the centuries after the Protestant Reformation, both Catholic and Protestant theologians tended to emphasize that we are saved *from sin*. They differed in their view of how this happened and what was its effect in our lives. But they were alike in their focus on the sin from which Christ saved us. In contrast, Bl. Josemaría taught that we are saved not merely from sin, but *for sonship*. Thus he could preach of divine filiation as the end of divinization, and of divinization as the reason for our redemption.[129]

---

125. Charles Baumgartner, "Grâce," in *Dictionnaire de spiritualité ascétique et mystique*, 6 (1967): col. 718. According to this author, the idea is found implicitly as early as Ignatius of Antioch, explicitly in Irenaeus, and "it especially governs the thought of Athanasius and of Cyril of Alexandria" (ibid.).

126. After distinguishing the generation of the Son from the substance of the Father and the creation of man, he teaches that God has justified us by divinizing us: making us his sons and daughters. "*Manifestum est ergo, quia homines dixit deos, ex gratia sua deificatos, non de substantia sua natos* [. . .]. *Iustificando, filios Dei facit. Dedit enim eis potestatem filios Dei fieri (Io 1,12). Si filii Dei facti sumus, et dii facti sumus: sed hoc gratiae est adoptantis, non naturae generantis*" (St. Augustine, *Enarrationes in Psalmos* 49, 2: PL 36, 565). See idem, *Contra Faustum*, III, 3, 2: PL 42, 215; *Ep. 140 ad Honoratum*, 4, 10: PL 33, 541).

127. See G. Bardy, "Divinisation (III. Chez les Pères latins)," in *Dictionnaire de spiritualité ascétique et mystique*, 3 (1957): col. 1395 ff.

128. See principally, *In III Sent.*, d. 10, q. 2; *S. Th.*, I, q. 33, a. 3; III, q. 23.

129. Scott Hahn, "Grace and Conversion in the Writings of Bl. Josemaría," in Paul O'Callaghan (ed.), *La grandezza della vita quotidiana*, vol. V/1 (Rome: Edusc, 2004), pp. 115–118.

The controversy around Luther implied a new and grave setback for the teaching on divine filiation. Theological debates at the time focus primarily on man's justification (the step from the state of sin into that of friendship with God) which the Reformers understood in purely extrinsic or "legalistic" terms, as the simple non-punishing for sin.[130] The key notion dispelling misunderstanding on this issue and clearly showing how the person is transformed in passing from one state to another is that of "created grace,"[131] distinct from "uncreated grace," which is the Holy Spirit dwelling in the Christian's soul. Even though the Council of Trent teaches that in justification man receives the gift of the Holy Spirit and "is born to the state of grace and of adoption as a son of God,"[132] the later debate was centered more on created grace rather than on uncreated grace. In fact, the result was "a certain eclipse of the doctrine about the inhabitation of the Holy Spirit."[133] Divine filiation, the result of the Holy Spirit being sent into souls (see Gal. 4:6), suffered the same fate.[134] Theology tended to place it among the "effects of created grace," without being more precise about what "effect" means. And this explanation would be indispensable when dealing with the different levels of an individual's ontological makeup.

We have to keep in mind that, in the teaching of St. Thomas, sanctifying grace lies at the level of essence or nature that it elevates, while adoptive filiation, being a personal property, is found at the level of the act of being, constitutive of the ontological personality.[135] If speaking about cause

130. See Council of Trent, *Sessio V: Decr. de peccato originali*: DS 1515.

131. The *gratia gratum faciens* in St. Thomas, or what later was called "sanctifying grace," or also "grace of justification."

132. Council of Trent, *Sessio VI: Decr. de iustificatione*: DS 1524; see DS 1515, 1529, 1531.

133. Baumgartner, "Grâce," col. 711. According to G. Biffi, the problem comes from further back: "Starting in the fourteenth century, [scholastic theology] ended up not giving to 'uncreated grace' (the indwelling of the three Divine Persons in the just) all the attention that it merits because it placed at the center of its research the concept of 'accidental grace' [or 'created grace']." *L'enigma dell'uomo e la realtà battesimale* (Turin 2006), p. 58. The author then continues to propose "returning to the dominant position of the earlier scholastics which took as its starting point the indwelling of the Holy Spirit also to justify the existence of a "supernatural newness" inherent in all the baptized" (ibid.). He refers to the position held by Alexander of Hales, St. Bonaventure, and St. Thomas (and in this last case, he mentions *In II Sent.*, d. 26. q. 1, a. 1).

134. Actually, the teaching about adoptive divine filiation is hardly present even in the Roman Catechism. See what we say in this regard in the Preliminary Part, section II.3. In contrast, the *Catechism of the Catholic Church* gives it a due prominence throughout the whole text.

135. Supernatural divine filiation and sanctifying grace are inseparable but distinct realities: divine filiation is a "personal property" (St. Thomas Aquinas, *S. Th.*, III, q. 23, a. 4, c) that elevates the person, while grace elevates his nature. The metaphysical distinction between person and nature (which is necessary to be able to speak of the mystery of Christ: one divine Person in two natures, the divine and the human) is also indispensable in order to speak of the Christian: a human person elevated to the dignity of a child of God with his

and effect between these two levels already requires great care in employing metaphysical terms accurately in the order of creation, all the more so is that the case in speaking about matters in the order of supernatural elevation.[136] That a Christian is a "son of God through grace" is not the same as saying that "adoptive filiation is an effect of the infusion of created grace." If one does not accurately explain this last statement, it can seem that adoptive filiation is a juridical reality like human adoption, when it is actually a true participation in the Subsistent Filiation that transforms the person into a son or a daughter of God.[137] The theology of the early post-tridentine era focused on nature healed and elevated by sanctifying grace more than on the person adopted as a child of God when he receives the Holy Spirit. It is reasonable to think that later on the controversy with Jansenism, centered on grace as a divine help (whether sufficient or efficient, etc.), still further contributed to postponing the reality of divine filiation from being dealt with in theological scholarship.

In the nineteenth century, there were signs of a recovery of the patristic notion of the gift of the Holy Spirit as the foundation of divine adoption and created grace: a recovery which, according to Rondet,[138] can be

---

human nature elevated by participating in the divine nature. In the following chapter where we explore human freedom, we will see the idea (that we are following here) that the essential constitutive feature of one's personality is the *actus essendi* (taken as intensive act of being). We point out in advance that this understanding of Thomistic metaphysics is not the only one possible within the general framework of Thomism.

136. One way to clarify this question is to consider the parallelism between the creation of man (his constitution in his natural being) and his "re-creation" (his supernatural elevation), which leads to the discovery of a certain correspondence of the relation between "form" and "esse" (being) which is given in the two cases. "By creation God constitutes things in their natural being through a natural form received in the very thing created, and also in elevation God constitutes the soul in a new being (esse gratiae) by means of a created form (grace)." St. Thomas Aquinas, *In I Sent.*, d. 17, q. 1, a. 1, ad 3. In both cases "*forma dat esse*" (*De Veritate*, q. 5, a. 8, ad 10), or what is the same, "*esse consequitur formam*" (*S. Th.*, I, q. 9, a. 2, c). In the case of creation, the expression means that the natural form determines the way of being, and also that it receives and limits the act of being. In the case of re-creation it only means the first: the form "grace" determines the supernatural way of being, which is "to be a child of God." In this sense we say that "by grace we are made children of God." Divine filiation is the same supernatural way of being as one who receives sanctifying grace. On this point one might look at the interesting reflections of Fernando Ocáriz, *Naturaleza, Gracia y Gloria* (Pamplona: Eunsa, 2000), pp. 95–100.

137. According to Stanislas Lyonnet, when St. Paul spoke of adoptive divine filiation, he did not take the term "adoption" from Greco-Roman legislation, as other authors affirm, or at least he did not take it exclusively from there, but rather from the Old Testament, where Yahweh adopts the people of Israel as his child (see Ezra 4:22; Hos. 11:1; Is. 63:7–16; Jer. 3:19; Wis. 8:13; etc.), the people of the Covenant (see *Quaestiones in Epistolam ad Romanos*, II, Roma 1956, p. 19). In the New Testament, the adoption of the Christian occurs within the framework of the New Covenant, which implies a new participation in the divine life.

138. See Henri Rondet, *Gratia Christi: essai d'histoire du dogme et de théologie dogmatique* (Paris: Beauchesne, 1948), p. 340.

attributed especially to Matthias Josef Scheeben (d. 1888). In the doctrinal foundation of St. Josemaría's message, one can perhaps discover a likeness to Scheeben with respect to the theme we are discussing here. But in any case, there is little probability of any direct influence.[139]

Passing on to the first half of the twentieth century, we find that the most important studies in Dogmatic Theology about the divine filiation of the Christian (like those of Émile Mersch[140] and Stanislas Dockx)[141] do not appear until the end of the 1930s and '40s, respectively, when this central point in St. Josemaría's message had already taken shape.

In the end, even though Josemaría Escrivá's teaching springs up in a booming era of theological reflection on divine filiation, it seems to us that the central place he gives to this topic in his spiritual teaching cannot be explained by the developments in systematic theology of his day, nor from their conclusions. On the other hand, it is not difficult to show that academic research has paid (and continues to pay) little attention to this topic, and that it is practically absent in the widely diffused works of major influence until most recent times.[142]

---

139. We have already noted in the Preliminary Part, section II.2.b), that the first Spanish edition of *Die Mysterien des Christentums* (Freiburg im Breisgau: Herder, 1865) was only published in 1950.

140. See Émile Mersch, "Filii in Filio," in *Nouvelle revue théologique* 65 (1938): 551–582; 681–702; 809–830.

141. See Stanislas Dockx, *Fils de Dieu par grâce* (Paris: Desclée de Brouwer, 1948).

142. To the extent that one can say that dictionaries of theology reflect the theological interests of an epoch, it is significant to point out that in the extensive lexicon directed by Karl Rahner (*Sacramentum mundi. Theologisches Lexikon für die Praxis*, 4 vols., Freiburg-Basel-Vienna: Herder, 1967–69) there are no headings for "divine filiation," "adoption," "children of God," nor have we seen others in which they deal with adoptive filiation to any great extent. Nor does it dedicate special attention to it within such headings as "grace," "holiness," and "baptism." Something similar happens in the encyclopedia of theology directed by Peter Eicher (*Neues Handbuch theologischer Grundbegriffe*, München: Kösel Verlag, 1984–85). The concept does not occupy a position of importance in these works. In the classic *Dictionnaire de Théologie Catholique* (begun under the direction of A. Vacant and consisting of eighteen volumes published between 1908 and 1972), the heading "divine filiation" does not exist, but its equivalent "*adoption surnaturelle*" is present, although the subject is not treated with the extension that one would expect today (see ibid., vol. I [1925]: cols. 425–437); there is also a brief reference to divine filiation under the heading of "*Grâce*" (see ibid., vol. VI/2 [1925]: cols. 1613–1615). In the *Dictionnaire de spiritualité ascétique et mystique* (13 vols. published between 1937 and 1994, begun under the direction of Marcel Viller) there is also no heading dedicated to divine filiation; in this case, the heading "*adoption divine*" is empty and refers to "*Divinisation*" and to "*Grâce*." Within this latter there is a section dedicated to adoptive filiation (see ibid., 1 [1965]: cols. 708–726, of Charles Baumgartner). Some recent dictionaries, much shorter than those referred to earlier, dedicate proportionally greater attention to the subject, as for example, in Louis Bouyer's entries "*Adoption surnaturelle*" and "*Filiation*" in *Dictionnaire Théologique* (Paris: Desclée, 1990); the entry heading "*Adozione divina*" in the *Dizionario enciclopedico di spiritualità*, directed by Ermanno Ancilli (3 vols., Rome: Città Nuova, 1990); the entry "*Abbá*" in the *Dizionario di Teologia fondamentale*, dirigido por R. Latourelle (Assisi: Citadella, 1990). A work of this genre that deals with the subject in greater depth (always in terms proportional to the total

On the other hand, it is very probable that beginning in 1931, St. Josemaría was familiar with the writings of some contemporary authors who had been emphasizing the importance of the divine filiation, among whom we find Bl. Columba Marmion (1858–1923) in his book *Jesus Christ in his Mysteries*, published originally in French in 1919 and translated immediately into several other languages.[143] In this work that was soon to be widely read, he writes that we will not understand anything about Christianity "as long as we are not convinced that what is fundamental consists in being 'children of God' through participation, by means of sanctifying grace, in the eternal filiation of the Word incarnate [. . .]. All of Christian life, as sanctity itself, is reduced to being through grace what Jesus Christ is by nature: Son of God."[144] It is clear that St. Josemaría coincides with this central idea of Bl. Columba. But the mere fact that he wrote about this earlier is not sufficient to conclude that he influenced St. Josemaría. Something similar may have occurred in his relationship to St. Thérèse of Lisieux, to whom he had great devotion as a young priest.[145] That he coincides with her "little way of spiritual childhood" is undeniable. Nevertheless, it is a coincidence that he only discovers after he himself received the lights that brought him to base his spiritual life on divine filiation with its own specific features. In his *Apuntes*, St. Josemaría has this to say: *I didn't learn in the books the path of childhood* [*of St. Thérèse*] *until after Jesus had me made me walk along this way*.[146] According to Pedro Rodríguez,

> the "spiritual childhood" that St. Josemaría lived and proposed to the readers [of *The Way*] is not only, nor above all, a matter of littleness, the humility of a creature before God, but more deeply, joy and sureness before the paternity of God the Father, and a way of living the divine

extension) is the recent *Diccionario de Teología* directed by César Izquierdo (Pamplona: Eunsa, 2006), pp. 415–420. See the entry "*Filiación divina*," by Antonio Aranda. Among the works of Moral Theology which give prominence to adoptive filiation, we can point out: Enrique Colom—Ángel Rodríguez Luño, *Scelti in Cristo per essere santi: elementi di teologia morale fondamentale* (Rome: Edusc, 2003); Tremblay Réal, Stefano Zamboni (dir.), *Figli nel Figlio. Una teologia morale fondamentale* (Bologna: Edizioni Dehoniane, 2008).

143. Bl. Columba Marmion, *Le Christ dans ses mystères* (Paris: Desclеé *de Brouwer*, 1922). See also, by the same author, *Le Christ, idéal du prêtre* (Maredsous: Les Éditions de Maredsous, 1951).

144. Idem, *Jesucristo en sus misterios*, III, 6 (p. 52 in the Spanish edition of Editorial Litúrgica, Barcelona 1948).

145. See Andrés Vázquez de Prada, *The Founder of Opus Dei*, vol. I, pp. 309 and 317, where there are citations of *Apuntes Intimos*, nos. 307 and 562 (of October 2, 1931, and of January 14, 1932, respectively).

146. *Apuntes íntimos*, no. 560, January 13, 1932; cited in Pedro Rodríguez, *Santo Rosario. Edición crítico-histórica* (Madrid: Rialp, 2010), p. 82.

filiation of a "child" (see in this sense no. 860 [of *The Way*] which is definitive), who sees in Jesus his older brother.[147]

> As Illanes observes, "several texts in which St. Josemaría speaks about divine filiation are situated in the context of the life of childhood."[148] Nevertheless the same author goes on to say that it is necessary to distinguish "the sense of divine filiation from the life of childhood even though they may have, and do have, many relations to one another. They are not identified either in general nor in the teaching of St. Josemaría."[149] One thing is to know oneself to be a "small child" of God (which is certainly a feature of the spirit of divine filiation), and another is to follow a way of spiritual infancy in one's interior life (for example the "little way of infancy" of St. Thérèse of Lisieux). St. Josemaría distinguished these two things and points out that the way to live as a small child of God is not one and the same for everyone. He first advises: *Become children before God. Only thus will we become men of great maturity here on earth, because God's hand will act through our simplicity, imparting his strength and security. Children before God, with complete trust, as a small child trusts his mother. He has no worry about tomorrow or any other concern, since his mother is watching over him. God watches over us, if we are simple.*[150] But in being more specific about this way of acting as small children, he points out: *Ordinarily I abandon myself; I try to make myself small and put myself in the arms of our Lady. I tell the Lord: Jesus, make a bit of room for me! Let's see if the two of us can fit in your Mother's arms! But you should follow your own path: mine doesn't have to be yours* [. . .]. *Long live freedom!*[151]

These brief considerations do not allow us to reach a conclusion about the influence of other authors on St. Josemaría. For example, we would also have to examine the magazine called "*Vida sobrenatural*," which was promoted by the Dominican Juan González-Arintero. Since its publication

147. Pedro Rodríguez, *The Way: Critical-Historical Edition*, p. 977 (introduction to the chapter "Spiritual Childhood").

148. José Luis Illanes, "Experiencia cristiana y sentido de la filiación divina," p. 468. According to this author, the fact is explained because "in the first years of the thirties and parallel to the experience that led him to the deep perception of the reality of divine filiation and to the living of its meaning, there occurred in the Founder of Opus Dei what one of the students of his thought, Pedro Rodríguez, has referred to as 'the dawn of spiritual childhood.' (*The Way: Critical-Historical Edition*, p. 975)." Ibid.

149. Ibid., p. 469.

150. Notes taken from preaching, August 25, 1968 (AGP, P01 XI-1968, p. 27).

151. Notes taken from preaching, December 20, 1974 (AGP, P01 XII-1974, pp. 29–30).

in 1921, it was focused on divine filiation, and St. Josemaría was well acquainted with it, as well as with other sources. Such a study exceeds our possibilities. In any case, what we have pointed out above suffices to show that any possible influences are to be sought more in contemporary spiritual authors than in the field of speculative theology. Regardless, the main source is clearly Sacred Scripture, read and meditated on with the lights that God gave him in order to open a way to sanctity in the middle of the world.

Before concluding, we want to point out that it is easier to indicate the influence that goes in the opposite direction: the teaching of St. Josemaría has awoken an interest for the theological study of adoptive divine filiation and the place it corresponds to in the spiritual life. There are several works that, without being dedicated to the message of St. Josemaría, owe their origin to him as those same authors point out.[152] Numerous, in fact, are the studies on divine filiation in his preaching.[153]

2.2. Doctrinal Elements in the Notion of Supernatural Divine Filiation

Let us now discuss the underlying principal, doctrinal elements of the spirit of Christian life based on divine filiation as transmitted by St. Josemaría.

152. Among the studies of systematic theology we mention: Alfredo García Suárez, "La primera persona trinitaria y la filiación divina adoptiva," in *XVIII Semana española de Teología* (Madrid 1961), pp. 69–114; Fernando Ocáriz, *Hijos de Dios en Cristo: Introducción a una teología de la participación sobrenatural* (Pamplona: Eunsa, 1972); Ramón García de Haro, *Cristo, fundamento de la moral: los conceptos básicos de la vida moral en la perspectiva cristiana* (Barcelona: Ediciones Internacionales Universitarias, 1990); Antonio Aranda, "*Llamados a ser hijos del Padre: Aproximación teológica a la noción de filiación divina adoptiva*," J.L. Illanes (dir.), *El Dios y Padre de Nuestro Señor Jesucristo*, pp. 251–272.

153. See Catalina Bermúdez Merizalde, "Hijos de Dios uno y trino por la gracia: La filiación divina, fundamento y raíz de una espiritualidad," in *Annales Theologici* 7/2 (1993): 347–368; eadem., "Hijos de Dios Padre en la vida cotidiana: El sentido de la filiación divina en las enseñanzas del Beato Josemaría Escrivá de Balaguer," in *Pensamiento y cultura* 1 (2002): 155–167; Jutta Burggraf, "El sentido de la filiación divina," in M. Belda, J. Escudero, J.L. Illanes and P. O'Callaghan, *Santidad y mundo* (Pamplona: Eunsa, 1996), pp. 109–127; María Caterina Calzona, "Filiación divina y cristiana en el mundo," in A. Sarmiento, T. Rincón, J.M. Yanguas, and A. Quirós (eds.), *La misión del laico en la Iglesia y en el mundo* (Pamplona 1987), pp. 299–308; José Luis Illanes, "Filiación divina: ontología y vivencia existencial," in idem (ed.), *El Dios y Padre de Nuestro Señor Jesucristo*, pp. 537–545; Ocáriz, "La filiación divina, realidad central en la vida y en la enseñanza de Mons. Escrivá de Balaguer," F. Javier Sesé, "La conciencia de la filiación divina, fuente de vida espiritual," in *Scripta Theologica* 31 (1999): 471–493; Johannes Stöhr, "La vida del cristiano según el espíritu de filiación divina," in *Scripta Theologica* 24 (1992): 879–893. In recent years, several works of spirituality on this subject have also seen the light of day (e.g., Francisco Fernández Carvajal and Pedro Beteta, *Hijos de Dios: la filiación divina que vivió y predicó el beato Josemaría Escrivá* (Madrid: Ediciones Palabra, 1995); Mercedes Eguíbar, *Vida de infancia espiritual* (Madrid: Ediciones Palabra, 2006); Andrea Mardegan, *Tra le braccia del Padre: scritti scelti sulla paternità divina* (Genova: Marietti, 2000). This is an anthology of writings of St. Josemaría, with an interesting 44–page preliminary study.

(1) *Orders of filiation.* The first and most basic point is his proclamation that *all men and women are children of God*,[154] that is, not only the baptized, nor only simply those who live in the state of sanctifying grace, but all men and women, because all have been created to the image and likeness of God (see Gen. 1:26–27; 5:1). This filiation is ordered to another still more perfect one: *we have been created to achieve the dignity of children of God.*[155] This is supernatural divine filiation, proper to those who share in the supernatural life, and that is not transmitted by human generation, but is a further subsequent gift. It is the filiation of those "who were born, not of blood, nor of the will of the flesh, nor of the will of man, but of God" (John 1:13). A Christian is born to this supernatural filiation when he receives the supernatural life in baptism. *By the grace of baptism we have been made children of God. With this free divine decision, man's natural dignity has been elevated in an incomparable way.*[156] The infusion of sanctifying grace confers on man a likeness to God of an absolutely superior order to that which he already had as a person through human nature. *Man, in the state of grace, is divinized.*[157] The most Blessed Trinity *makes us members of his family.*[158] We acquire the new status of children, and in this way we are able to *look at God the Father, God the Son, and God the Holy Spirit, and realize that we share in God's own life.*[159]

This supernatural filiation will reach its fullness in glory when each soul receives a new, higher likeness to God, according to the words of St. John: "Beloved we are God's children now; it does not yet appear what we shall be, but we know that when he appears we shall be like him, for we shall see him as he is" (1 John 3:2). That is why, sanctity in glory is none other than *the fullness of divine filiation.*[160]

As we can see, St. Josemaría considers three orders of divine filiation: that of every human being, another which is "supernatural," proper to those who are in the state of sanctifying grace, and a third which is its fullness in glory.

> St. Thomas explains these different orders of filiation in this way: "The perfect idea of paternity and filiation is to be found in God the Father,

154. *Christ Is Passing By*, no. 64.
155. Ibid., no. 133.
156. *Letter, March 19, 1967*, no. 93.
157. *Christ Is Passing By*, no. 103.
158. Ibid., no. 48. See Eph. 2:19.
159. *Christ Is Passing By*, no. 160. See John 1:12–13; 2 Pet. 1:4.
160. *Letter, February 2, 1945*, no. 8.

and in God the Son, because one is the nature and glory of the Father and the Son. But in creatures, filiation in relation to God is not found in a perfect manner, since the Creator and the creature have not the same nature; rather is it found by way of a certain likeness. The more perfect this likeness is, the nearer it approaches the true idea of filiation. God is called the Father of creatures [the irrational ones], by reason only of a trace [. . .]. Of the rational creatures He is called Father by reason of the likeness of His image [. . .]. But moreover He is Father of some of them by similitude of grace, and these are also called adoptive sons [. . .]. Lastly, He is Father of others by similitude of glory."[161] Elsewhere, St. Thomas shows that there is such a great difference between the filiation proper to every man as a rational creature and supernatural adoptive filiation, that the first is metaphorical, because human beings have not been "engendered" by the Father in a way analogous to the way the Son has been engendered in the heart of the most Blessed Trinity, but rather, they have been "created *ex nihilo.*"[162] On the other hand, supernatural adoptive filiation is filiation in the proper, analogous sense (that is, man is really engendered to the supernatural life, made *a son in the Son*, as we will now see).

(2) *Supernatural filiation: sons in the Son.* How is divine filiation in a Christian related to the filiation of the Word? Let us consider a passage that characterizes St. Josemaría's teaching on this subject:

> *By the grace of Baptism we have been made children of God. With this free divine decision, man's natural dignity has been elevated in an incomparable way: and if sin destroyed this marvelous work, the Redemption restored it in an even more admirable way* (Missale Romanum, Ordo Missae), *bringing us to share even more closely in the divine filiation of the Word.*[163]

This passage characterizes his teaching, as we have said, for two reasons:

(a) It refers to the divine filiation of the Christian as "participation" in the divine filiation of the Word. Here St. Josemaría does not cite St.

161. St. Thomas Aquinas, *S. Th.*, I, q. 33, a. 3, c; see *S. Th.*, III, q. 32, a. 3, c.

162. Ibid., q. 41, a. 3, c.

163. *Letter, March 19, 1967*, no. 93. The passage of the *Ordo Missae* to which he alludes is found in one of the prayers of the offertory of the Missal of St. Pius V: "*Deus, qui humanae substantiae dignitatem mirabiliter condidisti et mirabilius reformasti . . .*"

Thomas, but undoubtedly he depends on him. In effect, the Angelic Doctor explains that the Word "is called the only begotten Son of God by nature; but he is called the firstborn insofar as from his natural sonship, by means of a certain likeness and participation, a sonship is granted to many."[164] He understands supernatural divine filiation as participation in the subsistent Filiation (the Son) such that when we say that the Christian is a "son of God," we must not think that he is "at the Son's side," but rather more profoundly, that he is united to the Son, forming as it were one Son with him. The doctrine of St. Thomas on this point is of immense value for understanding that the Christian is a "son in the Son": a son who is "present in the Son," or a son "in whom the Son is present." This is an expression that bears biblical and patristic roots, and is also used by the Magisterium of the Church.[165]

According to scripture scholar Scott Hahn,

> [for St. Josemaría], "divinization is the process by which Christians become "sons in the Son"—sons of God through incorporation into the eternal Son of God. We are sons because Christ has shared his own divine sonship with us. Our sonship is more than mere imitation of Christ; it is more than a legal transfer of title; it is more than acting 'as if' we were sons. Ours is a metaphysical participation in Christ's only-begottenness."[166]

(b) The second reason for the special interest in the text we are commenting on is the affirmation that the redeeming Incarnation of the Son has enabled us to participate "even more fully" in the divine filiation of the Word. This evidently refers to a (hypothetical) way of being redeemed whereby God would have made us sharers in divine filiation without the Incarnation of the Word. In effect, in order to make us children of God the Incarnation was not necessary. The "motive" of the Incarnation is, for St. Josemaría, to redeem us from sin. Nevertheless,

---

164. St. Thomas Aquinas, *In Ioann. Ev.*, c. 1, lect. 8. Aquinas frequently noted that "*filiatio adoptionis est participata similitudo filiationis naturalis.*" *S. Th.*, III, q. 23, a. 4, c; see *S. Th.*, I, q. 33, a. 3, c; II-II, q. 45, a. 6, c; III, q. 3, a. 5, c and ad 2; q. 24, a. 3, c; *In Ep. ad Rom.*, c. VIII, lect. 6; *In Ioann. Ev.*, c. I, lect. 8; etc. On divine filiation as a participation in subsistent Filiation, see Ocáriz, *Hijos de Dios en Cristo*, pp. 93–111.

165. See Vatican II, Pastoral Constitution on the Church in the Modern World *Gaudium et Spes* (December 7, 1965), no. 22. "Through the grace received in Baptism, man participates in the eternal birth of the Son from the Father, since he is constituted an adoptive son of God." St. John Paul II, Homily (March 22, 1980). This expression is found in many of the texts of Pope John Paul II.

166. Scott Hahn, "Grace and Conversion in the Writings of Bl. Josemaría" in Paul O'Callaghan (ed.), *La grandezza della vita quotidiana*, vol. V/1 (Rome: Edusc, 2004), p. 117.

> the greatness of the gift of divine filiation is even more admirable thanks to the Incarnation, because the fact that the Son of God has assumed human nature allows us to participate "even more fully" in the divine filiation of the Word: with a co-naturalness or familiarity based not only on our sharing in the divine nature, but also on his sharing in our human nature.

(3) *"Adoptive" filiation.* Now, let us consider the fact that divine filiation in the Christian is "adoptive" (see Rom. 8:15, 23; Gal. 4:5; Eph. 1:5). St. Josemaría recalls this frequently, making reference to these and other texts.[167] It is "adoptive" because the Christian does not possess it by nature (as it is a gift that follows birth), and it is not identical, but rather analogous to the "natural" filiation of the only begotten Son.

But supernatural adoption completely transcends human adoption. This latter one is a legal act that does not entail transmission of (biological) life from parent to child. The adopted child is a son or daughter of the one who adopts him or her before the law. On the other hand, supernatural adoption really makes the adopted "members of God's family" (Eph. 2:19) because they are made capable of participating in the divine nature.[168] That is why adoptive filiation "has something of natural filiation," as Scheeben says. And he goes on: "But because we are not merely adopted sons, but members of the natural Son, we really share in the personal relation that the Son of God has to his Father."[169] Along the same vein, while glossing over St. Josemaría's teaching on divine filiation, Fernando Ocáriz states, "We are not only called children of God, but truly are. Not only does God, in an outpouring of love, want us to treat him *as* a father, but in an incomparably greater outpouring of his love, he adopts us as his children *in a strict sense* (although in a limited and partial sense); in other words, strictly speaking, we participate in the singular divine Filiation, which is the Second Person of the Blessed Trinity, the only begotten Son of the Father: 'See what love the Father has given us, that we should be called children of God; and so we are' (John 3:1)."[170]

---

167. See, e.g., *Christ Is Passing By*, nos. 65, 112, 118, 183; *Friends of God*, no. 2.

168. See St. Thomas Aquinas, *S. Th.*, III, q. 23, a. 1, c.

169. Matthias Josef Scheeben, *Die Mysterien des Christentums* (Freiburg: Herder, 1951), p. 318.

170. Ocáriz, "La filiación divina, realidad central en la vida y en la enseñanza de Mons. Escrivá de Balaguer," p. 184.

(4) *Sons of the Father, in the Son, through the Holy Spirit.* By its origin, supernatural adoption is the work of the *three divine Persons in the unity of God's substance, in the unity of his love and of his sanctifying action.*[171] Its effect on the adopted person is a "personal property"[172] consisting in a supernatural relation with God; a relation, in fact, with each of the divine Persons in their mutual distinction. St. Josemaría expresses this when he states that God has wanted to *bring all men and women to share in the divine life,*[173] or that *we have been called to penetrate into the intimacy of God, to know and love God the Father, God the Son, and God the Holy Spirit.*[174] This means that in the spiritual life of a son of God, he can *distinguish and adore each one of the divine Persons,*[175] and thus maintain a "personal" dialogue with the Father, with the Son, and with the Holy Spirit.

In order to illustrate this point of St. Josemaría's teaching, some authors make use of the theological concept that describes supernatural adoption as a certain "introduction" to the most Blessed Trinity. For example, Fernando Ocáriz writes, "The Father, the Son and the Holy Spirit, in the unity of their action *ad extra,* sanctify us and adopt us as children of God. But the *terminus* of this unique efficient divine action (that is, in us) is precisely our *divinization,* our being truly brought into the divine Life."[176] Johannes Stöhr uses similar terms when he states, "A Christian is in a certain sense brought into God's family community, that is, into the mystery of trinitarian life [. . .]. He takes on a personal relationship with each of the three divine Persons."[177]

If we consider the intimate life of the most Blessed Trinity as the eternal acting out of the intra-Trinitarian processions (the generation of the Son by the Father and the spiration of the Holy Spirit by the Father and the Son), we can conceive of the "introduction" of the Christian into this life as a mysterious sharing in these processions. In effect, the three Persons "come"

---

171. *Christ Is Passing By,* no. 86. The text refers to the Mass as an action of the Three Divine Persons, but the affirmation of the "unity of the efficacious sanctifying action of the three Persons" is of general validity and therefore we apply it to supernatural adoption.

172. "*Filiatio proprie convenit hypostasi vel personae, non autem naturae, unde in prima parte dictum est quod filiatio est proprietas personalis.*" St. Thomas Aquinas, *S. Th.*, III, q. 23, a. 4, c; see *De Veritate*, q. 29, a. 1, ad 1.

173. *Letter, January 9, 1932,* no. 29.

174. *Christ Is Passing By,* no. 133.

175. *Friends of God,* no. 306.

176. Ocáriz, "La filiación divina, realidad central en la vida y en la enseñanza de Mons. Escrivá de Balaguer," p. 191.

177. Stöhr, "La vida del cristiano según el espíritu de filiación divina," p. 884.

to dwell in the soul that is open to supernatural life, in keeping with the Lord's words: "If a man loves me, he will keep my word, and my Father will love him, and we will come to him and make our home with him" (John 14:23).[178] The divine Persons "come" to the soul because the Son and the Holy Spirit are sent by the Father to bring the Christian into the trinitarian community as *a son of the Father, in the Son, through the Holy Spirit.*[179]

Thus, in the first place, adoptive filiation is filiation to the Father. This means that in the spiritual life *we can talk things over with him and spend time with him, just as trustingly as a son does with his father.*[180] In the second place, it is participation in the Filiation of the Son that, in turn, gives rise to dealing with him as our brother. We are *children of God, brothers of the Word made flesh.*[181] In the third place, it also implies a personal relationship with the Holy Spirit. Since it is a birth, a supernatural generation as sons of the Father in the Son, divine filiation is given to us "through the coming of the Holy Spirit," and it implies a participation in the same Holy Spirit who proceeds from the Father and the Son as their mutual gift: "*non quomodo natus, sed quomodo datus,*" not as one born, but as one who is given, according to the expression of St. Augustine.[182] As St. Josemaría says (quoting some words from St. Cyril of Alexandria), the Third Person of the most Blessed

---

178. The fact that the Blessed Trinity is present in man does not mean, obviously, that man "contains" God, as if God were circumscribed in a place. One could apply to this supernatural presence what St. Thomas says in relation to the presence of immensity (the presence of God in all creatures): "Spiritual things contain those things in which they are; as the soul contains the body. Hence also God is in things containing them." (St. Thomas Aquinas, *S. Th.*, I, q. 8, a. 1, ad 2).

179. See Ocáriz, *Hijos de Dios en Cristo*, p. 132; idem, *Naturaleza, Gracia y Gloria*, p. 88. This expression indicates that the Son is sent by the Father into the soul so that man might be a son in the Son, through the sending of the Holy Spirit. That is to say, both the Son and the Holy Spirit are sent to the Christian ("invisible missions") to introduce him into the life of the divine processions as an adopted son, but there is an "order" in these missions: for the Son to be sent, the Holy Spirit is sent; or that is to say, through the sending of the Holy Spirit, the Son is also sent. St. Josemaría reflects this mysterious dynamic when he writes, e.g., that the Holy Spirit, *by making us brethren of Christ leads us to God the Father. Conversations*, no. 67.

It's useful to note that this other expression is also usual: "children of the Father through the Son in the Holy Spirit." The meaning of this is that by the sending of the Son-made-man, we have received the Holy Spirit (that is to say, in virtue of the Redemption worked by Christ, the Paraclete has been sent). St. Josemaría hence writes: *Through Christ and in the Holy Spirit, a Christian has access to the intimacy of God the Father. Christ Is Passing By*, no. 116. The two expressions reflect different aspects of the mystery of salvation. We use one or the other as the case requires.

180. *Friends of God*, no. 145. See Luke 11:2; *The Forge*, no. 71. A doctrinal study of the theme, in spiritual harmony with St. Josemaría, is that of Alfredo García Suárez, "La primera persona trinitaria y la filiación divina adoptiva," pp. 69–114.

181. *Christ Is Passing By*, no. 66. See Rom. 8:29.

182. "*Exiit enim, non quomodo natus, sed quomodo datus.*" St. Augustine, *De Trinitate*, V, 14, 15: PL 42, 921.

Trinity "marks the hearts of those who receive him as a seal upon wax [. . .] by the communication of his own life."[183] Through this communication of the Holy Spirit, a Christian becomes a gift by being made a son of the Father in the Son: the gift of the Father to the Son and of the Son to the Father (see Heb. 2:13) in the Holy Spirit. Hence the life proper to a son of God consists in the complete gift of himself: a life of love, "a participation in infinite charity, the Holy Spirit."[184] This comes about with man's free cooperation. To the extent that a Christian seconds the impulses of the Spirit, moved by love to hand himself over to the will of the Father, he becomes "more spiritual" in that he takes on a more intimate relationship with the Spirit. *If we have a constant relationship with the Holy Spirit, we will become spiritual ourselves, we will realize that we are Christ's brothers and children of God, and we will not hesitate to call upon our Father at any time.*[185]

(5) *Children of God in Christ.* A final point to consider is that the life of the children of God is given to us in Christ by means of his sacred humanity. It is sharing in the fullness of grace of Jesus Christ as man and brings with it a sharing in his priesthood.

When the first man sinned, he lost supernatural life and adoptive divine filiation. To this we can add the sins of all others. But "God, who is rich in mercy, out of the great love with which he loved us, even when we were dead through our trespasses, made us alive together with Christ"(Eph. 2:4–5).

> *Adam did not want to be a good son of God; he rebelled. But we also hear the echoing chant of that* felix culpa: *O happy fault* (paschal Praeconium), *which the whole Church will joyfully intone at the Easter vigil. God the Father, in the fullness of time, sent to the world his only begotten Son, to reestablish peace; so that by his redeeming men from sin,* adoptionem filiorum reciperemus, *we might become sons of God* (Gal. 4:5), *freed from the yoke of sin, capable of sharing in the divine intimacy of the Trinity. And so it has become possible for this new man, this new grafting of the children of God*

183. St. Cyril of Alexandria, *Thesaurus de sancta et consubstantiali Trinitate*, 34 (PG 75, 609), quoted by St. Josemaría in *Christ Is Passing By*, no. 134. In chapter six, note 20, we will explain that these words do not mean that the Holy Spirit communicates himself to the Christian as his "form" (it is not a matter of formal causality), but neither is it a merely extrinsic union.

184. *Letter, March 24, 1931*, no. 9 (citing *S. Th.*, II-II, q. 24, a. 7, c.; it is in italics in the text of St. Josemaría.

185. *Christ Is Passing By*, no. 136 (following this it refers to Gal. 4:6 and Rom. 8:15).

> (see Rom. 6:4–5), *to free all creation from disorder, restoring all things in Christ* (see Eph. 1:5–10), *who has reconciled them to God.* (see Col. 1:20)[186]

The divine plan to grant us supernatural filiation was effected through the Incarnation of the Son who *became man in order to bring all men and women to share in the divine life.*[187] Jesus Christ *has raised us to his level, the level of children of God, by coming down to our level, the level of the children of men.*[188]

The Son of God entered our human family by assuming our nature and in so doing "united himself in some fashion with every man."[189] In this way, he can give divine life to all because the Holy Spirit filled his humanity with grace (see John 1:14) and "from his fulness have we all received, grace upon grace" (John 1:16). Grace, or supernatural life that the Paraclete infuses in a Christian, is *gratia Christi*,[190] a participation in the grace of the humanity of the Word that the Holy Spirit communicates, "associating us to the fullness of Jesus Christ."[191] As such we are also made sharers in his priesthood; and it allows us to act as his members for the salvation of men.

Having been made children of God and sharers in the priesthood of Christ (no longer "next to him," or at his side, but "in him"), and having been vitally united to him through his sacred humanity (in a way similar to how the members of the body are united to the head), "in a certain way, we form with Christ and in him, *one same* Son of the Father."[192]

> The whole of divine intimacy is opened to us in him, and without him there can be no sharing in his filiation, because he, Christ (God and man) is that filiation insofar as he is God and he possesses it as man through his union *in Persona*. Christ is the only begotten son of the Father, and we are children of God to the degree that we are Christ himself, *ipse Christus*.[193]

This last expression (which was greatly loved by St. Josemaría as we will see in the next section) places us before the nucleus of his understanding of this mystery.

---

186. Ibid., no. 65.

187. *Letter, January 9, 1932*, no. 29.

188. *Christ Is Passing By*, no. 21.

189. *Gaudium et Spes*, no. 22.

190. See St. Thomas Aquinas, *In IV Sent.*, d. 43, q. 1, a. 2, sol. 1.

191. St. Cyril of Jerusalem, *Catecheses*, 22, 3 as cited in *Christ Is Passing By*, no. 87.

192. Scheeben, *Die Mysterien des Christentums*, p. 318.

193. Ocáriz, "La filiación divina, realidad central en la vida y en la enseñanza de Mons. Escrivá de Balaguer," p. 186.

2.3. The Christian: "Another Christ—Christ Himself"

Contemplating the mystery of adoptive divine filiation leads St. Josemaría to call the Christian "*alter Christus*" and even "*ipse Christus.*" These expressions recur frequently in his writings,[194] and, although there are many precedents in Christian tradition for them, they take on special characteristics in St. Josemaría's preaching. According to Antonio Aranda, author of the most detailed studies on this topic,[195] St. Josemaría's consideration of the Christian as "*alter Christus, ipse Christus*" has its specific origin in his "theological experience,"[196] and in this sense, "it proceeds only in part from the multifaceted Catholic tradition."[197]

2.3.1. "Not Simply Alter Christus, but Ipse Christus"

To call a Christian in the state of grace "another Christ"—*Christianus, alter Christus*—is a rather frequent affirmation in Christian literature.

> Even though literally it is not found in the Fathers, according to a study by R. Gerardi,[198] many authors say that it goes back to the patristic era. For example, Scheeben affirms that "an ancient Father of the Church said: *Christianus alter Christus* ['the Christian, another Christ']. And St. Cyprian wrote (*De idolorum vanitate*, 2): *Quod homo est, esse Christus voluit, ut et homo possit esse, quod Christus est*"[199] ["That which man is, Christ has wanted to be, so that man too can be what Christ is"]. As we can see, the quotation from St. Cyprian does not contain the expression

194. Referring to the Christian as "*ipse Christus*" appears, e.g., in *Furrow*, no. 166; *The Forge*, no. 74; *Christ Is Passing By*, nos. 11, 96, 104, 107, 115, 120, 121, 183, 185; *Friends of God*, no. 6; *Conversations*, no. 58; the homily "A Priest Forever," April 13, 1973, in *In Love with the Church*, London 1989, no. 38; *The Way of the Cross*, Sixth Station and Tenth Station, no. 5. The "identification with Christ" appears already in *Consideraciones espirituales*, Cuenca 1934, where we read: *[the saints] who would not be saints if each of them had not identified himself with Christ* (p. 100). The phrase was then taken up literally as no. 947 of *The Way*. The origin is a note of December 24, 1931, in *Apuntes íntimos*, no. 503; and the same expression—"identification with Christ"—is found in another note of the following day, December 25, 1931, in *Apuntes íntimos*, no. 511. See Rodríguez, *The Way: Critical-Historical Edition, ad loc.*

195. See Aranda, "*El bullir de la sangre de Cristo.*" *Estudio sobre el cristocentrismo del Beato Josemaría Escrivá* (Madrid: Rialp, 2000), pp. 227–254; idem, "En torno al 'alter Christus, ipse Christus,' de S. Josemaría Escrivá," in T. Trigo (ed.), *Dar razón de la esperanza* (Pamplona: Ediciones Universidad de Navarra, 2004), pp. 763–793.

196. Aranda, "*El bullir de la sangre de Cristo,*" p. 283.

197. Ibid.

198. See Renzo Gerardi, "'Alter Christus': La Chiesa, il cristiano, il sacerdote," in *Lateranum* 1 (1981): 116.

199. Scheeben, *Die Mysterien des Christentums*, p. 313.

literally. But closer to the "*alter Christus*" are other words from that same work: "*Quod est Christus erimus christiani, si Christum fuerimus imitati*"[200] ["That which Christ is, we Christians will be, if we have imitated Christ"].

An example of allusion to this expression in patristics can be found in the commentary of Cornelius a Lapide (d. 1637) on Romans 13:14 ("Put on the Lord Jesus Christ") in which he interprets a text of St. John Chrysostom in the following sense:

> *Unde S. Chrysostomus: "induire, ait, Christum, est undique in nobis per sanctimoniam et mansuetudinem Christum conspicuum esse. Homo enim indutus id esse videtur, quod indutus est: appareat itaque in nobis Christus." Christianus ergo quasi viva imago, viva forma, vivus habitus Christi sit oportet, imo sit alter quasi Christus ut in eius vita, gestu, habitu et moribus omnes se Christum videre putent.*[201]

In the masters of spirituality, it is not uncommon to find similar formulas. We will give only one example from the French school of the seventeenth century. St. John Eudes writes that "a Christian is a member or like an extension of Jesus, or better yet, another Jesus."[202] In the twentieth century, Bl. Columba Marmion rather frequently uses the expression "*christianus, alter Christus.*"[203] Another contemporary author, Raoul Plus, explains the meaning here:

> We say: *christianus, alter Christus*, a Christian is another Christ and nothing could be truer. But it is important not to make a mistake here. "Other" here does not mean "different." We are not another Christ different from the true Christ. We are destined to be the only Christ who exists: *Christus facti sumus*, according to St. Augustine. We must not become something different from him; we must be converted into him."[204] We will come back to this Augustinian text again when we speak about the precedents for the use of "*ipse Christus*" to refer to the Christian.

---

200. St. Cyprian, *De idolorum vanitate*, XV: PL 4, 603–604 (in some versions of the text, the word "*imitati*" is reported as "*secuti*," following the Migne edition).

201. Cornelius a Lapide, *Commentaria in Scripturam Sacram*, vol. 18, París 1880, col. 226.

202. St. Jean Eudes, *Le Cœur admirable*, in *Œuvres choisies*, vol. VIII (Paris: Lebrun, 1937), ch. 21, point 3.

203. See Bl. Columba Marmion, *Jesucristo vida del alma* (English edition, *Christ the Life of the Soul*), Barcelona 1955, p. 39.

204. Raoul Plus, *Cristo en nosotros*, Barcelona 1941, p. 2 (French original: *Le Christ en nous*, Toulouse 1922). A 1931 edition of this work is found in the library that St. Josemaría used, next to his bedroom, in Rome.

> Recent papal magisterium frequently applies the expression "*alter Christus*" to the priest. But it also applies it to every Christian. "If every baptized person is *alter Christus*, the priest is such by a new title [. . .]."[205]

The texts we have quoted offer us a guide to understand the meaning of "*christianus, alter Christus*" in the spiritual tradition. Speaking in this way emphasizes that a Christian is at the same time human and divine, like Christ, because he shares in his human and divine natures.[206] We can say that the Christian is "another Christ" given that, having been anointed in baptism and in confirmation, he partakes of the priesthood of Christ and cooperates in the redemption of human beings. But, even more precisely, we call the Christian "another Christ" when he, in fact, reflects the life of Christ in his behavior, and when he exerts himself to put his priesthood into practice in his apostolic mission. This is the sense of the expression we find in St. Josemaría. Kurt Koch observes that

> Escrivá deliberately uses this terminology that some lines of Catholic tradition had reserved to the ordained priesthood. Precisely in this way, he wanted to express the fact that all the baptized and confirmed are called to holiness and that in the Church there is no first or second class sanctity.[207]

St. Josemaría writes, in effect, that the Christian is *not simply* alter Christus: *another Christ, but* ipse Christus: *Christ himself!*[208] This concept

---

205. St. John Paul II, Address (May 1, 1988). See idem, Homily (July 2, 1980); Address (March 13, 1982); Homily (June 21, 1987).

206. There is a certain analogy between the supernatural elevation of the human person and the mystery of the Incarnation of the Word. This mystery, in effect, is the assumption of a human nature by the second Person of the Blessed Trinity. With this *assumptio*, Christ's human nature is *divinized*, introduced into the Blessed Trinity as the human nature of the Son, and is transformed into an instrument united to the Person of the Word in order to carry out our salvation. Something analogous takes place in the mystery of the supernatural elevation of man. St. Thomas does not hesitate to describe it with the same term, *assumptio*: "*Assumptio quae fit per gratiam adoptionis, terminatur ad quandam participationem divinae naturae.*" St. Thomas Aquinas, *S. Th.*, III, q. 3, a. 4, ad 3; see *Comp. Theol.*, II, 4. Of course, he does not use the word in the same sense, since in being elevated the human person is not *assumed* as is the human nature of Christ which is united hypostatically to the divine nature. But we could say that there is in the Christian an "impression" of this supreme mystery which enables us to say that he is "another Christ." We can contemplate "the Incarnation of the Son of God [. . .] considered as the *assumption* of the Human Nature of Christ by the Divine Person, as the *one and transcendent summit* of the supernatural elevation of the human." Ocáriz, *Naturaleza, Gracia y Gloria*, p. 82.

207. Kurt Koch, *Kontemplativ mitten in der Welt. Die Wiederentdeckung des Taufpriestertums beim seligen Josefmaría Escrivá*, in César Ortiz (dir.), *Josemaría Escrivá. Profile einer Gründergestalt*, Köln 2002, pp. 318–319.

208. *Christ Is Passing By*, no. 104.

is not new.[209] In a certain sense, we could say that it is present in many authors who have felt the need to emphasize that the Christian is not only "similar" to Christ, but, if in the state of grace, "is Christ." This can easily be seen because man's supernatural life is not distinct from that of the Lord, but is rather a participation in the very life of Christ's sacred humanity, and because, in some way, Christ is present in him. "It is no longer I who live, but Christ who lives in me" (Gal. 2:20), writes St. Paul. Echoing these ideas, St. Josemaría writes: *Christ is alive in Christians.*[210] Christ is present in a Christian. Hence, we can affirm that "a Christian is Christ."

The Christian's relation to Christ should not be thought of as mere adherence of the disciple to the master, nor as that of a follower to a human leader. Certainly, the Christian has to follow Jesus in response to his invitation—"Follow me" (Matt. 9:9), says the Lord—and the Christian has to take Christ as his model. But the biblical meaning of these terms shows that following Christ is more than simply imitation.[211] It implies a mysterious communion of life that exceeds the parameters of any simple moral relationship, no matter how deep it may be. It does not consist in merely applying the teachings of Jesus to one's own life either; nor is it limited to the Christian's decision to give himself over to sharing Jesus' own fate. Indeed, it embraces all these ambitions, but at the same time it goes further: it implies living his same supernatural life. And that is why St. Josemaría speaks of "identification with Christ" and says that the secret of the Christian life consists in "following Christ to the point of identifying oneself with him." Here is a text where he describes the nucleus of sanctity and apostolate:

> *To follow Christ—that is the secret. We must accompany him so closely that we come to live with him, like the first Twelve did; so closely, that we become identified with him. Soon we will be able to say, provided we haven't put obstacles in the way of grace, that we have put on, have clothed ourselves with our Lord Jesus Christ* (see Rom. 13:14). *Our Lord is then reflected in our behavior, as in a mirror. If the mirror is as it ought to be, it will capture our Savior's most*

209. See, e.g., the following text of Raoul Plus: "*Mais 'autre Christ,' le baptisé peut et doit l'être par bien mieux que cela: par une identification avec Lui qui devrait tendre à devenir la plus intime possible*" (*Dieu en nous*, Toulouse 1919, p. 54). This author cites in his support Ferdinand Prat who, commenting on Gal. 2:20, speaks of the "*identité mystique*" of the Christian with Christ (Raoul Plus does not indicate where, but he is surely referring to the work *La Teologia di San Paolo*, Torino 1961, vol. II, p. 289).

210. *Christ Is Passing By*, no. 103.

211. See Gerhard Kittel and Gerhard Friedrich, *Grande Lessico del Nuovo Testamento*, vol. I (Brescia, 1965), cols. 574–581; Gilbert Bouwman, *L'imitazione di Cristo nella Bibbia* (Rome, 1968), p. 91.

> *lovable face without distorting it or making a caricature of it; and then other people will have an opportunity of admiring him and following him.*[212]

A commentary by Fernando Ocáriz will help to penetrate the density of these words: "The way for us to enter into intimacy with the Father and the Son and the Holy Spirit is to follow Christ. But in such a way that we not only imitate him, but we identify ourselves with him. Only in this way does the Lord become the firstborn among many brethren without ceasing to be the only begotten of the Father. We are not sons of the Father, each one of us on his own, so to speak. We are sons of the Father because we are Christ, without ceasing to be our individual selves."[213]

From the above quotations, we can see that St. Josemaría employs the expressions "*ipse Christus*" and "identification with Christ" in two interconnected senses that we should distinguish in order to understand them better: (1) as a fact derived from baptism, and (2) as a process that demands correspondence to grace.

The first interpretation is factual: a Christian has been *identified with Christ, through Baptism.*[214] The transformation worked by baptismal grace is a christification that makes the person a son of God in Christ and can be called "identification with Christ." The second interpretation is a process: St. Josemaría speaks of this identification as taking on the virtues of Christ, his same sentiments, intentions, and desires. He says: *But we have to unite ourselves to him through faith, letting his life show forth in ours to such an extent that each Christian is not simply* alter Christus: *another Christ, but* ipse Christus: *Christ himself!*[215]

Consequently, for St. Josemaría a Christian "is" *ipse Christus* through baptism. But at the same time "he ought to be" *ipse Christus* through his free correspondence to grace, that is, through his response to Love. For St. Thomas, "through love [of friendship] the lover becomes one with the loved one."[216] And in this sense one can say that the friend is "*alter ipse.*"[217]

---

212. *Friends of God*, no. 299. An interesting and integrated commentary on the teaching of St. Josemaría on the notion of the imitation of Christ as identification with him can be seen in Paul Olivier, "La filiation divine: vocation et liberté," in Antonio Malo (ed.), *La grandezza della vita quotidiana*, vol. III, pp. 45–48.

213. Ocáriz, "La filiación divina, realidad central en la vida y en la enseñanza de Mons. Escrivá de Balaguer," p. 187. The last words are taken from Michael Schmaus. We will cite the text in a subsequent footnote.

214. *Letter, January 9, 1932*, no. 86. See *Christ Is Passing By*, no. 120.

215. *Christ Is Passing By*, no. 104. See *The Forge*, no. 74.

216. St. Thomas Aquinas, *In III Sent.*, d. 27, q. 1, a. 1, c.

217. See ibid.; *S. Th.*, I-II, q. 28, a. 1, c; q. 77, a. 4, ad 4; *In VIII Ethic.*, lect. 1, no. 6; etc.

Friendship with Christ leads to identification with him. This identification, which begins with the infusion of sanctifying grace, grows through love in a person who is docile to the Holy Spirit. *Docile to the Holy Spirit, the image of Christ will be formed more and more fully in us, and we will be brought closer every day to God the Father.* For whoever are led by the Spirit of God, they are the children of God (Rom. 8:14).[218] St. Josemaría emphasizes the need for cooperation on the part of a Christian in this process.

We cannot stay still. We must keep going ahead toward the goal St. Paul marks out: It is not I who live, it is Christ who lives in me (Gal. 2:20). *This is a high and very noble ambition, this identification with Christ, this holiness. But there is no other way if we are to be consistent with the divine life God has sown in our souls in Baptism.*[219]

In order to avoid misunderstanding, at the beginning of this chapter we felt it necessary to state that "identification with Christ" does not imply any confusion between Christ and a Christian. Now we can see that such is the case based on the quoted texts. In St. Josemaría, as we have already explained, it is clear that Jesus and the Christian are two distinct persons. Jesus Christ is the second Person of the Trinity; the Christian is a human person and besides, a sinner. There is an infinite distance between them. Nevertheless, this distinction does not keep us from speaking about a certain identification. *With all our personal defects and limitations, we are other Christs, Christ himself.*[220] We can say with Schmaus that "a Christian is Christ without ceasing to be himself."[221]

2.3.2. Basis and Precedents for This Expression

It is nothing new to affirm that a Christian "is Christ" or that he has to "identify himself with Christ." This was not invented by St. Josemaría, as we will see by means of several examples. When he expresses himself in this way, he is reflecting the Christian mystery, faithful to the sources of Revelation, and in continuity with tradition. What is "new"—if we may speak in

218. *Christ Is Passing By*, no. 135.

219. Ibid., no. 58.

220. Ibid., no. 106.

221. Michael Schmaus, *Katholische Dogmatik*, vol. 3, part 2, München 1951, S. 53. As basis for this affirmation, the author refers to St. Augustine, *Enarrationes in Psalmos*, 17, 51, and 90, as well as to *Sermo* II, 1 (according to the enumeration of Migne: PL 36, 154 and PL 37, 1159, respectively).

such terms—is that he preaches identification with Christ to all Christians, something that shows it is accessible in ordinary life, and teaches everyone to base his or her spiritual life on the awareness of being a son or a daughter of God: of being Christ.

In contemporary works of systematic theology, these expressions are not used that often. This might be due to the fact that, on the one hand, as already mentioned, divine filiation has not been that present in the theological studies of past centuries. On the other hand, we must remember that some ancient and recent authors have spoken about a Christian's union with Christ in a way that creates confusion.[222] And since this could cast a shadow on the appropriateness of these expressions, we want to show in greater detail their roots in Sacred Scripture and in the spiritual tradition of the Church.

In the New Testament, union with Jesus Christ is a vital union, like that of the vine and the branches (see John 15:1–7), and this implies a certain mutual connection. As the vine is present in the branches, and the branches are present in the vine, so too the Lord is in his members and they are in him. Christ gives them supernatural life and they receive it from him, allowing them to bear fruit in the measure of their union with the vine: "Abide in me and I in you [. . .]. He who abides in me, and I in him, he it is that bears much fruit" (John 15:4–5).

The reality signified by this image takes on its full import in light of the words that the Lord uses to compare the union of his disciples with him, to his own union with the Father in the heart of the Blessed Trinity: "I am in my Father, and you in me, and I in you" (John 14:20). We can say that this mystery is made "tangible" in Sacred Scripture: "He who eats my flesh and drinks my blood abides in me, and I in him. As the living Father sent me

---

222. It is worth recalling that on this subject there have been some errors as, for instance, the following proposition attributed to Eckhart and condemned by Pope John XXII in 1329: "We transform ourselves totally into God and we change ourselves into him. In a way similar to how in the sacrament the bread is changed into the Body of Christ; in such a way I convert myself into him, who himself makes me into a single thing with him, not a similar thing: because living by God it is true that there is no distinction at all" (DS 960). It is not clear that this proposition, taken, as it seems, from the preaching of Eckhart in German, really reflects his thought, which is much more nuanced in his writings in Latin. See documented article of Félix Vernet, "Eckhart," in *Dictionnaire de Théologie Catholique*, 4/2 (1924): cols. 2057–2081. In any case, it is erroneous to affirm that there is no distinction at all between the Christian and Christ. In the twentieth century, the Magisterium had to go out to meet other errors in this sphere, such as "*panchristism*," which dissolves the being of the Christian into that of Christ. See Pius XII, on the work of Karl Pelz, *Der Christ als Christus*: AAS 32 (1940): 502 and AAS 33 (1941): 24. On other confusions, see Pius XII, Encyclical *Mystici Corporis* (June 29, 1943): AAS 35 (1943): 234 (DS 3816).

and I live because of the Father, so he who eats me will live because of me" (John 6:56–57).[223]

> Jesus Christ is substantially present in the Eucharist with his humanity and he comes to the Christian who receives him. This presence lasts as long as the eucharistic species are present. When these disappear, the substance of his humanity ceases being present in the Christian. Consequently, this mode of presence cannot be the way in which a Christian "is Christ" at every moment. There must be another way, a different way (a presence that is not from the substance of his humanity, but instead by his action, as we will see later).[224]

The teaching on union with Christ and his presence in the Christian is found especially in St. John's Gospel. But we also discover particular aspects of it in St. Paul's letters. In order to show the intimate compenetration of the Christian with Christ, St. Paul frequently uses the expression "in Christ Jesus," or an equivalent expression, appearing more than 150 times in his epistles.[225] Christians have been "created in Christ Jesus" (Eph. 2:10), chosen in Christ (see Eph. 1:4) and "called in the Lord" (Phil. 3:14). "They

---

223. In fact, St. Hillary comments on the text "I am in my Father and you in me and I in you," referring it to the Eucharist: "He is in the Father by his divine nature, while we are in him through his human birth and he is in us by the celebration of the sacrament [the Eucharist]. 'The Father who lives has sent me, and I live through the Father; in the same way, he who eats me will live through me.' He lives then, by the Father, and in the same way as he lives by the Father, we live by his flesh [. . .]. Christ, by his flesh, lives among us, carnal beings, so that by him we can come to live in a way similar to the way he lives by the Father" (*De Trinitate*, 8,13–16).

224. As man or by his humanity, Jesus is substantially present only in heaven and in the Eucharist, not everywhere, as he is by his Divinity. There is a classic formula: "*Christus secundum humanitatem in coelo est; secundum divinitatem, ubique*." Hugh of St. Victor, *De Sacramentis*, lib. II, part. I, c. 13; see Peter Lombard, *Sent. lib. IV*, d. 10, no. 2. Already in the Second Council of Nicaea (787) the Church rejected as heretical the theory that the humanity of Christ is not circumscribed: "If anyone does not admit that Christ, our God, is circumscribed, let him be condemned." Session VIII: DS 606. The error that the humanity of the Lord is substantially present everywhere has been designated with the name of "ubiquism" of the humanity of Christ. See Albert Michel, "Ubiquisme," in *Dictionnaire de Théologie Catholique*, 15/2 (1950): col. 2042. In this article the author refers above all to the Lutheran error of "ubiquity" (col. 2034 ff.), in regard to the Eucharistic presence, which is also considered under the heading *Hypostatique* (*Union*) of vol. VII, cols. 542–549. Behind these ideas there is an evident error in regard to the "*communicatio idiomatum*" in Christ, which leads one to attribute to the human nature something which is proper to the divine nature. To a great extent this is due to not distinguishing clearly between nature and person.

225. Adolf Deissmann verified that the expression appears 164 times in the Pauline epistles (in all of them except for the Letter to Titus): see *Die neutestamentliche Formel "In Christo Iesu,"* (Marburg, 1892). The formula doesn't always have a *mystical* sense (i.e., one referring to the mystery of the union of the Christian with Christ), but it does have this meaning in most cases. For more on this expression, see Alfred Wikenhauser, *Die Christusmystik des Apostels Paulus* (Freiburg, 1956), 2.

live" in Christ (see Rom. 6:11; Gal. 2:20), and "they are" in Christ Jesus (see 1 Cor. 1:30; 2 Cor. 5:17; Rom. 16:7–11; Gal. 3:28). He likewise affirms that Christ "is" in the Christian (see Rom. 8:10; 2 Cor. 13:5; Col. 1:27) and "he is formed" in him (Gal. 4:19). On other occasions, this union is expressed with the terms "with Christ," "through him," and "for him." Thus, for example, "buried with Christ" (Rom. 6:4; Col. 2:12), "alive and risen with Christ" (Eph. 2:5–6), saved by Christ (see Rom. 5:9), created for him (see 1 Cor. 8:6; Col. 1:16), made children of God through Christ (see Eph. 1:5), etc. Finally, at other times he describes the union of a Christian with Christ by means of the image of the head and the body: Christians are "members of Christ" (1 Cor. 6:15; 12:27), "body of Christ" (Eph. 1:13; 4:12; 5:30; Col. 1:24; Rom. 12:5).[226] The presence of Christ in a Christian implied in this vital union is the nucleus of the "mystery" preached joyfully by the apostle: that "Christ [be] in you, the hope of glory" (Col. 1:27).

Let us now consider the patristic tradition. We recall in the first place, following chronological order, what was written by St. Ignatius of Antioch to the Christians in the second century: "You are bearers of Christ."[227] From the context, it is clear that he is not referring only to the moment of having received the Eucharist. Nor is he limiting himself to making the Christian a mere messenger of his Master's teachings. He says that the Christian is a "bearer of Christ" because Jesus is present in him, not as he is in the

226. These texts are just some examples without pretending to be exhaustive. As Fitzmyer points out, St. Paul mainly uses four prepositions to indicate distinct aspects of the influence of Christ in the Christian: "*dia*," "*eis*," "*syn*" and "*en*." The first ("*dia*" = by or through) generally expresses the mediation of Christ in propositions whose subject is the Father, as e.g., 1 Thess. 4:14; 5:9, and Rom. 1:5. The second ("*eis*" = in, with the idea of movement and insertion) is found above all in the context of the faith and of baptism in Christ, and indicates the beginning of the condition of the Christian "in Christ" (see 1 Cor. 10:2): going from his original state "in Adam" (see 1 Cor. 15:22) and "in the flesh" (Rom. 7:5), the believer is introduced formally "into Christ" through faith and baptism: *eis Christon* signifies therefore the movement of incorporation into Christ. The third preposition ("*syn*" = with) means either the identification of the Christian with the redemptive acts of the life of Christ (suffering with him; being crucified with him, dying with him; being buried with him; rising with him; being glorified with him; reigning with him), or the association of the Christian with Christ in future glory, his destiny of being "with Christ," "with the Lord" (see 1 Thess. 3:17; Rom. 6:8 and 8:32; 2 Cor. 4:14). Finally, the preposition "*en*" (= in) has been interpreted in the sense of finding oneself in a "space," so that "in Christ" means the immersion of the Christian in the milieu or the spiritual atmosphere, so to speak, of the glorified Christ and the Holy Spirit. The most frequent use of the expression "in Christ" is that which indicates the close union between Christ and the Christian: an inclusion or incorporation which means a certain symbiosis or community of life (see 2 Cor. 5:17); this vital union is also expressed with the formula "Christ in me." See Gal. 2:20; 2 Cor. 13:5; Rom. 8:10; Col. 1:27; Eph 3:17, and Joseph A. Fitzmyer, *Teología de San Pablo* (Madrid 1975), pp. 175–178.

227. St. Ignatius of Antioch, *Letter to the Ephesians*, 9, 2.

Eucharist (substantially), nor through his doctrine alone, but in another way, the explanation of which is left as an open-ended task for theology.

Something similar can be said about many patristic texts in different eras, both in the East and in the West. They affirm that Christ is present in the Christian and even that the Christian "is Christ." These passages have frequently been understood in a rather weak way, as if referring to a presence of the doctrine of Christ, or as a reflection of his virtues. But this reduction does not do justice to the force of the texts. Let us quote a few that will allow us to see that the expressions "*ipse Christus*" and "identification with Christ" move along the same line.

Commenting on the words "Behold, your son" (John 19:26) that Jesus addresses to his Mother from the Cross, Origen (d. ca. 255) writes, "If Mary did not have other children besides Jesus and Jesus said to his Mother: *Behold, your son*, and not *behold, another son* it is as if he were to say: *here is the Jesus to whom you have given life*. In effect, whoever is perfect, does not live for himself, but Christ lives in him (see Gal. 2:20). And since Christ lives in him, Jesus can say to Mary: *Behold, your son, Christ*."[228] This ancient text admirably testifies to the conviction that Christ is present in the Christian. (Evidently for Origen, St. John represents every disciple of Christ.)

St. Cyril of Jerusalem (d. ca. 386) considers that there is an image of Christ in the baptized person that is not separated from the exemplar, but rather one that exists precisely because the Christian is a *sharer in Christ*. Hence, he can be called "christ" without further need of any other name: "Baptized in Christ and clothed with Christ, you have been made like unto the Son of God. Because God predestined us to adoption and made us conform to the glorious body of Christ. Hence, made sharers in Christ, in all truth you call yourselves christs. And God himself said of you: do not touch my christs. You were converted into Christ when you received the seal of the Holy Spirit."[229] The basis for calling a Christian Christ ultimately is not the likeness, but an even deeper reality from which the likeness stems.

St. Gregory of Nyssa (d. 394) refers to this reality using the example of St. Paul who was granted a very intense awareness of the presence of Christ in him: "He imitated him in such a perfect way that he revealed in his person a reproduction of the Lord because through his great diligence in imitating

228. Origen, *Comm. in Ev. Ioann.*, I, 6.

229. St. Cyril of Jerusalem, *Catecheses*, 21 [Mystagogica 3], 1.

him he was so transformed into the exemplar that it no longer appeared to be Paul who spoke, but Christ. He himself, completely conscious of his own perfection could say: *You will have the proof that you seek: that Christ dwells in me*. And he also says: *I live, but it is not I, it is Christ who lives in me*."[230] An attentive reading of this quotation allows us to see that this text does not state that the presence of Christ in Paul consists only in his imitating Christ, but that in imitating him he reveals Christ's presence in him.

The author of the ancient homily "Sancto et magno Sabbato"[231] tries to imagine the dialogue between Jesus, who descends to the realm of the dead after his death on the Cross, and Adam, as the representative of every man awaiting liberation from sin and the new life in Christ. Thus, Jesus says to Adam, "I order you: O sleeper, to awake. I did not create you to be held a prisoner in hell. Rise up from among the dead, for I am the life of the dead. Rise up, work of my hands, you who were created in my image. Rise, let us leave this place, for you are in me and I am in you; together we form only one person and we cannot be separated."[232] These last words express a mysterious compenetration with Christ through which he is present in the Christian and the Christian in Christ.

St. Cyril of Alexandria (d. 444), commenting on the words "I am the vine, you are the branches" (John 15:5), considers the missions of the Son and the Holy Spirit, and speaks openly about a presence of Christ as man in the Christian. He writes, "Those who are united to him and inserted into his person, are like his branches and, in sharing in the Holy Spirit, they share in his very nature (for the Spirit of Christ unites us to him). The bond of those who are tied to the vine consists in a bond of will and desire. On the other hand, the union of the vine with us is a union of love and of presence [. . .]. And the way in which we are in Christ and Christ is in us is made clear by the evangelist John as he says: 'This is how we know that we are in him and he in us: in that he has given us his Spirit.'"[233] In other words, in some way, the Holy Spirit who is sent makes Christ present as man in those to whom he gives his grace.

---

230. St. Gregory of Nyssa, *De perfecta christiani forma*. This text is currently found in the Liturgy of the Hours under the title "*Christianus alter Christus*" (Monday of the Twelfth week of Ordinary Time, *Ad Officium lectionis*).

231. Found in PG 43, 439 ff. The homily was erroneously attributed to St. Epiphanius of Salamis. It is usually dated back to the fourth century (see Johannes Quasten, *Patrología*, vol. II, Madrid 1962, p. 413).

232. *Hom. in Sancto et magno Sabbato*: PG 43, 462.

233. St. Cyril of Alexandria, *In Ev. Ioann.*, 10, 2.

St. Augustine (d. 430), who so deeply expresses the mystery of the mystical Body ("*Christus totus, caput et corpus*"),[234] insists that Christ is present in the Christian and calls him simply "Christ": "We congratulate you and we give thanks because we have become not only Christians but Christ. Let us be in wonder, let us leap for joy, for we have become Christ."[235] In another place he writes, "Shedding his blood, the Immaculate Lamb redeemed us. He incorporated us into himself, making us his members so that in him we might also be Christ."[236] And commenting on John 17:26, he states, "'I in them,' as if he were to say: because I myself am in them. In a way, he is in us as in his temple. In another way because we are him [*quia nos ipse sumus*] insofar as by [Christ] becoming man to be our Head, we are his Body."[237]

Let us continue these patristic testimonies with some examples from the later theological literature. These come from the great masters of the spiritual life who were well known to Josemaría Escrivá. St. Thomas fits into a separate category and we will refer to him extensively in the next section.[238]

The following text from *The Life of Christ* of Nicholas Cabasilas (1320–1391 ca.) honors the oriental tradition. "[Union with Christ] is beyond any union that we might try to express in earthly symbols. That is why the Sacred Books make use of many symbols to signify this union, since no one sufficed: the guest and the house; the branches and vine; the betrothal; the head and the members. None of these is able to express this union entirely since they are all incapable of grasping its exact content [. . .]. The members are united to the head, they live bound to it, and being separated would mean death. But Christians live even more united to Christ than to their own head, and they live more truly from him than from the union that binds them to their head. We find an example of this in the Holy Martyrs who joyfully confronted death, and not wanting to hear about separation from Christ, they joyfully offered their head and members to the executioner

234. St. Augustine, *Sermo* 25, 7. *In Epistolam Ioannis ad Parthos*, 1, 2 (PL 35, 1979).

235. "*Ergo gratulemur et agamus gratias, non solum nos christianos factos esse, sed Christum* [. . .]. *Admiramini, gaudete, Christus facti sumus*" (idem, *In Ioann. Ev.*, 21, 8: PL 35, 1568).

236. "*Tamquam agnus immaculatus fuso sanguine suo redimens nos, concorporans nos sibi, faciens nos membra sua, ut in illo et nos Christus essemus*" (idem, *Enarr. in Psalmos*, 26, 2, 2: PL 36, 200).

237. "*Ideo subiunxit,* et ego in ipsis*; tamquam diceret, quoniam ego sum et in ipsis. Aliter enim est in nobis tamquam in templo suo; aliter autem quia et nos ipse sumus, cum secundum id quod ut caput nostrum esset, homo factus est, corpus eius sumus*" (idem, *In Ioann. Ev.*, 111, 6: PL 35, 1925).

238. For more on divine filiation and configuration with Christ in the spiritual life according to the thought of St. Thomas, see the excellent chapter by Jean-Pierre Torrell, *St. Thomas Aquinas, Spiritual Master* (Washington, DC: CUA Press, 1998), pp. 125–152.

[. . .]. But there is something still more admirable. Is there something more intimately united than a person with himself? Well, even this intimacy is far from that union. Every one of the holy souls is united and is identical to itself, and yet it is more united to the Savior than to itself."[239]

If Cabasilas experiences the limits of any metaphor when speaking about union with Christ, the same happens to St. Teresa of Ávila and St. John of the Cross (sixteenth century). They cannot find the words to express what they contemplate. The reader can verify this without need for us to include here the lengthy texts that refer to this mystery.[240]

In the seventeenth century, we find precedents of the expressions that St. Josemaría uses in the authors of the "French school." For Jean-Jacques Olier, "a Christian is Christ alive on earth."[241] St. John Eudes reflects an idea that is very common in this school of spirituality: "The Son of God decided to consummate and complete in us all the states and mysteries of his life. He wants to carry out in us the mysteries of his Incarnation, his birth, his hidden life, being formed in us and once again being born in our souls through the holy sacraments of Baptism and the Holy Eucharist and enabling us to live a spiritual, interior life hidden with him in God."[242]

We conclude this exposition of testimonies with two texts from authors contemporary to St. Josemaría who reveal the difficulty theologians faced in finding adequate terms to define union with Christ and his presence in the Christian. Émile Mersch states, "The Lord has revealed that between the Incarnate Word and the Christian there is something more than a union of love, even though it is ardent; there is something more than a relation of likeness, no matter how accurate it might be; there is something more than dependence, in spite of the fact that it is complete [. . .]; more than the always precarious inclusion of the members in an organism; more than a moral union, however extraordinarily intimate it might be. There is a physical union, we might say, as long as we do not put this word at the same level as simple natural unions. It is a real union in any case, an ontological union.

239. Nicolas Cabasilas, *De vita in Christo*, lib. 1. The text in Greek and in French (*La vie en Christ*) is found in "Sources chrétiennes," 361, Paris, 1989. In Spanish it was published by Ediciones Rialp (*La vida en Cristo*, Madrid, 1952), in a collection of books of spirituality ("Patmos") that St. Josemaría habitually made use of.

240. See St. Teresa of Jesus, *Vida*, c. 18, 2.14; St. John of the Cross, *Llama de amor viva*, 1 (among many other texts, in both cases).

241. "Un chrétien c'est le Christ vivant sur la terre" in Michel Dupuy, *Vivre pour Dieu en Jésus-Christ* (*textes de Mr. Olier*), Paris, 1995, p. 140.

242. St. John Eudes, *Le Royaume de Jésus* (1637), in *Œuvres choisies*, vol. I, *La vie et le royaume de Jésus dans les âmes chrétiennes* (Paris: Lethielleux, 1931), 3, 4.

Or better yet, for the traditional terms in this case are the most adequate: a mystical, transcendent, supernatural union that, in unity and in reality, is beyond the formulas that can be offered, and that only God can make known as only he can accomplish it."[243] On the other hand, according to Michael Schmaus, "we can call the union between Christ and Christians a *physical-dynamic* union. But we must not forget that Christ and Christians are not fused into one sole nature; this point is expressed when we call it a *physical-accidental* union. But then, it does not sufficiently emphasize that we are dealing here with a personal encounter. And if we call it a *personal-dynamic* communion, we do not accentuate sufficiently its vigor and intimacy. It would give the impression that we are dealing with a *moral* union; and that is certainly true because it is a communion of intentions and consequently, it has a very real character. But it is more than that because it is a participation in the life of Jesus Christ. Because of this, some theologians call it an *organic* union, but this runs the danger of being interpreted as a natural process and does not express the consistency and substantiality of the human *I*. It could suggest the idea that Christ and Christians are replete with the same current of celestial life, while in reality each continues to have his own life, with that of the Christian being a participation in the life of Christ. All these expressions then, have their pros and cons. Some accentuate the union and intimacy, but they place in danger the personal character. Others emphasize the personal character, but put at risk the intimacy. Perhaps it would be better to choose a word adapted to express its singularity. We might call it a *mystical-sacramental* unity though not using the word "mystical" in the sense of having a special experience of Christ, but rather of signifying the mysterious nature of this union: the union between Christ and Christians is a mystery. And this fact is stressed by denoting such a union as mystical-sacramental. A Christian is himself insofar as he exists in Christ and is independent and sovereign [. . .]. This is in essence the profound mystery of the Christian."[244]

In our opinion, these texts suffice to show that calling a Christian "*ipse Christus*" is not a pious exaggeration. They are examples taken from an uninterrupted spiritual tradition throughout the history of the Church. It stems more from the mystical experience of union with Christ and his presence in the Christian than from theological research. St. Josemaría adds to

243. Émile Mersch, *Le Corps Mystique du Christ* (Paris: Desclée de Brouwer, 1936), vol. II, pp. 376–377.
244. Schmaus, *Katholische Dogmatik*, vol. 2, Part 2, p. 53.

this tradition his own experience: that being a son of God is "to be Christ." He does not affirm anything new, but with his testimony, he corroborates the validity of this way of expressing the Christian mystery.

Being aware that this profound union with Christ is not reserved to a few souls, he proposes it in simple language and with living formulas that can be universally understood. The best way to show this would be to reproduce his homily entitled "Christ's Presence in Christians"[245] in its entirety. However, let us limit ourselves to quoting a few lines and invite the reader to meditate on the entire text at his or her leisure.

> Christ is alive in the Christian [. . .]. *That is why a Christian should live as Christ lived, making the affections of Christ his own* [. . .] *letting his life be manifested in ours to such an extent that each Christian is not simply* alter Christus*: another Christ, but* ipse Christus*: Christ himself!* [. . .] *The Christian knows himself to be grafted onto Christ through Baptism; empowered to fight for Christ through Confirmation, called to act in the world sharing the royal, prophetic and priestly role of Christ; made one and the same thing with Christ through the Eucharist, the sacrament of unity and love. And so, like Christ, he has to live for other men, loving each and every one around him and indeed all humanity* [. . .]. *With all our personal defects and limitations, we are other Christs, Christ himself, called too to serve all men* [. . .] *But to be* ipse Christus, *we must* see ourselves in him. *It's not enough to have a general idea of the spirit of Jesus' life; we have to learn the details of his life and his woldview* [. . .] *Thus, living in a Christian way among our equals, in a natural way consistent with our faith, we will be* Christ present among men.[246]

In summary, for St. Josemaría, being a son or a daughter of God is "to be Christ" because "Christ lives in the Christian," "he is present in the Christian." This presence is given by the grace of baptism. But when the Christian "lets Christ's life be manifested in his," when he strives "to live the life of Christ" in a conscious and free way, cooperating with his redeeming mission by exercising his priesthood, then the seed of the baptismal grace matures, and we can then say that he is *ipse Christus*, and speak about an identification with Jesus Christ which is compatible with being a distinct person.

---

245. See *Christ Is Passing By*, nos. 102–116.

246. Ibid., nos. 103, 104, 106, 107, 112.

In the first place, the reason why a Christian can be called *ipse Christus* is because Christ is in some way present in him; in the second place, because (beginning with his presence), he allows Christ to act through him, thereby exercising Christ's priesthood. The most basic aspect is the first one. We will study this in the following section.

2.4. Christ's Presence in the Christian: A Theological Explanation

St. Josemaría does not explain theologically what constitutes the presence of Christ in the Christian through grace. But from his texts we can deduce that:

1. He does not speak solely about Christ's presence as God, but *also as man* or through his humanity;
2. It is about a *permanent presence*, not limited to the moment of receiving the Most Holy Eucharist;[247]
3. It is *not a substantial presence*, that is, presence of the substance of Christ's humanity. But neither can it be reduced to a likeness to Christ derived from imitating him, even though certainly it is a presence that impels us to imitate him; and
4. It is a *presence of the "life of Christ" and of his action*, and not only of the knowledge of Christ or of the love we have for him, even though it is carried out through this knowledge and love, and is nourished by them.

Keeping these elements in mind, we can seek different theological explanations for this presence of Christ in the Christian. What we propose now is inspired by St. Thomas. We will make use of his teachings especially in regard to this question for two motives. The first motive is that in the mystery of the Christian's union with Christ, we find a direct reference to the notion of participation: through his Incarnation, the Son of God has willed to *participate* with all men in human nature; and the Christian has been made a *participant* in the divine nature by means of Christ and in Christ. Moreover, it is well known that the notion of participation is central to the thought of St. Thomas. The second motive is

247. In the Eucharist "there is contained truly, really, and substantially the body and blood together with the soul and divinity of our Lord Jesus Christ, and, therefore, the entire Christ" (the Council of Trent, *Session XIII: Canones de ss. Eucharistiae sacramento*, can. 1: DS 1651).

that St. Josemaría's message on this matter is in keeping with the doctrine of the Angelic Doctor for he speaks about adoptive filiation as *participation in the filiation of the Word*,[248] of grace as *participation in the divine nature*,[249] and of charity—expressly quoting St. Thomas—as *participation in the infinite love which is the Holy Spirit.*[250]

Our thesis is that the doctrine of St. Thomas allows us to affirm a presence of Christ in the Christian that has the four characteristics listed above, and that this presence is the most basic reason for being able to affirm that the Christian is "Christ himself." It seems to us that when St. Josemaría says that a Christian is *ipse Christus*, above all he is saying that Christ is present in the Christian, but also that it is necessary for the Christian to want to allow Christ to act through him. Then we could more precisely say that the Christian is "Christ himself."

We reiterate that the theological explanation we will now propose is solely one possible way of illustrating this point in St. Josemaría's teaching.

Sacred Scripture shows us that we have been created "in Christ," raised to the status of being children of God "in Christ," and also redeemed "in Christ." These are different divine works, but they are intrinsically ordered among themselves: man has been created in Christ insofar as Word, so as to be elevated to the supernatural life in Christ insofar as Son, and born again in Christ, God-made-man, in order to recover the life he had lost through sin. This is the path described in the Prologue of St. John's Gospel: "In the beginning was the Word [. . .]. All things were made through him [. . .]. To all who received him [. . .] he gave power to become children of God [. . .]. And the Word became flesh [. . .]. And from his fulness have we all received, grace upon grace" (John 1:1–16).

Creation, elevation and supernatural rebirth are man's way of "participating" in God's own Being and in his intimate Life. And since they are carried out "in Christ," they entail a certain presence of Christ in the Christian: a presence of Christ insofar as he is God and also, in a distinct way, insofar as he is man. We will first address his presence as God (i.e., through his divine nature) before seeing in what sense we can also speak about his presence as man (i.e., through his human nature).

---

248. See *Letter, March 19, 1967*, no. 93 (the text is cited above).

249. See ibid., no. 58.

250. See *Letter, March 24, 1931*, no. 9 (quotation from St. Thomas, *S. Th.*, II-II, q. 24, a. 7, c).

In creation, God who is Being by essence, makes creatures participate in his being and he maintains them in being with his permanent presence. "In him we live and move and have our being" (Acts 17:28). The *Catechism of the Catholic Church* teaches that "because he is [. . .] the first cause of all that exists, God is present to his creatures' inmost being."[251] This presence of the Being-in-essence in the beings-through-participation is usually termed *presence of immensity*.[252] It is necessary to maintain creatures in existence just as the presence of the sun is necessary for there to be light through the air.[253] In this sense, Christ is present in all creatures as the Word of God in whom all have been created.

In being elevated to the supernatural order, the human soul begins to host the divine presence in a new way. This is called *supernatural presence of [divine] indwelling*. The Father, the Son, and the Holy Spirit dwell in the soul in grace when it is introduced in the intimate life of the most Blessed Trinity (see John 14:23). We have already explained that supernatural elevation takes place when the human being is brought to share in the divine processions through the sending of the Son and the Holy Spirit to the soul.[254] The Son is sent by the Father and, thanks to his presence, the Christian is a "son in the Son." (In terms of the theory of participation, we would have to say that the presence of Subsistent Filiation gives rise to participated filiation.) The Holy Spirit is also sent, and thanks to his presence the Christian receives charity. (We will not deal directly with this topic now. We only want to note that through the supernatural elevation of becoming adopted children of God, Christ is made present in the soul as the only begotten Son of God.)

These two forms of presence to which we have referred stem from Christ as the Word (his presence in all creatures), and as Son (his supernatural presence in adopted children). Now, let us ask if we can also speak about a presence of Christ as man in the Christian. We will explain this in a very succinct way.[255]

In order to re-engender us to the supernatural life lost through sin, the Son of God assumed a human nature full of grace (see John 1:14), and

---

251. *CCC*, no. 300.

252. See Ps. 138; St. Thomas Aquinas, *In Ioann. Ev.*, I, 5.

253. See St. Augustine, *Super Gen. ad litt.*, c. 8; St. Thomas Aquinas, *S. Th.*, III, q. 7, a. 13 c.

254. See St. Thomas Aquinas, *S. Th.*, I, q. 38, a. 1, c; q. 43, a. 5, c.

255. A more detailed explanation can be found in Javier López Díaz, "La identificación con Cristo según Santo Tomás," in *Excerpta e dissertationibus in Sacra Theologia* (Pamplona: Ediciones Universidad de Navarra) 44 (2003): 104–127. See also: Ocáriz, *Naturaleza, Gracia y Gloria*, pp. 95–106.

we have all taken part of that fullness (see John 1:16).[256] Christ as man, or through his humanity, is the "instrumental" efficient cause of grace. St. Thomas affirms that "to give grace belongs to Christ as man, inasmuch as his manhood is the instrument of his Divinity."[257] Since Christ's humanity is hypostatically united to the Word, it possesses grace in all fullness, and in a certain way infinitely,[258] but it is not the Divinity (as there is no confusion of human and divine natures in Christ), and it is therefore not the principal cause of grace, but rather the instrumental one (i.e., the cause that "shares in the operation of the Divine Nature, as an instrument shares in the operation of the principal agent").[259]

The consequences that derive from this for the study of Christ's presence as man in the Christian are decisive. That the instrumental cause is a cause by participation implies that it is cause not through its being (as the principal cause, the Divinity), but through its action or "power," which Christ's humanity has in an indefectible way. This implies that Christ's presence as man in a Christian who receives grace is not like the presence of the principal cause, the Divinity, which dwells in the soul in grace. Instead, it is a presence through his action or "virtue." In this sense, it can be called "*virtual* presence," understanding this term as the presence of the action of Christ or of his *virtus* (i.e., his "power" or "force").[260] The *virtual presence* of Christ as man in the Christian is a true and real presence, but it is not substantial. It is a presence of the power or influence of the humanity of Christ,

---

256. "*De plenitudine eius nos omnes accepimus*" (John 1:16). St. Thomas comments on this verse of the prologue of St. John concentrating on three different meanings of the preposition "*de*" ["of," "from"]: efficiency, consubstantiality, and partiality. In the first place, he points out that receiving the grace "from" Christ (of his plenitude) means that he is the efficient cause of grace ("the grace comes 'from' Christ as light comes 'from' the sun," says St. Thomas in his commentary); in second place, it signifies that there is a consubstantiality between Christ and us (as when one says that the Son is "of the Father," one affirms that he is "of the same substance of the Father," consubstantial with him; thus, upon receiving grace "from Christ," we are consubstantial with him because we receive the Holy Spirit, uncreated grace, which is one and the same in Christ and in us); in the third place, receiving grace from the plenitude of Christ means that created grace is found in us in a partial and limited way, while in Christ it is found totally and fully (see *In Ioann Ev.*, c. I, lect. 10). In this commentary, together with the affirmation that the humanity of Christ is an "instrumental" cause, one finds all the necessary elements to be able to affirm a permanent virtual presence of Christ in the Christian in grace, as we will point out as follows.

257. St. Thomas Aquinas, *S. Th.*, III, q. 8, a. 1, ad 1. See St. John Damascene, *De Fide Orthodoxa*, lib. 3, c. 19.

258. On the sense in which one says that the grace of the human soul of Christ is infinite, see José Antonio Riestra, *Cristo y la plenitud del Cuerpo Místico* (Pamplona: Ediciones Universidad de Navarra, 1985).

259. St. Thomas Aquinas, *S. Th.*, III, q. 19, a. 1, c.

260. Hence, the term "virtual" is not used in the same sense as in the software field to refer to "virtual reality" since "virtual" in this latter sense is taken to mean "simulated," or "imaginary."

not of his substance. We are dealing here with a dynamic presence. Thanks to this, we can say that the actions of a child of God, which stem from his nature elevated by the grace of Christ, are also actions of Christ who acts through the Christian as one of his members: indeed, it is the life of Christ in the Christian.[261] And besides, it is a *permanent* presence, lasting as long the Christian is in the state of grace.[262]

Now we have to consider how this presence is produced (i.e., how it begins and how it grows in intensity). St. Thomas affirms that participation in the grace of Christ is a certain "transmission," somewhat akin to the way human nature is transmitted from parents to children.[263] For just as human nature is the same in the parents and in the children, so the Holy Spirit who descends from Christ to us is the same in him and in us.[264] Nevertheless this "transmission" does not occur in the same way, because the gift of created grace (the effect of the indwelling of the Holy Spirit) is not in us as it is in Christ: in him it is found in all its fullness, whereas in us only partially. If to this we add that "an agent must be joined to that wherein it acts immediately, and touch it by its power,"[265] we can conclude that Christ's humanity must in some way enter into "contact" with those on whom he confers the gift of the Paraclete so that they might share in his grace. St. Thomas affirms this explicitly in expounding on the efficacy of the Lord's Passion. He poses the following difficulty: "No corporal agent acts efficiently except by contact: hence we see that Christ cleaned the leper by touching him [. . .]. But Christ's Passion could not touch all mankind. Therefore it could not efficiently bring about the salvation of all men."[266] And he resolves it this way: "Christ's Passion, although corporeal, has yet a spiritual power due to its union to the divinity. And therefore it secures its efficacy by *spiritual contact*, namely, by faith and the sacraments of faith."[267]

---

261. On this subject in the teaching of St. Thomas, see Juan Larrú, *Cristo en la acción humana, según los comentarios al Nuevo Testamento de Santo Tomás de Aquino* (Rome: Lateran University Press, 2004); see especially chapter one: "Cristo en el horizonte de la acción humana como un *motus*."

262. See Ocáriz, *Naturaleza, Gracia y Gloria*, ch. 4.

263. St. Thomas Aquinas, *In III Sent.*, d. 13, q. 2, a. 1, ad 2. St. Thomas uses the term *traductio* to refer to both, participation in the grace of Christ and the transmission of human nature from parents to children (see idem, *In II Sent.*, d. 20, q. 2, a. 3, ad 3).

264. Idem, *In III Sent.*, d. 13, q. 2, a. 1, ad 2.

265. Idem, *S. Th.*, I, q. 8, a. 1, c.

266. Idem, *S. Th.*, III, q. 48, a. 6, arg. 2.

267. Ibid., ad 2. "*Passio Christi, licet sit corporalis, habet tamen spiritualem virtutem ex divinitate unita. Et ideo per spiritualem contactum efficaciam sortitur, scilicet per fidem et fidei sacramenta* [. . .]."

The "spiritual contact" between Christ and a Christian is brought about by drawing both together. On the one hand, the Son has come to us by assuming a human nature, thus entering into the human race, and in so doing "has united Himself in some fashion with every man."[268] This *natural* union with Christ as man, due to our participating in the same human nature, is the basis for the supernatural communion that is brought about by the "transmission" of the Holy Spirit from Christ to us.

But this basic reality is not enough for man in fact to receive the supernatural life of Christ. Man must be open to his action and *adhere* to Christ "by faith and the sacraments of faith,"[269] first, through a living faith informed by charity, as St. Paul describes, "that Christ may dwell in your hearts through faith; that you [may be] rooted and grounded in love" (Eph. 3:17). And second, by participating in the sacraments, in which Jesus Christ himself acts, especially and in a supreme way, in the Eucharist. The reference to "the sacraments of faith" can be extended to the other means of sanctification (prayer and Christian formation) that we will deal with in chapter nine.

By means of faith and the sacraments, a Christian establishes a relationship with Jesus Christ and consequently receives the Holy Spirit who descends from the Head to the members in order to initiate or give growth to supernatural life. In this way, St. Paul's words are fulfilled: "He who is united to the Lord becomes one spirit with him" (1 Cor. 6:17); as well as St. John's: "By this we know that he abides in us, by the Spirit which he has given us" (1 John 3:24). And it is the Holy Spirit, the Divine Guest of the soul, who makes present in the human spirit in a permanent way the *power* or *operation* of Christ's humanity through which the supernatural life develops fully as the life of Christ in the Christian, who in turn is progressively more and more identified with the Lord (see 2 Cor. 3:18).

> In the Encyclical *Mystici Corporis*, Pius XII teaches that Christ, the author and efficient cause of sanctity in the members of his mystical body "is in us through his Spirit whom he gives to us and through whom he acts in us in such a way that all the divine activity of the Holy Spirit in souls must also be attributed to Christ."[270] The presence of Christ in the Christian is not identical with the presence of the Holy Spirit, but it is brought about

---

268. *Gaudium et Spes*, no. 22. See St. John Paul II, Encyclical *Redemptor Hominis* (March 4, 1979), no. 8; St. Thomas Aquinas, *Comp. Theol.*, I, c. 196; *In Ioann. Ev.*, c. 14, lect. 5.

269. St. Thomas Aquinas, *S. Th.*, III, q. 48, a. 6, ad 2. See ibid., q. 68, a. 1, ad 1.

270. Pius XII, Encyclical *Mystici Corporis* (June 29, 1943): AAS 35 (1943): 192, 197, 230: DS 3813.

> by the Holy Spirit and is inseparable from him. St. John Paul II expressed this same idea in commenting on Jesus' words at the Last Supper: "I will pray the Father, and he will give you another Counselor, to be with you forever" (John 14:16). And St. John Paul II says, "This promise must be taken together with the others made by Jesus when going to the Father: 'I am with you always, to the close of the age' (Matt. 28:20). We know that Christ is the Word who 'became flesh and dwelt among us' (John 1:14). When going to the Father he said: 'I am with you always, to the close of the age' (Matt. 28:20). It follows that the apostles and the Church must continually find, by means of the Holy Spirit, that presence of the Word-Son which, during his earthly mission, was physical and visible in his incarnate humanity, but which, after his ascension to the Father, is completely immersed in mystery. The Holy Spirit's presence which, as Jesus said, is interior to souls and to the Church ['He dwells with you, and will be in you': John 14:17], will make the invisible Christ present in a lasting manner 'until the end of the world.' The transcendent unity of the Son and the Holy Spirit will ensure that Christ's humanity, assumed by the Word, will be present at work wherever the trinitarian plan of salvation is being put into effect through the power of the Father."[271]

This presence of Christ as man explains how we can affirm that a Christian is and ought to be *ipse Christus*. As we have already said, through the infusion of grace "he is" *ipse Christus* from the moment of baptism. But the presence of the life of Christ can grow, for we are dealing here with the influence of his action. And consequently we can also say that the Christian "must become" *ipse Christus*. Christian life is a progressive growth in identification with Christ, until one reaches the fullness of Christ (see Eph. 4:13). This growth occurs through the grace of the Holy Spirit and the correspondence on the part of the Christian.

In summary, this is the theological explanation we want to offer as the basis for the expressions "identification with Christ" and "the Christian, *ipse Christus*" that St. Josemaría uses. As we acknowledged earlier, other interpretations are possible; but in any case, it goes unquestioned that these ways of positing the relationship of the Christian with Christ open perspectives for future theological development and lead us to found the spiritual life on the awareness of "being Christ," or, that is, simply build the Christian life on the "sense of divine filiation."

---

271. St. John Paul II, General Audience (May 24, 1989), no. 4.

2.5. Sons and Daughters of God with an "Identical Adoptive Divine Filiation"

Since the gift of adoptive divine filiation is a sharing in the one substantial and uncreated filiation of the Word, it is identical in men and women. *Women have in common with men the same personal dignity and responsibility, and—in the supernatural order—[. . .] an identical adoptive divine filiation.*[272]

When St. Josemaría refers to *hijos de Dios* ["children of God" and/or "sons of God"],[273] he means to include both men and women. At times he expressly speaks about "sons and daughters of God" not because the gift of divine filiation is different, but because he wants to highlight that the subjects who receive divine adoption are both men and women. Regardless, for St. Josemaría, the equality between both men and women is radical and stands unquestioned:

> *All the baptised, men and women alike, share equally in the dignity, freedom and responsibility of the children of God. There exists in the Church that fundamental unity which St. Paul taught to the first Christians:* Quicumque enim in Christo baptizati estis, Christum induistis. Non est Iudaeus, neque Graecus: non est servus, neque liber: non est masculus, neque femina: *Now there is no distinction between Jew and Greek, nor between slave and freeman, nor between man and woman.* (Gal. 3:26–28)[274]

In the text of St. Paul quoted by St. Josemaría above, the difference between "man and woman" appears together with other differences like "Jew and Greek," "slave and freeman." What the faithful have in common is adoptive filiation received in baptism. "You are all sons of God [. . .]. For as many of you as were baptized into Christ have put on Christ" (Gal. 3:26 f.). In the moment of baptism, this gift is the same in everyone in a strict sense not only because it is identical (as happens, for example, in those who get the same amount of money), but because it is one and the same gift (i.e., a gift that while received in many, makes them one). This is in fact the conclusion the apostle reaches: "For you are all one in Christ Jesus" (Gal. 3:28).[275] We find ourselves facing the dialectic of the one and

272. *Letter, July 29, 1965*, no. 4.

273. Translator's note: In Spanish, the phrase "*hijos de Dios*" is ambiguous, as it can mean both "children of God" and/or "sons of God."

274. *Conversations*, no. 14.

275. St. Josemaría omits these last words in the citation probably because the idea is already present in the earlier ones.

the many, typical of transcendental participation.[276] While Subsistent Filiation is one (i.e., the only begotten Son), participated filiation, since it is received by many, enables many children to be "one in Christ Jesus."

Since divine filiation received in baptism is identical for man and woman, so too is the common priesthood identical for both. There are numerous daily (and even legal) implications that follow from this reality, which St. Josemaría noted and proclaimed ahead of his time.[277] As an example, we quote a text that contains also an observation on the ministerial priesthood:

> *For many reasons, including some derived from positive divine law, I consider that the distinction between men and women with respect to the juridical capacity for receiving Holy Orders should be retained. But in all other spheres, I think the Church should fully recognize in her legislation, internal life and apostolic action exactly the same rights and duties for women as for men. For example, the right to do apostolate, to found and direct associations, to give their opinion responsibly on matters which affect the common good of the Church, etc.*[278]

He states that the capacity to receive the ministerial priesthood must be reserved to men, and this "for many reasons, including some derived from positive divine law." Without going into an explanation, he simply refers to the doctrine of the Church.[279] But, more than this, what is of interest to us here is to point out that his words strongly emphasize the equality between men and women in what refers to the common priesthood. In fact,

---

276. See St. Thomas Aquinas, *Quodlibet.* II, q. 2, a. 3; Cornelio Fabro, *La nozione metafisica di partecipazione* (Torino: SEI, 1950) pp. 317 ff.; idem, "Elementi per una dottrina tomistica della partecipazione," in *Divinitas* 11 (1967): 559–586.

277. "It is important to put on record that at a historical moment in which equality between men and women was not accepted socially and juridically, St. Josemaría saw clearly that this was a mistake." Ángela Aparisi Miralles, "El feminismo de la complementariedad en el pensamiento de san Josemaría Escrivá," in J. Borobia et al. (ed.), *Trabajo y espíritu. IV Simposio internacional "Fe y cultura contemporánea,"* (Pamplona: Universidad de Navarra, 2004), p. 357.

278. *Conversations*, no. 14. This text is from 1968, but the ideas can be found much earlier in the preaching of St. Josemaría.

279. Later this doctrine has been expressed in magisterial documents. In chronological order these are: Congregation for the Doctrine of the Faith, Declaration on the question of the admission of women to the priestly ministry *Inter Insigniores* (October 15, 1976); St. John Paul II, Apostolic Letter *Mulieris Dignitatem* (August 15, 1988), nos. 26–27; *CCC*, no. 1577; John Paul II, Apostolic Letter *Ordinatio Sacerdotalis* (May 22, 1994); The Congregation for the Doctrine of the Faith, Response in regard to the teaching of the Apostolic Letter *Ordinatio Sacerdotalis* (October 28, 1995).

both receive divine filiation and both therefore share in the priesthood that is Christ's by his human nature (see 1 Tim. 2:5). Since men and women share the same human nature and have received the same baptismal character, they likewise possess the same royal priesthood, the same capacity to be mediators in Christ between God and men.[280] The ministerial priesthood, on the other hand, is a capacity to carry out specific priestly actions in representation of Christ, the head of the mystical body. And to function as a head is related to the condition of being male, as we see in creation (see Gen. 1:7.18 ff.), and which is also what St. Paul teaches: "But I want you to understand that the head of every man is Christ, the head of a woman is her husband, and the head of Christ is God." (1 Cor. 11:3; see Eph. 5:23). Hence, there are certain priestly functions that require the priest to be male. But those who receive the ministerial priesthood are not more children of God, nor better Christians, nor holier. They are only "more priests," and not because they exercise the common priesthood more or better, but because, in addition to those functions that are proper to all the baptized, they exercise other priestly functions.

> *In those who have been ordained, the ministerial priesthood is added to the common priesthood of all of the faithful. Therefore, although it would be a serious error to argue that a priest is more a member of the faithful than an unordained Christian is, it can, on the other hand, be said that he is more a priest: like all Christians he belongs to the priestly people redeemed by Christ, and in addition to this he is marked with the character of the ministerial priesthood which differentiates him* essentially and not only in degree (Second Vatican Council, Dogm. Const. *Lumen gentium*, no. 10) *from the common priesthood of the faithful.*[281]

Neither women nor the majority of men receive the ministerial priesthood, but all are called (whether ordained ministers or not) to the fullness

280. "*Character sacramentalis est quaedam participatio sacerdotii Christi in fidelibus eius*" (St. Thomas Aquinas, *S. Th.*, III, q. 63, a. 5, c). The baptismal character, being a reality different from sanctifying grace—"*aliter est in anima gratia, et aliter character*" (ibid., ad 1)—attests that the Christian has been made a child of God and participates in the divine nature through grace in baptism. Although afterward he might lose grace, there always remains the indelible imprint of the sacramental character that makes him capable of being a mediator between God and men, and which in a certain way urges him to return like the prodigal son (see Luke 15:11 ff.) to the house of the Father in order to live in communion with God. The baptismal character remains without sanctifying grace and yet it evokes it, or longs for it, tends toward it, and "demands" it.

281. Homily: "A Priest Forever," April 13, 1973, no. 41.

of divine filiation, which is sanctity. As children of God in Christ, all must strive to be like Christ, and consequently to have a *priestly soul*.[282] We will deal with this concept in greater detail shortly.[283] Now we simply want to point out that St. Josemaría, taking into account that the tendency to identify "priesthood" with the "ministerial priesthood" could lead people to think that "priestly soul" is something proper to ministers and only to them, he insists that women, as well as men who do not receive Holy Orders, are children of God in Christ, and that precisely because of that, they too have a "priestly soul." This was a central theme in his last conversation on earth, held on June 26, 1975, with a group of women, just a few hours before his transit to heaven: *You women have a priestly soul* . . .[284]

Let us now take a moment to look at the most specific aspect of St. Josemaría's teaching on divine filiation.

3. The Sense of Divine Filiation: The Basis for the Christian Life

"Knowing oneself to be children of God," or "knowing oneself to be Christ" is an extremely simple source for the spiritual life and at the same time, it has the inexhaustible richness of a deep ocean in which one can always discover new marvels. The multifaceted nature of this reality can be seen in the existing bibliography.[285] Here we will try to order the different implications of this in such a way as to emphasize this central idea: that the sense of divine filiation possesses a foundational characteristic when it comes to the Christian life.

First, however, we must clarify a terminological matter. St. Josemaría affirms at times that the basis for the spiritual life is "divine filiation" whereas at other times, he says that the basis is "the sense of our divine filiation." In our opinion, these expressions are equivalent. The first is only an abbreviated form of the second. When, for example, he says that *divine filiation is the basis of the spirit of Opus Dei*,[286] (that is, of his teaching), he is not simply recalling the dogmatic truth that a Christian is a child of God through

282. *Furrow*, no. 499; *The Forge*, no. 369; etc.

283. See upcoming section 3.1.2.

284. See Vázquez de Prada, *The Founder of Opus Dei*, vol. III, p. 563.

285. See the works cited at the end of section 2.1 of this chapter ("Theological Sources and Context").

286. *Christ Is Passing By*, no. 64.

grace, and that his supernatural life is objectively based on that. Nor is he merely affirming that Christian life is built on the doctrine of Jesus Christ according to the words of the apostle: "No other foundation can any one lay than that which is laid, which is Jesus Christ" (1 Cor. 3:ll). He is instead proposing a practical teaching that on many other occasions he expressed by saying *the foundation of our spiritual life is the sense of our divine filiation.*[287] In both cases, he is dealing with the same teaching, which in the latter case is presented explicitly from the perspective of the first person, indicating that the foundation is not the new reality of divine filiation, but rather the "sense" that one has of divine filiation.

3.1. The Meaning of the Expression "The Sense of Divine Filiation"

In speaking now of the "sense" of divine filiation, we are not referring simply to "what is understood" by divine filiation (taking "sense" to be the meaning of a term), but rather of the intimate perception or habitual awareness of being a child of God; an awareness that is not only an act of the intellect, but one that engages the person as a whole.

What type of quality is this "sense" of divine filiation in the Christian, and how does it configure his or her personality?

3.1.1. "The Thread of All the Virtues:" Relation with the Virtue of Piety and the Gift of Piety

We should be clear that one can be a child of God without having the "sense of divine filiation." Many people are in fact adopted children of God, but they do not know that or, in any case, it is a reality that does not conscientiously influence their behavior. St. Josemaría presents this "sense" as a quality that, to the degree it is possessed, leads a person to act spontaneously as a child of God. At times he calls it a "virtue," not because it is one more virtue, but because it is a quality that is present in all the virtues and gives a filial slant to their acts. On one occasion, responding to a woman's question about the "marvelous virtue of divine filiation," St. Josemaría commented, among other things, that *truly it is an extraordinary virtue. It is—I see that you are wearing a necklace—like the thread that unites the pearls of a great, marvelous necklace. Divine filiation is the thread tying together all the virtues,*

287. *Letter, January 25, 1961*, no. 54.

because they are the virtues of a child of God, of a Christian.[288] It is not just one more "pearl." It is the "thread of the necklace" of Christian virtues. "Divine filiation is not a particular virtue with its proper acts. Instead it is the permanent status of the subject of the virtues."[289] One does not act as a child of God performing some actions that are specified by their object. Each act can take on a particular shade if it is carried out with "the awareness of being a child of God." And this awareness should progressively determine all the conduct of a Christian: *we are children of God all day long.*[290]

Since divine filiation is *the deepest truth*[291] of the Christian (i.e., this new relation with God that a person receives on being raised to the supernatural level), the "sense" of this relation confers a self-awareness in the depths of one's being and, in consequence, a moral "personality": a way of thinking, loving, and wanting, proper to a child of God; a knowing, loving and feeling *in Christ Jesus.* Hence the advice of St. Josemaría: *You need to have your own personality, agreed. But you should try to make it conform exactly to Christ's.*[292] This is why he asks for himself, and teaches others to ask Jesus, to *make the foundation of my personality my identification with you.*[293]

The "sense of divine filiation" is to be found in all the faculties of the soul: in the intellect, in the will, and in the sensible faculties. It is not reduced to a theoretical knowledge of the teaching on supernatural adoption.[294] It also brings with it the practical judgment of what it means to be a child of God, and what this implies in life. It moves the will and the affections to appreciate that all of one's conduct must be based on this reality. Hence, St. Josemaría speaks of the "sense" of filiation: something that is not only known from the outside, but "felt" from within, and—to borrow Leonardo Polo's expression—something that is "configurating"[295] of the person.

---

288. Notes taken from preaching, July 6, 1974 (AGP, P04 1974, vol. II, p. 164).

289. Ocáriz, "La filiación divina, realidad central en la vida y en la enseñanza de Mons. Escrivá de Balaguer," p. 199.

290. *Conversations*, no. 102.

291. *Friends of God*, no. 26.

292. *The Forge*, no. 468.

293. *Christ Is Passing By*, no. 31.

294. As St. Thomas noted, it is common to employ in theology the term "*sentire*" to designate the certainty of the intellectual perception (which therefore is called "*sentential*," by analogy with the corporal senses). See St. Thomas Aquinas, *S. Th.*, I, q. 54, a. 5, ad 1.

295. Leonardo Polo, "Acerca de la plenitud," in *Nuestro Tiempo* 162 (1967): 642. [In Spanish, "*Configurador de la persona.*"]

Since it is found in all the faculties, the sense of divine filiation can influence all the virtues. In keeping with the simile used above, it is akin to the "thread" that supports them and enables them to form a necklace. When St. Josemaría mentions a specific virtue, he frequently adds: "of a child of God." He says, for example, "the love of a child of God," or the joy, the obedience, the loyalty . . . "of the children of God."

Nevertheless, the sense of divine filiation does not affect all the virtues in the same way. It has a special relationship with one of them: piety. *Piety is the virtue of children.*[296] This is the virtue that above all inclines a person to deal with God as Father, and to always behave as his children. Of course, it leads a person to give worship to God by means of certain "acts of piety." But a Christian glorifies his Father God with all his works. Piety, in the genuine meaning of the word, extends to everything in a person's conduct, both his internal and external acts. And since he is a son of God, he ought to live piously (see Titus 2:12).[297]

But St. Josemaría does not identify the "sense of divine filiation" with the virtue of piety. He says, rather, that it is *the marrow of true piety.*[298] It would be useless to attempt to distinguish between the virtue and its "marrow." What St. Josemaría means is that the sense of divine filiation is an essential aspect of what makes piety what it is, without implying thereby, however, that in every other aspect the sense of divine filiation is to be identified with the virtue of piety. The essence of piety is thus knowing oneself and feeling oneself to be a child of God. In other words, the relation of the sense of divine filiation to the virtue of piety is immediate, and through

296. *Christ Is Passing By*, no. 10. The context of these words shows that St. Josemaría is referring to the piety of the children of God toward their Father. He does not limit the virtue of piety to the manifestations of love and honor to one's earthly parents or to one's country, as does St. Thomas, who reserves the virtue of "religion" for the worship of God as Creator (see *S. Th.*, II-II, q. 101, a. 1, c). It is only when this worship is directed under the action of the Holy Spirit that St. Thomas includes it under "piety," understood as a gift of the Holy Spirit: "*exhibere cultum Deo ut Creatori, quod facit religio, est excellentius quam exhibere cultum patri carnali, quod facit pietas quae est virtus. Sed exhibere cultum Deo ut Patri est adhuc excellentius quam exhibere cultum Deo ut Creatori et Domino. Unde religio est potior pietate virtute, sed pietas secundum quod est donum, est potior religione*" (see St. Thomas Aquinas, *S. Th.*, II-II, q. 121, a. 1, ad 2). Various Thomistic authors amplify the notion of the "virtue of piety." For them, its primary meaning refers to the worship of God as Father (see Dominic M. Prümmer, *Manuale Theologiae moralis*, vol. II, [Barcelona: Herder, 1945], no. 569). For St. Josemaría, the virtue of piety does not have as its object only exterior worship, but in general, one's filial dealings with God.

297. See Burkhard Neunheuser, "Pietà," in Ermanno Ancilli (dir.), *Dizionario enciclopedico di spiritualità*, vol. 2 (Roma: Città Nuova, 1990), pp. 1954–1955. The author of this article emphasizes the extension of "piety," but does not mention its relation to filiation.

298. *Conversations*, no. 102.

piety, it is present in the other Christian virtues. We could think of piety as the clasp that closes the thread of the necklace of virtues and makes them all virtues of a child of God. Naturally, this is only a metaphor that shows the particular relation of the sense of divine filiation to the virtue of piety in a limited way.

Much stronger is the relationship to the "gift of piety," one of the seven gifts of the Holy Spirit, that perfects the virtue with the same name. It is the gift that disposes the soul to be docile to the impulse the Holy Spirit gives to deal with God the Father in a filial way.[299] The sense of divine filiation is not the result of a personal discovery, or of one's personal effort, as St. Josemaría himself points out when he talks about the events that gave rise to the invocation *Abba, Pater!*[300] in his soul. It is an outlook and a way of carrying out our lives that comes from the gift of piety. *Through the gift of piety, the Holy Spirit helps us to realise with certainty that we are children of God.*[301] In a prayer to the Holy Spirit that he composed in 1971, St. Josemaría states, *Grant us the gift of piety to teach us the meaning of our divine filiation, the joyful supernatural awareness of being children of God and, in Jesus Christ, brothers and sisters of all mankind.*[302]

According to these words, the sense of divine filiation is a consequence of the gift of piety. And yet they are not the same, because not everyone who has the gift of piety likewise possesses the vivid and actual "sense" of divine filiation that St. Josemaría preaches. The gift of piety is a readiness to be moved by the Holy Spirit to act like a child of God. The "sense of divine filiation" is the actual awareness of this gift, of what it represents in the Christian life, as well as the conscious cooperation it demands in conformity to the words of St. Paul: "For all who are led by the Spirit of God are sons of God" (Rom. 8:14). It is the desire to allow oneself to be led in everything by the Paraclete, and to correspond to the gift of piety. It means recognizing this gift and the eagerness to have the Paraclete activate this filial disposition. If we include the fact that correspondence to this gift is also aroused by the same Spirit who counts on our freedom, then we can say, with the words of Álvaro del Portillo, that the sense of divine filiation is the gift of piety.[303]

299. See St. Thomas Aquinas, *S. Th.*, II-II, q. 121, a. 1, c. We will study this in chapter six, section 5.1.

300. See *Letter, January 9, 1959*, no. 60 (text cited at the beginning of this chapter).

301. *Friends of God*, no. 92.

302. *Consecration to the Holy Spirit*, Solemnity of Pentecost, May 30, 1971 (AGP, P01 XII-1983, p. 10).

303. "This spirit of divine filiation, so proper to the Work, is the gift of piety, granted by the Holy Spirit" (Álvaro del Portillo, note 3 to *Instruction*, March 19, 1934, no. 1).

> Because of its close relationship with the gift of piety, the sense of divine filiation is also related to the other gifts of the Holy Spirit. In reaching the intimate core of the person (i.e., his being a child of God), this gift disposes the will[304] to act in conformity with this condition under the action of the Holy Spirit: with filial wisdom,[305] filial fortitude, filial fear, etc.[306]

In the last quotation of St. Josemaría, we have seen that the sense of divine filiation derives from the gift of piety: recall that he implores "the gift of piety to teach us the meaning of our divine filiation." Elsewhere, however, he writes: *piety* [. . .] *is born of divine filiation.*[307] This might seem like a contradiction, but it is only apparent if we distinguish between the "gift of piety" and a "life of piety." The latter expression does not refer to the gift, but rather to the life of piety that springs from divine filiation as a consequence of the gift of piety. That is, the gift of piety is the origin of the sense of divine filiation and from this stems the life of piety that influences all of one's conduct: *The piety which is born of divine filiation is a profound attitude of the soul which eventually permeates one's entire existence: it is there in every thought, in every desire, in every affection.*[308]

We must also note that the "sense of divine filiation" includes the "sense of fraternity in Christ." With words that we have already quoted, it is *the joyful supernatural awareness of being children of God and, in Jesus Christ, brothers and sisters of all mankind.*[309] Piety reaches out to others. It leads a person to respect in them the image of God and the call to be his children through supernatural grace.

In the end, in order to be theologically precise about what constitutes the "sense of divine filiation" we must at least distinguish between "divine filiation, "sense of divine filiation," "the gift of piety," and a "life of piety." Divine filiation is an entitative gift that enables the Christian to participate in Christ's filiation. The "sense of divine filiation" is an operative gift meant

---

304. According to St. Thomas, the gift of piety divinizes the acts that proceed from the will: see *S. Th.*, I-II, q. 68, a. 4, c.

305. St. Thomas relates divine filiation also with the gift of wisdom: "*Conformari Deo quadam filiatione divina adoptiva pertinet ad donum sapientiae*" (*S. Th.*, I-II, q. 69, a. 4 c). See Cruz González Ayesta, *El don de la sabiduría según Santo Tomás. Divinización, filiación y connaturalidad* (Pamplona: Universidad de Navarra,1998), pp. 173–178.

306. In chapter six, section 5, we will speak of the seven gifts of the Holy Spirit.

307. *Friends of God*, no. 146.

308. Ibid.

309. *Consecration to the Holy Spirit.*

to conform a Christian's way of acting to that of Christ. It derives from the "gift of piety," as the continuous awareness of being a son or a daughter of God and arouses the desire to be constantly guided by the Holy Spirit. Finally, from the sense of divine filiation comes the "life of piety," or the life proper to a child of God who tries to live honestly before God and men.

A Christian is guided in all his actions by the sense of divine filiation in a way similar to how we say that someone follows a path guided by his bodily senses (by hearing or smelling, etc.). To the extent that one feels the "sense of divine filiation," it directs his steps toward the goal guided by that "sense." Or put more precisely, he perceives all reality with that sense and possesses a particular "sensitivity" in dealing with God and others, an ease in discerning what is proper of a child of God, and a way of considering people, issues, events, etc. from the viewpoint of sanctity and apostolate. Thus, the Pauline exhortation to share the sentiments of Christ (see Phil. 2:5) becomes a reality in one's life.

The sense of divine filiation is so important that to lose it entirely in the spiritual life would mean to be left "without meaning" in life; it would be like "fainting," or even worse since the one who faints may not be responsible for the harm he causes others. However, the one who lacks the sense of divine filiation completely and does not deal with God as Father can become a person who does not know who he is, or one who is not in control of his own life. *Anyone who does not realize that he is a child of God is unaware of the deepest truth about himself. When he acts, he lacks the dominion and self-mastery we find in those who love the Lord above all else.*[310]

3.1.2. "Priestly Soul" with "Lay Mentality"

After having seen what type of quality we have in the "sense of divine filiation," we now ask how it configures the personality of a Christian who seeks sanctity in the middle of the world.

In order to respond to this question in the necessary depth, we would have to consider how the "sense of divine filiation" influences all the Christian virtues (especially charity and, through charity, the other virtues that it informs), and for which of those virtues the sense of divine filiation becomes like the "thread" that unites them. But now is not the moment to speak about the virtues. We will study them in chapter six. Here, we will

310. *Friends of God*, no. 26.

limit ourselves to pointing out something more basic: the two characteristic features of that "sense of divine filiation" that, because they are intrinsic to it, are manifested later in charity and in all the other virtues of a child of God called to sanctify himself by carrying out his earthly duties. These two features, typical and inseparable in the teaching of St. Josemaría, are "priestly soul" and "lay mentality."

These two features respectively correspond to two realities that we have addressed above and that come with divine adoption in baptism: priesthood and inheritance.[311] In effect, when a person is adopted as a child of God in baptism, he receives a share in Christ's priesthood and consequently has a "priestly soul." Besides this, he is made heir to glory, an inheritance that includes created realities purified from the consequences of sin. Already in this world, a Christian begins to possess them when he uses them as matter for his sanctification. This status of an heir requires, in the case of those faithful called to sanctify the world from within, the "lay mentality" St. Josemaría speaks about.

A Christian shares in Christ's priesthood so that he might be a mediator between God and men. And he has received the world as his inheritance in order to exercise his priesthood in temporal activities, sanctifying them, and carrying them out for the glory of the Father.[312] As an adopted child of God, he has to know that he is, with Christ and in Christ, priest and heir to the world. These two aspects are intimately united because a Christian takes possession of his inheritance by exercising his priesthood. Here we find the theological foundation for the compenetration of these two features ("priestly soul" and "lay mentality"), which are proper to the "sense of divine filiation.

St. Josemaría does not propose these as something secondary to his message. They are *the hinge and the foundation*.[313]

Always and in everything we need to have—both priests and laity—a truly priestly soul and a fully lay mentality.[314]

---

311. See sections 1.2.1. and 1.2.2.

312. See Vatican II, Dogmatic Constitution of the Church *Lumen gentium*, no. 31. See 1 Cor. 10:31.

313. *Letter, February 2, 1945*, no. 1.

314. Ibid. St. Josemaría used to say that the "axle" or "hinge" of the spiritual life is the sanctification of professional work, as we will study in chapter seven; and he also affirmed, as we know already, that its "foundation" is the sense of divine filiation. When he applies these two terms to "lay mentality" and to "priestly soul," respectively, he appears to be indicating that the first term ("lay mentality") is essential to sanctification in the middle of the world and, in particular, to sanctification of professional work, which is the "hinge." With

He addresses himself expressly in these terms to the faithful of Opus Dei. He presents the union of "priestly soul" and "lay mentality" as an essential characteristic of their mission to sanctify the world from within.[315] But since this mission is common to all the ordinary faithful and to secular priests, it is evident that he does not conceive these two features and their mutual connection as a characteristic exclusively for the members of Opus Dei. He proposes them in order to make them known among all the faithful who have received from God the calling to sanctify their professional, family and social duties.

Let us now examine yet another text of St. Josemaría taken from the same document as above in which he refers to priestly soul (even though he does not mention that expressly in these lines), to lay mentality, and to their connection:

> *Since each of us wants to be* ipse Christus*—realizing that He is the only mediator between God and men* (see 1 Tim. 2:5)*—we need to unite ourselves to our Lord and be mediators in Christ Jesus, in order to bring to him all earthly realities. Our vocation demands that we seek not only our own personal sanctity, but that we go out to all the pathways of the earth, in order to convert them into pathways of God. We are called to take part, as ordinary citizens, in all temporal activities, being leaven* (see Matt. 13:33) *that informs the whole dough* (see 1 Cor. 5:6). *But for our apostolic work to be fruitful, we also need to have a lay mentality, since, in order to be effective, the leaven has to penetrate, to disappear in the dough of human society, with naturalness.*[316]

---

regard to the second term (priestly soul) he is referring to what is essential for anyone who is seeking holiness based on the foundation of divine filiation. In other words, "lay mentality" and "priestly soul" do not form another "hinge" and another "foundation" besides those of sanctification of work and the sense of divine filiation, but rather they belong essentially to them.

315. Bishop Álvaro del Portillo saw the union of these two features reflected in the very seal of Opus Dei, the cross inscribed in a circle which represents the world. In the teachings of St. Josemaría, he writes, "These two features are inseparably linked, like the Cross in the heart of the world. The Cross reminds us that we must identify ourselves with Christ in order to co-redeem with him. As a result, the soul of one who is a son of God, regardless of whether he is a priest or not, must necessarily be a *priestly soul.* And, for us, the world is the "place" where we seek that identification: our work, our family life, our social relations, which all of us, priests and laity together, strive to sanctify, precisely by carrying out our temporal affairs or our ministerial priesthood with a *fully lay mentality:* without confusing the human and the divine elements, but without separating them either, since in Christ there is neither confusion nor separation, but rather intimate union, between his human and his divine nature" (*Pastoral Letter*, January 9, 1993: AGP, P 17, vol. III, no. 372).

316. *Letter, February 2, 1945*, no. 12. The priestly soul is implicit as he speaks of "being mediators in Christ Jesus."

As we can see in these words, beginning with "since each one of us wants to be *ipse Christus*," St. Josemaría points out that the sense of divine filiation leads the Christian to be a "mediator in Christ," that is, to put into practice his own priesthood. Immediately afterward, he refers to the exercise of this priesthood in temporal activities in order to offer them to God and to bring others to him, acting as leaven in a lump of dough. This intimate desire is the "priestly soul." But the leaven that St. Josemaría is thinking about has to be mixed in with the dough, be a part of it, and for this reason, it needs a "lay mentality."

To have a "priestly soul" is to conscientiously assume what the common priesthood entails (in the case of a layperson, or of the common priesthood and the ministerial priesthood in the case of a priest) in order to seek sanctity for oneself, for others, and for the world. It means seeing and dealing with temporal realities in a priestly way, offering them to God as mediators *in Christ*, who have surrendered their life on the Cross in order to unite men with God. It means generously embracing the cross of every day (see Luke 9:23). As Álvaro del Portillo explains, "It means having the same sentiments of Christ the Priest, seeking in every moment to fulfill the divine Will, and thus offering our entire life to God the Father in union with Christ, in order to co-redeem with him."[317] For St. Josemaría a priestly soul is recognized *in never saying enough*,[318] in not setting boundries when sacrificing oneself out of love for God and neighbor, just as Christ the Priest did not condition his own self-giving.

On the other hand, "lay mentality" consists essentially in understanding and assuming that earthly affairs have to be ordered to God, respecting and appreciating their proper autonomy (i.e., any work in the natural sciences, technology, the economy, social organization, art, etc., has to be carried out in accord with the laws governing each field and activity). Temporal activities, in effect, *have to be brought to God (and now, after sin, redeemed, reconciled), each in accord with its own nature, with the immediate end God has given it, but always keeping sight of our ultimate supernatural destiny in Christ:* Because in him, it hath well pleased the Father, that all

317. Álvaro del Portillo, *Pastoral Letter*, January 9, 1993, no. 375). See Marco Busca, *L'anima sacerdotale del cristiano* (Milan: Marna, 2010), pp. 67ff. According to this author, "the 'sentiments of Jesus' to which St. Paul refers, and the *priestly soul* of which the founder of Opus Dei reminds us substantially indicate the same reality, signifying it in the first case as more present in our Redeemer, and in the second case as present in the soul of the Christian" (ibid., p. 68).

318. Notes taken from preaching: cited by Álvaro del Portillo, *Pastoral Letter*, January 9, 1993, no. 377.

fullness should dwell; and through him to reconcile all things unto himself, making peace through the blood of his cross, both as to the things that are on earth, and the things that are in heaven (Col. 1:19–0).[319] "The autonomy and proper nature of temporal realities implies (in the writings of St. Josemaría) the command to know and respect their intrinsic dynamism, fruit of the rationality that the Creator's Wisdom placed in his works. Consequently the need for technical and professional expertise is an indispensable prerequisite for any apostolic endeavor that strives for the sanctification of the world *from within*."[320] This "legitimate autonomy of temporal realities"[321] allows for them to be ordered to God in a variety of ways. Consequently, God expects full respect for freedom in these matters and in the apostolic initiatives of the faithful who have to sanctify them.[322] Hence for St. Josemaría *freedom* [. . .] *is the key to this lay mentality*,[323] as he constantly preached.

Speaking about the "autonomy of temporal realities," the Magisterium of the Church points out that it is not a case of absolute but only relative autonomy, because the fact that they have their proper laws does not mean that they are independent of God. On the contrary, they can and ought to be ordered to him in accord with these laws.[324] St. Josemaría brings this to mind also when he writes that *the autonomy of the world is relative, and everything in this world of ours has as its ultimate meaning the glory of God and the salvation of souls*.[325] Under this perspective, a lay mentality leads a person to see his engagement in these temporal activities as the field he must cultivate and from which he can draw fruit with his "priestly soul."

The layperson's lay mentality needs a priestly soul, and vice versa. The two notions cannot be understood in St. Josemaría's preaching if one is

---

319. *Letter, March 19, 1954*, no. 7.

320. Ángel Rodríguez Luño, "*Cittadini degni del vangelo*" (*Phil. 1:27*). *Saggi di etica politica* (Rome: Edusc, 2005), p. 42. The third chapter is entitled: *La formazione della coscienza in materia sociale e politica secondo gli insegnamenti di san Josemaría Escrivá*.

321. See *Gaudium et Spes*, no. 36.

322. Moreover, in general, the Church recognizes and also protects the freedom of the faithful to practice apostolate. See CIC, can. 225 and 227.

323. *Letter, September 29, 1957*, no. 55. See Pierpaolo Donati, "Senso e valore della vita quotidiana," in *Annales Theologici*, 16/1 (2002), pp. 221–263 (in particular pp. 255 ff.: ". . . *verso una nuova "laicità civile* . . .").

324. See *Gaudium et Spes*, nos. 36 and 56.

325. *Letter, January 9, 1959*, no. 31.

isolated from the other. He never separates them. The "priestly soul" he speaks about is not a generic "priestly sense" that every Christian has to cultivate since he is a child of God and participates in Christ's priesthood. He speaks instead of the specific priestly spirit of those who have been called to sanctify the world from within. Theirs is a mission that requires a "lay mentality" and consequently, as we have seen, an awareness of the autonomy of temporal affairs that allows ample room for freedom. In a reciprocal way, this "lay mentality" that St. Josemaría teaches is not that of just any citizen immersed in the activities of the world. Instead it is that which is proper to a Christian who wants to sanctify those activities. "Priestly soul" and "lay mentality" are not united in an extrinsic way, like two independent qualities that happen to coincide in the same subject. They are attitudes that must go together. Arturo Cattaneo has rightly stated that, "a lay mentality that is not informed by a priestly soul would lead to *laicism* [. . .]; and vice versa, a priestly soul that did manifest itself according to a lay mentality could lead to *clericalism*."[326]

A faithful Christian lay person contributes to the work of Redemption at the same time that he works for temporal progress. He does not separate the one from the other as would someone who had embraced a *laicist* outlook and not a lay mentality. But neither does he confuse the two, imagining that the human solution to temporal affairs (economic systems, political organization, etc.) derive from the faith, or thinking that there is only one "Christian answer" to these problems. That would not be a sign of a priestly soul, but rather of *clericalism* given that thinking thus he would tend to place temporal activities under the direction of the ecclesiastical hierarchy, which in fact does not have that mission. (A different matter altogether would be the moral dimension of temporal matters. Church leaders, in fact, do have something to say about that.)[327] By contrast, a "priestly soul" united to a "lay mentality" allows one to *understand and live in our personal life the freedom that we enjoy in the sphere of the Church and in temporal matters,*

326. Arturo Cattaneo, "Priestly Soul and Lay Mentality: The Ecclesiological Relevance of an Expression of Bl. Josemaría Escrivá," in *Romana* 34 (2002): 170. See Busca, *L'anima sacerdotale del cristiano*, p. 69.

327. "It belongs to the Church always and everywhere to announce moral principles, even about the social order, and to render judgment concerning any human affairs insofar as the fundamental rights of the human person or the salvation of souls requires it" (*CIC*, c. 747). In the writings of St. Josemaría, there are "theological-moral reflections on the action of Christians in the social and political realm, but we do not find in them what is commonly understood as 'political ideas or opinions.' This fact corresponds to a line of conduct thoughtfully assumed and constantly respected" (Rodríguez Luño, "*Cittadini degni del vangelo*" (Phil. 1:27), p. 36 s.).

seeing ourselves at the same time as both citizens of the city of God (see Eph. 2:19) *and of the city of men.*[328]

In fact, in the personality of St. Josemaría one can clearly detect the compenetration of priestly soul and lay mentality which were reinforced from early on by some of the circumstances of his life. Without going into biographical details,[329] it is worth noting that toward the end of his studies at the seminary in Zaragossa, he was simultaneously taking courses in law at a civil university. This allowed him to have contact with ways of thinking different from those in the seminary. The witness of his colleagues during those years, gathered much later in view of his cause of canonization and published in a monograph,[330] point out how naturally he moved in lay circles with a priestly spirit. He seemed to be "like a fish in water."[331] On the other hand, in the ecclesiastical environment of the seminary, one could notice in him a way of thinking proper to a Christian layperson and an effort to foster the virtues expected in civic spheres. This union of the two aspects conferred a special feature on his personality and his apostolic work, which proved decisive in establishing a deep harmony for the necessary cooperation between priests and laypersons in order to carry out together the apostolic mission of sanctifying the world from within. Already in the first residence for students that he started in Madrid in 1934, the "DYA Academy-Residence," he wanted the director to be a layman, not a priest. He wanted a well-established professional in his field (he, in fact, chose an architect for that role), who was well versed in the work of running a residence, and at the same time had the apostolic zeal and formation that would allow him to give Christian formation to students.[332] The examples are many, given that throughout his lifetime there were numerous

328. *Letter, February 2, 1945*, no. 1. We will return to considering the union between "priestly soul" and "lay mentality" in chapter seven, section 1.5.1. There, we will more greatly emphasize what the "lay mentality" of the Christian requires from the "priestly soul," whereas now we have fixed our attention above all on what the "priestly soul" of the faithful called to sanctify themselves in the middle of the world demands of the "lay mentality."

329. See, for example, Vázquez de Prada, *The Founder of Opus Dei*, vol. I, ch. IV, pp. 153–160. In general, the mutual intertwining between "priestly soul" and "lay mentality" in the personality of St. Josemaría is accurately described and illustrated through events of his life in the book of Pilar Urbano, *The Man of Villa Tevere* (New York: Scepter, 2011).

330. See Ramón Herrando Prat de la Riba, *Los años de seminario de Josemaría Escrivá en Zaragoza (1920–1925)* (Madrid: Rialp, 2002), pp. 321–374 (Documentary Appendix). Some testimonials can also be seen in A. Vázquez de Prada, *The Founder of Opus Dei*, vol. I, pp. 157–160.

331. A. Vázquez de Prada, *The Founder of Opus Dei*, vol. I, p. 157.

332. This refers to Ricardo Fernández Vallespín: see ibid., p. 538.

laypersons and priests who learned from his example of how to combine a "priestly soul" and a "lay mentality" in their lives as proper features to the Christian's "sense of divine filiation."

3.2. The Basis for Tending toward the Ultimate End of the Christian Life

For ages men have noted that God draws his children to himself, moving them not only from the outside, but also from the inside. Men are, as it were, inclined by an interior instinct, in virtue of the principle of supernatural life with which they are endowed. A human being is not only *capax gratiae*, but once made sharer in the divine nature, has in himself a positive inclination to develop more and more this life of God in his soul. St. Augustine comments in this sense on Jesus' words, "No one can come to me unless the Father who sent me draws him" (John 6:44):

> Do not think that you are drawn against your will. The mind is drawn also by love. [. . .] I say it is not enough to be drawn by the will; you are drawn even by delight. [. . .] You hold out a green twig to a sheep, and you draw it. Nuts are shown to a child, and he is attracted; he is drawn by what he runs to, drawn by loving it, drawn without hurt to the body, drawn by a cord of the heart. If, then, these things, which among earthly delights and pleasures are shown to them that love them, draw them, since it is true that every man is drawn by his own pleasure, does not Christ, revealed by the Father, draw? [. . .] [F]or '*Blessed*,' says He, '*are they that hunger and thirst after righteousness*,' that is, here; '*for they shall be filled*,' that is, there. [. . .] I render unto him what he loves, what he hopes for: he will see what, not as yet by seeing, he has believed; he shall eat that which he hungers after; he shall be filled with that which he thirsts after.[333]

Many other works of spirituality mention this tendency of man toward God. At times these considerations are not presented as an active impulse. But there are other authors who teach souls to be aware of this interior inclination to union with God and to allow themselves to be led to him without placing obstacles. The classic work of Alonso Rodríguez, *Practice of Christian Perfection and the Virtues* (first published in 1614) begins by dealing

333. St. Augustine, *In Ioann.Ev.*, 26:4–6.

with the "desire for perfection" as the basis for the spiritual life, arguing that if that desire is lacking, it is difficult for the soul to be moved toward God and to employ all the means to attain sanctity.[334]

St. Josemaría states this even more radically. The desire for perfection must be based on the awareness of being a child of God, a dearly beloved child. This is the ultimate basis and the foundation for true sanctity. Let us return for a moment to the text of St. Augustine, for it can shed light on this point. It is reasonable to think that a child may not take the nuts that his father offers him (even though he might love them and want them), if he does not know that it is his father who is offering them, or if he does not feel loved by him. After all is said and done, desire is not enough. The child will only allow himself to be drawn to the nuts if he realizes that he is the son of a father who loves him and offers him his gifts. Applying this example to the spiritual life, we can say that when St. Josemaría teaches that *the foundation of our spiritual life is the sense of our divine filiation*,[335] he is referring to the essential backdrop for the Christian's response to God who calls him and offers him his gifts: nourishment of his supernatural life, familiarity with him as his son in Christ through the Holy Spirit, and the inheritance proper to a son. Thus, the "sense of his divine filiation" launches the child toward his Father God. He runs toward that union with him not only because his Father offers him a reward, but because he knows he is a beloved child of God: "We love, because he first loved us" (John 4:19).

This way of looking at things greatly simplifies the spiritual life.

> *To establish a building's foundation, at times it is necessary to dig very deep and sink huge iron beams, until they come to rest on bedrock. But there is no need to do so if solid rock is reached right away. Our "bedrock" is this: piety, divine filiation.*[336]

In reality, whenever we look for a solid basis for the spiritual life, we end up discovering divine filiation, because this is the truth of the Christian. St. Josemaría teaches us to "excavate" there where that firm foundation can be immediately found. His advice is very simple:

---

334. See Alonso Rodríguez, *Ejercicio de perfección y virtudes cristianas* (Madrid: Nabu Press, 2012), part I, treatise 1.

335. *Letter, January 25, 1961*, no. 54.

336. *Letter, March 24, 1931*, no. 7. See Matt. 7:24–25.

> *We must try to be children who realize that the Lord, by loving us as his children, has taken us into his house, in the middle of the world, to be members of his family, so that what is his is ours, and what is ours is his.*[337]

One does have to make an effort, but this "trying to realize" that we are children of God, is something not only accessible but heartwarming. It is nothing more than what a father asks of his son when he says to him: "look at me . . . I am your father who loves you so much." Thus, a Christian is gladly drawn to God. The panorama of the spiritual life, which comes along with the burden of carrying the cross in the footsteps of Christ, then becomes sweet and lovable. *Divine filiation is a joyful truth, a consoling mystery.*[338] *Words have not yet been invented to express all that one feels—in the heart and in the will—when one knows oneself to be a son of God.*[339]

There are numerous New Testament passages that can be read in this sense. For example, the apostle writes, "Do you not know that all of us who have been baptized into Christ Jesus were baptized into his death? [. . .] So that as Christ was raised from the dead by the glory of the Father, we too might walk in newness of life" (Rom. 6:3–4). It is as if he said, "If you were only more aware of having been born as children of God in baptism, you would strive to live as children of God." Or, in other instances, the apostle is more specific: "Do you not know that your bodies are members of Christ? [. . .] Shun immorality [. . .]. Glorify God in your body" (1 Cor. 6:15, 18, 20). This is as if he had said, "If you keep in mind that you are children of God, you would use your body to give glory to your Father God." There are exhortations of some of the Fathers of the Church that reflect these ideas as well. It would suffice to recall the famous words of St. Leo the Great: "O Christian, recognize your dignity and since you have been made a sharer in the divine nature, do not think of going back to the vileness of your former ways. Think instead who is your Head and of whose body you are a member [. . .]."[340] The tone of St. Josemaría's teaching fits perfectly well with this spiritual tradition. What he proposes is already found there, and, thanks to divine graces received, he has rightly taken stock of the transcendence of knowing that he is a child of God.

---

337. *Christ Is Passing By*, no. 64.

338. Ibid., no. 65.

339. *Furrow*, no. 61.

340. St. Leo the Great, *Sermo 1 in Nativitate Domini*, 3.

To expressly place the sense of divine filiation as the foundation of the spiritual life is a teaching that is valid for all Christians, because all can call God "Father" and see themselves as his children.[341] St. Josemaría's message is addressed to the masses of faithful who have received this dignity in baptism and are called to sanctity. It offers them a solid and accessible basis for identifying themselves with Christ.

The image of "foundation" or "basis" should not lead us to think that the sense of divine filiation is like the "inert" foundation of the building of our sanctity and apostolate. For St. Josemaría, it is a "living" foundation, a dynamic basis from which Christian life flows as a plant that rises from its roots. He writes that divine filiation is a *joyful reality that grounds all our spiritual life, and imbues our interior struggle and apostolic endeavors with hope.*[342]

On another occasion, St. Josemaría stresses the power of the sense of divine filiation to sustain and direct one's whole conduct to God:

> *For our apostolate, there is no firmer rock than divine filiation; for our work, there is no source of serenity outside of divine filiation;* [. . .]. *For our mistakes, even when we come face to face with our own wretchedness, there is no greater solace or a better path, if one truly wants to seek out forgiveness and amendment, than divine filiation.*[343]

The "sense of divine filiation" is, as we have said, a "living" foundation, a vital basis that leads a person to order all situations to God. It is a root that provides vital energy to direct all of one's actions to the ultimate end of the Christian life. As we already know, St. Josemaría proclaims that ultimate end in three expressions: "giving glory to God"; "striving for Christ to reign"; and "all with Peter to Jesus through Mary." These are generic expressions that in the teaching of St. Josemaría are translated into three more specific formulas as we have studied in Part I: "contemplating God in ordinary life"; "placing Christ at the summit of all human activities"; and "making the Mass the center and root

341. As a matter of fact, Benedict XVI has proposed this approach to all Catholics: "This is our greatest dignity: to be not merely images but also children of God. And it is an invitation to live our sonship, to be increasingly aware that we are adoptive sons in God's great family. It is an invitation to transform this objective gift into a subjective reality, decisive for our way of thinking, acting and being." (*Address*, November 15, 2006).

342. *Letter, March 11, 1940*, no. 2.

343. Notes taken from preaching (AGP, P01 VI-1969, p. 13).

of the interior life." Consequently, we will devote the following sections to showing that the "awareness of being a child of God" leads a person (1) to live for the glory of God, being a contemplative in the middle of the world; (2) to strive to make Christ reign by placing him at the summit of one's professional work; and (3) as a demand of God's glory and his kingdom, to build up the Church in ourselves and in others by making the Eucharist the center and root of the Christian life. We will also add a fouth point to show how the sense of divine filiation leads us to live a profound filiation to the Church and to Mary.

3.2.1. Being Contemplatives in the Middle of the World

In order to see how this new and dynamic foundation leads to the goal, the first point we will analyze is this: knowing oneself to be a child of God leads a person to live for God's glory, seeking to be a contemplative in ordinary life.

Let us recall that to give glory to God is the same as knowing and loving him, living supernatural life, fulfilling his will with deeds. In other words, it means transforming everything into prayer dealing with the Father, with the Son, and with the Holy Spirit. And this prayer can be contemplative if God so disposes. St. Josemaría teaches us in particular to strive to contemplate in ordinary activities, as we saw in chapter one. Now, we only add that the sense of divine filiation is the foundation for the spiritual life precisely because it leads to a contemplative life and to dealing with the three divine Persons as children of the Father in the Son through the Holy Spirit in everyday life. A person who is aware of his filiation strives "to live constantly immersed in God, *deified* [*endiosado*]"[344] And this is not done passively because in giving us his grace, God draws us into his divine life. And so, we participate with our intellect, our will, and our affections in this eternal act of knowing and loving that is the mystery of God One and Three.

Just as the foundation of a house "awaits" the house itself, or as the seed of a plant "begs" for growth, so too, the sense of divine filation is the basis and the motor for growth in sanctity because it expects and begs for that contemplative life that glorifies the most Blessed Trinity, and leads the Christian to his perfection and happiness:

---

344. Ocáriz, "La filiación divina, realidad central en la vida y en la enseñanza de Mons. Escrivá de Balaguer," p. 206.

> *Divine filiation* [. . .] *fills all our spiritual life, because it shows us how to speak to God, to know and to love our Father in heaven. And it makes our interior struggle overflow with hope and gives us the trusting simplicity of little children. And even more: precisely because we are children of God, that we can contemplate everything in love and wonder as coming from the hands of our Father God the Creator. And so we become contemplatives in the middle of the world, loving the world.*[345]

When Jesus' disciples asked him: "teach us to pray" (Luke 11:1), the Lord *reveals to them the great secret of God's mercy: that we are children of God and we can talk things over with him and spend time with him, just as trustingly as a son does with his father.*[346] St. Josemaría teaches us to cultivate that relationship: *God is a Father who is full of tenderness, of infinite love. Call him 'Father' many times a day and tell him—alone, in your heart—that you love him, that you adore him, that you feel proud and strong because you are his son. All this implies a genuine program of interior life.*[347] This "program of interior life" is a way of prayer and contemplation "in the middle of the world": *While being fully involved in his everyday work, among other men, his equals; busy, under stress, the Christian has to be at the same time totally involved with God, for he is a child of God.*[348]

In these last words ("for he is a child of God"), there lies the key to what we now want to consider. The awareness of being a child of God leads a person to be "immersed in God" at the same time that he is "immersed" in his professional or family affairs. And so, he converts them into prayer, a prayer that can reach the heights of contemplation, crowning his desires to give glory to God.

For the rest, the sense of divine filiation gives a particular tone to prayer. It *gives us the trusting simplicity of little children.*[349] It leads a person to begin and to continue a dialogue *with the same spontaneity and confidence with which a child abandons himself to his father's care.*[350] It is a prayer of children who know they are unworthy of everything and in need of forgiveness,[351]

---

345. *Christ Is Passing By*, no. 65.

346. *Friends of God*, no. 145.

347. Ibid., no. 150. See *The Forge*, no. 331.

348. *Christ Is Passing By*, no. 65.

349. Ibid.

350. Ibid., no. 135.

351. See ibid., no. 7; St. Thomas Aquinas, *S. Th.*, I, q. 21, a. 3, c.

but who are completely certain of the mercy of the Father who leads them to abandon themselves in his hands and to have the eagerness to *identify our will fully with God's will.*[352] This unlimited confidence glorifies God and at the same time gives joy to man. *Abandonment to the will of God is the secret of happiness on earth.*[353] The Christian life based on the sense of divine filiation is distinguished by its abandonment in the hands of God. And this bears the unmistakable seal of peace and joy, fruits of the Holy Spirit (see Gal. 5:22).

3.2.2. Placing Christ at the Summit of All Human Activities

In order to give glory to God, it is necessary to strive for Christ to reign. One cannot be a contemplative in the middle of the world (and thus give glory to God), if one does not strive to place Christ at the heart of all that one does, because it is only in this way that we allow him to reign in our life and help him to reign in society, sharing in his mediation. In summary, this is what we have already seen in chapter two. Now we only want to see how the sense of divine filiation, in fact, leads to placing Christ in the heart of the activity that each one carries out in the middle of the world.

The question is quite clear because a person who knows himself to be a child of God is also aware that *Christ's life is our life*,[354] and this necessarily moves us to seek to identify ourselves with him. The end result of this seeking is that Christ comes to reign in one's life ever more deeply. And just as *you cannot separate the fact that Christ is God from his role as Redeemer*[355] so neither is it possible to separate in a Christian who lives the life of Christ his status of a son of God from that of being called to take part in the intra-Trinitarian life and sharing in the priestly mediation of Christ through which he is called to co-redeem. The sense of divine filiation, which "requires" being identified with Christ, also demands and inflames apostolic zeal. It brings a person to allow Christ to reign in his life and to cooperate with him in spreading his kingdom, that is, to love him and seek for others to love him.

Let us take a look at the different aspects of this topic following the order we established in chapter two. We will do this in broad strokes without considering every point in detail.

---

352. *Christ Is Passing By*, no. 135.

353. *The Way*, no. 766.

354. *Christ Is Passing By*, no. 103.

355. Ibid., no. 106.

In the first place, wanting Christ to reign implies receiving his mediation: following him and imitating him. The awareness of divine filiation leads precisely to this: "St. Josemaría speaks to us about our effort to *imitate* Jesus, not because of a simple exterior likeness, but rather because he lives in us as the only begotten Son, in his unity and distinction with the Father."[356] *If we imitate Christ, we will attain the marvelous possibility of sharing in that current of love, which is the mystery of God, One in Three.*[357]

In the second place, wanting Christ to reign leads a person to exercise his priesthood, being with Christ and in Christ a mediator between God and men. The sense of divine filiation arouses and strengthens this awareness of the priesthood that a son (or daughter) of God is called to live, both in the ascending sense (offering prayers and the sacrifice of his own will to God the Father), as well as in the descending sense (being Christ's instrument to save men). The following words of St. Josemaría are a source of these ideas:

> *Each of us is to be* ipse Christus*: Christ himself. He is the one mediator between God and man* (see 1 Tim. 2:5). *And we make ourselves one with him in order to offer all things, with him, to the Father. Our calling to be children of God, in the middle of the world, requires us not only to seek our own personal holiness, but also to go out onto all the pathways of the earth, to convert them into roads that will lead souls over all obstacles and lead them to the Lord. As we take part in all temporal activities, as ordinary citizens, we are to become leaven* (see Matt. 13:33) *acting on the dough.* (see 1 Cor. 5:6)[358]

The sense of divine filiation in Christ implies that,

> *we consider ourselves to be sent, as he was,* peccatores salvos facere (1 Tim. 1:15), *to save all sinners, with the clear realization that we ourselves need to trust in the mercy of God more and more every day; hence, the vehement desire in us to live as coredeemers with Christ, to save all souls with him, because we are, we want to be,* ipse Christus, *Christ himself, as He gave himself as a ransom for all.* (1 Tim. 2:6)[359]

---

356. F. Ocáriz, "La filiación divina, realidad central en la vida y en la enseñanza de Mons. Escrivá de Balaguer," p. 187.

357. *Friends of God*, no. 252.

358. *Christ Is Passing By*, no. 120.

359. Ibid., no. 121.

The awareness of our divine filiation fosters the priestly meaning of our life, provoking a positive attitude in the face of sacrifice and sorrow that are seen as a means and occasion for co-redeeming with Christ. St. Josemaría states that *close to our Lord we are able to find joy in suffering, self-denial and sorrow. What a great source of strength it is for a son of God to know that he is so close to his Father!*[360]

> *This supernatural acceptance of suffering was, precisely, the greatest of all conquests. By dying on the cross Jesus overcame death. God brings life from death. The attitude of a child of God is not one of resignation to a possibly tragic fate; it is the sense of achievement of someone who has a foretaste of victory.*[361]

Here one can see a characteristic feature of the spirit of divine filiation: to make our joy "solid" or stable. A son of God knows that in order to be a mediator in union with Christ, he has to embrace the cross. He doesn't see this as contrary to joy and peace. His filial awareness leads him to recognize the redeeming value of physical or moral suffering, and he does not lose his joy when they come his way.[362]

In the previous paragraphs, we have essentially referred to our ascending mediation. Now, we want to note that the sense of divine filiation is also the basis for and the impulse that prolongs the descending priestly mediation, in view of being instruments of Christ in communicating supernatural life to others, and of transforming earthly realities according to the will of God. "To *divinize* the world and guide all things back to God as the result of our own *divinization*: all Christian apostolate, which is built upon divine filiation, has this as its aim because it is a necessary consequence of our being *ipse Christus*; and in Christ—the only Mediator—we are co-reedemers and mediators."[363]

"If children, then heirs, heirs of God and fellow heirs with Christ, provided we suffer with him in order that we may also be glorified with him" (Rom. 8:16–17). The inheritance of the adopted children is the vision of God face-to-face in future glory. But we must not forget, as we have already

---

360. *Friends of God*, no. 246.

361. *Christ Is Passing By*, no. 168.

362. An admirable example of this attitude is the life of María Ignacia García Escobar, one of the first women of Opus Dei, incorporated into the Work in 1932 when she was already gravely ill: see José Miguel Cejas, *La paz y la alegría: María Ignacia García Escobar en los comienzos del Opus Dei, 1896–1933* (Madrid: Rialp, 2001).

363. Ocáriz, "La filiación divina, realidad central en la vida y en la enseñanza de Mons. Escrivá de Balaguer," p. 210.

explained,[364] that created goods also form part of this inheritance once they have been fully ordered to God and reflect his glory without the shadows brought on by sin.[365] The sense of divine filiation leads a person to take possession of this inheritance: to contemplate God and to order all things to his kingdom.

For an ordinary Christian, filiation and inheritance are bound together in a special way because he is called to identify himself with Christ precisely by sanctifying his action in his ordinary, secular, and civil life. We can say that he is called to make heaven his own by taking possession of the earth, and in this sense we should read the following words:

> *We must, each of us, be* alter Christus, ipse Christus: *another Christ, Christ himself. Only in this way can we set about this great undertaking, this immense, unending task of sanctifying all temporal structures from within, bringing to them the leaven of the Redemption.*[366]

We are not saying that an ordinary Christian "first" ought to seek to identify himself with Christ and "then" sanctify temporal activities. What he must do is place the sense of divine filiation, the search for identification with Christ in ordinary life, as the basis for sanctifying earthly realities. Here is another text that shows this clearly:

> *Sacred Scripture teaches us that when he finished the marvelous work of creation, bringing forth heaven and earth with the splendid array of beings* (see Gen. 2:1), God saw everything that he had made, and behold, it was very good (Gen. 1:31). *It was Adam's sin that broke the divine harmony of creation. But God the Father, when the fullness of time came, sent his Only-Begotten Son into the world to re-establish peace: so that, by redeeming man from sin,* adoptionem filiorum reciperemus (Gal. 4:5), *we might be made children of God, able to share in the divine intimacy; and so that it would also be possible for this new man, this new branch of God's children* (see Rom. 6:4–5), *to free the entire creation from disorder, re-establishing all things in Christ* (see Eph. 1:9–10), *who has reconciled them with God* (see Col. 1:20) [. . .]. *God calls us to imitate him as dearly beloved children—* estote imitatores Dei, sicut filii carissimi (Eph. 5:1), *be imitators of God, as*

364. See section 1.2.1.

365. See *CCC*, nos. 299 and 1029; Ps. 15:5; Col. 1:12 and 3:24; Tit. 3:7; 1 Pet. 1:4.

366. *Christ Is Passing By*, no. 183.

> *his beloved sons and daughters—collaborating humbly and fervently in the divine plan to unite what is broken, to save what is lost, to put straight what man has put into disarray, to bring to its true goal what has gone astray: to restore divine harmony to all created things.*[367]

Psalm 2, which St. Josemaría urged people to meditate on frequently, expresses this relation between divine filiation and the inheritance of created things: "You are my Son, today I have begotten you. Ask of me, and I will make the nations your heritage, and the ends of the earth your possession" (Ps. 2:7–8). To possess earthly realities is to sanctify them. And this is only possible with God's grace. (The Psalm in effect exhorts us to ask for it: "Ask of me . . .") It is from the sense of divine filiation that there comes the urge to ask God for the inheritance of children. We ask him to enable us to sanctify earthly realities, and thus lead us to the fullness of divine filiation in glory.

3.2.3. Building up the Church by Making Holy Mass the Center and Root of the Interior Life

Let us recall, as a premise for this point, that the glory of God and the reign of Christ require that "all with Peter go to Jesus through Mary," that is, to build up the Church. But the Church is built with "living stones" (1 Pet. 2:5), or that is, Christians who seek personal sanctity and carry out apostolate. The sense of divine filiation urges us to do precisely this: seek personal sanctity (i.e., union with Christ in the Church, making use of the means that he offers us, and doing apostolate, knowing that we are members of Christ destined to draw all human beings to his body).

> *A Christian knows that he is grafted onto Christ through baptism. He is empowered to fight for Christ through confirmation, called to act in the world sharing the royal, prophetic, and priestly role of Christ. He has become one and the same thing with Christ through the Eucharist, the sacrament of unity and love. And so, like Christ, he has to live for other men, loving each and every one around him, and indeed all humanity.*[368]

---

367. *Letter, March 11, 1940*, no. 2. See *Christ Is Passing By*, no. 183; *Conversations*, no. 114. In chapter seven, we will deal with sanctification of earthly realities in depth; here, we are only trying to show that the foundation of that sanctification is the sense of divine filiation.

368. *Christ Is Passing By*, no. 106.

It is in the Eucharist that we achieve the highest degree of sacramental union with Christ, and where a Christian is sent forth to all souls in order to draw them into the Church or to unite them more fully with the Head. The communion of men with God in Christ—the Church—is formed and built up by means of the Eucharist. "We who are many are one body, for we all partake of the one bread"(1 Cor. 10:17), as the apostle writes. Whoever participates in the Eucharist and strives to bring others to share in it, builds up the Church. In the spiritual teaching of St. Josemaría, all this comes about by making Holy Mass the "center and root" of the interior life, as we saw in chapter three.

On the basis of these premises, we can now emphasize what we are most directly interested in: the sense of divine filiation as the solid foundation for building up the Church. Whoever is aware of being a child of God, of "being Christ," sees the Church as Christ sees her, as his body. This awareness moves him to care for her and to strengthen her, to develop her, and to build her up, "for no man ever hates his own flesh, but nourishes and cherishes it, as Christ does the church" (Eph. 5:29). This becomes even clearer when we bear in mind what the Eucharist means for the Church. The Christian who knows that he is Christ will want to unite himself to the Sacrifice of Christ, from which stems all the life of the Church. Isn't this what St. Paul says when, after declaring to the Colossians that Christ lives in every Christian (see Col. 1:27), he applies that to himself and writes, "In my flesh I complete what is lacking in Christ's afflictions for the sake of his body, that is, the church" (Col. 1:24)? The apostle, utterly enthused by his divine filiation, knows that Christ lives in him and consequently aspires to "complete" Christ's self-giving in his flesh. For us, this is carried out at Holy Mass, the sacramental renewal of the Sacrifice of Calvary, which allows the Christian to offer himself to the Father in union with Christ through the Holy Spirit in order to draw all men and women to his mystical body.

Thus, the sense of divine filiation moves the Christian to build up the Church, making the Holy Mass the *center and root of the Christian life.*[369] For a person who is aware of "being Christ," the Mass is not a ceremony in which he is present as a spectator or one that he witnesses from the outside. On the contrary, he feels implicated in the sacrifice with his whole being and perceives it as "his," precisely because he knows that he is *ipse Christus*. St. Josemaría says, *"Our" Mass, Jesus,*[370] and expresses the "need" for

369. Ibid., no. 102.

370. *The Way*, no. 533.

Eucharistic Communion by saying, *I can understand your keenness to receive the Holy Eucharist each day. Those who feel they are children of God have an overpowering need of Christ.*[371]

The Church was born from the open side of Christ crucified. A Christian who knows that he is one with him will want to unite himself to his sacrifice in order to cooperate in building up the mystical body.[372] He feels this way not only while sharing in the liturgical celebration, but throughout the whole day. He longs to convert the fulfillment of his duties into "a Mass." The basis for this grand longing is the sense of divine filiation.

(a) "My Mother the Church"

Filiation to the Church and filiation to Mary are not distinct. We will see this later. But the first question we need to deal with is a didactic one. Now, if we consider Mary to be the "Mother of the Church,"[373] we should first speak about filiation to Mary; however, if we consider that she is a member of the Church—a "preeminent and singular member,"[374] in fact—we should first consider filiation to the Church. We have chosen the latter approach because it is clearer in the context of this section on building up the Church.

The sense of divine filiation moves a Christian to look at the Church as a mother who gives supernatural life to her children and rejoices in her maternity. *What joy to be able to say with all the fervor of my soul: I love my Mother the holy Church!*[375] This tender expression, "my Mother the Church," is found everywhere in the preaching of St. Josemaría as we already saw at the beginning of chapter three. Filiation to the Church is a deep sentiment in the soul of a child of God because, "we are born from her and in

371. *The Forge*, no. 830.

372. In *Letter, March 19, 1967*, no. 66, St. Josemaría cites the Council of Vienne: "In order to carry out the salvation of all, the Word of God not only wished to be nailed to the cross and die on it, but allowed himself to be pierced by a lance after exhaling his spirit, so that as water and blood flowed from his side, the one Holy Mother Church, the immaculate and virginal spouse of Christ, should be formed just as Eve was formed from the side of the first man while fast asleep" (Concilium Viennense, 1312, Constitution *De Summa Trinitate et fide catholica*: DS 901). The comparison is of Patristic origin: see St. Ambrose, *Expositio Evangelii secundum Lucam*, 2, 85–89: PL 15, 1583–1586. This teaching was proposed again in Vatican II, Constitution on the Sacred Liturgy *Sacrosanctum Concilium* (December 4, 1963), no. 5. See also *CCC*, nos. 766 and 1067.

373. Paul VI, Address (November 21, 1964).

374. *Lumen gentium*, no. 53.

375. *The Way*, no. 518.

her to the life of grace through baptism, and our supernatural life always grows *ex Ecclesia*. Certainly, our birth as children of God is *ex Deo*, but also *ex Ecclesia*. And thus, we are children of God insofar as we are children of the Church, and vice versa: one presupposes and implies the other. The Church's motherhood is, in a certain way, an expression or manifestation of the divine fatherhood with respect to God's adoptive children."[376]

St. Josemaría repeats the well-known expression of St. Cyprian: "Whoever does not have the Church as his Mother, cannot have God as his Father."[377] Being aware of being a child of God entails being aware that one is son or daughter of the Church, the *family of the children of God*.[378] This is not a theoretical or intellectual awareness. It is, instead, a loving realization stemming from filial love that moves the Christian to be a good child of the Church, to "build up" the family of the children of God by striving to intensify his personal union with God the Father, in the Son, through the Holy Spirit, and to extend this union to other persons with the eager desire to embrace all of humanity. Filial love for the Church makes us feel the responsibility of being personally holy and of desiring holiness for all the members of the Church. It moves a person to draw all men and women to the Church, cooperating with the Holy Spirit in order to lead everyone to the means of sanctification through which our Mother the Church communicates supernatural life. The principal means to which all the others are directed is the Eucharist, the sacrament of the Body and Blood of Christ, "the bread of children,"[379] food that unites us intimately with him and enables us to grow as children of God. Inspired by St. Josemaría, Bishop Javier Echavarría writes, "The Eucharist is justly called 'the bread of children' because it develops and strengthens man's participation in the eternal filiation of the Word. The Eucharist is the sacrament that increases, perfects, and brings to perfection the Christian's participation in the divine filiation that Christ personally possesses in all its fullness."[380]

St. Josemaría frequently speaks not only of filiation to the Church, but also to the Pope. Oftentimes he mentions them together, encouraging souls

376. Ocáriz, "La filiación divina, realidad central en la vida y en la enseñanza de Mons. Escrivá de Balaguer," p. 195.

377. St. Cyprian, *De catholicae Ecclesiae unitate*, 6 (cited in the homily "The Supernatural Aim of the Church," May 28, 1972, in *In Love with the Church*, no. 29).

378. *Conversations*, no. 113. See *Christ Is Passing By*, no. 139.

379. Sequence *Lauda Sion*: expression cited in *Christ Is Passing By*, no. 152.

380. Javier Echevarría, *Eucaristía y vida cristiana* (Madrid: Rialp, 2005), pp. 31–32.

to be good *children of the Church and of the Pope*;[381] they are, in effect, one and the same, for the latter is nothing else than a visible and necessary sign of the former.

The sense of divine filiation, which leads to filiation to the Church, also moves the Christian to express it as filiation to the Pope. St. Josemaría writes,

> Ubi Petrus, ibi Ecclesia, ibi Deus. *We want to be with Peter, because with him is the Church, with him is God; and without him we will not find God* [. . .]. *Love the Holy Father a lot. Pray for the Pope often. Love him very much; yes, love him very much!*[382]

"Praying" for the Pope and "loving" the Pope are two aspects of filial love to which St. Josemaría refers in this text. At other times, he speaks about "supernatural and human" affection: a love that is supernatural because it is manifested, for instance, with prayer and sacrifice for the Pope, as well as human because it is expressed by means of various local customs and circumstances. Regardless, these are not just sentiments, but rather something that transcends them, for love is rooted directly in the will. Thus, in order for the Christian's love for the Pope to be truly filial love, we undoubtedly need obedience to the Pope's supreme authority and adherence to his Magisterium. In this sense, the forms of showing filiation to the Pope become the channel for living as children of God, and vice versa: *In order to be good children of the Pope, I don't have any other recipe than this: sanctity.*[383]

On the connection between divine filiation and filiation to the Pope, it is worth while to recall that "Father" is the proper name of the first Person of the Most Blessed Trinity. He is subsistent Paternity, and no one else can be called "Father" in this full and perfect sense. "Call no man your father on earth, for you have one Father, who is in heaven" (Matt. 23:9).[384] That paternity is present in the only begotten Son made man, because of the unity of the divine Persons in their relative distinction. The Lord says, "He who has seen me has seen the Father" (John 14:9). But in addition, God

381. *Letter, January 9, 1932,* no. 1. *We will be what our Lord wants, good children of the Church and of the Pope.* Notes taken from preaching, January 9, 1972 (AGP, P01 II-1972, p. 51).

382. Notes taken from preaching, May 11, 1965 (AGP, P01 I-1976, p. 113).

383. Notes taken from preaching, May 28, 1964 (AGP, P01 VII-1964, p. 47).

384. See *CCC,* no. 198.

wanted to reflect his paternity in his children in different ways (see Eph. 3:14–15). There is a natural, human engendering with its corresponding paternity, as well as a supernatural generation that gives rise to a spiritual paternity (see John 1:13). The apostles felt this spiritual paternity when the Lord sent them out as he himself had been sent by the Father (see John 20:21) to convey supernatural life, by teaching the Good News and baptizing (see Matt. 28:19). St. Paul also must have felt this paternity very deeply when he wrote, "For though you have countless guides in Christ, you do not have many fathers. For I became your father in Christ Jesus through the gospel" (1 Cor. 4:15). "My little children, with whom I am again in travail until Christ be formed in you!" (Gal. 4:19). After the apostles, this supernatural paternity corresponds to the bishops in the Church, and above all to their head, the successor of Peter, the universal shepherd. He is called "holy father" because he is the first depository of a truly holy, supernatural paternity. And he is the common father of all, as Vatican I teaches: "the Roman Pontiff is the successor of Blessed Peter, Prince of the Apostles, and is the true Vicar of Christ, and the Head of the whole Church, and Father and Teacher of all Christians."[385] At times St. Josemaría calls him the *common Father*[386] of Christians.

We briefly mention here that there is also a spiritual paternity proper to the other shepherds in the Church, and not only to the Pope and the bishops,[387] and of every Christian who, by exercising his common priesthood, can be said to engender Christ in others when he cooperates with the Holy Spirit in passing on supernatural life.

Filiation to the Church and the Pope, as a demand and sign of divine filiation, is something common to all Christians. Together with it (or, more precisely, "from within" it), St. Josemaría speaks about other aspects of divine filiation derived from his mission as founder of Opus Dei. We will briefly refer to them, because even though they only directly apply to those who form part of Opus Dei, they contain a more general teaching about filiation to the Church and in the Church.

385. Vatican I, Dogmatic Constitution *Pastor Aeternus*: DS 3059. The text has words from the Council of Florence: DS 1307.

386. Notes taken from preaching, November 21, 1958 (AGP, P01 II-1988, p. 44); November 30, 1964 (AGP, P02 XII-1964, p. 33); etc.

387. As the Second Vatican Council affirmed, the sacred ministers receive a "paternity in Christ" (Decree *Prebyterorum Ordinis*, no. 16), as shepherds of the Church. On the bishop as father, see St. John Paul II, Apostolic Exhortation *Pastores Gregis* (October 16, 2003), nos. 7, 10, 33, 37, 42, etc.

The founder frequently called Opus Dei [or, familiarly, "the Work"] "Mother." For example: *We have this most lovable Mother, the Work.*[388] He uses this expression because he knows that Opus Dei has to feed the spiritual life of its members with solid Christian formation. He exhorts them to "care for the Work" as caring for a mother, which for them is a specific way of fulfilling the duty to care for the Church, given that God entrusted that part of his family in a special way to them. St. Josemaría encourages the members of Opus Dei to seek sanctity by being faithful to their calling, and to *protect the sanctity of the Work, our Mother.*[389]

For the faithful of Opus Dei, the sense of divine filiation also includes a filial attitude toward the founder to whom God granted a spiritual paternity of which he was aware from the beginning: *I cannot fail to lift up my heart in gratitude to God,* from whom every family in heaven and on earth is named (Eph. 3:15–16), *for having given me this spiritual paternity, which I have taken on with his grace, fully aware of being on this earth only to fulfill it. And so I love you with the heart of a father and a mother.*[390] The purpose of this divine gift was not only to found Opus Dei, but also to direct it as the head of a family, exercising the role of the Good Shepherd. In this sense, the same paternity extends to his successors. Bishop Javier Echevarría explained this when he took over as the Prelate of Opus Dei in 1994, after the death of the Servant of God, Álvaro del Portillo: "Thanks to the very special paternity that God granted Blessed Josemaría to found Opus Dei [. . .], [Opus Dei] is a true family with supernatural ties. Based on the foundation of that paternity—in which all of the successors of our Father will participate until the end of time—with God's grace, in the Work we will always keep alive this family spirit that is essential to it."[391]

(b) "My Mother Holy Mary"

The "sense of divine filiation" necessarily entails the "sense of filiation to Mary." *My Mother Holy Mary*[392] is the way the Founder of Opus Dci often expresses it, as have many other saints. For him, it is an essential dimension of the sense of divine filiation because how can a person who is aware of

388. *Letter, March 28, 1955,* no. 29.

389. *Letter, June 16, 1960,* no. 27.

390. *Letter, May 6, 1945,* no. 23.

391. Javier Echevarría, Homilía, April 24, 1994, in *Romana* 18 (1994), 131.

392. *The Way,* no. 507; *The Forge,* no. 624; etc.

being a child of God—"another Christ, Christ himself"—not see himself as a son of Jesus' Mother? *It was on Calvary that Christ, her most blessed Son and our brother, gave her to us as our mother when he said to St. John:* Behold your mother (John 19:27).[393]

As we have said before, filiation to the Church and filiation to Mary are not two distinct filiations. The supernatural life that is given to us through Mary's mediation is received in and through the Church. Mary is not only the most eminent member of the Church, but also her "figure" (*typus*).[394] In a certain way, she represents the Church. Filiation to the Church can be somewhat of an abstract notion; however, with filiation to Mary, it becomes something entirely personal. In Mary, the Church takes on the features of a Mother on this earth. The sense of divine filiation and of filiation to the Church thus take on a warm, familiar tone. God has willed to introduce us into the Trinitarian life along a safe path, which invites us to have complete confidence, and which is fully tender and sweet. *Cor Mariae dulcissimum, iter para tutum!*[395] [Most sweet Heart of Mary, prepare a safe way for us!] Thus, St. Josemaría prayed many times because *her sweet heart knows the surest path for finding Christ.*[396]

> *I would recommend that, if you haven't already done so, you find out for yourself through personal experience the meaning of Mary's maternal love. It is not enough to just know she is our Mother and to think and to talk about her as such. She is your Mother and you are her son. She loves you as if you were her only child in this world. Treat her accordingly: tell her about everything that happens to you, honor her and love her. No one will do it for you or as well as you, if you do not do it yourself. I give you my word that, if you set out along this way, you will quickly discover all the love of Christ: and you will find yourself drawn into the ineffable life of God the Father, God the Son, and God the Holy Spirit.*[397]

St. Josemaría wanted to impress on souls an endearing conviction about the supernatural maternity of the most holy Virgin. With words that sprang from his experience of living divine filiation, he contemplated Mary as *a Mother with two sons, face to face: He . . . and you;*[398] and showed that her

393. *Christ Is Passing By*, no. 171.

394. See *Lumen gentium*, no. 63.

395. *Christ Is Passing By*, no. 38. See ibid., no. 178.

396. Ibid., no. 38.

397. *Friends of God*, no. 293.

398. *The Way*, no. 506.

maternal role is to cooperate with the Holy Spirit in uniting us to her first-born Son: *Our Lady, Holy Mary, will make of you* alter Christus, ipse Christus: *another Christ, Christ himself!*[399]

The words "she will make of you [. . .]." contain in some way his deep understanding of Mary's maternity in the economy of grace to which we have already referred.[400] Mary not only intercedes for us to obtain supernatural life, as do the saints; her mediation is truly "maternal" because, in some sense, she engenders us to that life. And this is the doctrinal background for the exhortations that St. Josemaría continually addresses to us, so that we might have recourse to the most holy Virgin as our mother.[401]

From the point of view of divine filiation, we can consider Mary also as a model, *speculum iustitiae*, a perfect reflection of Christ. And so it is natural to want to be more like her, as a child resembles his or her mother. Of course, this implies imitating her virtues. But the Christian must also follow Mary's example in cooperating with the Holy Spirit in forming the Church and in transmitting supernatural life. Mary shows us how to carry out our apostolic mission, how to draw others to Christ, and how to build up the Church in them. It is in this profound sense that a Christian has to be like Mary: *If we become identified with Mary and imitate her virtues, we will be able to bring Christ to life, through grace, in the souls of many who will in turn become identified with him through the action of the Holy Spirit. If we imitate Mary, we will share in some way in her spiritual motherhood.*[402]

(c) "St. Joseph, My Father and Lord" and "From the Trinity on Earth to the Trinity in Heaven"

Together with filiation to the most holy Virgin, St. Josemaría considers filiation to St. Joseph, whom he frequently calls *my father and lord,* or *our father and lord.*[403] A characteristic feature of his preaching is that of not "separating" Joseph from Mary. Even though St. Joseph's paternity with regard to Jesus is of an essentially different order than Mary's maternity, it

399. *Christ Is Passing By*, no. 11.

400. See chapter three, section 4.2.

401. See, e.g., the homily "Mother of God, Our Mother," in *Friends of God*, nos. 274–293.

402. *Friends of God*, no. 281. Here we can see how St. Josemaría uses the term "identification" in a flexibile way. In any case, although the "identification with Mary" of which he speaks here does not have the same meaning as the "identification with Christ," neither can it be reduced to an external imitation, precisely because she intervenes as mother in the infusion of supernatural life.

403. *The Way*, no. 560; *The Forge*, no. 624; *Friends of God*, no. 174; etc.

is not merely a legal title. It is an authentic paternity established by God, and it extends spiritually to those who are united to Christ.[404] Hence, the awareness of being "*ipse Christus*" also entails an awareness of being a child of Mary, as well as a son or daughter of St. Joseph.

St. Joseph's fatherhood toward the children of God is shown in that he is the protector and master of the interior life: a master who teaches the Christian how to become one with Christ.

> *Saint Joseph really is Father and Lord. He protects those who revere him and accompanies them on their journey through this life, just as he protected and accompanied Jesus when he was growing up. As you get to know him, you discover that the holy patriarch is also a master of the interior life, for he teaches us to know Jesus, to share our life with him, and to realize that we are part of God's family.*[405]

According to St. Josemaría, St. Joseph teaches us to go to Jesus through Mary. Put in such terms, filiation to Joseph acquires an exceptional importance. His intercession leads a person to deal with Mary as our mother, and both of them lead us to become more and more identified with Jesus.

> *I go to St. Joseph, who is my Father and Lord, and with him I go to his Spouse, the Virgin Mary, who is also my Mother. With Mary and Joseph I draw close to Jesus* [. . .]. *Then, knowing that he listens to us, that he loves us; knowing that we are Christ (because he assumes us in some way), we find joy in praising him in this way: glory be to the Father, glory be to the Son, glory be to the Holy Spirit.*[406]

This is the *itinerary* for the Christian life:

> *Through Jesus, Mary and Joseph, the* trinity *on earth, each of us will find our own way to draw close to the Father, the Son and the Holy Spirit, the Trinity in heaven.*[407]

---

404. St. Augustine writes that "both [Mary and Joseph] deserve to be called parents of Christ; not only that mother, but also that father as spouse of her who was his mother, both by means of the mind, not of the flesh" (*De nuptiis et concupiscentia*, I, 11, 12). St. John Paul II explains this mystery in the Apostolic Exhortation *Redemptoris Custos* (August 15, 1989), see especially, nos. 7–8 and 19.

405. *Christ Is Passing By*, no. 39. See Laurentino María Herrán, "La devoción a San José en la vida y enseñanzas de Mons. Escrivá de Balaguer, fundador del Opus Dei," in *Estudios Josefinos* 68 (1980): 147–189. Ignacio Soler, "San José en los escritos y en la vida de San Josemaría. Hacia una teología de la vida ordinaria," in *Estudios Josefinos* 118 (2005): 259–284.

406. Notes taken from preaching, May 1974 (AGP, P04 1974, vol. I, p. 65).

407. Notes taken from preaching, December 25, 1973 (AGP, P09, p. 205).

We find ourselves before a teaching that embraces the whole of the spiritual life. "From the *trinity* on earth to the Trinity in heaven," is a profound idea that we have not found expressed this way in any other master of the spiritual life. The goal is union with the most Blessed Trinity and the way is the *trinity* on earth. St. Josemaría sees in this *trinity* a reflection of the Trinity. The reflection does not consist in a one-to-one correspondence between the persons (as if, Jesus could be paired up with the Son, Mary with the Father, and Joseph with the Holy Spirit). It doesn't simply consist in there being three, but rather in there being *three hearts, but only one love.*[408] This is what makes the *trinity* on earth the way to the Trinity in heaven. In reality, only Jesus is the way (see John 14:6), but God has willed to give us Jesus in the family of Mary and Joseph. This family is the cradle of the Church, and is already the Church. That is precisely why it is also the way like Jesus is (i.e., not like a way that we leave behind when we reach the end, but rather like the "locus" where the end comes to us, that is, where we unite ourselves to the most Blessed Trinity). Thus we discover this fountain of our supernatural life that is near at hand, readily accessible, and also very sweet and cordial. Entering intimately into these three hearts that are really just one, the Christian is united to Christ through those persons chosen by God to welcome him lovingly on earth, and in such a way, begin to contemplate and participate in the intimate life of the most Blessed Trinity, the God who is love (see 1 John 4:7). Hence, St. Josemaría teaches us to go to Jesus through Mary, and to Mary through Joseph (who leads us to Jesus through Mary). This path is to be traveled not only in mental prayer, but also in carrying out one's family and professional duties, given that the family of Nazareth is also "Joseph's workshop" where the Christian learns to sanctify his professional work, as well as his family and social duties. In other words, the Christian learns to convert his ordinary duties into prayer, a dialogue with the three divine Persons through his dialogue with the *trinity* on earth.

3.3. From Baptism to Glory

We have seen that St. Josemaría considers the sense of divine filiation to be the foundation of the Christian life in its most radical dimension: the ultimate end of all one's actions. Being fully aware of being a child of God means that a person sees that the end goal of his life is to give glory to God,

408. Notes taken from preaching, March 19, 1971 (AGP, P09, p. 133).

with all that it entails (contemplating God in the middle of the world, placing Christ at the summit of all human activities, building up the Church), as we have studied in Part I.

Now we will pause to consider two questions that are basic for what we will see in Parts II and III (on the *subject* and on the *path* of the Christian life, respectively). We will see, first, that growing in identification with Christ means growing in the sense of divine filiation, in charity, and in the freedom of the children of God. In fact, the sense of divine filiation brings a person to seek this growth. Second, keeping in mind that the ultimate end of the Christian life and of the perfection itself of the Christian (his/her identification with Jesus Christ) is accomplished on this earth, as we will see in Part III, the awareness of divine filiation moves a person to undertake this path: to sanctify temporal realities, to struggle out of love against the obstacles that are opposed to sanctity, and to use the means for sanctity and apostolate that the Church offers.

3.3.1. The Growth of a Child of God

Let us recall some words of St. Josemaría that we have previously quoted in part: *Sanctity, both in priests and in laity, is simply the perfection of Christian life, the fullness of divine filiation.*[409] In this text, the terms "sanctity," "perfection," and "divine filiation" are intimately united. Undoubtedly, sanctity and perfection are realities that are meant to grow from the first infusion of grace until its culmination in glory. Can we say the same about adoptive divine filiation? The words of St. Josemaría quoted above indicate that this filiation has a "fullness." Hence, we are not dealing with a "static" reality that remains always the same. And since it is intended to become a fullness, it seems that there must be progressive growth and intensification. St. Josemaría does not affirm this explicitly, but in our opinion it is a logical conclusion from his earlier words, and in general, from the notion of divine filiation as a participation in the filiation of the Word.

However, this hypothesis seems to clash with what is normally understood by filiation. At first sight, filiation is an immutable relationship: whoever is a son is a son once and for all. He may be a better or worse son to his parents, but he is not more or less their son. Nor can he cease being their son, because the basis for this relationship (having been engendered by

409. *Letter, February 2, 1945*, no. 8.

them) is an unquestionable historical fact, and is in perfect conformity with human nature itself. This is clearly the case with human filiation. But is it the same with adoptive supernatural filiation? Is this filation identical with human filiation?

We must above all keep in mind a fundamental difference. Adopted divine filiation is, as we have seen in the teaching of St. Thomas to which St. Josemaría refers, a participation in a filiation that exists outside of the participants by essence: subsistent Filiation, which is the Second Person of the Trinity. On the other hand, human filiation exists only *in* men, not *outside* of them. That is why it is possible to participate in various degrees in subsistent Filiation (as also happens with participation in being), while human filiation is a relation that is always predicated in the same way and does not admit of degrees. Supernatural adoptive filiation is a relation that can become more intimate and grow in its formal being (i.e., the "*esse ad*" that constitutes every relation, which in this case is an "*esse ad Patrem in Filio per Spiritum Sanctum*"), to the point of reaching the transcendent fullness of glory (see 1 John 3:1). There exists, then, the possibility of growing in adopted divine filiation. Now, let us see that this possibility is bound with growth in the supernatural life.

We need to consider first that adoptive divine filiation can be lost, not because it is "adoptive" in the human sense, consisting of a legal relation that can cease or disappear, but because it is possible to lose the supernatural life of a child of God. In effect, divine filiation is called adoptive not in order to liken it to human adoption, but in order to distinguish it from the natural filiation of the only begotten Son. While human adoption is a legal reality that is not based on the transmission of biological life, in supernatural adoption there is a true engendering and therefore a true transmission of supernatural life (analogous to natural human filiation). In this sense Stanislas Lyonnet sustains[410] that St. Paul, in speaking about divine "adoption," does not take the term solely from the Greco-Roman legal cultural context. Rather, he also employs it according to Old Testament tradition, where the adoption of the people of Israel is a much richer reality, even though it does not yet possess the depth it would later acquire in the New Testament, where it is revealed as inseparable from the sending of Holy Spirit into the hearts of the faithful and from a true supernatural rebirth. According to Albert Vanhoye, the context of Gal. 4:5–7 (adoption as sons through the

---

410. See Stanislas Lyonnet, *Quaestiones in Epistolam ad Romanos*, p. 19.

sending of the Holy Spirit) "shows how St. Paul understands divine adoption. It is not a case of a simple juridical decision that would not interiorly change the adopted person, but a decisive divine intervention that confers a new life, a participation in the sonship of the risen Christ. 'It is no longer I who live, but Christ who lives in me' (Gal. 2:20)."[411]

This conferral of supernatural life takes place for the first time in baptism, when man is adopted as a son of God. However, through mortal sin, the adoption can be lost and then man, in a certain way, "dies" as an adopted son of God (i.e., he loses the adopted status received through the infusion of grace, given that the very supernatural life of a son of God ceases to exist). St. Josemaría expresses this also in another way. He says that whoever rejects the grace of God *stops being a son and becomes a slave*.[412] Certainly one does not lose the filiation to God that one has as a human creature because, as is obvious, the status of being a person made in the image and likeness of his Creator does not disappear. But whoever rejects the grace of God through mortal sin no longer shares the intratrinitarian supernatural life that had freed him from sin and the power of the devil. He is no longer a son of God in the same sense as when he was in the state of grace. He has lost the supernatural life and the freedom of a son of God: the "freedom [by which] Christ has set us free" (Gal. 5:1).[413] Hence, he "stops being a son and becomes a slave." In spite of all this and for as long as he is on earth, a baptized person retains the indelible seal of having received supernatural life. Even though it is not life in the proper sense, it remains a title for its recovery.

> A baptized person always conserves the *baptismal character* as an indelible sign that he shares in the priesthood of Christ because he was made a son of God through grace. If afterward he separates himself from God through mortal sin, if, that is, he ceases to participate in the intimacy of the divine life, he would then lose his dignity as a son, yet preserve the character that acts as a sign for him to know that he belongs to the family of God, as a call to return to the house of the Father, and as an incentive to do so with the assurance of not being rejected. In many cases, he may also conserve a "formless" faith and hope (as they would exist without charity). The prodigal son of the parable recovers

411. Albert Vanhoye, *Lettera ai Galati. Nuova versione, introduzione e commento*, p. 108.

412. *Friends of God*, no. 34.

413. In the following chapter, we will consider more fully this relationship between supernatural life and Christian freedom.

> his original dignity when he repents and goes back home (see Luke 15:11 ff). His father says of him to his other son "your brother was dead, and is alive" (Luke 15:32). The contrite sinner may even attain a greater intimacy with God than before. What he lost through sin, he recovers through a new infusion of supernatural grace, ordinarily through the Sacrament of Penance.

Although supernatural life can be lost, it can also be recovered, and then one also recovers the corresponding filial relationship to God: one's adoptive divine filiation. In other words, divine filiation is inseparable from supernatural life; it is received or lost with it. But supernatural life can also grow or diminish. It can be possessed more or less intensely as a participation in the intratrinitarian divine life that is the divine essence. (On the other hand, human life is either possessed or not. One can be more or less healthy, which is a quality of life, but one cannot be more or less alive.) As supernatural life grows, it increases the person's likeness to God, one's identification with the divine nature (see 2 Pet. 1:4). This similarity is precisely a likeness to the Son (see 2 Cor. 3:18), because whoever receives supernatural life is made "a son or daughter in the Son."

Consequently, one could think that whoever is more divinized by grace is also more a son or daughter of God "in the Son," that is, that divine adoptive filiation grows or diminishes with supernatural life. The letters to the Romans and the Galatians seem to point in this direction when they speak about different stages of divine filiation tied to those of grace. As Heinrich Schlier observes, the apostle mentions "a threefold way of 'being children of God' or better yet: there are three moments or states of being a child of God: (1) the state that begins with baptism in the faith (Gal. 3:26; 4:6); (2) the state that corresponds to our present existence under the guidance of the Holy Spirit (Rom. 8:14); and (3) the eschatological state in its definitive manifestation (Rom. 8:19, 23)."[414] The first state of divine filiation corresponds to the infusion of grace in baptism. The second one to growth in the supernatural life after baptism. For this same reason, it appears that we can speak about a development of adoptive filiation within this second state—the earthly existence of a Christian—to the extent that one grows in supernatural life.

St. Josemaría often refers to growth in the supernatural life, expressing this frequently in terms of growing in charity. We have selected one text in

414. Heinrich Schlier, *La Lettera ai Romani*, p. 417.

which, quoting St. Thomas, St. Josemaría bases the possibility of unlimited growth in charity on the fact of participating in the infinite charity that is the Holy Spirit:

> *A person develops little by little, but never develops all his capacities; he never attains all the human perfection his nature is capable of. He may become the best in a specific field compared to everyone else, and even attain a level that is humanly insuperable. Nevertheless, as a Christian his growth has no limits; he can always grow in charity, which is the essence of perfection.* For charity itself considered as such has no limit to its increase, since it is a participation in the infinite charity which is the Holy Spirit. In like manner, the cause of the increase of charity (i.e., God, is possessed of infinite power). Furthermore, on the part of its subject, no limit to this increase can be determined, because whenever charity increases, there is a corresponding increased ability to receive a further increase. It is therefore evident that it is not possible to fix any limits to the increase of charity in this life. (St. Thomas, *S. Th.*, II-II, q.24, a.7 c.)[415]

Growth in charity (and in sanctifying grace) implies a growth in divine filiation because this is nothing else than the relation of a person who has charity (supernatural life) to the three divine Persons. Adoptive filiation is a participation in the Son and charity is a participation in the Holy Spirit. Both are inseparable in the Christian, just as the Son and the Holy Spirit are in the heart of the Trinity. Sanctity in glory is, at one and the same time and inseparably, *fullness of divine filiation*[416] and *fullness of charity*.[417] When a Christian grows in charity, he also advances toward the fullness of the filiation he received in baptism. He grows in the most intimate aspect of his relationship to God, that is, in his being a child of God. Divine filiation is a relation based on the transmission of supernatural life, and its reality or "intensity" depends on the degree of that life. It will grow to the extent that there is an increase in identification with the divine nature that stems from the gift of supernatural life insofar as the person corresponds to the action of the Holy Spirit.

Growing as a child of God is not something that happens automatically as when a man grows in age. It only takes place if a Christian corresponds

415. *Letter, March 24, 1931*, no. 9.

416. *Letter, February 2, 1945*, no. 8.

417. *Furrow*, no. 739.

freely to the gift of the Paraclete and behaves as a child of God. In fact, acting as a child of God is precisely what leads to growing as a child of God. It is the free correspondence to the action of the Holy Spirit, the acts of charity and of the other virtues informed by charity, that bring about the person's growth in divine filiation. Therefore, the "sense of divine filiation," which is like an interior instinct to act as a child of God, is a sure foundation for intensifying the sense of divine filiation. Among those who are adopted as children of God in baptism, some act as children, and thus reach a greater identification with God, becoming in fact more "sons or daughters in the Son" than others. The supernatural divine filiation that arose from the baptismal waters is not an "historical" relation set once and for all by baptism. It is an actual participation in the eternal birth of the Son, engendered by the Father, and its intensity will follow upon the degree of participation in the divine life through grace and charity.

Our discussion on the first stage of growth in the Christian identifying himself with Christ has been characterized by the incremental growth or intensification of his adoptive filiation. In order to grow and mature as children of God, however, we face an apparent paradox: we must become little. "Unless you turn and become like children, you will never enter the kingdom of heaven" (Matt. 18:3). St. Josemaría points out that to become like little children before God has nothing to do with a lack of human maturity. On the contrary; it requires us to live solid virtues, the virtues of *children of that Love, that grandeur, that infinite wisdom, that mercy, that is our Father,*[418] the virtues that help us to live simple, childlike humility.

> Quasi modo geniti infantes (1 Pet. 2:3), *as newborn babes. It occurred to me that the Church's invitation today is very well suited to all of us who feel the reality of our divine filiation. It is certainly right that we be very strong, very solid, men of mettle who can influence our environment; and yet, before God, how good it is to see ourselves as little children!*[419]

We are little children before God, "and as such, we have to try to live," Fernando Ocáriz says, "without pretending to be 'of age' which, before God, would be simply absurd. But we can be 'of age' in another sense: fully

418. *Friends of God*, no. 146.

419. Ibid., no. 142. The text is from a homily from the Sunday after Easter, in which the Eucharistic liturgy begins with the text of 1 Pet. 2:2. Thus it refers to the "invitation of the Church."

identifying ourselves with Christ 'to the fullness of the perfect age of Christ' (Eph. 4:13), which we will only attain in Heaven if we are faithful."[420]

To be little, it is necessary to believe as children believe, to love as children love, to give yourself up as children give themselves up . . . to pray as children pray.[421] There are many ways of actualizing that "spiritual childhood" and St. Josemaría urged everyone to freely choose that which would be more fitting to one's way of being and one's circumstances. In any case,

> *We have to learn to behave like children* [niños], *we have to learn how to be God's sons* [hijos]. *At the same time, we have to pass on to others this outlook which amidst our natural weaknesses, will make us* strong in the faith (1 Pet. 5:9), *fruitful in good works, and certain of our way, so that no matter what kind of mistakes we make, even the most embarrassing ones, we will never hesitate to react and return to the sure path of divine filiation, which ends in the open and welcoming arms of our Father God.*[422]

3.3.2. The Way of the Children of God

From birth as children in baptism to the fullness of divine filiation in glory, there is a long path of growth to travel. Many, and probably all people, travel this path making progress at times, while going backward at others. Some travel at a more constant rate, although at a different pace at different stages of life. Others spend a great part of their lives far from the Father's house, and only at the end do they come back contrite. In any case, the "traveler" is always a child of God (with supernatural life or called to recover that life). It is under this perspective that St. Josemaría considers our journey through this world.

We can distinguish three aspects of this journey. The first is precisely the *terrain* along which the Christian travels: the temporal realities that he has to sanctify. The second is the *effort* necessary to travel this road of sanctity because as a consequence of sin, the path has become a steep upward incline. The third is the *means* we can count on in order to advance toward our heavenly goal. We will study these aspects in depth in Part III. For now we only want to note how they appear when seen from the point of view of the sense of our divine filiation.

---

420. Ocáriz, "La filiación divina, realidad central en la vida y en la enseñanza de Mons. Escrivá de Balaguer," p. 219.

421. *Holy Rosary*, "To the Reader."

422. *Friends of God*, no. 148. See *The Way*, no. 93.

1. *Seeing human realities through the eyes of a child of God.* The sense of our divine filiation enables the Christian to discover in all the circumstances of his ordinary life—his work and his rest, his family and social life—the place in which he has to live the life of Christ. *While being fully immersed in his everyday work* [. . .] *the Christian has to be at the same time totally immersed in God, for he is a child of God.*[423]

But work and other occupations are the "place" for meeting God, yet not like the backdrop of a play that does not change while the drama takes place. Rather, it is the setting that the Christian transforms by seeking sanctity, for he has received the command to perfect the world. A person who knows he is a child of God does not fail to realize that creation "awaits with eager longing for the revealing of the sons of God" (Rom. 8:19). He sees earthly realities as part of the "inheritance" that God the Father has entrusted to his children so that they might take "possession" of it. And this means *giving back to matter and to the most trivial occurrences and situations their noble and original meaning, placing them at the service of the Kingdom of God, spiritualizing them, turning them into a means and an occasion for a continuous encounter with Jesus Christ.*[424] Inspired by the sense of divine filiation, the Christian looks on the world as something that he has to order to God: "All are yours; and you are Christ's; and Christ is God's" (1 Cor. 3:22–23). St. Josemaría sums it all up in these words: *We should all realize that we are children of God, and should want to fulfill the will of our Father. We should do things as God wants them done.*[425] (He is referring here to temporal activities.)

2. *Confronting the struggle for sanctity with the spirit of children of God.* Along the path leading to the fullness of divine filiation, the Christian has to struggle to overcome the obstacles that come from sin.[426] The sense of divine filiation moves a person to struggle to please his Father God, always trying to have a right intention in that fight. It is a struggle carried on out of love for God, not love for self. It is a struggle that counts on the fatherly help of God and his mercy. Since there will be defeats, great and small, our spirit must have a readiness to convert. Precisely the *awareness that God is our Father brings joy to our conversion: it tells us that we are returning to our*

423. *Christ Is Passing By*, no. 65.

424. *Conversations*, no. 114.

425. *Christ Is Passing By*, no. 17.

426. See ibid., no. 75.

Father's house.[427] This filial sense makes St. Josemaría recall that *God is not scandalized by men. He can put up with all our infidelities. Our Father in heaven pardons any offense when his child returns to him, when he repents and asks for pardon. The Lord is such a good Father that he anticipates our desire to be pardoned and comes forward to us, opening his arms laden with grace.*[428] The spirit of penance must also be filial: *You ought to practice the spirit of penance: looking toward God and behaving like a son, like a little child who shows his father how much he loves him.*[429]

3. *Using the means that God offers his children in the Church.* In order to grow in identifying ourselves with Christ, the Christian must have recourse to the channels through which he receives the action of Christ and the Holy Spirit in the Church: first, participation in the sacraments, especially the Eucharist;[430] second, dedicating some time to prayer, a filial dialogue with God;[431] and third, formation and spiritual direction. Here we also include all those pastoral means that serve as the channel for the action of the Holy Spirit leading the faithful to identify themselves with Christ.[432] Chapter nine will be dedicated to these means. Here we simply want to note that the Christian who is conscious of his divine filiation sees in them a "vital need." For him they are not obligations that are added on to his duties, nor are they optional. The "filial sense" leads him to seek them eagerly, to make use of them and to care for them diligently.

Concluding this chapter, we could say that in St. Josemaría's teaching, the entire life of the Christian (i.e., his radical orientation to the glory of God as a son in Jesus Christ, with whom he struggles to identify himself through the Holy Spirit) has its foundation in the "sense of divine filiation."

Later studies in the history of spirituality will determine whether this is the first time that this spiritual doctrine, solidly based on Sacred Scripture and the Tradition of the Church, was proposed. On our part we can say that we have not found it in an explicit way prior to St. Josemaría.

❂ ❂ ❂

427. Ibid., no. 64.

428. Ibid.

429. *Friends of God*, no. 136.

430. See, e.g., *The Way*, no. 124; *The Forge*, nos. 119, 424, 643; *Conversations*, no. 115; *Christ Is Passing By*, nos. 78, 80, 169; *Friends of God*, no. 185.

431. See *The Forge*, no. 534; *Christ Is Passing By*, no. 13; *Friends of God*, no. 255; etc.

432. See *Christ Is Passing By*, no. 135.

Some Practical Applications[433]

(1) *Greatness and humility of the children of God.* "We have this treasure in earthen vessels" (2 Cor. 4:7). These words of St. Paul can be applied to divine filiation. It is proper to the sense of divine filiation to recognize the greatness of this gift without forgetting the lowliness of our condition. Only a person who strives to be humble can receive the gift and preserve it effectively. St. Josemaría states,

> *Together with humility, the realization of the greatness of man's dignity—and of the overwhelming fact that, by grace, we are made children of God—forms a single entity. It is not our own strength that saves us and gives us life; it is the grace of God. This is a truth which we can never forget, lest the* divinization *of our life be perverted and become presumption, pride, and sooner or later, lead to the breakdown of the spiritual life, when the soul experiences its own weakness and wretchedness.*[434]
>
> *I often give the example of dust that is lifted up by the wind until it forms a golden cloud high up in the sky because it allows the rays of the sun to shine through it. In the same way, the grace of God lifts us up high. And all this wonder of goodness, of wisdom, of effectiveness, and of beauty, that is God, reverberates in us. If you and I realize that we are but dust and misery—of no value—our Lord will do the rest. It is a consideration that fills my soul* [. . .].
>
> *Divinization is bad if it blinds, if it prevents us from seeing clearly that we have feet of clay, since the touchstone for distinguishing good divinization from bad is humility. Therefore, it is good as long as one doesn't lose the awareness that this divinization is God's gift, God's grace; and it is bad if the soul attributes to itself—to its deeds, to its merits, to its excellence—the spiritual greatness that has been given to it.*
>
> *Be humble, humble! Because we know that in part we are made of clay, and we know a bit about our pride and our wretchedness. . . . And we*

433. We include below a synthesis of the explanation on the content of this section that we have given in the corresponding section of chapter one (vol. I): The texts of St. Josemaría very frequently contain practical applications of the doctrine he teaches. Nevertheless, we have seldom stopped to comment on them, since our intention is to explain his spirit from a theological point of view. For this reason, at the end of each chapter we include a section with "some practical applications." We will limit ourselves to mentioning a few examples of the many that could be provided.

434. *Christ Is Passing By*, no. 133. In an earlier letter, he writes something similar: *My daughters and sons, I cannot conceal from you the fear that in some cases this divinization, without a deep basis of humility, could give rise to presumption, to the corruption of true hope, to pride, and sooner or later to spiritual ruin, on being faced with the unexpected experience of one's own frailty. Letter, March 24, 1931*, no. 4.

> *don't know it all. May we discover what is hindering our faith, our hope and our charity!*[435]

(2) *Cultivating the sense of our divine filiation. In the spiritual life, there is no new era to come. Everything is already there, in Christ who died and rose again, who lives and stays with us always. But we have to join him through faith, letting his life show forth in ours to such an extent that each Christian is not simply* alter Christus: *another Christ, but* ipse Christus: *Christ himself!*[436] In order to achieve the goal of identifying ourselves with Christ, St. Josemaría urges us to strive *to acquire virtues rather than fighting defects.*[437] And since we are not dealing here with a simply exterior imitation, he urges those who impart spiritual direction to follow this advice with those who come to them: *they will be encouraged to undertake this ascent, if you awaken in them the awareness of their divine filiation.*[438] Spiritual direction is a privileged place for fostering the sense of divine filiation. It can teach a person to see all things from the perspective of a child of God in Christ and to love, feel and act as Christ (see Phil. 2:5). But one must not forget that the sense of divine filiation is a gift from God. The person who wants it must ask for it perseveringly. And in order to prepare oneself to receive it, St. Josemaría recommends a daily exercise that requires some effort: *to consider frequently our divine filiation.*[439]

(3) *Being little children before God and the value of "little things." Before God, who is eternal, you are much more a child than, before you, the tiniest toddler. And besides being a child, you are a son of God. Don't forget it.*[440] To see oneself as a small child before God gives a special tone to the sense of divine filiation. St. Josemaría applies this to many aspects of the spiritual life: asking as little children ask, trusting as little children trust, getting up again after a fall with the agility of a child, etc. *In our interior life, it does all of us good to be* quasi modo geniti infantes, *like those tiny tots who seem to be made of rubber, who even enjoy falling over because they get up again right away and are once more running around; and also because they know their parents will always be there to console them, whenever they are needed.*[441]

---

435. *Letter, March 24, 1931*, nos. 4–6.

436. *Christ Is Passing By*, no. 104.

437. *Letter, August 8, 1956*, no. 40.

438. Ibid.

439. *Instruction*, May 1935/September 14, 1950, note 28.

440. *The Way*, no. 860.

441. *Friends of God*, no. 146.

St. Josemaría teaches us to live the piety of small children, a simple and strong piety, but not an "infantile" one. *Piety is the virtue of children. And if the child is to take refuge in the arms of his father, he must be, and know that he is, small, needy. I have often meditated on this life of spiritual infancy, which is not incompatible with fortitude, because it demands a strong will, proven maturity, an open and firm character.*[442] In particular it is characteristic of the piety of children to offer small things (sacrifices, pious gestures, etc.) that have their worth based on the love with which they are performed. One can find numerous examples of this in three chapters of *The Way*: "Little things," "Spiritual Infancy," and "Life of Infancy."

(4) *Firm foundation in difficulties.* In order to know whether the sense of divine filiation is truly the foundation of the spiritual life on which everything else is based, difficult moments in life, temptations, and contradictions are particularly important. It is in these situations that the need for a solid foundation in the spiritual life is felt. "The rain fell, and the floods came, and the winds blew and beat upon that house, but it did not fall, because it had been founded on rock" (Matt. 7:25). *For us, this is the rock: piety, divine filiation.*[443] *Divine filiation is the only secure place to attach the anchor, no matter what happens on the surface of the sea of life. And the result is joy, strength, optimism, and always victory* [. . .]. *In order to remain standing, and to get up, this is the consideration that makes us stronger: I am a son of God. Divine filiation: in order not to lose joy, or serenity, in order to feel secure; and in order to return if we have strayed from the right path in a skirmish of our daily struggle. Or when we have suffered a great defeat, since we can stray from the right path, and in fact sometimes do. The sense of our divine filiation gives us a great facility for returning with gratitude, sure of being received by our Father.*[444]

(5) *Steadfastness in prayer. By loving us as his children, God has taken us into his house, in the middle of the world, to be members of his family, so that what is his is ours, and what is ours is his, and to develop that familiarity and confidence which prompts us to ask him, like children, for the moon!*[445] In order to foster this filial steadfastness and daring in prayer, St. Josemaría frequently

---

442. *Christ Is Passing By*, no. 10.
443. *Letter, March 24, 1931*, no. 7.
444. *Instruction*, May 1935/September 14, 1950, note 28.
445. *Christ Is Passing By*, no. 64.

recalls the words of Psalm 2: "You are my son, today I have begotten you. Ask of me, and I will make the nations your heritage, and the ends of the earth your possession" (Ps. 2:7–8).[446] It is the very same teaching of Jesus: "What father among you, if his son asks for a fish, will instead of a fish give him a serpent; or if he asks for an egg, will give him a scorpion? If you then, who are evil, know how to give good gifts to your children, how much more will the heavenly Father give the Holy Spirit to those who ask him!" (Luke 11:11–13). The sense of divine filiation leads us to ask "in the name of Christ," knowing that we are *ipse Christus*. "If you ask anything of the Father, he will give it to you in my name" (John 16:23). That is why a son of God has to feel complete confidence in prayer. *Amen, amen dico vobis: si quid petieritis Patrem in nomine meo, dabit vobis* (John 16:23); *if we ask in Christ's name, be certain that the Father will grant it to us.*[447]

To know that we are children of God *in the Church* leads us to ask *with* all the People of God. "I say to you, if two of you agree on earth about anything they ask, it will be done for them by my Father in heaven. For where two or three are gathered in my name, there am I in the midst of them" (Matt. 18:19–20). *We never feel alone.*[448] The *ecclesial sense* [. . .] *leads us to live instinctively the reality of the Mystical Body of the Church.*[449] This same "sense" leads us to pray for the other members of the Body and to ask them for their prayers and to put our trust in those prayers.

(6) *The Holy Mass of a son of God.* The culminating moment in the day of a child of God is participating in the Eucharistic sacrifice. *Think now about the Holy Mass: about how we should celebrate it or attend it* [. . .]. *See how on the altar, Christ again offers himself for you and for me. And you will feel a great desire to imitate his humility, his self-abasement in the Host; and you will be filled with acts of thanksgiving, adoration, reparation, and petition. You will offer yourself, with your arms outstretched, like another Christ,* ipse Christus, *ready to be nailed to the sweet wood, for the love of souls.*[450]

(7) *The joy of the children of God.* This is an essential conviction: *God is my Father! If you meditate on it, you will never let go of this consoling thought.*[451]

---

446. See ibid., no. 186; *Friends of God*, no. 190; etc.

447. *Letter, February 14, 1944*, no. 18.

448. *Letter, May 31, 1954*, no. 30.

449. Ibid.

450. Notes taken from preaching, April 14, 1960 (AGP, P01 II-1965, p. 11).

451. *The Forge*, no. 2.

And it comes from experience: "*Happy?*"—*The question made me think. Words have not yet been invented to express all that one feels—in the heart and in the will—when one knows oneself to be a son of God.*[452]

The awareness of divine filiation is a source of a deep and lasting joy: *Let those who aren't God's children be sad!*[453] exclaims St. Josemaría. For a child of God *to lose one's good humor is something serious.*[454] There are never reasons for sadness, not even in the most harsh or difficult moments, because "in everything God works for good with those who love him" (Rom. 8:28). *But, have you again forgotten that God is your Father?—allpowerful, infinitely wise, full of mercy. He would never send you anything that is evil. That thing that is worrying you, it's good for you, even though those earthbound eyes of yours may not be able to see it now.* Omnia in bonum! *Lord, once again and always, may your most wise Will be done!*[455]

Even a person's wretchedness and that of others enter into the fatherly plans of providence. *Reasons for being cheerful? Realizing we are God's children; children, as well, of our Mother in heaven. And never becoming sad because of our own errors, which we have to strive to correct, by fighting with humility. Nor do we become sad because of others' errors, since we have to help them, by our example and prayer, to win out in the ascetical struggle.*[456]

God counts on the joy of his children so that the world will embrace the Gospel. *The cheerfulness of a man of God, of a woman of God, has to overflow: it has to be calm, contagious, attractive . . . In short, it has to be so supernatural, and natural, so infectious that it may bring others to follow Christian paths.*[457]

---

452. *Furrow*, no. 61.

453. Notes taken from preaching (AGP, P10, no. 202).

454. Notes taken from preaching (AGP, P10, no. 294).

455. *The Way of the Cross*, Ninth Station, no. 4.

456. Notes taken from preaching (AGP, P10, no. 296).

457. *Furrow*, no. 60.

CHAPTER FIVE

The Freedom of the Children of God

We should realize we are children of God, and live with the desire of fulfilling the will of our Father. We should do things as God wants them done, because we feel like it, which is the most supernatural of reasons.
(*Christ is Passing By*, no. 17)

It is uncommon to find a chapter on freedom in books on spiritual theology.[1] Freedom is usually considered a subject pertaining to moral theology.

1. We have verified this fact by reviewing a good number of manuals, monographs, and essays published up until 1975 (the year of St. Josemaría's death). These are cited in the volumes of the *Bibliographia internationalis spiritualis* of the Teresianum. In none of these have we found a chapter on freedom. More recently, some works of spirituality dedicated to this subject have appeared, such as Jacques Phillipe's *Interior Freedom* (New York: Scepter, 2007) [orig. French, 2002]. Of special note is the theological essay of Jutta Burggraf, *Libertad vivida con la fuerza de la fe* (Madrid: Rialp, 2006), a work that quotes St. Josemaría and is in harmony with his message.

With only some noteworthy exceptions, such as St. Augustine, the masters of the spiritual life do not deal with the subject. Freedom is taken for granted and is not given specific attention as a guide in the spiritual life.

In studying the teaching of St. Josemaría Escrivá, however, we cannot omit this topic without seriously undermining his message. Far from being a secondary subject, it is a "key concept in his teaching"[2] and, more radically so, his own personality is characterized by the "passion for freedom."[3] To justify the importance he gives to freedom, it would suffice to consider these words of his: *Without freedom we are unable to love.*[4]

The need for freedom to respond to the call to holiness in the middle of the world is for St. Josemaría a basic conviction and an unmistakable and deep characteristic of his very personality. "Freedom constitutes one of the characteristic features of his human spirit,"[5] writes Alejandro Llano. "He disliked any homogeneity that was imposed and considered different forms of conduct a positive value. He favored spontaneous originality while being suspicious of uniformity. He trusted the initiatives and decisions of people more than in the exact fulfillment of institutional policies. He disliked official formulaic protocols and preferred the simplicity of informal expressions. [. . .] He contributed in reaffirming the personal style of individuals and in furthering personal means of expression. He was a powerful catalyst for freedom: he lived with a spirit of freedom and encouraged others to do likewise."[6]

A reader can hardly miss his insistence on this point; it is present throughout his preaching.[7] Antonio García-Moreno affirms that the word freedom appears 239 times in his to-date published works[8] (without

---

2. Juan José Sanguineti, "La libertad en el centro del mensaje del Beato Josemaría Escrivá," in Antonio Malo (ed.), *La grandezza della vita quotidiana* (vol. III, p. 81). A pertinent selection of texts of St. Josemaría on freedom can be found in the volume written by Andrea Mardegan, *Una libertà da vivere. Brani scelti di Josemaría Escrivá. Presentazione di Javier Echevarría* (Milan: Edizioni Paoline, 2004).

3. Pilar Urbano, *The Man of Villa Tevere* (New York: Scepter, 2011), p. 211.

4. Notes taken from preaching, April 10, 1974 (AGP, P01 V-1974, p. 86). The idea is repeated in various ways in his works and in his preaching: see, for example, *Conversations*, no. 104; *Christ Is Passing By*, no. 131; *Friends of God*, nos. 24, 171; etc.

5. Alejandro Llano, "Libertad y trabajo," in *Trabajo y espíritu. Sobre el sentido del trabajo desde las enseñanzas de Josemaría Escrivá en el contexto del pensamiento contemporáneo* (Pamplona: Eunsa, 2004), p. 185.

6. Ibid.

7. Among his published homilies there are two expressly dedicated to freedom: *Freedom, a Gift of God* (see *Friends of God*, nos. 23–38) and *Christian Respect for Persons and their Freedom* (see *Christ Is Passing By*, nos. 67–72). But the presence of this subject in his preaching far exceeds those two writings.

8. Antonio García-Moreno, "Aspectos de la libertad en Josemaría Escrivá," in *El caminar histórico de la santidad cristiana* (Pamplona: Universidad de Navarra, 2004), p. 395.

including references to "liberation" or to the Christian as a "free" person, and not taking into consideration academic speeches and other newspaper articles, of which some focus on freedom).[9]

St. Josemaría shows a "special sensitivity and appreciation"[10] for freedom. He finds it throughout Sacred Scripture. Contemplating the scene of the Annunciation, he sees in Mary's response, "let it be to me according to your word" (Luke 1:38), *the fruit of the best freedom of all, the freedom of deciding in favor of God.*[11] He goes on to say: *This hymn to freedom is echoed in all the mysteries of our Catholic faith.*[12] It is a discovery that makes him feel a *deep love for freedom;*[13] a love that *is not something human, but divine, because it is the freedom Christ won for us on the Cross.*[14] It leads him to proclaim it, to promote it, and whenever necessary, to defend it. *More than preaching it, I shout out my love for personal freedom,*[15] he affirms, and on another occasion, he adds, *It is a treasure we never will appreciate enough.*[16] It is no surprise that he has been called a "pioneer of love for freedom within the Church."[17] And the Church is the salt of the earth.

His love for freedom is deeply connected with two central subjects of his teaching: the sense of divine filiation and the sanctification of professional work (which includes all ordinary life). Adoptive divine filiation is for him like the root from which freedom is born; and professional work and ordinary life are like the field where the it is cultivated and the yield harvested. This specific perspective explains why his doctrine on freedom was taken by Cornelio Fabro to be "the most brilliant and new dimension of his path to holiness."[18]

With respect to the binomial freedom-filiation, it is easy to verify that Josemaría Escrivá speaks a lot about *the freedom of the children of God*, thus

---

9. Especially the article "The Riches of the Faith" in *Life of Faith* (Scepter Booklet No. 5, 1974, originally published in "*ABC*," Madrid, November 2, 1969) and the interview on the political freedom of members of Opus Dei published in the same newspaper, *ABC*, on March 24, 1971.

10. J.J. Sanguineti, "La libertad en el centro del mensaje del Beato Josemaría Escrivá," p. 81.

11. *Friends of God*, no. 25.

12. Ibid.

13. *The Forge*, 144; *Conversations*, nos. 29, 59, 66, 67; *Christ Is Passing By*, nos. 17, 99; *Friends of God*, nos. 26 ff, 31, 169; etc.

14. *Instruction*, December 8, 1941, no. 59.

15. *Friends of God*, no. 32.

16. *Christ Is Passing By*, no. 184.

17. Martin Rhonheimer, *Changing the World: The Timeliness of Opus Dei* (New York: Scepter, 2009), p. 77.

18. Cornelio Fabro, "El temple de un Padre de la Iglesia," in *Santos en el mundo* (Madrid: Rialp, 1993), p. 42.

"emphasizing the relationship between freedom and divine filiation which God had shown him to be the foundation for his spiritual life."[19] Álvaro del Portillo holds that his entire spirit "is imbued by the great certainty of knowing himself to be a son of God, something closely linked with another fundamental note of our spirit: love for freedom."[20] Another privileged witness, Bishop Javier Echevarría, testifies that "he meditated throughout his life that each person should live in *libertatem gloriae filiorum Dei* (Rom. 8:21), in the freedom of the glory of the children of God, and he would encourage us to rejoice in this freedom, which is fruit of divine filiation."[21] Lluís Clavell holds that St. Josemaría considers freedom "under the light with which the Holy Spirit made him see and, in some sense, understand divine filiation. To be sons and daughters of God means to be free persons."[22]

With regard to the relationship between freedom and sanctification of ordinary life in the middle of the world, it has been rightly said that St. Josemaría sees "freedom as an essential characteristic of the secularity of the lay faithful,"[23] of their ordering temporal activities, which they must sanctify, and in which they must sanctify themselves. These activities have their own autonomy, and there are many legitimate ways of carrying them out. For this reason, St. Josemaría insists in respecting others' freedom—a responsible freedom—and in promoting conditions of social life which favor the practice and growth of freedom. Since the field of temporal pursuits is immense, we can only begin to intuit the "unsuspected influence"[24] this theme has in his preaching.

Divine filiation and the mission of sanctifying temporal realities are like the two tracks that this chapter will travel along. Both of them begin at baptism. It is there that the Christian is freed from sin, from the power of the devil and eternal death, so as to live, under the influence of grace, in the freedom of the children of God, and thereby direct all of creation to God's

---

19. Lluís Clavell, "The Freedom Won by Christ on the Cross: Theological Reflections on Freedom in Bl. Josemaría's Teaching," in *Romana* 33 (2001), p. 240.

20. Álvaro del Portillo, note 28 to *Instruction*, May 1935/September 14, 1950.

21. Javier Echevarría, *Memoria del Beato Josemaría Escrivá* (Madrid: Rialp, 2000), p. 148.

22. Clavell, "Personas libres," in Antonio Malo (ed.), *La grandezza della vita quotidiana*, vol. III, p. 116.

23. J.J. Sanguineti, "La libertad en el centro del mensaje del Beato Josemaría," p. 90. The same can be said with respect to secular priests. On the relation between the secularity of the laity and of secular priests, see the Preliminary Part, section 1.3.3. As we will see below, St. Josemaría preached a "lay mentality," common to secular priests and to the laity, which is characterized essentially by love for freedom in temporal affairs and in how it is actually put into practice.

24. Ibid., p. 98.

glory (see Rom. 8:21): this is the mission the lay faithful are called to carry out by sanctifying their work and all temporal activities.

In the first part of this chapter, we will study the principal elements of the notion of the freedom of the children of God in St. Josemaría. For him, Christian freedom is born from divine filiation received in baptism, and it is perfected with the growth of supernatural life. In the second part, we will study the genesis of the free act: the role of the intellect, the will, and the emotions in the exercise of freedom. Lastly, in the third part, we will deal with the issue of respecting freedom in society, something that Christians must foster as a fundamental dimension of their baptismal mission to sanctify the world from within.

Almost every study on the teaching of St. Josemaría dedicates some space to the subject of freedom. Not surprisingly, our preference will be to concentrate on the works whose primary aim and focus is the topic of freedom.[25]

1. Freedom in the Teaching of St. Josemaría

St. Josemaría considers his teaching a "catechesis" accessible to everyone regardless of background, including those who do not have specialized theological formation. But just because his doctrine is accessible to everyone, it does not mean that he simplifies the problems or eludes key issues. The reader should keep this in mind because behind the easily understandable assertions and explanations there is a theological vision of freedom, which we must unpack in order to present his teaching adequately.

25. They are principally the following, in alphabetical order: Clavell, "La libertad Ganada por Cristo en la Cruz"; Mónica Codina, "La libertad humana, don de Dios que es Padre. En torno a una homilía del Beato Josemaría Escrivá," in *El Dios y Padre de Nuestro Señor Jesucristo* (Pamplona: Universidad de Navarra, 2000), pp. 633–642; Ricardo Crespo, "El concepto de libertad en Mons. Josemaría Escrivá de Balaguer," in *Un mensaje siempre actual* (Buenos Aires: Universidad Austral, 2002), pp. 259–265; Cornelio Fabro, "El primado existencial de la libertad," in *El temple de un padre de la Iglesia* (Madrid: Rialp, 2002) pp. 171ff. Antonio García-Moreno, "Aspectos de la libertad en los escritos de San Josemaría Escrivá," pp. 393–406; Mireille Heers, "La liberté des enfants de Dieu," in *La grandezza della vita quotidiana*, vol. I (Rome: Edusc 2002), pp. 199–219; Juan Larrea Holguín, "El amor a la libertad en el pensamiento y la conducta del Beato Josemaría Escrivá de Balaguer," in *Un mensaje siempre actual* (Buenos Aires: Universidad Austral, 2002), pp. 617–626; Juan José Sanguineti, "La libertad en el centro del mensaje del beato Josemaría Escrivá," in *La grandezza della vita quotidiana*, vol. III (Rome: Edusc, 2003), pp. 81–99. We mention also the article by Fernando Ocáriz, "El Espíritu Santo y la libertad de los hijos de Dios," in Idem., *Naturaleza, Gracia y Gloria* ((Pamplona: Eunsa, 2000), ch. 5, pp. 107–121; although the author does not directly propose to consider the teaching of St. Josemaría, he offers a theological basis to go deeply into it.

The title of the homily "Freedom, the Gift of God" expresses the starting point.[26] Freedom is a gift which has its origin and foundation in God. The human person possesses this gift in virtue of the spiritual dimension of his nature composed of soul and body. He has received this gift with a purpose: union with God by means of love and the perfecting of himself and the world according to God's will. This purpose, which is in some way the horizon for our freedom, has been illuminated and enlarged by our supernatural adoption. In the divine plan, human freedom is the freedom of the children of God: freedom to love God the Father, in the Son, through the Holy Spirit. When sin separated man from God reducing him to slavery, the Son, who became man to rescue us from this state through the donation of his life on the Cross, has obtained for us the gift of the Holy Spirit who makes us children of God and free once again, with "the freedom that Christ gained for us" (Gal. 5:1). Now the reason for freedom is to live according to our condition as God's children in Christ, that is, to seek identification with Christ through love and to direct creation toward the Father's glory.[27]

In a nutshell, these are the subjects that we will present in this section. After some considerations regarding the context, we will look at the principal elements of the concept of Christian freedom in St. Josemaría; then, we will examine the relation between grace and freedom in order to conclude with the importance of cultivating a lively "awareness of the freedom" that arises from the sense of divine filiation.

1.1. Context and Sources

In St. Josemaría's social and cultural environment, freedom is a key subject.[28] *People have never spoken so much about freedom as now,*[29] he writes at the beginning of one of his letters. He comments that, on the one hand, *we see, in some countries that have just emerged from tyranny, and in others that have fallen under the despotic and materialistic yoke of Communism, a strong and holy desire for Christian freedom* [. . .]. *On the other hand, the general environment in many countries is marked by an intemperate zeal for a false freedom: everyone is crying out for freedom, for greater concessions in every*

26. In *Friends of God*, nos. 23–38.

27. See ibid., no. 299.

28. We refer to what was said in the Preliminary Part, section I.3.a), about freedom as a central theme of modern thought.

29. *Letter, April 30, 1946*, no. 1.

sector. We observe a disordered desire, since, rather than freedom it's about a lack of restraint, a loss of the Christian meaning of life.[30]

There are two extremes that threaten freedom: tyranny and licentiousness; the first one can be understood not only as political despotism but, in general, as an abuse of power that thwarts others' freedom, whether at home, or in one's social and professional relations. Escrivá writes, *We detest tyranny as being opposed to human dignity;*[31] *we detest tyranny* [. . .]. *We love plurality.*[32] As always, his attitude is rooted in the sense of divine filiation, which in this case, confirms his conviction that *your Father-God is not a tyrant.*[33] With the same vigor with which he opposes tyranny, he confronts the other enemy of freedom: licentiousness, which he describes as, *an aimless freedom, one without objective principles, one that is lawless and irresponsible.*[34] Undoubtedly it is a more insidious enemy because it does not offer a direct opposition to freedom, and yet it undermines its very roots.

These two dangers, tyranny and licentiousness, which at first seem to be opposites, have a common root: the desire to impose one's will as the one and supreme norm of behavior for others (the case of tyranny), and for one's self (the case of licentiousness, inasmuch as it is freedom without moral truth). This is the enemy threatening the cause of freedom in today's society. The problem is not vindicating freedom of thought, of expression, or of conscience, which constitute a noble and just cause, if such freedoms are understood as civic liberties. From the moment that Jesus manifested the link between freedom and knowledge of the truth—"you will know the truth, and the truth will make you free" (John 8:32)—the Christian notion of freedom has borne abundant fruits in civic understanding throughout history, in spite of human failings, and it could also give the necessary response to this need in modern and contemporary times. A sector of the dominant culture, however, presented these freedoms as emancipation from faith, according to anthropological foundations irreconcilable with the Christian vision of the human being and the world. For this reason, St. Josemaría warns against a notion of freedom, which "rather than freedom is the lack of restraint, the loss of the Christian meaning of life." He does not fear

30. Ibid., no. 2.

31. *Conversations*, no. 53.

32. Ibid., no. 35.

33. *The Way*, no. 435.

34. *Friends of God*, no. 32.

freedom, but rather its dissolution in the hands of tyranny or licentiousness. His position will be that of facing the crisis by fostering authentic freedom.

St. Augustine distinguished between "*liberum arbitrium*," or the capacity to choose, which everyone has, and "*libertas*," the effective governing of one's own actions in view of one's good.[35] In the context of the contemporary culture in which St. Josemaría was living, this conceptual distinction had been darkened or at least blurred. Part of contemporary thought—the philosophies of emancipation (from religion and faith)—denied freedom its foundation in God and did not view it as directed toward an end. In so doing, they reduced freedom to merely *freedom of choice*, or that is, the capacity to choose without any constraints. There thus arose a crisis in the notion of freedom that would have important consequences. It soon became clear that those who (metaphorically speaking) raised high the flag of freedom on the pole of a reason emancipated from faith did so on a pole that was no longer grounded in truth, not even on truth accessible through reason (even though in theory it could have been possible). Various ideologies were then embraced with the hope of securing the flagpole; but soon enough it was put at the mercy of the wind of those with a will to power, frustrating the hopes of many who yearned for true liberation. At last, after many painful experiences, the flagpole of reason was substituted by the easily bent reed of *weak thought*, and each person was offered a twig with a part of the old flag to take wherever he wished, and without much company, since the majority was no longer interested in "freedom" as such but only in its "freedom of choice."

The intense debate regarding freedom in the modern age explains in some way why St. Josemaría gives it so much importance. He notes, *Not without the guiding hand of divine Providence, modern times seem especially sensitive to the natural values of freedom, which, only when elevated to the order of grace, find their full realization and perfect fulfillment.*[36] As we can see, St. Josemaría perceives the demands of freedom and the need for a response in Christian terms.

The currents of thought that sought to emancipate reason from faith and freedom from truth and good are undoubtedly the context that motivates his preaching on freedom. However, it would be very difficult to determine causal relations between one author and St. Josemaría or to draw

35. See St. Augustine, *De libero arbitrio*, 2, 13, 37.

36. *Letter, April 30, 1946*, no. 3.

meaningful comparisons.[37] In any case, these authors cannot be considered "sources" for the ideas that he transmits. "His message about freedom," Sanguineti writes, "is not inspired by the reading of certain authors; rather, it is directly tied to his charism."[38] In some way, he conveys this in his preaching:

> *Some of you listening to me have known me for a long time. You can bear out that I have spent my whole life preaching personal freedom, with personal responsibility. I have sought freedom throughout the world and I'm still looking for it, just like Diogenes trying to find an honest man. And every day I love it more. Of all the things on earth, I love it most.*[39]

In the midst of a culture that praises freedom, St. Josemaría is conscious of the treasure that God has given to Christians and that the Church's Magisterium guards and dispenses. The popes, especially since the Leo XIII's encyclical *Libertas praestantissimum* (June 20, 1888), had addressed the problems surrounding the notion of freedom, and their teaching on this subject gradually developed until Vatican Council II. All of this body of doctrine is found in St. Josemaría's writings and is frequently cited.[40] The pontifical Magisterium of the twentieth century is not only the context for his preaching, but also a source.

We must keep in mind, however, that the spirit of sanctification in the middle of the world that he teaches and the apostolic activity that he fosters differ from other realities within the Church that are also in conformity with the Magisterium. As we have explained before, such is the case of Catholic Action, promoted by the hierarchy to make the Church present in society, imbue society with a Christian spirit, and inspire and direct the apostolic actions of the laity.[41] St. Josemaría, instead, considers it natural to appeal to their free initiative as children of God, as they are called to sanctify the world from within, without the need for further tasks or mandates.

---

37. A critical comparison of freedom in the teachings of St. Josemaría and in various authors of modern thought can be found sketched in the following article, which gives an idea of the complexity of the subject: Enrique Cases, "La libertad en el beato Josemaría," in *El cristiano en el mundo. En el centenario del nacimiento del Beato Josemaría Escrivá (1902–2002)* (Pamplona: Universidad de Navarra, 2003), pp. 137–155. See also, Fernando Inciarte, "Die Bedeutung der Freiheit für den seligen Josemaría Escrivá," in César Ortiz (ed.), *Josemaría Escrivá. Profile einer Gründergestalt* (Köln: Adamas Verlag, 2002), pp. 419–432.

38. J.J. Sanguineti, "La libertad en el centro del mensaje del Beato Josemaría Escrivá," p. 81.

39. *Christ Is Passing By*, no. 184.

40. For instance, he quotes the encyclical *Libertas* in *Friends of God*, no. 32 and in the *Letter* of *March 19, 1967*, no. 84. References to later documents related to freedom are numerous.

41. We refer to the Preliminary Part, section 1.3.b.

This determination to strengthen freedom sometimes was received with suspicion in the ecclesiastical circles of his time, as he himself bears witness:

> *Throughout my years as a priest, whenever I have spoken, or rather shouted, about my love for personal freedom, I have noticed some people reacting with distrust, as if they suspected that my defence of freedom could endanger the faith. Such fainthearted people can rest assured. The only freedom that can assail the faith is a misinterpreted freedom, an aimless freedom, one without objective principles, one that is lawless and irresponsible. In a word, licentiousness.*[42]

The tone of this text suggests that the cause for these reservations was not primarily the suspicion that Escrivá may have been proclaiming an erroneous idea of freedom, similar to the promoters of radical liberalism, but rather the fear that a preaching exalting the role of freedom in Christian life could endanger the traditional recognition of the primacy of obedience.

Cornelio Fabro, author of important studies on freedom, has keenly noted this point. He called St. Josemaría a "master of Christian freedom,"[43] indicating his role in history: "A new man for the new times of the Church of the future, Josemaría Escrivá de Balaguer has captured the original notion of Christian freedom through a sort of connatural approach, as well no doubt through supernatural light. Immersed in the Gospel proclamation of freedom, understood as freedom from the slavery of sin, he trusts in the believer in Christ, and after centuries of Christian spiritualities based on the priority of obedience, he inverts the situation, making obedience an attitude and consequence of freedom, like the fruit of the flower, or, more deeply, of its root."[44]

Fabro insightfully notes that what is characteristic of St. Josemaría is how he orders the concepts at hand. Naturally, one will not find a spiritual master who writes about an obedience that is not free, but, in general, priority is given to obedience, whereas freedom is placed at its service. This is true if obedience is exercised out of love, but it can lead one to think that as long as one obeys, freedom does not count for much. In fact, some

42. *Friends of God*, no. 32.

43. Fabro, "Un maestro di libertà cristiana: Josemaría Escrivá de Balaguer," in *L'Osservatore Romano*, July 2, 1977. On the thought of this author, see Ariberto Acerbi, "La libertà in Cornelio Fabro," (Rome: Edusc, 2005).

44. Fabro, "El primado existencial de la libertad," pp. 186–187.

traditional expressions such as 'to obey blindly,' or 'to obey like a cadaver,' sometimes have been understood as *voluntarist* (i.e., acting out of sheer will-power), which undermines the role of the intellect and free will in the act of obeying. It is clear that this way of understanding the expressions quoted above are far from the minds of their authors, who only wished to underline the value of heroic obedience within a precise context: a just command. In fact, we do not quote them because we are not referring to any given master of the spiritual life; rather, we are making reference to the vulgar deformation of these doctrines. In any case, St. Josemaría poses the problem in a different manner: *I do not think there can be such a thing as true Christian obedience unless that obedience is voluntary and responsible. The children of God are not made of stone. Nor are they corpses. They are intelligent and free beings. And they all have been raised to the same supernatural order.*[45] For him, a Christian must always act freely because he is a son of God, as St. Paul asserts, "you are no longer a slave but a son" (Gal. 4:7). It is precisely for this reason that the Christian should obey the divine will out of love for Christ, making himself "obedient unto death, even death on a cross" (Phil. 2:8); this obedience will free him and make him more of a son of God.

Naturally, freedom and obedience are on different planes. Obedience is a moral virtue while, freedom is a property of the person based on his or her spiritual nature (a topic to which we will return). There is no opposition, but there is an order between them. On the plane of nature, freedom is the foundation for the operations and virtues. When Fabro refers to centuries of spiritualities based on the priority of obedience, we think that he is not leveling a criticism at those spiritualities because he is referring to Christian obedience, which is essentially a free obedience out of love. But this obedience can be understood in two ways: either teaching persons to submit freely, or teaching them to engage all the potential of their freedom in obeying. The difference may appear subtle, yet it deeply affects the spiritual life. With divine filiation as his starting point, St. Josemaría fosters a way of acting that is imbued with the awareness of the freedom of the children of God, leading to a loving obedience of the divine will. Other authors do not lay down this foundation explicitly, and in their writing the priority of freedom is not so clearly shown.

45. *Conversations*, no. 2.

The various circumstances of the nineteenth and twentieth centuries revealed an urgent need for the laity to act in order to fulfill the Church's mission in modern societies. These only uncovered the problem, however. Centuries of spiritualities that are based on the priority of obedience and that have been duly retrofitted for the laity have given rise in them to a certain passivity in obeying. It is not surprising how difficult it is for them now to assume their ecclesial mission with the freedom and personal responsibility that the very mission itself requires, and to cease to expect mandates and directives from the hierarchy in the ambit of temporal affairs. It is likewise not surprising how difficult it is for the clergy to foster the free and responsible initiatives of the laity and to abstain from directing them in the fields of their legitimate autonomy.

This freedom and responsibility, instead, is the one that St. Josemaría promotes. His message concerning freedom "forms part of a living charism,"[46] which leads him to discover within the sources of Revelation new lights on freedom: a *freedom which is the key to the lay mentality*[47] necessary to foster the sanctification of the world from within.[48]

In addition to the sources of Revelation and to his "living charism," St. Josemaría bases his teaching on freedom on the common theological doctrine of St. Augustine and St. Thomas,[49] so often invoked by the Magisterium of the Church. These are the bases of his teaching in this field: Christian Revelation and the theology of these two great doctors, understood under the light of the charism that he himself received.

1.2. Aspects of St. Josemaría's Notion on Freedom

St. Josemaría does not offer an explicit definition of freedom, nor do we propose to arrive at one based on his teaching. We only wish to present some reflections on the concept of freedom that underlies his teaching, both on

46. J.J. Sanguineti, "La libertad en el centro del mensaje del Beato Josemaría Escrivá," p. 98.

47. *Letter, September 29, 1957*, no. 55. See Pierpaolo Donati, "Senso e valore della vita quotidiana," in *La grandezza della vita quotidiana*, vol. I, pp. 221–263 (in particular pp. 255 ff.: ". . . *verso una nuova 'laicità civile'* . . .")

48. In ch. 7, section 1.5.1, we will see that the "Christian lay mentality" that St. Josemaría preaches is inseparable from a "priestly soul."

49. One can see this, for example, in the homily "Freedom, a Gift of God." Of the fourteen footnotes that are not references to Sacred Scripture, five refer to St. Augustine and four to St. Thomas. According to Alejandro Llano, the vision of freedom rooted in the Augustinian and Thomistic tradition enables St. Josemaría to understand the insufficiency of a culture that absolutizes freedom and deprives it of its foundation in God. See Llano, "La libertad radical," in *Acto de homenaje al Beato Josemaría Escrivá de Balaguer, Fundador de la Universidad de Navarra* (Pamplona: Universidad de Navarra, 1992), p. 97.

human freedom in general, as well as on the freedom of the Christian who lives a supernatural life (i.e., who is in the "state of grace").

St. Josemaría's notion of freedom is theological. As we have just noted, it arises from Revelation and includes what a believer's reflection is able to reach. When he wishes to explain one of its components, he usually quotes a biblical passage or evokes events of the history of salvation that manifest the mystery of freedom. The following quotation contains the principal elements of his teaching on freedom that we will use as a reference for our subsequent analysis:

> *We have learned with gratitude, because it makes us realize the happiness we are being called to, that all creatures have been created out of nothing by God and for God: both men and women, who are rational creatures (although we so often act unreasonably) and irrational creatures,* [. . .]. *But in all this wonderful variety, it is only we men and women (I am not referring now to angels) who can unite ourselves to the Creator by using our freedom. We are in a position to give him, or deny him, the glory that is his due as the Author of everything that exists. This possibility makes up the lights and shadows of human freedom. Our Lord invites us, urges us to choose the good—so tenderly does he love us!* 'See, I have set before you this day life and good, death and evil. If you obey the commandments of the Lord your God which I command you this day, by loving the Lord your God, by walking in his ways, and by keeping his commandments and his statutes and his ordinances, then you shall live [. . .]; choose life, that you [. . .] may live.' (Deut. 30:15–16, 19)[50]

With an eloquent simplicity, this passage contains three elements of freedom that we briefly enumerate below in order to have a prelimary picture of the whole:

(1) First, God created man with the capacity of choosing between one thing and another, having dominion over his own acts without being moved by necessity. As we will see, for St. Josemaría this basic element of the notion of freedom is completed and clarified under the light of man's supernatural elevation to the condition of children of God. The "freedom of the children of God" is the fullness of human freedom. From this fullness, St. Josemaría understands the gift of freedom that God has granted to man, creating him in his image.

50. *Friends of God*, no. 24.

(2) Second, in the present life, the capacity to choose has before it good and evil, but the capacity is not neutral, because it has an intrinsic end, which is to choose the good to give glory to God. The exercise of this choice, oriented toward this direction and under divine inspiration is man's path toward perfection and happiness. St. Josemaría's texts develop at length this second element of freedom. Starting from the belief that union with God out of love is the good toward which freedom should be directed, he insists that freedom exists for the sake of one's self-giving to God: to love and fulfill his will. There is always, however, the possibility of losing one's path. For this reason, he speaks of the "adventure" of freedom and says that God has wished to run "the risk of our freedom," something that indicates the greatness of this divine gift.

(3) Third, there is an implicit reference in the text to man's situation after sin. Man has used his freedom poorly, not always choosing "life and good," but instead from the beginning and on many other occasions, choosing "death and evil," as the text from Deuteronomy cited by St. Josemaría says. Man has offended God and, consequently, has lost supernatural life. He has remained subject to death and has misused his freedom as a son of God. He has contracted an inclination toward evil, making it difficult for him to use his freedom for the good; he has made himself a "slave of sin" (Rom. 6:17), and he finds himself under the power of the devil who tempts him to continue to do what is evil. In order to free him, God has shown him the path of goodness by means of the Law in the Old Testament. When the fullness of time came, he sent his Son, who, in giving his life on the Cross, has atoned for the offense against God and obtained for us the gift of the Holy Spirit. The Paraclete, in turn, makes the one who receives him an adopted son once again and gives him the strength to conquer the inclination toward evil. This is the principal basis for the "confidence in freedom" that characterizes all of St. Josemaría's preaching. It is confidence in the Christian's capacity to conquer evil with goodness, confidence in divine grace that heals and enlivens human freedom. At this point, a discussion on the relationship between grace and freedom would be in due order. However, we will leave the development of this topic for another section.

From a practical perspective of the spiritual life, the points of most interest are the second and the third. The former element (section 1.2.1) is more theoretical or speculative than the latter, but it is not absent from

St. Josemaría's preaching, for he always invites his audience to return to the foundation of divine filiation.

1.2.1. "The Gift of Freedom"

Sacred Scripture teaches that all creatures exist as a result of God's freedom. God has created them out of nothing to communicate his goodness.[51] This applies especially to man, created *in a free outpouring of love.*[52] God made man in his image and likeness and therefore a free being. In words of St. Josemaría, he granted him *the splendid gift of freedom which gives us power over our own actions.*[53] It can be said that the first element of human freedom as a reflection of divine freedom is dominion over one's acts, the possibility of choosing between one thing and another without being compelled by necessity. This basic, and at the same time traditional, idea is found throughout St. Josemaría's writings.[54]

The capacity to choose implies the capacity to love. St. Josemaría points out that the verb *diligere* (which is used in the Latin version of the New Testament in Mark 12:33 and John 13:34 to translate the Greek verb *agapé*, meaning love of benevolence and love of friendship), does not refer to love as a blind impulse; instead it implies a choice, an act of the rational will: *Sacred Scripture uses the Latin word* dilectio, *to make us understand clearly that it does not simply mean the feeling of affection. It signifies, rather, a firm determination on the part of the will.* Dilectio *comes from* electio, *choice.*[55] Fundamentally, "love is none other than the free affirmation of the good,"[56] the free choosing of the good. Because of this relation between choice and love, man's freedom can be described as his capacity to choose autonomously, which allows him to love as God loves; and in virtue of man's *potentia oboedientialis,* he does so by allowing God to elevate him to participate in the intimacy of the divine life, which is a life of love.

St. Josemaría considers human freedom within the perspective of his participation in divine life for which man has been created. At the beginning of the homily "Freedom, a Gift from God," he quotes some words of

51. See Vatican I, Dogmatic Const. *Dei Filius,* ch. 1: DS 3002 y 3005; Jer. 18:6; Rom. 9:21; etc.

52. *Friends of God,* no. 25.

53. *Christ Is Passing By,* no. 99.

54. See, for example, *Friends of God,* nos. 24 and 27. The traditional teaching can be seen in St. Thomas Aquinas, *S. Th.*, I, q. 83.

55. *Friends of God,* no. 231.

56. Rodríguez Luño, *Ética general,* 4th ed. revised (Pamplona: Eunsa, 2001), p. 205.

St. Augustine that *sound like a wonderful ode to freedom*: God who created you without you, will not save you without you.[57] The meaning of these words is that salvation (of an adult, obviously) demands the exercise of that person's freedom; or, in other words: freedom is ordered to salvation given that God created man free so that he could reach happiness by freely fulfilling God's will. In this Augustinian *dictum*, however, we can find a deeper meaning. If salvation (as a state already reached) is considered the full participation in intra-Trinitarian life, these words not only mean that man should cooperate with grace in order to be saved; in a more profound sense, they also mean that freedom pertains to the state of salvation, that is, to the full participation in the life of God in glory. The life of God's children is thus essentially one of freedom because it is a participation in the divine life of love. Employing a Pauline expression (see Rom. 8:21), St. Josemaría constantly speaks of *the glorious freedom of the children of God*.[58] He considers freedom to be something proper to the condition of a son of God whose perfection is reached in glory.[59]

For this reason, we will deal first with the "freedom of the children of God" (the freedom of a Christian with supernatural life), which is a redeemed freedom: "the freedom for which Christ has set us free" (Gal. 5:1). This freedom presupposes human freedom, the freedom that every human person has by virtue of being created in the image and likeness of God. We will deal with this kind of freedom later and see how St. Josemaría's teaching on "the freedom of the children of God" is contained implicitly in the notion of "human freedom."

We begin with "the freedom of the children of God." For St. Josemaría the relationship between divine filiation and freedom is essential. He asserts that on earth the Christian enjoys greater freedom to the extent that he is aware of being a child of God and lives as a child of God. He develops this idea by taking as a starting point some words of Jesus from the fourth Gospel:

---

57. *Friends of God*, no. 23. The quotation of St. Augustine is: *Sermo* 159, 13.

58. Ibid., no. 38. See *Via Crucis*, introduction; *Christ Is Passing By*, no. 130.

59. The close relationship between adoptive filiation and freedom can be seen reflected in the words of Jesus: "the sons are free" (Matt. 17:26). As the context is that of payment of taxes, many versions translate: "The sons are exempt. Nevertheless it seems that our Lord is applying a general affirmation to a particular situation: since "the children are free (ἐλεύθεροι)," they are exempt from paying taxes. For an exposition of biblical Theology on the notion of "freedom of the children of God," see Ceslas Spicq, *Teología moral del Nuevo Testamento*, vol 2 (Pamplona: Eunsa,1970), ch. 9.

> Veritas liberabit vos (John 8:32), *the truth will set you free. What truth is this which opens for us the way to freedom and gives it meaning throughout our lives? I will sum it up for you, with the joy and certainty of creatures who have a close relationship with God: knowing that we have come from the hands of God, that the Blessed Trinity looks upon us with predilection, that we are children of so great a Father. I ask my Lord to help us decide to take this truth to heart, to savor it day after day; only then will we be acting freely. Don't forget: anyone who does not realize that he is a child of God is unaware of the deepest truth about himself, and lacks in his behavior the dominion and self-mastery proper to those who love the Lord above all things.*[60]

In analyzing the main idea of this text, we can see that the awareness of being a child of God (i.e., the loving knowledge of this truth) leads to the awareness that "the Blessed Trinity looks upon us with predilection," (we who are "children of so great a Father," and we might add, "brothers and sisters of Jesus Christ," as well as "temples of the Holy Spirit"), which drives us to love God above all things in order to correspond to his love. And this love is not only the exercise of freedom; it is the source of a greater freedom, because it predisposes the person to exercise his freedom in the direction where it finds its fullest meaning, thus affirming dominion and self-mastery of his behavior.

As we can see, the relation between divine filiation and freedom has a specific order to it whose consequences are significant. One is not a child of God because one is free; rather, one is free because he or she is a person; and, in a new way if he or she is a child of God. St. Josemaría speaks of *the dignity and freedom that derive from the divine filiation of Christians.*[61] Thus, in his view, Christian freedom "proceeds" from divine filiation, and not the other way around—assuming, of course, we are dealing with the freedom of a Christian living in the state of grace that presupposes human freedom (i.e., the freedom of man created in God's image and likeness). What makes a person an adopted child of God is the gift of supernatural filiation—his being engendered by the Father, in the Son, through the sending of the Holy Spirit—not the gift of a new freedom. This gift necessarily accompanies or "follows" (ontologically, not chronologically) upon supernatural adoption,

---

60. *Friends of God*, no. 26.

61. *Conversations*, no. 22.

because this adoption takes place through grace that elevates human nature, giving it a new supernatural life that makes it "more spiritual" and "more free."[62] This new freedom is a gift for the sake of acting in accord with the dignity of our supernatural adoption and growing as a child of God. We can affirm with Lluís Clavell that "divine filiation allows one to understand and to live out his freedom."[63] This is most definitely the order of ideas according to St. Josemaría. The freedom of the children of God "originates" in divine filiation. This is the source of the "new freedom" that grows in the measure in which it is lived according to the truth of divine filiation: *veritas liberabit vos* (John 8:32). By contrast, *anyone who does not realize that he is a child of God is unaware of the deepest truth about himself, and lacks in his behavior the dominion and self-mastery proper to those who love the Lord above all things.*[64]

At the base of the relation between divine filiation and the freedom of the children of God (which is proper to the supernatural order), there lies the relation (proper to the order of creation) between the human person and freedom.[65] St. Josemaría refers to the latter relationship, although less explicitly than the former, as he considers it from the point of view of faith:

> *Christian faith makes us see the world as God's creation and appreciate all its nobility and beauty, recognizing the dignity of each person made in the image of God. It makes us admire the splendid gift of freedom which gives us power over our own actions and enables us—with heaven's grace—to build our eternal destiny.*[66]

Just as St. Josemaría, in referring to the supernatural plane, placed the condition of adoption as children as the basis for a new freedom ("freedom which originates from divine filiation"), now, in referring to the created plane, first speaks of the "person made in the image of God" as the basis for

62. On the subject of sanctifying grace making one "freer" because it makes one "more spiritual," see section 1.3.a.

63. Clavell, "Personas libres," p. 115. It is obvious that when he affirms that divine filiation "allows one to understand" freedom, he is referring to understanding the fullness of its meaning (which one finds in living as children of God). It does not mean that human freedom cannot be understood with the light of reason alone.

64. *Friends of God*, no. 26.

65. Recall that adoptive filiation is a "personal property" (St. Thomas Aquinas, *S. Th.*, III, q. 23, a. 4, c). See chapter four, section 2.2.

66. *Christ Is Passing By*, no. 99.

"the splendid gift of freedom."[67] In an analogous way as to when we said that for St. Josemaría, a Christian is free (with a "new freedom") because he is a son of God (and not that he is a son of God because he is free), so too, it can be affirmed that man is free because he is a person, and that he is not a person because he is free. At least in our opinion, the ontological priority of being a person over freedom is presupposed in the writing of St. Josemaría, at least according to our understanding of these notions.[68]

St. Josemaría considers freedom as *gift from God*,[69] a *wonderful human gift*.[70] For Lluís Clavell, "this is perhaps the radical theological point of his reflection [on freedom]."[71] If it is a gift to the person, it means that in each person there exists an ontological reality "prior" to the gift. In man's ontological makeup, freedom is not first; it does not constitute a person in his or her essence. At the same time, there is no doubt that freedom is an essential dimension of the person due to the spiritual nature of the person. In this

---

67. The same can be seen, for example, in the homily "Passionately Loving the World," in which St. Josemaría says: *You would not be able to carry out this program of sanctifying your everyday life if you did not enjoy all the freedom which proceeds from your dignity as men and women created in the image of God and which the Church freely recognizes. Personal freedom is essential to the Christian life* (*Conversations*, no. 117). This concatenation of the concepts of "image of God," "dignity," and "freedom" of the human person is present throughout his homilies "Freedom, a Gift of God" and, "Christian Respect for the Person and His Freedom," as well as in other texts such as, for example, *Conversations*, nos. 5, 14, 22.

68. We have referred to the terms "person," "nature," and "freedom." We have said that the teaching of St. Josemaría presupposes the priority of being a person over freedom "according to our understanding of these notions," because this understanding is not the only one possible within the thought of St. Thomas, which is the conceptual frame of reference for the teaching of St. Josemaría.

For example the philosopher Leonardo Polo established a distinction between metaphysics and anthropology based on the distinction between the being dealt by metaphysics and the being in the case of man (the being of the human person); this last one implies in the thought of Polo a "transcendental freedom" that explains moral freedom. See L. Polo, *La libertad transcendental* (Pamplona: Eunsa, 2005), chapter 2; Idem, *Persona y libertad* (Pamplona: Eunsa, 2007). Here we do not adopt the concept of freedom of the human being as transcendental, but rather, starting from the distinction between "act of being" (*esse ut actus*) and essence (or nature) (following the thought of thinkers like Étienne Gilson and Cornelio Fabro), we will say that freedom belongs to the human person essentially not through his act of being, but through the spiritual dimension of his essence or nature. It is possible that the notion of "transcendental freedom" of Polo is not irreconcilable with that of freedom in the thought of those other authors, but this is not the place to elucidate this. In any case, the potentiality of the thought of Polo to explain the spiritual doctrine of St. Josemaría is clearly shown in the various studies that he has dedicated to this and which we have cited throughout the present chapter. According to Concepción Naval, Polo's anthropology contains "the conceptual elements necessary to go more deeply into the doctrine of Bl. Josemaría Escrivá de Balaguer on freedom as a gift of God," as quoted in "La confianza: exigencia de la libertad personal," in Antonio Malo (ed.), *La grandezza della vita quotidiana*, vol. III, p. 237; she refers in particular to the work of Polo, *Antropología trascendental*, vol. I: *La persona humana* (Pamplona: Eunsa, 1999).

69. *Friends of God*, no. 35.

70. *Christ Is Passing By*, no. 184.

71. Clavell, *Personas libres*, p. 104.

sense, it belongs necessarily to the nucleus of the human person: there is no human person without feedom, just as there is no human person without a human nature, and specifically, without a spiritual soul.[72]

Human freedom is an essential characteristic of human nature: it is the active capacity to pursue the good of the person in an autonomous way. It is the freedom of a created person with a finite nature capable of further perfection: a freedom, therefore, that is limited according to its human condition.[73] Freedom is not the power to do whatever one is capable of doing (in

---

72. This subject can be clarified somewhat by recalling the distinction between person and nature, a distinction that is not a superfluous fancy but something indispensable to speak of the mystery of Jesus Christ—a (divine) Person in two natures (the divine and the human)—and for the whole of Christian anthropology. The individual of the human species is denominated in a singular mode: "person," because it is not "something" but "someone" whom God loves for himself. The human person is the singular and concrete man or woman in his or her real totality, while his or her nature is the formal substantial element of the person (see St. Thomas Aquinas, *S. Th.*, III, q. 2, a. 2; *De unione Verbi Incarnati*, a. 3). Each person is distinguished from others not only by his or her formed matter, as the animals of the same species are, but rather by his or her substantial form, the human soul, which is spiritual and subsistent. The act that gives being to that spiritual form (*actus essendi*) and through it the whole individual human nature, soul and body substantially united, is what constitutes the personality in the ontological sense (not the psychological one). "Given its spiritual nature, what is it that is constitutive of the personality? In accord with St. Thomas, the answer is immediate: the act of being, which is the final perfection and the founding actuality of nature" (Ocáriz, *Naturaleza, Gracia y Gloria*, p. 47).

These are the indispensable elements to understand what we want to say in affirming that freedom pertains essentially to the human person by reason of his spiritual nature—or more precisely, by reason of the spiritual dimension of his nature composed of body and soul—but it is not that which makes a person into "this (singular) person." This last notion (i.e., that which ontologically constitutes one's personality) is not human nature, nor therefore the freedom that belongs essentially to human nature, but the "act of being" (*actus essendi*) of the person itself. Every human person is autonomous and essentially free because his act of being is the act of an essence or nature that is not only material but also spiritual and therefore free. "It is the ontological autonomy of the person that is the basis of his practical freedom" Joseph Rassam, *La Métaphysique de Saint Thomas* (Paris: Presses Universitaires de France, 1968), p. 118. Freedom is also an originating principle, but in the order of existence, insofar as it is constitutive of dominion over one's own acts and, in this sense, of one's personality in the psychological sense, of one's own "I." See Fabro, *L'io e l'esistenza e altri brevi scritti* (*a cura di Ariberto Acerbi*) (Rome: Edusc, 2006), p. 79.

73. To understand what is at risk, it is worth noting that if we inverted the previously mentioned conceptual order and were to ask ourselves first about freedom and then about the human person, we would run the risk of thinking of freedom as an impersonal kind of freedom, that is, as an absolute with no limits other than those one wants to place on oneself (for example: "my freedom ends where that of others begins"). The thought of an absolute freedom that coexists with other freedoms that limit it, or that mutually limit each other, is an attitude which is absent in thinkers like Leonardo Polo; on the other hand, it is typical of a sector of existentialist thought that, starting with an idealistic basis, places the goal of freedom in its "emancipation," first from God and then from all that seems like a limit that is not autonomously established. Thus, they have unchained an interminable process of emancipation, presided over by a dialectical conflict and without a point of reference that permits one to focus freedom on the good of the person. On this subject, see José María Barrio, *Los límites de la libertad: su compromiso con la realidad* (Madrid: Rialp, 1999). An overcoming of these conflicts can be seen in the works of that Leonardo Polo himself, which we cited above through a path that parts from the thought of St. Thomas and offers a possible and interesting development of the notion of person as a "free person."

which case, we would be talking about an "absolute freedom"); rather, it is a power with a meaningful finality; it is a power relative to the good that befits the human person, his or her own perfection, and the perfection of other persons and the world. St. Josemaría emphasizes that freedom is a gift of God that aims toward the supernatural end of the human person. He is convinced that *to attain this supernatural end, men need to be and to feel personally free,*[74] and he points out that defending freedom is not a problem for the Christian faith, but rather an internal necessity. *The only freedom that can assail the faith is a misinterpreted freedom, an aimless freedom.*[75] "Freedom," writes Cornelio Fabro, "is given to man so that he can form himself, forge himself, become himself according to the form of his finality; the form of his finality is the *choosing of the ultimate end*, and the ultimate end is God."[76]

> God created each person in his image and likeness as a being open to communion with him and with men. He also conferred upon man the gift of freedom, a power to determine oneself, thanks to which man can develop the image of God in his being and move toward his ultimate end. Certainly, being able to determine one's own acts means that one's faculties and being are subject to him, or, "being the cause of oneself"[77] in the moral sphere, as the ancient philosophers would say. But this does not mean that one has the power to create oneself, as if freedom were the first principle of a personal being in an ontological sense, a being independent of God the Creator. Alejandro Llano writes, "Human freedom is not an isolated *a priori*, because it does not constitute its own foundation. God's freedom is the foundation for ours."[78] Human freedom is the power to open oneself up to God and others in an autonomous way in accord with the very structure of the created person: it is the power to welcome the gift of another and to

---

74. *Conversations*, no. 34.

75. *Friends of God*, no. 35.

76. Cornelio Fabro, *Momenti dello spirito* (Assisi: Edizioni Sala Francescana di Cultura, 1982), p. 204. The quotation continues, "not the abstract God of the philosophers (the God of Aristotle, the God of Plato, the God of Epicurus), but the *God of Christ*, because it is a historical fact that Christ became man, that the Word was made flesh" (ibid.).

77. "*Liber est causa sui,*" St. Thomas Aquinas, *S. Th.*, I, q. 96, a. 4, c, quoting the *Metaphysics* of Aristotle.

78. Alejandro Llano, "Libertad y trabajo," p. 188. On the same line there has also been written, reflecting on the teachings of St. Josemaría, that "he who does not discover God in the heart of his freedom, does not know himself." Paul Olivier, "La filiation divine: vocation et liberté," in Antonio Malo (ed.), *La grandezza della vita quotidiana*, vol. III, p. 55.

> give oneself, to be loved and to love.[79] Lourdes Flamarique notes that mastery over one's own acts "reveals an essential structure characterized by an original capacity to dispose onself to be open [to others]."[80] This basic structure of personal beings explains how freedom is the person's power of self-determination as a being in relation: in relation with God first and foremost, the beginning and ultimate end of man whereby "choosing God existentially becomes *the foundation* of freedom itself."[81] "Being the cause of oneself" does not refer to being in the ontological sense (self-creation), but rather to the configuration of the person as a being in relation to others, capable of freely assuming the condition of a creature with its own finality: its origin and end (and ultimately its supernatural end). In this sense, freedom is indeed an principle of origin.[82]

As will be noted later, St. Josemaría praises freedom as the capacity to love proper to man's nature, but he does not make it an absolute, identifying the person with his freedom. This is perhaps the clearest consequence of what we just described. Man's freedom is not absolute; rather, it is relative to his limited and finite nature. It is "human freedom" which should be distinguished from divine freedom. Its finiteness is not an imperfection; instead

79. "We have a freedom that needs love [it is a gift of God's love] and directed toward love, which necessarily takes us out of ourselves and turns us toward another person, in a sense which requires free reciprocity. This is especially so in regard to God." Sanguineti, "La libertad in el centro del mensaje del Beato Josemaría Escrivá," p. 82.

80. Lourdes Flamarique, "Realidad histórica, libertad, *amor mundi*," in *El cristiano en el mundo*, p. 110.

81. Fabro, "El primado existencial de la libertad," p. 179 (italics is in the original). "The essence of existence is the reality of freedom, just as the essence of freedom is the possibility of elevating itself to the Absolute." Idem, *La preghiera nel pensiero moderno* (Rome: Edizioni di Storia e Letteratura, 1979), p. 23.

82. In the same article on the teachings of St. Josemaría about freedom, Cornelio Fabro observes that "in the existential sphere, which is the field of action and, therefore, of the formation of the "I" and of the person, the first principle is the will, whose dynamic center is freedom. It is well known that modern thought has exalted freedom as the unique constituent of man and as the foundation of himself [. . .]. In reality, the natural primacy of freedom does not mean that this is founded in itself, as if it was something originating in the absolute sense [. . .]. The true primacy of freedom means that, by its very nature, the primary energy of the will tends to the formation of the person." Ibid., pp. 342 and 344.

Leonardo Polo has shown how powerful St. Josemaría's notion of freedom is by contrasting it with the weakness of the attempt to base freedom upon itself, that is, to maintain an absolute autonomy with respect to God. According to Polo, St. Josemaría's idea of freedom "is properly framed in the vital unity based on the idea of gift. [. . .] To be a child of God implies the disappearance of the subjective *a priori.* An adequate approach to the question of the human person, central for anthropology, comes from the discovery of the value of freedom as a gift." Polo, "El concepto de vida en Mons. Escrivá de Balaguer," in *La personalidad del Beato Josemaría Escrivá de Balaguer* (Pamplona: Eunsa, 1994], p. 173. The human person develops his freedom by responding to the divine initiative "which supports it by anticipating its very own intimacy." Ibid., p. 193.

it is a logical expression of its created condition. St. Josemaría recounts a common happening in order to explain this further:

> *By choosing something specific, many other things that are also good are excluded. But this doesn't imply a lack of freedom; it's a consequence of our finite nature, which is limited in scope.*[83]

"Many other good things are also excluded" from the sphere of the exercise of our freedom. "The good" (i.e., the specific object of our freedom) is the one God desires (and which he manifests to us in diverse ways, including through our own personal circumstances). It would be absurd, however, to consider God as a limit to human freedom, since freedom is his gift, and has its origin and end in God. A freedom "emancipated from God" would be a freedom emancipated from man himself, which would develop outside of his true integral good. In the operative sphere (which we will discuss in the next section) the meaning of freedom is nothing else than choosing God, that is, loving him by fulfilling his will. Far from being a restriction, it is a path for putting freedom into action and realizing it fully. St. Josemaría thus adds: *By choosing God at each moment, one in some way attains everything in him.*[84]

In our opinion, this is the "position" behind St. Josemaría's teaching on human and Christian freedom. We emphasize that this is *our opinion* because we do not think it is the only possible stance on the matter. It is the one which seems most fitting to us within our understanding of the doctrinal framework within which St. Josemaría's thought moves, which, as we have argued, is the Angelic Doctor's doctrine.[85]

In any case, this notion of freedom provides a solid basis to argue in favor of the radical dignity of every human person, including those who cannot exercise their freedom or do not use it well. There is an essential dignity which does not derive from the use of freedom, although undoubtedly it flourishes when used well. Jesús Ballesteros has noted the emphasis with which St. Josemaría highlighted *the greatness of man's dignity.*[86] Citing various texts, he comments that St. Josemaría foresaw and warned of "the risks of a dehumanization which would occur decades later marked by the tendency

83. Notes taken from preaching, June 25, 1972 (AGP, P01 VII-1972, p. 9).

84. Ibid.

85. See Preliminary Part, section II.1.

86. *Christ Is Passing By*, no. 133.

[. . .] to separate 'persons' (i.e., those considered worthy, given their condition of self-awareness and freedom) from mere 'human beings,' or, that is, those considered to be unworthy, given their lack of self-awareness."[87]

1.2.2. "The Adventure of Freedom"

> *I like to speak of the adventure of freedom, because that is how your lives and mine unfold. I insist that it is freely, as children and not as slaves, that we follow the path which our Lord has marked out for each one of us. We relish our freedom of action as a gift from God.*[88]

These words serve as an introduction to the second aspect of freedom we would like to focus on: namely, freedom in its dynamic or practical aspect seen as having an intrinsic finality, that of choosing the good in order to give glory to God.

The second account of creation in Genesis (see Gen. 2: 4–24) indicates that God entrusted man with the task of prolonging his loving creative act by means of work and the formation of the family and society. Man was not given freedom to do whatever he pleased; rather, he was given freedom to do the good desired by God. It is proper only of God to do all that he wishes, since his will is the source of all good. Man, on the other hand, has the gift of freedom to direct himself toward fulfilling God's will for the sake of love, and to reach his own perfection and happiness thereby. "The freedom of a son," notes Leonardo Polo, "does not consist in independence (for independence is contradictory to being a son), but rather in taking charge of one's destiny."[89] The perfect model of filial freedom is Jesus Christ who surrendered his life in order to fulfill the Father's will. The Christian follows in his footsteps as a son of God in Christ when he uses his freedom to fulfill the divine will in a loving way. As we hope to show, this exercise of freedom requires effort because man must overcome the inclination to evil, which sin has left in his heart.

When we take up in our person the finality of freedom, employ all of our energies for the good without going off track, and walk toward God in the footsteps of Christ, we indeed live out an "adventure," as does the

---

87. Jesús Ballesteros, "Toda persona es digna. No toda opinión es válida," in Antonio Malo (ed.), *La grandezza della vita quotidiana*, vol. III, p. 72.

88. *Friends of God*, no. 35.

89. Polo, "El hombre como hijo," in Juan Cruz (ed.), *Metafísica de la familia* (Pamplona: Eunsa,1995), p. 324.

character in the Gospel who negotiates with the talents he received instead of burying them (see Matt. 25: 15 ff). Freedom is an "adventure" because, in order to bear fruit, we need to take a risk and choose some things while rejecting others: *putting our lives on the line, giving ourselves completely, so as to answer to the love and the confidence that God has placed in us.*[90]

(a) "God Has Willed to Run the Risk of Our Freedom"

St. Josemaría explains that *freedom is used properly when it is directed toward the good; and that it is misused when men are forgetful and turn away from the Love of loves.*[91] Human freedom is a "freedom for," not simply a "freedom from." It is a freedom to do good, not merely a freedom from constraints when deciding or doing something. Let us return to the text in which St. Josemaría recalls the biblical teaching: *Our Lord invites us, urges us to choose the good, so tenderly does he love us!* See, I have set before you this day life and good, death and evil. If you obey the commandments of the Lord your God which I command you this day, by loving the Lord your God, by walking in his ways, and by keeping his commandments and his statutes and his ordinances, then you shall live [. . .]; choose life, that you [. . .] may live' (Deut. 30:15–16, 19).[92] In the face of this alternative, man's position is not neutral. God invites him with his grace to freely choose the good to which he is already naturally inclined. In fact, human nature is dynamically oriented toward its own good (ultimately, to the highest good of union with God), and freedom is the capacity to realize and direct that inclination on one's own. The use of freedom thus has an intrinsic purpose, the same one proper to human nature: to seek the highest good, which consists in the knowledge and love of God, and which leads to the service of others for the sake of love.

Man is naturally inclined to the good, but it is not sufficient for a thing to appear desirable to him for that thing to be good here and now for the person. The good is what God desires for man. In paradise, God said to Adam, "You may freely eat of every tree of the garden; but of the tree of the knowledge of good and evil you shall not eat" (Gen. 2:16). For Eve's eyes,

---

90. *Christ Is Passing By*, no. 129.

91. *Friends of God*, no. 26.

92. Ibid., no. 24. In the same sense he brings up on various occasions the following words from Vatican II: "For God has willed that man remain under the control of his own decisions, so that he can seek his Creator spontaneously, and come freely to utter and blissful perfection through loyalty to Him" (*Gaudium et Spes*, no. 17): see *Conversations*, no. 104; *Friends of God*, no. 36; etc.

that fruit seemed good, but God had told them that they would die if they ate it (see Gen. 2:17); their true good lay in obeying him. It was for this reason that they had received the gift of freedom. Their first and fundamental act, according to Carlos Cardona, is to make a decision with an elective love that seeks the good-in-itself, transcending the natural love that seeks the good-for-me.[93] At least implicitly, this act consists in choosing God, the Highest Good, whereas the contrary consists in rejecting him. That is what Adam and Eve did. They did not simply err about an earthly good (as the fruit was indeed good); rather, they placed their own will over God's will. They desired to "be like God" (see Gen. 3:5) and rejected his sovereignty.[94]

This transcendence of freedom is a notion that is very much present in St. Josemaría's thought. He does not conceive of freedom as a simple capacity to choose limited to choosing among the goods of this earth; rather "he sees it as something that has been instilled with an essential orientation to God [. . .], [it is] above all, freedom in the eyes of God."[95] *We are answerable to God for all the actions we freely perform. There is no room here for anonymity. Each one finds himself face to face with his Lord, and he can decide to live as God's friend or as his enemy.*[96] Each person can *give him, or deny him, the glory that is his due.*[97] This notion of freedom surpasses the one that views it as the mere capacity to choose the means for an end.[98] For St. Josemaría, "human choice lies, in the final analysis, not only in choosing the proper *means*, but the also the right 'content' of the final end, that is, the choice of God himself. This implies *an act of complete acceptance of the will of God: 'Is that what you want, Lord? . . . Then, it's what I want also!'* (*The Way*, no. 762)."[99]

---

93. See Carlos Cardona, *Metafísica del bien y del mal* (Pamplona: Universidad de Navarra, 1987), pp. 105 ff. The summary of this aspect of the thought of Cardona has been taken from Clavell, "Personas libres," p. 107.

94. See St. Augustine, *De Genes. ad litt.*, 8, 6, 12 (text cited in a subsequent note).

95. Clavell, "Personas libres," p. 106.

96. *Friends of God*, no. 36.

97. Ibid., no. 24.

98. This is the classic definition of free will as "*vis electiva mediorum servato ordine finis.*" Dominic M. Prümmer, *Manuale Theologiae Moralis* (Freiburg: Herder, 1935), vol. I, p. 41. This author attributes the definition to St. Thomas Aquinas, *S. Th.*, I, q. 83, a. 4; actually it is not found there literally, but that is a possible interpretation of two affirmations of Aquinas: that free will "*nihil aliud est quam vis electiva*" (ibid.) and that "*Eligere autem est appetere aliquid propter alterum consequendum, unde proprie est eorum quae sunt ad finem*" (ibid.).

99. Álvaro Pezoa Bissières, "La libertad moral en las enseñanzas del Beato Josemaría Escrivá de Balaguer: la noción de finalidad," in Antonio Malo (ed.), *La grandezza della vita ordinaria*, vol. III, p. 121. "To choose the final end" means that man can place his end in God or in something else (such as pleasure, power, etc.)

St. Josemaría writes that God *has willed* to run the risk of our freedom.[100] In this world, freedom is the freedom of the *homo viator*, of man on the path toward perfection in the heavenly home. There, man will see God as he is (see 1 John 3:2), and far from distracting him from God as the highest good, created goods will lead man to him. While he is *in via*, however, man can choose the creature over the Creator (see Rom. 1:25) and thereby reject God. Nonetheless, in an absolute sense, this possibility of evil is not an imperfection of freedom. God, whose works are perfect (see Deut. 32:4), does not create man in a defective manner when placing him on a path that points to an ulterior perfection given that God grants him the capacity to attain it. Neither is our freedom imperfect because we have the possibility of choosing evil. Our freedom is simply that which is proper to one who needs to move toward his final end and has yet to do so. For St. Augustine, the possibility of acting wrongly is precisely the reason for merit such that God can grant us eternal life as a reward for our free correspondence to grace.[101] For St. Josemaría, the possibility of going off the path reveals an amazing aspect of God's love: his trust in each man, since it is proper to love to desire correspondence and to trust in the beloved. This is the reason why he says that God "has willed to run the risk of our freedom" and other similar expressions, such as, *God does not want slaves, but children. He respects our freedom.*[102] This manifestation of the authenticity of God's love and the real weight that he confers on human freedom prompts St. Josemaría to utter expressions of jubilee. Thus,

---

in rejection of God, although he will not really find happiness in any created good. Seen from outside the subject, freedom presupposes a determination with respect to the final end, which is God; but seen from the perspective of the subject himself, it is self-determination with respect to the end, since he can propose it to himself or not as the final end. "Not infrequently people have insisted in a unilateral way in freedom as a capacity to choose the means, leaving aside the fact that, in first place, it is the power or proposing to oneself [. . .] the final end." Clavell, *Metafisica e libertà* (Rome: Edusc, 1996), p. 184.

100. *Christ Is Passing By*, no. 113.

101. Reflecting on the commandment against eating from the tree of the knowledge of good and evil (see Gen. 2:16–17), which God gave to Adam and Eve, the Bishop of Hippo commented, "I, who have considered this matter a lot, do not have words to praise how much I am pleased by the sentence that said that that tree was not harmful because of its food, for he who made all things exceedingly good did not place any bad thing in paradise, but that the evil for man came from his transgression of the commandment. For it was good for man that something be prohibited to him, so that placed below the Lord God, he could merit the possession of his Lord through the virtue of obedience. Obedience which one can say with certainty is the virtue proper to the rational creature who acts under the power of God; and also that the first and greatest of all vices is pride, which leads man to want to use his power for ruin, which has the name of disobedience" (St. Augustine, *De Genesi ad litteram*, 8, 6, 12). See 1 Thess. 2:12.

102. *Christ Is Passing By*, no. 129.

> *Once again I raise my heart in thanksgiving to my God and Lord, because there was nothing to stop him from creating us sinless, irresistibly drawn toward the good. Nevertheless,* he judged that his servants would be better if they served him freely (St. Augustine, *De vera religione*, 14, 27). *How great is the love, the mercy of our Father! Whenever I think of his divine extravagance for us his children, I wish I had a thousand tongues, a thousand hearts and more, with which to be constantly praising God the Father, God the Son, and God the Holy Spirit. Just think: the Almighty, who through his Providence rules the whole universe, does not want the forced service of slaves; he prefers to have children who are free.*[103]

(b) Freedom to Love

St. Josemaría sees in Jesus Christ the paradigm of human freedom. It could not be any other way because Christ is *perfect man, like us in everything except sin.*[104] His freedom is revealed already in the Incarnation. *The Word comes down from heaven and takes on our flesh, an act which bears the splendid mark of freedom in submission:* Behold I have come to do thy Will, O God, as it is written of me in the scroll of the book (Heb. 10:7).[105] As soon as he assumes our flesh, the Word shows that he has true human freedom which, in virtue of the mystery of the hypostatic union, is the human freedom of a divine Person. In a certain sense, it is the seal of God's own freedom impressed upon the human nature he assumed. By obeying the Father, Jesus will employ this freedom to atone for the disobedience of Adam and his descendants. It is true that insofar as Jesus is a man, he is not only *viator*, but also *comprehensor.*[106] And yet, in spite of the fact that the freedom he possesses through his human nature is absolutely unique, it is still the real freedom of a man on the path to future glorification. It is for this reason that Christ's freedom can serve as a model for our own. It is a perfect human freedom and its perfection is manifest by virtue of the fact that Jesus does not employ it to obtain his own glory; rather, he uses it to fulfill the will of the Father out of love by becoming "obedient unto death, even to death on a cross" (Phil. 2:8). From this, St. Josemaría concludes that [*w*]*e must especially value obedience* [. . .]. *Freedom is very close to my heart—that is*

103. *Friends of God*, no. 33.

104. *Christ Is Passing By*, no. 61. See Heb. 4:15.

105. *Friends of God*, no. 25.

106. St. Thomas Aquinas, *S. Th.*, I. q. 62, a. 9, ad 3. See *CCC*, no. 474.

precisely why I so love the Christian virtue of obedience. We should all realize that we are children of God, and should want to fulfill the will of our Father.[107] "The opposition between freedom and obedience, when the latter refers in one way or another to God's will, is often the sign of an impoverished vision of freedom as the capacity to choose, removed from its meaning and finality. Christ's freedom, manifested in his obedience to the Father during his entire existence, is the key to his biography on earth from Nazareth to the Cross, and it illumines the meaning of our own freedom as a loving response to divine freedom."[108]

The Lord said, "I lay down my life, that I may take it again. No one takes it from me, but I lay it down of my own accord" (John 10:17–18). In his book *Jesus Christus*, Karl Adam comments on these words: "Never and nowhere on earth there happened something so thoroughly free, something so completely one's own will and one's own deed, as the deed of Jesus on Golgotha."[109] For his part, contemplating the scene of the Crucifixion, St. Josemaría writes, *We will never fully understand Jesus' freedom. It is immense, infinite, as is his love.*[110] However, the light of Christ's sacrifice on Calvary illumines the meaning of human freedom because man has received it to love God *as* Jesus Christ did, and *in union with him.*

Christ's freedom is completely at the service of Trinitarian love. Out of love for the Father, Jesus exercises mastery over his own life *to save mankind from the slavery of sin.*[111] *He spontaneously and unconditionally accepts the sacrifice which the Father is asking of him.*[112] *He gives himself up to death with the full freedom of Love.*[113] This self-giving is the sublime exercise of his human freedom. It is here where St. Josemaría finds answers to the questions concerning the meaning of freedom:

> *Lord, why have you given us this power? Why have you entrusted us with the faculty of choosing you or rejecting you? You want us to make good use of this power. Lord, what you do want me to do?* (see Acts 9:6). *His reply is precise, crystal clear:* Thou shalt love the Lord thy God with thy whole heart and

107. *Christ Is Passing By*, no. 17.

108. Clavell, "La libertad ganada por Cristo en la Cruz," p. 254.

109. Karl Adam, *Jesus Christus*, 7th edition (Düsseldorf: Patmos Verlag,1946), p. 246.

110. *Friends of God*, no. 26.

111. Ibid., no. 25.

112. Ibid.

113. *The Way of the Cross*, Tenth Station.

> with thy whole soul and with thy whole mind (Matt. 22:37). *Don't you see? Freedom finds its true meaning when it is put at the service of the truth which redeems, when it is spent on seeking God's infinite Love.*[114]

Jutta Burggraf points out that the human person is a being "born to respond;"[115] the person is given freedom to respond to the Love of God with love. But *if I say "yes" to this exclusive Love, might I not lose my freedom?*[116] No! he emphatically replies: *It is utterly false to oppose freedom and self-surrender, because self-surrender is a consequence of freedom.*[117] Lluís Clavell comments, "We come to a very important point. Freedom is for the sake of self-surrender in such a way that self-giving is in itself freedom's most proper and fitting act."[118] In the one who makes the gift of self to God and to others, freedom becomes *more active than ever, because love is not content with a routine fulfillment of duty. Love is incompatible with boredom or apathy. To love means to renew our dedication every day, with loving deeds of service.*[119] St. Josemaría wishes to emblazon in people's souls this conclusion:

> *Freedom and self-surrender are not contradictory. They sustain one another. Freedom can only be given up for love; I cannot conceive any other reason for surrendering it. And I am not just playing with words or phrases. In self-surrender, at every moment freedom renews love; and to renew oneself in that way is to be always young, generous, capable of high ideals and great sacrifices.*[120]

"Freedom" and "love" encounter each other constantly: we need freedom to love God and love to move freedom. Antonio Millán Puelles notes that in St. Josemaría Escrivá, "love for freedom is rooted in love for God, and the fullness of its meaning is only perceived in light of this love."[121]

---

114. *Friends of God*, no. 27.

115. Jutta Burggraf, *Libertad vivida: con la fuerza de la fe*, p. 8. The author cites St. Josemaría on this subject, emphasizing the value of his teaching on freedom.

116. *Friends of God*, no. 28.

117. Ibid., no. 30.

118. Clavell, "La libertad ganada por Cristo en la Cruz," p. 255. See Javier Echevarría, "Maestro, Sacerdote, Padre. Perfil humano y sobrenatural del Beato Josemaría Escrivá de Balaguer," in *La grandezza della vita quotidiana*, vol. I, p. 80.

119. *Friends of God*, no. 31.

120. Ibid.

121. Antonio Millán Puelles, "Amor a la libertad," in *Homenaje a Mons. Josemaría Escrivá de Balaguer* (Pamplona: Eunsa, 1986), p. 26.

Since love for God implies identification with his will and obedience to his commandments, the pair "freedom-love" is often translated as "freedom and fulfillment of the divine will," or as "freedom and obedience," and also as "freedom and the law of Christ," (as will be discussed in the following section). It is clear that for St. Josemaría the latter element of this binomial pair does not constrain the former; rather, it gives it its true object by giving meaning to freedom, and taking it to its fullness: that of directing its proper acts to the ultimate end, the glory of God and happiness of man.

When meditating on the mystery of freedom, St. Josemaría contemplates along with Christ's freedom, the freedom of Mary, the pure image of her Son. He pauses especially on the moment of the Incarnation: *the sublime moment when the archangel Gabriel announces to the Virgin Mary the plans of the Most High. Our Mother listens, and asks a question to understand better what the Lord is asking of her. Then she gives her firm reply:* Fiat! (Luke 1:38). *Be it done unto me according to thy word! This is the fruit of the best freedom of all, the freedom of deciding in favor of God.*[122] This is the full meaning of a man's freedom on his path to the heavenly home; it consists in fully giving himself in doing good and in seconding the will of God. Love of God *marks out the way of truth, justice and goodness.*[123]

The figure of St. Joseph is also like a mirror that reflects the intertwining of freedom and obedience. This is manifested in the ease and initiative with which the Patriarch moves within the divine plans because he has made them his own.

> *His docility is not a passive submission to the course of events. For the Christian's faith has nothing whatsoever to do with conformity, inertia or lack of initiative. Joseph entrusted himself unreservedly to the care of God, but he always reflected on the events* [. . .]. *In the different circumstances of his life, St. Joseph never refuses to think, never neglects his responsibilities. On the contrary, he puts his human experience at the service of faith. When he returns from Egypt,* learning that Archelaus had succeeded his father Herod as ruler of Judea, he was afraid to go there (Matt. 2:22). *In other words, he had learned to work within the divine plan. And to confirm that he was doing the right thing, Joseph received an instruction to return to Galilee.*[124]

---

122. *Friends of God*, no. 25.

123. Ibid., no. 38.

124. *Christ Is Passing By*, no. 42.

1.2.3. Freedom and the Inclination to Evil; Freedom and Law

The third element of freedom to which we referred eariler is that the exercise of freedom in the present life falls under the influence of the inclination to evil, traditionally called concupiscence, which appeared in human nature as a consequence of evil.

St. Josemaría takes this into account very carefully: *We should never forget that we bear within us a principle of opposition, of resistance to grace: the wounds of original sin, perhaps deepened by our personal sins.*[125] He frequently refers to this inclination which can lead man to various forms of slavery, yet he does not exaggerate the inclination to sin. Often he reminds his audience that, *although we are born* proni ad peccatum, *inclined to sin, due to the fall of our first parents,* [*God*] *has placed in the soul of each and every one of us a spark of his infinite intelligence, an attraction toward the good.*[126] Inclination to evil has not snuffed out the light, which permits us to recognize moral truth, nor has it destroyed the original inclination to good. Both remain present in human nature, and human freedom, which has not been destroyed by sin, sinks its roots in both.

Inclination to evil is a complex reality studied in Moral Theology. St. Josemaría studies it in the framework of traditional doctrine.[127] While *in via*, man finds within himself not only the possibility of using freedom wrongly, but also the difficulty of using it well (to love God and neighbor), and the tendency to change the order of goods, placing creatures before God (see Rom. 1:25; 7:14 ff). Therefore, in man's present condition, the good use of freedom requires him to fight against the inclination to evil by cooperating with grace (which we will see later on). When a Christian does not do this, and instead allows that inclination to control him, *he stops being a son and becomes a slave;*[128] he becomes a slave of sin (see Rom. 6:17), a slave of concupiscence. He becomes a servant of that which has defeated him: *Some stoop down before riches; others worship power; some, the relative*

---

125. *Letter, March 24, 1931*, no. 10. He speaks here of a "principle of resistance to grace." This is equivalent to a principle of resistance to the good use of freedom under the action of grace. We now focus on the resistance to the good use of freedom; however, in the next section, which will deal with the relation between grace and freedom, we will see that that resistance is a resistance to grace.

126. *Friends of God*, no. 33.

127. Among the texts of St. Josemaría, one can see, for example, *The Forge*, no. 11; *Christ Is Passing By*, no. 18, and *Friends of God*, no. 33. On traditional moral teaching, see *CCC*, no. 1264; Council of Trent, *Session 5: Decree on original sin*: DS 1515; St. Thomas Aquinas, *S. Th.*, I-II, q. 77, a. 2 c. In chapter eight we will speak extensively on this subject (section 2.2.1) and of other aspects of the Christian struggle.

128. *Friends of God*, no. 34.

tranquility of skepticism, and there are those who discover in sensuality their golden calf.[129]

Freeing oneself from the slavery of sin and withdrawing from the inclination to evil, implies allowing oneself to be guided by the love of God. Thus, a Christian makes himself a "slave to God's love," like the Virgin Mary, who calls herself "the handmaid of the Lord" (Luke 1:38). But that slavery is actually a falling in love, a filial submission to God's love that does not supress freedom; instead it gives it meaning. Thus, St. Josemaría states,

> *There is nothing better than recognizing that Love has made us slaves of God. From the moment we recognize this we cease being slaves and become friends, children.*[130]
>
> *I tell you once again: I accept no slavery other than that of God's Love. This is because, as I have told you on other occasions, religion is the greatest rebellion of men, who refuse to live like animals, who are dissatisfied and restless until they know their Creator and are on intimate terms with him. I want you to be rebels, free and unfettered, because I want you—it is Christ who wants us!—to be children of God. Slavery or divine sonship: this is the dilemma of our lives. Children of God or slaves of pride, of sensuality, of the fretful selfishness which seems to afflict so many souls.*[131]

"These words," Millán Puelles comments, "contain in a nutshell a complete theology of freedom."[132]

In addition to the slavery of sin discussed above, there is another one: the "slavery to the law," also present in Pauline doctrine (see Rom. 2; Gal. 3). This takes us to a teaching of St. Josemaría that we wish to consider more carefully now.

In the Old Testament, in order to free man from the slavery of sin, God shows man the path of goodness that had been darkened in his conscience. God does so by revealing a law which includes both the natural moral law (in essence, the Ten Commandments), as well as a code of precepts whose purpose is to determine the law in particular historical circumstances and to establish Israel as God's people with a specific form of worship, rites of

129. Ibid., no. 34.

130. Ibid., no. 35.

131. Ibid., no. 38.

132. Millán Puelles, "Amor a la libertad," p. 27.

purification from sin, and style of life that prepared it for the coming of the Messiah (see Ex. 20 ff.)

The Old Law was meant to be a "pedagogue" leading to Christ (see Gal. 3:24). Nevertheless, as time went on, many believed that belonging to the Chosen People and fulfilling the prescribed rituals—to which many other prescriptions had been added (Matt. 15:1 ff; Mark 7:3–4)—was sufficient to consider themselves righteous before God, ignoring all along however, the conversion of heart required by the prophets (Is. 1:10; Hos. 6:6; Hab. 2:4). Instead of using their freedom to love God and fulfill his will, they sought salvation by simply belonging to the People of the Covenant, and by observing the "works of the law" (Rom. 3:20, 28; Gal. 2:16; etc.). In the end, this led them to what we can call "slavery to the law."

The inertia of this deformity reached the nascent Church. St. Paul had to fight so that Gentile converts would not have circumcision imposed on them and with it, submission to all the precepts of the Old Law. He argued that salvation comes from a living faith in Jesus Christ through their incorporation to the Church by means of baptism: "faith working though love" (Gal. 5:6).[133]

This doctrine has a reach that transcends the historical problem at its origin because there is always the temptation to reduce the Christian life to the observance of some practices and the fulfillment of some laws that supposedly guarantee salvation at the cost of renouncing freedom. St. Josemaría warns us about this danger by preaching the value of good works carried out with a spirit of freedom because God wishes *exterior deeds to be the reflection of a spirit and not the result of coercion:* no man is justified before God by the law; for he who through faith is righteous shall live (Gal. 3:11).[134] As we can see, St. Josemaría applies the well known Pauline doctrine to our present-day circumstances. Thus, the "law" is no longer the set of precepts of the Old Testament and the added traditions referred to earlier, but rather any body of laws and behavioral norms in whose mere external observation salvation is thought to be found.

In order to refute this "slavery to the law," St. Josemaría alludes to the figure of St. Joseph, whose attitude toward the angel's messages about his

133. See Schlier, *La Lettera ai Romani* (Brescia: Paideia, 1982), p. 207; Vanhoye, *Lettera ai Galati* (Milan: Figlie di San Paolo, 2000), p. 124; Rodríguez Luño, "Introduzione allo studio della morale in san Paolo," in *Annales Theologici* 21 (2007): 417–450.

134. *Letter, May 6, 1945*, no. 39.

marriage to the Virgin, the flight to Egypt, and/or their return to Israel, reveals a marvelous example of a free obedience ready to take initiatives to carry out God's will. This is an important lesson indeed:

> *He didn't fulfill the will of God in a routine or perfunctory way; he did it willingly and wholeheartedly. For him, the law which every practicing Jew lived by was not a code or a cold list of precepts, but an expression of the will of the living God. So he knew how to recognize the Lord's voice when it came to him so unexpectedly and so surprisingly.*[135]

St. Joseph, the obedient man, comes across in St. Josemaría's teaching as an example of a free man who uses his freedom to grow, love, and serve God, without seeking refuge in the reduced limits of some precepts. Rather than a simple abider of precepts, he is a "just" man (Matt. 1:19), because *to be just is not simply a matter of obeying rules. Goodness should grow from the inside; it should be deep and vital—for* the just man lives by faith (Hab. 2:4).[136] He is a man who embraces the "adventure of freedom," guided by a living faith.

This example is just as pertinent as the opposite deformity. As St. Josemaría points out: *There are those who are afraid of exercising their freedom. They would rather be given ready-made formulas for everything. It's paradoxical, but often people demand rules—renouncing their freedom—out of fear of taking a risk.*[137] When freedom is not cherished it is easy to substitute it for the servile fulfillment of some rules that give security. Failure to appreciate interior freedom leads people to place their trust in external deeds in order to "fulfill" their duties toward God. St. Josemaría's preaching decisively challenges this attitude. *A Christian is not a neurotic collector of good behavior reports.*[138] His religion is neither a rulebook nor a moral code. Once again, God *does not want the forced service of slaves; he prefers to have children who are free.*[139]

"For freedom Christ has set us free; stand fast therefore, and do not submit again to a yoke of slavery" (Gal. 5:1). Jesus Christ has freed us from

---

135. *Christ Is Passing By*, no. 41. Earlier we stated that St. Josemaría interpreted Gal. 3:11 in a spiritual sense, but the literal meaning is not absent, as can be seen in the reference to "the law that every practicing Jew lives." On other occasions he speaks of St. Joseph as the heir of the promises made to Abraham, Jacob, and Moses (see ibid., no. 42) and of the traditions of Israel, as a man who *came from a noble line—the house of David and Solomon (Christ Is Passing By*, no. 40).

136. Ibid., no. 41.

137. *Letter, January 9, 1959*, no. 59.

138. *Christ Is Passing By*, no. 75.

139. *Friends of God*, no. 33.

the "slavery to sin" and the "slavery to the law." He has paid the debt for our sins "having canceled the bond which stood against us with its legal demands [. . .] nailing it to the cross" (Col. 2:14). He has obtained for us the gift of the Holy Spirit, who divinizes us and makes us children of God through grace; in a word, we become "more spiritual" and "more free," (a topic which we will discuss later on). The same Spirit pours out charity into our hearts together with faith and hope, so that an "interior law" inclines the children of God from the innermost sanctum of their soul to use their freedom to love God and others for his sake. "Love is the fulfilling of the law" (Rom. 13:10), says St. Paul. Through grace and charity, a Christian enjoys the "glorious liberty of the children of God" (Rom. 8:21).

St. Josemaría applies this teaching on law, love, and freedom to the Christian called to holiness in the middle of the world, for it is the Christian who must use his freedom to love God and others, fulfilling the divine mandate to work and build up the family and society in accord with God's design. That basic design is expressed in God's law, which marks out the path for us to love him while we accomplish the task of perfecting the world. For this reason, St. Josemaría reminds us that the Lord *has gratuitously given us a great supernatural gift, divine grace, and another wonderful human gift, personal freedom. To avoid this degenerating into license, we must develop integrity, we must make a real effort to conform our behavior to divine law.*[140]

The divine law is the law of Christ that, on the one hand, contains the natural moral law inscribed in every person's heart and illuminates it with the light of supernatural Revelation, thus permitting it to be known with the certainty of faith. On the other hand, the divine law inclines the person to order freely his behavior along the path of God's will out of love for God.

> *On the one hand, we have the natural law; through it, the divine will and designs are made known to us by the light of reason which grasps human nature and the nature of created things, as well as their natural and essential relations, especially the relation of order to their Creator and final end, on which everything else depends. On the other hand, we have Revelation which we come to know through the light of faith; through it, we come to better understand the natural law itself, and the divine positive law is made known to us. This divine law (which is proper to the supernatural order to*

140. *Christ Is Passing By*, no. 184. On the notion of divine law see Ernst Burkhart, *La grandeza del orden divino. Aproximación teológica a la noción de ley* (Pamplona: Universidad de Navarra, 1977), ch. 1 and 2.

> *which we have been raised) has restored, reaffirmed, perfected, and elevated the natural moral life of mankind to a higher plane and end.*[141]

Underlying these words is St. Thomas Aquinas' notion of natural law.[142] It is not only a "law of nature" that man can simply discover, but rather the "light of reason which grasps human nature and the nature of created things," and which discovers "their natural and essential relations." St. Josemaría recognizes the correspondence that exists between the human spirit and the structures of these earthly realities. He has a keen sensibility concerning the sanctification of the world from within temporal activities–in fact, he does not tire of repeating that *it is in the midst of the most material things of the earth that we must sanctify ourselves.*[143] With this in mind, he emphasizes that "human nature and the nature of created things" are significant for the moral order. By means of his freedom, man transforms the world and "cultivates" it. But the result of his actions will only yield a true "culture" (i.e., cultivation or perfection of creation for the good of man), as long as he employs his freedom within the moral order according to the demands he discovers instilled in human nature and in the nature of created things. Fernando Inciarte notes that if man were to lose awareness of these demands, he would also lose sight of the distinction between good and evil.[144]

St. Josemaría speaks of divine law as the path for freedom, pointing out that within it there is wide space for one to give order to the things of the world. Many ways exist to resolve social, economic, and political problems, and *all of these will be Christian, as long as they respect those basic principles which one cannot set aside without violating the natural law and Gospel teaching.*[145]

---

141. *Letter, March 19, 1967,* no. 83. At the end of the first sentence about the natural law he includes the following reference: See Pius XII, Encyclical *Summi Pontificatus* (October 20, 1939): AAS 31 (1939): 423.

142. See St. Thomas Aquinas, *In duo praecepta caritatis et in decem legis praecepta, Prologus*; *S. Th.*, I-II, q. 91, a. 2. The Pontifical Magisterium refers to this notion of law in various documents; see, e.g., St. John Paul II, Enc. *Veritatis Splendor* (August 6, 1993), nos. 12 and 44; *CCC*, no. 1955.

143. *Conversations*, no. 113.

144. See Fernando Inciarte, "Derecho natural o derecho racional: treinta tesis y una propuesta," in Idem, *Liberalismo y republicanismo. Ensayos de filosofía política* (Pamplona: Eunsa, 2001), p. 185. This was strongly emphasized by St. John Paul II in his encyclical *Veritatis splendor* (August 6, 1993), nos. 46–50, where he refutes both the "physicalist" and the "idealistic" conceptions of the natural law. Both have negative consequences for freedom. In the first case, freedom would be determined by the corporal nature of man and physical laws while in the second, these laws would lack significance for freedom, laying aside the substantial union of body and spirit which is proper to human nature. Neither of these extremes is found in St. Josemaría.

145. *Letter, January 9, 1959*, no. 35.

In his preaching, he is concerned with emphasizing the importance of natural law, but he is even more insistent on the specific nucleus of the "law of the Gospel" or the "law of Christ" that is summed up in love of God and love of others with deeds of service: "Bear one another's burdens, and so fulfill the law of Christ" (Gal. 6:2).[146] God's law is not a long series of precepts. It is summed up in one commandment: to love Jesus Christ and serve him with deeds. As noted earlier, it contains the natural law, and in this sense, it marks out the path for freedom to fulfill the divine will, but without making further indications for particular cases, as there is an infinite number of ways to tred along the path to God by ordering temporal realities. The novelty of the law of Christ is that it is carried out with love, the love of the children of God. It is a law of love, "the perfect law, the law of liberty" (Jas. 1:25). What God desires is for men to act freely out of love. He does not prescribe what man must do in temporal activities to please him; the natural moral law leaves wide room for action. What he must not do has been said and is impressed on his conscience. Christ's disciple should not await further instructions; he should not behave as a slave who only moves when ordered to do so. St. Augustine said "*Dilige, et quod vis fac*,"[147] love and do what you please. This attitude imbues St. Josemaría's entire life.

> *You shouldn't be concerned about anything, so long as you are acting out of love for God. It is easy to understand why St. Augustine said: love and do what you will. For in loving God our Lord, we can be sure of doing good.*[148]

1.3. Grace and Freedom in the Spiritual Life

According to St. Josemaría, the Christian life leads us *to admire the splendid gift of freedom which gives us power over our own actions and enables us—with heaven's grace—to build our eternal destiny.*[149] These words are quoted again with the intention of focusing on the clause "with heaven's grace," which is present in many of St. Josemaría's texts. Supernatural grace heals

146. See, e.g., *Friends of God*, nos. 44, 69, 173, 236.

147. St. Augustine, *In Ep. Ioannis ad Parthos*, VII, 8. In another place he writes that "*in recte faciendo ideo nullum est vinculum necessitatis, quia libertas est Caritatis*" (idem, *De natura et gratia*, 65, 78: PL 44, 486). This does not mean that there are no moral duties, but that one who loves will fulfill them freely and will exceed them through love.

148. Notes taken from preaching, January 1, 1965 (AGP, P02 I-1965, p. 16).

149. *Christ Is Passing By*, no. 99.

and raises human nature, enabling freedom to open its wings with an unexpected power to love God.

Supernatural life (sanctifying grace) is always a gift, a gift that is meant to grow, but it only grows with the cooperation of freedom, under the impulse of actual grace. A Christian can thwart its growth, but he cannot cause it with his strength alone.

Grace and freedom together build up Christian holiness. Scheffczyk writes that the relation between grace and freedom "is worked out well [in the works of Josemaría Escrivá]. He highlights the dominant and prior role of grace which decides everything without interpreting the universal efficacy (*Allwirksamkeit*) of divine grace in the same way as the sole efficacy (*Alleinwirksamkeit*) of the evangelical [Protestant] Theology."[150] It is neither grace alone nor freedom alone, but grace and freedom, with priority on the former. Josemaría Escrivá, continues Scheffczyk "fully places himself in the spiritual line of Catholic thought on grace which unites the unmerited strength of grace with human correspondence. He is aware of the objection and the danger of a Pelagian 'righteousness through works,' [. . .] as can be noted, for example, in the following words: *People have often drawn attention to the danger of deeds performed without any interior life to inspire them; but we should also stress the danger of an interior life—if such a thing is possible—without deeds to show for it* (*Forge*, no. 734). In this manner he decisively confronts the supposed Catholic principle of '*sola gratia*,' which states that, since the origin of every salvific action lies in grace and through the causality of grace, human co-causality can be done away with. He thus offers a determined and correct development of the Augustinian principle *qui te creavit sine te, non te iustificat sine te* [He who created you without you, will not justify you without you] (*Sermo* 169,13)."[151] St. Josemaría emphasizes the importance of human cooperation, but always within the context of a spiritual life based on divine filiation, and therefore, one based on the priority of grace.

As the reader will note, the reference to grace is a reference to both sanctifying grace and actual grace. Both play a role in the exercise of freedom, yet each in a distinct manner. Christian freedom is a "new" freedom whether because of the new elevation of our nature, or because of the

---

150. Leo Scheffczyk, "Die Gnade in der Spiritualität von Josemaría Escrivá," in Ortiz (dir.), *Josemaría Escrivá, Profile einer Gründergestalt*, p. 64.

151. Ibid., p. 68. See *Friends of God*, no. 23.

impulses through which the Holy Spirit moves us to act. In order to understand this newness it is useful to make the following distinctions:

- Freedom understood as "freedom of choice" (*liberum arbitrium*, according to St. Augustine). This is the power to direct oneself toward the good; of desiring or not desiring something; of desiring one good or another. It is "freedom for." In this sense, freedom's primary characteristic is self-determination.
- Freedom as the "condition or state of being free" (*libertas*, according to St. Augustine). This refers to the state of the person that permits him to decide with more or less self-mastery; it is "freedom from." This includes freedom from external coercion, on the one hand, and freedom from sin and slavery to disordered passions on the other. A person is "more free" when he is not subject to coercion, and "less free" when he is in some way oppressed. More specifically, he has more freedom when he is free from the guilt of sin, and has control over his passions; whereas he has less freedom when he is removed from God due to sin and is blinded by passions.[152]

In Sacred Scripture, there are references to both of these aspects of freedom in different books. Examples of "freedom of choice" are found in passages such as: "See, I have set before you this day life and good, death and evil [. . .]. Therefore, choose life, that you and your descendants may live, loving the Lord your God, obeying his voice" (Deut. 30:15, 19–20). Or, "It was he [God] who created man in the beginning, and he left him in the power of his own inclination. If you will, you can keep the commandments, and to act faithfully is a matter of your own choice. He has placed before you fire and water: stretch out your hand for whichever you wish. Before a man are life and death, and whichever he chooses will be given to him" (Sir. 15:14–17).

Examples of "state of freedom" are found in many passages that speak of freedom from slavery and its consequences.[153] The following are some

152. "One who sins against God preserves free will insofar as freedom from coercion is concerned, but has lost it in regard to freedom from guilt" (St. Thomas Aquinas, *De Malo*, q. 6, ad 23). St. Josemaría cites this text in *Friends of God*, no. 37. For a more detailed explanation of the previous distinction, see: Rodríguez Luño, *Ética general*, pp. 201–210. On the first meaning, see St. Thomas Aquinas, *In Ep. ad Rom.*, c. 2, lect. 3.

153. The term that the Greek version of the Old Testament uses for the concept of freedom is "*eleutheria.*" In the classical Greek culture there is no direct reference to the interior freedom of the person, but rather to his state of freedom with respect to his situation *in society*, which is opposed to slavery. But in the New Testament "*eleutheria*" does not refer to an external, legal state, but rather to the freedom of the children of God, who are not subject to certain prescriptions of the old Law because they have been freed by Christ.

examples: "Jesus then said to the Jews who had believed in him, 'If you continue in my word, you are truly my disciples, and you will know the truth, and the truth will make you free.' They answered him, 'We are descendants of Abraham, and have never been in bondage to any one. How is it that you say, "You will be made free?"' Jesus answered them, 'Truly, truly, I say to you, every one who commits sin is a slave to sin. The slave does not continue in the house forever; the son continues forever. So if the Son makes you free, you will be free indeed'" (John 8:31–36). "Let not sin therefore reign in your mortal bodies, to make you obey their passions [. . .]. But thanks be to God, that you who were once slaves of sin have become obedient from the heart to the standard of teaching to which you were committed, and, having been set free from sin, have become slaves of righteousness" (Rom. 6:12, 17–18). St. Paul also refers to freedom in this sense in his Letter to the Galatians (see Gal. 4:1, 5, 21–31; 5:1, 13; 6:2).

The following text from the Magisterium sums up these two aspects: "For its part, authentic freedom is an exceptional sign of the divine image within man. For God has willed that man remain under the control of his own decisions, so that he can seek his Creator spontaneously, and come freely to utter and blissful perfection through loyalty to Him. Hence man's dignity demands that he act according to a knowing and free choice that is personally motivated and prompted from within, not under blind internal impulse nor by mere external pressure. Man achieves such dignity when, emancipating himself from all captivity to passion, he pursues his goal in a spontaneous choice of what is good, and procures for himself through effective and skilful action, apt helps to that end."[154]

Both aspects are interdependent: depending on how a person employs one's "freedom of choice" (with God's grace), there is a corresponding "state of freedom" (which is also God's gift). And vice-versa, such "state of freedom" has a profound influence on how the person makes use of his or her freedom.

The freedom of the children of God is "new" with respect to the freedom of a man without supernatural life in both senses of freedom explained above. This is so in the latter sense, because *sanctifying grace* brings about a new situation of freedom; and in the former sense, because *actual graces* give a new impulse to the person in view of the positive use of freedom. Let us now consider in more detail these two aspects of freedom in the following sections.

---

154. *Gaudium et Spes*, no. 17.

1.3.1. Grace and the "Situation of Freedom"

Taking up the doctrine of the Council of Trent, the *Catechism of the Catholic Church* teaches that through sin, human nature "is wounded in the natural powers proper to it, subject to ignorance and the dominion of death, and inclined to sin."[155] All this brings with it a situation of slavery (see John 8:34). But "Justification *detaches man from sin* [. . .], it frees from the enslavement to sin and it heals."[156]

Sanctifying grace places man in a new situation of freedom: "For freedom Christ has set us free" (Gal. 5:1).[157] When man is "justified," he moves from the state of sin to that of friendship with God, and the successive increase in grace frees him more and more from the slavery to sin. This is why *we must go to Jesus, so that he will make us truly free.*[158] Although the outpouring of grace does not change the essence of self-determination, which is a free act, we can truly say that it makes a person "more free" because it frees him from sin and enables him to perform supernatural actions according to the condition he enjoys as a child of God.

> This can be understood better by considering that through rebirth in the Holy Spirit, a Christian receives "a new spirit" (Ez. 36:26; see John 3:5). This is the sanctifying grace, which according to St. Thomas, makes a person *more spiritual*,[159] and consequently *more free*, because as stated above, freedom belongs to human nature by virtue of its spiritual dimension.[160] Just as nature once elevated by divine grace is a *new nature*, it has a corresponding *new situation of freedom*: the one proper to the children of God.

"Christ has set us free." By redeeming us, he has set us in a new situation just as when the doors of a jail are opened for a prisoner, or, as St. Paul mentions, when someone pays the ransom for a slave. Christ has paid for

155. *CCC*, no. 405. See ibid., no. 1264; Council of Trent, *Session 5: Decree on original sin*, no. 2: DS 1512.

156. *CCC*, no. 1990.

157. This "new nature" is not new in the sense that it "substitutes" human nature or that it is "superimposed" on it, but rather that it is elevated by grace, which deeply renews it. Human nature is not annihilated nor replaced, but perfected. In the same way, the "new freedom" is not another freedom, but human freedom itself which is proper to the "new nature."

158. *Christ Is Passing By*, no. 17. The words refer, in an immediate way, to man's tendency to "defend himself" in the face of the divine requirements in such a way as to remain imprisoned by his own egoism.

159. Sanctifying grace "*addit spirituale*" (St. Thomas Aquinas, *De Veritate*, q. 27, a. 6, ad 1); by the infusion of grace, God grants to the human person an "*esse spirituale gratuitum*" (ibid., q. 27, a. 1, ad 3).

160. See section 1.2.1.

our liberation with the price of his blood (see 1 Cor. 6:20; 7:23) and has obtained for us the Holy Spirit who heals and raises our nature with sanctifying grace so "that you are no longer a slave but a son" (Gal. 4:7).

What is the reason for our liberation? Christ's words are an eloquent answer: "No longer do I call you servants, for the servant does not know what his master is doing; but I have called you friends" (John 15:15). He has liberated us so that we can become *friends of God*: so that we can know and love him in accord with our dignity of adopted children. Christ has freed us so that we may love in such a way. In elevating our nature through grace, God also elevates the operative powers of the soul (i.e., the intellect, will, and sensible faculties) through charity, the other supernatural virtues, and the gifts of the Holy Spirit. Thanks to these virtues and gifts, the use of freedom "flows" spontaneously from the "new nature" by means of the powers, which have been elevated and healed not only from the inclination of the will to evil, but also from the darkening of reason and disordered passions. The one who participates more in divine nature through grace and has greater charity finds himself in a situation of greater freedom. In this sense, it can be said that one who is "more holy" is also "more free."

In addition to the consequences of sin *within the person*, such as our being inclined to evil and experiencing disorder in our passions, there are consequences *over the person*, namely, the power of the devil (his temptations), pain, and death.[161] Christ's grace frees us from these consequences even though this liberation will only fully manifest itself at the end of history when the power of the devil over the children of God will be destroyed (see Rev. 12:9–10). The Lord "will wipe away every tear from their eyes, and death shall be no more, neither shall there be mourning nor crying nor pain any more, for the former things have passed away" (Rev. 21:4; see 1 Cor. 15:26).

Though only incipient, the liberation wrought by Christ is, however, already a reality that is present in the following aspects:

- We are liberated from Satan's power because *temptation can easily be rejected*. Even the slightest degree of grace is sufficient to resist any concupiscence and to merit eternal life (St. Thomas, *S. Th.*, III, q. 62, a. 6, ad 3).[162] *We are not exempt from temptations* (*Christ himself, in fact, allowed*

161. See Council of Trent, *Session 5: Decree on original sin*, no. 1: DS 1511; Heb. 2:14–15; *CCC*, no. 407.

162. *Letter, March 24, 1931*, no. 21. The struggle against temptations will be discussed in chapter eight, section 3.

the devil to tempt him), but we can overcome them and take advantage of them to show our love and trust in God (see 2 Cor. 12:7–10).

- *We are also liberated from pain, not because it disappears through the outpouring of grace, but because Christ has given to it a new meaning and worth, liberating us from the fear of suffering. This is not a "pious consolation" for those who suffer. Rather it is an essential aspect of the freedom of the children of God. The great Christian revolution has been to convert pain into fruitful suffering and to turn a bad thing into something good. We have deprived the devil of this weapon; and with it we can conquer eternity.*[163]
- *Finally, we are liberated from death because Christ came to* "deliver all those who through fear of death were subject to lifelong bondage" (Heb. 2:15). He has freed us from fear of death and has gained for us a glorious future resurrection. Death has lost its threatening character; it has become a path to eternal life. Jesus tells us, "Do not fear those who kill the body but cannot kill the soul; rather, fear him who can destroy both soul and body in hell" (Matt. 10:28). And St. Paul writes, "For to me to live is Christ, and to die is gain" (Phil. 1:21). Liberation from fear of death is based on the objective reality of what death means for a child of God: *For "others," death is a stumbling block, a source of terror. For us, death—Life—is an encouragement and a stimulus. For them it is the end: for us, the beginning.*[164]

In summary, we can say that the supernatural life (or sanctifying grace), which Christ has won for us on the cross, frees us from sin and its consequences. "For the law of the Spirit of life in Christ Jesus has set me free from the law of sin and death" (Rom. 8:2). Therefore, the life of a Christian should not be that of a slave who behaves well out of fear of punishment, but that of a son who acts out of love for his father, trying to do what pleases him with a free and joyful interior obedience.[165]

The state of being free with the freedom of the children of God is, in a certain sense, an anticipation of the perfect freedom in the state of glory. In this world, however, liberation is not yet definitive.

---

163. *Furrow*, no. 887.

164. *The Way*, no. 738.

165. See Ramón García de Haro, *La vida cristiana* (Pamplona: Universidad de Navarra, 1992), pp. 248–255. The author, a professor of Moral Theology who died in 1994, dedicated various articles to the study of the teachings of St. Josemaría. In the pages just cited, the author proposes an approach to the moral life saturated with a consciousness of freedom in tune with St. Josemaría's message.

> *We Christians carry the great treasures of grace in vessels of clay* (see 2 Cor. 4:7). *God has entrusted his gifts to the weakness and fragility of human freedom. We can be certain of the help of God's power, but our lust, our love of comfort and our pride sometimes cause us to reject his grace and to fall into sin.*[166] *Each one finds himself face to face with his Lord, and he can decide to live as God's friend, or as his enemy. This is the beginning of the path of the interior struggle which is a lifelong undertaking because, as long as we are on this earth, we will never achieve complete freedom.*[167]

1.3.2. Grace and the "Exercise of Freedom"

As God's creature, man depends completely on God for his being and acting. Being "cause of something" and being "cause of oneself" through the use of freedom is always founded on divine causality.

Through supernatural elevation, dependence on God is already of another order. Not only do we need sanctifying grace that divinizes our nature to carry out actions of a supernatural character, but also *actual graces* that move us to carry out each of those actions as children of God regardless of how small they may be (see 1 Cor. 12:3).

St. Josemaría conveys the traditional doctrine on actual graces when he says that they consist in *motions of our will, in clear insights of our mind, in affections of our heart.*[168] On another occasion, he gives some examples: *It is as if [God] were saying to us: fight continuously in the apparently unimportant things which are to my mind important; fulfill your duty punctually; smile at whoever needs cheering up, even though there is sorrow in your soul; devote the necessary time to prayer, without haggling; go to the help of anyone who looks for you; practice justice and go beyond it with the grace of charity. These and many others are the inspirations we feel inside us every day.*[169] Every one of these motions and inspirations are "actual graces."

Although nature elevated by grace is the principle for supernatural actions, the Christian needs these divine motions prompting him to act

166. *Christ Is Passing By*, no. 131.

167. *Friends of God*, no. 36.

168. *Christ Is Passing By*, no. 13. "*Actual graces* refer to God's interventions, whether at the beginning of conversion or in the course of the work of sanctification." *CCC*, no. 2000. Unlike sanctifying grace, these are not a "habitual" gifts, or permanent qualities; they are "actual" motions of the Holy Spirit, by which we know, desire, or act (see St. Thomas Aquinas, *S. Th.*, I-II, q. 110, a. 2, c).

169. *Christ Is Passing By*, no. 77.

because, given that sanctifying grace is a completely supernatural gift not required by human nature, the determination to act does not come in the first place from one's own initiative, but rather from God by means of actual graces to which the Christian may freely correspond.[170] He would not be able to carry out any supernatural action if, in addition to sanctifying grace, God did not move him with actual graces: "God is at work in you, both to will and to work for his good pleasure" (Phil. 2:13).

The primacy of grace is absolute, not only in the sense that God's action is the foundation for man's acts, but also in the sense that, in the order of sanctification, man's acts are the fruit of grace. The greatness of the Christian lies in his seconding that which God wishes to carry out within him. For this reason, in the work of sanctification the Christian, like a needy child, should always ask for the grace of Christ, who said, "*Sine me nihil potestis facere*" (John 15:5). In fact, he needs the Holy Spirit to move him even to ask for this (see Rom. 8:26). Thus, St. Josemaría insists,

> *Seek, always and in everything, the help and support of God. Be convinced that, without him, nothing worthwhile is accomplished. Aspire, therefore, to his mercy, and pray:* dirigat corda nostra, quaesumus Domine, tuae miserationis operatio, quia tibi sine te placere non possumus. *We need to be governed by God's mercy, because without his help we can neither please him nor serve him joyfully. We have to rely on him for everything, opening up our heart, so that he can lead us along the paths of interior life and apostolate in a supernatural and paternal way.*[171]

All this, however, should not make us forget that God always counts on man's freedom, both for the passage from the state of sin to that of grace (justification), as well as for his growth in holiness (sanctification). St. Augustine teaches that God acts in us in an invincible manner (*gratia invicta*), but with the gentleness of love (*suavitas amoris*), fully respecting our freedom.[172] Grace thus solicits our cooperation.[173] *We cannot, properly*

170. It is traditionally said that "the divine initiative in the work of grace precedes, prepares, and elicits the free response of man." *CCC*, no. 2022.

171. *Letter, February 14, 1974*, no. 22. The prayer "*dirigat . . .*" was from the eighteenth Sunday after Pentecost. In the current Roman Missal it is the collect for the Saturday of the fourth week of Lent.

172. On the notion of "*gratia invicta*," see St. Augustine, *De correptione et gratia*, 12, 38; and on the "*suavitas amoris*," see Idem, *Enarrationes in Psalmos*, 13.

173. See *CCC*, no. 2022.

speaking, move ahead of grace. But in all that does depend on us, we have to prepare the way and cooperate when God grants grace to us.[174]

> The Lord compares the growth of the kingdom to the growth of a seed. The seed tends to grow on its own: "if a man should scatter seed upon the ground, and should sleep and rise night and day, and the seed should sprout and grow, he knows not how" (Mark 4:26–27). This parable points to the primacy of grace in sanctification, but it does not claim that man has nothing to do on his part. Jesus also speaks of the seed, which falls on the path, among rocks, among weeds or in good soil; some receive the seed and others do not, and not every seed bears the same fruit. The fruit also depends on human correspondence to grace (see Mark 4:9–20). Likewise, the parables of the "talents" and the "pounds" show the need to cooperate with divine grace. (see Matt. 25:14–28, Luke 19:11–27)[175]

The positive exercise of freedom on the part of a child of God thus consists in accepting sanctifying grace and seconding actual graces by being docile to the guidance of the Holy Spirit. As an example of a shining exercise of freedom, St. Josemaría looks to the the Virgin Mary's response to the archangel Gabriel. From the beginnning, she was full of grace (see Luke 1:28); and at the moment of the Annunciation, she receives the necessary actual graces—the light and divine motions—conveyed through the archangel's words, informing her how the Incarnation would take place. In the end, she gives her reply: "Behold, I am the handmaid of the Lord; let it be to me according to your word" (Luke 1:38). Her freedom is manifested in this reply. Her decision is a "yes;" it is the result of grace, but grace working through her freedom. She acknowledges herself to be a "handmaid" because everything that occurs is God's initiative; and then she pronounces her *fiat* (her "let it be done"), since it is through her that it will happen. As we can see, we exercise our freedom when, with God's grace, we accept what God himself carries out.[176]

---

174. *Furrow*, no. 668.

175. We are not mentioning here many other aspects of the relation between grace and freedom that are studied in Dogmatic Theology. It is sufficient to recall that, on this subject, Catholic doctrine is as distant from the Pelagian posture (which tends to prescind from grace and count on purely human strength to attain salvation) as from the Lutheran position, according to which man cannot do anything for his salvation except trust in God (see *CCC*, no. 406).

176. See *Christ Is Passing By*, no. 173.

1.3.3. From the "Exercise of Freedom" to a "State of Freedom"

When the Christian carries out a free act corresponding to an actual grace, he merits an increase in sanctifying grace and a strengthening of his supernatural virtues, both of which lead him to a better situation (or state) of freedom.[177] "God has given us freedom so that we love him, and freedom grows in the measure that one loves more."[178] If, on the contrary, we act wrongly, we compromise our freedom. [*W*]*e can still say 'no' to God, rejecting this source of new and permanent happiness. Anyone who does so stops being a son and becomes a slave.*[179] *Evil is an enslavement, not a liberation.*[180] In the case of having committed a mortal sin, man is deprived of the life of grace and loses the freedom of the children of God, which belongs to the state of those who are justified. In this situation, he is unable to carry out meritorious acts and his moral weakness is greater. Nonetheless, someone who sins mortally does not lose the power of freedom, which he has as a person. He can always convert, responding to the actual graces offered to him by Divine Mercy, and once again attain the freedom of the children of God.

No concrete action of the Christian is morally indifferent or without significance for the spiritual life. All, including the most basic ones, such as eating and drinking, can be carried out either out of love of God and for his glory (see 1 Cor. 10:31), which is the goal toward which actual graces move the person, or out of selfishness and vainglory. It is love that sets freedom in motion. If it is love of God and love of neighbor out of love of God, that act contributes to the freedom of the Christian; if, on the other hand, it is a disordered self-love, the act will enslave him in one way or another. Freedom turns against itself, in other words.

St. Gregory the Great affirms, "Not to go forward on the path to God is to go backward."[181] By means of every free act, a person grows or diminishes as a son or daughter of God; and the state of freedom improves or worsens. In the end, there is a Christian freedom, with which we are born to

---

177. See *CCC*, no. 1828.

178. Cecilia Echevarría Falla, "Libertad y estructura de las virtudes en el Beato Josemaría," in *Hacia una educación más humana. En torno al pensamiento de Josemaría Escrivá* (San Jose, Costa Rica: Promesa, 2002), p. 65.

179. *Friends of God*, no. 34. Following these words, St. Josemaría cites an explanation of St. Thomas that concludes with these words: "When [man] sins, he works outside of reason, and then lets himself be led by the impulse of another, subject to foreign limits, and by this he who accepts sin is a servant of sin (John 8:34)." *In Ioann. Ev.*, c. 8, lect. 4.

180. *Friends of God*, no. 37. See John 8:34.

181. "*In via Dei stare retrocedere est.*" St. Gregory the Great, *Regula pastoralis*, p. 3, c. I.

the supernatural life at baptism, and there is a "state of freedom," which we win over by corresponding to actual graces. When we use the freedom we received at baptism to love God, we grow in holiness and freedom. "Freedom is obtained at the beat of every free-step: it expands through its very exercise," writes Alejandro Llano when commenting on the teaching of St. Josemaría.[182] Antonio Millán Puelles expresses the same idea in different words when he states, "Without freedom we cannot love God [. . .]; without love of God we cannot be free."[183] This is not circular reasoning. When he says that "without freedom we cannot love God," he is speaking of the freedom with which we are born; whereas when he affirms that "without love of God we cannot be free," he is referring to the freedom that is won by corresponding to grace: the freedom of the one who is his own master, and not of the one who is a slave of things, of his passions, or of his very self.

Christian life can be described as a process of "liberation" whereby little by little we receive and conquer a more perfect freedom every time. St. Thomas wrote, "the more charity one has, the more freedom one has."[184] St. Josemaría also expresses this decisive truth with great liveliness: [*o*]*nly when we love do we attain the fullest freedom.*[185]

1.4. The "Awareness of the Freedom of the Children of God"

In St. Josemaría's teaching, the Christian life is proposed as a constant putting into action of freedom. Thus, he states, *In order to persevere in following in the footsteps of Jesus, you need a continuous freedom, a continuous willing, and a continuous exercise of your own freedom.*[186]

When St. Josemaría writes these words, just as when more generally speaking he had said that we *unite ourselves to the Creator by using our freedom,*[187] he does not wish to simply recall a basic truth of Christian anthropology. Rather, he wishes to transmit the conviction that, for the sake of sanctification and apostolate in the midst of daily activities, *we need to be and to feel personally free with the freedom that Christ won for us.*[188] It is

182. Llano, "Libertad y trabajo," p. 185.

183. Millán Puelles, "Amor a la libertad," p. 33.

184. ". . . *quanto aliquis plus habet de caritate, plus habet de libertate.*" St. Thomas Aquinas, *In III Sent.*, d. 29, a. 8, qla. 3, s.c..

185. *Friends of God*, no. 38.

186. *The Forge*, no. 819.

187. *Friends of God*, no. 24.

188. *Conversations*, no. 34.

not only about "being free" but also of "feeling free" or "having a sense of being free" [*sentirse libres*]. St. Josemaría's goal is to foster in souls the *awareness of freedom* as the proper and necessary manifestation of the "sense" [*sentido*] of divine filiation. His message "is not theoretical; instead, it seeks for each person to come to the awareness of a full and responsible freedom."[189]

If the sense of divine filiation is the "foundation" of the spiritual life in St. Josemaría's teaching, the awareness of freedom is the conviction that this foundation is something "alive," as if it were more of a beating heart than a motionless rock. Awareness of this freedom is the intimate and permanent conviction that personal sanctity and apostolate require "a continuous exercise of your freedom" as a child of God who wants to correspond to divine grace. This is more than a mere knowing that being a child of God through grace implies a new freedom; rather, it is a passionate appreciation for freedom that translates into a zeal for defending it and a desire to foster it in oneself and others. St. Josemaría would sometimes summarize this profound awareness that he wished to transmit with the expression "*love for freedom.*"[190]

Becoming more fully conscious of freedom is a central part of having an awareness of divine filiation. And living in accord with this sense means exercising this freedom. Whoever abuses his freedom, turning it into "a pretext for evil" (1 P 2:16), certainly does not behave as a son of God; but neither is the one who does not exercise his freedom, which amounts to burying his talent (see Matt. 25:18): *Let us not forget*, says St. Josemaría of the man who buried his talent, *this man's sickly fear of putting to honest use his capacity for work, his mind, his will, his whole being.*[191]

The connection between divine filiation and freedom is so profound that from an existential perspective, the Christian not only feels free because he knows he is a son of God; he is also conscious of being a son of God because he feels free when he loves God.

> *We Christians perceive with a particular clarity all the wealth of our divine filiation when we realize that we are fully free, because we are doing our Father's work.*[192]

189. Sanguineti, "La libertad en el centro del mensaje del Beato Josemaría Escrivá," p. 85.

190. Ibid., p. 81.

191. *Friends of God*, no. 30.

192. *Christ Is Passing By*, no. 138.

What are the manifestations of this awareness of freedom? And what demands does it have on Christians? The manifestations and demands are as many as those corresponding to a spirit of divine filiation, but there are two that stand out in St. Josemaría's preaching: a sense of responsibility and trust.

1.4.1. "Sense of Responsibility"

Personal freedom is essential to the Christian life. But do not forget, my children, that I always speak of a responsible freedom.[193] Freedom is a gift that enables a person to "respond" to God's gift with his own self-giving. It is precisely because our free actions belong to us (in fact, we say they are "ours") that we are accountable for them. Freedom makes man *responsible* for his acts, and first of all responsible to God. "Freedom, according to the founder of Opus Dei, is, in its primary and most radical sense, freedom before God and for God, and therefore responsibility is inseparably united to it."[194] Willem Onclin indicates that one of Escrivá's relevant personality traits is "his love for freedom, a word he never said without adding another word: responsibility."[195] In fact, the words 'freedom' and 'responsibility' occur together in numerous writings of his.[196]

It is not necessary to dwell on the notion of responsibility to reach what is of most direct interest to this disscussion: the sense of responsibility as a manifestation of consciousness of one's freedom. Whoever knows himself to be free (with a Christian freedom) feels the obligation of responding for the use of his freedom.

> *This freedom will give rise to a healthy sense of personal responsibility that will make you serene, upright and friends of the truth, and prevent you from falling into error. For you will sincerely respect the legitimate opinions of other people, and you will not only know how to change your opinion when you see it is not in accord with the truth, but you will also be able to take on another viewpoint, without feeling humiliated because you have changed your mind.*[197]

---

193. *Conversations*, no. 117. See *CCC*, no. 1734.

194. Clavell, "Personas libres," p. 108.

195. Willem Onclin, "Msgr. Escrivá de Balaguer: un grand fondateur disparu," in *La Libre Belgique*, July 2, 1975.

196. See, e.g., *Conversations*, nos. 14, 26, 28, 38, 60, 65, 66, 77, 78, 84, 98, 100, 118; *Christ Is Passing By*, nos. 27, 99, 124, 184; *Friends of God*, nos. 11, 32.

197. *Letter, January 9, 1951*, no. 25.

Commenting upon St. Josemaría's preaching, José María Barrio states that, "a responsible freedom is no less freedom; it is a freedom which owns up to its acts, which is more conscious, and if I may say so, more free."[198]

The idea of the "sense of responsibility," with these or similar terms, appears constantly in St. Josemaría's writings. To show this, let us take a closer look at two quotations; the first is a point from *The Way*. Note the tone of his preaching from the onset:

> *Many great things depend—don't forget it—on whether you and I live our lives as God wants.*[199]

It is significant that this point appears in the chapter "The Will of God." The chapter does not mention the expression "sense of responsibility," but it is clear that it wishes to foster responsibility in the use of one's freedom in order to fulfill the will of God. "Many great things depend" on this freedom. From the context, it is apparent that he is thinking about sanctification and apostolate that includes Christianity's edifying influence in society, and the consequent building up of the temporal common good. This is a responsibility before God and men, the world, and history.

The other text is of special interest because it is autobiographical:

> *If my own personal experience is of any help, I can say that I have always seen my work as a priest and shepherd of souls as being aimed at helping each person face up to all the demands of his life and to discover what God wants from each in particular—without in any way limiting that holy independence and blessed personal responsibility which are the features of a Christian conscience. This way of acting and this spirit are based on respect for the transcendence of revealed truth and on love for the freedom of the human person. I might add that they are also based on the certainty that history is undetermined and open to a variety of human options—all of which God respects.*[200]

St. Josemaría does not wish to offer preconceived solutions to those who come to him with very important questions about their lives. He respects their independence and wishes for them to take responsibility for

198. José María Barrio, "Educar en libertad. Una pedagogía de la confianza," in Paul O'Callaghan (ed.), *La grandezza della vita quotidiana*, vol. V/1, p. 97.

199. *The Way*, no. 755.

200. *Christ Is Passing By*, no. 99.

their decisions. He acts in this manner "out of love for freedom," a freedom with which they must write history, "open to a variety of options," especially in the case of those called to live holy lives in temporal realities.

1.4.2. Trusting in God and in Others

Whereas a sense of responsibility clearly manifests the "awareness of one's freedom," it manifests "trust" less so. This subject in St. Josemaría's teaching is the object of an interesting study by Concepción Naval, titled "Trust: a requirement of personal freedom."[201]

Assuredly, "trust" is a recurring theme in St. Josemaría's writings. Before all else he advises to trust in God: *In your heart and soul, in your intelligence and in your will, implant a spirit of trust and abandonment in the loving Will of your heavenly Father.*[202] *Trust fully in God and have a greater desire each day never to run away from him.*[203] He also counsels his audience to trust others and thus he writes to his children in Opus Dei, *How proper to our way of being is trust!*[204] In particular, concerning spiritual direction he writes, *In the spiritual life you have to let yourself be led with complete trust, single-mindedly and without fear.*[205] Even though he does not mention freedom in these or other texts,[206] it can be noted that trust arises from an awareness of the value of the freedom of the children of God. Concepción Naval wonderfully sums up St. Josemaría's train of thought from awareness of divine filiation to awareness of freedom and trust: "Through a lived out experience of divine filiation—and not just one that is thought up or proclaimed—the full sense of human freedom is discovered that, as personal freedom, is seen as a gift from God. Thanks to freedom, we are capable of giving and of giving ourselves: freely do we give the freedom we have been given. In human dealings, this gift-response appears to be nothing other than trust."[207] If, however, human freedom is understood as having no reference whatsoever to its origin and end, and if it is reduced to the power to

201. See Concepción Naval, "La confianza: exigencia de la libertad personal," in Antonio Malo (ed.), *La grandezza de la vita quotidiana*, vol III, p. 229–242.

202. *Furrow*, no. 850.

203. *The Forge*, no. 214.

204. Notes from his preaching (AGP, P10, no. 197).

205. *Furrow*, no. 145.

206. In other cases, it is mentioned with specific applications that we are not dealing with now: see *Conversations*, no. 100; *Christ Is Passing By*, no. 79, 129; *Friends of God*, no. 35; etc.

207. Concepción Naval, "La confianza: exigencia de la libertad personal," p. 240.

act, then it will lead man to "mistrust trust," as Naval also goes on to explain. Instead, when it is considered a gift from God that allows the person to give of himself, then its full value emerges. Only within a context of trust is it possible to give oneself to God and to others out of love for God. In summary, mistrust leads freedom to recoil upon itself in a self-referential way.

It is true that trusting God is not the same as trusting others: God alone never fails. Yet, in order to trust God we need to trust others. "While clearly distinguishing between trust in God and trust in men, Bl. Josemaría does not separate them at the root level."[208] The others deserve to be given a certain trust primarily because God trusts them: God trusts the way they will make use of the freedom he gave them. The notion of freedom as a gift from God demands trusting in others "because only thus can they effectively be helped to live their freedom as a gift, allowing them (and encouraging them) to act and manifest themselves freely."[209] This trust is given to them based on who they are (free persons) and not on how they have used their freedom. If they have used their freedom well, it will be an additional motive to trust in them; however, if they have not used it well, a complete loss of trust in them would not be justified. This would be tantamount to negating the positive possibilities of their freedom. Inspired by a noble realism, St. Josemaría invites people *to be prudent, yes; but not suspicious.*[210]

In addition to these two expressions of awareness of Christian freedom, briefly outlined, we should speak about fostering freedom. Whoever is aware of how valuable freedom is does what he can to promote it. For St. Josemaría, this was of such import that we will discuss it in detail later on in this chapter.

2. Will, Reason, and Sentiments in the Exercise of Freedom

We will now study the role of the different human faculties in the exercise of freedom. What is the influence of reason, will, and sentiments? It is common to find one-sided explanations to this, both in theory and in practice. When one of these elements is given more importance than the others, the result is voluntarism, rationalism, or sentimentalism. A Christian vision of

208. Ibid., p. 239.

209. Ibid., p. 240.

210. *Friends of God*, no. 159.

man and his freedom can only reflect the harmony present in Christ, who is perfect man. St. Josemaría's vision is at the same time balanced (for it is rooted in Revelation as developed throughout the centuries), as well as specific to his spirit of divine filiation and sanctification in the middle of the world. Before delving into this topic, however, let us make two terminological observations.

The first one regards the title of this section: "Will, Reason, and Sentiments in the Exercise of Freedom." This threefold set seems to be heterogenous because, while will and reason are "faculties" or spiritual powers, sentiments are considered "acts" or "states" (of varying duration) of the sensible faculties. It would have seemed more appropriate to write: "Will, Reason, and Sensible Faculties," but this could have given the impression that freedom arises from the sensible faculties just as much as from reason and will, which is not the case. The chosen title, "Will, Reason, and Sentiments," reflects real distinctions: will and reason, as spiritual faculties of human nature, are the twofold source of the person's freedom. Sentiments, on the other hand, proceed from the sensible faculties and, even though they exert a significant influence on the exercise of freedom due to the substantial unity of body and soul, they are not its source, or at least not in the same way.[211]

The second observation refers to the absence of the word "heart" in the title. Does not this word commonly express sentiments and sensible affections? It certainly does, but if mentioned together with will and reason, it may be understood as another faculty different from the two spiritual faculties. This would introduce a notion that differs from the biblical sense of the term "heart" used by St. Josemaría:

> *When we speak of a person's heart, we refer not just to his sentiments, but to the whole person in his loving dealings with others. In order to help us understand divine things, Scripture uses the expression "heart" in its full human meaning, as the summary and source, expression and ultimate basis, of one's thoughts, words and actions. A man is worth what his heart is worth* [. . .].[212]

---

211. On the basic concepts of this section, you might see Martin Rhonheimer, *La perspectiva de la moral* (Madrid: Rialp, 2000), pp. 169–197.

212. *Christ Is Passing By*, no. 164. On this subject, see José María Yanguas, "Loving 'with all your mind' (Deut. 6:5): Christian Love in the Teachings of Bl. Josemaría Escrivá," in *Romana* 26 (1998): 144–157; Carmen Vidal Montecinos, "El corazón humano en las enseñanzas de san Josemaría," in Helena Ospina (ed.), *Colección Centenario*, no. 9 (San Jose, Costa Rica: Promesa, 2003).

> Juan Fernando Sellés comments that "for some [twentieth-]century thinkers (such as Von Hildebrand, Stein, Haecker, Guardini, etc.) the bipolar exclusivity of *reason* and *will* as the only superior faculties of the soul which has characterized modern and contemporary philosophy is not only open to debate but also deficient. These authors frequently assert that the heart is a *faculty* that is different and not inferior to the others. Instead, Escrivá thinks of the heart, as we have seen, as the *person*, and it is clear that the person is greater than his or her powers."[213]

In summary, when speaking of the "heart," we seem to point to the intimate nucleus of human activity in the widest sense possible, which includes thinking, loving and feeling. It is a term that manifests the unity of that nucleus and, in a particular way, evokes the fact that the spiritual life is not the life of a bodiless spirit, but rather that of man made up of "flesh and bones," with affections, sentiments, and emotions. *God does not say: "In exchange for your own heart, I will give you a will of pure spirit." No, he gives us a heart, a human heart, like Christ's.*[214]

2.1. Freedom, Will, and Reason

Let us begin with the role of the will and of reason. Christian tradition teaches that "By virtue of his soul and his spiritual powers of intellect and will, man is endowed with freedom [. . .]."[215] Free choice is an act of the will because it is a kind of desire, but it also stems from reason because the will can only aspire to its object guided by reason with knowledge of the end.[216] As a result, freedom has a twofold root: "The root of freedom is the will as the subject thereof; but as far as its cause, it is reason."[217] The free act is an expression of both powers.

> Here we should recall that we are referring to the Christian in the state of grace who seeks holiness. The "will" refers to that of a person who possesses charity, and "reason" refers to a reason enlightened by faith. Since the freedom of a child of God stems from faith informed by charity, it

213. Juan Fernando Sellés "La verdad del corazón," in "Tres estudios sobre el pensamiento de san Josemaría Escrivá," *Cuadernos de Anuario Filosófico* 158 (2003), p. 27.

214. *Christ Is Passing By*, no. 166.

215. *CCC*, no. 1705. See *Gaudium et Spes*, no. 17.

216. See St. Thomas Aquinas, *S. Th.*, I-II, q. 6, a. 1, c.

217. Idem, *S. Th.*, I-II, q. 17, a. 1, ad 2.

> is able to do many things that, on a purely human plane are not "reasonable," and that go further than an earthly love. A clear example of this is the zeal of the apostles after they received the Holy Spirit at Pentecost. Along a similar vein, St. Josemaría too accomplished many feats during his lifetime, which humanly speaking were "acts of madness inspired by divine love."[218]

What we have just explained above is necessary for understanding an expression frequently employed by St. Josemaría to describe freedom: acting "because one feels like it" [*porque a uno le da la gana*]: *I love you, Lord, because I feel like loving you.*[219] *You hold out your hand to me lovingly, and I, with your grace, strive to take hold of it because I feel like it* [porque me da la gana]*: because I want to! Because I love you!*[220] He thus describes someone acting with mastery over his own choices, who acts neither out of fear nor coercion. St. Josemaría does not endorse acting without reason ("just because") in a voluntaristic way (i.e., by sheer will power), or by instinct ("doing whatever I please"). He deliberately rules out these attitudes. For example, he comments: *many times we will come to "feel like it" when we don't feel like doing anything: because we are doing it for love, entirely for Love, for a love filled with loyalty.*[221]

It is the will, the power to love, that "feels like it," and that is why it is the first root of freedom. But it needs to be guided by reason enlightened by faith, which indicates what is good: knowing and loving God and fulfilling his will.[222]

> *Freedom finds its true meaning when it is put at the service of the truth which redeems; when it is spent in seeking God's infinite Love* [. . .]. *This is what is meant by a* good will, *which teaches us to pursue* good, after having distinguished it from evil. (St. Maximus the Confessor, *Capita de caritate*, 2, 32)[223]

---

218. See, e.g., *The Way*, no. 479. See the explanation of this point in Pedro Rodríguez, *The Way: Critical-Historical Edition* (London-New York: Scepter, 2009), *ad loc.* See also *Furrow*, no. 2; *The Forge*, no. 870.

219. *Te amo Señor, porque me da la gana de amarte.* Notes from a meditation, November 21, 1954 (AGP, P09, p. 19).

220. *Letter, March 19, 1967*, no. 134.

221. Notes taken from preaching, September 27, 1967 (AGP, P03 XII-1967, p. 19). See also *Friends of God*, no. 32.

222. See St. Thomas Aquinas, *Summa contra gentiles* III, c. 109.

223. *Friends of God*, no. 27.

God has given man freedom so that man can love him. Freedom allows man "to give" glory to God, "to give" him something: one's will, one's love. Obviously, man cannot "give" anything to God if by "giving something to God" we mean adding some perfection to God. But man can love God because he is free. He can give himself to God; he can give his very being to him. Commenting on the teaching of St. Josemaría, Leonardo Polo writes that "through freedom, the divine gift (of being and life) becomes, so to speak, reversible."[224] By means of our freedom we can correspond to God properly speaking; we can give our life to God. Hence, Polo adds, "To give oneself to God is doubly free: we freely give the freedom we ourselves have received."[225]

This is not an illusion. Jesus says it: "You shall love the Lord your God with all your heart [. . .]" (Matt. 22:37). *He himself points out what he desires from us. He does not care for riches, or for the fruits or the beasts of the earth, nor for the sea or the air, because they all belong to him. He wants something intimate, which we have to give him freely:* My son, give me your heart" (Prov. 23:26).[226] The Lord shows Peter that he seeks his love: "Simon, son of John, do you love me?" (John 21:16); and he accepts the reply: "Yes, Lord; you know that I love you" (ibid). He seeks not only Peter's love, but also the love of every man in spite of being a creature and a sinner.

The love that gives meaning to freedom is not a futile desire, but rather the giving of oneself completely to the fulfillment of the divine will. St. Josemaría uses the expression "because I feel like it" precisely to describe this act of personal self-giving. *I opt for God because I want to, freely, without compulsion of any kind. And I undertake to serve, to convert my whole life into a means of serving others, out of love for my Lord Jesus.*[227] It is in this self-giving to God (and to one's neighbor out of love for God) that freedom finds its ultimate meaning. *Gaudium et Spes* states that man, "the only creature on earth which God willed for itself, cannot fully find himself except through a sincere gift of himself."[228] Apropos of one of St. Josemaría's homilies, Leonardo Polo notes that "fulfilling the greatest of all commandments (to love God with all one's heart and all one's mind) becomes the preeminent vital

224. Polo, "El concepto de vida en Mons. Escrivá de Balaguer," p. 173.

225. Ibid.

226. *Christ Is Passing By*, no. 35.

227. *Friends of God*, no. 35.

228. *Gaudium et Spes*, no. 24.

need [of man]. The tightly woven union between the commandment and one's impetus for existence constitute Christian freedom."[229]

A decision to embrace a life of love of God is not a blind choice. Both human and supernatural reasons exist for this choice. Giving oneself to God is undoubtedly the most reasonable thing to do, but the will is not necessarily determined to do so by reasons alone. The more light it receives, the more inclined it is to follow reason; but in this life, no light is compelling enough if one does not want to follow suit. One can always "close his eyes." If in the end the person wills to give himself, the will is certainly guided by those reasons, but it is not absolutely coerced by them. A Christian places himself in God's hands and freely permits him to be master of his entire life. That is why St. Josemaría qualifies the motive for this action as the "most supernatural of reasons":

> *For me and for my children, the most supernatural of reasons for self-giving and Love is this one:* because I feel like it [porque me da la gana], *because I want to, because there is nothing in the world that can separate me from Christ's charity.*[230]

> *Freedom of choice* comprises both *freedom of exercise* (i.e., the power of self-determination to love or not to love), and *freedom of specification* (the power of loving this or that, of choosing one thing or another which is known and measured by reason). In the free act, *freedom of exercise* (or of self-determination) is absolutely key.[231] Thus, in the spiritual life, it is essential for one to decide to give glory to God and to love his will even without knowing the particulars. Afterward one must discover God's will and choose these or those means to follow it with this or that intention. But above all, the spiritual life requires *making up one's mind to want/love* what God wants/loves. St. Josemaría points out that God does not ask his children to achieve this or that goal; rather, he asks them to struggle, because what he looks for is where our hearts are rather than what the results are. Later on he adds that even if there are moments of weakness in which it seems we are not strong enough to fight, we can always "want to want" to do so.

229. Polo, "Acerca de la plenitud," in *Nuestro Tiempo* 162 (1967): 632.

230. *Letter, April 30, 1946*, no. 1. See Rom. 8:35, 38, and 39. On "because I feel like it" as the "most supernatural" motive, see Juan Bautista Torelló, "Was ist Berufung?" in Ernst Burkhart and J.B. Torelló, *Berufung und Elternhaus* (Vienna, 1989), pp. 1–13.

231. See St. Thomas Aquinas, *De Malo*, q. 6.

> This is the essence of what it means to "love the will of God." *We want to want to. At least we have desires to desire. Children, this means that we are fighting already.*[232]
>
> Our decision to give ourselves to God is like a first step that is then followed by other steps. Hence, the spiritual life is not the result of pure inertia: *Renew your firm resolution to live your Christian life* right now, *at every moment and in all circumstances.*[233]

To get to heaven we must commit ourselves freely, with a wholehearted, constant and voluntary determination. By itself, however, freedom is insufficient: it needs a guide, a polestar.[234] Freedom does not only reside in the will because the will does not move without the light of reason. The will is not a blind force; rather it *aliqualiter rationem participat* [In some way it participates in reason].[235] However, we only know if we wish to know. Reason and will are not two independent powers or simply juxtaposed; instead they are intimately intertwined.

> In the spiritual life, it is of great importance a use of freedom which fully involves the intellect and the will, avoiding both a "voluntaristic" attitude (acting or omitting action in disregard of good reasons) as much as a "rationalistic" one (understanding clearly the reasons but not trusting in those that should be trusted, or not accepting that moments of darkness may arise, or that one has insufficient light to understand, etc.).

Sin has injured the "twofold root" of freedom. St. Paul transmits his experience when he writes, "I do not understand my own actions. For I do not do what I want, but I do the very thing I hate [. . .]. For I do not do the good I want, but the evil I do not want is what I do [. . .]. So I find it to be a law that when I want to do right, evil lies close at hand. For I delight in the law of God, in my inmost self, but I see in my members another law at war with the law of my mind and making me captive to the law of sin which dwells in my members" (Rom. 7:15, 19, 21–23). St. Josemaría speaks of this inner tension by quoting a text of St. Thomas and commenting on it as follows: Since the object of the will is the good, or at least the apparent

232. Notes taken from preaching, February 1972 (AGP, P09, p. 154).

233. *The Forge*, no. 396. See *The Way*, no. 293.

234. *Friends of God*, no. 26.

235. St. Thomas Aquinas, *In III Sent.*, d. 35, q. 1, a. 1, sol. 4.

good, the will is never attracted by evil unless it appears to have an aspect of good about it (St. Thomas, Aquinas, *S. Th.*, I-II, q. 77, a. 2 c.). *The passions, or the disordered will, force the intellect to assent precipitously, or to overlook certain opposing aspects, in order to embrace others that favor—that adorn with goodness—that inclination.*[236]

It would be naive to ignore or undervalue this fact; yet realism should not lead to doubt the possibility of always being able to freely respond to grace. *Let us say with John and James:* possumus! (Matt. 20:22). Omnia possum in eo qui me confortat (Phil. 4:13). *I can do all things in Him who strengthens me. Be filled with trust, because* he who began the work will bring it to completion (Phil. 1:6). *We will be able to, if we cooperate, because we are assured of God's strength:* quia tu es, Deus, fortitudo mea (Ps. 42:2).[237] The experience of one's weaknesses does not justify giving in to them. On the contrary, it should lead to cooperation with grace, which heals the twofold root of freedom.

In what does this cooperation consist? Or, stated differently, if the right use of freedom depends on the health of reason and the will, how can this twofold root be strengthened and cultivated? The answer is none other than to nourish reason with the knowledge of truth, and the will with the love of God. St. Paul shows the importance of these two aspects in the path of identification with Christ when he writes, "living the truth in love, we are to grow up in every way into him who is the head, into Christ" (Eph. 4:15). St. Josemaría often refers to the following two aspects:

(1) In the first place, reason is nourished by the knowledge of truth. "You will know the truth, and the truth will make you free" (John 8:32).[238] But which truth is our Lord referring to? As we discussed, St. Josemaría commented on these words and stated in essence that the truth that makes us free is our divine filiation: *How great a truth is this, which opens the way to freedom and gives it meaning throughout our lives. I will sum it up for you* [. . .] *that we are children of so wonderful a Father.*[239] A Christian who knows that he is a son of God, called to be "another Christ, Christ himself"; one who does not

---

236. *Letter, March 24, 1931*, no. 36. We will discuss the influence of the passions later on.

237. Ibid., no. 49.

238. For a biblical-theological study of the meaning of this text, against the background of the teachings of St. Josemaría, see Antonio García-Moreno, "*'Veritas liberabit vos'* (John 8,32)," in *El cristiano en el mundo*, pp. 113–136.

239. *Friends of God*, no. 26.

ignore the reality of sin and its consequences, but is conscious of having been redeemed by Christ; and one who knows his path of sanctification and the means to follow it, has a powerful light to guide his freedom. This knowledge of the truth is the root of freedom because it liberates from ignorance and error, and it shows the will the true good so that it decides to seek after it.[240]

This knowledge of the truth is designated with the term "wisdom" (*sapientia*). It is a "knowledge that is tasteful" (*sapientia* being a derivation of *sapida scientia* [tasteful science] in Latin); it is knowledge of the one who loves that which he knows. It is not simply personal speculation, but a gift from God. As the apostle Paul prays, "that the God of our Lord Jesus Christ, the Father of glory, may give you a spirit of wisdom and of revelation in the knowledge of him, having the eyes of your hearts enlightened, that you may know what is the hope to which he has called you, what are the riches of his glorious inheritance in the saints" (Eph. 1:17–18).

In effect, the Paraclete is the Spirit of truth (see John 14:17; 15:26) who guides us to the complete truth (see John 16:13). In addition to assisting the Church's Magisterium in the transmission of the Gospel, he moves the faithful interiorly to accept the truth which makes them free.[241] *It is he* [the Holy Spirit] *who leads us to receive Christ's teaching and to assimilate it in a profound way. It is he who gives us the light by which we perceive our personal calling.*[242] He does this by connaturalizing the Christian with the Word of God through the gift of wisdom that is a fountain of freedom in the innermost part of the heart. Indeed, it *makes us know God and rejoice in his presence, thereby placing us in a perspective from which we can judge accurately the situations and events of this life.*[243]

This wisdom, which is nourishment for the root of freedom, is a gift from God. However, we must not forget that the action of the Holy Spirit bears fruit counting on the person's cooperation. The Spirit himself moves us with his grace to employ the means to know the truth that guides the exercise of freedom. St. Josemaría often insists in these means: study and

240. See St. Thomas Aquinas, *In Ioann. Ev.*, c. 8, lect. 4.

241. "Just as the effect of the mission of the Son was to lead us to the Father, so the effect of the mission of the Holy Spirit is to lead the faithful to the Son. Now the Son, once he is begotten Wisdom, is Truth itself: 'I am the way, and the truth, and the life' (John 14:6). And so the effect of this kind of mission [of the Spirit] is to make us sharers in the divine wisdom and knowers of the truth. The Son, since he is the Word, gives teaching to us; but the Holy Spirit enables us to grasp it." St. Thomas Aquinas, *In Ioann. Ev.*, c. 14, lect. 6; see *Summa contra gentiles* IV, c. 21.

242. *Christ Is Passing By*, no. 135.

243. Ibid., no. 133.

doctrinal formation. [*N*]*o one can use his intelligence and freedom properly* [. . .] *unless he has acquired an adequate Christian education.*[244] "His love for freedom" writes Lluís Clavell, "leads him to generously employ himself in providing well thought out formation to others, including in the theological sphere, so that each lay faithful could then act freely in the sanctification of work and in apostolic enterprises without waiting for orders."[245] At the same time, love for freedom completely envelops his understanding of theological formation: "It is a question of education *in* freedom (as its climate and proper context), and *for* freedom (as an end in helping to form free and responsible persons)."[246]

(2) Formation of the will also strengthens the twofold root of freedom. Since love for God and for others is what gives meaning to free choice, formation of the will consists in orienting it to the gift of self, giving oneself to God and one another out of love for God.

I don't understand freedom without self-giving, or self-giving without freedom: the one underscores and strengthens the other.[247]

The first words convey this idea directly: freedom is reached or lived in its full sense with the gift of oneself to God (i.e., with the love for God that is manifested in dedicating one's life to fulfilling his will). This dedication nourishes the root of freedom:

> *When we make up our minds to tell our Lord,* I put my freedom in your hands, *we find ourselves loosened from the many chains that were binding us to insignificant things, ridiculous cares or petty ambitions. Then our freedom, a priceless treasure, a wonderful pearl that it would be a tragedy to cast before swine* (see Matt. 7:6), *will be used by us entirely to learn how to do good.* (see Is. 1:17)[248]

---

244. *Conversations*, no. 2; see *Furrow*, no. 389.

245. Clavell, "La libertad ganada por Cristo en la Cruz," p. 267. On the subject of "formation," explains Rodríguez Luño: "When one speaks here of formation, one does not understand the communication of specific prefabricated and irreformable solutions which are closed to constructive dialogue. Rather, to form is to promote a sensibility toward the demands of the common good, as well as to stimulate thought that, in the light of faith, permits one to progress in an understanding of reality and of social change" ("*Cittadini degni del vangelo*" *(Fil 1,27). Saggi di etica politica*, c. III: "La formazione della coscienza in materia sociale e politica secondo gli insegnamenti di san Josemaría Escrivá," Roma 2005, p. 50).

246. Clavell, "La libertad ganada por Cristo en la Cruz," p. 271. Christian formation will be discussed in chapter nine, section 4.

247. *Letter, May 31, 1954*, no. 24.

248. *Friends of God*, no. 38.

The second part of the phrase quoted above ("I don't understand [. . .] self-giving without freedom") emphasizes the first. The gift of oneself to God must be free: free not only upon the initial commitment but permanently. In this sense, as noted earlier, St. Josemaría invites people to serve God with *an ever-renewed willingness.*[249] This disposition of the will nourishes the root of freedom.

Some people think that giving oneself to God and in the service of others is tantamount to "losing one's freedom" and therefore wish "to preserve it." Instead of choosing to give themselves out of love, such people prefer to keep their freedom as the possibility of giving or not giving of themselves. St. Josemaría points out to them that by acting in such a way they are converting their freedom into an end in itself and thus transform it into a kind of object to be locked up in a "safe place." But far from keeping it intact, in the end, they are actually end up damaging it. *Such people barricade themselves behind their freedom. My freedom! My freedom! they cry. They have their freedom, but they don't use it. They look at it, they set it up like a clay idol for their petty minds to worship.*[250] Along these lines he warns those who decided to give their lives generously to fulfill the divine will of the temptation of "lowering" their self-giving as the years go by. *Do you know what the worst enemy is for souls dedicated to God? A half-hearted dedication!*[251] It can rightly be said that, given that freedom is ordered for giving oneself to God and that self-giving liberates, placing limits on one's self-giving to God is tantamount to placing limits on freedom.

Instead of fostering growth in freedom by nourishing its roots, these types of behavior weaken it. When a person does not choose God, freedom is not kept "intact" because he chooses "not to love God," and *where there is no love of God, the individual and responsible use of personal freedom becomes impossible.*[252] And these are the consequences:

> *[D]espite appearances to the contrary, the individual is coerced at every turn. The indecisive and irresolute person is like* modeling clay *at the mercy of circumstances. Anyone and anything can mold him according to its whim, and especially his passions and the worst tendencies of his own nature wounded by sin.*[253]

249. *The Forge*, no. 396. See *The Way*, no. 293.

250. *Friends of God*, no. 29.

251. Notes taken from preaching, June 21, 1972 (AGP, P01 VII-1972, p. 13).

252. Ibid.

253. Ibid.

Lastly, it is noteworthy to state that knowledge of revealed doctrine and love are sources of freedom, though not separately. The knowledge of truth is knowledge of the good, and therefore faith is a condition for love. On its part, love is a source of knowledge (see 1 John 4: 7–8). "*Per ardorem caritatis datur cognitio veritatis* [Through the ardor of love knowledge of the truth is given], " writes St. Thomas.[254] Making use of our own efforts to correspond to grace, the Holy Spirit carries out in us a mutual reinforcement of love and knowledge as the source of greater freedom.

2.2. Sentiments and Freedom

The spiritual life is obviously not the life of a pure spirit with knowledge and will alone. It is the life of a person composed of body and soul, with sentiments or affectivity that profoundly influence the exercise of freedom.[255] *There is just one life, made of flesh and spirit. And it is this life which has to become, in both soul and body, holy and filled with God.*[256] St. Josemaría does not have a *spiritualistic* or *dis-incarnate* notion of the Christian life. He underlines the importance of affectivity without giving into *sentimentalism,* which would allow the affections to usurp the helm of the spiritual life from the intellect and the will. Arturo Blanco points out the importance that St. Josemaría gives to the "connection of the intellect and the will, emotions and human sentiments,"[257] fostering a harmonious integration of all the faculties in the formation of personality and growth in identification with Christ.

Before delving futher into the subject matter, we need to make some observations about the terminology of St. Josemaría's conceptual framework.

Due to his corporeal dimension, the human person has sensible powers (appetites or inclinations), that are directed toward objects perceived

254. St. Thomas Aquinas, *In Ioann. Ev.*, c. 5, lect. 6. See Id., *De caritate*, a. 6 s.c.

255. See Antonio Malo Pé, *Antropología de la afectividad* (Pamplona: Eunsa, 2004); Francisca R. Quiroga, *La madurez afectiva* (San Jose, Costa Rica: Promesa, 2003), which has a select bibliography; Dietrich von Hildebrand, *The Heart: An Analysis of Human and Divine Affectivity* ((Chicago: Franciscan Herald Press, 1977); Ricardo Yepes, *La persona y su intimidad* (Pamplona: Ediciones Internacionales Universitarias, 2004); Juan Luis Lorda, *Para una idea cristiana del hombre* (Madrid: Rialp,1999); Polo, *La persona humana y su crecimiento* (Pamplona: Eunsa, 1996). These works, of which we are citing only recent editions, offer interpretations of affectivity that differ from one another, and they cite St. Josemaría, with the exception of the work of Dietrich von Hildebrand.

256. *Conversations*, no. 114. See *CCC*, no. 365.

257. Arturo Blanco, "Alcuni contributi del beato Josemaría alla comprensione dei rapporti tra fede e ragione," in Paul O'Callaghan (ed.), *La grandezza della vita quotidiana*, vol. V/1, p. 256.

by the senses and exert influence over reason and the will.[258] The movements of these powers are usually called "passions" because they are experienced by reason and the will. (The latin "*passio*" is derived from "*pati*" [to suffer], but these movements are called "passions" not because there is "pain" involved but because they affect the person from the outside in.)[259] Often they are distinguished by various nuances and can be called *sentiments*, [*feelings*], *emotions*, or *affections*. This is a traditional terminology employed, for example, in the *Catechism of the Catholic Church*.[260] Some authors distinguish between these terms while others do not. In any event, in St. Josemaría's writing, as in common usage, they have a similar connotation.[261] For the purposes of our present work, we will use these terms almost synonymously.

Notwithstanding further elaborate distinctions made in Moral Theology, it is good to remember that these inclinations originate in what is classically called the "sensible appetites" (or faculties that tend toward a sensible good). The "concupiscible appetite" is the inclination toward sensible pleasure, while the "irascible appetite" is the inclination to overcome the obstacles that keep us from attaining a good perceived by the senses.[262]

Passions or emotions are movements that arise from a good or an evil that is grasped by the senses. These may arise before a person is aware of them, that is, before his reason takes note and the will intervenes; in fact, passions can arise in a relatively independent way from one's reason and will. These are referred to as the "antecedent passions" because they precede the free act; they are felt without consent. Antecedent passions are not free acts and therefore are neither good nor evil.[263] Thinking particularly about

---

258. The authors of moral theology who follow St. Thomas generally understand that the sentiments have a direct influence on the judgment of reason and, through it, on the will.

259. See St. Thomas Aquinas, *S. Th.*, I-II, q. 22, a. 1, c; ibid., q. 22, a. 2, c. and ad 2.

260. "Feelings or passions are emotions or movements of the sensitive appetite that incline us to act or not to act in regard to something felt or imagined to be good or evil." *CCC*, no. 1763.

261. "Sentiment" is an affective state produced by some kind of impression; "emotion" is an affective reaction produced by some kind of sensation, memories, or ideas; and "affection" is an inclination or feeling of sympathy toward something or someone. In general, sentiment refers to something more lasting, while an emotion usually designates that which is momentary or passing.

262. St. Thomas Aquinas speaks of eleven passions: six that proceed from the concupiscible appetite and five from the irascible (see *S. Th.*, I-II, q. 23, a. 4, c).

263. "In themselves passions are neither good nor evil. They are morally qualified only to the extent that they effectively engage reason and will. Passions are said to be voluntary, 'either because they are commanded by the will or because the will does not place obstacles in their way.' (St. Thomas Aquinas, *S. Th.*, I-II, q. 24, a. 1)." *CCC*, no. 1767. The antecedent passions are neither good nor bad in the sense that by themselves they do not constitute sin; but to have antecedent passions that incline one to evil, is an evil, and to have passions that incline one to the good, is a good.

these passions, St. Josemaría writes: *Whatever happens, there is no need to worry as long as you don't consent. For only the will can open the door of the heart and let that corruption in.*[264] Nonetheless, antecedent passions play an important part in the spiritual life because they influence the judgments (made by reason), and indirectly affect the will.

Passions also arise as a consequence of voluntary acts, and they are duly called "consequent" passions because they are provoked, consented to, or foreseen by our knowing their cause and desiring it. They have great importance in the spiritual life. It is not necessary to note the implications of "performing evil with passion," (since Moral Theology already deals with it), but it is of interest to point out the influence of passions that separate from the good as well as the importance of "carrying out the good in a passionate way" instead of acting in a cold manner. Reason and will need to be helped in some sense by the strength of the passions.[265] While it is undeniable that they can darken the light of reason, it is likewise true that they can facilitate the knowledge of the good and help reason direct the will better. This is why Rafael Alvira, commenting on the teaching of St. Josemaría, writes, "When we must carry out a duty which we do not like, we should do it, first because we wish to fulfill our duty but then, making an effort to like it."[266] The fact that the fulfillment of a duty "is not initially pleasing" (antecedent passion), does not mean that it should not be fulfilled because pleasure is not the rule. St. Josemaría sometimes joked, referring to those who take as rule of conduct the "law of the pleasurable" [*la ley del gusto*]. But human perfection demands the far greater standard of "accomplishing duties with pleasure," in such a way that the person should even seek to provoke in the soul the consequent pleasurable passion (by considering, for example, that the effort is well worth the good that will be done to others). St. Josemaría often uses the adverb "*gustosamente*" ("willingly," "gladly," "with pleasure"), applying it to those things that by their nature are not pleasing. For instance, he speaks of *gladly being a man of penance*,[267] and encourages *being able to gladly give oneself a hard time*

264. *The Way*, no. 140.

265. Perfection implies "that man is moved to the good not only by his will, but also by his sensitive appetite. As Psalm 83 says: 'my heart and my flesh rejoice in the living God,' where 'heart' refers to the intellectual appetite [the will] and 'flesh' to the sensitive appetite" (St. Thomas Aquinas, *S. Th.*, I-II, q. 24, a. 3, c).

266. Rafael Alvira, "Hacer Cristo al mundo," in Paul O'Callaghan (ed.), *La grandezza della vita quotidiana*, vol. V/1, p. 41.

267. *The Way*, no. 548.

for the love of Christ.[268] He asks people to gladly embrace small annoyances or lack of means,[269] and to gladly give their lives to others,[270] etc.

After these preliminary explanations, we can look at the subjects, which allow us to understand how St. Josemaría sees the influence of sentiments in the exercise of freedom, and therefore their importance in the spiritual life.

2.2.1. Ordering the Sentiments through Reason and Will

The Gospels reveal Jesus' sentiments: *They tell us of his compassion for the sick, of his sorrow for those who were ignorant or in error, his anger when faced with hypocrisy. Jesus cries for the death of Lazarus, he becomes angry at the money changers who profaned the temple; his heart is moved by the sorrow of the widow at Naim.*[271] These are only some examples highlighting the role of sentiments in the life of the Lord, and by extension, in the life of a child of God. If a Christian wishes to identify himself with Christ, he should try to have "the sentiments of Christ" (Phil. 2:5; see Phil. 3:15). He should try to do this, not because identification with Christ consists in having the same sentiments, but because these undeniably help him to exercise his freedom to love God and others, which is the essence of holiness or identification with Jesus Christ.[272]

> Among the sentiments proper to a Christian, St. Josemaría sometimes highlights three for those who follow the path of holiness he proposes. He calls these dominant passions[273] and are the following: to teach Christian doctrine; to guide others along the path of holiness by example and word; and to love unity. (In addressing members of Opus Dei, he refers specifically to the unity of the Work, but this can be applied in general to love for unity in the Church).
>
> He speaks of "passions" to emphasize that these sentiments should be vigorous and natural. He calls them "dominant" not because they should dominate a person's will and reason, but because they should guide the soul's energies along the same path of faith and love for God and souls.

268. *The Forge*, no. 519.
269. See *Furrow*, no. 411.
270. See ibid., no. 750.
271. *Christ Is Passing By*, no. 108. See ibid., no. 146.
272. See *CCC*, no. 1762.
273. Notes taken from preaching (AGP, P10, no. 18).

> The three "dominant passions" refer to the different aspects of a Christian's mission. A certain correspondence is noticeable with the *munera Christi*: passion for giving doctrine in the service of the *munus docendi*; for guiding souls in the service of the *munus regale*; and for unity in the service of the *munus sanctificandi*, since unity is a sign of a supernatural life and the condition for transmitting it. Passion for unity is passion for life.
>
> In any event, the "dominant passions" are ordered to carry out the mission of Christ and to further imbue the Christian with the sentiments of the Lord.

While it is undeniable that sentiments can influence powerfully in the growth of the spiritual life, it is also true that they can obstruct it and even divert its course and corrupt it. For them to contribute to identifying onself with Christ, they must be under the control of the will guided by reason and enlightened by faith.[274] However, as a consequence of sin, sentiments tend to rebel from the order of reason and to distort judgment. *Human passions have a facility to obscure reality*[275] and if they are not controlled, the helm is left to whims, preferences or moods, and behavior easily deviates from the human and Christian path (see 2 Tim. 4:3).

This disorder is vividly described in the following point of *Furrow.* It is clear that the protagonist is a person who, though fully committed to living his Christian vocation, is experiencing the loss of control of his sentiments:

> *In your life, there are two things that do not fit together: your head and your heart.*
>
> *Your intelligence—enlightened by faith—shows you the way clearly. It can also point out the difference between following that way heroically or stupidly. Above all, it places before you the divine greatness and beauty of the undertakings the Trinity leaves in our hands.*
>
> *Your feelings, on the other hand, become attached to everything you despise, even while you consider it despicable. It seems as if a thousand trifles were awaiting the least opportunity, and as soon as your poor will is weakened, through physical tiredness or lack of supernatural outlook, those little things flock together and pile up in your imagination, until they form*

274. See *CCC*, no. 1767.

275. *Letter, October 24, 1965*, no. 28.

> *a mountain that oppresses and discourages you. Things such as the rough edges of your work, your resistance to obedience; the lack of proper means; the false attractions of an easy life; greater or smaller but repugnant temptations; bouts of sensuality; tiredness; the bitter taste of spiritual mediocrity . . . And sometimes also fear; fear because you know God wants you to be a saint, and you are not a saint.*
>
> *Allow me to talk to you bluntly. You have more than enough "reasons" to turn back, and you lack the resolution to correspond to the grace that he grants you, since he has called you to be another Christ, ipse "Christus!"—Christ himself. You have forgotten the Lord's admonition to the apostle: "My grace is enough for you," which is confirmation that, if you want to, you can.*[276]

From among the various teachings contained in these words, it is worthwhile to highlight the danger of an illness in Christian life called "sentimentalism," the overamplification of the sentiments that threaten to take over a person's behavior, removing it from the order of reason and faith. The remedy is not the suppression or neutralization of the sentiments, which would be like the amputation of a vital organ; rather, it would be to combat the disorder of the sentiments. This is the motive for a prayer arising from a deeply human and holy heart: *I don't ask you to take away my feelings, Lord, because I can use them to serve you: but I ask you to put them through the crucible.*[277] And from this, St. Josemaría derived the following counsels imbued with the richness of personal experience:

> *Be upright persons by your struggle. Strive to reconcile the two brothers we all carry inside: our intellectual faculties, aided by the grace of God, and our sensuality. These two brothers are with us from birth and accompany us throughout our whole life. We must get them to live together in harmony, even though they tug in different directions. We try to get the superior one, the intellect, to steer the lower one, the senses. Following the dictates of faith and reason with the help of God's grace, our soul will aspire to the greatest of gifts: paradise, eternal happiness. And we need to guide our little brother, our sensuality, so that he may enjoy God in heaven too.*[278]

---

276. *Furrow*, no. 166.

277. *The Forge*, no. 750.

278. Notes taken from preaching, June 1972 (AGP, P09, p. 181. In this passage, St. Josemaría uses the term "sensuality" as equivalent to "sensibility," or that is, to refer to the tendencies of the sensible appetites in general.

The Holy Spirit enlightens the intellect and moves the will to order the sentiments or affections under the guidance of reason. In such a way, the sentiments will not only not obstruct our knowing the good and our carrying it out, but also contribute positively in doing so. "Good sentiments" thus not only provide keen insights to discover what one ought to do but will also provide the strength one needs in order to accomplish it.

2.2.2. Character Formation

Reason and will can certainly give rise to sentiments (e.g., one can voluntarily remember something that provokes a sentiment of hatred). But anything from sense perception (which can include one-time events such as a success or a failure, a health problem, fatigue, joy, sadness, etc.), to more lasting factors such as temperament and character also exert a considerable influence over one's sentiments.

All of these factors are important. Sometimes their significance is exaggerated, as would occur if one were to think that they determine the state of the spiritual life, or if one allows them to do so (as for example, if one were to abandon one's duties simply because he felt discouraged or apathetic). However, it is also possible to undervalue them, as would occur if one thought of his spiritual life as belonging to someone who did not possess a body and soul. St. Josemaría teaches the need to value all of these "sentimental factors" in their just measure, which can be reached by understanding all things human in light of the mystery of the Incarnation. Two points from *The Way* expound upon this:

> *Physical collapse. You are worn out. Rest. Stop that exterior activity. Consult a doctor. Obey, and don't worry. You will soon return to your normal life and, if you are faithful, to new intensity in your apostolate.*[279]
>
> *So you couldn't care less? Don't try to fool yourself. This very moment, if I were to ask you about certain people and undertakings in which for God's love you put your soul, I know that you would answer me eagerly, with the interest of one speaking of what is his own. It's not true that you don't care. It's just that you're not tireless, and that you need more time for yourself: time that will also be for your activities since, after all, you are the instrument.*[280]

279. *The Way*, no. 706.
280. Ibid., no. 723.

"Character" has a unique influence on the sentiments and hence the importance of its formation. In general, by "character" we mean the set of psychological qualities of a person. These depend on his or her makeup, the way he or she has assimilated formation, and the influence exercised on the person by family and social circumstances.[281]

Varying according to character, people are more or less reflective, active, phlegmatic, passionate, impulsive, apathetic, reserved, open, etc. In reality, none of these types of character exists in its pure form. People are complex and that is why it would not make sense to label someone as if that person could be reduced to a single aspect of his or her character. On the other hand, it should not be forgotten that God's grace and the effort to practice the virtues profoundly mold one's character and give it *the smooth and regular finish, the firm flexibility of charity, of perfection*,[282] a shape which is diverse and unrepeatable in each one.

Among the distinguishing marks which a child of God should look for, St. Josemaría points out *a calm and balanced character*,[283] that is, possessing the diverse features that configure one's character in a harmonious way. Naturally, the equilibrium point is different for each person depending on his masculinity or her femininity and personal qualities. In any case, there are countless ways to identify oneself with Christ and for St. Josemaría diversity is a richness:

> *You have to be different from one another, as the saints in heaven are different, each having his own personal and special characteristics. But also as alike to one another as the saints, who would not be saints if each of them had not identified himself with Christ.*[284]

The goal of character formation is for each one to reach his proper equilibrium point or harmony in the positive aspects of his personality. From the first chapter of *The Way*, St. Josemaría refers to character formation as a fundamental demand of the spiritual life: *Don't say: "That's the way I'm made . . . it's my character." It's your lack of character: Be a man—"esto*

281. Although the terms "temperament" and "character" are very close in common parlance, they are not identical. By temperament we understand here a whole of one's own personal inclinations that spring from the psychosomatic constitution of the individual. Temperament (or whatever one wants to call this psychosomatic foundation) does not change, while character can be corrected and improved.

282. *The Way*, no. 20.

283. *Furrow*, no. 417; see ibid., no. 440.

284. *The Way*, no. 947.

vir."[285] This formation requires self-knowledge. *Each one should look at himself, to see if he is or is not the instrument that God wants.*[286] With these words, he is not inviting persons to psychological introspection, but to a sincere self-examination before Christ: to see oneself in him[287] through personal prayer and with the help of spiritual direction in order to become *ipse Christus.*

From self-knowledge one must go on to practice the virtues, especially those that each one needs to develop so as to reach the equilibrium mentioned above and thus achieve the ordering of the sentiments under reason and will. In particular, we need fortitude and temperance, and their many associated virtues which perfect the sensible powers of the person (see chapter six).

As a whole, for the philosopher Carlos Ortiz de Landázuri, St. Josemaría's teaching on the equilibrium of character, and harmony between the sentiments, the will and reason, reached through the practice of Christian virtues "is an efficacious antidote to the 'corruption of character,' a result of an ethics of feelings (Hume) and of duty (Kant) that today translates into an ethics of success and an ethics of power."[288] St. Josemaría's teaching leads to the formation of the image of Christ in free men and women who have a lively awareness of the treasure of the freedom of the children of God.

By way of conclusion on the role of the different faculties of the soul in the exercise of freedom, we can affirm that the freedom of a child of God is greater or lesser depending on the degree of harmony between the will, reason, and sentiments. And this harmony depends on charity, knowledge of the truth, and growth in the moral virtues.

It can also be said that charity is the compendium of all that implies knowledge of the truth, a right ordering of the will, and the good governing of the passions. We recall St. Thomas's words, "the more charity one has, the greater freedom one possesses."[289]

Perfect charity and perfect knowledge of truth can only be attained in heaven. Therefore freedom can only reach its fullness in the beatific vision. In the mean time, the degree of freedom depends on a loving vision of God:

---

285. Ibid., no. 4. This point, as well as all those in *The Way*, is addressed to both men and women. The words "*esto vir*" (see 1 Sam. 18:17; 2 Sam. 10:12; 1 Kings 2:2; etc.) refer to the virtue of fortitude, as Pedro Rodríguez explains in *The Way: Critical-Historical Edition, ad loc.*

286. Notes taken from preaching, October 2, 1962 (AGP, P09, p. 60).

287. *Christ Is Passing By*, no. 107.

288. Carlos Ortiz de Landázuri, "La reinvención innovadora del carácter en 'Camino,' 'Surco' y 'Forja,'" in *Tres estudios sobre el pensamiento de san Josemaría Escrivá*, pp. 79–115.

289. St. Thomas Aquinas, *In III Sent.*, d. 29, a. 8, qla. 3, s.c.

contemplation. The intrinsic relationship between Christian freedom, charity, and knowledge of the truth allows us to affirm that the one who has greater freedom is the one who is more contemplative.

> Et reducam captivitatem vestram de cunctis locis (Jer. 29:14). *I will free you from captivity, no matter where you are. With prayer we cease to be slaves. We feel free and we are free, flying on the wings of a nuptial poem of a soul in love—carried by a love song toward union with God! It is a new way of living on earth, one that is divine, supernatural, marvelous.* [. . .] *We need to live a long time, but in this way, in freedom:* in libertatem gloriae filiorum Dei (Rom. 8:21), qua libertate Christus nos liberavit (Gal. 4:31), *with the freedom of the children of God, which Christ won for us by dying on the wood of the Cross.*[290]

2.2.3. Developing One's Personality as Man or Woman

As we noted before, being man or woman deeply influences one's character and therefore also personality, which when understood as "psychological personality" is practically synonymous to "character." This is the case in St. Josemaría's preaching and in common language, and as we will see, being man or being woman will also have a profound influence on the exercise of one's freedom.

There is no doubt that St. Josemaría "addresses himself from the start to both men and women, preaching to all the same human and Christian virtues and the same ideal of life in Christ. However since his language, which is tied closely to the biblical text and to his pastoral experience, [. . .] he frequently employs masculine words"[291] which "require an analogical reading on the part of women,"[292] just as the biblical expressions on which he bases his thoughts and which he often uses: "*Esto vir*" (1 Kings 2:2),[293] "*Viriliter age*" (Ps. 26:14),[294] etc.

St. Josemaría, however, also emphasizes that men and women have distinctive characteristics of their own.[295] He avoids the general tendency to uniformity that he observes, and insists concretely that *a woman has*

290. Notes taken from preaching, November 26, 1967 (AGP, P09, p. 79). See *Friends of God*, no. 297–299.

291. Rodríguez, *The Way: Critical-Historical Edition*, p. 219.

292. Ibid., p. 239.

293. See *The Way*, no. 4.

294. See *Friends of God*, no. 94.

295. See Blanca Castilla, "Consideraciones sobre la antropología 'varón-mujer' en las enseñanzas del Beato Josemaría," in *Romana* 21 (1995): 434–447.

to develop her own personality and not let herself be carried away by a naive desire to imitate[296] the masculine way of being because *that would not be a victory, but rather a loss for women, not because they are better than men or worse, but because they are unique.*[297] Women should *fully develop their own potentialities: the ones they have as persons and those they have as women.*[298]

When he refers to what is particular to each, rather than speaking about men, St. Josemaría highlights the characteristics proper to women to counter perhaps the common tendency of erasing the differences. He does this in a positive manner, asking, for example, *Who slandered women by saying that discretion is not a woman's virtue?* And he then adds, *There are many men—yes, full-grown men—who have yet to learn!*[299] Reflecting on what happened on the morning of the Resurrection when the women went to the sealed and guarded tomb of Christ, St. Josemaría comments, *difficulties, great and small, can be seen at once. But if there is love, one pays no heed to those obstacles: one goes ahead with daring, with conviction, with courage. Don't you have to confess your shame when you contemplate the drive, the daring and the courage of these women?*[300] He, moreover, often repeats, *women can be stronger than men, if determined to be so.*[301] *I like to remind you that you women—as you well know—have a great strength, which you know how to envelop with a special gentleness, so that it goes unnoticed.*[302]

St. Josemaría underlines that in women the interaction between reason, will and sentiments has its unique forms, giving their way of acting a special value. The following text could be considered paradigmatic:

> *Women are called to bring to the family, to society, and to the Church, characteristics which are their own and which they alone can give: their gentle warmth and untiring generosity, their love for detail, their quickwittedness and intuition, their simple and deep piety, their constancy . . . A woman's femininity is genuine only if she is aware of the beauty of this contribution for which there is no substitute and if she incorporates it into her own life.*[303]

---

296. *Conversations*, no. 87.
297. Ibid.
298. Ibid.
299. *The Way*, no. 652.
300. *The Forge*, no. 676.
301. *Christ Is Passing By*, no. 26.
302. *The Forge*, no. 690.
303. *Conversations*, no. 87.

These are not qualities that are a product of culture; rather, they are true characteristics of "femininity," that is, of the feminine way of being a person, which each woman must assume in a unique manner in her own life by means of character formation.

Some of the elements characteristic of the feminine personality noted by St. Josemaría, such as a "gentle warmth," "intuition," and "constancy" are undoubtedly related to a more emotional way of acting. Compared to men, sentiments have greater influence on reason and will in women's exercise of freedom. This is not a defect. It is something unique to women; a different point of equilibrium.

This uniqueness entails the danger of falling into passivity, preferring security to the risk of undertaking large enterprises in the human sphere, and even more radically in the sphere of holiness. St. Josemaría addresses this reticence in the following words:

> *You shouldn't think that, as women, you can't do great things. I am convinced that you can achieve as much as you want to in your dealings with Christ. You have the qualities, talents, and dispositions needed. You have a facility for sacrifice and for work and for joy. What a great work you can do! And how much confidence I have in you!*[304]

When referring to the excellence of some of women's qualities over those of men, while alluding to some of the correlative defects, he gives great importance to the apostolic mission, as was noticeable in some of the texts already quoted:

> *Woman is stronger than man, and more faithful, in the hour of suffering: Mary of Magdala and Mary Cleophas and Salome! With a group of valiant women like these, closely united to our Lady of Sorrows, what work for souls could be done in the world!*[305]

3. Conditions for Expanding One's Freedom

In the first part of this chapter, we discussed St. Josemaría's understanding of freedom, and attempted to show that, above all else, it is a "freedom for" the sake of seeking the good with self-determination; in other words, the

304. Notes taken from preaching (AGP, P02 VIII-1974, p. 36).

305. *The Way*, no. 982.

capacity to love or the "freedom to love." A requirement of this capacity is "freedom from:" freedom from the guilt of sin, freedom from a slavery to passions, and finally, freedom from coercion, obstacles, and external impediments to the exercise of freedom itself.[306] Liberation from sin and from disordered passions is connected with the practice of virtues and will be the topic of chapter six. In this section, however, we will deal primarily with freedom from coercion and impediments from the outside, that is, we will examine the external conditions that permit freedom to expand or develop.

Some currents of thought have reduced freedom to this aspect, namely, to liberation from certain social structures considered oppressive; they identify freedom with political and social freedom. The Christian notion of freedom surpasses this reductive understanding and puts the idea of liberation in its proper place, that is, as a requirement for the expansion of one's freedom for the sake of acting.

Above all, one should keep in mind that the exercise of personal freedom is also possible in the most adverse circumstances of oppression. St. Josemaría provides an extreme example to show that unless someone is deprived of his interiority through psychological torture or other types of aggression which destroy his capacity to love, it is not possible to completely eliminate freedom. *A person can be a prisoner in the most horrible and inhuman cell, and be free, accepting God's will and loving sacrifice, with a concern for all souls on earth. How many martyrs for the faith in our days have soared aloft like eagles, with their body in chains and their soul free to love God without limits!*[307]

This way of speaking does not make sense for those who identity freedom with liberation. At the same time there is the opposite danger based on a spiritualist way of thinking: that of relegating liberation (the conditions necessary for one's freedom to expand) to an inferior place and being content with interior freedom. More than just a few who think in this manner allow others to easily take away their freedoms or do not defend their rights with determination.

Conscious of the value of divine filiation and the freedom of the children of God, St. Josemaría demands respect for all human beings and their freedom, and promotes an authentic Christian liberation. For him, the

306. Although this has already been mentioned, let us recall that it does not make sense to speak of "freedom from" in respect to the natural moral law, which precisely indicates the good of the person and is constitutive of his nature and of his freedom.

307. Notes taken from preaching, June 25, 1972 (AGP, P01 VII-1972, p. 9).

gift of freedom requires the best conditions possible if it is to expand in all spheres of human existence.

These conditions can be summarized in two ways:

(1) First, nothing should impede the legitimate use of freedom: there should be no unjust coercion, neither interiorly nor externally. This implies that a Christian must defend and promote respect for his own freedom and that of others. Both kinds of freedom go together. A basic attitude of consistency must lead the Christian to understand that *only if he defends the individual freedom of others—with the personal responsibility that must go with it—can he also then defend his own with human and Christian integrity.*[308] This first condition covers various aspects which are summarized by the title of one of St. Josemaría's homilies: "Christian Respect for the Person and His Freedom."[309]

(2) Second, each person should accept and faithfully keep the commitments freely made to direct the exercise of freedom toward the fulfillment of God's will. For a Christian, this entails the baptismal promises and other commitments acquired in response to one's personal call to follow a specific path toward holiness. These commitments favor the expansion of one's freedom. When they are cast aside, the vigor freedom brings with it is dispersed rather than intensified. This second condition also includes different aspects that could be summarized in the phrase: "Christian commitments as a path to freedom."

3.1. "Christian Respect for the Person and His Freedom"

The reader who looks at the book *Christ is Passing By* will not be astonished by finding titles such as "The Eucharist, a Mystery of Faith and Love" or "The Ascension of Our Lord into Heaven." However, it is possible that he will be surprised by the subject of the seventh homily mentioned earlier: "Christian Respect for the Person and His Freedom." At first it may not seem to be a subject of preaching; however it will suffice to begin reading it to realize its importance for the spiritual life, especially for those whose mission consists in sanctifying the world from within.

In St. Josemaría's teaching, it is therefore a subject of extraordinary importance; and in our opinion, it is the most important one in which we

308. *Christ Is Passing By*, no. 184.

309. See ibid., nos. 67–72.

perceive the consequences of the awareness of divine filiation (along with the topic of interior freedom which we dealt with at the beginning of this chapter). A person who knows that he is a son of God knows that he is free and feels the duty of respecting others' freedom as well as of demanding respect for his own, both in his interior life and in his external behavior within the limits imposed by the person's social and historical conditions. Whereas divine filiation is the foundation of the spiritual life, respect for a person's freedom, according to St. Josemaría's teaching, is like the air that a son of God needs to breath normally.

The texts we have to study deal mainly with three aspects. We will enumerate them now in the order that seems the most logical. First, he refers to respect for people's freedom inasmuch as it is required *by their dignity;* here he speaks of "freedom of consciences" in general, and specifically of respect for a faithful's freedom and rights within the Church. Second, he refers to respect for freedom *in virtue of the object* of the free choice; here he insists at length on "freedom in matters of opinion." Third, he refers to freedom *in virtue of the an authority not having the competence* to judge over certain matters, even though in themselves such matters are not matters of opinion; here he is dealing primarily with "religious freedom," or social and civic freedom in religious affairs. The whole of these three aspects offer a general vision of St. Josemaría's teaching on this important subject.

3.1.1 "Freedom of Consciences"

The expression "freedom of consciences" is typical of the teaching of Pius XI although it originated with Leo XIII.[310] It is emblematic of Catholic doctrine regarding each person's right not to be obliged to act, either with physical or moral coercion, against his conscience, and furthermore, the right to be positively respected, defended and helped to act in conscience.

St. Josemaría often uses this expression, starting from papal teaching, but as we will see, he opens it up to new ideas which will take shape in Vatican Council II.

> It should be noted from the outset that following the terminology of Leo XIII and Pius XI, St. Josemaría distinguishes between "freedom of consciences" and "freedom of conscience." The latter, understood as freedom

310. See Pius XI, Encyclical *Non Abbiamo Bisogno* (June 29, 1931), part III, §7: AAS 23 (1931): 301 ff. The concept is already found explicitly in Leo XIII, Encyclical *Libertas Praestantissimum* (May 20, 1888), in *Acta Leonis*, vol. VIII, p. 237 s.

to do whatever one decides without taking into account the moral order established by God, denotes a notion that is incompatible with a Christian outlook. In this sense, he writes that *it is inaccurate to speak of* freedom of conscience [. . .]. *I defend with all my strength the* freedom of consciences. (Leo XIII, *Enc. Libertas praestantissimum*, 20-VI-1888, ASS 20 [1888], 606)[311]

> Later on the meaning of the term "freedom of conscience" changed. Today, it is frequently used as equivalent to "freedom of consciences," which is understandable as the expression itself is ambiguous and thus, currently it does not have a negative connotation. What is important is for the underlying doctrine to remain intact. When St. Josemaría took the expression "freedom of conscience" in a negative manner, he wished to reject the error the papal Magisterium then rejected (and continues rejecting), and not what is meant by it in more recent documents.

After this premise, St. Josemaría's use of this notion is evident.

> *I have always defended the freedom of individual consciences. I do not understand violence. I do not consider it a proper way either to persuade or to win over. Error is overcome by prayer, by God's grace, and by study; never by force, always with charity.*[312]

The text expresses well St. Josemaría's character. He is a man of firm convictions and a brave spirit whose personality as a son of God is marked by a delicate respect for freedom. This characteristic leads him to reject any type of coercion of consciences, and in a positive way, to use all the means (prayer, study, charity as mentioned in the above quotation) to help others use their freedom in the right manner. In this latter sense, his appreciation for freedom of consciences goes much further that a simple respect for privacy, a praiseworthy yet insufficient attitude for Christian apostolate; this certainly requires refraining from an abusive intrusion into others' intimacy, but far from being satisfied with that, it seeks a positive fostering of their freedom.

> *If my own personal experience is of any help, I can say that I have always seen my work as a priest and shepherd of souls as being aimed at helping each person face up to all the demands of his life and to discover what God wants from*

311. *Friends of God*, no. 32.

312. *Conversations*, no. 44.

> *him in particular—without in any way limiting that holy independence and blessed personal responsibility which are the features of a Christian conscience. This way of acting and this spirit are based on respect for the transcendence of revealed truth and on love for the freedom of the human person.*[313]

The following text (the opening words of which were already quoted) offers an explanation of how he understands this concept:

> *I defend with all my strength the* freedom of consciences (Leo XIII, *Enc. Libertas praestantissimum*, 20-VI-1888, ASS 20 [1888], 606), *which means that no one can licitly prevent a man from worshipping God. The legitimate hunger for truth must be respected. Man has a grave obligation to seek God, to know him and worship him, but no one on earth is permitted to impose on his neighbor the practice of a faith he lacks; just as no one can claim the right to harm those who have received the faith from God.*[314]

It is noticeable that here he applies respect for freedom of consciences to the sphere of religion. In other texts he employs the expression in general to refer to the respect for the intellectual and moral convictions of others. In any case, since religious convictions are the highest type of convictions, what is said of them applies to other types. We should also point out that in the previous text, he seems to refer only to the case of conversion to the Catholic faith or incorporation into the Church. At other moments, as in the following quotation, we can see that he thinks of apostolate in general and not only of apostolate ad fidem:

> [*It is necessary*] *to eliminate any form of intolerance, coercion and violence in the mutual dealings among men. Also in our apostolic activity (better: principally in our apostolic activity), we want to prevent even the least hint of coercion. God wants to be served in freedom, and therefore any apostolate that failed to respect* the freedom of consciences *would not be rightly ordered.*[315]

After again rejecting unjust coercion, violence, and intolerance[316] St. Josemaría mentions the most significant sphere for the defense of freedom of

---

313. *Christ Is Passing By*, no. 99.
314. *Friends of God*, no. 32.
315. *Letter, January 9, 1932*, no. 66.
316. The word "unjust" must be correctly understood in the words just cited. Obviously St. Josemaría does not exclude cases of "just" coercion, as happens when the public authorities imprison an offender.

consciences: the sphere of apostolic endeavors. Dealing with an activity that seeks to communicate truth and the good (the full Gospel truth and the excellent good of supernatural life), someone might think that a certain coercion is justified. In effect, throughout history there have been some who have tried to impose the Gospel through coercive means. However, by acting in such a way, they have not acted according the Christian spirit. Here we cannot enter into the complex question of "Christian States" with intermingling of civil and ecclesiastical authorities, and practical confusions of diverse kinds. We can recall some words of Vatican II that propose the constant teaching of the Church: "It is one of the major tenets of Catholic doctrine that man's response to God in faith must be free: no one therefore is to be forced to embrace the Christian faith against his own will. This doctrine is contained in the word of God and it was constantly proclaimed by the Fathers of the Church. The act of faith is of its very nature a free act. Man, redeemed by Christ the Savior and through Christ Jesus called to be God's adopted son, cannot give his adherence to God revealing Himself unless, under the drawing of the Father, he offers to God the reasonable and free submission of faith."[317] St. Josemaría's teaching (offered above) is in complete harmony with this perennial doctrine and extends to all moments of the journey of faith, not only to conversion to the faith or full incorporation into the Church (to which the Council text refers directly), but also to every step in a person's following of Christ. The decision to embrace the faith and every decision of the life of faith must always be free.

The conclusion is a strong one: *Therefore, if anyone were ever to attempt to mistreat those in error, rest assured that I will feel urged to stay by their side and share their lot out of love for God.*[318] St. Josemaría refers specifically to respect for the convictions of non-Catholics, but it is clear that this is only an example for radically transmitting a spirit of freedom rooted in the dignity of a person called to supernatural divine adoption. It is never morally justified, nor therefore acceptable, to coerce anyone's conscience because this would be to disregard his freedom and offend his dignity as a person and son of God. In St. Josemaría's teaching, it is not licit "to sacrifice a person's freedom on the altar of truth."[319] Without rejecting truth, he prefers to suffer with those unjustly treated for their convictions before forcing anyone to reject error.

---

317. Vatican II, Declaration on Religious Liberty *Dignitatis Humanae* (December 7, 1965), no. 10.

318. *Letter, May 31, 1954*, no. 19.

319. Rodríguez Luño, "Relativismo, verdad y fe," in *Romana* 42 (2006): 153.

This way of thinking applies to all spheres of life. For instance, when he speaks of the relations of a Christian (both as a faithful member of the Church and citizen) with civil and ecclesiastic authorities, he makes clear that authorities must not discriminate unjustly:

> *In the Church and in civil society there are no second-class faithful or citizens. Both in the apostolic terrain and in the temporal, limitations to the freedom of the children of God, to the freedom of consciences or to legitimate initiatives, are unjust and arbitrary. They are limitations that stem from the abuse of authority.*[320]

In the sphere of the relations between parents and children (and in formation in general) he fosters trust, precisely as a demand of the freedom of the children of God. This has been discussed earlier with reference to a study by Concepción Naval. To offer a specific example, it is good to recall his advice to parents regarding decisions children take concerning their own lives:

> *Parents can, and should, be a great help to their children. They can open new horizons for them, share their experiences and make them reflect, so they do not allow themselves to be carried away by passing emotional experiences. They can offer them a realistic evaluation of the world* [. . .]. *Advice does not take away freedom, but rather provides elements with which to judge* [. . .]. *After hearing the opinions of others and taking everything into consideration, there comes a moment in which a choice has to be made and then no one has the right to force a young person's freedom.*[321]

The area of personal spiritual direction is also suffused with this spirit of freedom. The following is the advice that St. Josemaría offers to those who provide spiritual direction:

> *Always allow souls a great freedom of spirit. Remember what I have told you so many times:* Because I feel like it [porque me da la gana] *seems to me to be the most supernatural of reasons. The function of the spiritual director is to help the soul to want to, to "feel like" fulfilling the will of God. Don't command, counsel* [. . .], *may each one sense his personal freedom and corresponding responsibility.*[322]

---

320. *Letter, March 11, 1940,* no. 65.

321. *Conversations,* no. 104.

322. *Letter, August 8, 1956,* no. 38. On the educational dimension of freedom in St. Josemaría, see J.J. Sanguineti, "La libertad en el centro del mensaje del Beato Josemaría Escrivá," pp. 85–89.

These are examples from various spheres of life. From them we can conclude that freedom of consciences, based on the dignity of the person, is a characteristic seal of St. Josemaría's teaching. It serves as a guiding principle to channel different subjects that were not directly considered in the Magisterium of Popes who used the same expression.

3.1.2. "Freedom and Pluralism in the Matters of Opinion"

Let us now explore the respect due to freedom of consciences in virtue of the very object of the free choice, and not only from the point of view of the dignity of the person. We will consider this freedom in matters of opinion not in an abstract manner, but in the way in which it is found in St. Josemaría, that is, closely related to the vocation and mission of the lay faithful. Reflecting on St. Josemaría's teaching, Ana Marta González states, "Pluralism is an essential characteristic of the secular manner of being in the world which extends to all realms of life."[323]

His sensitivity to these matters is acute because they touch upon the very nerve center of the meaning of sanctifying oneself in the middle of the world, the very core of his ecclesial mission. As we noted in the Preliminary Part and at the beginning of this chapter, St. Josemaría considers it essential that the autonomy of the lay faithful in professional life, culture, politics, the economy, etc. be recognized by the Church because only thus can they live the spiritual life and carry out apostolate with the initiative and responsibility required by the gift of divine filiation and the royal priesthood received through baptism.

> *The personal freedom of Catholic lay people in these questions is limited only by God's law and faithfulness to the Holy Church. Rather than limits, these are a precious gift, which bestows value on human actions and makes them worthy of a child of God.*[324]

---

323. Ana Marta González, "El trabajo filosófico a la luz del Beato Josemaría," in Giorgio Faro (ed.), *La grandezza della vita quotidiana*, vol. IV (Rome: Edusc, 2003), p. 178. The author's considerations about how the Christian faith forms the doctrinal basis for pluralism in matters of opinion are interesting: "Faith is not a philosophy, but a gift [. . .]. That gift gives us the criteria that in a certain way frees us from giving absolute value to our human accomplishments, including our theoretical accomplishments [. . .]. Faith frees us, not from love for the truth, but from the danger of identifying truth with our own theories, with our proper and personal path [. . .]. Faith makes us capable of carrying out a special detachment without which all pluralism is fictitious, a detachment which is shown, among other things, in the readiness to receive any kind of criticism. From here on, all the difficulties in living pluralism are purely moral: one's lack of humility, love for one's own excellence." Ibid.

324. *Letter, January 25, 1961*, no. 41.

An explanation of his teaching in this area calls for a useful preliminary distinction. As a member of the Church, every Christian has *certain fundamental rights, duties and powers within ecclesiastical society related to his juridical status as baptized: active participation in the liturgy, the possibility of cooperating directly in the hierarchy's apostolate, and of offering advice to the hierarchy in its pastoral task if invited to do so, etc.*[325] In addition to this which is common to all the faithful, the lay faithful have a specific mission; it *consists precisely in that of sanctifying secular reality, the temporal order, the world,* ab intra, *in an immediate and direct way.*[326] *And they know that this mission comes from the very fact of their being Christian and not necessarily from a mandate from the Hierarchy; although they obviously ought to fulfill it in a spirit of union with the Hierarchy following the teaching authority of the Church.*[327] While in the first case (cooperation with the hierarchy's apostolate) every faithful, including laypersons, must use his freedom to second the mandates of the hierarchy and to act in keeping with them, in the second case (that of a laity's specific apostolate in temporal matters), the apostolic mandate derives directly from Christ through baptism. It implies a series of rights and duties within ecclesial life in relation to sanctification and apostolate that must be recognized and respected so that the freedom of the children of God can grow and bear fruit.

For this reason, the defense of freedom in the temporal activities constitutes a key point for St. Josemaría. Without fostering this freedom, the laity would not be able to carry out their proper mission. It is a matter of freedom with all its consequences, the clearest one being that of pluralism. *When the value of freedom is fully understood and the divine gift of freedom is passionately loved,* the pluralism that freedom brings with it is also loved.[328] Any defense of freedom seeking (or secretly hoping) for everyone to use his/hers in same way would amount to a charade.

The scope of application of one's freedom is as vast as the temporal activities over which it is exercised. It goes without saying that the moral dimension that all human activities possess insofar as they are human acts implies that it is within the scope of the Magisterium of the Church to offer guidance regarding certain aspects of such activities according to the light

325. *Conversations*, no. 9.

326. Ibid.

327. Ibid., no. 59.

328. Ibid., no. 98.

of the Gospel. But there will also always necessarily be other aspects pertaining to the proper autonomy of each science or art (or of any temporal activity in general) where room for a plurality of opinions, views, and solutions exists.[329]

St. Josemaría does not exclude any temporal activity from this pluralism. He defends such pluralism even in a field so closely tied to the Magisterium as theological research. In this sense, referring concretely to Opus Dei, he lays down as a principle that *we do not all think the same way because we admit the greatest possible pluralism in all temporal matters and in debatable theological questions.*[330] This pluralism is not an obstacle to the unity of faith; it only considers respect for freedom as an important factor for unity. In Opus Dei, for instance, *a diversity of opinions is and always will be a sign of good spirit.*[331]

Nonetheless, no matter how significant his position on free theological research may be, the majority of St. Josemaría's texts on freedom of opinion do not regard this matter; rather, they refer to another topic which requires particular attention: that of the political choices of the Christian faithful.[332] In this field, the danger of considering pluralism negatively is always present, whether it is because someone suffers from an authoritarian mentality, whereby anything that falls out of the person's control is held in contempt; or from a herd mentality, whereby the person is afraid of diversity and only feels secure with uniformity.

In St. Josemaría's writings, "there exist abundant theological reflections on the action of Christians in the social and political sphere, but we do not find what is commonly called 'political ideas and opinions.' This is

---

329. One can see in St. Josemaría a precedent for the teaching that one finds at the basis of the following canon of the Code of Canon Law of 1983: "The lay faithful have the right to that freedom which belongs to all citizens in earthly things. However, in using that freedom, they have to take care that their actions are inspired by the spirit of the Gospel, and have to pay attention to the teachings proposed by the Magisterium of the Church, avoiding at the same time presenting their own criteria in opinionable matters, as the doctrine of the Church" (*CIC*, can. 227).

330. *Conversations*, no. 30.

331. *Letter, March 11, 1940*, no. 27. In this respect one can see some biographical events that illustrate this teaching, in Pilar Urbano, *El hombre de Villa Tevere*, pp. 259–282 (English trans. *The Man of Villa Tevere*).

332. See Fernando Inciarte, "Die Bedeutung der Freiheit für den seligen Josemaría Escrivá," in César Ortiz (dir.), *Josemaría Escrivá. Profile einer Gründergestalt*, Köln 2002, pp. 419–432. The interest of this excellent article derives also from the references that the author makes to the historical circumstances in which St. Josemaría had to defend the political freedom of the lay faithful (above all those of Spain, between 1940 and 1975). Here we center on his teaching on freedom; we cannot stop to comment on that historical framework. A significant testimony is that of Manuel Aznar, "Amigo de la libertad," in Rafael Serrano (ed.), *Así le vieron: testimonios sobre monseñor Escrivá de Balaguer* (Madrid: Rialp, 1992), pp. 25–31.

due to a conduct that he adopted upon significant reflection and by which he always abided."[333] According to Ángel Rodríguez Luño, if one were to express concisely the thinking of St. Josemaría on social and political action, "the formula would be no other than the indissoluble link between personal freedom and a corresponding personal responsibility."[334] Antonio García-Moreno comments that "love for freedom always led him to the highest respect for the political ideas of the laity. With regard to their public life, he considers them completely free in choosing a political party, naturally in keeping with the binding doctrine of the Church."[335] This same author closes his remarks with the following quotation that attests to the importance given by St. Josemaría to this subject: *This doctrine of civic freedom, of understanding, of living together in harmony, forms a very important part of the message Opus Dei seeks to spread.*[336]

The insistence on this point is historically related with very different situations. One of these is the establishment of totalitarian governments in various countries, especially in twentieth-century Europe. His point of view was clear:

> *We need to love freedom. Avoid an abuse that seems especially aggravated in our days, one that is evident and can be seen in nations all over the world. This is the desire, contrary to the licit independence of men, to oblige everyone to form a single group in questions open to opinion, to make temporal doctrines into dogma, and to try to defend this false position with scandalous propaganda, attacking those who have the nobility not to submit.*[337]

Another factor is the tendency within the Church to promote the unity of Catholics in politics as well as in various professional spheres out of the need to resist a secularist and Marxist pressure. This topic was addressed in the Preliminary Part. Gabriel Zanotti holds that, in practice and with certain frequency, the basic principles of the Church's social doctrine have been "adopted and lived as just one more political and economic policy with concrete applications and solutions [. . .] [that would be] the only possible

---

333. Ángel Rodríguez Luño, "*'Cittadini degni del vangelo'* (Phil. 1:27)," p. 36 f.

334. Ibid., p. 45.

335. Antonio García-Moreno, "Aspectos de la libertad en Josemaría Escrivá," p. 397. The author refers to *Conversations*, nos. 12 and 48.

336. *Conversations*, no. 118.

337. *Letter, January 9, 1932*, no. 1.

temporal position for a Catholic."[338] Zanotti adds that there have been undoubtedly clear rebuttals to this "temporalism," and he holds the opinion that "if there is someone who has not been confused on this matter it is Josemaría Escrivá de Balaguer."[339] In the biography by Andrés Vázquez de Prada, there is ample historic documentation that shows how much St. Josemaría strove to defend the legitimate pluralism of Christians in politics.[340]

St. Josemaría persistently defended the *absolute freedom* [of the lay faithful] *in temporal matters, because there is no single Christian formula for ordering worldly affairs.*[341] His writings contain a refrain that effectively conveys this idea: *There are no dogmas in temporal affairs.*[342] It is a principle laden with consequences that he illustrates in the following citation:

> *Trying to impose dogmas in temporal affairs leads inevitably to forcing other people's consciences, to lacking respect for one's neighbor.* [. . .] *A Christian needs to make his eagerness for civic and social progress compatible with an awareness of the limitations of his own opinions, thereby respecting the opinions of others and loving genuine pluralism.*[343]

Juan José Sanguineti comments that, "By this he did not pretend to uphold a sort of 'Christian liberalism' in the sense of separating secular activities (politics, sciences, arts, etc.) from the faith, which would [in turn] be reduced to a life of piety and theology. Nothing could be further from his thought. As part of his message on sanctification of work and secular structures, he strongly held that the Christian faith should enlighten all temporal problems, and that a Christian cannot put aside his faith when he works as a legislator, a doctor, an architect, etc. (see *The Way*, 353) because he must sanctify his work and the world in order to take them to Christ [. . .]. He must not do this, however, with a fundamentalist attitude, but rather with a *spirit of freedom*, without equating the Christian faith to his personal solutions and choices regardless of how noble and successful they may be."[344]

---

338. Gabriel J. Zanotti, "La libertad en el orden temporal según el pensamiento de Escrivá de Balaguer," in *Un mensaje siempre actual*, p. 65.

339. Ibid., p. 67.

340. See Vázquez de Prada, *The Founder of Opus Dei: Life of Josemaría Escrivá*, vol. III (New York: Scepter, 2005), pp. 360–382.

341. *Letter, January 9, 1959*, no. 35.

342. "The Riches of the Faith." See *Conversations*, nos. 11, 77.

343. "The Riches of the Faith."

344. J.J. Sanguineti, "La libertad en el centro del mensaje del Beato Josemaría," p. 90.

St. Josemaría fosters unity among Christians in the faith, but he has in mind,

> *a unity and not uniformity, which does not consist in everyone thinking in the same way or of forming just one party: that is not God's will. He not only respects our personalities and inclinations, he has created them in their diversity. He wants people to grow and mature by exercising their freedom; he desires human history to run its course. The unity Christ wants is much deeper than all this, because it belongs to another order: the divine order, the order of faith and charity.*[345]

For him, *spiritual unity is compatible with variety in temporal matters when fanaticism and intolerance are shunned.*[346] Fanaticism consists in denying that matters of opinion are open to opinion. In this sense, it is a "gnoseological error"[347] which leads to attitudes that are foreign to the Christian spirit of freedom even though they are dressed up with an apparent zeal for unity.

> *A true Christian never thinks that unity in the Faith, fidelity to the Magisterium and Tradition of the Church, and concern for the spreading of the saving message of Christ run counter to the existence of a variety in the attitudes people have regarding the things which God has left* [. . .] *to the free discussion of men. In fact, he is fully aware that this variety forms part of God's plan. It is something desired by God, who distributes his gifts and his lights as he wishes. The Christian should love other people and therefore respect opinions contrary to his own, and live in harmony and full brotherhood with people who do not think as he does.*[348]

These words seem to encapsulate rather well the teaching of St. Josemaría that we have attempted to summarize in this section and in the preceding one. They harmonize two motives for respecting freedom of conscience that we have already discussed: the dignity of the person, which calls for a love that is not conditioned by differing convictions; and a positive assessment of pluralism in matters of opinion. The most important motive is the first:

---

345. *Letter, October 24, 1965*, no. 52.

346. *Conversations*, no. 67.

347. Sanguineti, "La libertad en el centro del mensaje del Beato Josemaría," p. 96.

348. *Conversations*, no. 67.

The root of respect for freedom lies in love. If other people think differently from me, is that a reason to regard them as enemies?[349]

Love leads to a careful respect for freedom, and this respect is, for St. Josemaría, *a condition for coexistence* [convivencia].[350] This is so because he is not referring to a kind of "respect" that leads to personal isolation and the isolation of others in their opinions (as when someone who "respects" someone else's ideas, says, "You can think whatever you like; your ideas are your problem not mine . . ."). Rather, it is a true appreciation for responsible freedom and pluralism. It is understandable why Josemaría Escrivá has been called "a master of getting along with others" [*maestro de la convivencia*].[351]

The next subject we will now discuss, freedom in civil society, precisely dovetails from what we have analyzed above.

3.1.3. Freedom in Civil Society: "Religious Freedom" and the "Liberation of the Children of God"

Through a variety of ways, St. Josemaría supported and encouraged each Christian in his or her task to be a protagonist in improving the conditions which facilitate the exercise of freedom (such as laws, customs, and various other structures), promote the dignity of the children of God, and favor the human perfection of all citizens. And the first dimension of freedom that must be protected and defended by virtue of its very nature is "religious freedom."

It is well known that since Vatican II's declaration on religious liberty *Dignitatis Humanae*, the Magisterium holds "religious freedom" to be synonymous with "social and civic freedom in religious matters." Thus citizens ought to enjoy a freedom from being coerced by society or the State in religious matters, safeguarding the limits of public order imposed by the common political good entrusted to the State.[352]

> We should recall that "religious freedom" does not mean that it is the same to choose one religion or other, or that conscience is independent from religious truth. It means that each person deserves respect for the

349. "The Riches of the Faith."

350. Ibid. Let us transcribe the passage at greater length: *Awareness of the limitations of human judgment leads us to recognize freedom as a condition for living together. But this is not everything; it is not even the most important thing. The root of respect for freedom lies in love* [. . .] *because each person has an infinite price and an eternal destiny in God. Jesus Christ has died for each one of us.*

351. Sanguineti, "La libertad en el centro del mensaje del Beato Josemaría," p. 98.

352. See *Dignitatis Humanae*, nos. 2 and 7.

> right to seek religious truth and to profess it without being coerced by society or the State. This does not mean religious indifference (*Dignitatis Humanae*, in fact, rejects it from the start by affirming that the "one true religion"[353] is the Catholic one), but rather the limitations of the State's authority.

St. Josemaría does not employ the expression "religious freedom," but the concept was not foreign to him. In order to understand it, we should keep in mind that the right to religious freedom has two aspects. On the one hand it is necessary in order to respect freedom of consciences (and in this sense, there are texts of St. Josemaría on freedom of consciences referring to religious freedom). On the other hand, it is a consequence of "juridical constraints to civic powers [. . .] with regard to the free exercise of religion in society."[354] The Magisterium, in fact, points out that as long as civil order is respected, civic authorities cannot coerce anyone in religious matters because it would mean violating their competency. The State does not have the mission of expounding on supernatural revelation, nor of telling citizens which acts of worship they must practice, nor of guiding them in any such matters. "Civil authority, whose proper end is to protect the temporal common good should acknowledge and foster the religious practice of its citizens. But it must be clear that it exceeds its limits if it pretends to direct or impede religious acts."[355]

This second aspect is also present in St. Josemaría although less often than that of religious freedom as needed to respect freedom of consciences. Sometimes it is found only implicitly and tied to the first aspect. For instance, St. Josemaría was once asked about what he thought about the Spanish government policy of "teaching religion at universities." (During the 1960s, Spain was governed by a confessional state and religion was a compulsory part of the curriculum at all public universities.) He affirmed then that *no one may violate the freedom of students' consciences. Religion has to be studied voluntarily, even though Christians know that, if they want to live their Faith well, they have a grave obligation to receive a sound religious training.*[356] He thus holds that the State cannot impose obligatory classes on a given religion for anyone attending State-run schools; that would

---

353. Ibid., no. 1.

354. Ibid.

355. Ibid., no. 3. The state should "help create conditions favorable to the fostering of religious life" (ibid.).

356. *Conversations*, no. 73.

"violate the freedom of consciences" of those who do not adhere to such religion. Rightly so, Martin Rhonheimer indicates that, by understanding the expression "freedom of consciences" in its deepest and most essential sense, St. Josemaría "breaks through the traditional formulas and opens a wider understanding of the subject."[357] By demanding respect for freedom of consciences, also on the part of the State, he is implicitly supporting the principle of "social and civic freedom in religious matters" contained in *Dignitatis Humanae.* For this reason it has been asserted that "Josemaría Escrivá de Balaguer defended religious liberty [. . .] understood as a deepening of Catholic doctrine and a harmonic development of the same."[358] He also specifically manifested his appreciation for this Vatican II document in a 1966 interview with *Le Figaro*: *From the first moment, this is the spirit we have lived. You can understand, then, how the Council's teaching on this subject could only make me happy.*[359]

On other occasions, he expressly refers to the distinction between the responsibilities of the Church and the State. In one of his letters, after citing Matt. 22:21 ("Render therefore to Caesar the things that are Caesar's, and to God the things that are God's."), he comments,

> *Christ distinguished the areas of jurisdiction of the two authorities: the Church and the State. By doing so he forestalled the harmful effects of* caesarism *and* clericalism [. . .] *and he clarified the autonomy of God's Church and the legitimate autonomy of civil society in its laws and technical structures.*[360]

For him, defending the State's autonomy is instinctive; however, he is also careful to define the scope of the State's authority thereby rejecting *caesarism* and demanding respect for the Church's authority in matters pertaining to its public jurisdiction.

Such a demarcation of the State's authority does not imply that *Dignitatis Humanae* or St. Josemaría accept religious indifference on the part of the State. The State should not impose or direct the religious life of its

357. Martin Rhonheimer, "Truth and Politics in Christian Society, Josemaría Escrivá and Love for Freedom: Presented in a Historical-Theological Perspective," in Idem, *Changing the World*, p. 108. "Undoubtedly, Josemaría Escrivá was a pioneer of the rediscovery of this spirit of profound respect for freedom marked by rejection of all forms of coercion of consciences." Ibid., pp. 106–107.

358. Cristóbal Orrego Sánchez, "La libertad religiosa y la continuidad doctrinal del Concilio Vaticano II. El testimonio cualificado del Beato Josemaría Escrivá de Balaguer," in *Un mensaje siempre actual*, p. 460.

359. *Conversations*, no. 44.

360. *Letter, January 9, 1959*, no. 31.

citizens, but it should "foster the religious life of its citizens."[361] What does this mean? How does Josemaría Escrivá understand the difference between "not directing" and "fostering" the religious life of its citizens?

In relation to this point, St. Josemaría quotes a passage from the Council's declaration, which states that since religious freedom has to do with freedom from coercion in civil society, it leaves intact the traditional Catholic teaching on the moral duty of individuals and societies toward the true religion and the one Church of Christ (Vatican II, Decl. *Dignitatis humanae*, no. 1). *On our part, to this duty of each person and of society there corresponds a correlative apostolic duty, of which God will ask us to give an account, since he also gives us the grace to fulfill it.*[362]

As we can see, he emphasizes the duty of the individual and of society toward the true religion. It is clear that each person must search for it and embrace it once he has found it.[363] Furthermore, as a member of society, he is bound by this obligation not only as an individual, but also as a social being. The words "Render unto Caesar the things that are Caesar's, and unto God the things that are God's" must be properly understood because,

> *the distinction established by Christ does not in any way mean that religion should be confined to churches and sacristies, or that human affairs should be carried out in complete separation from God's law or Christian law. That would be to deny one's faith in Christ, which demands the obedience of the whole person, body and soul, as an individual and as a member of society.*[364]

Therefore, while respecting the freedom of those who do not share the same faith, Christians should offer to God the *public worship that society is obliged to render unto God.*[365] Of note, St. Josemaría speaks here of society, not the State. It is society, and specifically Christians as its members, who should offer worship to God. The State should not direct this public worship, but it should certainly favor the members of society to offer it to God.

Without dwelling further on other questions of Catholic doctrine on matters regarding the State, it seems opportune to comment briefly on

---

361. See *Dignitatis Humanae*, nos. 3 and 6 (passages cited above).

362. *Letter, March 19, 1967*, no. 39.

363. "All men are bound to seek the truth, especially in what concerns God and his church, and to embrace the truth they come to know, and to hold fast to it." (*Dignitatis Humanae*, no. 1).

364. *Letter, January 9, 1959*, no. 31.

365. Ibid., no. 38.

the previous quotations. The starting point is that the State should not impede the public worship of any religion within the limits of public order and morality. So far this does not present any difficulties. A doubt may arise with respect to "fostering" public worship. Should the State equally foster the public worship of all religions? In order to answer this question we must keep in mind that it belongs to the responsibilities of the State to promote in its actions the principles of the natural law that affect social well-being. These principles do not pertain exclusively to any one religion. Among these, for example, are: defending innocent human life, promoting the unity and stability of marriage, protecting private property and the consonant social use where appropriate, etc. We ought to note, however, that these principles are not equally recognized by all religions. The Catholic religion teaches the entire natural law and educates people to live according to it. A government keeping to its own specific mission can legitimately support the Church's action in this sense. Considering other religions, the State should not impede what remains within public order and should support whatever contributes to the common good (not what does it harm). Such a position should not be construed as arguing in favor of a Catholic confessional state, which the Church is not asking for.[366] Instead, it is a demand to respect the natural law, accessible to reason, in matters of social relevance. "The Catholic faithful can and should expect society's customs and laws to uphold these requirements for all, not as purely religious preferences which should be protected by being granted immunity from coercion [. . .] but rather, in virtue of the values rooted in the same human nature."[367]

A different matter is how natural law, especially regarding social life in humanity's present situation, can be known with certainty. Here, Christians have an important apostolate to carry out: in addition to reaching these principles through reason, they count on the certainty that comes from the faith and the Church's teaching. St. Josemaría encourages people to carry out this apostolate with complete respect for freedom of consciences and of the social right to religious freedom.

Let us now turn last of all to another subject often present in St. Josemaría's writings, which is closely tied to the previous one. Fostering freedom

---

366. See *Dignitatis Humanae*, nos. 6 and 13.

367. Orrego Sánchez, "La libertad religiosa y la continuidad doctrinal del Concilio Vaticano II," p. 464 (the author refers in regard to this point to St. John Paul II, Apostolic Letter *Novo Millennio Ineunte*, January 6, 2001, no. 51).

also demands removing unjust structures that are present in society as a consequence of sin because they impede or make difficult the exercise of freedom. For this reason the subtitle of this section partially reads, "Liberation of the Children of God."

> *Your task as a Christian citizen is to help see Christ's love and freedom preside over all aspects of modern life: culture and the economy, work and rest, family life and social relations.*[368]
>
> *You, as a Christian and, perhaps, as a research worker, writer, scientist, politician or laborer, have the duty to sanctify those things. Remember that the whole universe—as the apostle says—is groaning as in pangs of labor, awaiting the liberation of the children of God.*[369]

This subject is related to religious freedom since it deals with "public morality," that is, with effort to foster just relationships among citizens, and between them and the State. These relationships are an essential element of the political common good, and therefore a necessary condition for people to be able to exercise their freedom in society, beginning with religious freedom.

Structures contrary to public morality are, for example, customs that discriminate based on race, sex or socioeconomic standing; situations of poverty and misery arising from injustices; laws contrary to human life and the dignity of marriage; moral corruption in economics and politics; etc. The attempt to substitute those structures for other ones that are just is an important element in promoting freedom on behalf of the children of God because *freedom is a strong and healthy plant which does not grow well among stones and brambles or on the roadway, trodden underfoot* (see Luke 8:5–7).[370]

At the same time, we should not forget that a Christian must at times learn to suffer injustice with interior freedom by uniting himself to Christ's Passion. St. Paul reproves some who, seeking to uphold their own rights, denounce their brothers before pagan courts. "Why not rather suffer wrong? Why not rather be defrauded?" (1 Cor. 6:7). Without dwelling on the context of these words and explaining what it meant to go before a pagan judge, we can still affirm that the main idea is that in temporal matters, a Christian should not demand his rights "at all costs." In some situations, charity will

368. *Furrow*, no. 302.

369. Ibid., no. 311.

370. *Christ Is Passing By*, no. 185.

prompt him to suffer injustice, whereas in others, charity will move him to stand up against it. St. Peter teaches, "But even if you do suffer for righteousness' sake, you will be blessed [. . .]. For it is better to suffer for doing right, if that should be God's will, than for doing wrong. For Christ also died for sins once for all, the righteous for the unrighteous, that he might bring us to God" (1 Pet. 3:14, 17–18). Above all, Christian freedom is interior freedom. To achieve it, its first requirement is to be liberated from sin. Physical pain, poverty, or injustice can be suffered out of love and do not impede interior freedom.

In 1974, during a gathering for catechetical instruction in a South American country at the time that Liberation Theology with its Marxist connotations was spreading,[371] St. Josemaría was asked, "Would you please tell us what liberation means?" And he replied in the following manner:

> *Liberating oneself from sin! Liberating oneself from the chains of evil passions! Liberating oneself from vices! Liberating oneself from bad company! Liberating oneself from laziness! Liberating oneself from ugliness in the soul and in the body!* [. . .] *But suffering is a blessing from God. Blessed be suffering! Beloved be suffering! Sanctified be suffering! Glorified be suffering! Where would the world be without suffering? It would be in bad shape! A painting without shadows isn't a painting. Are there only lights? No, you also need shadows. And suffering, borne out of Love, is something very savory, marvelous. All mothers know this. All husbands and wives know it. All fathers know that suffering is very good. It's wonderful to want to free ourselves from pain, from poverty, from misery; but that's not liberation. Liberation is something else. Liberation is . . . to bear poverty joyfully! To bear suffering joyfully! To bear sickness joyfully!*[372]

371. The Magisterium would later pronounce itself critically on these tendencies. See Congr. for the Doctrine of the Faith, Instruction *Libertatis Nuntius* (August 6, 1984), and Instruction *Libertatis Conscientia* (March 22, 1986). "Liberation Theology reacted against a bourgeois and individualistic religiosity, promoted action by Christians [in the social, political and economic spheres] [. . .]. This led to seeing the Church as an instrument for the reconstruction of secular society and not as a means of salvation. Salvation—the growth of the Kingdom of God—was to be carried out by means of that reconstruction of secular society [. . .]. Liberation Theology put the Church at the service of the kingdom that would attain its plenitude with the liberation of the oppressed." Miguel de Salis, *Concittadini dei santi e familiari di Dio. Studio storico-teologico sulla santità della Chiesa* (Roma: Edusc, 2009), p. 226. The author points out that Liberation Theology put the emphasis on the mission of Christians to contribute to the restoration of social justice and, in general, to temporal progress, but it did so by confusing this goal, fruit of human effort, with salvation, which is a supernatural gift from God (see ibid., p. 227).

372. Notes taken from preaching, July 29, 1974 (AGP, P04 1974, vol. II, p. 427). See *The Way*, no. 208.

The fact that suffering can be offered up to God, however, does not mean that people should not do everything within their power to remedy it. The same should be said with regard to injustice. St. Josemaría's teaching does not admit conforming oneself to structures of sin that have become institutionalized. *A person or a society that does not react to suffering and injustice and makes no effort to alleviate them is still distant from the love of Christ's heart.*[373] These words contain a keen sensitivity to the defense of the rights that protect people's dignity and freedom, a defense always made out of love of God like that of Christ who demands justice on earth but does not make it an end in itself. In such a way, Jesus is able to suffer injustice by ordering it to the one necessary end, and thereby able to bestow a redemptive value on it.

3.1.4. "Holy Intransigence, Holy Coercion, and Holy Shamelessness"

Respect for freedom is the indispensable basis for understanding the meaning of three surprising and paradoxical expressions used in *The Way*.

> *The plane of holiness that God asks of us is determined by these three points: Holy intransigence, holy coercion and holy shamelessness.*[374]

This text has been misinterpreted at times. Specifically considering the term "holy coercion," Martin Rhonheimer notes that the critics "have fallen into a hermeneutical error,"[375] identifying "holy coercion" with "coercion for holy motives." The same can be said about "holy intransigence," which they interpret as "intransigence for holy motives." The author's intent is quite different. Rhonheimer explains that the word "coercion" in the expression "holy coercion" is used in an analogical sense. Whoever were to take it in a univocal sense "could be likened to certain Pharisees in the Gospel"[376] who distorted the meaning of Jesus' words in order to accuse him.

Let us now take a closer look at these expressions that St. Josemaría used in his preaching at least since 1931.[377]

---

373. *Christ Is Passing By*, no. 167.

374. *The Way*, no. 387.

375. Rhonheimer, *Changing the World*, p. 108.

376. Ibid., p. 120, note 47.

377. See Rodríguez, *Critical-Historical Edition of "The Way," ad loc.*

(1) "Holy intransigence" consists in confessing and keeping whole the truths of the faith.

> *By the grace of God, who led us to be born in his Church through Baptism, we know that there is only one true religion, and we refuse to cede on this point: we are intransigent, with a* holy intransigence. *As I often tell you, would anyone with common sense cede on something so simple as the sum of two plus two? Could he concede that two plus two might be three and a half? Ceding, in the doctrine of faith, is a clear sign of not having the truth, or not knowing that one possesses it.*[378]

This attitude is not opposed to tolerance with others, but rather demands it. Christian formation should manifest itself, *in being understanding, in being transigent with people who defend contrary ideas, even while being intransigent toward these ideas, when they are opposed to the Church's doctrinal or moral teaching.*[379]

"Holy intransigence" in matters of doctrine is therefore not opposed to respect for freedom. It entails defending and protecting truth as the root of freedom. The Church's Magisterium teaches that "an elevated form of charity for souls is not to diminish in anything the saving doctrine of Christ [. . .]. He was intransigent with evil but merciful toward people."[380]

In his study on this subject, Jesús Ballesteros notes that in St. Josemaría's teaching "the universal equality of respect toward every human being is united in a coherent manner with the rejection of relativism [. . .]. On this point, it could be said that the writings of the Founder of Opus Dei anticipate future developments because they hold a critique *avant la lettre* of what could be called a decadent post-modernity; in other words, the worldview whereby 'anything goes' or where 'all opinions are equally valid,' makes the individual and society incapable of defending themselves from errors and atrocities. He expresses this point graphically in *Forge*: *When we Catholics defend and uphold the truth, without making concessions, we have to strive to create an atmosphere of charity, of harmony, so as to drown all hatred and resentment*. In the same book he writes: *Error does not only darken our understanding: it also divides wills. But* "veritas liberabit vos": *the truth will*

---

378. *Letter, July 16, 1933*, no. 7.

379. *Letter, May 6, 1945*, no. 34.

380. Paul VI, Encyclical *Humanae Vitae* (July 25, 1968), no. 29. Text quoted again by St. John Paul II, Encyclical *Veritatis Splendor* (August 6, 1993), no. 95.

set you free from the partisan spirit that makes charity wither (no. 842). This is the proper way of understanding what he courageously called 'holy intransigence.'"[381] Ballesteros concludes that there is a need to harmonize "respect for the dignity of persons with the just defense of the truth, defending truth with charity (see Eph. 4:15)."[382]

Juan José Sanguineti points out that Josemaría Escrivá also received the diametrically opposite criticism. Given how much he respected the opinions of others and his insistence on not bringing dogmas into matters of opinion, some attempted to link his thought with that of recent philosophers such as Karl Popper, who held that a democratic society would only be possible if all matters anthropological were exclusively matters of opinion (where "there are no dogmas"). The reason for this is that in Popper's view, if someone were to believe to possess the truth in this realm, it would necessarily lead to imposing it on others in a dictatorial manner. The similarity with St. Josemaría is very weak because, on the one hand, he held the dogmas proposed by the Church, while on the other hand, "he did not think that belief in intangible dogmas leads to intolerance or violence. Were that to happen it would be an abuse, something contrary to the Christian faith itself. He always urged people to respect the freedom of those who do not hold the Catholic faith, teaching them to be 'intransigent' with regard to the truths of faith that cannot be held as mere opinions open to discussion, while on the other hand, to be forgiving and understanding with all persons, regardless of their religious creed."[383]

> *We are great friends of freedom. This is the foundation of all our apostolate, and especially the apostolate* ad fidem, *for which we have a special predilection. Faith cannot be imposed by force. God's grace and human freedom have to work together in intimate harmony. This approach is far removed from indifferentism or a subjective relativism.*[384]
>
> *Respect others' freedom and the freedom of grace; and, at the same time, make known your faith with deeds and with words.*[385]

---

381. Jesús Ballesteros, "Toda persona es digna. No toda opinión es válida," pp. 75–76.

382. Ibid., p. 77.

383. Sanguineti, "La libertad en el centro del mensaje del Beato Josemaría Escrivá," pp. 93–94.

384. *Letter, March 19, 1967*, no. 39.

385. *Letter, October 24, 1965*, no. 62.

(2) The expression "holy coercion" (in reference to apostolate) has likewise nothing to do with lacking respect for the freedom of others. Doing apostolate requires others' freedom.

In the parable of the guests invited to the wedding feast, Jesus says, "*Compelle intrare*" ("Compel them to come in," Luke 14:23). For St. Josemaría this is *an invitation, a help to decide, and never—not even remotely—is it coercion.*[386] He takes Jesus' words very differently from the way they were understood in centuries past in the struggle against heresies.[387] He explains that the "*compelle intrare,*" *is not a physical push but an abundance of light, of doctrine. It is the spiritual stimulus of your prayer and work, which bear authentic witness to doctrine. It is all the sacrifices you offer. It is the smile that comes to your lips because you are children of God* [. . .]. *Add to this your human bearing and warmth, and here we have the content of the* compelle intrare.[388]

> *In the parable of the wedding feast, when the master of the house finds out that some guests have declined his invitation with poor excuses, he tells his servant,* Go out into the highways and hedgerows and compel people to come in (Luke 14:32). *Isn't this coercion, an act of violence against the legitimate freedom of each individual conscience? If we meditate on the Gospel and reflect on the teachings of Jesus, we will not mistake these commands for coercion. See how gently Christ invites:* If you have a mind to be perfect . . . If any man would come after me . . . *His* compelle intrare *implies no violence, either physical or moral. Rather, it reflects the power of attraction of Christian example, which shows in its way of acting the power of God:* See how the Father attracts. He delights in teaching, and not in imposing necessity on men. That is how he attracts men toward himself. (St. Augustine, *In Ioannis Evangelium tractatus*, 26, 7)[389]

(3) Lastly, we have "holy shamelessness." This is an aspect of reason's mastery over feelings or sentiments: the mastery necessary to defend one's freedom to behave in a Christian manner, without being conditioned by one's surroundings or allowing them to impede apostolic activity.

---

386. *Letter, October 24, 1942*, no. 9.

387. See Max Seckler, "*Compelle intrare,*" in *Lexikon für Theologie und Kirche*, 3rd ed. (Freiburg: Herder, 1994), vol. 2, col. 1285 ff.

388. *Letter, October 24, 1942*, no. 9.

389. *Friends of God*, no. 37.

> *Laugh at ridicule. Despise the bogey of what people will say. See and feel God in yourself and in your surroundings. And you will acquire the holy shamelessness that you need—what a paradox!—in order to live with the refinement of a Christian gentleman.*[390]
>
> *If you have holy shamelessness, you won't be worried by the thought of "what people will say" or "what they may have said."*[391]

In the point of *The Way* we quoted at the beginning of this section, St. Josemaría affirms that the three attitudes of "holy intransigence," "holy coercion," and "holy shamelessness" *determine the plane of* [*our*] *holiness*. They can be understood therefore as points of reference to evaluate whether or not freedom is exercised along that plane. In effect, "holy intransigence" in doctrine is a clear sign that *reason* is perfected by the knowledge of truth. "Holy coercion" indicates that *the will* has the firm intention of directing itself to God with the desire that other persons will freely unite themselves to him. And "holy shamelessness" shows that *feelings* or *sentiments* are at the service of our reason and will, the twofold root of freedom. These three points "determine the plane of our holiness" because they manifest that the freedom of God's children is truly exercised.

3.2. Christian Commitments: A Path toward Freedom

In general, a "commitment" is an acquired obligation. In baptism, each Christian acquires some commitments that are strengthened by confirmation and renewed on different occasions throughout one's life. Furthermore, when someone discovers his personal call to holiness and the mission entrusted to him by God, he can acquire other commitments to fulfill that call, as for instance, those proper to marriage.

The following section will deal with the commitments that St. Josemaría frequently speaks or writes about: those that an ordinary Christian can acquire to further specify the commitments he already has through baptism without changing his condition in the Church.

How is the freedom of the children of God (which is proper to the Christian vocation), compatible with taking on further commitments at the service of that same vocation? A general answer to this question is easy.

---

390. *The Way*, no. 390.

391. Ibid., no. 391.

It is sufficient to recall the distinction between "freedom from" and "freedom for." If freedom is understood as the possibility of doing various things, then it is clear that any commitment limits freedom because it obliges one to omit certain other options. However, we know that a freedom that tries to keep open all possible options (or as many as possible) does not serve the good of the person. It is a freedom that edifies little or nothing. If, instead, freedom is understood as a freedom to choose the good (to love God and to act out of love for God), then, taking on commitments is not necessarily a limitation on one's freedom. It will depend on the nature of the commitments. If they are attachments which get in the way of Christian freedom, it is obvious that they should be removed. St. Josemaría refers to them when he writes: *I want you to be rebels, free and unfettered, because I want you—it is Christ who wants us!—to be children of God.*[392] On the other hand, there are commitments that strengthen freedom; and these should not be feared. Cecilia Echevarría Falla comments on St. Josemaría's teaching on this point by saying, "Though causing sacrifice, 'allowing oneself to be conditioned' by the commitments taken in one's personal life project and renouncing some partial good implies a strengthening in the good use of freedom which facilitates growth in an ethical manner."[393]

St. Josemaría comments on the attitude of those who flee from commitment out of fear of losing their freedom with a bit of irony as follows,

> *What use is this treasure to them, if there is no commitment guiding their whole lives? Such behavior goes against their very dignity and nobility as human beings. They are left aimless, with no clear path to guide their footsteps on this earth. You and I have met such people. They then let themselves be carried away by childish vanity, by selfish conceit, by sensuality.*
>
> *Their freedom turns out to be barren, or produces fruits which even humanly speaking are ridiculous. A person who does not choose, with complete freedom, an upright code of conduct, sooner or later ends up being manipulated by others. He will lead a lazy, parasitic existence, at the mercy of what others decide. He will let himself be blown to and fro by any wind whatsoever, and it will always be others who make up his mind for him* [. . .].
>
> *'No one is forcing me!' they obstinately repeat. No one? Everyone is coercing their make-believe freedom which will not run the risk of accepting*

392. *Friends of God*, no. 38.

393. Cecilia Echevarría Falla, "Libertad y estructura de las virtudes en el Beato Josemaría," p. 65.

> *responsibility for the consequences of its own free actions. Where there is no love of God, the individual and responsible use of personal freedom becomes impossible. There, despite appearances to the contrary, the individual is coerced at every turn. The indecisive and irresolute person is like plasticine at the mercy of circumstances. Anyone and anything can mold him according to whim, especially his passions and the worst tendencies of his own nature wounded by sin.*[394]

As can be inferred from these words, St. Josemaría preaches a "committed freedom" that is enriched by noble commitments that manifest a determined will to respond to the Christian vocation and lead to its fulfillment.

3.2.1. The Baptismal Promises: "Renouncing Sin" and Living as Children of God

During the Easter Vigil, the celebrant asks the assembly of the faithful: "Do you renounce sin so as to live in the freedom of the children of God? [. . .] Do you renounce Satan, the author and prince of sin?"[395] By replying "I do," a Christian commits himself to fighting Satan in a radical manner, rejecting sin as a condition to live in the freedom of the children of God.

This "renunciation" is not the giving up of a good, but rather the giving up of an evil that leads to slavery. For this reason, renouncing sin does not entail losing one's freedom. It is not about giving up doing things *because I want to* [*No es dejar de obrar* porque me da la gana]—as acting with a desire to act is an essential aspect of freedom—but rather it is about giving up doing *what I feel like doing* [*evitar hacer* lo que me da la gana], in case it is not something good. The good for man consists in the use of his freedom to reach perfection and happiness that resides in love of God through the fulfillment of his will. The person who decides not to use his freedom in a way that contradicts the moral law does not lose his freedom. In renouncing *that*, he only gains. Instead, "by separating himself from the moral law, man acts against his very freedom; he ties himself with chains."[396]

"Renouncing sin" certainly implies foregoing to carry out certain actions, and in this sense, it is a limitation to freedom. But this is a limit to its abuse, not to its perfection. Anything outside of this limit would not be

394. *Friends of God*, no. 29.

395. *Roman Missal*, Easter Vigil: The Renewal of Baptismal Promises.

396. *CCC*, no. 1740.

Christian freedom, but rather lawlessness. St. Paul teaches us to distinguish terms: "For you were called to freedom, brethren; only do not use your freedom as an opportunity for the flesh, but through love be servants of one another" (Gal. 5:13).

Each person's freedom is limited by loyalty to their Christian vocation.[397] "The first stage of liberty, then," writes St. Augustine, "is to be free from crimes [. . .] such as, murder, adultery, any uncleanness of fornication, theft, fraud, sacrilege, and others of that sort. When a man has begun to be free from these (and every Christian man ought to be so), he begins to raise his head to liberty; but that is liberty begun, not completed."[398] Committing onself to renouncing sin does not harm one's freedom, but rather benefits it and ensures its existence.

Naturally, baptismal commitments are not satisfied simply by renouncing grave sin or by respecting the prohibitions of the moral law. Those commitments incline Christian life in a positive manner toward its final end, holiness, and apostolate. That is why when they are renewed, the Church not only exhorts the faithful to renounce sin, but also to live as children of God and, more specifically, "to live in the freedom of the children of God,"[399] since "for freedom Christ has set us free" (Gal. 5:1). St. Paul, who on other occasions describes the work of redemption as "redemption from evil" (see Gal. 3:13), presents it in this last text as a "liberation" (or a "setting free"). By this he means that Christ bestows us with a precious gift, the good of freedom.[400] On our part, the rejection of sin is only the first step toward freedom. This must be followed by another step, that of living as God's children. Both of these steps or interior moments are clearly perceived in Jesus' encounter with the rich young man. First, Jesus teaches him that the life of a disciple demands, "fulfilling" the commandments; afterward he adds, "come, follow me" (Luke 18:22). Jesus does not exhort him only to avoid evil, but rather invites him to surrender his life with him. And just as renouncing sin is not a loss of freedom, neither is committing oneself to follow Christ.

Freedom and Christian commitments do not oppose each another. A commitment to follow Christ makes a person freer because it channels freedom toward the love of God. [*S*]*ince God is Love* (see 1 John 4:8), *and the*

397. *Letter, May 31, 1954*, no. 24.

398. San Augustine, *In Ioann. Ev.* 41, 10 (passage quoted by St. John Paul II, Enc. *Veritatis splendor*, August 6, 1993, no. 13).

399. *Roman Missal*, Easter Vigil: The Renewal of Baptismal Promises.

400. See Albert Vanhoye, *Lettera ai Galati*, p. 123.

obligations that stem from Love ennoble and liberate all of one's life, to let oneself be conditioned by our God is to enter on the marvelous path of those who share in his Love.[401]

3.2.2. Specifications to Our Baptismal Commitments

The commitment to follow Jesus Christ can be specified in many ways according to each one's vocation and mission. It is possible to commit oneself in the intimacy of one's conscience to practice in a particular way the means of sanctification (e.g., frequent reception of the sacraments, times dedicated to prayer and to Christian formation, etc.)[402] and thus, to follow a specific path of holiness and apostolate.

In exhorting the faithful not to be afraid to embrace commitments of this type and to be faithful to them, St. Josemaría points out that for a Christian called to holiness and apostolate in ordinary life, accepting obligations proper to professional, family, and social life belongs to the essence of the baptismal commitment to live as a son or daughter of God. The following quotation is, on the one hand, an invitation to see these human obligations in a positive way without the fear of losing one's freedom when ones embraces them; in fact, it is the one who does not embrace them who is most at risk of losing his freedom. On the other hand, the quotation below provides us with a kind of parable about the specific Christian commitments we just mentioned:

> *If a man doesn't let himself be bound by noble and clean ties, through which he accepts the obligations of a family, his profession, his civic duties . . . , if a man has no initiative to make these decisions, life itself will take care of imposing them on him against his will. Then there will come a reaction of rebellion, of violence, of letting himself go along a way that is not Christian. When all this happens, that person is left even more limited than if he had voluntarily accepted certain commitments which apparently curtailed his freedom. I say apparently, because in fact at the moment of his commitment he was free and he would continue to be free by his loyalty to this commitment. Don't forget my children that otherwise, the soul becomes more enslaved with chains that at times may seem to be made of gold, but are chains nonetheless. And at other times, they are made of rusty iron.*[403]

401. *Letter, February14, 1974*, no. 8.

402. We will study these means in chapter nine.

403. Notes taken from preaching, June 25, 1972 (AGP, P01 VII-1972, pp. 10–11).

In the quotation above, St. Josemaría implies that there are not just simply professional, family and social commitments, but others as well that are specifically Christian. He expresses this in the paragraphs that follow. First, he recalls a sad impression he once had as follows,

> [*I once saw*] *an eagle shut up in an iron cage, clutching in its claws a piece of carrion. That fettered bird, born to soar the skies majestically and gaze at the sun, was both disgusting and pitiful at the mercy of some children that taunted it.*[404]

And he concludes,

> *Believe me, all our disordered rebellions lead us into the cage and to the carrion, to degradation, to losing the power of rising high above. Only by giving ourselves with humility will we be able to say with St. John of the Cross:* I soared aloft so high, so high, that in the end I reached my prey.[405]

For St. Josemaría, giving ourselves wholeheartedly to our baptismal commitments does not represent a limit; on the contrary, it is a path toward freedom. Addressing the faithful of Opus Dei, he uses two analogies. The first one involves highway signs that provide indications for the road:

> *It's only logical, my daughters and sons, that there be limits to our behavior as children of God, while we also feel and truly are free. The limits and barriers on a highway that prevent cars from going off the road could only seem opposed to the freedom of one who really didn't want to get to where the highway leads. Only an irrational person wants his path to have no limitations, like a driver who says, 'Why are these barriers here?' and then crosses over to the other side of the road. This person is not freer for doing so; moreover, he violates the freedom of others, and will end up badly.*[406]

---

404. Ibid.

405. Ibid. Here, St. Josemaría makes an implicit reference to the commitment of self-giving to God that the faithful of Opus Dei make (these words, in fact, were addressed to them). This commitment entails an effort to strive for holiness and to carry out an apostolic mission in the middle of the world with a specific spirit whose central aspect is sanctifying work with a foundation of divine filiation. It requires employing the means of sanctification and apostolate in a particular way, and of forming part of Opus Dei. The object of this study, however, is not a detailed look at the commitment to Opus Dei, which, as a specific type of baptismal commitment, also favors freedom. The only reason for referring to it here is to indicate that St. Josemaría invites all Christians to activate their baptismal commitments in a manner that is not generic, but rather in one that is tailored to their personal circumstances. Each should have the resolute determination to give themselves totally to God in the state proper to each person, living the Christian vocation in a manner clearly defined by divine light.

406. Notes taken from preaching, June 25, 1972 (AGP, P01 VII-1972, p. 8).

The second analogy refers to the wings that enable birds to fly:

> *Consider those birds with a majestic, lordly flight, who soar to unseen heights. They don't feel the weight of their wings, which are quite large and heavy. If their wings were cut off, or if they could free themselves from them, they would weigh less but wouldn't be able to fly. Always live the spirit of Opus Dei with the conviction that your obligations are not a burden or something negative. On the contrary, they are a continuous affirmation of authentic Love. And by our faithful fulfillment we will fly high, very high. For even though each of us is of such little worth, we will live the life of God; we will reach very near to the sun, as the eagles do when they soar upward.*[407]

In the end, the person who keeps his baptismal commitments will be helped by them and will live in the freedom for which Christ has freed us (see Gal. 5:1).

Some Practical Applications

(1) *Formation in freedom.* Spiritual direction is the appropriate setting to help people gain greater freedom with the help of grace. In order to form persons in freedom, one's will, intellect, and affectivity need to be formed so that they freely desire what God desires, thereby reaching greater interior freedom without the obstacles of a servile mentality, poor doctrinal formation, and/or disordered passions. The following three points illustrate how:

- It is essential to strengthen good will to be able to live as free persons: *will-power. A very important quality. Don't despise little things, for by the continual practice of denying yourself again and again in such things—which are never futile or trivial—with God's grace you will add strength and resilience to your character. That way, you will first become master of yourself, and then a guide, a chief, a leader: to compel and to urge and to inspire others with your word, with your example, with your knowledge, and with your authority.*[408]

---

407. Notes taken from preaching (AGP, P10, no. 19). The image is already found in St. Augustine: "The burden of Christ is so light that it raises one [. . .]. May this burden be for you the same as the weight of their wings is for the birds; if they have them they take off, if they lose them they remain on the ground" (*Sermo* 68,12).

408. *The Way*, no. 19. Recall what we said in the Preliminary Part, section I, 4 about this point of *The Way*. In speaking of "a chief" or of "a leader" (*caudillo*). St. Josemaría is not thinking of politics, and much less of any specific leader. He is thinking of apostolic activity. His image of the leader, which is inspired by the person of Jesus Christ, absolutely transcends that of any political leader.

- Doctrinal formation, the deep knowledge of revealed truth is also a vital root for freedom: Veritas liberabit vos (John 8:32). *Only a true freedom, based on the knowledge and practice of Christ's doctrine, will make us free.*[409] In spiritual direction, in addition to clarifying doubts, possible errors of conscience, etc., it is important to know how to awaken the sense of responsibility that leads to the necessary doctrinal and moral formation. This formation is also indispensable to free others from the slavery of ignorance: *the greatest enemy of God.*[410] Carrying out apostolate is collaborating with Christ's redeeming and (therefore) liberating mission. Forming others in doctrine is an essential part of this work. *Christ won this freedom for us and counts on our cooperation in exercising it. And he counts on our help to bring it to all mankind, communicating his word, his saving doctrine.*[411]
- Sentiments should be a great help for us to "passionately" love and carry out the good and that is why sentiments and feelings should be governed by reason. Otherwise, they darken it and intensify our inclination toward evil. Through spiritual guidance, a person can learn to place his heart on whatever God wishes for him, though always ruling with the head so as not to conform to an often ephemeral and sentimental enthusiasm. Álvaro del Portillo comments on this aspect of St. Josemaría's doctrine by stating that, "Our heart and sentiments can help us to be more generous with God, but they should not be the only nor the main engine moving us to be faithful, since that would mean falling into sentimentalism, a truly dangerous deformity of love. Many people overvalue their moods. They rely a lot on the heart and less on the head. If they feel like it, if it pleases them, they consider themselves capable of doing everything, relying too much on their enthusiasm; if not, they collapse. We should be on guard against such deception; we should consider that *the heart alone is not enough to follow God* [. . .]. *The first thing we need to use is our head without letting ourselves be taken adrift by feelings.*"[412]

(2) *Freedom and spontaneity.* When educating in freedom, it is important to teach people from the initial stages of their spiritual life to distinguish

409. *Letter, April 30, 1946*, no. 2.

410. *Letter, March 11, 1940*, no. 47.

411. *Letter, March 19, 1967*, no. 134.

412. A. del Portillo, *Pastoral Letter*, March 19, 1992 (AGP, P17, vol. III, no. 321). The final quotation comes from notes taken from St. Josemaría's preaching, October 2, 1972.

within themselves between what is "natural" and what is the consequence of original sin and personal sins. Thus, one will avoid deeming as "free" that which is simply "spontaneous." Sexuality, for instance, is natural and good, but in the fallen state of man, its inclinations are disordered so that not everything which is "spontaneous" is natural, that is, in accord with human nature. Hence, to give in to a temptation against chastity, for example, is not "liberating onself," but rather offending God and enslaving oneself. Likewise, struggling against temptation is not "repressing oneself," but rather attempting to achieve self-possession or self-mastery. Something similar occurs with other disordered passions. The lack of harmony that people experience within themselves is overcome by corresponding to grace so that choosing what is good and virtuous becomes increasingly more spontaneous and truly free. Temptations will always exist because evil inclinations never disappear completely, but with the grace of God it is possible to overcome them.

A clear error would be to call temptations "natural inclinations" as a justification to giving in to them. Referring to spiritual direction, St. Josemaría says, *We have to teach* [*people*] *that a Catholic can have clear doctrine, can have faith . . . and be weak. The temptation to justify our passions, trying to accommodate the faith to them, is diabolical: there is no way to justify what cannot be justified. While being understanding, we have to prevent them from throwing everything overboard and show them what they ought to keep practicing, despite their weakness.*[413]

A defect closely related with the above is that the experience of freedom (the power of self-determination) may lead a person to trust in his own power excessively, thus forgetting the wounds of sin. Through spiritual direction we can come to realize that we absolutely need God's help. The Lord says, "Apart from me you can do nothing" (John 15:5). On the other hand, with his grace, it is always possible to reject temptations and to do all the good each one must do: "I can do all things in him who strengthens me" (Phil. 4:13). A Christian needs to ask for grace and thus recognize that the motivation itself and the decision to humbly ask for God's help is already the fruit of divine grace which precedes our actions and leads to their perfection (see Phil. 2:13).

(3) *Love for freedom and optimism.* St. Josemaría affirms that *one of the most evident characteristics* [of the Christian spirit of Opus Dei] *is love for*

413. *Letter, May 6, 1945*, no. 37.

freedom and understanding.[414] And he adds: *In the human plane, I want to leave you love for freedom and good humor as an inheritance.*[415] This connection between love for freedom, understanding, and good humor is typical of St. Josemaría's "temperament." In suffering harm resulting from others' abuse of freedom, some people can experience anger and reject those who caused them harm as well as give in to pessimism with regard to freedom. St. Josemaría's reaction is quite different. Love for freedom—the true freedom of man who is fallen yet redeemed by Christ—leads him to a profound understanding of the human heart and to trust that, with the help of grace, the good use of Christian freedom (i.e., love) is stronger than its corrupted use. This is the explanation for his good humor with its solid foundations. *Christian optimism is not a schmaltzy optimism; nor is it a mere human confidence that everything will turn out all right. It is an optimism that sinks its roots in an awareness of our freedom, and in the sure knowledge of the power of grace. It is an optimism which leads us to make demands on ourselves, to struggle to respond at every moment to God's calls.*[416] In the end, the legacy that St. Josemaría wishes to transmit is none other than the one received from St. Paul: "Do not be overcome by evil, but overcome evil with good" (Rom. 12:21).

---

414. *Letter, May 31, 1954,* no. 22.

415. Ibid.

416. *The Forge,* no. 659.

CHAPTER SIX

The Love of the Children of God

The Christian Virtues

The price paid for each Christian is the redeeming Blood of our Lord and he, I insist, wants us to be both very human and very divine, struggling each day to imitate him who is perfectus Deus, perfectus homo.
(*Friends of God*, no. 75)

1. THE CHARITY OF THE CHILDREN OF GOD
    1.1. Love for God with All One's Heart: "The Style of Contemplative Souls"
    1.2. Love for One's Neighbor
    1.3. Love for Oneself Out of Love for God
2. LIFE OF FAITH AND HOPE
    2.1. Life of Faith
    2.2. Life of Hope
3. HUMILITY: THE FOUNDATION OF ALL THE VIRTUES
    3.1. The Humility of the Children of God
    3.2. Aspects of Humility
    3.3. Sincerity, Docility, and Simplicity
4. THE HUMAN VIRTUES OF A CHRISTIAN
    4.1. In the Image of Christ, "*Perfectus Deus, Perfectus Homo*"
    4.2. Prudence, Sound Judgment, and Realism
    4.3. Justice, Faithfulness, and Obedience
    4.4. Fortitude, Patience, and Perseverance
    4.5. Temperance, Chastity, and Poverty
    4.6. Virtuous Heroism in "Little Things"

Continued

We have examined divine filiation and freedom, two very important aspects of the identity of a Christian in the teaching of St. Josemaría. The former is a perfection of the person, the latter an essential characteristic of human nature composed of body and soul. In order to complete the description, it is necessary to consider the virtues that perfect man's faculties: the intellect, will, and sensible faculties, which enable him to act as a child of God (i.e., to be "Christ himself"). We thus need to take into account all the levels that constitute the person according to the anthropology presupposed in St. Josemaría's preaching: the level of the person, the level of nature, and that of the faculties or powers.

St. Josemaría dedicated a considerable part of his preaching to the subject of practicing virtues. Nine of the eighteen homilies in *Friends of God* deal with virtues: three are on the theological virtues, one is on virtues in general, and five are on specific virtues. The rest of the homilies in this work (as, in fact, in all his works), moreover, deal with the topic of virtues in one way or another. In practice, a list of works by or about St. Josemaría on this topic would be equivalent to a complete bibliography on St. Josemaría.[1]

---

1. We are mentioning here only a few specific studies: Manuel Belda, "La pedagogía de la humildad en 'Camino,'" in J.I. Saranyana (ed.), *El caminar histórico de la santidad cristiana* (Pamplona: Universidad de Navarra, 2004), pp. 285–295; Vicente Bosch, "Para una 'Teología de la sinceridad,' a través de los escritos del Beato Josemaría Escrivá," in *Annales Theologici* 16 (2002): 165–183; José María Casciaro, "Magnanimidad en la vida del beato Josemaría Escrivá de Balaguer," in J.L. Illanes et al., *El cristiano en el mundo. En el centenario del nacimiento del Beato Josemaría Escrivá (1902–2002)* (Pamplona: Universidad de Navarra, 2003), pp. 331–346; Rafael Corazón González, "La virtud de la sinceridad en la espiritualidad de San Josemaría Escrivá," in Juan F. Sellés et al., *Tres estudios sobre el pensamiento de San Josemaría Escrivá*, in *Cuadernos de Anuario Filosófico* 158 (2003): 55–77; Cecilia Echeverría Falla, "Libertad y estructura de las virtudes en el Beato Josemaría," in Asociación ADEC, *Hacia una nueva educación más humana. En torno al pensamiento de Josemaría Escrivá* (San Jose, Costa Rica: Promesa, 2002), pp. 55–65; Cornelio Fabro, "Virtù umane e soprannaturali nelle omelie di mons. Escrivá. Ascetica e teologia in 'Amici di Dio'," in *Studi Cattolici* 265 (1983): 181–185; José Luis Illanes, "Trabajo, caridad, justicia," in Cornelio Fabro et al., *Santidad y mundo* (*Actas del simposio teológico de estudio en torno a las enseñanzas del beato Josemaría Escrivá*), Pamplona: Eunsa, 1996, pp. 211–248. We refer also to an extensive study of moral theology on the moral virtues as a whole, where St. Josemaría is frequently quoted: Ramón García de Haro, *La vida cristiana* (Pamplona: Eunsa, 1992), ch. 7 (especially pp. 615–670).

The studies on St. Josemaría's personal practice of charity and the other virtues are also numerous. One testimonial recounts that "he was very virtuous [. . .] because he put everything on the line for Love."[2] In this regard, the most authoritative text is the decree of the Congregation for the Causes of Saints on the heroicity of his virtues, published on April 9, 1990 with the approval of the Roman Pontiff.[3] Among the testimonials concerning his life gathered for his cause of canonization, the ones that stand out the most are those of Álvaro del Portillo and Javier Echeverría, who for decades closely collaborated with the founder of Opus Dei and have provided many examples of how he practiced the virtues.[4] In our present study, however, we have limited ourselves to analyzing his written works and preaching, as it is has not been possible for us to analyze the numerous testimonials of how he lived the virtues, even though arguably his example is also a source of his teaching. In fact, many people testify that they learned the meaning of virtues by observing how St. Josemaría lived them.[5]

St. Josemaría's concept of virtue is the classical one found in the catechisms of Catholic doctrine. The Catechism of St. Pius X defined virtue as "a quality infused by God into the soul by which the latter acquires inclination, facility, and promptness to know the good and do it [. . .]."[6] The current Catechism of the Catholic Church defines it thus: "a virtue is an habitual and firm disposition to do the good."[7] It is a habit that inclines one toward the good so as to choose an appropriate course of action, or simply a habit to use freedom well.[8] The virtues, in effect, have an intrinsic relation

---

2. Echevarría Falla, "Libertad y estructura de las virtudes en el Beato Josemaría," p. 65.

3. See AAS 82 (1990): 1450–1455.

4. See Álvaro del Portillo, *Immersed in God* (Princeton: Scepter, 1996); Javier Echevarría, *Memoria del Beato Josemaría* (Madrid: Rialp, 2000). To the testimony of these two exceptional witnesses we have to add that of many others whose declarations constitute the documentary basis for the *Positio super vita et virtutibus* of the Cause of Canonization (Rome, 1988), the text of which is in the archive of the Congregation for the Causes of Saints.

5. "On seeing them lived [the virtues] one knows in a spontaneous and intuitive way that 'for me it is good to be industrious and it is evil to be lazy': 'the good is to be generous and the evil to be egoistic.'" Echevarría Falla, "Libertad y estructura de las virtudes en el Beato Josemaría," p. 64.

6. *Catechism of St. Pius X*, no. 856 (part 5, ch. 1, §1).

7. See *CCC*, no. 1803.

8. We could elaborate more on the relation between "choosing well" and "using one's freedom well." We would have to distinguish the *intentio finis* and the *electio mediorum*, and their mutual relation. "Moral virtue is a firm and stable intention to virtuous ends [. . .] and also the choice and realization of those actions which here and now incarnate those ends. Thus, the moral virtues have an intentional act and an elective act." Ángel Rodríguez Luño, *Ética general*, 4th ed. (Pamplona: Eunsa, 2001), p. 218. See Martin Rhonheimer, *La prospettiva della morale* (Rome: Edusc, 1994), pp. 177–182.

to freedom. "Far from being reflex acts that diminish the freedom of our actions, they are qualities that strengthen and perfect them," writes Ángel Rodríguez Luño.[9] They cannot be reduced to positive character traits. "Virtue is a *habitus* (a habit), a term that should not be translated as a 'custom' because it is not a stereotype way of acting or a reflex."[10] It is a stable quality, the fruit of free acts that ensures the good use of freedom "inasmuch that the ends of the virtues (the goods of justice, fortitude, etc.) become the principle of freedom."[11] Virtues increase a person's mastery over his or her actions and provide strength, confidence, ease, and spontaneity to choose and carry out the good.

In the study of the virtues, a distinction is commonly made between the *object* (the good to which they are directed) and the *subject* (how they exist in the person, or the faculty in which they reside). Here, we have chosen to study them as perfections of the subject that configure the intellect, will, and affectivity to Christ. Our purpose for doing so in Part II is to depict the whole of what it means to be a child of God as *ipse Christus* in one's effort to identify oneself with Jesus Christ, "*perfectus Deus, perfectus homo*," (to use the formula of the *Athanasian Creed* so dear to St. Josemaría). If the virtues were considered under their object, then they should have been dealt with separately looking at the theological virtues in Part I, since their object is God, leaving the human virtues for Part III, since their object is created goods that are found on the path to holiness. But separating them in this manner would not underscore the figure of the Christian as image of Christ. This methodological choice of ours is not entirely free from difficulties since we have already discussed some aspects of theological charity in Part I when we considered our last end and therefore we will not go over them again. There are also some virtues such as industriousness that we will deal with in Part III when we discuss sanctification of work instead of doing so here. Each option has its advantages and difficulties, but it seems more coherent for our present scope to study the virtues in the present Part which is dedicated to the subject.

We would like to point out that although we will discuss the topic of virtues before that of sanctification of ordinary life, St. Josemaría's texts will

9. Rodríguez Luño, *La scelta etica. Il rapporto fra libertà e virtù* (Milan: Edizioni Ares, 1988), p. 156. "Moral virtue is not an automatic mechanism which leads one to always do the same without needing to choose. Virtue does not suppress choice, but perfects it. It does not spare us making the decisión, but it permits us to choose well in the most varied circumstances." Idem, *Ética general*, p. 214. See also Carlo Caffarra, *Viventi in Cristo* (Milan: Jaca Book, 1981), p. 143.

10. Jean Porter, "Virtù," in Jean-Yves Lacoste (ed.), *Dizionario critico di Teologia* (Rome: Città Nuova, 2005), p. 1469.

11. Rodríguez Luño, *La scelta etica. Il rapporto fra libertà e virtù*, p. 160.

lead from the onset to a vision of the practice of the Christian virtues in the middle of the world (in secular and civic life) given that that is the field of sanctification he contemplates.

In order to view the virtues as perfections of the subject in an organically structured way, scholars differ as to the best arrangement.[12] The one we follow here is based on the distinction between charity and the other virtues (see 1 Cor. 13:1 ff). Charity is not just one more virtue, but neither is it sufficient to say that it is the most important one. Charity "gives life to the soul formally, as the soul does to the body."[13] Just as the spiritual soul is the *substantial form* of the body, the spiritual and subsistent principle of unity that allows for one to carry out operations beyond matter, analogously, charity is the *form* of all the other virtues, the vital principle that unifies them and allows for acts in the realm of supernatural life to be carried out.

In St. Josemaría, moreover, *charity toward God* [. . .] *is marked by a strong sense of divine filiation.*[14] For him, the life of a child of God is necessarily presided by charity because supernatural filial adoption (i.e., participation in the Son) is inseparable from charity (i.e., participation in the Holy Spirit). This inseparability is a reflection of the unity between the Son and the Holy Spirit. Thus, a study on the virtues of a son of God, according to the teaching of St. Josemaría, must not only situate charity in a preeminent place; it must also be thoroughly structured by it from top to bottom. This will be our approach in the present chapter.

A second distinction that is also indispensable for understanding the organization of this subject is the difference between the "theological" and "human" virtues. The theological virtues (i.e., faith, hope, and charity) refer directly to God (hence the name "theological"). Charity presupposes faith and hope, since only he who believes in God and hopes to find happiness in union with him can also love him. Human virtues have as their object created realities that should be ordered to God. Without them, charity would not be able to express itself in the wide array of human circumstances. In addition, human virtues are of special interest for this study because St. Josemaría's teaching is expressly directed to ordinary Christians called to live holy lives in the middle of the world, and thus to carry out to perfection

12. A good systematization can be seen in Tomás Trigo, "Virtud," in César Izquierdo (ed.), *Diccionario de Teología* (Pamplona: Eunsa, 2006), pp. 1023–1033.

13. St. Thomas Aquinas, *S. Th.*, II-II, q. 23, a. 3, ad 2.

14. *Letter, December 8, 1949*, no. 35.

their professional, family, and social activities, requiring the exercise of human virtues informed by charity.

When referring to human virtues, St. Josemaría at times assumes the classical structure that categorizes them under the four cardinal virtues of prudence, justice, fortitude and temperance. We will do the same here. In his teaching, however, humility occupies a unique place that does not fit within this scheme, as we shall later explore.

On a terminological note, we should point out that with St. Josemaría and other authors, besides the expressions "theological" and "human" virtues, we frequently find others such as "moral," "cardinal," "infused," "supernatural," and "Christian" virtues.

By "human virtues," we mean the same as "moral virtues," which are those that reside in the appetitive powers (the will and the "appetites," or that is, faculties by which one is attracted to sensible goods). Here we do not consider the intellectual virtues as "human virtues," since they belong to the speculative or practical intellect (e.g., science and art) with the exception of the virtue of prudence since, even though it belongs to the practical intellect, it is a moral virtue because of its object.[15]

The "infused virtues" are those that God infuses in the soul. The theological virtues are always infused, whereas that is not always the case for the human virtues. Specifically, the human virtues of someone who does not enjoy the state of grace are not infused, whereas in someone who does, they are enlivened by infused charity and are thus "supernatural virtues." (In this sense they are infused, though not "directly" as the theological virtues are; they are infused only because they are informed by charity.) Consequently, charity and the all other virtues it enlivens are called "supernatural" (i.e., the theological virtues of faith, hope, and charity, as well as the human virtues of a Christian in the state of grace).

Lastly, all the virtues of a Christian are called "Christian virtues," both the theological and the human. Generally speaking, the expression "Christian virtues" refers to the Christian who is in the state of

15. See Rodríguez Luño, *Ética general*, p. 213. It is usually held that prudence is not properly a moral virtue because it perfects the intellect. But insofar as it perfects it in regard to moral action, one can include it among the "moral virtues." Its mission is not only that of judging but also of directing the other faculties in a way that conforms to the demands of the moral virtues (see St. Thomas Aquinas, *S. Th.*, I-II, q. 58, a. 3, ad 1).

> grace and is then synonymous with "supernatural virtues." All the virtues of a Christian, including the human ones, are supernatural because they have been elevated by charity and develop with the aid of grace.[16]

St. Josemaría frequently teaches that the human virtues are *the foundation for the supernatural virtues.*[17] By this affirmation, he does not mean to say that Christians have two types of virtues: ones purely human and others supernatural. Rather, he uses the expression in order to encourage Christians to exercise all the virtues required by human perfection (under the movement of grace) because *the price of living as Christians is not that of ceasing to be human or of abandoning the effort to acquire those virtues which some have even without knowing Christ.*[18] That does not mean that we should "first" seek to practice human virtues without counting on grace (as if we were not Christians), and "afterward," upon this basis, practice the supernatural ones. To think in this way would be to split the Christian life in two: "human life" up to a certain level, and "supernatural life" above that. But that would be tantamount to ignoring the reality of the Incarnation. A Christian should always practice the human virtues informed or enlivened by charity.

These observations allow us to understand the outline of this chapter. The first section will deal with charity itself followed by faith and hope, two virtues required and informed by charity. Next, we will discuss the virtue of humility and the other human virtues of the Christian. We will conclude the chapter with a section on the gifts of the Holy Spirit. They raise human activity to a perfection that is higher than that achieved by the virtues and dispose the Christian to a higher contemplative life in human activities.

All of these qualities (Christian virtues and the gifts of the Holy Spirit) sketch a portrait of a child of God. They are like Christ's "features" in the Christian. But far from being akin to external contour lines, they are more like internal "powers" or "strengths" (as indicated by the etymology of the word "virtue") that conform the Christian to Christ as they are enlivened by Christ's own charity. By means of the virtues, a Christian is an image of

---

16. See *CCC*, no. 1810.

17. *Friends of God*, no. 74. See ibid., no. 91. At other times he said that *we must be very human, for otherwise we cannot be divine*" (*Christ Is Passing By*, no. 166). Leo Scheffczyk comments that this principle "certainly shows the organic union between nature and grace and has to be considered a powerful defense against any kind of extrinsicism in the docrine of grace." "Die Gnade in der Spiritualität von Josemaría Escrivá," in César Ortiz (ed.), *Josemaría Escrivá. Profile einer Gründergestalt* (Köln: Adamas-Verlag, 2002), p. 71.

18. *Friends of God*, no. 75.

Christ. Furthermore, thanks to the theological and human virtues and to the gifts of the Holy Spirit, the same Christ can easily act in the Christian.

Although we will discuss the virtues as a whole and will remember the classical definition of each one as well as indicate the "subject" or power of the soul where each is rooted, our goal is not to give a systematic exposition of the virtues as in a moral theology textbook. Our purpose, instead, is to show how the virtues appear in St. Josemaría's teaching and how he characterizes each of them. We will thus explain the core of each virtue by relying heavily on St. Josemaría's own writings.

1. The Charity of the Children of God

In a classic sense, charity is defined as "the theological virtue by which we love God above all things for his own sake, and our neighbor as ourselves for the love of God."[19] This virtue is often designated by its act, which is love. In fact, in St. Josemaría's texts it is found more often as "love" than as "charity."

St. Thomas provides another definition of special interest here because St. Josemaría quotes it verbatim. Commenting on St. Paul's words "God's love [*caritas Dei*] has been poured into our hearts through the Holy Spirit which has been given to us" (Rom. 5:5), St. Thomas affirms that charity is "a certain participation of the infinite charity which is the Holy Ghost."[20]

---

19. *CCC*, no. 1822.

20. St. Thomas Aquinas, *S. Th.*, II-II, q. 24, a. 7, c. The definition is repeated various times in his works (see *Summa Contra Gentiles*, IV, cc. 17 y 21; *In Ep. ad Rom.*, c. 5, lect. 1; etc.). St. Josemaría cites it in *Letter, March 24, 1931*, no. 9; we reproduce the text below.

The Vulgate and the Neo-Vulgate in various places employ the term "caritas" to translate the Greek "*agape*," whose biblical significance is very rich. It designates the love between the Father and the Son within the heart of the Blessed Trinity, and also the love with which God loves us and the love with which the Christian loves God and his brethren. See Gerhard Kittel et al., *Theologisches Wörterbuch zum Neuen Testament*, vol. I (Stuttgart: Kohlhammer, 1933), pp. 20–55. We can also see the considerations of Benedict XVI, in his encyclical *Deus Caritas Est*, December 25, 2005, nos. 2–8. There are three different applications of the term. Specifically, our love for God is not the Holy Spirit, but the charity which the Holy Spirit infuses. St. Josemaría here avoids two positions: (1) The first is that of considering that the Spirit acts in the soul as "from without." In this sense he cites on one occasion the following text of St. Cyril of Alexandria: "The Holy Spirit is not an artist who paints the divine substance in us, as if he were alien to it; it is not in that way that he leads us to the likeness of God, but it is he himself, who is God and proceeds from God, who imprints himself in the hearts who receive him like a seal on wax and, in this way, by the communication of himself and his likeness, reestablishes the nature according to the beauty of the divine model and restores man to the image of God." *Thesaurus de sancta et consubstantiali Trinitate*, 34; cited in *Christ Is Passing By*, no. 134. (2) The opposite idea would be to think that the Holy Spirit unites himself to the Christian as his "form," thus misinterpreting the preceding text of St. Cyril. St. Josemaría avoids this reading by recalling numerous times

This definition has the value of indicating that charity is based on divine filiation. In effect, since the Holy Spirit is the mutual gift of Father and Son, it must be said that charity inclines a Christian to give himself completely to the Father in union with the Son. Thus, charity is love based on divine filiation, the friendship of a son with his Father God. The Angelic Doctor says as much, commenting upon a scriptural text: "'God is faithful, by whom you were called into the fellowship of his Son, Jesus Christ our Lord' (1 Cor. 1:9). Love founded upon this fellowship is charity."[21]

Love in the depths of the Trinity is poured out on men by the love in the heart of Christ.[22] Just as sanctifying grace is a participation in the fullness of grace of Christ's humanity, so too the charity bestowed on souls by the Holy Spirit is a communication of the "infinite treasures"[23] of the Sacred Heart of Jesus. In such a way, charity enables us to love as Christ loved (see John 13:34). And for this same reason, the process of identification with Jesus Christ consists essentially in the growth of charity: "*per amorem amans fit unum cum amato*."[24] As we said earlier, holiness (which is the *fullness of divine filiation*[25] or full identification with Christ) is also *fullness of charity.*[26]

> *The main thing we are asked to do, which is so much in keeping with our nature, is to love* [. . .]. Thou shalt love the Lord thy God, with thy whole heart, and with thy whole soul, and with thy whole mind' (Matt. 22:37), *holding back nothing for ourselves. This is what sanctity is all about.*[27]

In which faculty does charity reside? Traditional doctrine teaches that this virtue "purifies our human ability to love, and raises it to the supernatural perfection of divine love."[28] And since love is an act of the will, charity

---

that the Paraclete dwells in the Christian as in a temple and pours into the soul the created gift of charity (see *Christ Is Passing By*, no. 49). He distinguishes with precision between created charity and that which is uncreated (the Holy Spirit). His conception is along the line of the following words of St. Thomas Aquinas: "The act of charity is not caused by the Holy Spirit by moving the human mind as if it is only moved and in no way the principle of movement," but rather, "in order to realize the act of charity, it is necessary for there be in us an habitual form added to the natural potency." *S. Th.*, II-II. q. 23, a. 2, c.

21. St. Thomas Aquinas, *S. Th.*, II-II, q. 23, a. 1, c.
22. *Christ Is Passing By*, no. 169.
23. *Roman Missal*, Solemnity of the Sacred Heart of Jesus, Opening Prayer.
24. St. Thomas Aquinas, *In III Sent.*, d. 27, q. 1, a. 1, c.
25. *Letter, February 2, 1945*, no. 8.
26. *Furrow*, no. 739.
27. *Friends of God*, no. 6.
28. *CCC*, no. 1827.

resides in the will as in its "subject."[29] St. Josemaría affirms this on various occasions because he wishes to make it clear that *charity cannot be content with just nice feelings.*[30] *The charity of Christ is not merely a benevolent sentiment for our neighbor; it is not limited to a penchant for philanthropy. Poured out in our soul by God, charity transforms from within our mind and will.*[31] Speaking about the first commandment he asks, *What kind of love are we talking about?*[32] And he replies, *Sacred Scripture uses the Latin word* dilectio, *to make us understand clearly that it does not simply mean the feeling of affection. It signifies, rather, a firm determination on the part of the will.* Dilectio *comes from* electio, *choice*[33] (which is an act of the will). This does not mean that charity puts sentiments aside. In fact, St. Josemaría refers more often to the "heart" as the locus of charity, rather than the will.[34]

If the will is good the person is, strictly speaking, good because the will moves and governs the other faculties. And that which makes the will good is charity. Other qualities that perfect man such as having a keen intellect, broad learning, or other aptitudes, only make him relatively good under a certain aspect.[35] Therefore, Christian perfection consists essentially in the "perfection of charity."[36] The person who loves more is more perfect (and holier or participates more in divine life); the person who loves less is less perfect even though the latter may stand out for other qualities. "If I speak in the tongues of men and of angels, but have not love, I am a noisy gong or a clanging cymbal. And if I have prophetic powers, and understand all mysteries and all knowledge, and if I have all faith, so as to remove mountains, but have not love, I am nothing. If I give away all I have, and if I deliver my body to be burned, but have not love, I am nothing" (1 Cor. 13:1–3). St. Josemaría sums this up: *sanctity is not a matter of doing things that are more difficult each day, but rather of doing them each day with more love.*[37]

---

29. See St. Thomas Aquinas, *S. Th.*, II-II, q. 24, a. 1, s.c.

30. *Christ Is Passing By*, no. 173.

31. Ibid., no. 71.

32. *Friends of God*, no. 231.

33. Ibid. See *The Forge*, no. 100.

34. See *Christ Is Passing By*, no. 166; *Friends of God*, no. 117.

35. "*Simpliciter autem et totaliter bonus dicitur aliquis ex hoc quod habet voluntatem bonam, quia per voluntatem homo utitur omnibus aliis potentiis; et ideo bona voluntas facit hominem bonum simpliciter; et propter hoc virtus appetitivae partis secundum quam voluntas fit bona, est quae simpliciter bonum facit habentem.*" St. Thomas Aquinas, *De virtutibus in communi*, q. 1, a. 9, ad 16. See Idem, *In III Ethic.*, lect. 6, no. 4.

36. *Lumen gentium*, no. 40.

37. Notes taken from preaching (AGP, P10, no. 25).

> Sometimes this supreme importance of charity is deformed by separating it from human virtues. People say that "what is important is to love," but behind this phrase may lie hidden the lack of some virtue. As we show, the other virtues that perfect a person's faculties are also necessary "to do things with love." St. Josemaría insists on this point. *Recalling an expression of the prophet Isaiah*—discite benefacere (Is. 1:17)—*I like to say that we have to learn to live every virtue.*[38] Charity leads to the development of human virtues because these are particularly necessary to sanctify temporal activities. If the effort in developing these virtues is lacking, it is difficult for love to be authentic.

Charity resides in the will as an interior law. In the Old Testament, the first and principal commandment was love for God, which summed up all other precepts (see Deut. 6:5) and led toward the final end. But the old law was only an external help, coming from outside the person. Instead, charity is "the fulfilling of the law" (Rom. 13:10) because God, in addition to clearly revealing in Christ the requirements of love, has engraved his law "not on tablets of stone but on tablets of human hearts" (2 Cor. 3:3). For a Christian who is in grace, charity is like the will's interior and supernatural inclination to love God. This idea is present throughout St. Josemaría's writings, beginning with the first point of *The Way* in which he speaks of "the fire of Christ that you bear in your heart."[39]

As far as the "object" of charity is concerned, St. Josemaría echoes Christian doctrine by affirming that charity is always directed to God as filial love. But he includes love for those whom God loves, that is, love for others and for oneself out of love for God.[40] "You shall love the Lord your God with all your heart, and with all your soul, and with all your mind. This is the great and first commandment. And a second is like it, You shall love your neighbor as yourself" (Matt. 22:37–39).

> God also loves all the irrational creatures of the world, which are his handiwork. But he does not love them "for themselves,"[41] as he loves human persons; rather, he loves them for his children's sake, as a means for them to reach holiness and happiness. Consequently, the charity that moves a person to love God's will leads to the love of created

38. *Conversations*, no. 110.
39. *The Way*, no. 1.
40. See *CCC*, no. 1822.
41. See *Gaudium et Spes*, no. 24.

> things not "for their own sake" or absolutely, but rather as a means to holiness. The human person, by contrast, should not be loved only as a means.

Within the object of charity there exists an order. *This is the order of Charity: God, the others and myself.*[42] These words offer the scheme that will be employed to study different aspects of charity: love for God, love for others, and love for oneself out of love for God.

It is important to keep in mind that the act of love for God has been already amply studied in the three chapters of Part I when we discussed our final end. Here, we wish to focus on how this aspect of the virtue of charity configures the subject. For this reason, the first section is short even though it is the principal one.

By contrast, we will dedicate more space to the two other acts of charity: love for others and love for oneself out of love for God, which are not the "first commandment" but rather the "second," and that is why even though we mentioned them in Part I, they have not been discussed in as much detail as love for God.

1.1. Love for God with All One's Heart: "The Style of Contemplative Souls"

The title of this section describes the love for God with the words "with all one's heart" (and we could have added "with all one's mind and all one's strength") because what we will discuss is not the *act* of love for God, but rather the effect of the *virtue* of charity in the Christian, that is, how it configures one's personality. In essence, this virtue supernaturally produces an inner unity of all of a person's faculties: the intellect, the will, and the senses, directing them to union with God. It shapes the Christian into a contemplative soul who lives with his eyes directed toward God like Christ, and who lives toward the redemption of mankind because this is the will of his Father.

In order to understand how charity resides in the subject, we should keep in mind that it does not consist in the elevation of an already existing human virtue. A prior "human charity" does not exist as it would be an "uninformed charity" or a "charity without charity." Human justice (without charity) can exist, human fortitude (without charity) can exist, and other such virtues can exist and are the foundation of the corresponding

42. Notes taken from preaching (AGP, P10, no. 155).

Christian virtues inasmuch as they can be shaped by charity. Instead, "charity without charity" is not possible.

It is noteworthy to clarify this point. This does not mean that an unbaptized person is unable to love God. If such a person truly loves him by fulfilling his will as expressed in the moral law, then he loves God with supernatural charity even though he does not know the Gospel and is not baptized. In other words, he does not love God with a "natural charity" that, theologically speaking, does not exist.

Loving God above all things (which means fulfilling his will before all else) is a precept accessible to human reason. As St. Josemaría emphasizes, it is *the first and most important duty of the natural order*.[43] In fact, the Law of Moses commands love for God. The just of the Old Testament and every unbaptized person who loves God with his whole heart, loves God because he is already mysteriously united to Christ and his Church through a life of grace. A virtue of charity that is not supernatural does not exist. A man who is in the state of sin and thus lives without a fundamental orientation toward union with God (which constitutes the essence of love), can be an upright man in many aspects of his life (with the uprightness that the human virtues produce), but he cannot love God with his whole heart. He does not have charity although his right intention disposes him in some manner to receive it.

Charity, St. Thomas affirms "is not founded principally upon a human virtue."[44] He says "principally" because that which is principal to charity is love for God, the "first commandment," and this love is not founded on "human charity," as we have just explained. Instead, "the second commandment," love for others, which also belongs to charity, does take up and elevates human friendship even though it is not primarily founded on it. Principally, it is founded on the fact that others are God's children or are called to be so.

---

43. *Letter, March 19, 1967*, no. 84. In regard to the natural love of God, Aquinas says, "*Diligere autem Deum super omnia est quiddam connaturale homini* [. . .]. *Unde homo in statu naturae integrae dilectionem sui ipsius referebat ad amorem Dei sicut ad finem, et similiter dilectionem omnium aliarum rerum. Et ita Deum diligebat plus quam seipsum, et super omnia. Sed in statu naturae corruptae homo ab hoc deficit secundum appetitum voluntatis rationalis, quae propter corruptionem naturae sequitur bonum privatum, nisi sanetur per gratiam Dei. Et ideo dicendum est quod homo in statu naturae integrae non indigebat dono gratiae superadditae naturalibus bonis ad diligendum Deum naturaliter super omnia; licet indigeret auxilio Dei ad hoc eum moventis. Sed in statu naturae corruptae indiget homo etiam ad hoc auxilio gratiae naturam sanantis.*" St. Thomas Aquinas, *S. Th.*, I-II, q. 109, a. 3.

44. Charity "*non fundatur principaliter super virtute humana, sed super bonitate divina.*" St. Thomas Aquinas, *S. Th.*, II-II, q. 23, a. 3, ad 1.

Charity is not the elevation of a virtue that already exists in the will, but rather the elevation of the will itself. It is casually said that charity constitutes a new "supernatural faculty" and therefore is not just a "supernatural virtue of a human faculty," as would be the case of the human virtues in the Christian. Properly speaking, however, charity is not a new "faculty," but a virtue whose subject is the will. Nonetheless, it does not exist in the will as a human virtue in its faculty because it provides not only the "facility" but the very "possibility" of carrying out certain acts such as loving God as his children and giving a supernatural meaning to the other virtues. Thus, charity is like a "supernatural empowering" of the will that configures it with the human will of Christ. It is the defining quality of the will of a child of God.

> Charity elevates and gives supernatural power to the will to the point that surprisingly it can be affirmed, *as holy Scripture reminds us, even our sleep should be prayer.*[45] Charity enables a person to love God even without carrying out an act of the will because it not only elevates its acts but the will itself. Naturally, we should not confuse this quietism, which holds that in order to love God "there is no need to do anything at all"—as is the case with someone sleeping. Rather, it means that he who seeks to do everything that God wills can actually love even when God does not wish him to do anything. Before God we are small children, and just as a child loves his father without being aware of it, we can *analogously* love God just by resting in him when he wishes that we do just that (and nothing else).

The charity that the Holy Spirit infuses leads us to exclaim: "Abba! Father!" (Rom. 8:15), not as a mere formulation of words or a simple

45. *Christ Is Passing By*, no. 119 (refers at the foot of the page to Deut. 6:6–7). In the same paragraph, he cites other texts of Scripture: "*The just man's* delight is in the law of the Lord, and on his law he meditates day and night" (Ps. 1:2). "*Through the night I meditate on you*" (see Ps. 62:7) *and* my prayer comes to you like incense in the evening (see Ps. 140:2). *Our whole day can be a time for prayer—from night to morning and from morning to night.* Ibid. A Father of the Church refers to prayer during one's sleep as follows: "When the Holy Spirit establishes his dwelling place in a man, he cannot stop praying because the Holy Spirit never stops praying in him. Whether he is sleeping or awake, prayer never leaves his soul. While he eats or drinks, when he is in bed immersed in sleep, or on the contrary, is working, the perfume of prayer arises spontaneously from his soul. He no longer prays only at particular times, but continually" St. Isaac of Nineveh, *Tractatus*, 35. St. John Chrysostom holds that prayer is a supplication "that is not limited to a specific time or certain set hours, but which is prolonged day and night without interruption" (*Hom. 6: De precatione*). St. Jerome writes that "St. Paul commanded us to pray always, and for the saints sleep itself is prayer" (*Ep. ad Eustochium*, 22, 37). It's possible that St. Josemaría was referring to these words when he commented: *You don't know what a consolation it was to me when, after repeating for years and years that for a contemplative soul even sleep is prayer, I came across a text of St. Jerome which said the same thing.* Notes from a meditation, November 26, 1967: AGP, P09, p. 82.

declaration of a truth more or less felt, but rather as a clamor expressing the decision of giving one's life to the fulfillment of the will of the Father as Christ in the Garden of Olives: "Abba, Father, [. . .] yet not what I will, but what thou wilt" (Mark 14:36). For a son of God, *charity is not something abstract. It entails a real, complete selfgiving to the service of God and all men.*[46] It implies the determination to carry out the will of our Father God without any reservation, obediently "unto death, even death on a cross" (Phil. 2:8) because *relations with God necessarily demand self-giving and acquire a sense of totality.*[47] Charity enables man to love God through and through, with a "sense of totality:" "with all your heart, and with all your soul, and with all your mind, and with all your strength" (Mark 12:30). It is the virtue that unifies the different energies of a subject directing them to the final end, thus conferring on the person a supernatural interior unity. It unifies all the acts of the will, focusing them on the fulfillment of the divine will, and through the will, it also unifies the other faculties ordering the acts of the other virtues to God. *By living charity—Love—you live all the human and supernatural virtues demanded of a Christian. These virtues form a unity.*[48]

From this "totality" of love for God, we can derive two consequences respectively related with the other two dimensions of love (love for others and love for oneself). The first is that in a Christian who wishes to love God "with all his heart" every human love should be ordered to the love of God. In other words, no human love should be placed above God: "He who loves father or mother more than me is not worthy of me; and he who loves son or daughter more than me is not worthy of me" (Matt. 10:37). St. Josemaría expresses this vividly when he writes: *The only real love is God's Love!*[49] This exclamation does not only mean that "there is no greater love than Love of God." Rather, it means, above all, that for a Christian there can be no true love that excludes the love of God, places it on a secondary plane, or is independent of it. This necessary "subordination" of human love will be discussed later in the section on friendship.

The second consequence is that love of God requires renunciation of all self-love that is not for love of God: "If any man would come after me, let him deny himself and take up his cross and follow me. For whoever would save his life will lose it, and whoever loses his life for my sake will find it"

46. *Conversations*, no. 62.

47. *Christ Is Passing By*, no. 46.

48. *Conversations*, no. 62.

49. *The Way*, no. 417.

(Matt. 16:24–25). The need to purify self-love is developed later in the context of self-denial.

Complete or total love for God ("with all your heart") is something dynamic. It is open to growth without limits. St. Josemaría explains it, quoting St. Thomas:

> *A person develops little by little, but never develops all his capacities; he never attains all the human perfection his nature is capable of. He may become the best in a specific field compared to everyone else, and even attain a level that is humanly insuperable. Nevertheless, as a Christian his growth has no limits; he can always grow in charity, which is the essence of perfection.* For charity itself considered as such has no limit to its increase, since it is a participation in the infinite charity which is the Holy Spirit. In like manner the cause of the increase of charity, viz., God, is possessed of infinite power. Furthermore, on the part of its subject, no limit to this increase can be determined, because whenever charity increases, there is a corresponding increased ability to receive a further increase. It is therefore evident that it is not possible to fix any limits to the increase of charity in this life. (St. Thomas, S. *Th.*, II-II, q.24, a.7 c.)[50]

In light of this "growing" totality intrinsic to love for God, any love which is at the margins of charity, whether it be love for others or oneself, is an "attachment" or "fetter." It is an obstacle to progress. St. Josemaría uses these terms often. He also notes, evoking the mystical doctor, that in this sphere, a *subtle thread* has the same effect as a *wrought iron chain.*[51]

In the measure that love pervades the soul of a child of God, his activities are transformed into prayer. St. Josemaría exclaims: *We acquire the style of contemplative souls, in the midst of our daily work!*[52] A soul that is shaped by charity and the gifts of the Holy Spirit is a contemplative soul. Thus, if one asks, how does charity configure the soul? The reply would be: by making it contemplative in such a way that it tries to see and love God in everything it does.

---

50. *Letter, March 24, 1931*, no. 9.

51. *The Way*, no. 170. For the precedents of this comparison in St. John of the Cross, see Pedro Rodríguez, "*The Way*" *Critical-Historical Edition* (London/New York: Scepter, 2009), *ad loc.*

52. *Friends of God*, no. 67. This refers specifically to work converted into prayer, but it seems to us obvious that it can be applied to all of one's doings that one tries to turn into dialogue with God. 52 *Christ Is Passing By*, no. 120.

Someone who is thinking about God does not forget the children of God: *the contemplative soul is filled with apostolic zeal.*[53] The charity infused by the Paraclete leading to a contemplative life is always a *priestly charity* that moves a person to give himself to Christ for the salvation of souls. The same Holy Spirit who bestows charity on the soul anoints the Christian at baptism with Christ's priesthood. Even though priesthood does not require charity (the priestly character remains when a person loses grace and charity through sin),[54] they go together. Since the priesthood has a power to unite men with God, it should be lived out with love for God; it is a power that demands charity. St. Josemaría sums up the close connection between divine filiation, charity, and priesthood with the expression "*priestly soul.*"[55] A child of God, with all his thoughts, intentions, and affections enlivened by charity, ought to be a contemplative soul dedicated with Christ and out of love for God to *the work of Redemption, the coredemption of the whole human race.*[56] A person who loves God with all his heart is necessarily "an apostolic soul," an expression frequently used by St. Josemaría in *The Way*.[57]

In sum, being a contemplative and priestly (or apostolic) soul are key features of a child of God who loves God—who desires to love him—with all his heart and all his strength.

1.2. Love for One's Neighbor

The virtue of charity also leads a person to love those whom God loves as his children (see 1 John 4:20–21). St. Josemaría's teaching on this topic is quite extensive.

Above all, he emphasizes that *charity toward our neighbor is an expression of our love of God.*[58] This is the traditional doctrine maintaining that "the aspect under which our neighbor is to be loved, is God, since what we ought to love in our neighbor is that he may be in God [. . .]. Consequently the habit of charity extends not only to the love of God, but also to the love of our neighbor."[59] When recalling this truth his words

53. *Christ Is Passing By*, no. 120.

54. See *CCC*, no. 1121.

55. *Furrow*, no. 499. See *The Forge*, no. 369; etc.

56. *The Way of the Cross*, Eleventh Station.

57. See *The Way*, nos. 161, 321, 578, 737, etc.

58. *Friends of God*, no. 232.

59. St. Thomas Aquinas, *S. Th.*, II-II, q. 25, a. 1, c.

powerfully convey something not only known but personally experienced and lived out: *What respect, veneration and affection we should feel for every single soul when we realize that God loves it as his very own!*[60]

Jesus Christ speaks of love of neighbor as a "new" commandment: "A new commandment I give to you, that you love one another; even as I have loved you, that you also love one another. By this all men will know that you are my disciples, if you have love for one another" (John 13:34). Love for God and neighbor was already prescribed in the Old Testament; however, Jesus calls this commandment "new" because he asks to love "as I have loved you." *Love with the love of God,*[61] St. Josemaría often said. This is possible thanks to the gift of the Holy Spirit who makes us children of God and pours into our hearts the charity of Christ.

Awareness of divine filiation enabled him to understand deeply this newly discovered truth and to help many persons live with "the charity of the children of God": the charity proper to those who know that they must be for the others in ordinary life other Christs, Christ himself. Thus, St. Josemaría states,

> *I would like to help you realize that, even after twenty centuries, the Master's commandment is still as strikingly new as ever. It is, as it were, a letter of introduction proving that one is truly a son of God.*[62] *It is indeed still a new commandment because very few people have taken the trouble to practice it* [. . .]. *Our love is to be measured in terms of Jesus' own conduct.*[63]

1.2.1. "Behaving as God's Children toward God's Children"

All of St. Josemaría's teaching on charity with one's neighbor can be summarized in the following phrase: *We have to behave as God's children toward all God's sons and daughters.*[64]

It is worthwhile quoting more of this text, which is especially representative of his thought on this subject:

> *Be mindful of what others are—and first of all those who are at your side: children of God, with all the dignity that that marvelous title entails. We*

60. *The Forge*, no. 34.

61. *Instruction*, 9-I-1935, no. 41 (in italics in the original).

62. *Friends of God*, no. 44.

63. Ibid., no. 223.

64. *Christ Is Passing By*, no. 36.

> *have to behave as God's children toward all God's sons and daughters. Our love has to be a dedicated love, practiced every day and made up of a thousand little details of understanding, hidden sacrifice, and unnoticed selfgiving.*[65]

In this text, the awareness of divine filiation is shown as the foundation for the development of charity that enables a full vision of the diverse aspects of this virtue: those that derive from the personal awareness of being a child of God and those that derive from the consideration that others too are children of God, or called to become children of God.

When speaking of behaving "as God's children toward God's children," charity is understood within the context of radical equality that requires a certain reciprocity. It is not only about giving oneself as a son or daughter of God, like Christ, but seeing the others as children of God, recognizing them as another Christ, Christ himself. It is not only about giving oneself to the other, but also about receiving the other as Christ, as a gift from the Father (see John 3:16). Knowing oneself to be a child of God, and others to be God's sons and daughters, leads to considering oneself as Christ who has come to give his life for his brothers and sisters and, at the same time, to receiving them as gifts from the Father, uniting them to himself as the Letter to the Hebrews states, "Here am I, and the children God has given me" (Heb. 2:13). The mission of the Son is to incorporate into himself God's adopted children to take them to the Father. St. Josemaría's teaching enters deeply into the Christian sense of fraternity based on divine filiation; it leads us to keep in mind that, in some sense, "Christians, more than being many brethren are one: *ipse Christus*."[66] By teaching that the charity of a child of God does not seek his own good but the good of others (see Luke 6:32–35), the awareness of divine filiation takes him to the foundation: charity seeks the good of others because we are "all one in Christ Jesus" (Gal. 3:28), and the others are the brothers and sisters whom "God has given me."

This enables the Christian to detect grave and deep errors that could go unnoticed by someone who is not aware of his divine filiation. For instance, it would not be true charity if someone were to dedicate himself to the service of others but think that he does not need them and does not receive anything from them. This is the "charity" of someone who wishes to feel useful

65. Ibid.

66. Fernando Ocáriz, "La filiación divina, realidad central en la vida y en la enseñanza de Mons. Escrivá de Balaguer," in Idem, *Naturaleza, Gracia y Gloria* (Pamplona: Rialp, 2000), p. 196.

and is more interested in himself than in the good of his brothers. On the outside, his attitude resembles charity, but it is far removed from it because it considers the others as objects. St. Josemaría warns us of this deformity when he writes that the charity of God's children should not be confused *with that somewhat questionable zeal to help others in order to convince ourselves of our superiority. Rather, it means living in peace with our neighbor, venerating the image of God that is found in each and every human being.*[67]

In light of this argument, it is easier to understand the meaning of St. Josemaría's simple affirmation: *Charity does not consist so much in "giving" as in "understanding."*[68] Charity toward others is not addressed to something but to someone, to a child of God. It is not sufficient to give a person what he needs; I need to "understand" his real condition and make it my own. "Understanding" is more than intellectually perceiving a grave need or difficulty even though this is already a lot; it means "embracing" the whole person in his unique circumstances, empathizing with his pain and rejoicing with his joy. Charity is not about giving something to someone while seeing the need of the other as "foreign" to me. Rather, it is about giving myself by giving the things that I can give, all the while perceiving the other's need as my own; and, in recognizing the other as a child of God, I consider him as a gift to me.[69]

Rightly so, St. Josemaría stresses that charity is opposed not only to hatred (to will some evil to another), but also to a more frequent and subtle form of the same sin, which is indifference or, as he emphatically says to describe its evil, the *cruelty of indifference.*[70] This is the attitude of the one who completely neglects a person, acting as if he did not exist, thereby rejecting the gift God has made to us in the others as his children.

Following these basic considerations regarding the subject of charity, let us now discuss the goods that form the object of charity.

Charity moves a person to desire the integral, temporal, and eternal good of the others. This "good," to which all other goods should be

67. *Friends of God*, no. 230.

68. *The Way*, no. 463.

69. This subject has been admirably presented by Pope Benedict XVI in his encyclical *Deus Caritas Est* (December 25, 2005), nos. 34–35. "My deep personal sharing in the needs and sufferings of others becomes a sharing of my very self with them: if my gift is not to prove a source of humiliation, I must give to others not only something that is my own, but my very self; I must be personally present in my gift" (n. 34). "Those who are in a position to help others will realize that in doing so they themselves receive help" (n. 35).

70. *Instruction*, December 8, 1941, no. 64.

ordered, is that the others be holy, that they know and love God on earth, and afterward in heaven (for in this lies the glory of God and man's happiness). St. Josemaría expresses this in various ways. He writes, for example, *For Christians, loving means* [. . .] *working for the good of souls, without discrimination of any kind; trying to obtain for them, before any other good, the greatest good of all, that of knowing Christ and falling in love with him.*[71] This is nothing other than apostolate, to which charity leads: "For the love of Christ urges us [. . .]. We beseech you on behalf of Christ, be reconciled to God" (2 Cor. 5:14, 20).

In consequence, charity fosters helping people to have the necessary means to behave according to the dignity of the children of God called to live holy lives. On the one hand, charity offers them Christian doctrine, the possibility of receiving the sacraments, and guidance from pastors. In a nutshell, it offers them access to the specific means of sanctification (which we will study in chapter nine). On the other hand, it helps them procure living conditions, and conditions of freedom, work, culture, etc., required by human dignity, which are fitting for the sake of holiness. These conditions do not sanctify in themselves, as the sacraments do when received with the proper dispositions, but they are fitting because supernatural life is the elevation of human life. St. Josemaría's teaching, thus, sharply breaks from "spiritualist" errors that the genuine Christian spirit confronted early on.[72] It distinguishes supernatural and eternal goods from temporal human goods, but rather than separating them, it integrates them under the one final end, which is holiness.

Among these means there is an order that should be kept in mind. Considered in themselves, the supernatural means are higher and more important than the natural ones. Among the latter, the spiritual means are superior to the material ones: *Christian charity cannot be limited to giving things or money to the needy. It seeks, above all, to respect and understand each person for who he is in himself, in his intrinsic dignity as a man and child of God.*[73] At the same time, it is obvious that what is noble or important is not always what is more urgent. Many times it is more necessary to provide human means instead of

---

71. *Friends of God*, no. 231.

72. Even St. Augustine, in his day, countered those distortions: "He who loves his neighbor does good to his body as well as his soul, and this does not consist only in going to the doctor, but also in taking care of one's food, drink, clothing, and dwelling place and protecting his body against anything that could be troublesome." *De moribus Ecclesiae catholicae et de moribus manichaeorum*, 1, 28, 56.

73. *Christ Is Passing By*, no. 72. This order is shown in many other texts. See, for example, *The Way*, no. 467.

supernatural ones. However, in thus acting, the Christian does not limit himself to humanitarian action. Charity will prompt him to procure for others the human means in view of what is best for his holiness.[74]

Along this same line of thinking, two opposing defects can be pointed out. The first is to restrict charity to a zeal for providing supernatural means while disregarding the human means. St. Josemaría strongly reproaches such an attitude. He thus states, *Some people tend to see Christianity as a collection of devout practices, failing to realize the relation between them and the circumstances of ordinary life, including the urgency to meet the needs of other people and remedy injustice. I would say that anyone who has that attitude has not yet understood the meaning of the Incarnation. The Son of God has taken the body and soul and voice of a man; he has shared our fate, even to the extent of experiencing the excruciating anguish of death.*[75] It is true that misery, illness, or injustice can be the means and occasion for people to grow in holiness, but it is no less true that he who has the ability to alleviate someone's misery, suffering, or injustice and fails to do so does not advance in holiness.

The second error consists in limiting charity to providing human means, and at times only material ones such as food, housing, healthcare, etc., delaying the supernatural ones from the beginning, or even disregarding them altogether. This would be a heartless charity that does not treat the others as children of God.

Having considered the subject and object of charity, let us now look at its extension. As it is universal, it requires order.

(a) Charity with All: "There Is Only One Race: The Race of the Children of God."

As indicated in a text by St. Josemaría cited earlier, charity does not know discrimination of any type. It has a universal reach because it is based on the love of God who loves all men to the point "that he gave his only Son, that whoever believes in him should not perish but have eternal life" (John 3:16).

> *Like Christ,* [a Christian] *has to live for other men, loving each and every one around him and indeed all humanity.*[76] Charity excludes no one

74. See *Friends of God*, no. 236.

75. *Christ Is Passing By*, no. 98.

76. Ibid., no. 106.

> because *Christ has died for everyone, so that all men and women can come to be children of God and brothers and sisters of ours.*[77]
>
> *So there is only one race, the race of the children of God. There is only one color, the color of the children of God. And there is only one language, the language which speaks to the heart and to the mind, without the noise of words, making us know God and love one another.*[78]

God "who desires all men to be saved" (1 Tim. 2:4) has entrusted his children with a participation in the priesthood of Christ so that they cooperate in the work of Redemption. For St. Josemaría, *charity with everyone means, therefore, apostolate with everyone.*[79] It is a desire for all people to have the spiritual and material means of sanctification and the human means required by human dignity.

The zeal of this charity is not based on a generic "love for mankind" or philanthropy consisting of feelings of solidarity for our fellow human beings.[80] Rather, it is based on a deeper motive: God's personal love for each person. For this reason, as God's children, *we have the strength to love all mankind in a new way.*[81] Philanthropy, however, can be raised to a higher plan by charity, and also serves as a preparation for charity itself. St. Josemaría notes that there are *many upright individuals pursuing noble ideals, even though their motives are often not supernatural, but merely philanthropic. These people face up to all kinds of hardship. They generously spend themselves serving others, helping them overcome suffering and difficulties.*[82] In itself this is a good step on the path to the discovery of Christian charity that gives solidity to the human ideals of fraternity and elevates them.

The universal reach of charity is not just a "good wish," as it would seem to anyone who considers how in real life it is impossible to serve humanity as a whole. This impossibility only exists with respect to direct material services. Going beyond these, there is St. Paul's exhortation "that supplications, prayers, intercessions, and thanksgivings be made for all men" (1 Tim. 2:1). The Christian can and should live universal charity,

---

77. *Letter, March 11, 1940,* no. 7.
78. *Christ Is Passing By,* no. 106.
79. *Friends of God,* no. 230.
80. See *The Way,* no. 280; *Christ Is Passing By,* no. 71; *Friends of God,* no. 235.
81. *Friends of God,* no. 230.
82. Ibid., no. 208.

especially with *prayer that rises to heaven for all mankind,*[83] interceding for the temporal and eternal good of all people. *A Catholic, with his heart open to all men, will pray for all men, because no one can be excluded from his love.*[84] St. Josemaría writes these words referring specifically to the Holy Mass that the Church always offers, not only for the living "*sed etiam pro defunctis*" [also for the dead].[85] Thus, those who have departed from the world are not excluded from this universal charity. *The holy souls in purgatory. Out of charity, out of justice, and out of excusable selfishness—they have such power with God!—remember them often in your sacrifices and in your prayers. May you be able to say when you speak of them, "My good friends the souls in purgatory."*[86]

A child of God, called to sanctify the world through his civil activities, can also practice charity "with all" through his work and the fulfillment of his family and social duties because these activities carried out with a Christian spirit are a service to society as a whole and can be converted into prayer.

> *As you go about your work, doing your job in society, each of you can and should turn your occupation into a real service. Your work should be done well, mindful of others' needs, taking advantage of all advances in technology and culture. Such work fulfills a very important function and is useful to the whole of humanity, if it is motivated by generosity, not selfishness, and directed to the welfare of all, not our own advantage, if it is filled with the Christian sense of life.*[87]

St. Josemaría frequently advises people to carry out their personal work keeping in mind all of humanity,[88] but without forgetting that, *[we] are Christians when we are capable not only of loving humanity in the abstract, but also each person who comes our way* [. . .]: *being kind in a practical way toward those who work alongside us, trying to be a true friend to our colleagues, being concerned about someone's specific need.*[89]

---

83. *Furrow*, no. 518.

84. *Christ Is Passing By*, no. 90.

85. Council of Trent, *Sessio* XXII, *Doctrina et canones de ss. Missae sacrificio*, cap. 2: DS 1743.

86. *The Way*, no. 571.

87. *Christ Is Passing By*, no. 166.

88. See *Friends of God*, no. 118.

89. "The Riches of the Faith," in *Life of Faith* (Scepter Booklet, no. 5 [New York: Scepter, 1974]).

(b) Charity "Especially with Our Brothers and Sisters in the Faith"

St. Paul writes, "let us do good to all men, and especially to those who are of the household of faith" (Gal. 6:10). In one sense, charity leads a person to love all men and women equally and in another sense to love them differently.

As regards *the final end*, charity desires the same for all: their holiness and therefore their happiness, here on earth and afterward fully in heaven.

> This is not opposed to the fact that charity inclines a person to love especially those who have already begun a supernatural life because they are living in the state of grace, and because God loves them more than those who are not his friends (for God loves in us the supernatural life that he has bestowed). Generally speaking, charity desires men to convert from a state of mortal sin to one of sanctifying grace, and that they pass from the state of grace to one of greater friendship with God by means of subsequent conversions.

> "There will be more joy in heaven over one sinner who repents than over ninety-nine righteous persons who need no repentance" (Luke 15:7). The conversion of a sinner who repents from sin (also from venial sin, that is, from all lack of love for God) is a cause for joy in heaven. It produces joy in the blessed and in those who through grace have a foretaste of heaven, because the forgiveness of sins is the greatest manifestation of the love of God, the God who sent his Son saying: "I have not come to call the righteous, but sinners to repentance"(Luke 5:32; see Rom. 5:6–8). That joy is an act of charity.[90]

As regards *the means for the spiritual life*, charity does not seek the same for everyone because the Christian should first seek to make these means available to his brothers in the faith (see Gal. 6:10). The reason for this is that God wishes that they who are formally part of the Church should receive the care of their brethren. The children of God should mutually help one another to live holy lives, just as the members of the body help one another. Charity thus offers the faithful preference in receiving the supernatural and human means that suit their condition as Christians.

Regarding the supernatural means, it is easy to understand that charity inclines a person to help first a child of the Church before someone who is not, as for instance by teaching Christian doctrine to catechumens (or to those

90. St. Thomas Aquinas, *S. Th.*, II-II, q. 28, a. 4, c.

already baptized) before doing so to those who are not.[91] As far as the human means are concerned, from the beginning Christians have helped the neediest among the community such as widows (see Acts 6:1 ff) in material ways. St. Paul organizes a collection "for the poor among the saints at Jerusalem" (Rom. 15:26; see 1 Cor. 16:1–3), and points out that he does this as an act of charity (see 2 Cor. 8:7 ff).[92] Christians should offer assistance to their brothers in need, but no one should claim assistance for what he could obtain through his own effort. The apostle is emphatic on this point: "If any one will not work, let him not eat" (2 Thess. 3:10). A Christian should not take advantage of the Church to obtain material gain: *he must not make use of the sublimity and greatness of the Gospel to further his own interests or human ambitions.*[93] As an early Christian document states, whoever were to do this would be "trafficking upon Christ."[94] The same line in the text warns, "Beware of such men."[95]

Following the Pauline teaching, St. Josemaría fosters charity with a heart open to all, especially toward Christians spread throughout the world. He encourages people to take interest in knowing their situation, initiatives, difficulties, etc. This attitude is the complete opposite of indifference:

> *It is an essential part of the Christian spirit* [. . .] *to feel at one with the rest of one's brothers and sisters in the Faith. For a long time I have thought that one of the worst ills affecting the Church today is the ignorance many Catholics have concerning what Catholics in other countries or sectors of society are doing and thinking. We must rekindle the sense of brotherliness which was so deeply felt by the early Christians.*[96]

---

91. We must not conclude, obviously, that the apostolote *ad fidem*—directed toward non-Catholics so that they might become incorporated into the Catholic Church—should be postponed as long as there are Catholics who are not receiving formation. That would be a simplification, since there are many who refuse that formation while there are non-Catholics who wish to receive it. When Paul and Barnabas preached the Gospel they directed it first of all to the Jews, but when these opposed it, they preached to the pagans. "It was necessary that the word of God should be spoken first to you [the Jews]. Since you thrust it from you, and judge yourselves unworthy of eternal life, behold, we turn to the Gentiles" (Acts 13:46).

92. Along the lines of what we said in the previous footnote, it is worth noting that one might have Christians who are poor because they do not want to work. To these, one might sometimes be more helpful by inviting them to work than by giving them something to eat (see 2 Thess. 3:10). On the other hand, there are many non-Christians in need of material assistance and without the possibility of providing for themselves, whom charity leads one to aid materially without ignoring them because of their ideas or their religion. This is not opposed to the fact that charity inclines one to be especially concerned for Christians, and even more so if they suffer need because of their faith (i.e., because they are persecuted or discriminated against because of their faith).

93. *Christ Is Passing By*, no. 62.

94. *Didaché*, XII, 5.

95. Ibid.

96. *Conversations*, no. 61.

(c) Love for the Poor and the Sick

Besides the supernatural bond of faith, there is a general human bond that justifies a preferential order of charity: the care we ought to have for the poor and the sick. This is an integral and indispensable aspect of true Christian charity.[97]

Solidarity is the name given to that unique relationship of each person with the poor and the infirm, and with those who suffer injustice and loneliness or who are not educated or cultured, etc. In general, there exists an "ontological solidarity" among all men and women based on their membership in the human family, but more specifically, solidarity refers to the bond with persons in need and the virtue that inclines us to establish this bond (i.e., to associate ourselves with others' needs and to seek to remedy those needs).[98] Solidarity refers to the needs of individual persons, not to those of people in general; in other words, solidarity does not consist in having a "social conscience" about poverty overall but little actual concern for the poor person at my doorstep.

St. Josemaría constantly teaches that a Christian cannot live with his back turned to human suffering. *We are not only concerned about the problems of each person; we also feel a full solidarity with our fellow citizens in the calamities and misfortunes that affect the whole society, which affect us in the same way.*[99] In these words, the fact that the suffering is due to "public calamities and misfortunes" is only secondary. The same would hold if the causes were other. What is important is solidarity with those in need, to feel personally affected by them considering them as something personal, and not looking at others' difficulties as something foreign to me.

"Let brotherly love continue [. . .]. Remember those who are in prison, as though in prison with them; and those who are ill-treated, since you also are in the body" (Heb. 13:1–3). There is a special relationship between the Christian and those suffering from pain, ignorance, injustice, poverty, etc. that inspires charity to seek to remedy those needs. This relationship can

97. See *Lumen gentium*, no. 8. The Pontifical Magisterium speaks of "a preferential option for the poor": see, for example, St. John Paul II, Encyclical *Sollicitudo Rei Socialis* (December 30, 1987), no. 42.

98. The term *solidarity* has various connotations. Here it is enough to point out its most general acceptance as knowing and feeling oneself to be in "solidarity," that is linked to others *in solidum* by a common cause which brings with it certain obligations. It is opposed to individualism and lack of interest in the problems of others.

99. *Letter, February 14, 1950*, no. 20. See also, for example, *The Forge*, no. 453, and *Christ Is Passing By*, no. 146.

be described in various ways,[100] but at the core, it is based on a common participation in human nature and the reality of sin, for which we all are responsible and which is the reason why pain and death exist in the world. Without an underlying objective foundation, acts of charity would depend on our response to unreliable feelings and would thus run the risk of being neglected if those feeling are absent or, on the contrary, of leading to the neglect of other perhaps even grave duties.

St. Josemaría warns us of these dangers, especially the first. As a way to foster the character growth of youth, he recommends visiting the poor and sick:

> *The visits to the poor and the sick are a manifestation of charity toward our neighbor and also a marvelous means of formation* [. . .]. *Our friends who take part in our tasks of Christian formation, and we ourselves as well, learn to discover and love in the poor and the sick the human and divine figure of Jesus Christ.*[101]

The last sentence in the above quotation indicates why these visits provide Christian formation: through them, people learn to see Christ in those in need (see Matt. 25:34–40), and thus an essential dimension of love of neighbor is engraved in their hearts. Even though it may not be possible to remedy their material poverty, spending time with the poor is not worthless for it provides the means of practicing the essence of charity, which consists in "understanding" more than in "giving," and in making one's own the

---

100. A traditional method begins with the consideration that the fact of sharing the same human nature implies a certain union among men. One speaks of "the human community" or of "humanity," not only as a simple assemblage of all mankind, but as "the human family," which is formed by generation and education since our first parents and implies certain links to everyone. Inspired by a principle enunciated by Porphyry (s. III-IV), according to which "by their participation in the same species, all men form as it were a single man," St. Thomas Aquinas commented, "Just as in a person there are many members, so in human nature there are many persons." *Comp. Theol.*, c. 196; see *In Ep. ad Rom.*, c. 5, lect. 4. He uses this parallelism above all to explain the transmission of original sin, because participation in the same human nature creates a solidarity of everyone with Adam. "All men born of Adam can be considered a single man insofar as they possess the same nature [. . .] as many members of one same body." *S. Th.*, I-II, q. 81, a. 1, c. And St. Paul teaches that in Adam in some way we have all sinned (see Rom. 5:12–19). The miseries that the other members of the human family suffer as a result of the first sin—such as pain, ignorance, injustices, etc.—have to be seen in some way as our own and caused, to a certain degree, also by personal sins. Something similar is true for the solidarity of all with Christ, the new Adam, the head of redeemed humanity, because he assumed our nature to redeem all who form with him the human race (see Rom. 5:17–21; *In III Sent.*, d. 18, q. 1, a. 6, sol. 1). We have not been saved from outside of human nature, but from within it. Thanks to this we can be coredeemers with Christ, contributing to the repair of the miseries that proceed from sin.

101. *Letter, December 8, 1949*, nos. 192–193. In Opus Dei, these "visits to the poor" (and the sick) are a specific means of formation for young people, practiced and established by the founder in honor of the Blessed Virgin since the beginnings of its foundation.

problems of others. By thus caring for the poor, the Christian acquires the essential outlook that will enable him to address the many needs in the people he encounters, whether spiritual or material. He will be in a position to serve others to the best of his ability and according to his possibilities while at the same time avoiding the error of carrying out "charitable works" without true "charity" and compassion. Someone unable to have compassion with his neighbor's poverty would not carry out true charitable works for the needy; instead of lifting them up, he would end up humiliating them. St. Josemaría laments referring to such attitudes: *How many we have caused to be disaffected among those who are spiritually or materially in need!*[102]

Many Gospel passages show the care employed by the Lord as the one anointed by the Holy Spirit "to preach good news to the poor" (Luke 4:18; see Matt. 11:5).[103] One example is sufficient: "As he landed he saw a great throng, and he had compassion on them, because they were like sheep without a shepherd; and he began to teach them many things" (Mark 6:34). St. Matthew's parallel text reads that he "healed their sick" (Matt. 14:14). Jesus cures illnesses and teaches. He has compassion for the needs of men, his brothers. By assuming our nature "he has borne our griefs and carried our sorrows" (Is. 53:4; see Matt. 8:17).

Being compassionate (making one's own the suffering of others) is the basic attitude needed to remedy those situations materially (where possible) in a way that respects the dignity of the person. It is also the fundamental outlook required to aid others in bearing their pain by helping them understand the redemptive meaning of suffering, a true liberation.[104] Furthermore, a person who exercises Christian compassion can offer to God the suffering of men and women, his brothers and sisters, uniting suffering to Christ's sacrifice. This was St. Josemaría's personal experience in the years following the foundation of Opus Dei, years in which he dedicated himself in large measure to the care of the poor and sick. In addition to offering them human consolation and teaching them the Christian meaning of suffering, St. Josemaría offered up their suffering to God as a precious sacrifice so as to strengthen his petition for the development of the Work that God had entrusted to him:

---

102. *Furrow*, no. 228.

103. When Holy Scripture speaks of the "poor," it is referring at times to those who are oppressed or humiliated but who trust in God (the "poor of Yahweh"); at other times it includes all mankind for, because of sin, we are all indigent.

104. See chapter five, section 3.1.3.

> *Hours and hours going everywhere, day after day, on foot from one place to another among the shamefully and wretchedly poor, so poor that they had not a thing to their name* [. . .] *and in the hospitals, and the homes with sick people* [. . .]. *The human strength of the Work has been the sick people in the hospitals of Madrid: the most forsaken ones; those who lived in their houses having lost the last vestige of human hope; the most ignorant in the remotest corners of the city.*[105]

In order to conclude this section, it is fitting to quote Álvaro del Portillo as he comments on the parable of the Good Samaritan. His intention is to show the evangelical root of St. Josemaría's teaching by explaining how those called to sanctify themselves in their professional, family, and social duties live charity with the poor and the sick.

> The Good Samaritan who interrupts his journey in order to attend to the wounded man and take him to the inn (see Luke 10:30 ff) is "an image of Christ, model of the priestly soul, because suffering is not only a means of sanctification in the person who endures it, but also in the one who has compassion on the sufferer and who is prepared to suffer also to look after their needs. [. . .] Then, once he has personally brought the sick man to the inn, what does the Samaritan do? "He took out two denarii and gave them to the innkeeper, saying, "Take care of him; and whatever more you spend, I will repay you when I come back" (Luke 10:35). He sets off again because he still has other duties he cannot neglect. It is not an excuse, it is not an evasion. He would not have done the right thing if he had stayed longer. He would have been indulging in sentimentality, leaving other obligations unattended. The same charity which formerly made him stop now makes and resume his journey. It is Christ who offers us this example. [. . .] The desire to tend to the material needs of one's neighbor and, where possible to find a remedy for them, without neglecting one's other obligations, like the Good Samaritan did, is a distinguishing feature of the fusion between priestly soul and lay mentality. [. . .] To look after the wounded man the Samaritan enlisted the help of the innkeeper. How could he have managed without him? [St. Josemaría] admired this man, the owner of the inn: he passed unnoticed, yet he

105. Notes taken from preaching, March 19, 1975 (AGP, P09, pp. 217–218).

> did most of the work, acting in his professional capacity. Looking at what he did you rightly conclude, on the one hand, that by carrying out your work you can all do as well as he did, because every occupation offers many opportunities to help the needy, either directly or indirectly. [. . .] On the other hand, concern for the poor and the sick should lead you, inspired by the priestly soul and lay mentality which characterize our spirit, to cooperate in or initiate social programs which aim to remedy, in a truly professional manner, many of mankind's needs.[106]

1.2.2. "Making the Path to Holiness Appealing to Others"

We have discussed how the supernatural bond of the faith and the human bond of solidarity influence the order of charity. Now, let us look at other specific bonds that give rise to obligations of charity, such as family, professional and social relations. St. Josemaría does not hesitate to point out the *false and hypocritical zeal that leads some to be friendly toward those who are far away from us, while they trample on or despise those who share our same faith.*[107] The former exposition is a preparation for what follows: *In the same way, I don't believe that you are genuinely concerned about the poorest of the poor, if you persist in mortifying the people you live with; if you are indifferent to their joys, sorrows or grief.*[108]

Charity is not based primarily on human friendship due to family ties or professional contacts, similar personalities, tastes, or ambitions. Rather, it is founded on the love of God, on the truth that God loves all. This, however, does not mean that friendship has little relevance for charity. On the contrary, there is a very close relation between charity and human friendship. "I have called you friends" (John 15:15); Jesus calls friends those whom he loves with supernatural charity. St. Josemaría states that charity,

> *becomes even more affectionate when its object is* [. . .] *those who, by God's will, are close beside us: our parents, husband or wife, children, brothers and sisters, friends and colleagues, neighbors. Without this affection, which is a noble and pure human love directed toward God and based on him, there would be no charity.*[109]

106. Del Portillo, *Pastoral Letter*, January 9, 1993 (AGP, P17, vol. III, nos. 385–388).

107. *Friends of God*, no. 227.

108. Ibid.

109. Ibid., no. 231.

According to St. Josemaría's teaching, the relation between charity and human friendship can be formulated as follows: when there is pre-existing friendship, charity elevates it, and when friendship does not exist, charity tends to establish it. In both cases, *poured out in our soul by God, charity* [. . .] *provides the supernatural foundation for friendship.*[110] As a result, *in a Christian, in a child of God, friendship and charity are one and the same thing.*[111]

In a meditation, referring to people of the same household (and not to one's "brothers" in the faith in general), St. Josemaría asks, *And how should charity be shown toward your brothers?*[112] And he replies that it should be *by making the path to holiness appealing* [amable] *to them.*[113] The "charity-friendship" preached by St. Josemaría is such that it seeks not only the holiness of one's friends but makes their path to holiness "appealing" or "lovable." This has various manifestations that will be examined in the following sections.

(a) Charity and Friendship

Without defining terms in great detail, as this is a vast topic, let us describe human friendship as a mutual inclination between two persons that leads one to seek the good of the other, not out of self-interest nor simply out of justice, but rather freely and moved also by the sentiments or affections ordered by the moral virtues.

> This is called "virtuous friendship" as it seeks the good of the other and entails the practice of all the virtues. More specifically, prudence and justice are needed to know and to will the true good for the friend (and therefore at least implicitly what God's will is for that person), as well as temperance and fortitude to pursue it.[114] Concerning friendship, Sacred Scripture says, "A faithful friend is a sturdy shelter: he that has found one has found a treasure." (Sir 6:14)
>
> There also exists a friendship that is not virtuous because it does not put into practice the moral virtues and is hence incapable of willing the true good of the other. The latter happens when God is excluded from the friendship. This occurs especially when something

110. *Christ Is Passing By*, no. 71.

111. *The Forge*, no. 565.

112. Notes from a meditation, March 29, 1956 (AGP, P01 VIII-1962, p. 16).

113. Ibid.

114. See St. Thomas Aquinas, *De virtutibus in communi*, a. 5, ad 5.

> that offends God or separates one from him is willed for someone. St. Josemaría refers to this when he asks, *Tell me: is that . . . a friendship, or is it a fetter?*[115] Such a "friendship" is not authentic and cannot be elevated by charity.

When friendship is authentic ("virtuous"), charity elevates it. It is love for others out of love for God that moves a person to will for his friends what God wills for them: that they know and love him as his children, which is the greatest good. It is impossible for charity to "use" friendship as means to an end because it does not seek any other good other than that of the person; on the contrary, it bestows on human friendship a higher foundation, which is more noble and solid. It leads to its fullness since it seeks not only temporal, but eternal happiness. Charity purifies friendship from selfishness because whoever loves in this manner does not seek to be loved for himself, but rather aspires to be loved for God's sake.

Charity also unveils the limits of friendship. *We have to be ready to accompany people, if necessary, to the very gates of hell. But not further, for there no one can love Jesus Christ.*[116] A rightly ordered love for others, which forms part of charity, can only exist when love for God is maintained.

> The parable of the "prudent virgins" (Matt. 25:1 ff) teaches that each person must prepare what is necessary ("the oil") for the encounter with Christ, and that those virgins act rightly by not giving their oil to the "foolish" ones if it means losing it themselves. It goes against charity to offer some help that entails removing oneself from God. A "help" to others that leads to the loss of one's friendship with God cannot be charity. *We can't give away our oil if our own lamp is in danger of going out. This is how the prudent virgins acted: they refused to give their oil to the foolish ones* (see Matt. 25:1 ff.). *So if our soul is in danger, we have to flee, to cut with that person. But if no danger exists, we have to give, to give a lot of oil.*[117]

When a friendship does not previously exist, charity inclines toward establishing it. The Christian should not be satisfied with what St. Josemaría calls an official charity, *something dry and soulless.*[118] He should see in each person a child of God, known and loved by him in a unique manner,

115. *The Way*, no. 160.

116. *Letter, January 9, 1932*, no. 77.

117. Notes taken from preaching, September 15, 1971 (AGP, P01 X-1971, p. 43).

118. *Christ Is Passing By*, no. 167 (the words *official charity* are in italics in the original text).

and for this reason, he should seek to love each one as God loves him, with a rightly ordered affection that always *passes through the Most Sacred Heart of Jesus*[119] as he seeks the good willed by Jesus Christ.

Due to human limitations, it is impossible for anyone to establish a friendship with everyone he or she knows. An important part of the exercise of charity is directed necessarily not to single individuals, but to many people at the same time by means of the service provided to them through professional work, social and educational activities, etc. And yet, it remains undeniably true that *in itself,* charity "seeks" personal one-on-one dealings and friendship with others as it wishes the good of each person. It leads us *to sow understanding and friendship. We should accompany others so that no one is left, or can feel, abandoned.*[120]

(b) "Apostolate of Friendship and Trust"

The apostolic mission to which charity inclines can be carried out in many ways. St. Josemaría emphasizes a specific one: *apostolate of friendship and trust* [confidencia].[121] It becomes visible in the behavior of Jesus, who calls the apostles friends and opens his heart to them, introducing them thus into divine life: "I have called you friends, for all that I have heard from my Father I have made known to you" (John 15:15).

The relationship between charity and friendship described earlier allows us to understand better the value of this form of apostolate in which friendship is enriched and elevated: *When I speak to you about "apostolate of friendship," I mean a personal friendship, self-sacrificing and sincere: face to face, heart to heart.*[122]

Apostolate of friendship and trust fully responds to the spirit of divine filiation. It is a fitting expression of "the love of God's children for God's children," personally loved by God in a unique manner. The friendship that ensues is, therefore, of the deepest kind as it is the most fitting given the dignity of the person, which calls for a dialogue with an open heart and an open mind: it is, in other words, a friendship based on trust. *Friendship fosters trust; and thus it makes possible the apostolate of doctrine, bringing those souls to God, those friends whose good we seek.*[123] The Spanish term "*confidencia*" [which is

---

119. *Letter, February 14, 1974,* no. 23.

120. *Christ Is Passing By,* no. 36.

121. *Furrow,* no. 192. See *Conversations,* no. 62.

122. *Furrow,* no. 191.

being generally translated as "trust" here] indicates two things: communicating something confidential or intimate, and trusting in another person.

This type of apostolate also responds well to the call to sanctify temporal activities in daily dealings with professional colleagues and others in social and family life:

> *You will find in this human fellowship an opportunity to draw souls closer to Christ Jesus, so it's only natural that you won't avoid it. Rather, you need to seek it out, to foster it, because you are apostles, with an apostolate of friendship and trust* [confidencia], *and* [. . .] *your noble and sincere interaction with everyone is the human means for your work with souls.*[124]
>
> *Through personal dealings with your workmates, relatives, friends and neighbors, what I've often called the apostolate of friendship and trust, you will rouse them from their slumber. You will open up to them broad horizons above their selfish and comfort-seeking existence. You will "complicate" their lives, helping them to forget about themselves and understand the problems of those around them. And rest assured that by complicating their lives, you will lead them—you have already experienced it—to* gaudium cum pace, *to joy and peace.*[125]

According to St. Josemaría's teaching, the "apostolate of friendship and trust" is not the only way of living the apostolic mission. Other ways of sowing faith and love for God exist; they differ from the former because they address a number of persons at the same time by means of classes or other activities through which the Christian spirit is spread. But as mentioned earlier, in these circumstances St. Josemaría also encourages as much personal contact as possible, seeking to draw others to God, one by one.

It should be noted that, in general terms, St. Josemaría discourages apostolate of friendship and trust between persons of the opposite sex outside of the realm of family relations or those normally established between a man and a woman looking toward marriage or the possibility of marriage. The reason for this is that, objectively speaking, this apostolate implies the sharing of thoughts, hopes, difficulties, etc. that in persons of opposite sex usually favor mutual attraction. Keeping in mind the disorder of concupiscence, this attraction (outside the realm of the family or of a possible future family) can alter the right intention of the apostolate and even pose a threat

---

123. *Letter, March 11, 1940*, no. 54.
124. *Letter, July 16, 1933*, no. 13.
125. *Letter, January 9, 1959*, no. 16.

to chastity and faithfulness to God (and in the case of a married person to the faithfulness in marriage). Experience bears out the need for this advice. The above does not refer to the general subject of friendship between persons of opposite sex (a subject that is much wider), but specifically rather to "the apostolate of friendship and trust" that St. Josemaría teaches in the context of professional work and social life.

From the same perspective it can also be understood that the group activities of Christian formation such as monthly and yearly retreats, etc. which St. Josemaría promoted and taught others to promote are held separately for men and women because these activities are closely tied to the personal apostolate of friendship and trust (from which they have their origin and toward which they lead). This is so in addition to other reasons of convenience such as that of adapting the content of the formation to the specific needs of the participants.

The spiritual direction provided by priests to women is not an exception to the above because it is not "a personal apostolate of friendship and trust," but rather an exercise of ministry in which the exchange of confidential information is not mutual.

(c) "Human and Supernatural Affection"

In common language, the term "charity" has unfortunately been reduced in significance. To avoid misunderstanding, St. Josemaría teaches that *our charity has to be affectionate, full of human warmth.*[126] He means to point out that charity with those around us should necessarily integrate human affection by elevating it to the spiritual realm. It should be *human and supernatural affection* [cariño], *the authentic charity of Christ.*[127]

To make his point clear he would recall the complaint of a sick woman toward those taking care of her: *they treat me with "charity" here, but my*

---

126. *Christ Is Passing By*, no. 36.

127. Notes taken from preaching (AGP, P01 IX-1955, p. 58). The word "*cariño*" (affection) indicates an affectionate, "human" love that is not an act exclusively and purely of the will, but of the whole person: it arises from the heart (the will, reason, and feelings, as has already been said in chapter five), which does not mean that it is dominated by feelings or that it responds only to them, because then it would not be truly "human" love. In this chapter we will use this term frequently because it serves to transmit the idea that charity includes the feelings and is not something "dry," "cold," "formal," "official," etc. There is also the contrary danger, that "affection" might be interpreted as something sickeningly sweet or sentimental, and perhaps for that reason St. Josemaría frequently used expressions such as "noble and strong affection."

mother used to look after me with affection[128] [*cariño*]. He commented that it is not Christian to separate "charity" from "affection:"

> *A love that springs from the Heart of Christ could never countenance such distinctions* [. . .]. *We do not have one heart with which to love God and another with which to love men. This poor heart of ours, made of flesh, loves with an affection which is human and which, if it is united to Christ's love, is also supernatural. This, and no other, is the charity we have to cultivate in our souls, a charity which will lead us to discover in others the image of our Lord.*[129]
>
> *As Christians we must show that affection of this kind is in fact possible whatever the cynics or skeptics, those disappointed in love, or those with a cowardly outlook on life might say.*[130]

Moreover, St. Josemaría invites us to contemplate the behavior of Christ's first disciples as an example of this profoundly "human" way of living supernatural charity:

> *How well the early Christians practiced this ardent charity which went far beyond the limits of mere human solidarity or natural kindness. They loved one another, through the heart of Christ, with a love both tender and strong. Tertullian writing in the second century tells us how impressed the pagans were by the behavior of the faithful at that time. It was so attractive both supernaturally and humanly that they often remarked, "See how they love one another."* (Tertullian, *Apologeticum*, 39)[131]

The external expressions of affection with those who are closest vary with each person. Naturally there are some external manifestations that are proper in a family setting that would not be proper outside of it. There are other manifestations proper to friendship that involve daily interaction that would be inappropriate in other circumstances. Nonetheless, family relations and the relations of close friendship are the point of reference for the "human affection" proper to charity. *It's not enough to have an official, cold charity. Affection! Human and supernatural. We need to have Christ's*

128. *Friends of God*, no. 229.

129. Ibid.

130. Ibid., no. 233.

131. Ibid., no. 225.

affection, inflamed with love for all mankind, for his Mother, for the apostles, for Lazarus.[132]

For its part, charity gives new meaning to human affection. It purifies it, ennobles it, and frees it from subtle forms of selfishness covered up by politeness or tenderness. Thus St. Josemaría states,

> *When our affection passes through the Most Sacred Heart of Jesus and the Most Sweet Heart of Mary, fraternal charity takes on all its human and divine strength. It makes burdens bearable, it soothes pains, it ensures a cheerful struggle. It's not something that ties us down: it strengthens the wings of the soul to soar higher. Fraternal charity, which doesn't seek its own interest* (see 1 Cor. 13:5), *enables us to fly, to praise God with a spirit of joyful sacrifice.*[133]

Many of St. Josemaría's exhortations about not separating charity from human affection are directed specifically to the faithful of Opus Dei who deal with one another directly in matters of formation and apostolate. For the most part in these cases, human friendship has not previously existed, nor does there necessarily exist affinity of personality, opinions, or tastes. They have been united by a divine call to follow the same specific path of sanctification and apostolate for love of Christ, and this is the foundation for a special *fraternity filled with affection,*[134] which makes it clear that *we are united also by human affection.*[135] He sees in the experience of this reality another example of how the fraternity of the early Christians lives on in the Church. The Scriptures depict it with moving words: "The company of those who believed were of one heart and soul" (Acts 4:32).[136] With joy and gratitude to God, St. Josemaría writes that *more than a few people have discovered the Gospel in the Christian warmth of our home, where no one can feel alone, where no one can suffer the bitterness of indifference.*[137]

(d) "Loving Others with Their Defects"

If you love only the good qualities you see in others—if you do not know how to be understanding, to make allowances for them and forgive them—you are

132. Notes taken from preaching, November 1, 1964 (AGP, P01 I-1966, p. 12).

133. *Letter, February 14, 1974,* no. 23.

134. *Letter, June 16, 1960,* no. 21.

135. *Letter, September 29, 1957,* no. 76.

136. See *The Forge,* no. 632.

137. *Letter, March 11, 1940,* no. 7.

an egoist.[138] Such an attitude is not charity but self-centeredness. St. Josemaría often said that one should love others *with their defects, with their way of being.*[139]

In this context, what does St. Josemaría mean by a "defect"? He certainly does not mean the involuntary absence of a natural quality as for example, a physical limitation, or poor memory, or absence of another natural trait, and even less so, the simple spontaneity of many who lack manners or culture. Regarding this last point, St. Josemaría says, *don't try to change their way of speaking, their way of acting, that delightful and noble lack of sophistication.*[140] By "defect," St. Josemaría refers to the absence of a moral quality that would help the person fulfill his duties better, a quality that in theory he could acquire with the aid of God and personal effort. Examples of such qualities are determination, a spirit of service, cheerfulness, etc. We could explain this concept futher, but it is not necessary to do so to assert that charity leads persons to love others "with their defects." The reason for this is that God does not cease to love people because they have defects, but rather, he loves them "with their defects" insofar as the very defects are or can become an occasion for the person to fight against them out of love for God.

It may appear that "loving others with their defects" contradicts the fact that charity enables one to will the good of the beloved person, precisely because those moral deficiencies that can be remedied are not good in themselves. But St. Josemaría does not teach that charity loves defects in themselves. Rather, charity loves those who (following God's will) behave well in relation to their defects. This implies that they recognize them and seek to overcome them so as to please God and better serve others.

Sanctity consists in struggling, in knowing that we have defects and in heroically trying to overcome them. Sanctity, I insist, consists in overcoming those defects—although we will still have defects when we die; for if not, as I have told you, we would become proud.[141] It is always possible for a person to struggle to improve with more or less success, or to do so later on. For this reason, people should be loved just as they are, even when they do not recognize their faults and do not wish to avoid them. St. Josemaría, writes

138. *The Forge*, no. 954.

139. Notes taken from preaching (AGP, P01 IV-1971, p. 64).

140. *Instruction*, December 8, 1941, no. 95.

141. *The Forge*, no. 312.

José María Barrio, teaches that Christians "should be loved as saints and also loved with their defects. Despite appearances, the two things are not incompatible. In fact, true love means loving the *reality* of the beloved, and this reality includes both positive and less positive aspects. I cannot love someone *because of* his defects, but I can love him *with* his defects. Christian charity truly entails loving others who are fighting against their imperfections and helping them in their struggle, both in a human and supernatural way."[142]

Jesus Christ chose as apostles men who had evident deficiencies. He loved them with a tender affection, even though he knew they would deny him and needed to pray to the Father for their conversion (see Luke 22:31–34). St. Josemaría reminds us that God calls to holiness people *with miseries.*[143] He adds, *I too have them, and have fought and am fighting to overcome them.*[144] The experience of personal human miseries and those of others is no reason for a dampening of charity; on the contrary it is a reason for growing in a deeper charity that is more human and supernatural.

> *Pray for me. I pray for you, and I understand your defects, and I love you as you are, with defects. You should have a big heart, in order to love everyone on this earth with their defects, with their way of being.*
>
> *Father, do you love our defects?*
>
> *When you struggle to get rid of them, I love them, because they are a reason to be humble. As the first Castilian author said, humility is the foundation for all the virtues, and without it there is no true virtue. That is why I love your defects.*[145]

According to these words, it is not a matter of loving a person "in spite of his defects" but of loving him "with his defects," not because they are acceptable, but rather because they lead or can lead him to struggle out of love for for God with humility. In this sense, St. Josemaría even "loves" the defects in themselves. But what if they are conspicuous and disagreeable? Precisely in such cases the unmistakable features of charity stand out since true love for God does not pay attention to the fact that a certain behavior

142. José María Barrio, "Educar en libertad. Una pedagogía de la confianza," in Paul O'Callaghan (ed.), *La grandezza della vita quotidiana*, vol. V/1, pp. 96–97.

143. *Instruction*, May 1935/September 14, 1950, note 84.

144. Ibid.

145. Ibid. The "first Castilian author" is Miguel de Cervantes.

is disagreeable; a person's taste should not be the measure of what is good. Only that which is displeasing to God is in fact "disagreeable." Charity's gaze is able to see what is inside the heart of a neighbor. That is why charity gives little importance to some obvious defects while it gives a lot of importance to others that are less visible and perhaps not socially unacceptable but are displeasing to God. St. Josemaría graphically explains the different manner that an uncouth gesture of a child is viewed by a mother or a stranger. The episode is quoted in a later section since it bears another teaching that we will later discuss. For now the conclusion is sufficient: *Don't show repugnance for small spiritual or material faults that don't have too much importance. Look on your brothers lovingly!*[146]

Another notable characteristic of charity is to love one's neighbor not only when he recognizes his faults and struggles to improve, but also when he does not recognize them or does not wish to change. Charity is love for others with their defects for the main reason that God wishes them to fight to overcome them; he calls them to do so even though they may not presently respond. God gives them time to decide to struggle, and in the meantime counts on the human and supernatural affection of those who are close to them. St. Josemaría advises, *Be filled with joy and be assured that the Lord has granted to all the capacity to become holy precisely by fighting against their own defects.*[147]

At the same time, in teaching to love others with their defects, St. Josemaría does not fail to add: *if they* [the defects] *don't offend God.*[148] Sin cannot please God who said, "You, therefore, must be perfect, as your heavenly Father is perfect" (Matt. 5:48), where being perfect consists in being perfect in love. Therefore the person with defects can please God if he struggles out of love, regardless of whether he gradually overcomes them or whether he spends his life fighting to do so. Sin, on the contrary, is the opposite of love of God: it offends God and cannot be loved. Thus, charity only inclines to desire a person's conversion because that is what God desires. We ought to love the person even if he may offend God, but we cannot love that God be offended.

Loving others with their defects also manifests the profound dimension of charity that enables one to see others as a gift from God. In fact,

146. *Letter, September 29, 1957*, no. 35.

147. *Furrow*, no. 399.

148. Notes taken from preaching, November 18, 1972 (AGP, P11, p. 21).

the others' defects can become an occasion for discovering and correcting one's own. *Diamonds are polished with diamonds, and souls with souls.*[149] In general, this quotation (and the one that follows) refers to the potential that different temperaments and characters have for purifying a person: *Without that friction produced by contact with others, how would you ever lose those corners, those edges and projections* [. . .] *of your character, and acquire the smooth and regular finish, the firm flexibility of charity, of perfection?*[150] Undoubtedly, it applies to defects as well. Our neighbors are a gift from God not only for their positive qualities, but also for their defects. Withdrawing from someone because of his faults would thus be contrary to charity for two reasons: on the one hand, we would not be "giving" the person the help he needs, and on the other hand, we would not be "receiving" what God wishes to give us through that person.

Naturally, if charity leads a person to love others with their miseries, it also leads him to be pleased with their virtues as they reflect the glory of God. The charitable person loves the others with "their good qualities" of health, intelligence, charm, material goods, etc. However, he does not love them for what they have, but for who they are. Charity helps admire more those who use these qualities than those who only possess them. It helps people use their qualities as administrators of goods they have received from God. Charity "is not jealous" (1 Cor. 13:4): it rejoices always for the true good of others.

(e) Understanding, Mercy, and Fraternal Correction

With regard to our neighbor's faults, charity inclines us both to be understanding and to make fraternal corrections.

As far as being understanding, we have already said that charity does not consist only in giving ourselves, but in receiving and making ours the "things of others." If these "things" are miseries, our being understanding with others is called "mercy" because it consists in bearing in one's heart the spiritual and material needs of others.[151] Christ's love is a "merciful love" since he had taken up our sorrows and carried our miseries (see Is. 53:4–5;

---

149. *Furrow*, no. 442.

150. *The Way*, no. 20.

151. See St. Thomas Aquinas, *S. Th.*, I, q. 21, a. 3, c. "Do you not know that having mercy means making oneself miserable, sympathizing with the other person?" (St. Augustine, *De moribus Ecclesiae catholicae et de moribus manichaeorum*, 1, 28, 56).

Matt. 8:17). The love of a Christian should also be merciful: a love that "understands" others' miseries in the sense that it embraces or comprehends them. They should not be foreign to us, but rather be something that is borne as personal and with the clear awareness of the proper need for divine mercy while keeping in mind the Lord's words: "Blessed are the merciful, for they shall obtain mercy" (Matt. 5:7).

Mercy is a form of charity proper to parents just as the parable of the prodigal son shows (see Luke. 15:20–24). God the Father is "rich in mercy" (Eph. 2:4). Mercy, however, is also proper to children with regard to their siblings, toward whom they should have the heart of a father, like that of Christ, who being "the first-born among many brethren" (Rom. 8:29), calls his disciples "sons" or "my little children" (see John 13:33) because he is in the Father and the Father is in him (see John 14:10–11).[152] To show this aspect of charity in a graphic way, St. Josemaría evokes the affection of mothers who see defects in a positive light. Thus, St. Josemaría says,

> *Seeing our Lord's example, show understanding for your brothers with a very big heart, which is not shocked by anything. Truly love them. I love you as your mothers do: because you are trying to be saints and because you are so "charming"* [. . .]. *By being very human, you will know how to pass over small defects in others, and with motherly understanding you will always see the good side of things. In a graphic, joking way, I've pointed out the different impressions people have of the same event depending on whether they look on it affectionately or not. And I told you—forgive me because it's very graphic—about the child who goes about with his finger in his nose. Visitors remark, "How dirty!;" while his mother says, "He's going to be a researcher!" My children, you understand what I'm trying to say: we have to forgive. Don't show repugnance for small spiritual or material faults that don't have too much importance. Look on your brothers lovingly and you'll reach the same conclusion, full of charity, that* we're all researchers![153]

God's merciful love manifests itself not only in not rejecting any of his children; he also corrects them so that they conform to the image of his Son. It is a correction done for our good, which Sacred Scripture exhorts us to receive as a sign of love: "My son, do not regard lightly the discipline of the Lord, nor lose courage when you are punished by him, for the Lord

152. See chapter four, section 1.2.3.

153. *Letter, September 29, 1957*, no. 35.

disciplines him whom he loves, and chastises every son whom he receives" (Heb. 12:5–6). Jesus corrects the apostles on various occasions, sometimes even energetically, as when Peter tries to oppose the prediction of his Passion: "Get behind me, Satan! You are a hindrance to me; for you are not on the side of God, but of men" (Matt. 16:23). He corrects him to impede him from turning him from the good or tempting him to evil that is proper to Satan. He corrects him for love for the Father as well as because he loves Peter.

On another occasion, Jesus teaches his disciples that they should know how to correct others when necessary. "If your brother sins against you, go and tell him his fault, between you and him alone. If he listens to you, you have gained your brother" (Matt. 18:15).[154] Charity is understanding and it inclines a person to make fraternal correction, when the good of souls requires it. Understanding and making one's own others' miseries does not mean justifying them or calling good what is evil. *To understand and forgive doesn't mean to accept things that are unjust, because that would also be a disorder and would cause harm.*[155] Understanding should not be confused with the attitude of the "goody-goody friend" who approves of everything. More than true understanding, it is lack of concern and neglect for the true good of the other.

St. Josemaría clearly saw the importance of practicing fraternal correction as *a clear sign of the supernatural virtue of charity,*[156] as *a proof of supernatural affection and trust*[157] and *the best way to help next to prayer and good example.*[158] The greatness of fraternal correction consists in that *at that moment you are God's instrument.*[159] It has a clear priestly character that is recognized by the sacrifice it demands: *You may find it hard, for it's easier to be reticent. It's easier to behave that way, but it's not supernatural. And you will have to render an account to God for such omissions.*[160] In addition to reminding people of the value of this custom, St. Josemaría fostered the practice of fraternal correction

154. Although charity corrects what separates us from God, in this text Jesus says, "if your brother sins *against you,*" and not "if he sins *against God.*" A way of understanding this is to consider that the correction refers to faults that can be noticed by others, not those that only God knows, such as the intentions of the heart. The correction is not to be made by judging the person's intentions, but only the deeds that are manifested externally. I correct the one who sins "against me" because I recognize something that I can note as a fault, but I correct it because it is displeasing to God.

155. *Letter, September 29, 1957,* no. 34.

156. *The Forge,* no. 146.

157. Ibid., no. 566.

158. Ibid., no. 641.

159. Ibid., no. 147.

160. Ibid., no. 146.

as a sign of loyalty toward others, and as a means of safeguarding unity with one another and with ecclesial authorities (see Gal. 2:14).

Nonetheless, St. Josemaría warns of the danger of subjectivism. *What we see as defects in others are often the product of our defective vision.*[161] And for this reason he advises people to examine themselves on the same point before correcting someone else. Perhaps it is something which is not objectively a fault but only displeasing.

The defects you see in others are perhaps your own. "Si oculus tuus fuerit simplex . . ."—If your eye is clear, the whole of the body will be lit up; whereas if the eye is diseased, the whole of the body will be in darkness. Moreover: "How is it that you can see the speck of dust in your brother's eye, and are not aware of the beam that is in your own?"[162]

In order to ensure objectivity and right judgment, St. Josemaría taught people to consult the person who has authority and prudence to discern the appropriateness of the correction before making it.

(f) Knowing How to Forgive: "Drowning Evil in an Abundance of Good"

When St. Josemaría wishes to show the greatness of the love of God, Creator and Redeemer, he finds the greatest expression in the forgiveness of sins. *A God who forgives! Isn't that marvelous?*[163] *To forgive is something divine.*[164] This is why it is so characteristic of the children of God to do so. *The character of a person who knows how to forgive is marked by something divine, because only God can teach us to forgive in that way.*[165]

"You have heard that it was said, 'You shall love your neighbor and hate your enemy.' But I say to you, Love your enemies and pray for those who persecute you, so that you may be sons of your Father who is in heaven" (Matt. 5:43–45). St. Josemaría comments on these words as follows:

> *We might not feel humanly attracted to those who would reject us were we to approach them. But Jesus insists: we must not return evil for evil; we must not waste any opportunities we have of serving them wholeheartedly, even if we find it difficult to do so; we must never cease keeping them in mind in our prayers.*[166]

---

161. Notes taken from preaching, May 4, 1968 (AGP, P02 October-1968, p. 48). See *Furrow*, no. 644.
162. *Furrow*, no. 328. See Matt. 6:22–23; 7, 3–5.
163. Notes taken from preaching, April 13, 1972 (AGP, P01 VI-1972, p. 45).
164. Notes taken from preaching, April 7, 1974 (AGP, P01 V-1974, p. 72).
165. Notes taken from preaching, May 18, 1974 (AGP, P01 October-1974, p. 97).
166. *Friends of God*, no. 231.

A Christian should not consider himself an enemy of anyone because this would mean willing evil to someone, and whoever follows Christ should always will good to all. *Have no enemies. Have only friends: friends on the right—if they have done or have wished to do you good; and on the left—if they have harmed or tried to harm you.*[167]

It can happen that others consider a Christian their enemy out of human motives such as differing in opinion, having opposing interests, experiencing envy, etc., or precisely for being a disciple of Christ, who himself announced, "you will be hated by all nations for my name's sake" (Matt. 24:9).

Charity also leads us to love these "enemies," and to implore God's forgiveness for them, just as Christ did on the Cross, "Father, forgive them; for they know not what they do" (Luke. 23:34). A Christian ought to desire their conversion, not primarily so that he will cease to suffer at their hands, but rather so that they cease to offend God and live as his good children. Referring to love toward one's enemies, the Lord teaches, "To him who strikes you on the cheek, offer the other also; and from him who takes away your cloak do not withhold your coat as well" (Luke. 6:29). Clearly what counts least is to be offended and to suffer ill treatment; if that were the only harm we suffered, charity would tolerate and endure it. What is grave is that that kind of behavior goes against God because his children are treated unjustly.

St. Paul sums up this Christian attitude in the following manner: "Repay no one evil for evil, but take thought for what is noble in the sight of all. If possible, so far as it depends upon you, live peaceably with all. Beloved, never avenge yourselves, but leave it to the wrath of God; for it is written, 'Vengeance is mine, I will repay, says the Lord.' No, 'if your enemy is hungry, feed him; if he is thirsty, give him drink; for by so doing you will heap burning coals upon his head.' Do not be overcome by evil, but overcome evil with good" (Rom. 12:17–21). From these words St. Josemaría concludes,

> *We have to understand everyone; we must live peaceably with everyone; we must forgive everyone. We shall not call injustice justice; we shall not say that an offense against God is not an offense against God, or that evil is good. When confronted by evil we shall not reply with another evil, but rather with sound doctrine and good actions: drowning evil in an abundance of good.* (see Rom. 12:21)[168]

---

167. *The Way*, no. 838.

168. *Christ Is Passing By*, no. 182.

Charity with such persons may at times require doing everything within our power to impede their wrongdoing while at other times it may lead to tolerating it. Jesus occasionally hid from those who sought to kill him (see John 8:59; 12:36), but when his hour came, he did not impede his crucifixion, and he asked the Father to forgive his executioners. The path for others to convert does not always mean preventing them from committing an injustice (see 1 Pet. 3:14–17), especially when someone acts wrongly and does harm, yet thinks he is doing good. It may even happen *that people dedicated to God are the instrument for doing evil,* putantes se obsequium praestare Deo, *thinking they are serving God.*[169] St. Josemaría suffered much in this manner and gave example of heroic charity by praying for those who persecuted him and using those attacks as an occasion for personal purification and penance. In the case of both those who wished to do him ill for the sake of going against God and those who thought to serve God, he taught people to love their persecutors, and to consider persecution as an occasion of identifying oneself with Christ. For St. Josemaría, this attitude was the source of a joy and peace that were humanly inexplicable.[170]

1.3. Love for Oneself Out of Love for God

Charity denotes "man's friendship with God in the first place, and, consequently, with the things of God, among which things is man himself who has charity. Hence, among these other things which he loves out of charity because they pertain to God, he loves also himself out of charity."[171] Let us use these words of St. Thomas Aquinas as a springboard to present St. Josemaría's teaching.

1.3.1. Seeking One's Own Holiness

Above all, we should mention the relationship between upright love of self and love of God. For St. Josemaría, charity moves a person to address God in a trusting, filial manner telling him, *I want what You want, in everything.*[172] And what God desires for everyone is for the person to be united with him. In a word, this is the essence of holiness that produces perfect happiness.

---

169. *Letter, September 14, 1951,* no. 11. See John 16:2.

170. See Vázquez de Prada, *The Founder of Opus Dei,* vol. I, pp. 168 ff.; vol. II, pp. 334 ff.; vol. III, pp. 136 ff. and 402 ff.

171. St. Thomas Aquinas, *S. Th.*, II-II, q. 25, a. 4, c.

172. *The Forge,* no. 529.

Rightly ordered love of oneself, therefore, seeks holiness and the means to achieve it. This is the supreme good that should be desired for oneself and to which all other desires should be subordinated. *All that which worries you for the moment is of relative importance. What is of absolute importance is that you be happy, that you be saved.*[173] This point merits closer inspection.

Charity seeks to be what God wants us to be: saints, perfect in love (see Eph. 1:4) with a perfection that includes all the Christian virtues. As a result, charity fosters employing all the necessary means to achieve that goal: the supernatural ones (e.g., the sacraments and prayer) and the human ones among which we can distinghuish spiritual ones (culture, civic freedoms, etc.) and material ones (health and material well-being).

It is noteworthy to point out that the material conditions of life are important because they are meant to foster human and Christian perfection. St. Josemaría asserts that it is fitting to have *a minimum of well-being in order to practice the Christian virtues, to be able to work and to develop the human personality with dignity and without undue tensions.*[174] This material well-being was evident in an exemplary way in *the simplicity of the home at Nazareth which was the witness to Jesus' hidden life.*[175] At other times, St. Josemaría refers to a *minimum of well-being indispensable for the ascetical struggle and for apostolate,*[176] and *for being able to work earnestly for years in the service of God and souls.*[177] Of course, material well-being is not an absolute necessity strictly speaking, since even the privation of basic material conditions can be transformed into a means for union with Christ. Under normal circumstances, however, it is a relative need for sanctifying oneself from within civil and secular activities.

In this sense it is important for a person to care for his health and to be in good physical shape, not out of vanity or self-praise, but out of love for God.

> *We joyfully accept sickness, when God sends it to us; but we should do all we can to be healthy and strong, in order to work for Christ, for the Church, and for souls.*[178] *You should therefore take care of yourselves, so that you die old, very old, squeezed out like a lemon, accepting from now on the Will of the Lord.*[179]

---

173. *The Way*, no. 297.
174. *Letter, May 6, 1945*, no. 22.
175. Ibid.
176. *Letter, July 29, 1965*, no. 34.
177. Ibid., no. 45.
178. *Instruction*, 31 May, 1936, no. 67.
179. Ibid., note 95.

> St. Thomas holds that "man ought to love his own body out of charity," and he offers the following explanation: "Our bodies can be considered in two ways: first, in respect of their nature, secondly, in respect of the corruption of sin and its punishment. Now the nature of our body was created, not by an evil principle, as the Manicheans pretend, but by God. Hence we can use it for God's service: 'Present your members as instruments of justice unto God' (Rom. 6:13). Consequently, out of the love of charity with which we love God, we ought to love our bodies also."[180] This reflection lies at the foundation of the teaching of St. Josemaría just mentioned. The words that follow help us to understand how for Christians, corporal mortification does not contradict love for the body (see chapter eight): "We ought not to love in the body the evil effects of sin and the corruption of punishment; we ought rather, by the desire of charity, to long for the removal of such things."[181]

Jesus' triumphal entry into Jerusalem seated on a donkey prompted St. Josemaría to make the following comparison with the Christian who should also serve God with his body:

> *For our body is, at the same time, both the friend and the enemy of our supernatural life. If we "kill" it, our Lord won't have a donkey to ride on. We have to strive to ensure that the little donkey is docile, but also that it is strong and healthy, so it can carry out its task of serving God.*[182]

Above we concluded that a rightly ordered love of self is an integral part of charity, inseparable from the love we have for God. However, a rightly ordered love of self is also inseparable from the love we ought to have for others. A person who does not love himself in an upright manner would be unable to enter into friendship with others because in both cases what is loved is that which God loves. Furthermore, the measure of love of neighbor is love of self according to the words of Scripture: "you shall love your neighbor as yourself" (Lev. 19:18; see Matt. 22:39; Mark 12:31).

It may be useful to mention one of St. Thomas's explanations to understand these words of Scripture and the affirmation we cited earlier: "we should behave as children of God with the children of God." Taking as a starting point that friendship is the foundation for charity with others,

---

180. St. Thomas Aquinas, *S. Th.*, II-II, q. 25, a. 5, c.

181. Ibid.

182. *Letter, July 29, 1965*, no. 46.

Aquinas notes, "A man is not a friend to himself, but something more than a friend, since friendship implies union, for 'love is a unitive force' [. . .] and everybody has a union with himself that is greater than every other union."[183] Therefore, the precept "you shall love your neighbor as yourself" indicates that love for others should be such that it establishes a union with them that is analogous to the union that one has with himself. This is possible through Christ's grace, which repairs the inner disintegration produced by sin and unites all in the unity of the Blessed Trinity (see John 17:23, 25–26).

St. Josemaría speaks of the need for this love of oneself for the sake of loving others in speaking especially of the apostolate. A disciple of Christ must be concerned with seeking his own holiness, using the necessary means, if he really wishes to help others to live holy lives. Thus, he states, *Apostolic soul: first of all, yourself.* [. . .] *God forbid—says Saint Paul—that I, who have preached to others should myself be rejected.*[184]

On the other hand, a person who does not love others is unable to love himself because this love implies seeking for oneself the good willed by God, and an integral part of this good is being in communion with others, especially one's closest neighbors. In order to reach one's own perfection, it is necessary to give oneself to others.[185]

1.3.2. Rejecting "Self-love": "Self-denial" and "Self-forgetfulness"

At the same time that the Lord teaches love for oneself, he also declares that if someone "does not hate his own life" he cannot be his disciple (see Luke 14:26). At first sight this seems contradictory, but it is not if one considers that next to an ordered love for oneself there is another love of self that stands in opposition to charity. This is not only a "lack of love of God," but rather "love for oneself instead of love for God," a disordered "self-love" or "selfishness," which is the most basic expression of idolatry. A Christian should not love himself in this manner; he should flee from idolatry and hate it. True charity seeks one's perfection and happiness because God wishes it, and it rejects or hates a self-fulfillment that turns its back on God. St. Josemaría expresses this in a very strong manner saying, *If life's purpose were not to give glory to God, how contemptible, how hateful it would be.*[186]

183. St. Thomas Aquinas, *S. Th.*, II-II, q. 25, a. 4, c.

184. *The Way*, no. 930.

185. Man "cannot fully find himself except through a sincere gift of himself." *Gaudium et Spes*, no. 24.

186. *The Way*, no. 783.

A disordered self-love is evident when a person wishes for himself things that are clearly opposed to God's law. But there can also be selfishness when something licit in itself is pursued without regard to God's will in that specific matter. A selfish person is not a person who wishes something for himself, but rather one who wishes it in a disordered manner. That is why good things, which can arguably be chosen out of love for God, can also be sought out selfishly. Those deliberately seeking holiness are more exposed to this type of distorted self-love. St. Josemaría describes it in a point of *Furrow* that helps to unmask veiled forms of this disorder:

> *You fulfill a demanding plan of life: you rise early, you pray, you frequent the sacraments, you work or study a lot, you are sober and mortified, but you are aware that something is missing.*
>
> *Consider this in your conversation with God: since holiness, or the struggle to achieve it, is the fullness of charity, you must look again at your love of God and your love of others for his sake. Then you may discover, hidden in your soul, great defects that you have not even been fighting against. You may not be a good son, a good brother, a good companion, a good friend, a good colleague. And, if you love your "holiness" in a disordered manner, you are envious.*
>
> *You "sacrifice" yourself in many small personal details, and so you are attached to yourself, to your own person. Deep down you do not live for God or for others, but only for yourself.*[187]

These words are meant to warn of a danger that is always at bay because it is not sufficient for our actions to be good in virtue of their object; they should also be good in virtue of their proximate and final end. If it is for self-love rather than love of God, even the holiest of actions are corrupted; personality develops in a manner contrary to Jesus Christ, who is the model of perfect love of self precisely because he has come to give himself completely for others.

> *Turn your gaze constantly to Jesus who, without ceasing to be God, humbled himself and took on the nature of a slave* (see Phil. 2:6–7) *in order to serve us.* [. . .] *Christ brings us face to face with the ultimate choice: either we spend our life in selfish isolation, or we devote ourselves and all our energies to the service of others.*[188]

---

187. *Furrow*, no. 739.
188. *Friends of God*, no. 236.

"If any man would come after me, let him deny himself and take up his cross and follow me" (Matt. 16:24). In everyday language, "to deny oneself" or "to practice self-denial" is to renounce self-interests and to be ready to sacrifice oneself for the good of another. Christian self-denial is a much deeper reality; it is an aspect of charity and hence principally refers to God. It is a denial of oneself before God, a renunciation of being something by oneself without God, a rejection of disordered self-love, and an affirmation of the love of God united to the desire of following Christ by carrying the cross.

Only by grasping this radical meaning of self-denial can we understand its positive value in the Christian tradition and in the form St. Josemaría expresses it in the following personal testimony:

> *Looking at my life, I see quite honestly that I myself am nothing, am worth nothing and have nothing, that I can do nothing and, even more, that I am nothingness itself! But he is everything and, at the same time, he belongs to me and I to him because he does not reject me and has given himself up for me. Have you ever seen a greater love than this?*[189]

Affirmation of one's "nothingness" does not contradict the truth that God has communicated his being to us. "I am nothing" does not mean "I am absolutely nothing," but rather, "I am nothing on my own," that is, there is no being or good in me because of myself and therefore I should love myself for God's sake, rather than for my own sake. This is St. Paul's own teaching: "What have you that you did not receive? If then you received it, why do you boast as if it were not a gift?" (1 Cor. 4:7). Christian "self-denial"—the self-denial practiced by a child of God—implies the affirmation that all the good within that person is a gift from God and that it should be loved for God's sake. A Christian denies any personal good that does not come from God whereby the denial becomes a greater recognition of his dignity as a child of God. With this radical awareness of being "nothing," man stops seeking his own interest and sacrifices himself out of love for God and others.

Ordinarily, renouncing to commit a sin (i.e., an action whose moral object is evil) is not called "self-denial." But even if it were, Christian self-denial is not limited to rejecting sin; it is the renunciation of things that are good and licit for love of God and neighbor and for the service of others.

---

189. Ibid., no. 215. See *The Way*, no. 731.

> *"What do I have to do to maintain my love for God and make it increase?" you asked me, fired with enthusiasm. Leave the "old man" behind, my son, and cheerfully give up things which are good in themselves but hinder your detachment from yourself. You have to repeat constantly* [with words] *and with deeds, "Here I am, Lord, ready to do whatever you want."*[190]

Under this light, it becomes clear that Christian "self-denial" is not a negative attitude, but one rather that is charged with the love of God. There is nothing in the spiritual life that is pure self-denial, not even as a condition for a subsequent affirmation (as in denying oneself in order to be able to love God later). Self-denial is already love for God; it is an affirmation. Jesus' invitation, "If any man would come after me, let him deny himself and take up his cross and follow me" (Matt. 16: 24) does not mean that in following Christ there is first a negative "step" (denying onself) followed by a positive one (taking up the cross); rather denying onself out of love has in itself a redemptive value (it is to take up the cross), and every "taking up of the cross" implies self-denial. It means to *become less selfish and let Christ grow in us, for* illum oportet crescere, me autem minui (John 3:30), *he must become more and more, I must become less and less.*[191]

"Self-forgetfulness" is another term frequently used by St. Josemaría. It is the deepest expression of self-denial. It is not only about leaving behind any selfish interest; it is not even thinking about oneself so as to be only concerned in loving and serving God and others. It is self-denial taken to what is most intimate: to thoughts, memories, imagination, etc., so that they will not revolve around one's ego. To forget oneself means to put God at the center.

Every person has a tendency toward having an interior monologue in which the self is usually exalted. Self-forgetfulness out of love for God tends to substitute this monologue with a dialogue with God the Father, the Son, and the Holy Spirit who is present in the soul in grace. It is an attitude of absolute love for God, a recognition that he is the origin, end and center of everything; it means living in a radical manner on God, in God, and for God, without allowing oneself to occupy the place that only belongs to him.

St. Josemaría goes as far as to say that *we don't love God if we are concerned only about our own sanctity: we have to be concerned about the others, about the sanctity of our brothers and all souls.*[192] A Christian should not be

190. *The Forge*, no. 117.

191. *Christ Is Passing By*, no. 58.

192. Notes from a meditation, March 3, 1963 (AGP, P09, pp. 63–64).

self-centered, not even in what refers to "his" own path to holiness because charity leads a person to holiness for the sake of God, not for "the sake of being holy."

Self-forgetfulness is also necessary in order to live charity fully with others. *Charity, holy affection, consists in forgetting about yourself and being concerned about the others. You aren't anything. The others are everything in Christ.*[193] This attitude should imbue the soul in such a way that it constitutes a sort of "prejudice," the "*psychological prejudice*" *of thinking habitually about the others.*[194]

When the life of a child of God has God, Christ, and the Church as its center, the personality is centered on a solid foundation while that of a selfish person is for the same reason off-center, self-absorbed, and subject to conflicts.[195]

> *Almost all those who have personal problems, have them because they selfishly think about themselves. What we have to do is to give ourselves to others, to serve others for the love of God: that's the way to make our sorrows disappear. Most of our difficulties stem from forgetting about the service we owe to others and getting caught up in our own ego.*[196]

In the end, for St. Josemaría, the growth in charity, and therefore in the Christian life, is recognized by self-forgetfulness and a corresponding concern for others.

> *When at night you do that small exam and you have to say at the end: Lord, but I haven't thought about myself! I've been concerned about the others . . . That day you have done very well, because you have lived like St. Paul, and you can say that it is not you who lives, but Christ who lives in you.*[197]

---

193. Notes taken from preaching (AGP, P01 III-1970, p. 10).

194. Notes from a meditation, March 3, 1963 (AGP, P09, pp. 63–64).

195. We are not speaking of pathological cases. The citation of St. Josemaría that we reproduce begins prudently with the words "Almost all" because not all of those who have "personal problems"—and he is not referring to the preoccupations or concerns that are never lacking in anyone who loves, but to those conflicts which show a lack of interior unity—have them because of egoism. There are those who suffer psychological sicknesses which have those effects and, nevertheless, love God with all of their heart and sanctify those difficult situations. St. Josemaría was not speaking here of those cases, but of interior conflicts in persons with sufficient personal health issues that proceed from the "egoism of thinking of oneself." Much less is he saying that all "personal problems" can be resolved simply with good will. At times he would refer certain cases to doctors (see *The Way*, no. 706).

196. *Letter, March 24, 1931*, no. 15.

197. Notes taken from preaching, April 9, 1974 (AGP, P01 V-1974, p. 134).

2. Life of Faith and Hope

The entire life of a child of God must be presided over by charity, but there is no charity without faith and hope. Charity presupposes both virtues since God cannot be loved without knowing him (faith) or aspiring to be united with him (hope).[198]

At the same time faith and hope must be *informed* by charity; only in this way are they "alive" and unite the Christian to God.[199] The same Holy Spirit who infuses charity guides us "into all the truth" (John 16:13) and communicates a hope that "does not disappoint us" (Rom. 5:5). Thanks to charity, both faith and hope acquire the perfection of love and are converted into a force at the service of charity itself. We can thus say that, *to live according to the Holy Spirit means to live by faith and hope and charity.*[200]

Since these pages refer to the spiritual life of those in the state of grace, we will limit our discussion to a "living" faith and hope, informed by charity, and we will not discuss the so-called "dead" faith and hope. To be accurate, the topic of our discussion will continue to be simply charity because every act of living faith and hope is also an act of charity. When we say that the Christian life is a "life of faith," we mean that charity is not a "blind" love, but rather one enlightened by faith. Similarly, when we commonly say that the Christian life is a "life of hope," it means that charity is not a love that "despairs," but rather one joyfully filled with the hope of heaven.

Faith and hope are virtues for this life, not for the future life. In glory, faith will be substituted by the vision of God and hope by blessedness in God. In the "beatific vision," charity will no longer need the other theological virtues (see 1 Cor. 13:8–13).

2.1. Life of Faith

"Without faith it is impossible to please [God]" (Heb. 11:6); it is impossible to love him. Charity, which resides in the will, "is not foreign to reason."[201] For Christian life to be presided by charity, it must be enlightened by faith.

---

198. "*Caritas est radix fidei et spei, inquantum dat eis perfectionem virtutis. Sed fides et spes, secundum rationem propriam, praesupponuntur ad caritatem, ut supra dictum est. Et sic caritas sine eis esse non potest.*" St. Thomas Aquinas, *S. Th.*, I-II, q. 65, a. 5, ad 2; see q. 62, a. 4, c.

199. See ibid., q. 65, a. 5, ad 1.

200. *Christ Is Passing By*, no. 134. On the biblical terms corresponding to these three virtues, see Mieczyslaw Lubomirski, *Vita nuova nella fede, speranza e carità* (Rome: Cittadella, 2000), pp. 19–185. He studies faith and hope in greater depth.

201. St. Thomas Aquinas, *S. Th.*, II-II, q. 24, a. 1, ad 2.

It has to be a "life of faith," a "faith working through love" (Gal. 5:6).[202] A living faith is not only something of the intellect. As Arturo Blanco points out, St. Josemaría has "an understanding of the faith that brings it in relation with the whole person, not only the intellect."[203]

"To believe" is *credere aliquid alicui*, to believe something said by someone. It always implies these two aspects: to believe a truth and to believe the person who communicates it. In the case of supernatural faith, it calls for "belief in revealed truth" and "belief in God who reveals it." But in addition it includes a third aspect: to try to live according to that truth. St. Augustine synthesizes these three dimensions of the faith with the well-known expression *credere Deo, credere Deum, credere in Deum*:[204] "to believe God" or to trust in him, "to believe what he has revealed" (to hold the doctrine he has revealed as true) and "to believe in God" (to go toward him by living according to what he has revealed).

St. Augustine's notion embraces the essential characteristics of faith[205] and can therefore aid in expounding what St. Josemaría teaches since he too refers to all the aspects of faith, as can be seen in his homily "Life of Faith."[206] There, he comments on two Gospel passages that narrate the cure of two blind men: the one Jesus sent to the pool of Siloam after having touched his eyes with clay and spittle (see John 9:6–7); and the one who begged at the gates of Jericho (Mark 10:46–52). In both cases, St. Josemaría compares faith with the eyesight they lack, emphasizing thus that faith is knowledge of the truth: *credere Deum*. Furthermore, in the first case he emphasizes the

---

202. The statement that "charity presupposes faith" can be understood as referring to a dead faith or to a living faith. The first case refers to those who are not in the grace of God and the expression means that in order to receive charity and to begin to love God, it is necessary "first" (temporally) to believe in him. The second case refers to the one who enjoy the grace of God and thus the expression means that the love of God "presupposes" a *living faith*, not in a temporal sense but in the very act of believing. Here we employ the expression in this second sense.

203. Arturo Blanco, "Alcuni contributi del beato Josemaría alla comprensione dei rapporti tra fede e ragione," in Paul O'Callaghan (ed.), *La grandezza della vita quotidiana*, vol. V/1, p. 259.

204. St. Augustine, *Sermo de Symbolo*, c. 1. St. Thomas Aquinas uses this expression: see, for example, *S. Th.*, II-II, q. 2, a. 2, c.

205. For reasons of space, here we will not be able to discuss some other aspects of importance for the spiritual life such as the *motives of credibility* which make it reasonable to believe; the *voluntary character of the act of faith*, which, under the action of grace, makes it possible for us to believe in the very foundation of the faith (i.e., we believe everything God has revealed because we believe in God who has revealed it): this is not contrary to reason but rather surpasses it, and that is why believing implies a voluntary self-surrender to God. On these subjects, see Fernando Ocáriz and Arturo Blanco, *Revelación, fe y credibilidad* (Madrid: Palabra, 1998), ch. 7; Arturo Blanco and Antonio Cirillo, *Cultura e Teologia. La Teologia come mediazione specifica tra fede e cultura* (Milan: Edizioni Ares, 2001), ch. 3.

206. See *Friends of God*, nos. 190 ff.

blind man's trust; he trusts in the Lord and goes to wash where he is told: an example of faith as *credere Deo.*

> *What an example of firm faith the blind man gives us! A living, operative faith. Do you behave like this when God commands, when so often you can't see, when your soul is worried and the light is gone? What power could the water possibly contain that when the blind man's eyes were moistened with it they were cured? Surely some mysterious eye salve, or a precious medicine made up in the laboratory of some wise alchemist would have done better. But the man believed; he acted upon the command of God, and he returned with eyes full of light.*[207]

In the case of the other blind man, Bartimaeus, who says to Jesus, "Master, let me receive my sight!" (Mark 10:51), St. Josemaría underscores that faith leads people back to God (*credere in Deum*). Jesus asks the people to call the blind man, and *some of the better people in the crowd turned to the blind man and said,* Take heart. Rise up, he is calling you (Mark 10:49). *Here you have the Christian vocation! But God does not call only once. Bear in mind that our Lord is seeking us at every moment: get up, he tells us, put aside your indolence, your easy life, your petty selfishness, your silly little problems. Get up from the ground, where you are lying prostrate and shapeless. Acquire height, weight and volume, and a supernatural outlook.*[208]

This "going toward God," proper of faith, consists in adopting the *logic of faith*, of the complete surrender (self-giving) to God. St. Josemaría comments on this, drawing attention to the reaction of the blind man: "And throwing off his mantle he sprang up and came to Jesus" (Mark 10:50):

> *He threw aside his cloak!* [. . .] *Never forget that Christ cannot be reached without sacrifice. We have to get rid of everything that gets in the way: greatcoat, haversack, water bottle. You have to do the same in this battle for the glory of God, in this struggle of love and peace by which we are trying to spread Christ's kingdom. In order to serve the Church, the Pope and all souls, you must be ready to give up everything superfluous, to be left without a cloak to shelter you from the bitter cold of night, without your much loved family souvenirs, without water to refresh you. This is the lesson taught us by faith and love. This is the way that we must love Christ.*[209]

---

207. Ibid., no. 193.
208. Ibid., no. 196.
209. Ibid.

These texts highlight the three dimensions of the faith that are the framework for this section. We should keep in mind that they are three aspects of the same reality. The texts by St. Josemaría that will be cited refer at times specifically to one or the other aspects, but it is important not to lose sight of their unity.

2.1.1. Knowledge of Revealed Truth

Love for God presupposes the first aspect of faith, which is to accept as true what God has revealed of himself and his designs (*credere Deum*); and in turn, the same love becomes a spur to acquire an even deeper knowledge of God. In other words, the deeper the knowledge of God one has by faith, the greater one is able to love him; and the greater that love is, the deeper one's knowledge of him becomes. Faith is both a prerequisite and a consequence of love, precisely because "God is love" (1 John 4:8). Whoever knows and believes in God's love for us is drawn to love him, and whoever loves him knows and believes more deeply in his love (see 1 John 4:16). Let us now examine the first motion that goes from faith to love, where faith is a prerequisite of love, keeping in mind that the second motion is implicitly contained in the first, given that love enkindles the light of faith more intensely.

We should point out that in addition to being a prerequisite for the love of God, faith is also a prerequisite for the love we have for others. It suffices to consider the need of doctrinal knowledge to fulfill the Lord's mandate that represents the greatest sign of charity: "Go therefore and make disciples of all nations [. . .] teaching them to observe all that I have commanded you" (Matt. 28:19–20).

(a) "For Sanctity, Doctrine; For Apostolate, Doctrine"

St. Josemaría encapsulates the function of faith as a prerequisite of love for God and neighbor thus: *For our sanctity, doctrine; and for the apostolate, doctrine.*[210] Naturally, by "doctrine" he means "doctrine of faith," a doctrine that *is fully in accord with the mind of the Church and that follows the Magisterium of Peter with full fidelity.*[211]

Let us examine these two points:

210. Notes taken from preaching, November 21, 1954 (AGP, P09, p. 21).

211. *Letter, March 28, 1955*, no. 7.

(1) "For sanctity, doctrine." St. Josemaría teaches people to foster a "doctrinal piety," urging them to nourish their loving relationship with God by means of doctrine. The very notion of "filial piety" refers to the Son's love for the Father. This "filial piety" (see Heb. 5:7) is the love of the Word who knows the Father, and who, in joining us to himself as the Father's adopted children, makes us partakers of that knowledge: "No one knows the Father except the Son and any one to whom the Son chooses to reveal him" (Matt. 11:27). Holiness (or more strictly speaking, authentic filial piety) includes the real concern to go deeper and deeper in the knowledge of God, which is "never exclusively an intellectual process, but simultaneously also an intellectual and spiritual progressing in union with God in whose reality and love a person believes."[212] Doctrine is not something "added" to the spiritual life to enrich it, but rather a constitutive element of it, and even more so if this life is explicitly based on a person's awareness of his divine filiation. *We need to have the doctrine of theologians and the piety of children.*[213]

The expression "piety of children" implies simplicity in one's relationship with God and refers to a kind of piety that is neither sentimental nor voluntaristic according to St. Josemaría. It is about a kind of piety that rests on the "doctrine of theologians." He states,

> *Be pious, then, as children, but not ignorant. Insofar as possible, each of us should study the faith seriously, rigorously—all of which means theology. Ours should be the piety of children and the sure doctrine of theologians.*[214]

Piety safeguards good doctrine. When piety is missing, doctrine is easily corrupted as St. Josemaría points out in the following text commenting on a passage from St. Paul:

> Take heed to yourself and to your teaching; hold to that, for by so doing you will save both yourself and your hearers (1 Tim. 4:16). *Be pious: a person who is truly pious can make a mistake, but without piety it is impossible to be faithful, both in doctrine and in one's conduct.*[215]

---

212. José Luis Illanes, *Tratado de Teología espiritual* (Pamplona: Eunsa, 2007), p. 362.

213. *Letter, March 19, 1967*, no. 43. See Pilar Río, "Doctrina y unidad de vida a la luz de las enseñanzas del Beato Josemaría Escrivá," in Paul O'Callaghan (ed.), *La grandezza della vita quotidiana*, vol. V/1, pp. 271–311 (especially pages 281–292, where the author studies the cited expression of St. Josemaría).

214. *Christ Is Passing By*, no. 10.

215. *Letter, March 28, 1955*, no. 7.

(2) "For the apostolate, doctrine." Knowledge of the doctrine of faith is necessary for apostolate just as it is for holiness because apostolate is *the overflow of your life "within."*[216] St. Josemaría illustrates this with a direct reference to Opus Dei:

> *Our personal mission comes down to this: to give doctrine, to place the seed of good doctrine, this divine light, in the heads and hearts of all men and women* [. . .]. *You have heard me so often say that the greatest enemy of Christ and of the Church is ignorance, and that therefore we have the obligation to acquire formation, to have a sound knowledge of doctrine, in order to be able to give it to others, without disfiguring it, despite our personal mistakes.*[217]

St. Josemaría's understanding of the doctrine of faith "should not be interpreted as being a paralyzed and inert element that only yields dull intellectual and spiritual considerations that bleed the Christian soul dry. On the contrary, it should be viewed as lively and dynamic, constantly aimed at stimulating new evangelizing endeavors, inspiring new vitality for the Church, and expanding the Kingdom of God to new frontiers."[218]

> *We have a pressing need to acquire doctrine, and to live a life of faith, in order to be able to give it to others. Thus we can keep souls from falling into the errors of ignorance or into "pietism," which disfigures the face of true piety with its empty, sentimental or superstitious devotion.*[219]

It does not make sense to expound doctrine with sophisticated addresses that are incomprehensible to people. Doctrine should be "communicated" and made easier to assimilate. St. Josemaría encourages people to adapt to the personal and cultural circumstances of those receiving the doctrinal formation. He calls this "the gift of tongues," which he did not take so much to be the ability of speaking different languages as the art of communicating well with people from differing mindsets, education, and culture.

---

216. *The Way*, no. 961.

217. Notes taken from preaching, February 4, 1962 (AGP, P01 XII-1968, pp. 79–80).

218. Álvaro del Portillo, "Discurso conclusivo del Convenio teológico de estudio sobre las enseñanzas del Beato Josemaría Escrivá" (Roma, 12–14 octubre 1993), in Manuel Belda et al. (ed.), *Santidad y mundo*, p. 292. See Ethel Tolansky, "The Dynamic Role of the Intellectual in the Message of Bl. Josemaría," in Fernando de Andrés (ed.), *La grandezza della vita quotidiana*, vol. V/2, pp. 237–249.

219. *Letter, May 31, 1943*, no. 8.

> *We have to give doctrine in all social settings. And to do so we need to adapt ourselves to the mentality of those who listen to us: with the "gift of tongues." This gift of tongues obliges us to ensure our words are filled with content:* Now, brethren, *writes St. Paul,* if I come to you speaking in tongues, how shall I benefit you unless I bring you some revelation or knowledge or prophecy or teaching? (1 Cor. 14:6). *Therefore, we have an obligation to acquire formation: an obligation to get to know doctrine very well, with the preparation needed so that others will understand us, and so that they too in turn will be able to pass on what they have heard.*[220]

(b) Faith and Personal Vocation: Faithfulness

In addition to faith in revealed truth, another requirement for love of God is knowledge of his will for one's life, which is primarily knowledge of one's personal vocation. In the Preliminary Part we asserted that God calls everyone to holiness by different paths with specific missions within the singular mission of the Church. Knowledge of one's own vocation and mission (that is, the path to holiness and apostolate desired by God for each person) has a lot to do with the virtue of faith.

Faith and vocation are often found together in St. Josemaría's thought, as can been seen, for instance, in the following text:

> *Our vocation enkindles a light which allows us to recognize the meaning of our existence. It means being convinced through the splendor of faith of the "why" of our life on earth* [. . .]: *we come to understand where God wants to lead us, and we stand in awe by the mission entrusted to us.*[221]

Here vocation is described as a "light" (which ultimately is also a force) that makes up part of the "splendor of faith." Certainly faith and vocation are not synonymous, and in fact, St. Josemaría distinguishes both in many texts.[222] Yet their mutual relation is very close; and in order to understand it, we need to keep in mind that when theology talks about the assent to the truths of faith, it usually distinguishes between "external" revelation (i.e., the revealed and public deposit of faith, protected, and expressed by the Church), and "internal" revelation (i.e., the light of faith that God grants us to be able to assent to

---

220. *Letter, January 9, 1932*, no. 28.

221. *Christ Is Passing By*, no. 45.

222. See, for example, ibid., no. 32, and, in general, the homily "The Epiphany of Our Lord" (in *Christ Is Passing By*, nos. 31–38).

those truths). This interior light is a divine gift that "connaturalizes" our intellect with the supernatural truths so as to be able to judge not only that those truths are *able* to be believed, but also that they *ought* to be believed.

The distinction between public revelation and interior light allows us to see in what sense the conviction of having received a specific divine vocation belongs to the realm of supernatural faith. It is clear that the truth of having received a determined divine vocation is not a revealed truth. It is a revealed truth that all are called to holiness and that God grants different gifts to each person in order to reach it, but it is obviously not a "truth of the deposit of faith" that a specific person has received a given vocation. Nonetheless, it can be said that the conviction of having received such a vocation is due to a sort of interior revelation. God freely grants the gift of a calling (a gift of his love surpassing human reason), and manifests it to each person by means of an interior grace that enlightens the intellect and urges the will. This light is similar to that of the interior light of faith. It is not called *lumen fidei* because it does not fall on a truth publicly revealed, but it does provide a *conviction of faith* concerning a truth that God manifests interiorly as a gift of his love for which he gives some exterior signs allowing it to be recognized. For this reason, theologians state that the light of one's own vocation comes as the result of a certain "maturing in the faith."[223] Thus, it is about a light that enables a person to take the step from knowing of the possibility that "God may be calling me to holiness through a determined path," to affirming "God is actually calling me along this path." In addition to this light, God grants an impulse to the will so that it can freely assent to his call. Both the light and the impulse allow the person to see that it is right to recognize God's call and not to doubt that such a call has been received. God wishes to be loved by everyone and marks out for each his or her own personal vocation. This vocation is a gift of God's love and the response to this gift (i.e., our correspondence to divine love) presupposes faith in having received it (understanding "faith" to mean an interior light that enables the assent to a truth—a design of love—which God manifests to us in a personal way).

Let us now take a look at some texts by St. Josemaría. When he speaks on this subject, he refers specifically to the call to Opus Dei. Nonetheless, his teaching also has a more general application because it can be extended

---

223. See Ocáriz, "Vocation to Opus Dei as a Vocation in the Church," in Pedro Rodríguez, Fernando Ocáriz, and José Luis Illanes, *Opus Dei in the Church* (Princeton: Scepter, 1994), p. 77; Claudio Moreschini, *Vocazione e realtà ecclesiale*, in *Vocazione e società* (Padua: Ed. Laurenziane, 1970), p. 63.

to any divine vocation within the Church, especially to the vocation of everyday Christians that the majority of the faithful receive.

> Let us briefly recall something already mentioned in the Preliminary Part. Every Christian has a divine call: he or she has been called to holiness on a specific path willed by God. It is not just priests and religious who "have a vocation," but rather all Christians. The path by which God calls the great majority is one of total self-giving love for God and others in ordinary life without changing one's place or state in life. It is a call to sanctify one's activities with a specific spirit and set of means, as is the case, for example, with the faithful of Opus Dei, or in the way that each person discovers with the light of God. Every person has a personal divine vocation and everyone can discover it. The Lord invites people to use the proper means to discover it: "Ask, and it will be given you; seek, and you will find" (Matt. 7:7). He manifests himself to those who sincerely look for the path to fulfill his will. The means to find it are the normal ones in the Christian life, which we will discuss in chapter nine: prayer, the sacraments, and Christian formation.

A divine vocation is an eternal project of God. It exists before it is discovered. It is a gift bestowed from eternity and forever. St. Josemaría applies to the personal call of each person what St. Paul affirms of everyone's call to holiness: *From all eternity our Creator has chosen us for a life of complete self-giving:* elegit nos in ipso ante mundi constitutionem (Eph. 1:4), *he chose us before the creation of the world.*[224] Whoever believes that he is called to holiness (a truth corresponding to public revelation) and sincerely desires to respond to this call finds himself in the best interior disposition to discover the specific path through which God wishes to lead him. This is because his good disposition to receive the light of faith in revelation ensures that he is well prepared to receive the light of his specific and personal vocation.

Although throughout one's life the circumstances in which a personal vocation is lived can change, the unconditional disposition to correspond to God's will implies having in mind that the essential element of a vocation is an immutable reality. Once one has discovered God's invitation to follow a determined path to holiness, one can be sure that God will continue to grant the assistance needed to follow it. Moments of fatigue or trial can arise in which

224. *Letter, March 24, 1931*, no. 47.

the light of the vocation is perceived dimly, and it may even seem to have been extinguished. Something similar can occur with faith in public revelation; the interior *lumen fidei* that leads to assent to revealed truth can be darkened and the soul left in shadows. But God does not abandon those who do not voluntarily separate themselves from him. Some interior clarity always remains along with the visible reality of the ever shining faith of the Church (see Matt. 16:17–18). Similarly, in reference to one's personal vocation, God does not abandon the person moved by the desire to respond to his call. God is faithful and does not extinguish the light he has bestowed on the person to guide him along the path of love. However, since God asks for a response based on faith, and not one based on one's own decision and strength, he *wants his Omnipotence to be accompanied by our weakness: next to his light, the shadows of our poor nature.*[225] It is not uncommon to experience one's own miseries. Taking into account these circumstances, St. Josemaría says: *no matter what happens, none of us has the right to place in doubt his divine calling.*[226] Since one's vocation is permanent, it follows that God grants the necessary graces to correspond to it at every moment in life, and whenever necessary, to rectify any infidelities, and even grave ones. In short, God does not wish man to begin building without being able to finish (see Luke 14:9–30).

> *Therefore it would be absurd, after a fall, to say: I've had a defeat, so I don't have a vocation! On the contrary, we have to reason in this way: because I have been chosen with this vocation, I will win out, I will be humble and, with God's grace—which I am assured of having:* ubi autem abundavit delictum, superabundavit gratia (Rom. 5:20), *where sin increased, grace abounded all the more—I will be faithful from now on.*[227]

The decision to remain always on the path toward holiness that one has discovered with God's light after looking for it with a sincere and upright intention is an act of "faithfulness" (or "fidelity"), a virtue derived from "*fides*" or "faith." It is about being faithful to a divine interior light akin to being faithful to revealed doctrine. Like faith, it involves the assent of the intellect enlightened by God and of the will moved by grace. For this reason, in referring to giving oneself to God as a response to a divine call, St. Josemaría affirms that, it *isn't a "state of mind," a passing situation, but rather,*

---

225. Ibid.

226. Ibid.

227. *Letter, March 28, 1955*, no. 26.

in the intimacy of each one's conscience, a definitive state in order to seek perfection in the middle of the world.[228]

It is a "definitive state" because it is the assent to an eternal call, to a divine interior light that by its very nature requires the adjective "definitive," just as by analogy the assent of faith also requires it. Both are closely related; one strengthens the other, and the weakness of one affects the other. Experience confirms that a weak response to one's specific vocation often follows from a weak faith, just as a weak faith produces a wavering in faithfulness to one's path to holiness and apostolate.

Whoever is faithful to the Christian vocation will receive the reward that Jesus Christ has promised to those who follow him: "he who endures to the end will be saved" (Matt. 24:13). St. Josemaría often conveys the connection between "perseverance" and "salvation" with another binomial when he speaks of *a fidelity* [fidelidad] *that is happiness* [felicidad].[229] If salvation means receiving full and everlasting happiness, for him it is no less obvious that final perseverance is made up by daily acts of faithfulness to the Christian vocation in "little things."

> *Let us listen to our Lord:* He who is faithful in a very little is faithful also in much; and he who is dishonest in very little is dishonest also in much (Luke 16:10). *It is as if he were saying to us: fight continuously in the apparently unimportant things which are to my mind important; fulfill your duty punctually; smile at whoever needs cheering up, even though there is sorrow in your soul; devote the necessary time to prayer, without haggling; go to the help of anyone who looks for you; practice justice and go beyond it with the grace of charity.*[230]

St. Josemaría considered Jesus' words to those he received in glory as a formula for canonization: "Well done, good and faithful servant; you have been faithful over a little, I will set you over much; enter into the joy of your master" (Matt. 25:21).[231]

---

228. *Instruction*, April 1, 1934, no. 20.

229. *Instruction*, December 8, 1941, no. 61.

230. *Christ Is Passing By*, no. 77.

231. *You will not sanctify yourselves if you spend your life awaiting a great occasion to be heroic* [. . .], wrote St. Josemaría to his daughters in Opus Dei. *On the other hand, there are a multitude of little things that require heroism: some of them, because of their continuity; others, precisely because of their human littleness. For that reason our Lord used this formula of canonization:* quia super pauca fuisti fidelis, super multa te constituam, intra in gaudium domini tui (Matt. 25:21); *because you have been faithful over a little, I will set you over much; enter into the joy of your master." Letter, July 29, 1965*, no. 55.

2.1.2. Trust in God

Another integral element of faith is to believe what God reveals because it is he who is revealing it (*credere Deo*). Even before believing something, faith implies believing a person, which translates to: believing God who reveals himself, trusting him, and going on his word. And since he has revealed that he is love, to believe God means "to believe the God who loves us," and therefore, above all, "to believe that God loves us" and "to trust in his love for us."

This aspect of the faith is an essential requirement in order to love God. Whoever does not believe that God loves him and does not trust in his love is unable to love him. It is understandable that after St. John writes "we know and believe the love God has for us" (1 John 4:16), he would add, "we love, because he first loved us" (1 John 4:19). A point from *Forge* vividly expresses this relationship between believing in God who loves us and loving him with all our heart:

> *God loves me. And John the Apostle writes, "Let us love God, then, since God loved us first." As if this were not enough, Jesus comes to each one of us, in spite of our patent wretchedness, to ask us, as he asked Peter: "Simon, son of John, do you love me more than these?" This is the moment to reply: "Lord, you know all things, you know that I love you!"—adding, with humility: Help me to love you more. Increase my love!*[232]

Believing in the love that God has for us is also a requirement for love of neighbor, and especially for its most proper and fitting manifestation: apostolate. To carry out our apostolic mission among our fellow men and women, it is necessary to believe that God loves them and wants each of us to be an instrument to unite them with him.

This attitude is essential for the Christian life. Let us recall the Gospel scene in which the apostles try unsuccessfully to cure a boy possessed by an evil spirit. Jesus intervenes by expelling the demon. "Then the disciples came to Jesus privately and said, 'Why could we not cast it out?' He said to them, 'Because of your little faith. For truly, I say to you, if you have faith as a grain of mustard seed, you will say to this mountain, "move from hence to yonder place," and it will move; and nothing will be impossible to you" (Matt. 17:19–20; see Luke 17:5–6). Among other lessons that can be learned from this Gospel passage, a clear teaching is that faith is necessary if

---

232. *The Forge*, no. 497.

one is to be the channel of the wonders of God's love. In other words, faith in his love is necessary to act as the instruments God uses to bestow his gifts and graces to his children. With this passage in mind, St. Josemaría puts forth the following exhortation:

> *"Omnia possibilia sunt credenti."—Everything is possible for anyone who has faith. The words are Christ's. How is it that you don't say to him with the apostles: "Adauge nobis fidem!"—Increase my faith!?*[233]

(a) Filial Trust: "Omnia in Bonum"

When faith is imbued by divine filiation, its determining feature is the lively belief in God's fatherly love: a *filial trust* with many implications for charity. The faith of a child of God is a requirement for filial love, the charity of children.

St. Josemaría writes: *I know you will always keep very much in mind those words:* omnes enim filii Dei estis per fidem (Gal. 3:26), *you are all children of God through faith. What power we have! The power of knowing we are children of God and actually being so.*[234] St. Paul affirms that we are children of God "through faith" in the sense that we adhere to Christ with a faith informed by charity[235] in order to receive supernatural life, according to the words of the same apostle: "May Christ dwell in your hearts through faith; that you be rooted and grounded in love" (see Eph. 3:17).[236] Christ dwells in a Christian "through faith" not because his presence is only intentional (as a thing known is present in the knower), but because faith opens the doors to the presence of Christ's life and action in a Christian. Thus, one can understand the exclamation by St. Josemaría just quoted: "*What power we have! The power of knowing we are children of God and actually being so.*" Jesus teaches that whoever asks "in his name," that is, whoever is identified with him "through faith," will receive what he asks for: "Truly, truly, I say to you, if you ask anything of the Father, he will give it to you in my name" (John 16:23). Imbued with this spirit, St. Josemaría encourages people to seek holiness and carry out their apostolate with the boldness of a son or a daughter of God like a little child would do:

---

233. *The Way*, no. 588.

234. *Letter, October 24, 1942*, no. 68.

235. See Albert Vanhoye, *Lettera ai Galati*, p. 98.

236. See St. Thomas Aquinas, *S. Th.*, III, q. 68, a. 1, ad 1.

The greatest daring is always that of children. Who asks for . . . the moon? Who is blind to dangers in getting what he wants? To such a child add much grace from God, the desire to do his Will, great love for Jesus, all the human knowledge he is capable of acquiring, and you will have the likeness of the apostles of today such as God undoubtedly wants them.[237]

Filial trust is a profound attitude of the soul in all circumstances, not just when making petitions. This is manifested beautifully in one of St. Paul's texts: "We know that in everything God works for good with those who love him, who are called according to his purpose" (Rom. 8:28). St. Josemaría would reduce this phrase into a short aspiration: *omnia in bonum!*[238] "All for the good!," which he used to express a conviction of faith: out of his omnipotent love for his children, God the Father ordains that even what is evil can work unto the good if they love him (because then, they are open to receiving all his gifts).

Woes? Setbacks deriving from one thing or another? Can't you see that this is the will of your Father God, who is good and who loves you—loves you personally—more than all the mothers in the world can possibly love their children?[239]

Filial trust in God's fatherly love renders the Christian life with a characteristic tone: a positive approach to every circumstance, a serene and cheerful disposition, and a readiness to spend oneself, because all in all, it is about a trust that goes together with a struggle to use all the means at one's disposal:

My children, go forward with joy, with effort. Nothing will stop us in this world, when we serve God, because everything works for the good of those who love God: diligentibus Deum, omnia cooperantur in bonum (Rom. 8:28). *Everything in life can be fixed except death, and for us death is life.*[240]

(b) Faithfulness to God's Love

Trust in God makes love secure because to trust is to lean and rest on God's faithfulness to his children. "For God so loved the world that he gave his

---

237. *The Way*, no. 857.

238. *Friends of God*, no. 119; *Furrow*, no. 127; *The Way of the Cross*, Ninth Station, no. 4.

239. *The Forge*, no. 929.

240. *Letter, March 24, 1931*, no. 55.

only Son, that whoever believes in him should not perish but have eternal life" (John 3:16). God is faithful to his love, and a Christian knows that nothing by itself can impede us from loving him. "Who shall separate us from the love of Christ? Shall tribulation, or distress, or persecution, or famine, or nakedness, or peril, or sword? [. . .] No, in all these things we are more than conquerors through him who loved us" (Rom. 8:35, 37). Not even the scandal of persons who should give witness to the faith and fail to do so can dampen the charity of a Christian who places his faith on the authority of God who reveals himself through Christ and not on that human conduct. St. Josemaría states,

> *I believe* per Dominum nostrum Iesum Christum!*—because of the authority of God who reveals, because of our Lord Jesus Christ, and as the Church teaches. And that's enough. I would rather have everyone in the world behave well; if they don't do so, I am very sorry, but that doesn't undermine my faith. So when I speak to you in this way, I do so with the intention of strengthening your faith, in case you see things that aren't going well. Have faith* per Dominum nostrum Iesum Christum, *because of our Lord Jesus Christ.*[241]

Believing the God who loves us (which is the basic condition for loving him), is a conviction of faith that comes from the "head," that is, one that comes from the intellect. This is also why correspondence to God's love through the path of one's vocation is called "faithfulness." It is true that faithfulness is an act of love, but it is not only a decision of the will (the faculty in which charity resides); it is also an act of the intellect because it involves belief in God. The decision to be faithful to God presupposes believing in the love that he has for us and trusting that his love is made manifest in the specific vocation of each person to holiness.

St. Josemaría emphasizes this especially when talking about moments when faithfulness is challenged. These moments of trial are precisely due to blindness concerning the content of faith or one's personal path toward holiness. Thus, he writes,

> *We have to live by faith, and make it more theological, less dependent on reasons other than God himself. As St. Thomas says,* A person with scant learning is far surer of something he hears from an expert than he is of any insight of his own. Thus anyone is far surer of what he hears from

241. Notes taken from preaching (AGP, P04 1974, vol. II, pp. 600–601).

> God, who is infallible, than of what he sees with his own fallible reason (*S. Th.*, II-II, q. 4, a. 8 ad 2) [. . .]. *If that soul lets itself be led, if he obeys, if he wholeheartedly accepts purification, if he lives by faith, he will see with unimagined light, and afterward think with amazement that till then he had been blind from birth.* Again Jesus spoke to them, saying, I am the light of the world; he who follows me will not walk in darkness, but will have the light of life. (John 8:12)[242]

It is clear from this text that periods of blindness can lead to growth in trust placed in God. When a person "tries to live by faith" and "to make his faith less dependent on reasons other than God himself," God intensifies the virtue of faith in that person, making use of those trials when the person experiences his shortcomings. Turning to the Gospel passages that show how "little faith" Jesus' disciples have and how much it needs to grow (Matt. 8:26; 14:31; 16:8, etc.), St. Josemaría affirms, *How humbly and simply the Gospels relate incidents that manifest the weak and wavering faith of the apostles! So that you and I won't lose hope of some day achieving the strong unshakable faith those first few afterwards had.*[243]

2.1.3. "Vision of Faith" and "Supernatural Outlook"

So far, we have touched upon two aspects of faith required by charity. A third one remains to be examined because in addition to presupposing faith in what God has revealed and believing because he is the one who reveals it, charity requires taking truth as a guide to direct all of our behavior toward God (*credere in Deum*). The Letter to the Hebrews mentions great examples from salvation history such as Abel, Abraham, Moses, and others.[244] This is the dimension of faith referred to in the following point of *The Way*:

Faith.—It is a pity to see how abundantly many Christians have it on their lips, and how sparingly they put it into their actions. One would think it a virtue to be preached only, and not one to be practiced.[245]

---

242. *Letter, March 24, 1931*, nos. 16–17.

243. *The Way*, no. 581.

244. "By faith Abel offered to God a more acceptable sacrifice than Cain [. . .]. By faith Abraham obeyed when he was called to go out to a place which he was to receive as an inheritance; and he went out, not knowing where he was to go [. . .]. By faith Abraham, when he was tested, offered up Isaac [. . .]. By faith Moses, when he was grown up, refused to be called the son of Pharaoh's daughter, choosing rather to share ill-treatment with the people of God than to enjoy the fleeting pleasures of sin. He considered abuse suffered for the Christ greater wealth than the treasures of Egypt" (Heb. 11:4 ff.).

245. *The Way*, no. 579.

St. Paul refers to this aspect of the faith with the expression "obedience of faith" (Rom. 1:5; 16:26; see 1 Pet. 1:22). Here the term "obedience" is understood as a complete submission of a person's behavior to the Word of God, an orientation of a person's entire life to the will of God. Many times St. Josemaría speaks of a "life of faith" in the sense of faith guiding one's life. Precisely in his homily entitled "Life of Faith," St. Josemaría refers to this dimension of faith with expressions such as "supernatural outlook," "a vision of faith," and/or "a Christian outlook."[246] They convey an invitation to see reality from the perspective of faith in order to redirect everything toward God.

St. Josemaría is not satisfied with a purely human outlook. That would imply *a two-dimensional, flat and too earthly an outlook.*[247] He urges people to acquire *the third dimension: height, and with it, perspective, weight and volume.*[248] He encourages an attitude that corresponds to the supernatural elevation by grace, the attitude of children who see their life with *the logic of God,*[249] or that is, the logic of faith. Charity presupposes a supernatural outlook that imbues a person's entire way of acting, making it clear that there is little room except for a life of complete self-giving. Love for God calls for the same way of thinking (or logic) that led the apostles to leave everything and follow Christ (see Matt. 4:18–21; Luke 5:11); that led the blind man to throw down his cape and run to Jesus (see Mark 10:50); and, that led Zacchaeus to change the course of his life (see Luke 19:8). This "divine logic" stands in contrast to the "human logic" of the rich young man, who rejected Jesus' invitation "for he had great possessions" (Matt. 19:22). God's logic reverberates in the parables of the kingdom: the pearl of great price and the hidden treasure: he who finds them sells everything to obtain them (see Matt. 13:44–46). In this sense, St. Josemaría underscores the importance of love: [*T*]*he supernatural value of our life does not depend on accomplishing great undertakings suggested to us by our overactive imagination. Rather, it is to be found in the faithful acceptance of God's will, in welcoming generously the opportunities for small, daily sacrifice.*[250]

---

246. See, for example, ibid., no. 664; *Furrow*, nos. 166, 447, 774, 756; *The Forge*, nos. 657, 730, 996; *Conversations*, no. 16; *Christ Is Passing By*, no. 174; *Friends of God*, nos. 196, 200, 206.

247. *The Way*, no. 279.

248. Ibid.

249. *Christ Is Passing By*, no. 172.

250. Ibid.

The contrast between "supernatural" and "human" outlooks is particularly clear in the attitude toward the Cross: "For the word of the cross is folly to those who are perishing, but to us who are being saved it is [. . .] the power of God and the wisdom of God" (1 Cor. 1:18.24). Living faith teaches that the path of love entails sacrifice. This is the faith needed to love without limits, with Christ and in union with him, as each one fulfills the mission inherent to his vocation.

The logic of faith guides a Christian along the path of his personal divine vocation. If the interior light of the vocation has revealed to him the loving design of God, the response cannot be a cold assent; it must be inflamed by divine love. And faithfulness to that calling should be a permanent response. *The dedication of each of us was a generous, detached act of self-giving. And because we maintain that dedication, our faithfulness is a continuous gift of self: an ongoing love, generosity, and unselfishness, and not just the result of inertia.*[251] St. Josemaría often repeated the phrase *Vale la pena* [It's worth it]. It is worth being faithful to one's divine vocation, persevering in a loving response to God's call. *It is worthwhile giving oneself completely, dedicating one's life to God's service.*[252]

2.2. Life of Hope

God wishes his children to be happy loving him, and he fills them with the hope of reaching that love which begins to satiate the desire for happiness here on earth and will fully realize it in heaven: "What no eye has seen, nor ear heard, nor the heart of man conceived, what God has prepared for those who love him" (1 Cor. 2:9). Hope is the virtue that responds to the desire for happiness that God has placed in the heart of every man. It is usually defined as the theological virtue by which we aspire to eternal life as our happiness.[253] Thus, hope is a requirement for charity because unless a person hopes that the love for God will make him happy, that person would not be able to love God, and vice versa: the greater a person's hope that happiness is found in having love for God, the greater that person's inclination to love God will be.

It is difficult to exaggerate the importance of hope in the Christian life. However, when dealing with the theological virtues, works of spiritual

251. *Letter, March 24, 1931*, no. 12.

252. *Conversations*, no. 67.

253. See *CCC*, nos. 1817–1818.

theology often relegate it to a second plane, focusing their attention on faith and charity.[254] There are different reasons for this, none of which will be discussed here. It is important to note that this is not the case in the writings of St. Josemaría. It suffices to read the homily "The Christian's Hope"[255] to see the prominent role he attributes to this virtue. It is a role different from faith, but not subordinated to it. Both faith and hope appear as requirements of charity, and when informed by charity, they are like parallel tracks that lead the Christian to the goal of his existence, that is, to the glory of God and his own perfection, a loving knowledge of the Holy Trinity, and joy in union with the Father, the Son, and the Holy Spirit.

Hope presupposes faith, and gives a right to love.[256] With these words St. Josemaría summarizes the relation of hope with the other theological virtues. Let us now analyze their meaning:

- "Hope presupposes faith" because "faith is the assurance of things hoped for, the conviction of things not seen" (Heb. 11:1). Faith resides in the intellect and has God as its object inasmuch as he reveals the truth to us. Under the light of faith, hope (which resides in the will)[257] has God as its object inasmuch as he is the principle of all that is good and is the source of our complete happiness.
- "Hope gives a right to love" because the Christian disposes himself to receive the love that the Holy Spirit pours into his heart in the measure that he seeks this love, placing his desire for happiness in union with God.[258]

At the same time, charity gives life to hope moving the Christian to desire happiness not out of a sort of selfishness but out of love for God, that is, because it is God's will. This is how the three theological virtues work together here on earth. "We are justified by faith [. . .], we rejoice in our

254. Nevertheless we have to point out that we are recovering the importance of this virtue today thanks in part to the encyclical *Spe Salvi* of Benedict XVI (November 30, 2007).

255. See *Friends of God*, nos. 205–221.

256. Notes taken from preaching, January 9, 1971 (AGP, P01 II-1971, p. 39).

257. See St. Thomas Aquinas, *S. Th.*, II-II, q. 18, a. 1, c. St. Josemaría indirectly affirms this in *Furrow*, no. 780.

258. St. Thomas Aquinas explains it in this way: "Charity makes us adhere to God for his own sake [. . .]. On the other hand, hope and faith make man adhere to God as to a principle wherefrom certain things occur to us. Now we derive from God both knowledge of truth and the attainment of perfect goodness. Accordingly faith makes us adhere to God, as the source whence we derive the knowledge of truth [. . .] while hope makes us adhere to God, as the source whence we derive perfect goodness, insofar as, by hope, we trust to the divine assistance for obtaining happiness" (*S. Th.*, II-II, q. 17, a. 6, c.; see ibid., q. 18, a. 1, c.).

hope of sharing the glory of God [. . .]. Hope does not disappoint us, because God's love has been poured into our hearts through the Holy Spirit who has been given to us" (Rom. 5:1, 2, 5). In heaven, however, charity will need neither faith nor hope. Instead of faith there will be a loving vision, face to face, and instead of hope there will be possession of true happiness.

Awareness of one's divine filiation is the foundation for hope. St. Josemaría testifies that *the certainty I derive from feeling—from knowing—that I am a son of God fills me with real hope.*[259] To know ourselves to be children of God, to know that it is "Christ who lives in me" (Gal. 2:20) and that therefore we are called to be seated with him in the heavenly places (see Eph. 2:6) is a source of hope: "Christ in you, the hope of glory" (Col. 1:27). To know that we are loved by God as his children leads to the joyous conviction that he wishes our happiness. This entails seeing oneself and others as heirs of heaven and of all goods created for our happiness, once we are purified from sin (see Rom. 8:16–17; Ps. 2:8). Divine filiation *imbues our interior struggle and our apostolic tasks with hope.*[260]

Next to the general theological reasons that justify the importance of hope in the Christian life, there is also a motive which is intrinsic to the spirit that St. Josemaría preaches. In order to reach sanctification in everyday life, we especially need the theological virtue of hope. Only thus can we firmly rest our desire for complete happiness on union with God, and not on the possession of created goods that merely offer the attraction of human satisfaction. We also need theological hope in order not to give up activities that must be sanctified even when these do not offer any satisfaction. Whether these activities are pleasing, difficult, or taxing, whether they fulfill or excite the aspirations of the heart, or whether they produce boredom and distaste, the theological virtue of hope inclines the person to find union with God in whom happiness is to be found by means of these activities, allowing persons to love the world without becoming worldly. Hope protects the ideal of sanctifying secular realities from the danger of secularism to which the ordinary Christian is exposed. This is the reason for its importance in St. Josemaría's spiritual doctrine.

With this in mind, let us now examine the role of this virtue as a condition for charity in its triple aspect of love for God, love for others, and love for oneself out of love for God. As we have previously done, we will limit

259. *Friends of God*, no. 208.

260. *Letter, March 11, 1940*, no. 2. See *Christ Is Passing By*, no. 65.

our analysis to the case of the Christian in the state of grace. This means we will only discuss the role of hope as informed by charity.

2.2.1. The Hope of Becoming Saints

Hope that complete happiness is found in union with God in heaven and "leads to charity, inasmuch as a man through hoping to be rewarded by God is encouraged to love God."[261] We would be unable to love God if we did not hope that such love would make us happy. St. Josemaría conveys this truth when he preaches: *I have seen many souls with such hope in God that it has set them marvelously ablaze with love, with a fire that makes their heart beat strong.*[262] Hope nourishes love for God without diminishing its purity. Hence his advice: *Do everything unselfishly, for pure Love, as if there were neither reward nor punishment. But in your heart foster the glorious hope of heaven.*[263]

In addition to hope in eternal life, a Christian should consider that *God, who will one day be everything for us, already lets us share in his goodness here on earth.*[264] Through grace and charity, Christians already possess a foretaste of glory in such a way that in this life they are able to enjoy the beginnings of God's love and the happiness of heaven. Supernatural hope does not belittle such foretaste, but rather delights in it as a seed of eternal life. It not only desires the future blessedness in glory, but also blessedness in the present by seeking union with God by means of grace. This is so to the extent that hope does not renounce to the blessedness of union with God under any circumstances, even where suffering is involved. A Christian who lives with hope does not allow present-day sufferings to lead him to despondency; rather, in those hardships he experiences *happiness in the Cross.*[265] The hope of happiness in God sustains charity when it requires sacrifice, especially when one is tempted to exchange the desire for complete happiness with a created good. *At the time of temptation think of the Love that awaits you in heaven: foster the virtue of hope—it's not a lack of generosity.*[266] A man with hope can say along with St. Augustine, "You have made us for yourself, O

---

261. St. Thomas Aquinas, *S. Th.*, II-II, q. 17, a. 8, c.

262. *Friends of God*, no. 205.

263. *The Way*, no. 668. See *The Forge*, no. 1008; Rom. 5:2.

264. Notes taken from preaching (AGP, P01 I-1969, p. 66).

265. *The Way*, no. 758. We have commented on this expression of St. Josemaría in chapter two, section 2.

266. *The Way*, no. 139.

Lord, and our heart is restless until it rests in you."[267] And as a result, he will be able to say to himself: the more I love God without rejecting sacrifice, the happier I will be already here on earth.

St. Josemaría clearly affirms the superiority of love of God over hope, but he encourages people to find happiness precisely in love: God wishes us to be happy loving him. He objects to the deformed vision of Christian life as a painful path, which is made bearable only by the thought that at the end of it all, there is heaven. Thus he eloquently remarks, *Every day, I'm more and more convinced that happiness in heaven is for those who know how to be happy on earth.*[268] This is one of the fixed points of his teaching.[269] Naturally he does not deny that earthly happiness is relative; we do not see God face to face yet. Love is accompanied by sorrow [on earth]; our present life is like a pilgrimage along a *vale of tears.*[270] However, the tears of a child of God can always be tears of love, of reparation for sin, of purification and petition to our Father God.[271] They can be tears of a loving obedience to the divine will like those of Christ (see Heb. 5:7); they leave God's consolations in the soul: "Blessed are those who mourn, for they shall be comforted" (Matt. 5:4).

If at times we fail to emphasize the desire for joy in Christian life, it may be due to fear of being selfish or tarnishing the purity of God's love.[272] However, the desire for happiness that characterizes hope has precisely the opposite effect: "Buoyed up by hope, he is preserved from selfishness and led to the happiness that flows from charity."[273] With a weak hope, charity would be lacking in joy. And since charity informs the moral virtues, there would be the risk of *long faces*[274] that do not reflect the image of Christ.

---

267. St. Augustine, *Confessions*, 1, 1, 1. St. Josemaría cites this text in his homily "The Christian's Hope": see *Friends of God*, no. 208.

268. *The Forge*, no. 1005.

269. See Paul O'Callaghan, "La virtù della speranza e l'ascetica cristiana in alcuni scritti del beato Josemaría Escrivá," in *Romana* 23 (1996): 262–279.

270. Hymn *Salve Regina*.

271. See *Friends of God*, no. 302.

272. We are not entering into the historical debate about the so-called "pure love" in the seventeenth century between Bossuet and Fenelon. St. Josemaría does not refer to this debate. Nevertheless, a conception of love of God that prescinds from theological hope of happiness in union with him is foreign to his thinking. See, for example, *The Way*, no. 668.

273. *CCC*, no. 1818.

274. *The Way*, no. 661.

> *Christ's enemies never tire of using the diabolical ploy of spreading the rumor that the people who give themselves to God are all wrapped up in themselves. And, unfortunately, some of those who wish to be "good," echo those words, with their "sad virtues." We give you thanks, Lord, because you have chosen to count on our cheerful, happy lives to erase that false caricature.*[275]

God's children must live with joy, *the indescribable joy which comes from the theological virtue of hope.*[276] The apostle says, "Rejoice in your hope" (Rom. 12:12). Christian life has this unmistakable tone. Its essence is charity, and charity contains, so to speak, the hope of "running into" the love of God. It is a *blessed life which is to love his Will,*[277] because happiness is to be found in that love, and hope desires it: *You need a heart which is in love, not an easy life, to achieve happiness.*[278]

Earlier we said that hope leads us not only to desire future blessedness in glory, but also blessedness in union with God through grace in the present life. St. Josemaría teaches us to find that union in temporal affairs. For this very reason, hope does not separate us from these activities. It is true that the object of hope is not happiness through the possession of temporal goods, but rather through union with God. However, we can find God while carrying out those activities if we order them toward his glory. Hope is a "theological" virtue, but it is not for that reason divorced from real life:

> *Far from separating me from the things of this earth, hope draws me closer to these realities in a new way, a Christian way, which seeks to discover in everything the relation between our fallen nature and God, our Creator and Redeemer.*[279]

If union with God in everyday civil affairs is possible, then the beginning of an authentic happiness can be found in carrying them out for love of God and of others. For this reason, theological hope moves a person to fulfill his own duties out of love.

But this is not all. Just as hope of heaven includes not only the vision of God but also the possession of created goods—"we wait for new heavens and a new earth in which righteousness dwells" (2 Pet. 3:13; see Rev. 21:1 ff)—so

275. *Furrow*, no. 58.
276. *Friends of God*, no. 206.
277. *The Forge*, no. 617.
278. *Furrow*, no. 795.
279. *Friends of God*, no. 208.

too the hope of blessedness in union with God through grace includes the beginnings of the possession of the goods of the earth (see 1 Cor. 3:23). To "possess" these goods does not mean to dispose of all of them in human terms, but rather to ordain them to God. It consists in carrying out one's activities in accord with God's will, offering them to the Father in union with Christ through the Holy Spirit. Hope, in the words of an author reflecting on St. Josemaría's teaching, leads one to value "the weight of eternity that can be given to each moment. The present moment must be open, not only to the future; above all it must be open to eternity. A full appreciation of the present can only be reached in the measure that it is opened from within (through work well done and with the proper intention) to what transcends the temporal, toward that which by virtue of being offered up to God, acquires an eternal dimension."[280] Jesus Christ has promised, "Truly I say to you, there is no one who has left house or brothers or sisters or mother or father or children or lands, for my sake and for the gospel, who will not receive a hundredfold now in this time, houses and brothers and sisters and mothers and children and lands, with persecutions, and in the age to come eternal life" (Mark 10:29–30). He who follows Christ in a radical way will possess not only the divine goods, but also all the human goods for the simple reason of ordaining them to the one for whom all things have been created (see Col. 1:16).

On the other hand, if happiness is sought in temporal goods such as success, pleasure, riches, etc., rather than in God, hope would be corrupted and charity would be lacking because these goods would be loved more than God. This is the attitude of the character of the parable who told himself, "'Soul, you have ample goods laid up for many years; take your ease, eat, drink, be merry.' But God said to him, 'Fool! This night your soul is required of you; and the things you have prepared, whose will they be?'" (Luke 12:19–20). It is the attitude rejected by the Book of Revelation when it states, "For you say, I am rich, I have prospered, and I need nothing; not knowing that you are wretched, pitiable, poor, blind, and naked" (Rev. 3:17). Without undermining a highly positive view of created goods, St. Josemaría energetically rejected a "worldly" hope that would attempt to fill the desire for blessedness with these goods:

280. Jorge Peña Vial, "'Mística ojalatera' y realismo en la santidad de la vida ordinaria," in Giorgio Faro (ed.), *La grandezza della vita quotidiana*, vol. IV, p. 133. On the expression "*mística ojalatera*," see in this same chapter, section 4.2.2.

> *Some people, alas, whose aims are worthy but limited and their ideals only perishable and fleeting, forget that Christians have to aspire to the highest peaks of all, to the infinite. Our aim is the very Love of God, to enjoy that Love fully, with a joy that never ends. We have seen in so many ways that things here below have to come to an end for all of us when this world ends; and even sooner, for each individual, when he dies, for we cannot take wealth and prestige with us to the grave. That is why, buoyed up by hope, we raise our hearts to God himself and have learned to pray,* in te Domine speravi, non confundar in aeternum (Ps. 30:2), *I have placed my hope in you, O Lord: may your hand guide me now and at every moment, for ever and ever.*[281]

The lack of love of God can have its roots in a certain "deficit" of hope; man has little desire for the blessedness of the union with God and places his heart on creatures, forgetting that only God is the source of all that is good. "For what will it profit a man, if he gains the whole world and forfeits his life? Or what shall a man give in return for his life?" (Matt. 16:26). St. Josemaría encourages a determined opposition to this type of temptation in saying, *Stop building castles in the air. Make up your mind to open your soul to God, for only in our Lord will you find a real basis for your hope.*[282]

2.2.2. The Hope of Bearing Fruit

Before delving into this section, we first need to keep in mind that union with God only happens in communion with others and, for this reason, it is part of hope to desire the joy of being united to God together with our neighbor. The happiness of the members of the mystical body does not exist in an isolated manner: "If one member suffers, all suffer together; if one member is honored, all rejoice together. Now you are the body of Christ and individually members of it" (1 Cor. 12: 26–27). Thus the object of hope is not the happiness of an "individualistic holiness," but rather the happiness of holiness in union with the entire mystical body, for "there is one body and one Spirit, just as you were called to the one hope that belongs to your call" (Eph. 4:4).

Second, we should recall that each member of the mystical body of Christ is an instrument for others to be united with Christ. It is in this union where they find happiness, an integral part of which is the happiness

---

281. *Friends of God*, no. 209.

282. Ibid., no. 211.

of others. Thus, hope includes the desire to share one's Christian life with others and to bear apostolic fruit in them. It implies the desire of being God's instruments for others' holiness and happiness in union with Christ and ourselves.

In this way, we can now understand that charity toward one's neighbor presupposes hope because, when we place happiness in union with God, we are led to the essence of charity: to desire the greatest good for others: to be united with God in whom lies the greatest and most abundant joy. *A person who possesses happiness, and the good, will always seek to give it to others.*[283] A Christian must *be concerned about all men and women, fighting for their eternal happiness and well-being.*[284] Precisely the virtue of hope leads him to help others to be happy loving God. Charity toward one's neighbor presupposes hope because we would not be able to desire others to love God (as charity calls for) unless we truly hoped that such love would make them happy.

Theological hope leads not only to apostolate but also to Christian proselytism (which we have already discussed),[285] namely to encourage others to follow Christ along the same path we have followed where we have experienced a foretaste of heaven. St. Josemaría eloquently puts it this way in his opening point in the chapter on proselytism in *The Way*: *Don't you long to shout to those young men and women all around you: Fools, leave those worldly things that shackle the heart and very often degrade it . . . , leave all that and come with us in search of Love?*[286]

St. Josemaría refers to proselytism in general that can be carried out by any Christian who is happy on his path of holiness. The following words from his preaching capture this idea:

> *How much it hurts me to see a priest or religious who fails to seek vocations for the diocesan seminary or for his novitiate. It's almost always a sign that they themselves aren't pleased with their vocation, that they aren't happy, or even that they feel unlucky in life. In contrast, when one loves this sign of predilection by God, who invites us to assist him, to co-redeem, then* [. . .] *more than a desire, one has a real hunger to spread this madness to others! It is something that happens without effort, like the beating of our heart* [. . .].

283. *The Forge*, no. 914.

284. *Friends of God*, no. 173.

285. See chapter three, section 2.3.

286. *The Way*, no. 790.

> *Those who aren't concerned about winning others give me the impression that they are a failure. For the good, of itself, is diffusive. If I have received something good, I will necessarily also have the desire, shown in deeds, to get others to share in my happiness.*[287]

Writing on St. Josemaría's teaching, José Luis Illanes states that, "Christian hope refers in the first place to the kingdom of heaven and to Christ's triumph which will be fully manifest at the end of time, beyond history; yet, it also refers to present history because the fruits of the Cross are anticipated in the today of our lives."[288] Just as the blessedness of heaven consists in seeing God in union with all the saints such that each person is also a channel of God's love for others (each being a gift for the others), the anticipation of this blessedness on earth consists in loving God and in others loving him, while we are mediators "in Christ" for them to be united to God. Jesus thus tells us, "I chose you and appointed you that you should go and bear fruit and that your fruit should abide" (John 15:16). Bearing apostolic fruits forms part of one's happiness in God and is thus an object of the theological virtue of hope.

Through parables that make use of farming imagery, Jesus teaches that apostolic fruitfulness is a reason for happiness, and thus an object of hope and a requirement for charity. The farmer hopes to reap the fruit of what he has sown and rejoices watching the seed grow. "Do you not say, 'There are yet four months, then comes the harvest'? I tell you, lift up your eyes, and see how the fields are already white for harvest. He who reaps receives wages, and gathers fruit for eternal life, so that sower and reaper may rejoice together" (John 4:35–36).

"By this my Father is glorified, that you bear much fruit" (John 15:8). Jesus encourages the desire to bear fruit in order to give glory to God. It would not make sense to cease to aspire for apostolic fruitfulness out of fear that satisfaction would sully one's upright intention. God himself purifies those who bear fruit, precisely to be more effective: "Every branch of mine that bears no fruit, he takes away, and every branch that does bear fruit he prunes, that it may bear more fruit" (John 15:2). Purification consists in "dying to one's self," to one's disordered self-love and hence this condition

287. Notes taken from preaching, December 29, 1959 (AGP, P01 1977, pp. 1324–1326).

288. José Luis Illanes, *Existencia cristiana y mundo. Jalones para una reflexión teológica sobre el Opus Dei* (Pamplona: Eunsa, 2003), p. 241.

for fruitfulness: "Unless a grain of wheat falls into the earth and dies, it remains alone; but if it dies, it bears much fruit" (John 12:24).

The importance of bearing fruit for love of God is such that St. Josemaría begins *The Way* by fostering that desire. He states,

> *Don't let your life be barren. Be useful. Make yourself felt. Shine forth with the torch of your faith and your love. With your apostolic life, wipe out the trail of filth and slime left by the corrupt sowers of hatred. And set aflame all the ways of the earth with the fire of Christ that you bear in your heart.*[289]

In order to understand these words well, it is necessary to keep in mind that human criteria are not good for measuring apostolic fruits. Sometimes God allows for a Christian not to reap any fruits and counts on others to reap them. And when he allows someone to reap apostolic fruit, God wishes for that person to realize that others have sown the seed before him. "For here the saying holds true, 'One sows and another reaps.' I sent you to reap that for which you did not labor; others have labored, and you have entered into their labor" (John 4:37–38). In the work of evangelization, God's children must always be conscious that they participate in the one priesthood of Christ and that they are instruments of his grace.[290]

In any event, apostolic hope should not waver if on occasion fruits are not visible. Hope is about our happiness and that of others in God, not about the satisfaction of reaching tangible results. St. Josemaría exhorts people to persevere with determination when the fruit is slow to arrive. He states,

> Work filled with hope: *plant* [and] *water, trusting in God, who is the one who gives the increase (see 1 Cor. 3:7). And when discouragement comes, should God permit that temptation, in the face of apparently adverse circumstances; when you see, in some cases, the ineffectiveness of your apostolic work of formation; when someone were then to ask you, as was asked the elder Tobias,* ubi est spes tua? *Where is your hope? . . . , raise your eyes above the wretchedness of this life, which is not our final goal, and tell them, like that Old Testament character, who was strong and full of hope* quoniam memor

289. *The Way*, no. 1.

290. The fruits always come from Jesus, but at times he wants to rely on hidden instruments. These are they "who have labored beforehand." Just as the action of Christ is not seen and nevertheless is the most important, so too it happens that fruits proceed from instruments that are not seen either (i.e., they come from those who have sown, more than from those who reap).

> fuit Domini in toto corde suo (*Tob. 1:13*), *because he always remembered the Lord and loved him with all his heart:* filii sanctorum sumus, et vitam illam expectamus, quam Deus daturus est his, qui fidem suam nunquam mutant ab eo, *we are the children of saints, and we look to that life which God will give to those who never lost their faith in him.* (*Tob. 2:18*)[291]

An important part of the fruit to which the common faithful should aspire in the middle of the world is to configure society in accord with human dignity, imbuing it with a Christian spirit. The virtue of hope also concerns this type of fruitfulness. It presupposes the conviction (which is part of faith) that such a configuration contributes to the temporal happiness of men and helps them to attain eternal beatitude. If a Christian were not convinced that a social life in which the good of the person and family is fostered in accord with the natural moral order favors these goals, then he would not have the hope of reaching them and he would be lacking the indispensable moral strength to seek those goods as charity demands. On the contrary, when this conviction is present, *hope makes us powerful.*[292] It provides the necessary spiritual strength to strive for the high goals that faith presents and charity requires.

In other words, a Christian should desire to imbue society with the spirit of Christ.[293] And he will do so as an exercise of charity if he knows with the certainty of faith that only such a society is worthy of man, and if he aspires, with the strength of hope, to foster those conditions of life that God desires and that in themselves contribute to the happiness of all.

> *God did not create us to build a lasting city here on earth* [. . .]. *Nevertheless, we children of God ought not to remain aloof from earthly endeavors, for God has placed us here to sanctify them and make them fruitful with our blessed faith, which alone is capable of bringing true peace and joy to all men wherever they may be* [. . .]. *In this way all human occupations will be lit up by a new hope that transcends time and the inherent transience of earthly realities.*[294]

The work proper to the children of God who have received the world as an inheritance (see Ps. 2:7–8; Rom. 8:17) is to free creation "from its

291. *Instruction*, January 9, 1935, no. 19.

292. *Friends of God*, no. 221.

293. See *Lumen gentium*, no. 31.

294. *Friends of God*, no. 210.

bondage to decay and obtain the glorious liberty of the children of God" (Rom. 8:21). Hope leads us to carry out this work with a realistic optimism which, without ignoring the presence of evil, avoids the pitfall of sadness because it relies on the supernatural outlook of faith.

> *Our Lord, I insist, has given us the world for our inheritance. It is up to us to keep our souls and our minds wide awake. We have to be realistic, without being defeatist. Only a person with a callous conscience, made insensitive by routine or dulled by a frivolous attitude, can allow himself to think that evil—offense to God and harm, at times irreparable harm, to souls—does not exist in the world he sees. We have to be optimistic, but our optimism should come from our faith in the power of God who does not lose battles, and not from any human sense of satisfaction, from a stupid and presumptuous complacency.*[295]
>
> *If we beg our Lord to grant us an ever increasing hope, we will possess the infectious joy of those who know they are children of God:* If God is with us, who can be against us? (Rom. 8:31). *Let us be optimists. Moved by the power of hope, we will fight to wipe away the trail of filth and slime left by the sowers of hatred. We will find a new joyful perspective to the world, seeing that it has sprung forth beautiful and fair from the hands of God. We will give it back to him with that same beauty.*[296]

During St. Josemaría's lifetime in the twentieth century, diverse materialistic ideologies attempted to construct a society without God whereby man's desire for happiness would be satiated by excellent conditions of material well-being, by technical and scientific progress as well as social achievements. While many of these human goals are positive in themselves, they failed to bring about their desired goals because they passed themselves off as the highest horizon of hope. As such, they are "false substitutes for hope" that degrade mankind instead of making it more noble.

> *If we transform our temporal projects into ends in themselves and blot out from our horizon our eternal dwelling place and the end for which we have been created, which is to love and praise the Lord and then to possess him for ever in heaven, then our most brilliant endeavors turn traitor, and can even become a means of degrading our fellow creatures* [. . .]. *Perhaps there is no greater tragedy for man than the sense of disillusionment he suffers when he*

295. *Christ Is Passing By*, no. 123.
296. *Friends of God*, no. 219.

> *has corrupted or falsified his hope by placing it in something other than the one Love which satisfies without ever satiating.*[297]

It is understandable that the experience of evil in society can weaken the hope of transforming it. But to think that the reign of Christ in the world is an unreachable utopia because there is no "human hope" of reaching it, means risking the loss of the strength of theological hope. The Scriptures underline the example of Abraham who in the midst of trials knew how to hope with theological hope when there was no place for human hope: *contra spem in spem* [In hope (. . .) against hope] (Rom. 4:18; Vulgate). Commenting on these words of Scripture, St. Josemaría exhorted Christians to *live in certain hope, against all hope. Rely on that firm rock which will save you and spur you on.*[298] He also encouraged people to look beyond the shadows of the present situation of society or of individuals to recognize what is positive with all of its significance. This optimistic and hope-filled vision is an impetus for putting into practice the apostle's teaching: "Do not be overcome by evil, but overcome evil with good" (Rom. 12:21).

Thinking of the sowing of this Christian spirit in society by his children in Opus Dei throughout time and sanctifying the most diverse professions, he wrote,

> *We will help in an effective way to create a climate of mutual understanding and fellowship, with a broad and universal vision, which drowns all hatred and resentment through charity: without any class struggle, or nationalism, or discrimination. Dream, and your dreams will fall short.*[299]

This last expression, "Dream and your dreams will fall short" had a "solid mooring to reality; it was not a utopian dream, but rather an ideal filled with faith and hope that each day becomes a reality in time and in concrete situations."[300]

---

297. Ibid., no. 208.

298. *Furrow*, no. 780. In this text he cites Rom. 4:18 according to the Vulgate. The Neo-Vulgate translates it as: "*contra spem, in spe.*"

299. *Letter, October 24, 1942*, no. 58. [Translator's note: The Spanish expression "*Soñad y os quedaréis cortos*," which in the quotation above has been literally translated as "Dream and your dreams will fall short," is not meant in a pessimistic sense, but rather in a sense that conveys optimism and excitement as if to say, "Dream. But the reality will be beyond your wildest dreams."]

300. Peña Vial, "'Mística ojalatera' y realismo en la santidad de la vida ordinaria," p. 133. This expression of St. Josemaría inspired the witness of one of the first members of Opus Dei: Pedro Casciaro, *Dream and Your Dreams Will Fall Short* (New York: Scepter, 2001).

2.2.3. The Security of Hope

As we stated in discussing charity, a Christian should love himself as God loves him. But he would not be able to love himself in this way if, in addition to placing his desire for happiness in that which God wishes for him (to be a saint and to produce fruits of holiness), he did not also hope that such a goal is attainable. This hope is founded on the truth that God himself gives him the necessary means and does not cease to love him despite his failures when he struggles to overcome them.[301]

Christian hope is not only the desire for some *bonum futurum* [future good] regardless of the possibility of attaining it. The good to which the Christian aspires (blessedness in union with God in heaven and its anticipation here on earth, for oneself as well as for others) is a *bonum possibile* [a possible good],[302] a good that can be attained with the help of God, *who gives us all the means we need.*[303] If we thought it impossible to obtain, there would be no hope, and charity would be absent. If union with God were considered a utopia, the Christian would cease to love him. And it would really be a utopia if the Christian counted on his strength alone. Thus, it is also the object of hope that God will always provide his grace to become saints and bear fruit.[304]

> *We can never lose hope of becoming holy, of accepting the invitations of God, of persevering until the very end. God, who has begun in us the work of our sanctification, will bring it to completion* (see Phil. 1:6). *Because if the Lord* is with us, who is against us? He who did not spare his own Son but gave him up for us all, will he not also give us all things with him? (Rom. 8:31–32)[305]

Proof that we count on God's assistance is the very self-giving of his Son. Another proof is the reality of the means of sanctification and apostolate that Christ has left his Church in order for his priestly mediation to reach all men: the sacraments, authentic preaching of the Gospel, and pastoral guidance. The object of hope is not the recognition of the existence of these means in general (that is a matter of faith), but rather their availability to us.

---

301. See St. Thomas Aquinas, *Quaestio disputata "De spe,"* a. 1; *S. Th.*, II-II, q. 17, a. 4, c.

302. "*Obiectum enim spei est bonum futurum arduum possibile haberi. Ad hoc ergo quod aliquis speret, requiritur quod obiectum spei proponatur ei ut possibile. Sed obiectum spei est uno modo beatitudo aeterna, et alio modo divinum auxilium, ut ex dictis patet*" (Idem, *S. Th.*, II-II, q. 17, a. 7).

303. *Friends of God*, no. 218.

304. See *CCC*, no. 1817.

305. *Christ Is Passing By*, no. 176.

Hope aspires to a "possible good," a good that can be obtained by whoever uses the appropriate means. It is not a simple wish such as the carefree dream of someone who buys a lottery ticket and "hopes" to win the jackpot. That person knows that it is "possible" to win though very unlikely, and he does nothing further to obtain it. *The firm hope of our personal sanctification is a gift from God, but we cannot remain passive.*[306] It is not the virtue of those who *say that hope is merely an illusion, a utopian dream, a bit of relief from the anxieties of a hard life. For these people, hope has become frivolous wishful-thinking, leading nowhere. What a false idea of hope!*[307] Limiting oneself to "hope" in the happiness that God wishes to give us without applying the means that he offers to reach holiness and bear fruit would be *confusing hope with comfort.*[308] Christian hope implies a conditional assurance: we will obtain the prize if we correspond—with God's help—to the graces he grants to us.

The good to which hope aspires is a *bonum arduum,* a demanding good that requires fighting against sin and the inclination to evil, which are opposed to union with God within ourselves. As will be discussed later on,[309] this is a matter of fighting out of love, and hope is absolutely necessary for this combat. St. Paul writes, "For to this end we toil and strive, because we have our hope set on the living God" (1 Tim. 4:10). It is clear that it would not make sense to fight without the hope of attaining the good for which one is fighting and without the certainty that such a good is worthwhile because it contains the fullness of happiness. St. Josemaría encourages people not to lose sight of this as follows,

> *Let us bear all the difficulties of our voyage over the seas of this life, in the hope of heaven. Our goal, and that of everyone who wants to love, is to reach God and the glory of heaven. Otherwise, nothing is worthwhile. In order to get to heaven, we must be faithful. And to be faithful we have to struggle.*[310]

Hope puts in the soul the determination of "beginning and beginning again" the interior battle without getting discouraged.

---

306. Ibid.

307. *Friends of God*, no. 207.

308. Ibid., no. 207.

309. See chapter eight, section 2.3.

310. *Letter, March 24, 1931*, no. 55. On the *bonum arduum* as an object of hope, see St. Thomas Aquinas, *Quaestio disputata "De spe,"* a. 1.

> *Make more acts of hope. Let me remind you that in your interior life you will suffer defeats and you will have ups and downs—may God make them imperceptible—because no one is free of these misfortunes. But our all powerful and merciful Lord has granted us the precise means with which to conquer. As I have already mentioned, all we have to do is to use them, resolving to begin again and again at every moment, should it prove necessary.*[311]

Hope is not dimmed when a noticeable improvement is not reached because it leads a person to fight for love of God rather than for the satisfaction of reaching some goals. And to fight for love is already to love. An unexpected fruit is gained: *Hope shows us that without him we cannot carry out even the most insignificant duty.*[312] Awareness of our own weakness, *the realization that we are made of clay, and cheap clay at that, has to lead us, above all, to strengthen our hope in Christ Jesus.*[313] St. Josemaría insists in a special way that the persistence of temptations should not weaken our hope; it should be the occasion to practice it. *Far from discouraging us, the difficulties we meet have to spur us on to mature as Christians.*[314] Not even sins should lead us to despair as St. Josemaría points out:

> *How great is the virtue of hope! Judas recognized Christ's sanctity, and repented for the crime he had committed. So much so that he took the money that was the price for his treason and threw it down in front of those who had given it to him as his reward. But . . . he lacked hope, which is the virtue needed to return to God. If he had possessed hope, he still could have been a great Apostle* [. . .]. *So never lose hope, never despair, even if you have done the most foolish thing possible.*[315]

If sin should not shatter our hope, even less so our difficulties, failures, illnesses, and whichever other circumstances that are not an offense against God. These, instead, are the Cross of Christ, occasions to grow and identify ourselves with him. The Cross is precisely *the central point upon which to rest our hope of being united with our Lord.*[316] We should "consider that 'the sufferings of this present time are not worth comparing with the glory about

---

311. *Friends of God*, no. 219.
312. Ibid., no. 215.
313. Ibid.
314. Ibid., no. 216.
315. Notes taken from preaching, December 8, 1968 (AGP, P01 I-1969, pp. 25–26).
316. *Friends of God*, no. 212.

to be revealed to us' (Rom. 8:18; see 2 Tim. 2:11–12), and remain strong in the faith 'while we wait for the blessed hope and the manifestation of the glory of our great God and Savior, Jesus Christ' (Tit. 2:13)."[317]

3. Humility: The Foundation of All Virtues

The theological virtues are not the only Christian virtues. Many of our acts do not have God as their immediate object; their object is the diverse human goods such as work, rest, cultivating friendship, etc. For them to be directed to God as the last end, they must be enlivened by charity; that is possible only if they are rightly ordered. And so, where does this right order come from? It comes from the "human virtues" (the moral virtues), habits that allow us to act well by inclining our faculties to choose what is good and to carry it out. This is why they are necessary.

In the next section, we will make some general remarks about the human virtues, starting with humility. In the teaching of St. Josemaría, this virtue plays such a particular role that it deserves further study going beyond our scope.[318]

3.1. The Humility of the Children of God

The spiritual tradition is practically unanimous in assigning a singular importance to this virtue.[319] Church Fathers from St. Clement of Rome to St. Augustine "have their moral teaching converge on humility after the theological virtues."[320] By humility they understand the virtue proper and characteristic of those whom the Bible calls "poor in spirit" (see, for instance, Matt. 5:3), that is, those who recognize themselves as indigent before God and place all their hope in him. After the Patristic Age, the great spiritual teachers reiterate these intuitions and develop them while always looking at Jesus Christ who is "humble of heart" (Matt. 11:29).[321] It would

317. *Lumen gentium*, no. 48 (text cited by St. Josemaría in his *Letter, March 19, 1967*, no. 96).

318. See Manuel Belda, *La pedagogía de la humildad en "Camino,"* pp. 285–295. Before St. Josemaría, various authors had pointed out the unusual nature of humility with respect to the other human virtues.

319. For a historical review, see Pierre Adnès, "Humilité," in *Dictionnaire de spiritualité ascétique et mystique*, 7 (1969): 1136–1187.

320. Patrizio Sciadini, "Umiltà," in Ermanno Ancilli (dir.), *Dizionario enciclopedico di spiritualità*, vol. 3 (Rome: Vita Nuova Edizioni, 1990), p. 2580.

321. The text says "meek and humble of heart." However, tradition does not consider meekness to be a foundation of all the virtues. On the relationship between meekness and humility, see section 4.4.2.

suffice to recall the central place that humility occupies in *The Imitation of Christ*. According to Daniel-Rops "it is the prominent virtue to which its [*The Imitation of Christ*'s] phrases constantly return."[322] At the time of distinguishing where its prominent place lies, there are varied replies which cannot be summarized here. St. Josemaría echoes this tradition but offers a new and specific outlook, closely relating humility to divine filiation and to sanctification in the middle of the world.

Although it may seem obvious, first we should point out that humility is a *human* virtue and not a theological one. Its object is not God; it is, rather, the elimination of the obstacles within us that prevent our union with him. St. Josemaría summarizes these obstacles in a few words: *What can block charity? Pride.*[323] The object of humility is to combat pride, the first and principal vice. For the same reason, humility is also the most important human virtue.

With regard to its "subject" or the human faculty in which this virtue resides, there are varied replies. For St. Thomas, it resides in the "sensible appetite" and is part of temperance.[324] St. Theresa of Ávila describes humility as "walking in the truth"[325] and seems to underscore, instead, its relation to the practical intellect. Considering the different teachings of the saints, it is not possible to place it under one or another faculty because in some sense, it is found in all; it is an inclination of the whole person. Undoubtedly humility lies in the intellect because it leads us to recognize the truth of what we are before God, before others, and before ourselves (and therefore its close relation to sincerity, as we will see later on). But it also lies in the will and in the sensible faculties in which it places its aspiration to live in accord with that truth. One could say, in keeping with a broad spiritual tradition, that humility resides in the *heart*, if this word is understood in its biblical sense as the intimate nucleus of the person.[326]

This is also the way in which St. Josemaría understands humility. The following text significantly situates it within all of the person's faculties as an element that disposes each one of them in accord with its "truth" (i.e.,

---

322. Henri Daniel-Rops, Preface to *L'Imitation de Notre Seigneur Jésus-Christ* (Paris: Librairie Arthème Fayard, 1961), p. 13.

323. Notes taken from preaching (AGP, P01 III-1962, p. 7).

324. See St. Thomas Aquinas, *S. Th.*, II-II, q. 161, a. 2 and 4.

325. St. Teresa of Jesus, *The Interior Castle*, VI, 10, 8.

326. See *Christ Is Passing By*, no. 164. In chapter five, section 2, in speaking of the influence of the intellect, will and feelings on freedom, we have briefly explained what the Bible means by the term "heart."

its specific nature), so that afterward each faculty can be perfected by other virtues.

> Prayer *is the humility of the man who acknowledges his profound wretchedness and the greatness of God. He addresses and adores God as one who expects everything from him and nothing from himself.*
> Faith *is the humility of the mind which renounces its own judgement and surrenders to the verdict and authority of the Church.*
> Obedience *is the humility of the will which subjects itself to the will of another, for God's sake.*
> Chastity *is the humility of the flesh, which subjects itself to the spirit.*
> Mortification *is the humility of the senses.*
> Penance *is the humility of all the passions, immolated to the Lord.–Humility is truth on the road of the ascetic struggle.*[327]

There is a certain "omnipresence" of humility that is understandable if it is considered to be the foundation of all the virtues.[328] This position that humility has traditionally been given brings it closer to the realization of one's *divine filiation*, which for St. Josemaría is, as we know, the basis or foundation of the spiritual life. He in fact also affirms that *humility is the foundation of our life.*[329] The relation between humility and the awareness of our divine filiation can be seen, for instance, in the following text:

> [*Humility*] *is the deep realization that God our Father is the one who does everything, making use of the poor instruments that each of us are:* servi inutiles sumus (Luke 17:10). *He plays with each of us as with children:* ludens in orbe terrarum et deliciae meae esse cum filiis hominum. (Prov. 8:31)[330]

The link between humility and the awareness of our divine filiation can be understood better when we reflect on the significance of the Incarnation of the Son of God in order for us to be divinely adopted. It is true that if we

---

327. *Furrow*, no. 259.

328. This is a classic statement. St. Josemaría repeats it, mentioning other authors at times. For example, in his *Letter, March 24, 1931*, no. 33, he cites St. Augustine (*Sermo* 69, reproduced below); on another occasion he recalls the words of Cervantes: *[Cervantes] has said that humility is the basis and foundation of all the virtues, and without it there is no virtue. Letter, March 24, 1931*, no. 34. The etymology of the Word *humility*, moreover, is significant: it comes from the Latin *humus*, the organic substratum that allows plants to grow.

329. *Letter, March 24, 1930*, no. 20.

330. *Letter, May 6, 1945*, no. 31.

consider only the filiation of the Word, man's humility has nothing to do with it, because according to the etymology of the term and its traditional use, "humility" denotes "lowliness," "smallness" or a certain inferiority,[331] and the Only-begotten and consubstantial Son is not inferior in any way to the Father. But in the Incarcation, he "emptied himself, taking the form of a servant, being born in the likeness of men. And being found in human form he humbled himself and became obedient unto death, even death on a cross" (Phil. 2:7–8). St. Athanasius notes that "terms such as 'humbled' and 'exalted' refer only to the human dimension. In fact only what is humble can be exalted."[332] Humility corresponds to the Son only inasmuch as he is man. And given that the Christian participates in divine filiation through the humanity of the Lord, we can affirm that "being humble" pertains essentially to man's adopted filiation, for this latter condition is an exaltation that presupposes the lowliness of the human condition with respect to the divinity. Hence, the "awareness of our divine filiation" must necessarily include an awareness and acceptance of this lowliness (i.e., humility).

Situating the awareness of divine filiation as the foundation of the spiritual life means above all to consider it as the basis for growth in charity, because charity is the essence of the Christian life. Stated in other words, it means fostering "the charity of God's children": filial love for the Father and fraternity in Christ. Now if the awareness of our divine filiation necessarily includes humility, it follows that humility is also the foundation for charity and that by means of charity (the "form" of all the other virtues), humility is the foundation for the rest of the virtues as well.

Everything we have discussed above thus far refers to *Christian* humility, informed by charity and pertaining to the awareness of our divine filiation. St. Josemaría also posits a natural or human humility (not informed by charity) and in so doing, he makes humility a requirement of the other moral virtues: *The first step to be prudent is to acknowledge our own limitations. This is the virtue of humility.*[333] Prudence is the guiding cardinal virtue that directs the other virtues. If humility is its "first step," it means that it is in some sense at the very foundation of prudence and therefore of the other virtues as well. But only when it is informed by charity does it become the humility of an adopted child of God. In referring to humility, St. Josemaría

331. See Adnès, "Humilité," col. 1136.

332. St. Athanasius, *Oratio contra Arianos*, 1, 41.

333. *Friends of God*, no. 86.

once called it a "living" humility (as it is enlivened by charity) and one that *stems directly from the contemplative dialogue that we have with God* sine intermissione (1 Thess. 5:17).[334] Thus, it is no longer the first step of prudence, but rather the foundation of charity itself and of all the virtues enlivened by charity. Humility is the first virtue that is informed by charity and on which charity "rests." This foundation becomes stronger in the measure that charity grows.

> At first sight it may seem contradictory that charity informs its very foundation, humility. But this is only a consequence of the fact that the adopted filiation of the Christian is, as it were, pervaded by the redemptive Incarnation. In the Incarnation, there is both humiliation (abasement) and elevation: the abasement of God and the elevation of the human nature assumed. It is the humiliation of Christ as God and his glorification as man (see Phil. 2:5 ff). In the mystery of the Son-of-God-made-man, humiliation is the basis for his elevation, and this elevation gives his humiliation meaning. In a like manner, there is also an inseparable link between the divinization of the Christian and his humiliation, and therefore between charity and humility: "For all who exalt themselves will be humbled, and those who humble themselves will be exalted" (Luke 14:11; see 18:14). Both the infusion of grace and its growth are realized on the basis of humility. "God opposes the proud, but gives grace to the humble." (1 Pet. 5:5; Jas. 4:6)[335]

Between charity and Christian humility there is a necessary mutual connection. St. Augustine teaches that "the home of charity is humility"[336] and in another place he writes, "Do you wish to construct a building that reaches to heaven? Think first of laying the foundation of humility. The greater the size of the structure that is to be raised and the height of the building, the deeper must its foundations be [. . .]. Before going up the

---

334. *Letter, May 6, 1945*, no. 31.

335. If this text is applied to the life of one who is in the grace of God, as we have done here, it means that the more a child of God delves deeper in humility (with the help of actual graces), the more he or she is disposed to receive new graces and thus grow in holiness. One can also apply this to a person who is not in the state of grace, and then it means (at least for what we are dealing with now) that he could prepare himself of herself to receive grace, trying to be humble (with a "human" humility that is the foundation of Christian humility), recognizing his sins, etc. God does not deny his grace to the humble, and anyone who makes an effort to practice this human virtue will have, when he or she receives sanctifying grace, a good basis for growing in the Christian life.

336. St. Augustine, *De Sancta virginitate*, 51.

building is humbled and its highest part is raised after its humiliation."[337] When mentioning this teaching, St. Thomas says that humility is the "negative" foundation of the supernatural edifice because it removes the obstacles that are opposed to the action of grace.[338] Along these lines St. Josemaría writes,

> *God* [. . .] *wants us to be humble and to empty ourselves, so that he can fill us. He wants us not to put obstacles in his way so that—humanly speaking—there will be more room for his grace in our poor hearts.*[339]

He frequently repeats the classical aphorism:

> *If you want to be holy, be humble; if you want to be more holy, be more humble; if you want to be very holy, be very humble.*[340]

3.2. Aspects of Humility

Humility removes pride, the main obstacle to loving God, neighbor, and oneself. We now discuss various aspects of this virtue with regard to charity: humility before God, in relation with others and with respect to oneself.

3.2.1. Humility before God: "May Jesus Alone Shine Forth"

"Humble yourselves before the Lord, and he will exalt you" (Jas. 4:10; see 1 Pet. 5:6). Humility and self-praise are incompatible. Any glory that is not directed to God and any vaunting before God should be rejected. St. Paul says, "For you have died, and your life is hidden with Christ in God" (Col. 3:3). Viewed from the precise context of "a new life in Christ," these words have a profound meaning for humility: namely, that it is necessary to "die to oneself," to die to the quest for glory so as to live in Christ for the glory of God. Humility does not impede our divinization; on the contrary, humility makes it possible. It allows a person "to live in Christ with God." St. Josemaría expressed this attitude with words that he used as the theme for his life:

---

337. Idem, *Sermo* 69. There is a handwritten note of St. Josemaría in which he copies this text of the holy bishop of Hippo in Latin (see Rodríguez, *The Way, Critical-Historical Edition*, commentary to point 590).

338. The basis is "*ut removens prohibens*." St. Thomas Aquinas, *S. Th.*, II-II, q. 161, a. 5, ad 2.

339. *Friends of God*, no. 98.

340. Notes taken from preaching, June 7, 1975 (AGP, P01 VII-1975, p. 219). St. Josemaría points out that he took those words from St. Joseph of Calasanz.

> *Mine is to hide and disappear, so that only Jesus may shine forth.*[341]

Seeking "to hide and disappear" is humility before God, and its purpose is so that "only Jesus may shine forth" in one's life because Christ lives in the Christian and God's glory requires that his life manifest itself in the Christian. Humility removes self-love and selfishness so that Christ's presence may shine forth.

This teaching opens vast horizons for humility in practical matters for those who are called to holiness in the middle of the world and wish to place Christ at the pinnacle of all human activities. St. Josemaría unfolds the consequences of this in a text that is well worth quoting at length:

> *Let us be humble, let us seek only God's glory. Our life of dedication, silent and hidden, ought to be a constant manifestation of humility* [. . .]. Vita vestra est abscondita cum Christo in Deo (Col. 3:3). *Live with your eyes fixed on God, not on men* [. . .]. *This should also be the aspiration of each one of us, my children: to pass unnoticed, to imitate Christ, who remained hidden for thirty years, being simply* the carpenter's son (Matt. 13:55); *to imitate Mary who, being the Mother of God, likes to be called a servant:* ecce ancilla Domini. (Luke. 1:38)
>
> *Our Lord wants us to be humble. But this doesn't mean that you fail to reach the level you should in your profession, in your ordinary work, and of course in your spiritual life. It is important to be competent, but with a right intention, without seeking oneself. We do not live for this life only, nor for our own glory. Rather we live for the glory of God, for the service of God: this alone moves us.*
>
> *God has wanted to make use of our struggle to reach holiness, and also of our human talents. Always keep in mind Christ's command:* Let your light shine before men, so that they may see your good works and give glory to your Father who is in heaven (Matt. 5:16). *All the glory to him, all the honor:* soli Deo honor et gloria in saecula saeculorum (1 Tim. 1:17). *Only to God are we to give honor and glory forever and ever.*[342]

One of the aspects that these paragraphs highlight is that humility counteracts the tendency to seek one's glory in virtuous acts, and in other

341. *Letter, January 28, 1975* (AGP, P01 VII-1975, p. 158). See José María Casciaro, "Fundamentos bíblicos del lema 'ocultarme y desaparecer' de San Josemaría Escrivá," in Juan Chapa (ed.), *Signum et Testimonium* (Pamplona: Eunsa, 2003), pp. 273–295.

342. *Letter, March 24, 1930*, nos. 20–21.

cases, it removes whatever impedes repentance: self-justification and resistance in recognizing offenses against God.

> *If we are not humble, deeply humble, it is easy for our conscience to become deformed. Perhaps in our life we may do something wrong through weakness. But let us have clear ideas, a clear conscience. What we can never do is to do things that are wrong and say that they are holy.*[343]

In paving the way for contrition, humility prepares the soul for the outpouring of grace that divinizes it. And this "divinization" leads in turn to a deeper recognition that all that is good is a gift from God.

> *When night falls, and I examine my conscience, I review the balance for the day and conclude:* Pauper servus et humilis! *And I repeat many times:* Cor contritum et humiliatum, Deus, non despicies! (Ps. 50:19). *This is not play-acting either. If God sees that we sincerely consider ourselves poor and useless servants, that we are humble and contrite of heart, then he will not turn us away. He will draw us very close to himself, to all the richness and strength of his most lovable Heart. And we will attain a good divinization: we will recognize that all the good we possess comes from God, since left to ourselves we are nothing, we have nothing, we can do nothing.*[344]

3.2.2 Humility in Relation to Others: "Naturalness"

Whereas charity leads to loving others for love of God with acts of service, humility removes the most radical obstacle: that of thinking oneself superior to others. In this regard, Jesus imparts his teaching in word and deed. When the mother of James and John asks for a place of honor in the kingdom of God for her sons and the other disciples become indignant, Jesus calls them and says to them, "Whoever would be great among you must be your servant, and whoever would be first among you must be slave of all. For the Son of man also came not to be served but to serve, and to give his life as a ransom for many" (Mark 10:43–45). At the Last Supper he preaches to them by washing their feet: "For I have given you an example, that you also should do as I have done to you" (John 13:15). Moreover, St. Paul describes the attitude that a Christian should have through the following words: "Do nothing from selfishness or conceit, but in humility count

343. *Letter, March 24, 1931*, no. 37.

344. Ibid., no. 29.

others better than yourselves" (Phil. 2:3). Humility, hence, allows charity to overflow in deeds of service.

The Lord teaches that no one should place himself above others. He publicly censures the attitudes of the Pharisee who considers himself better than the tax collector, as he even seems to offer "proof" of his superiority: "I am not like other men, extortioners, unjust, adulterers, or even like this tax collector. I fast twice a week, I give tithes of all that I get" (Luke 18:11–12). Instead, Jesus praises the tax collector who "beat his breast, saying, 'God, be merciful to me, a sinner!'"(Luke 18:13). "I tell you, this man went down to his house justified rather than the other; for every one who exalts himself will be humbled, but he who humbles himself will be exalted" (Luke 18:14).

Yet, would it not be contrary to the reality of things (as well as to humility) to consider as superior he who has less human qualities than oneself? In reference to the merely human, it is evident that some people stand out for some qualities, but probably not for all. Humility enables a person to discover those qualities in which others excel. St. Josemaría makes this point by means of a meaningful quotation:

> In any man, *writes St. Thomas Aquinas*, there is an aspect under which others can consider him superior to themselves, according to the Apostle's words, "Each of you must have the humility to think others better men than himself" (Phil. 2:3). It is in this spirit that all men should honor one another (*S. Th.*, IIII q. 103, a. 2, ad 3). *Humility is the virtue that teaches us that the signs of respect for others—for their good name, their good faith, their intimacy—are not external conventions, but the first signs of charity and justice.*[345]

In any event, the main motive for which a Christian can consider others superior to himself lies in the quality that makes a person "good" in the strict sense of the word: God's love (as it makes the will good).[346] And in this no one can affirm that he is superior to another; only God knows that. In fact, whoever thinks that he loves God cannot say that he is superior to the one who is far removed from God, because that "superiority" would only make sense with regard to the whole of a person's existence and therefore would need to include the final moment of a person's life on earth. Until that

345. *Christ Is Passing By*, no. 72.

346. See St. Thomas Aquinas, *De virtutibus in communi*, q. 1, a. 9, ad 16 (quoted at the beginning of this chapter).

moment, any person can convert, purifying in an instant his entire past, and love God more than another. St. Josemaría offers the following rationale: *It's true that he was a sinner. But don't pass so final a judgment on him. Have pity in your heart, and don't forget that he may yet be an Augustine, while you remain just another mediocrity.*[347]

Charity is such that a person becomes "all things to all men" (1 Cor. 9:22) and humility removes obstacles so that this can become a reality. *Humility leads us as it were by the hand to treat our neighbor in the best way possible, that is, being understanding toward everyone, living at peace with everyone, forgiving everyone.*[348]

This dimension of humility has diverse manifestations according to each person's vocation. The everyday faithful should serve others for the most part through their professional work and the fulfillment of duties in their family and society; this also implies the exercise of rights. It has been noted that "frequently people interpret humility to mean lowering oneself, giving up what is one's due or what one deserves, but true humility is not that. A humble person does not renounce anything; rather, he simply recognizes who he truly is, which is not easy to do."[349] It is not contrary to true humility to act in accord with one's position in society.

> *As our sanctity hinges on our work, we will need to achieve prestige in our profession, and each person will find that he has around him, in his own job and social sphere, the dignity and good name he has won by his merits, gained in honest competition with his professional colleagues.*
>
> *Our humility doesn't entail being timid and shy, or lacking in daring in the noble field of human endeavor. With a supernatural spirit and a desire to serve—with a Christian spirit of service—we must strive to be among the first among our peers.*
>
> *Some people without a genuine lay outlook on life understand humility as a lack of confidence, a kind of indecision that impedes action, a waiving of rights (sometimes even the rights of truth and justice) in order to avoid friction and disagreements and to be nice to everyone. Thus, there will be some who won't understand our way of living a deep—and genuine—humility; they may even call it pride. The Christian concept of this virtue has been*

347. *The Way*, no. 675.

348. *Friends of God*, no. 233.

349. Rafael Corazón González, "La virtud de la sinceridad en la espiritualidad de San Josemaría Escrivá," p. 63.

> *much deformed, possibly because of attempting to live it within secular society in ways more suited to convents than to Christians who are called to be at the crossroads of the world.*[350]

St. Josemaría often uses the term *naturalness* to designate a virtue that can be considered as part of humility with respect to one's neighbors.[351] Naturalness in fact leads one to act before others in conformity with one's condition as a Christian and as a citizen.

> *When we behave this way, acting quite normally (just the same as our fellow men do) and with a supernatural outlook, we are simply following the example set by Jesus Christ who is true God and true Man. See how full of naturalness his life is. For thirty years he passes unnoticed as just another worker, without calling attention to himself, and he is known in his village as the son of the carpenter.*[352]

This is a virtue that shines forth in a special manner in the behavior of the first Christians. *They lived their Christian vocation seriously, seeking earnestly the holiness to which they had been called by their Baptism. Externally they did nothing to distinguish themselves from their fellow citizens.*[353] It is

---

350. *Letter, May 6, 1945*, nos. 30–31.

351. See *The Way*, nos. 376 ff.; *Furrow*, nos. 555 ff.; *The Forge*, nos. 140, 508; *Conversations*, no. 119; *Christ Is Passing By*, nos. 53, 148; *Friends of God*, nos. 89–90; etc. Just in the works so far published, he speaks of naturalness more than forty times. We will not stop to study the sense in which this is "a part" of humility. St. Thomas Aquinas speaks of the parts of a virtue in three senses: as *integral, subjective* and *potential parts* (see *S. Th.*, II-II, q. 48, a. 1, c). Here it is enough to say that naturalness possesses the essence of humility but does not include all of its manifestations. Therefore we say that it is "a part."

352. *Friends of God*, no. 121. As you can see, in this text he speaks of "normality" and of "naturalness;" it seems to us that for St. Josemaría these are equivalent terms. In another homily also included in *Friends of God* (nn. 89–90), he refers, together with naturalness, to simplicity. He mentions them, on one occasion as two distinct virtues, and, at another time, as just one. Simplicity in dealing with others is practically identified with naturalness; but, on the other hand, it has aspects that do not necessarily refer to the others, and in this sense it is a distinct virtue (see section 3.3.3).

353. *Conversations*, no. 24. The Light of Christ that they have taken into their hearts leads them to sanctify their activities, not to abandon nor to change them, if they are honorable. "We do not cease to frequent the forum, the market, the baths, the stores, the offices, the inns and fairs; we do not give up relationships, living together with you in this world. We sail with you, we take part in the army, we cultivate the earth and market its fruits. And we sell to the people for your use the products of our efforts and fatigue." (Tertullian, *Apologetics*, ch. 42, 1–3). "Christians," we read in another document of the second century, "are not distinguished from other men neither in their country, nor in their language, nor in their customs. For they do not inhabit cities that are exclusively theirs, nor speak a strange language, nor live a kind of life apart from others [. . .]. They adapt themselves in dress, food, and other ways of life to the customs and usage of each country, giving an example of a way of acting which is admirable and, as all confess, surprising" *Ep. ad Diognetum*, ch. V, 1 ff. They are of the world without being worldly: they live with Christian naturalness.

well known that St. Josemaría sees in these first disciples of Christ the clearest precedent for his message of holiness in the middle of the world.[354] In fact, he points out that those who seek to follow the path of holiness that he teaches *are ordinary people. They work like everyone else and live in the middle of the world. They live like any other Christian citizen who wants to respond fully to the demands of his faith.*[355] This is the reason for the importance that he gives to naturalness as the norm of behavior that reflects secularity.

In general, Christian naturalness moves persons to live the faith in a coherent manner, behaving in their relations with others in accord with each person's condition with varying external manifestations. There is a naturalness proper to priests that leads them to carry themselves in a manner in keeping with their sacred ministry, which is a public office. There is a naturalness proper to members of religious congregations that prompts them to give public witness of the supreme value of the eternal goods in a way that corresponds to their vocation. And there is a naturalness proper to the lay faithful that consists in coherently living the faith in their professional and social milieu, also giving witness of Christ yet not like those who have a public office in the Church (as is the case of priests and religious), but rather in accord with their condition as citizens and professionals like the rest. When St. Josemaría speaks of naturalness he refers especially to the naturalness of the lay faithful. He affirms that *to show that one is a Christian, there is no need to wear a bunch of badges. Christianity will manifest itself with simplicity in the life of those who know the faith and struggle to put it into practice, in their effort to behave well, in the joy with which they approach the things of God, in the eagerness with which they live charity.*[356]

On another occasion, St. Josemaría completes the idea, addressing those who have made the decision to fully respond to the Christian vocation:

> *Isn't Christ teaching us that we should live alongside our peers, our professional colleagues, as one more, unnoticed? Unnoticed not because of your reputation or work, nor because of your talents. Unnoticed, rather, because there is no need for others to know you are souls dedicated to God, striving to imitate Jesus Christ; that you are the salt of the earth, other Christs. May they experience it; may they feel themselves helped to be clean and noble, when they see your conduct filled with respect for the legitimate freedom of*

354. See the Preliminary Part, section I.1.

355. *Conversations*, no. 24.

356. *Letter, March 24, 1930*, no. 8.

> *everyone; when they hear your words filled with doctrine, backed up by your consistent example. But your dedication to God's service should be hidden, unnoticed, as Jesus' life was hidden in his first thirty years.*[357]

In order to understand this teaching of St. Josemaría well, we need to keep in mind that what is "natural" or "normal" for a lay faithful is neither always nor in principle "to do what others do;" "to hide within the crowd so as to not attract attention;" or "to settle for the prevailing fads," etc. What is natural for the lay person is to live the faith integrally without the ostentation that is not proper to his state and condition, that is, to the divine call to holiness and apostolate he has received. *Naturalness. Let your lives as Christian men, as Christian women—your salt and your light—flow spontaneously, without anything odd or silly.*[358] In principle, a Christian should not seek to behave "the same as others," when others do not behave well. He must behave in a manner that is in keeping with the faith being one more "among his peers"[359] in the professional and social life, that is, like any ordinary citizen who wishes to be consistent with his Christian faith. For this reason, it is "natural" that those who are in contact with a Christian seeking holiness in ordinary life will notice his effort to grow in virtue, to practice his faith (also publicly) without "hiding" himself, and will receive the influence of his apostolate even though all this may visibly contrast with the environment that surrounds him. "*And in a paganized or pagan environment when my life clashes with its surroundings, won't my naturalness seem artificial?" you ask me. And I reply: Undoubtedly your life will clash with theirs; and that contrast—faith confirmed by works!—is exactly the naturalness I ask of you.*[360] These quotations demonstrate that the absence of external badges of a person's interior commitment to seek holiness has nothing to do with secrecy. On the contrary, it is discretion, a natural manifestation of the right of protecting one's intimacy. *Discretion is neither mystery nor secrecy. It is simply naturalness.*[361]

---

357. Notes taken from a meditation, January 9, 1959 (AGP, P18, p. 90).

358. *The Way*, no. 379.

359. See *Christ Is Passing By*, nos. 21, 111–112; *Friends of God*, no. 121.

360. *The Way*, no. 380. See ibid., no. 842.

361. *The Way*, no. 641. In this point of *The Way* and, in general, in the teaching of St. Josemaría, "discretion" is situated "in the life of ordinary Christians, of citizens equal to the others, who strive to sanctify their work and give unequivocal witness to their Catholic faith, but without 'advertising,' and trying to live a 'life hidden with Christ in God' (Col. 3:3)" (Rodríguez, *The Way, Critical-Historical Edition*, commentary to point 641). Later St. Josemaría decided to stop using the word "discretion" to avoid being misunderstood (see ibid.).

3.2.3. Humility in Considering Oneself: "Our Wretchedness and Our Greatness"

"I bid every one among you, not to think of himself more highly than he ought to think" (Rom. 12:3). In the context of the Pauline letter, the meaning of these words is that each person has received from God certain gifts for the sake of their use in the Body of Christ. Humility removes whatever makes their use difficult in fulfillment of the proper mission, according to the will of God. It impedes "thinking of himself more highly than one ought to think," not recognizing that all good things come from God (see 1 Cor. 4:7), and failing to accept one's limits. This is why St. Josemaría affirms that humility is *the virtue which helps us to recognize, at one and the same time, both our wretchedness and our greatness.*[362] He adds that *self-knowledge is a prerequisite for true humility.*[363]

When he speaks of humility, these two aspects ("our wretchedness and our greatness") usually go together in such a way that when he mentions one he refers also to the other. To realize what it means to be a child of God leads to a "good divinization" and to a certain "superiority complex"; at the same time, consciousness of our own deficiency as creatures who experience falls and miseries precludes forgetting that left to ourselves we are "nothing." The Christian is "dust from the earth," "a vessel of clay," fragile even though full of divine treasures; a "little donkey" whose sole dignity derives from being one who transports Christ; "a simple instrument," like a paintbrush in a painter's hands. When speaking of humility these are, among others, the expressions and images St. Josemaría uses. The following are some of his texts.

- "Superiority complex" and awareness of one's "nothingness":

  When we're working for God, we have to have a superiority complex, I told you. But isn't that a sign of pride? you asked me. No. It is a consequence of humility; the humility which makes me say: Lord, you are who you are. I am nothingness itself. You have all the perfections: power, strength, love, glory, wisdom, authority, dignity . . . If I unite myself to you, like a child who goes to the strong embrace of his father or sits on his dear mother's knee, I will feel the warmth of your divinity, I will experience the light of your wisdom, I will sense your strength flowing through my veins.[364]

362. *Friends of God*, no. 94.
363. *Letter, May 6, 1945*, no. 32. Self-knowledge is a "condition" for humility as long as it is not united to the acceptance of what one is. When it includes that acceptance it is true humility.
364. *The Forge*, no. 342.

- "Divinization" and awareness of being "dust of the earth." It is important *that we know how to distinguish "true godliness" from "false godliness."*[365] The former is the humble attitude of him who is aware that he is "immersed" in God through divine filiation; the latter is the pride of him who forgets his own miseries.

  I cannot conceal from you the fear that in some cases this "divinization," without a deep basis of humility, could give rise to presumption, to the corruption of true hope, to pride, and sooner or later to spiritual ruin, on being faced with the unexpected experience of one's own frailty.

  I often give the example of the dust that is lifted up by the wind until it forms a golden cloud high up in the sky because it receives the rays of the sun. In the same way, the grace of God lifts us up high, and all this wonder of goodness, of wisdom, of effectiveness, of beauty that is God, reverberates in us. If you and I realize that we are but dust and misery—of no value—our Lord will do the rest. It is a consideration that fills my soul.[366]

- Being clay but counting on God's strength:

  Humility leads each soul not to get discouraged when faced with its own faults. God our Father well knows the clay of which we are made (see Ps. 102:14). *Though the clay vessel might crack at times or even break, if we are humble, it is repaired with staples that make it more charming, and that no doubt are pleasing to God. Men's weaknesses, my children, give our God a chance "to shine," to show his omnipotence by excusing and forgiving.*[367]

  Humbly acknowledge your weakness so that, with the Apostle, you can say: "It is when I am weak that I am strong."[368]

- God's instruments:

  Get rid of those proud thoughts: you are but the brush in the hand of the artist. And nothing more. Tell me, of what use is a brush, if it won't let the painter do his work?[369]

  Humility will spur us on to carry out great tasks, but only on condition that we never lose sight of our inadequacy, and that we are convinced, and more so each day, of our own helplessness.[370]

---

365. *Friends of God*, no. 94.
366. *Letter, March 24, 1931*, no. 4. See *The Way*, no. 599; *Christ Is Passing By*, no. 133.
367. *Letter, May 6, 1945*, no. 32. See *Friends of God*, no. 108.
368. *The Way*, no. 604.
369. Ibid., no. 612.
370. *Friends of God*, no. 106.

3.2.4. "Collective Humility"

By "collective humility" St. Josemaría does not designate the "humility of a group," that is, the virtue exercised by a group (for in that case, the term 'virtue' would only apply metaphorically). Rather, what he means is an aspect of personal humility that should be practiced by those who form part of the group or collectivity, specifically the Church or an institution of the Church.

This is, in our opinion, the sense in which the following exhortation should be understood: *Besides personal humility, indispensable for all the faithful, love and practice "collective humility."*[371] There does not seem to be a contrast between "personal humility" and "collective humility," but rather between the individual aspects of personal humility and those that derive from the fact of forming part of a group within the Church or, more in general, from the Church itself. In either case, it is evident that St. Josemaría is talking about aspects of personal humility. Thus, he writes *if John and Peter and Andrew, as individuals, have the duty to be humble, I don't understand why they should think they have the right to be as proud as peacocks when they are all together.*[372] Individual humility and collective humility are inseparable. The same persons called to practice humility individually should do likewise when they are united among themselves for the sake of holiness and apostolate.

In various parts of Sacred Scripture, examples of this type of humility can be found. When the apostle John tells the Lord: "Master, we saw a man casting out demons in your name, and we forbade him, because he does not follow with us" (Luke 9:49), Jesus replies, "Do not forbid him; for he that is not against you is for you" (Luke 9:50). To these apostles who are tempted to form a closed group that claims an exclusive possession of the good, and to feel superior because they form part of that group, the Lord answers by inviting them to rejoice with a right intention for every good thing others do. The apostles should not rejoice for having been called to be part of the Apostolic College, using this honor to shine personally given they are only instruments of divine action. Each one of the apostles should be humble, not only individually but collectively, that is, as far as each is a member of the college of the Twelve. This is one of the Gospel passages on which St. Josemaría apparently bases his teaching on collective humility.

---

371. *Letter, December 24, 1951*, no. 42.

372. *Letter, May 31, 1954*, no. 13.

In the following words he refers indirectly to the object of this aspect of humility:

> *This collective humility, so pleasing to God, guards against an excessive esprit de corps, fanaticism, forming a little club* [. . .]. [*With collective humility*] *one rejects the thought that what is ours is good simply because it's ours; and what the others have is mediocre or bad.*[373]

Here, St. Josemaría is specifically addressing the faithful of Opus Dei with the intention of forming in them a humility that excludes the defects he mentions. Nonetheless, his teaching has a general application, valid for any Christian who, by the very fact of belonging to an institution within the Church, should practice collective humility. The Church (including the vital manifestations the Holy Spirit inspires within it) has a supernatural end that surpasses human prestige. Thus, neither should the Christian use the Church's good name, nor the merits of other Catholics for his own earthly or temporal good (thereby placing a human motive above the Church's supernatural end). Likewise, it would neither be in accord with truth and humility to undervalue the good carried out by another simply "because he is not one of us" (see Luke 9:49).

Certainly, an enterprise with temporal ends such as a car factory or a firm that seeks markets for its products and services needs to advertise in order to reach its proper objectives. St. Josemaría, however, makes it clear that it would be very harmful to apply these same practices to an institution with supernatural ends because the spread of the Gospel does not respond to market criteria.

> *It is reasonable for an association with earthly aims to publish impressive statistics as to the number, social standing, and qualities of its members. And, in fact, organizations in search of temporal prestige usually do so. But when the sanctification of souls is the aim, to act in such a way would encourage "collective pride," whereas Christ wants each individual Christian, personally, and the whole Christian body, collectively, to be humble.*[374]

Collective humility has so much importance for St. Josemaría that he presents it as an essential characteristic of the spirit of Opus Dei from

373. *Letter, December 24, 1951*, no. 42.

374. *Conversations*, no. 40.

the very beginnings of its foundation. He would have liked for the apostolic work that God entrusted to him on October 2, 1928, to have had no name in order to avoid any danger of vainglory, and because he only sought to spread a Christian spirit of sanctification in the middle of the world, a mission which is in reality the ordinary task of the Church. But it was not possible to operate without a name lest his work be misinterpreted as secretive. Even so, as can be gathered from the following text, he leaves a written expression of his inclination "to hide" so that others may understand how much he values collective humility:

> *To live facing God, not men. This has been and always will be the ambition of the Work: to live without human glory. And don't forget that, at the outset, I would have liked the Work not to have any name, so that its history would be known only to God. But since we detest secrets and always want to work within the confines of the law in each country, we will need to have a name.*[375]

He thus seeks neither praise nor human gratitude. His motto is *Deo omnis gloria!* ("All the glory to God"). His ambition is *to work as three thousand, while making the noise of three.*[376] What is at play is not the "humility of the Work of God" in some abstract sense, but the personal humility of each person, which removes the person [the member of Opus Dei in this case] from corporate vanity and from seeking human glory for Opus Dei. The purpose is *to not want to receive oneself the esteem and appreciation that the Work of God and the holy lives of one's brothers and sisters merit.*[377]

On the other hand, he also affirms that *the glory of God* [. . .] *is the only reason that leads us not to allow the beauty and good name of Opus Dei to be tarnished even in the slightest.*[378] By affirming that the motive for his conduct "is the glory of God," it is clear that to defend "the good name of the Work" is not a human end; rather, it is a demand of the building up of the Church. For this reason, these words have a general significance. Every Christian should behave in the same manner with the Church, striving to keep its beauty and good name from being tarnished.

The above notwithstanding, St. Josemaría appears to have contradicted himself: on the one hand, he does not wish human glory for the Church (or

375. *Letter, March 24, 1930*, no. 20.

376. *Letter, January 9, 1932*, no. 66.

377. Ibid., no. 64.

378. *Letter, September 14, 1951*, no. 49.

for the Work); yet on the other hand, he exhorts Christians to defend her good name. In reality, these are two requirements of collective humility that harmonize with each other in the same way that personal humility harmonizes with seeking the glory of God, according to the Lord's exhortation: "Let your light so shine before men, that they may see your good works and give glory to your Father who is in heaven" (Matt. 5:16).

Just as when speaking of personal humility the desire "to hide and disappear" (St. Josemaría's life motto)[379] is not opposed to the desire "that only Christ shine forth" (and is in fact its condition), so too, the behavior that leads St. Josemaría to shun human glory for Opus Dei is the condition that allows him to give glory to God, which has nothing to do with secrecy. Thus, he strongly asserts, *I find secrets repugnant. The only secrets I accept are the secret of Confession and those strictly defined by moral theology, since they are based on a good reason.*[380] In a graphic way, he points out the clear and insurmountable distance between a secret and collective humility: *The discreet reserve—never a matter of "secrets"—that I advise you to have, is simply the antidote against boasting; it is the defense of a humility that God wants to be lived collectively as well.*[381]

As with every moral virtue, collective humility has a "just medium" (a point between two vices). On the one hand, there is the defect that St. Josemaría calls "fanfare" (using the Castillian slangword "*faroleo*"). This consists in vainglory for being part of the Church or some institution for the sake of shining in a determined situation or of obtaining certain privileges (as for example, obtaining professional backing for one's reputation or advancing in social relations simply because one belongs to the Church). At the opposite end, there exists the defect of hiding one's condition as Catholic and one's practice of the Faith out of fear, shame, or human respects.

---

379. See section 3.2.1.

380. *Letter, December 8, 1949*, no. 195.

381. *Letter, January 9, 1932*, no. 66. In *Conversations*, no. 30, the founder responded to those who had maliciously suggested that, with the excuse of collective humility, he was trying to cover up secrets. That calumny–and this is what he called it–had its origin in the difficulty that some found in understanding that the faithful of Opus Dei are ordinary faithful and that their incorporation in the Work does not change their condition in the Church and/or in civil society in contrast to what happens in the case of members of religious orders. Therefore, they do not introduce themselves officially as belonging to the Work or use any distinctive signs; on the side of Opus Dei, moreover, it does not publish data and statistics about their professional, family, or social life. There is nothing secretive here, but rather simply proper and corresponding behavior to the reality of things which demands humility in order to respect what the bond with Opus Dei represents. On the other hand, the faithful of Opus Dei do manifest their bond with Opus Dei naturally in the realm of their personal relationships with family, friends and colleagues (see also *Conversations*, nos. 34 and 41).

In sum, we can state that St. Josemaría encourages people to keep the right intention; to avoid vainglory in their apostolate; to seek only God's glory without looking for satisfaction as a result of success, or the consolation of statistics, and without attributing to themselves others' merits. At the same time, it is necessary not to be afraid to stand up for Christ and to suffer the hardships that arise when working for him. Jesus was dishonored and ill-treated. His disciples faced the same fate (see 1 Cor. 4:8–13) when they were united in the Faith; they in fact "were of one heart and soul" (Acts 4:32); and they carried out the mission that Christ entrusted to them. Like the Lord, they should be able to say, "I do not receive glory from men" (John 5:41; see John 7:18 and 8:50).

3.3. Sincerity, Docility, and Simplicity

Before studying other human virtues, we should look at three virtues that are closely united to humility in St. Josemaría's writings. Theologically they could be considered as "integral parts of humility" in a way similar to how the walls and roof of a house are integral parts of the house. Humility can be understood as consisting in recognition of truth (sincerity), obedience to the truth recognized (docility), and the habit of choosing the straightest and simplest path to act according to the truth (simplicity). Since these three virtues form part of humility, they also participate in its foundational character.

In the following section, we will limit ourselves to commenting on the principle aspects of these virtues. We should keep in mind that what we said about humility in general can be applied to each one of these three virtues.

3.3.1. "Being Sincere with God, with Others, and with Oneself"

Humility requires acceptance of the truth concerning what one is before God, before others, and before oneself. The proper act of sincerity is this acknowledgment. *To be humble let us be sincere: sincere with God, with ourselves, and with those who guide our soul.*[382]

> Sincerity and humility are not the same. Sincerity lies in the intellect. Humility, instead, also requires the will to be disposed to live according to the truth that is known. As we will later expore, this leads to docility. Nonetheless, St. Josemaría sometimes speaks of sincerity in a broader sense

382. *Letter, March 24, 1931*, no. 34.

as "sincerity of life" that includes docility. He writes, for instance, that sincerity means *to align your thoughts, words and deeds with the Truth.*[383]

Overall, St. Josemaría gives great importance to sincerity even to the point of affirming that *the first human virtue a Christian needs is to be sincere, a friend of the truth.*[384] His teaching on sincerity is abundant, and what follows will be only a summary of fundamental points.[385]

As noted earlier, he teaches persons to live this virtue in three dimensions: *It is good that you be sincere with God in the intimacy of your heart, with yourself, and with the others to the extent that Christian refinement permits it.*[386]

These are the same three areas of charity and humility. It is logical that this be the case because for St. Josemaría sincerity, humility, and charity are intimately tied by the same thread: sincerity increases humility, and humility increases charity. *If we want to persevere, let us be humble. To be humble, let us be sincere.*[387]

The three spheres of sincerity flow into one another. Even though priority corresponds to sincerity with God, the first existential step is usually *sincerity with oneself.* "It can seem strange," notes Rafael Corazón González, "that man can lie to himself; and even stranger, that he can believe his own lies."[388] Indeed, when it comes down to specific actions, he explains, it is possible that under the influence of emotions, passions, or simple whims, man can deliberately leave aside considerations that would lead him to act differently. For this reason, according to this author, St. Josemaría understands sincerity with oneself as "right conscience,"[389] or the habit of judging one's own moral conduct according to the truth. Sincerity with oneself is an essential condition for sincerity with others and with God.[390] At the same time, St. Josemaría has texts which indicate that sincerity with God and

---

383. *Letter, March 11, 1940,* no. 60.

384. Notes taken from preaching, April 8, 1971 (AGP, P01 V-1971, pp. 43–44).

385. See Vicente Bosch, "Para una 'Teología de la sinceridad,' a través de los escritos del Beato Josemaría Escrivá"; Rafael Corazón González, *La virtud de la sinceridad en la espiritualidad de San Josemaría Escrivá.*

386. Notes taken from preaching, April 8, 1974 (AGP, P01 V-1974, pp. 130–131).

387. *Letter, March 24, 1931,* no. 34. By "persevering" he refers here to perseverance in one's dedication to God in Opus Dei, but it can be extended, in general, to perseverance in love for God, which is always dynamic, that is to say, it implies a constant growth in charity.

388. Corazón, *La virtud de la sinceridad en la espiritualidad de San Josemaría Escrivá,* p. 59.

389. Ibid., p. 56.

390. See, for example, *The Forge,* no. 710; *Conversations,* no. 93.

with others helps a person to be sincere with himself in the moral judgment of specific actions.[391] Clearly both aspects complement each other.

With regard to *sincerity with others*, the insistence of St. Josemaría on the importance of this habit in spiritual direction is notorious. Sometimes when speaking of manifestations of this virtue, he singles it out. He says, *sincerity: with God, with the director, with your brothers.*[392] In spiritual direction, sincerity has special attributes insofar as it deals with deep aspects of a person's intimacy that need to be communicated if a person wishes to receive guidance. In this context, he employs a strong adjective to describe what he considers decisive: *savage sincerity in spiritual direction.*[393]

Sincerity with God obviously does not consist in manifesting to him something that he does not already know, but rather in addressing him as a son or daughter, opening one's heart to recognize the truth in his presence and in light of one's relation with him. "The truth that each man should embrace as the truth about his own being is the acceptance of being a creature and the recognition that life has no meaning other than giving oneself to God."[394] For the Christian, it is an attitude imbued with the consciousness of being an adopted child of God in need of his mercy. "Sincerity with God in man's fallen and redeemed condition essentially consists in recognizing one's own faults, and in confessing oneself to be a sinner."[395] In such a way, the Christian finds himself on the path of humility and of growth in charity.

3.3.2. Docility: "Like Clay in the Potter's Hands"

St. Josemaría prays: *Lord, help me to be faithful and docile toward you,* sicut lutum in manu figuli, *like clay in the potter's hands. In this way it will not be I that live, but you, my Love, who will live and work in me.*[396]

It does not suffice to know the truth for the sake of advancing in humility and charity. It is important to desire to live according to it like Jesus Christ who, having assumed our nature, behaved in accord with the truth of his human condition and his redemptive mission: "And being found in human form he humbled himself and became obedient unto

391. See *Friends of God*, no. 141.

392. *Furrow*, no. 325. See *The Forge*, no. 328.

393. *The Forge*, no. 127. In chapter nine, section 4, spiritual direction will be discussed as a means of sanctification.

394. Corazón, *La virtud de la sinceridad en la espiritualidad de San Josemaría Escrivá*, p. 63.

395. Ibid., p. 65.

396. *The Forge*, no. 875. The text of Scripture is Jer. 18:6. See Sir. 33:13.

death, even death on a cross" (Phil. 2:8). Sincerity would be insufficient without the disposition of wishing to obey God, to obey the persons who as his instruments guide us, and to obey right conscience. This good disposition is called docility.[397]

Sincerity needs to be accompanied by docility to the Paraclete, the interior Master who guides us toward holiness through the path of the truth (see John 16:13). *Christian tradition has summarized the attitude we should adopt toward the Holy Spirit in just one idea: docility.*[398]

> *First of all docility, because it is the Holy Spirit who, with his inspirations, gives a supernatural tone to our thoughts, desires and actions. It is he who leads us to receive Christ's teaching and to assimilate it in a profound way. It is he who gives us the light by which we perceive our personal calling and the strength to carry out all that God expects of us. If we are docile to the Holy Spirit, the image of Christ will be formed more and more fully in us, and we will be brought closer every day to God the Father.* For whoever are led by the Spirit of God, they are the children of God. (Rom. 8:14)
>
> *If we let ourselves be guided by this lifegiving principle, who is the Holy Spirit in us, our spiritual vitality will grow. We will place ourselves in the hands of our Father God, with the same spontaneity and confidence with which a child abandons himself to his father's care. Our Lord has said:* Unless you become like little children, you will not enter the Kingdom of Heaven. (Matt. 18:3)[399]

In spiritual direction, sincerity also requires the help of docility.[400] Spiritual direction is a means of holiness, a channel for the action of the Holy Spirit to guide persons along the path of truth. Its effectiveness depends on the disposition of accepting the advice and suggestions received.

Lastly, sincerity with oneself also calls for docility to one's conscience rightly formed, in order to live according to the truth without remaining at the level of good desires.

---

397. St. Thomas Aquinas discusses docility as a part of prudence (see *S. Th.*, II-II, q. 49, a. 3); here we are considering it as a part of humility. The difference has its origin in the conception of humility that St. Thomas presents within temperance, which perfects the concupiscible faculty (see *S. Th.*, II-II, q. 161, a. 4), while for us it is rooted in all of the faculties of the soul. This different conception of humilty also affects the organization of other virtues.

398. *Christ Is Passing By*, no. 130.

399. Ibid., no. 135.

400. See *The Way*, no. 56; *The Forge*, no. 427; etc.

> We have discussed docility with hardly any mention of obedience, a virtue that we will study later. We should note, however, that these two terms are sometimes used synonymously (docility being the "spirit of obedience") given that obedience is taken in a general sense, including obedience to God. However, if the more restricted sense of "obedience to human authority" is used, then its subject is more restricted. In this work, obedience is set in the context of justice because it refers to relations with others. The connection between docility and obedience consists in that docility, being part of humility, is the foundation for obedience. Docility facilitates obedience by making possible the virtuous fulfillment of advice or orders given by those in authority.

3.3.3. Simplicity

Just like sincerity and docility, simplicity appears throughout St. Josemaría's preaching. He speaks about simplicity more than fifty times in published works, more than a hundred times in his letters, and many other times in his oral preaching. This virtue is directly related with the more characteristic elements of his doctrine. He often speaks of *the trusting simplicity of little children*[401] and of *the simplicity of the ordinary.*[402] For example, he exhorts his audience *to become like children, in simplicity of spirit*[403] and furthermore advises to *always act with simplicity, a virtue so appropriate for a good child of God.*[404] He sees in the ordinary life of Jesus, Mary, and Joseph the model for this virtue.[405]

In common language, "simple" describes something or someone that does not have any pretense or complication, or lacks ostentation and adornment. Based on this, the notion of Christian simplicity transmitted by St. Josemaría must be deduced from the practical applications that he proposes since he does not stop to define it. It is certainly related to the classical idea of *simplicitas*; however, it cannot be completely identified with it.

Most certainly, simplicity forms an indispensable part or "ingredient" of humility. St. Josemaría often mentions both virtues together and, on occasion, he even identifies them as is the case when a part is taken for the whole or vice

401. *Christ Is Passing By*, no. 65. See *The Way*, nos. 868, 887, 893.

402. *Conversations*, no. 110. See ibid., no. 112; *Christ Is Passing By*, no. 18.

403. *Christ Is Passing By*, no. 180.

404. *Friends of God*, no. 160.

405. See *Christ Is Passing By*, no. 20.

versa.[406] The relationship with the other parts of humility is equally strong; the set of terms "sincere and simple" or "docile and simple" go well together. It is made up of elements that complement each other and require each other.

Nonetheless, simplicity adds something to sincerity and docility. It indicates the shortest path possible in order to live according to the truth with charity (see Eph. 4:15), avoiding artificial complications in thoughts, words, and deeds. It is the virtue that opens a path to sincerity and docility, which would become twisted if it were missing. On the other hand, simplicity should not be confused with naivete: *Our Christian faith, which teaches us to be simple, does not bid us be simpleminded.*[407] A simple person is a realist, whereas a naive person is immature, and runs the risk of withdrawing within himself, ending up with interior complications.

This concludes our considerations on humility and the elements that integrate it. The rest of the virtues that we will analyze necessarily rely on humility. From St. Josemaría's doctrine, there emerges the figure of a Christian as a child of God who, having his gazed fixed on heaven through the theological virtues and being firmly anchored through humility, strives to cultivate the human virtues that reflect in him the image of Christ and allow him to sanctify all earthly realities according to God's will.

4. The Human Virtues of a Christian

In reading the writings of St. Josemaría, we quickly notice the abundant references to human virtues, whether it is about their need, the effort to acquire them, or the manner of practicing them in ordinary life. If a reader expected to hear St. Josemaría speak only of what refers immediately to God (e.g., about faith, charity, and prayer), he would remain rather baffled by questions that he brings up concerning the human condition and the effort to cultivate and develop many attitudes that perhaps one had not considered as being connected to holiness, such as order, joy, and industriousness, among others. The reason is that *our faith does not ignore anything on this earth that is beautiful, noble and authentically human.*[408] For St. Josemaría, *it is inconceivable that a Christian, in order to fulfill his task, should have to turn his back on the world and become fatalistic with regard to human nature.*[409]

---

406. See *Friends of God*, no. 102; *The Way*, no. 581; *Furrow*, no. 434; *Christ Is Passing By*, no. 18.

407. *Christ Is Passing By*, no. 34.

408. Ibid., no. 24.

409. Ibid., no. 125.

On the contrary, *being a Christian means incorporating all the nobility of what is human.*[410] And in order to do so, it is indispensable to cultivate the human virtues, for only he *who strives to be truthful, loyal, sincere, courageous, temperate, generous, serene, just, hardworking, patient*[411] is truly human.

The scope of these virtues is to embody charity in daily actions. *The Paraclete, who is Love, teaches us to saturate our life with the virtue of charity,*[412] but that "fusion" with charity would be impossible without the human virtues. Charity itself leads to their development and does not allow them to be left behind. St. Josemaría is convinced that *union with God, supernatural virtue, always brings with it the attractive practice of human virtues.*[413] He says "always" because he thinks of all Christians. Human virtues are not for the elite; they should be practiced by all the faithful and in all circumstances, including difficult environments. Wherever Christian life develops, there people's virtues blossom and they are able to experience a more dignified and ultimately more intensely human life.

In an essay on St. Josemaría's teaching, Giuseppe Tanzella-Nitti underscores that "the relationship between nature and grace should be understood as a movement in two directions, an ascending and a descending one. According to the first, the practice of human virtues constitutes *the foundation* of the Christian virtues. The descending movement represents the relationship between grace and nature arising from the principle of the Incarnation; it tells us that everything that Christ proposes to man is, by the very fact of the Incarnation, an authentic recognition of all that is profoundly human. [. . .]. The believer is conscious that knowledge of his condition as someone *created in Christ* has definitively unveiled for him the truth about human nature."[414] With this in mind, let us first look at the general exposition of the human virtues according to St. Josemaría, followed by an analysis of some of those virtues in particular.

---

410. Ibid., no. 52.

411. *Friends of God*, no. 90.

412. *Christ Is Passing By*, no. 87. When we say that the Paraclete is charity, we are referring to infinite (uncreated) charity, not to the charity that he pours out on the Christian.

413. *Furrow*, no. 566.

414. Giuseppe Tanzella-Nitti, "'Perfectus Deus, perfectus homo:' The Mystery of the Incarnation and Its Exemplarity for Christian Life in the Teachings of Bl. Josemaría Escrivá," in *Romana* 25 (1997): 360 ff.

4.1. In the Image of Christ, "*Perfectus Deus, Perfectus Homo*"

What is the origin of the idea that, as referenced above, *union with God always brings with it the attractive practice of human virtues*? An idea frequently repeated by St. Josemaría gives us the general answer: Christians must be *both very human and very divine, struggling each day to imitate him who is* perfectus Deus, perfectus homo.[415] How could human virtues be lacking in him who is called to be "another Christ," an image of the perfect man, the model of all the virtues? Furthermore, how could they be absent from a Christian if Jesus Christ *wishes to become incarnate in our deeds, to vivify from within even our most insignificant actions?*[416]

St. Josemaría often employs the expression *perfectus Deus, perfectus homo*,[417] taken from the ancient *Quicumque* Creed.[418] He did so not so much to comment on the *perfectus Deus* (the consubstantial nature of the Son, a central subject in the Arian controversy), but rather to underline the *perfectus homo* (the complete human nature assumed by the Word). This important clarification of the Christological dogma also implies that Jesus fully possessed all the human virtues. Man's perfection does not reside primarily in his physical or intellectual qualities, but rather in his moral goodness, which derives from the use of his freedom. Jesus Christ is "perfect man" even though he suffered hunger, thirst, fatigue, and other weaknesses that are part of human nature in the present state.[419]

On other occasions, St. Josemaría refers to the congruence between Jesus being "perfect God" and "perfect man." He offers two reasons. The first is that since the divinity should manifest itself through his humanity, the humanity should be perfect: *Christ is God become man: a complete, perfect man. And through his human nature, he shows us what his divine nature is.*[420]

The second reason is that as our Redeemer, he had to assume and raise up all the values that are proper to man:

---

415. *Friends of God*, no. 75.

416. *Christ Is Passing By*, no. 174.

417. It appears 25 times in his published works alone; most frequently in *Furrow* and in *Friends of God*.

418. See DS 76.

419. See *The Forge*, no. 290; *Friends of God*, nos. 176, 201. The intellectual and physical gifts that Jesus possessed in an excellent way also formed part of his human perfection, but human perfection is principally moral perfection.

420. *Christ Is Passing By*, no. 109.

> *Christ is* perfectus Deus, perfectus homo. *He is perfect God, the Second Person of the Blessed Trinity, and perfect man. He comes to save, not to destroy nature.*[421]
>
> *Christ, who is perfect man, did not come to destroy what is human, but to make it noble by taking on our human nature, except for sin: he came to share all man's yearnings, except for the sad experience of willful evil.*[422]

From this, we can draw direct consequences for the Christian life. If human virtues are part of man's perfection and Christ has assumed them, then the Christian should aspire to acquire them so as to identify himself with him. He will be "very divine" only if he is "very human." The awareness of being a child of God in Christ (the sense of his divine filiation) naturally leads to a deeper appreciation of everything that is authentically human and as such can be divinized. *Our faith brings out the full meaning of these human virtues, which no one should ever neglect. Christians should be second to none as human beings.*[423]

In addition, when a Christian seeks identification with Christ in the middle of the world (in similar conditions to those of Jesus when he lived in Nazareth), the importance of these virtues becomes even clearer. Sanctification of family and social life as well as of professional work requires them. For instance, with respect to professional work, St. Josemaría writes:

> *A complete range of virtues is called into play when we set about our work with the purpose of sanctifying it: fortitude, to persevere in our work despite the difficulties that naturally arise and to ensure that we never let ourselves be overwhelmed by anxiety; temperance, in order to spend ourselves unsparingly and to overcome our love of comfort and our selfishness; justice, so as to fulfill our duties toward God, society, our family and our fellow workers; prudence, to know in each case what course to take, and then to set about it without hesitation . . . And all this, I emphasize, is for the sake of Love.*[424]

This need for human virtues for holiness in everyday life leads St. Josemaría to reject contrary views: an other-worldly or pietistic spirituality that undervalues those virtues on the one hand, and a secularist vision that

---

421. *Friends of God*, no. 73.
422. *Christ Is Passing By*, no. 125.
423. *Friends of God*, no. 93.
424. Ibid., no. 72.

considers faith an obstacle to the affirmation of human values, on the other. He thus states,

> *There is a certain type of secularist outlook that one comes across, and also another approach which one might call* pietistic, *both of which share the view that Christians somehow are not fully and entirely human. According to the former, the demands of the Gospel are such as to stifle our human qualities; whereas for the latter, human nature is so fallen that it threatens and endangers the purity of the faith. The result, either way, is the same. They both fail to grasp the full significance of Christ's Incarnation; they do not see that* the Word was made flesh, *became man,* and dwelt amongst us. (John 1:14)[425]

Far from mistrusting human values, St. Josemaría proclaims their nobility. They should reflect the luminous image of Christ. Everything that is human should be assumed and raised by the divine. The "logic of the redemptive Incarnation" leads him to discover *the divine value of what is human.*[426]

4.1.1. "The Human Virtues as the Foundation of the Supernatural Ones"

St. Josemaría speaks of the human virtues without stopping to define them. He simply uses traditional language. Among the different formulations for the notion of "human virtues," we believe he would appreciate the one employed by the *Catechism of the Catholic Church* that describes them as "firm attitudes, stable dispositions, habitual perfections of intellect and will that govern our actions, order our passions, and guide our conduct according to reason and faith."[427] We hold that he would appreciate this definition in a special way because it applies both to those who are in the state of grace and those who are not, as well as because it acknowledges that the virtues of those who are not Christian are also true human virtues.

---

425. Ibid., no. 74.

426. *El valor divino de lo humano* ("The divine value of what is human") is the meaningful title of a well-known book by Jesús Urteaga (1921–2009), published in 1948, that has had many editions and printings in various languages. It was one of the works that tried to transmit the teachings of St. Josemaría about the Christian life. It was published in English with the title *Man the Saint*, later changed to *Saints in the World* (New York: Scepter, 2009).

427. *CCC*, no. 1804. While this definition of the Catechism is traditional, it also represents a certain novelty in referring to the "human virtues," which in the Christian are elevated by grace. This point of view is already present in the teaching of St. Josemaría.

A terminological clarification can be helpful here. Unlike the theological virtues, which do not have a "golden mean" or "measure" (as man can neither love God as much as God deserves to be loved, nor believe or hope in him as much as man ought to do so),[428] human virtues do have a *medium virtutis* since they have created goods as their object and the tendency toward these goods should avoid excess or defect. A Christian discovers this measure not through reason alone, but through reason illumined by faith, sustained by hope, and enlivened by charity; and, in order to put the human virtues into practice in such measure, he needs further divine assistance. This is why his human virtues are also supernatural. They are human by reason of their object and supernatural by reason of the subject (i.e., man raised by supernatural grace), origin, and end. Because of this, they are called Christian virtues in the sense that they are the "human virtues of a Christian" or "supernatural moral virtues."

When St. Josemaría speaks of *the human and supernatural virtues of a Christian*,[429] he does not wish to say that there are two types of virtues: ones that are purely human and others that are supernatural, but rather that the human virtues of a person in the state of grace are also supernatural. As is logical, the expression "the human and supernatural virtues of a Christian" can also be understood as including the theological virtues, thus including all the virtues.

St. Josemaría expresses the relationship between "human virtues" and the corresponding "supernatural virtues" explaining that *human virtues constitute the foundation for the supernatural virtues.*[430] This is a traditional concept, but the importance it acquires in the context of the sanctification of earthly realities is noteworthy because there, the spiritual life calls especially for the exercise of those virtues.

The word "foundation" suggests continuity and discontinuity with what is constructed. When St. Josemaría states that human virtues are the "foundation" of the supernatural ones, there is a recognition that discontinuity exists between them; there is a leap from one order to another having to do with supernatural grace. However, if they are a "foundation," it is because there is also continuity between them. The supernatural virtues

428. St. Thomas Aquinas, *S. Th.*, I-II, q. 64, a. 4, c.

429. *Conversations*, no. 62.

430. *Friends of God*, no. 74; see ibid., no. 91.

are by their object and by their nature the same human virtues; but when imbued by charity, they are raised to a transcendental fullness. Tanzella-Nitti comments that "the grace and light obtained through Revelation are not something juxtaposed with nature, and much less something superfluous. Christian virtues reveal their foundation (i.e., the *natural* virtues, which is their origin and end [*telos*] in the sense that they indicate their fulfillment and complete meaning)."[431]

St. Josemaría refers to three hypothetical scenarios that can help us understand better that human virtues are the foundation of the supernatural ones.

The first scenario is that of a person who does not have faith but practices the human virtues. For such a person, the human virtues are a foundation for the supernatural ones in the sense that he is prepared to receive grace, and when he opens up to the light of faith and converts, he will have a sound foundation for leading a coherent Christian life. St. Josemaría states,

> *In this world of ours there are many people who neglect God. It may be that they have not had an opportunity to listen to his words, or that they have forgotten them. Yet their human dispositions are honest, loyal, compassionate and sincere. I would go so far as to say that anyone possessing such qualities is ready to be generous with God, because human virtues constitute the foundation for the supernatural virtues.*
>
> *It is true that in themselves such personal qualities are not enough, for no one is saved without the grace of Christ. But if a man fosters and cultivates the seeds of virtue within him, God will smooth out his path, and such a person will be able to become holy because he has known how to live as a man of good will.*[432]

The second hypothetical scenario is that of a Christian who does not make an effort to cultivate human virtues. He lacks the necessary foundation to lead a life of faith in his daily circumstances. In his priestly work, St. Josemaría met people who reduced their following of Christ to some pious practices without imitating his human virtues; consequently, they did not advance spiritually. Thus, St. Josemaría comments,

---

431. Tanzella-Nitti, "Perfectus Deus, perfectus homo": Reflexiones sobre la ejemplaridad del misterio de la Encarnación del Verbo en las enseñanzas del Beato Josemaría Escrivá, *Romana* 25 (1997), p. 372.

432. *Friends of God*, nos. 74–75. Cornelio Frabro comments, referring to this text, that "this page is worth a treatise on asceticism and mysticism" ("Virtù umane e soprannaturali nelle omelie di mons. Escrivá," p. 184).

> Iesus Christus, perfectus Deus, perfectus Homo—*Jesus Christ, perfect God and perfect Man. There are many Christians who follow Christ and are astonished by his divinity, but forget him as Man. And they fail in the practice of supernatural virtues, despite all the external paraphernalia of piety, because they do nothing to acquire human virtues.*[433]

The last scenario has more bearing on this discussion. It is the case of a person in the state of grace who seeks holiness, that is, of the Christian who truly wishes to live the life of Christ, *perfect God and perfect man.* In this case, the phrase "the human virtues are the foundation of the supernatural ones" means above all that he must make the *effort to acquire those virtues which some have even without knowing Christ.*[434] It is not a matter of practicing the virtues by first applying reason alone and counting on his own natural strength (as someone who does not know Christ), only to later "add" what faith demands. No; from the start that person has to make an effort to live these virtues with a lively faith, counting on the help of grace. A child of God does not possess two types of virtues, ones that are purely human and others that are supernatural, but rather human virtues raised by grace, or that is to say: supernatural virtues. *These in turn provide us with constant encouragement to behave as good human beings.*[435] They allow the Christian to act in accord with what is proper to human dignity and perfection, something which is not possible for a person to achieve with his natural strength in the present condition of mankind. Grace must heal the weakness due to sin so that the Christian can act with the agility of a healthy person and in a supernatural way.

4.1.2. Charity and Human Virtues: "To Be Useful, Serve"

Identification with Jesus Christ essentially consists in charity, but in the present life charity "needs" the human virtues to be able to produce good works. In other words, human virtues are necessary for charity to manifest itself in the actions which have the realities of the world as their object.

Some acts of charity do not require the exercise of these virtues, but in ordinary social life *you cannot have charity without justice, solidarity, family and social responsibility, poverty, joy, chastity, friendship . . .*[436] If a Christian

433. *Furrow*, no. 652.

434. *Friends of God*, no. 75.

435. Ibid., no. 91.

436. *Conversations*, no. 62.

is lacking these virtues, he would be like a soul in a lifeless body; he could think and love, but he would be incapable of expressing his love through works.

Contemplating the reality of the Incarnation is the best way to grasp this concept: *I am moved when I contemplate how wonderful it is for God to love with a man's heart.*[437] Jesus Christ expresses his infinite love through his human actions when he works, when he smiles, when he listens, etc., in a word, when he lives all the human virtues. They are so united to charity that St. Augustine thinks that they are none other than "various sentiments of the same love [. . .], different functions of love."[438] In this sense, they remain in the saints after this life in some way when charity is perfected in glory in ways that can be likened to how they are found in the sacred Humanity of the glorified Christ, although in that case they are manifested in a different manner.

> "Love is patient and kind; love is not jealous or boastful; it is not arrogant or rude. Love does not insist on its own way; it is not irritable or resentful; it does not rejoice at wrong" (1 Cor. 13:4–6). These words reflect the idea that patience, goodness, modesty and so many other human virtues enumerated in the New Testament (see Col. 3:8–12; Eph. 4:2 ff., etc.) are necessary for charity to shape the Christian's behavior.
>
> Commenting on this passage of the First Letter to the Corinthians, St. Gregory the Great wrote that charity "includes the acts of all the virtues."[439] For instance, a slothful person will omit acts of service that charity demands one perform for others not because that person has an evil will, but simply because he is lazy. In fact, omissions in charity are often due to a lack of human virtues.

The "need" of human virtues for certain acts of charity to be manifest is expressed with a sentence often used by St. Josemaría:

> *Remember: in order* to be useful, serve [para servir, servir] [. . .]. *We need to strive to be good instruments, with a sound knowledge of our job or profession, being people who are competent.*[440]

437. *Christ Is Passing By*, no. 107.

438. St. Augustine, *De Moribus Ecclesiae*, lib. I, c. 15, no. 25. We will cite this shortly in more detail in speaking of the connection among the virtues.

439. St. Gregory the Great, *Moralia in Iob*, lib. 10, 7.

440. *Letter, October 15, 1948*, no. 30. [Translator's note: The Spanish expression "*para servir, sevir*" can also be translated in English as "in order to be of service, serve."]

> *As the motto of your work, I can give you this one:* If you want to be useful, serve [para servir, servir] [. . .]. *It's not enough to want to do good; we must know how to do it.*[441]

To be able "to be of service" or to be "useful," that is, in order to actually put charity into practice with works, people need to have the proper qualities. They must "be of service" in the sense of "being competent" or "have abilities for a given task." This suitability derives from human virtues. A person who is hardworking, orderly, educated, etc. is in a condition to respond to the demands of charity in the exercise of his duties. The expression "if you want to be of service, serve" is, therefore, a call to acquire and cultivate the necessary qualities and virtues that allow a person to render a useful service to others.

At the same time, human virtues "require" charity in order to be fulfilled, that is, to be the virtues of those who recognize that their ultimate end is to give glory to God. Since this is a supernatural end, it demands a perfection that human virtues do not possess without grace. Tanzella-Nitti expresses it well when he writes that "the insistence of the founder of Opus Dei on human virtues [. . .] should not be read from a *naturalistic* point of view. It would be a false interpretation, a semi-Pelagian error, to think that a nature that is more noble and robust constitutes a better basis for the action of grace, justifying a certain care of nature as if it were an end itself. This kind of outlook on virtue could be easily interpreted as a mere form of equilibrium or of human effectiveness. Instead, when nature is set on a path toward a fulfillment that is greater than itself, and human qualities toward a perfection that goes beyond the individual interests of the one who exercises them, then human virtues implicitly recognize their *telos* [end] not in nature itself but in something which transcends them, opening up to the gratuitous action of divine grace."[442]

Without charity, human virtues would be sterile for holiness. St. Paul affirms, "If I [. . .] have not love, I am nothing" (1 Cor. 13:2) and he exhorts, "Let all that you do be done in love" (1 Cor. 16:14). Charity should inform all of a person's works directing him to the last end of Christian life. Even though the virtues in themselves are perfections of the person, they reach their full meaning if they are enlivened by charity which gives them

441. *Christ Is Passing By*, no. 50.

442. Tanzella-Nitti, "'Perfectus Deus, perfectus homo,'" p. 372.

their final perfection, converting the proper act of each virtue into an act of love of God.

For this reason they should not be considered simply a preparation for charity nor should they be cultivated separately. It is precisely love that should lead to their development with the aid of grace. "The practice of all the virtues is animated and inspired by charity."[443] It is a question of being faithful out of love of God, courageous out of love, patient out of love, well-tempered, chaste, etc., out of love. "Put on then, as God's chosen ones, holy and beloved, compassion, kindness, lowliness, meekness, and patience [. . .]. And above all these put on love, which binds everything together in perfect harmony" (Col. 3:12, 14).

4.1.3. Classification of the Human Virtues: Distinctions and Relations

St. Josemaría sometimes uses the classical categorization of the cardinal virtues: prudence, justice, fortitude, and temperance, which perfect the intellect, the will, the irascible and the concupiscible appetite.[444] The other human virtues can be considered "parts"[445] of these, with the exception of humility to which he assigns a unique role. In the homily entitled "Human Virtues,"[446] he does mention this fourfold classification, which he uses as a frame of reference. We too will use it shortly as a framework to speak with a certain order of the virtues that appear most frequently in his works.

In St. Josemaría's teaching the *connexio vitutum* [theory of mutual dependence of the virtues] is very much present.[447] There exists an intimate,

443. *CCC*, no. 1827.

444. See, for example, *Friends of God*, no. 72. This is the division that the *Catechism of the Catholic Church* uses: see nos. 1805 and 1834. The four virtues are mentioned and connected in Wis. 8:7. As we know, the division is found in Plato (*The Republic*, IV, 427 e; 433 b-c; etc.) and was adopted by a number of Fathers of the Church.

445. See St. Thomas Aquinas, *S. Th.*, II-II, q. 48, a. 1, c.

446. See *Friends of God*, nos. 73–93.

447. See, for example, St. Thomas Aquinas, *S. Th.*, I-II, q. 65. It was masterfully explained by St. Augustine: "The inseparability of the virtues has been proposed by all of the philosophers who proclaim the virtues as necessary for life [. . .]. The reason why they think that if one possesses one virtue, one possesses all and, if one is lacking, one doesn't possess any, is that prudence cannot be weak, nor unjust, nor intemperate: well if you have any of these defects, you are not prudent. And if prudence is such when it is strong, just, and temperate, where it is, the others are also. In the same way, courage cannot be either imprudent, intemperate, nor unjust; in the same way, temperance should be prudent, courageous, and just; and so justice is not such if it is not at the same time prudent, courageous, and temperate. So that when one of those virtues exists, the others are also there; and when the others are lacking, that one is not authentic, even though for some reason it might appear so" (*Epistula* 167, 2, 4–5).

mutual relationship between the Christian virtues enlivened by charity such that the perfection of one does not exist without the others.[448] For earlier writers, virtue is one: good habits demand each other; while vices are many. In a Christian outlook, this natural reality has a new and deeper foundation. Charity does not unite them "from the outside," but rather from within the subject, raising the will that directs them toward God. This explains why, when speaking of one virtue, St. Josemaría often refers to others and he presents them as inseparable or mutually dependent. For instance, he ties faithfulness to fortitude, to purity, or to generosity, etc. Here, it is not possible for us to expound upon the richness of these relationships; however, we will show how charity is their root and for each human virtue, we will study its relation to charity. We will explain how it is that charity "requires" each virtue as well as how too the virtues "require" charity for them to be shaped as "Christian" virtues, that is, for them to reflect the virtues of Jesus Christ.

Before delving into some of the virtues, we note that we will limit ourselves to discussing some basic aspects of each as well as some of their quintessential applications, leaving aside many others. Furthermore, we will limit our discussion to the virtues, not the vices; and the virtues inasmuch as they are habits of a Christian. We will address the necessary ascetical struggle to improve them while combating defects in chapter eight.

4.2. Prudence, Sound Judgment, and Realism

The object of every human virtue is a created good, and created goods should be sought with measure. The virtue of prudence leads us to discern between good and evil in specific actions and *inclines us to act well: to shed light on the end, and to help us seek the most suitable means of achieving it.*[449] It points out the "golden mean" or "just measure" of the other virtues, distinguishing between excess and defect, as for example between cowardice

---

448. St. Augustine even thought that the "quadruple division [of the virtues] did not express anything more than various affections of a single love, and this is why he did not hesitate in defining these four virtues as different functions of love [. . .]. Temperance is love that gives itself totally [body and soul] to the thing loved; fortitude is love that easily endures everything for that which it loves; justice is love which is only enslaved by its beloved, by which it is an upright nobility; prudence is love which wisely chooses the most adequate means and rejects the contrary." *De moribus Ecclesiae*, I, 15, 25.

There is also a connection between the moral virtues by reason of prudence (see St. Thomas Aquinas, *De virtutibus in communi*, a. 12), but this is a subject that we do not need to look at in detail because when prudence itself is informed by charity, the connection has a new basis, which is that proper to the spiritual life.

449. *Friends of God*, no. 85.

and fear when considering the virtue of fortitude. For this, *not without good reason has prudence been called* genitrix virtutum (St. Thomas Aquinas, *In III Sententiarum, d. 33, q. 2, a. 5*), *the mother of virtues, and also* auriga virtutum (St. Bernard, *Sermones in Cantica Canticorum*, 49, 5), *the guide of every good habit.*[450] Following traditional doctrine, St. Josemaría is careful to note that prudence is not mediocrity. The *medium virtutis* is *a summit, a peak: the best course of action, as indicated to us by prudence.*[451]

Charity cannot do without this virtue: *to protect our Love we need prudence.*[452] At the same time, prudence "requires" or "demands" charity for it to be Christian prudence. In effect, after recalling what this virtue consists in, St. Josemaría adds, *We should ask ourselves always: Prudence, for what?*[453] The "for what" is not indicated by prudence itself, but by charity that orders it to its final end: to holiness and apostolate. *The highest goal of prudence is not social harmony or the peace which results from not provoking friction. The fundamental motive behind prudence is to fulfill the will of God* [. . .]. The prudent heart shall possess knowledge (Prov. 18:15), *the knowledge given by God's Love.*[454] St. Josemaría sees a reflection of this notion of prudence imbued with charity in a definition by St. Augustine that he quotes *because of the rich spiritual content it possesses.*[455] According to the Bishop of Hippo, prudence is "the love which knows how to distinguish what is useful in going to God from what separates from him."[456]

4.2.1. "Sound Judgment"

St. Josemaría's teaching on prudence is sometimes found under different names. Often he calls the discernment proceeding from love, which we just mentioned, "Christian judgment" [*criterio cristiano*]. He speaks of "having judgment" [*tener criterio*], "uprightness in judgment" [*rectitud de criterio*],

---

450. Ibid., no. 164. A synthesis of the traditional conception of prudence can be seen in *CCC*, no. 1806. Among the studies of this virtue, St. Josemaría probably knew that of Josef Pieper, *Traktat über die Klugheit* (Munich: Kösel, 1949).

451. *Friends of God*, no. 83.

452. Ibid., no. 180. The context of this sentence is the virtue of chastity: prudence teaches us not to put ourselves in danger of sin and in this way to guard our love of God. But the sentence has a more general application, because prudence indicates in each concrete situation the "measure" of the other virtues, making possible that they be informed by charity. In this way "it watches over love."

453. Ibid., no. 85.

454. Ibid., no. 88.

455. *Letter, December 24, 1951*, no. 4.

456. St. Augustine, *De moribus Ecclesiae*, I, 15, 25.

or of being "a person of judgment" [*alma de criterio*].[457] To guide one's behavior or that of others, it is not sufficient to know some rules and to have experience. A deeper habit that prudently marks out a path is needed. *Sound judgment* [criterio] *requires maturity, firm convictions, sufficient doctrinal knowledge, a refined spirit and an educated will.*[458] As we see, all the virtues converge to provide sound judgment. A person who is just, strong, temperate, etc. will find a good path to be prudent, capable of rightly deciding what is good in each case and to put it into practice. Christian judgment is a *wisdom of heart*[459] that enables a person to "prove what is the will of God, what is good and acceptable and perfect" (Rom. 12:2) and to apply moral principles to specific situations. It is a practical knowledge in the light of faith, guided by the impulse of love of God.

With this in mind, St. Josemaría recalls that, *St. Thomas points out three aspects of this good habit of the intellect. They are: to seek advice, to judge correctly and to decide.*[460]

- "To ask for advice" or "seek counsel" means to acquire the necessary knowledge to act in an upright way. It entails looking for the needed clarity without presumptuously relying solely on one's intuition. *A truly prudent person is ever attentive to God's promptings,*[461] using the adequate means required in each circumstance: thinking matters through and asking for advice. Before making decisions, the prudent person obtains any pertinent information; he does not act in a precipitated manner, nor is carried away by excessive self-confidence. *So, we look for advice; but not from just anyone. We go to a person with the right qualities, to someone who wants to love God as sincerely as we do and who tries to follow him faithfully.*[462]
- *Next we have to judge, because as a rule, prudence demands that we come to a suitable decision, and promptly,*[463] while avoiding rashness at the same time. *Urgent matters can wait, and very urgent ones should wait.*[464] St. Josemaría always defended this practice of good government.

---

457. *The Way*, introduction; see ibid., nos. 33, 384; *Furrow*, no. 595; *The Forge*, nos. 450, 713, 840; etc.

458. *Conversations*, no. 93.

459. *Friends of God*, no. 87.

460. Ibid., no. 86. Refer to St. Thomas Aquinas, *S. Th.*, II-II, q. 47, a. 8.

461. *Friends of God*, no. 87.

462. Ibid., no. 86.

463. Ibid.

464. *Instruction*, May 21, 1936, no. 43.

- Finally, a decision must be reached. A prudent person does not *give in to an easygoing "do nothing" attitude* [. . .]. *He will run the risk of his decisions. Fear of failure will not make him give up in his effort to do good.*[465] *Though at times it is prudent to delay a decision until all the factors that should influence our judgment have been brought together, on other occasions it would be very imprudent not to begin to carry out immediately what we see needs to be done. This is especially true when the good of others is at stake.*[466]

4.2.2. Christian Realism and "Tin-Can Mysticism": Interior Order

An integral element of prudence is what is commonly called "realism": knowing and presenting things as they are. A prudent man knows the ground on which he stands. In this sense *to be prudent, the first step is to acknowledge our own limitations.*[467]

There is a realism that forms part of human prudence and a realism proper to Christian prudence. With an outlook of faith, the latter discovers new aspects of reality, but it fully counts on reality. The Christian *is a realist. His supernatural and human realism helps him appreciate all the aspects of his life: sorrow and joy, his own and other people's suffering, certainty and doubt, generosity and selfishness.*[468]

This is an attitude that is connatural for St. Josemaría because, as Jorge Peña observes, "the santification of ordinary life requires this dose of realism and love for reality."[469] His preaching is not abstract; it moves persons to seek union with God in the midst of the real circumstances of life. It opens people up to the great ideal of holiness and Christian transformation of the world but without any utopias. *I ask you simply that your head be in heaven: you have a right, since you are children of God. But your feet should be firmly planted on the ground, in order to glorify God our Creator, in the realities of this world and human work.*[470]

One of the dangers faced by a healthy realism is what St. Josemaría called "tin-can mysticism" [*mística ojalatera*]. He describes it in one of his homilies:

465. *Friends of God*, no. 88.

466. Ibid., no. 86.

467. Ibid.

468. *Christ Is Passing By*, no. 60.

469. Peña Vial, "'Mística ojalatera' y realismo en la santidad de la vida ordinaria," p. 121.

470. *Letter, January 9, 1932*, no. 4.

> *Stop dreaming. Leave behind false idealism, fantasies, and what I usually call "tin-can mysticism": if only I hadn't married, if only I hadn't this profession, if only I were healthier, if only I were young, if only I were old . . . Instead focus seriously on the most material and immediate reality, which is where our Lord is.*[471]

"Tin-can mysticism" [*mística ojalatera*] is a newly coined word by St. Josemaría that results from combining the Spanish words *ojalá* [oh, if I only had . . .] and *hojalata* [tinplate] into a pun. Indicating the nice appearence but inferior quality of an alloy, it serves as a metaphor of a spitirual illness. "Tin-can mysticism" is a wishful thinking that lacks realism. It flees from real life, forgetting that it is the place of encounter with God, and instead finds refuge in the imagination. And it sets its desire for fullfillment in the hope of doing things, which though good in themselves, fall outside the scope of a person's calling. This is a deformity that, unless stopped, can lead to *frenzy for change.*[472] This "changing for the sake of changing," a desire for starting something better, is really only an excuse for not persevering in the good that one is doing.

This danger is an insidious one, especially in later years in life; it is the temptation to doubt the acquired commitments and their consequences. St. Josemaría warns of this danger and teaches how to help a person suffering from it *by trying to rejuvenate and strengthen their piety, treating them with special affection.*[473] In these situations the spirit of divine filiation (i.e., the piety and fraternity of the children of God) are also the firm rock that serves as the foundation for holiness in the midst of hardship (see Matt. 7:24–25). Together with this, it is necessary to develop the virtue of prudence because at the root of "tin-can mysticism" there is always "a problem of realism."[474] The exhortation to focus on "the most material and immediate reality, which is where our Lord is," is a good sign of the importance of this virtue on the path to a contemplative life. It is, as St. Josemaría puts it, to live *in heaven and on earth, always. Not between heaven and earth, because we are in the world. In the world and in heaven at the same time!*[475]

---

471. *Conversations*, no. 116; see ibid., no. 88.

472. *The Way*, no. 837.

473. *Letter, March 24, 1931*, no. 22.

474. Peña Vial, "'Mística ojalatera' y realismo en la santidad de la vida ordinaria," p. 130.

475. Notes taken from preaching, March 27, 1975 (AGP, P09, p. 230).

Another aspect of prudence on which St. Josemaría places great importance is that of order: "interior order" in one's thoughts, intentions, and affections from which derives the "exterior order" of conduct (understood as virtue, rather than as a predetermined response to stimuli).

In the field of human activity,[476] order entails setting priorities: actions should result from principles. Here we have two elements. The first element is that there should be order in every act. *The Way* reads, *Virtue without order? Strange virtue!*[477] St. Josemaría holds that order is necessary for an act to be virtuous, and this is precisely what is proper to prudence, whose object is to identify the right measure in all action. In this sense, order is an aspect of the virtue of prudence, which consists in pointing out the "place" that corresponds to each action, or, that is, in "ordering" them.

The second element is the organizing (or ruling) principle of conduct. For a Christian, this principle is charity, the love of God. St. Josemaría insists that the life of the ordinary faithful above all demands searching *for the true center of human life, which can give priority, order and meaning to everything. We find this center in our relations with God by means of a genuine interior life.*[478] Only from this central source of light can the proper place of each thing be discovered and can the order of goods sought by the will both in the affections and actions be found. Thus, each must determine what is priority and what should be put on hold. Ultimately, order is an act of the virtue of prudence informed by charity.

For an ordinary Christian pulled in different directions, this is an important virtue. *When there are lots of things to do you have to establish priorities, to get* organized. *Many difficulties stem from downright disorder.*[479]

Among the practical pieces of advice offered by St. Josemaría regarding this virtue, the most important and the most frequent one is to give priority throughout the day to the practices of piety that each person has decided upon. The first thing should be a person's relationship with God which is usually manifested (when charity does not demand something different) in placing the loving fulfillment of one's own spiritual plan of life before other habitual concerns.[480] There are many other considerations that we cannot

---

476. We will not detain ourselves for inquiries over other uses of the term order. One can see, St. Thomas Aquinas, *In I Sent.*, d. 20, q. 1, a. 3, sol. 1; *S. Th.*, II-II, q. 26, a. 1.

477. *The Way*, no. 79.

478. *Conversations*, no. 88.

479. Ibid. Emphasis ours.

480. We will speak about the "plan of life" in chapter nine, sections 5.1. and 5.3.

discuss here such as punctuality, material order with instruments of work, and even a person's attire: *Let your outward conduct reflect the peace and order of your soul.*[481]

St. Josemaría sums up the consequences, both internal and external, of the exercise of this virtue in the following point of *The Forge:*

> *Order will bring harmony to your life, and lead you to perseverance. Order will give peace to your heart, and gravity to your manner.*[482]

4.3. Justice, Faithfulness, and Obedience

One of the facets of charity is seeking the good for others out of love for God. The virtue of justice, which inclines the will to give each person his due, is indispensable to achieve this charity.[483] Without the right intention, it is impossible to practice charity, which also resides in the will.[484] St. Josemaría points out the sad mistake made by those who *leave aside justice and limit their actions to a bit of welfare work, which they define as charitable, without realizing that they are doing only a small part of what in fact they have a strict duty to do.*[485] By not paying attention to justice, they fail completely in charity.

But justice, guided by reason alone, is insufficient for a Christian. It *is not enough,*[486] because *however much a particular person deserves to be given, we must be ready to give him more, because each single soul is a masterpiece of God's making.*[487] St. Josemaría thus warns: *When justice alone is fulfilled, don't be surprised if people are hurt. The dignity of man, who is a son of God, requires much more. Charity must penetrate and accompany justice because it sweetens and deifies everything: God is love* (1 John 4:16). *Our motive in everything we do should be the Love of God.*[488] In Christian life, justice must be shaped by charity and should be guided by reason illumined by faith. This is why St. Josemaría notes that charity should be "packaged within" justice.

---

481. *The Way*, no. 3.

482. *The Forge*, no. 806. "Perseverance" here is perseverance in love of God, on the path of one's own vocation to holiness.

483. See *Friends of God*, no. 83; St. Thomas Aquinas, *S. Th.*, II-II, q. 58, a. 1, c.; *CCC*, no. 1807.

484. Since the two virtues are rooted in the will, their mutual relation is particularly close. In Sacred Scripture holiness is called "justice" (see Mark 6:20; etc.). A "holy man" is a "just man," one who is "adjusted" to God and to others, which is only possible by charity that enables us to act in a divine way, as children of God.

485. *Friends of God*, no. 172.

486. Ibid., no. 83.

487. Ibid.

488. Ibid., no. 172.

He also says that charity must "accompany" justice because Christian behavior toward others is not only regulated by justice. Charity that, properly speaking, is directed to God has higher demands. *Justice requires that we learn to recognize the rights of the others. Charity, however, demands that we comprehend not only the rights but also the needs of our neighbors.*[489] On various occasions he uses the following expression: *The best way of living charity lies in generously outdoing the demands made on us by justice.*[490] "This highlights the way of connecting the two virtues that is demanded by their mutual relation. Justice, a moral virtue, seeks the golden mean, but since it is united to charity, a theological virtue, it moves it out from its strict limits and brings it to fulfillment. Thus it is strengthened through its relationship with charity and is taken to completeness."[491] At the same time, charity extends itself, following the path indicated by justice as we can gather from the following text:

> *Charity, which is like a generous overflowing of justice, demands first of all the fulfillment of one's duty. The way to start is to be just; the next step is to do what is most equitable . . . ; but in order to love, great refinement is required, and much thoughtfulness, and respect, and kindliness in rich measure. In other words, it involves following the Apostle's advice:* carry one another's burdens, and thus you will fulfill the law of Christ (Gal. 6:2). *Then indeed we shall be living charity fully and carrying out the commandment of Jesus.*[492]
>
> *We need to forget about ourselves and aspire to no other honor than that of serving others, in the same way as Jesus Christ, who preached that* the Son of man has not come to be served but to serve (Matt. 20:28). *This requires the integrity of being able to submit our own will to that of our divine model, working for all men, and fighting for their eternal happiness and well-being. I know of no better way to be just than that of a life of self-surrender and service.*[493]

This is the way St. Josemaría considers the relationship between justice and charity for a son of God. Charity with one's neighbor is an "overflowing

489. *Letter, December 8, 1949*, no. 187. See *The Way*, no. 440.

490. *Friends of God*, no. 83.

491. Vicente Ferrero Muñoz, "La plenitud de la justicia," in Jon Borobia et al., *Trabajo y espíritu. Sobre el sentido del trabajo desde las enseñanzas de Josemaría Escrivá en el contexto del pensamiento contemporáneo* (Pamplona: Eunsa, 2004), p. 367.

492. *Friends of God*, no. 173.

493. Ibid.

of justice," but it does not substitute it or make it superfluous. Without justice, charity would substantially lack "matter" to vivify.

A just person has a lively "sense of obligation;" he is conscious that there are things that others have the right to demand,[494] and he acts with the firm determination of assuming and fulfilling those obligations. But for the Christian, this determination must be shaped by charity; one should fulfill duties out of love for God. At the same time, charity needs that "sense of duty" that is indispensable to urge others to act according to justice and to defend those who cannot defend their rights.[495]

Justice implies an inclination to exert one's personal rights in one's relations with others. Regarding "personal" rights, that is, rights that are inherent to the person, there can be reasons based on charity not to exercise them. St. Paul makes this point when referring to such situations: "Why not rather suffer wrong? Why not rather be defrauded?" (1 Cor. 6:7). On the other hand, as far as rights that are inherent to an office or position are concerned, their exercise is frequently a duty, because the good of other persons or the common good may require it. *Let's not confuse the rights of the office you hold with your rights as a person. The former can never be waived.*[496] St. Josemaría underscores that those who should sanctify social and professional relations cannot ordinarily omit the exercise of these rights. *Carry out all your duties as a citizen. Do not try to get out of any of your obligations. Exercise all your rights, too, for the good of society, without making any rash exceptions. You must give Christian witness in that also.*[497]

We will analyze other aspects of justice in professional and social relations in chapter seven when dealing with the sanctification of temporal realities.

4.3.1. Faithfulness to Commitments: Loyalty

A part of justice is faithfulness to morally upright commitments that have been assumed: the firm decision of fulfilling the duties derived thereof.

This is not a reference to "faithfulness to God" as an act of the theological virtues already studied in virtue of the faith, but rather "faithfulness to commitments acquired" with a person or an institution. This faithfulness

---

494. See ibid., no. 172.

495. See *Christ Is Passing By*, no. 167.

496. *The Way*, no. 407.

497. *The Forge*, no. 697. See *Conversations*, no. 117.

is a human virtue, also called "loyalty," because a person's word and an acquired commitment become a "law" for one's behavior.

A Christian can acquire different types of commitments to live his vocation for love of God. For instance, he can acquire a commitment with an institution of the Church to receive specific Christian formation and participate in certain apostolic initiatives dedicating his time and resources, or a commitment to remain celibate for love of God and to expand the kingdom of God—"*propter regnum caelorum*" (Matt. 19:12)—as a response to a divine call that is recognized as permanent. The love of God, which prompts persons to assume this commitment, calls for the human virtue of faithfulness so that it lasts in time without being altered by mood swings, external difficulties, or the attraction of goods left behind in order to attain others (as occurs when someone receives the gift of celibacy without for that matter ceasing to have an inclination for the good of marriage). At the same time, faithfulness requires charity to constantly renew "the first love" (Rev. 3:4) that led them to acquire those commitments not in a provisional but rather a permanent manner. Although St. Josemaría explains this concept in the following quotation in reference to one's self-giving to God in Opus Dei, given the theological content of his explanation, his words have a greater application:

> *It's only logical that we feel the attraction, not of sin, but of those noble earthly realities that we have left behind for love of Jesus Christ, without thereby losing the inclination toward them. Because we felt this tendency, our self-giving was truly generous and detached. And because we preserve our self-giving, our fidelity is a continual offering: a love, unselfishness, and magnanimity which lasts and which is not just the result of inertia. St. Thomas says:* eiusdem est autem aliquid constituere, et constitutum conservare (*S. Th.*, II-II, q.79, a.1 c.). *What gave rise to your self-giving, my son, will also maintain it.*[498]

When faithfulness to these commitments is informed by charity (as would be the case of faithfulness out of love for God), then, perseverance, as the corresponding human virtue, reaches its perfection and fulfillment. In *The Way* we read, *And what is the secret of perseverance? Love. Fall in Love, and you will not leave him.*[499] At the same time, given that the human virtue of faithfulness (i.e., loyalty) has its own object and value, even when supernatural charity is lacking, it retains its reason for being. Remaining loyal

498. *Letter, March 24, 1931*, no. 12.
499. *The Way*, no. 999.

in those moments is a way of recovering the love in which its perfection resides. This is why Álvaro del Portillo would explain that this point of *The Way* "also has meaning when it is read backwards: 'don't leave him and you will fall in love; be loyal and you will end up madly in love with God.'"[500]

4.3.2. Obedience "With All the Vitality of the Intellect and the Will"

Jesus Christ obeys the will of his heavenly Father as well as the will of Mary and Joseph. The first is obedience to God, and it can be identified with charity; the second, by its very object, is the human virtue of obedience.[501] We will now discuss it in the context of justice given that obedience, like justice, refers to others, to one's parents, or to the legitimate authority.

Obedience to God and obedience to human authority are intimately related. Jesus obeys Mary and Joseph out of love for the will of the Father, who established human power and authority. *Let us learn from Jesus how to obey. He wanted the Evangelist to record that marvelous biography which in Latin is expressed in only three words:* erat subditus illis (Luke 2:51), *he was obedient to them. Look how necessary obedience is for a son of God: God himself came to obey two people who, though perfect, were still creatures: Holy Mary—greater than she only God—and St. Joseph! And Jesus obeyed them.*[502] Sacred Scripture manifests that God wishes man to obey legitimate human authority (see John 19:11; Rom. 13:1–2; Heb. 13:17; 1 Pet. 2:13). His voice resounds in any just prescriptions of such authority. *It is not a man who is being obeyed, but God.*[503] Love of God requires this virtue: obedience in the family, in civil society and in the Church. On the other hand, Christian obedience should be shaped by charity; it should be obedience out of love.

Obedience perfects the will, but for a son of God the act of the will can only be virtuous if he follows the dictates of reason illumined by faith. This is why *God does not impose a blind obedience on us. He wants us to obey intelligently.*[504] Virtue does not consist in obeying like a robot, but with *all the vitality of our intellect and will,*[505] and with complete freedom, *with your*

---

500. Del Portillo, *Pastoral Letter*, March 19, 1992 (AGP, P17, vol. III, no. 348).

501. See St. Thomas Aquinas, *S. Th.*, II-II, q. 104, a. 2, ad 3.

502. *Letter, March 19, 1967*, no. 41. See *Christ Is Passing By*, no. 17.

503. *Furrow*, no. 374.

504. *Christ Is Passing By*, no. 17. These words do not contradict the *blind obedience to your superior* (*The Way*, no. 941), but serve to explain it. "Blind obedience" does not mean "obedience without using one's intelligence," but rather full trust in God who is guiding us by means of the persons who have the mission of directing us in our spiritual life (it being obvious that the mandate we have received is not an offense against God).

505. *Letter, May 6, 1945*, no. 39.

heart and your mind.[506] Therein lies the need to identify oneself with what is asked: *You do not love obedience if you do not really love whatever you have been asked to do,*[507] and the logical acceptance of *the consequent responsibility in each act of obedience.*[508]

> As is well known, the Greek (as well as the Latin) root for "obedience" in Sacred Scripture is related to "hearing" in the sense of "lending an ear," to listen to the manifestations of another's will for the sake of giving an answer to it and carrying it out.[509] Obedience is not the same as acting like a robot, an inanimate instrument; rather, it means putting one's intelligence at work ("listening") and then carrying out what one understands.
>
> In the act of obedience, the will must be enlightened by the intellect. That is why there must be "reasons" to obey. For St. Augustine, obedience "is the virtue proper to a rational creature."[510] An obedience based on sheer willpower, without reason intervening, cannot be a human virtue.[511] This, however, does not mean that the virtue of obedience cannot be exercised if the intellect is not satisfied because it has not fully understood the reason for a command. This would be another extreme, a sort of intellectualism, a type of tyrannical rule of reason. On the contrary, reason must subject itself to the will once it has enlightened it whereby it is possible to obey in a virtuous manner, trusting in the reasons of the person who commands, if there are good reasons to trust that person.

St. Josemaría drew many practical consequences from these premises which are applicable for those who exercise authority as well. He states,

> *One needs to learn how to command. Knowing how to command with all the power of authority—of an authority that is service—but keeping in mind that those who have to obey do so by employing their intellect and will: as free beings, not as cadavers* [. . .]. *Commanding with gentleness, respecting people's freedom, respecting the intellect and will of the one who obeys.*

506. *Furrow*, no. 374.

507. Ibid., no. 375.

508. *Letter, May 31, 1954*, no. 22.

509. See Horst Balz et al., *Dizionario Esegetico del Nuovo Testamento*, vol. II, col. 1719.

510. St. Augustine, *De Genes. ad litt.*, 8, 6, 12.

511. "*Virtus moralis habet rationem virtutis in quantum participat virtutem intellectualem*" (St. Thomas Aquinas, *S. Th.*, II-II, q. 47, a. 5, ad 1; see I-II, q. 55, a. 4, ad 3).

> *Otherwise, it would be an obedience* perinde ac cadaver, *and as I've told you, with cadavers I can't do anything.*[512]

St. Josemaría presents the Blessed Virgin at the moment of the Annunciation as an example of an intelligent and free obedience:

> *In Mary we don't find the slightest trace of the attitude of the foolish virgins, who obey, but thoughtlessly. Our Lady listens attentively to what God wants, ponders what she doesn't fully understand and asks about what she doesn't know. Then she gives herself completely to fulfilling the will of God:* Behold the handmaid of the Lord, be it done unto me according to your word (Luke 1:38). *Isn't that marvelous? The Blessed Virgin, our teacher in all we do, shows us here that obedience to God is not servile, does not bypass our conscience. We should be inwardly moved to discover the* freedom of the children of God. (see Rom. 8:21)[513]

> Let us consider this point further, taking note of another moment of Mary's life. This will allow us to discover how intelligent obedience is possible even when we do not understand the reasons to carry out what someone in authority is asking, yet there are sufficient motives to trust that what he or she is commanding is reasonable and good. This is the case when Mary finds her son among the Elders in the Temple after three days of a worrisome quest. She asks him, "Son, why have you treated us so? Behold, your father and I have been looking for you anxiously" (Luke 2:48). Just as at the Annunciation, here too the Virgin Mary desires to identify herself completely with the will of God (which she believes would be revealed in the words of her Son), and that is why she poses the question. But this time, she does not understand the reply: "And they did not understand the saying which he spoke to them" (Luke 2:50). "God permitted her not to understand Jesus' words, but she certainly understood that they had a message hidden from her at that moment; that there were some higher motives, and hence she accepted the will of God and identified herself with it without understanding it. In general this teaches us that it is possible to obey (by means of an intelligent obedience) 'without understanding,'

512. Notes taken from preaching (AGP, P01 XI-1966, p. 12).

513. *Christ Is Passing By*, no. 173. The text refers to obedience to God, but in this case it presents the attitude of Mary also as an example of the human virtue of obedience.

> though knowing that the command is intelligible and that it has a meaning known to the one who commands, not the one who obeys given a personal limitation or whatever other reason."[514] The person obeying does not discard reason, therefore; on the contrary, each one accepts his own limits and entrusts himself to the one who holds the authority to advise or power to command, trusting that the person in authority will do so with the light of reason and faith. In this case, the one obeying can rest assured that it is reasonable to obey.

The supreme model of obedience is Jesus on the Cross. Here again we are confronted with a question: "My God, my God, why hast thou forsaken me?" (Mark 15:34; Ps. 21[22]:2). Biblical commentators usually note that by quoting this psalm from the Cross, Jesus was indicating how at that moment the prophecies contained in other verses of the psalm were being fulfilled. "They have pierced my hands and feet [. . .] they divide my garments among them, and for my raiment they cast lots" (Ps. 21[22]:16–18). This is undoubtedly true, but it should not relegate to second place the initial question posed by the psalm that Jesus pronounced: "My God, my God, why have you forsaken me?" A biblical scholar has pointed out the relationship between these words and the virtue of obedience, recalling that at Calvary we are before the climactic moment of that obedience "unto death, even death on a cross" (Phil. 2:8) by which Adam's disobedience was repaired (see Rom. 5:19): "In the midst of the blinding light of the mystery of Christ who poses [this] question to the Father, we are able to catch a glimpse of the inscrutable depth of the identification of his human will (illumined by the beatific vision) with the divine will. Christ, who sees the Father face-to-face, knows the divine plans which include his death on the Cross for the salvation of men. His question, however, shows that the understanding of this divine plan is inaccesible to human understanding and reveals to us the fullness of Jesus' filial obedience that places all its trust in God's fatherhood: "Father, into thy hands I commit my spirit!" (Luke 23:46).[515] Quoting St. Josemaría, the same author notes that it is through obdedience that *we respond to God's marvelous fatherhood*.[516]

---

514. Ignacio de Celaya, "Libertad y obediencia en la formación sacerdotal," in Lucas Francisco Mateo-Seco (dir.), *La formación de los sacerdotes en las circunstancias actuales: XI Simposio internacional de teología de la Universidad de Navarra* (Pamplona: Eunsa, 1990), p. 703.

515. Ibid., pp. 703–704.

516. *Christ Is Passing By*, no. 17.

Assuming just reasons to trust in the righteousness of those exercising authority, when the intellect is placed at the service of obedience, it provides clear insights that often preclude the need for explicit commands; a suggestion is enough. That is why St. Josemaría often gave the following guideline to the faithful of Opus Dei: *A "please," and we head right for what we are being asked. It's the strongest way we have of commanding: please.*[517]

4.4. Fortitude, Patience, and Perseverance

We know that feelings have a deep influence in the exercise of our freedom. Their influence is positive when they are "virtuous," that is, when they arise from the sensitive faculties (i.e., the irascible and the concupiscible appetites) as perfected by the virtues of fortitude and temperance. The role of these, in their turn, is to shape the appetites according to an order established by a reason enlightened by faith so that they can be placed at the service of charity. In such a way, they enable the Christian to love with all the faculties of his soul.[518]

By means of these virtues, a Christian can make his heart grow to have the same sentiments of Jesus Christ (see Phil. 2:5): a heart overflowing with affection (see 1 Cor. 13:4) that knows how to overcome difficulties with fortitude and to use created goods temperately in the service of others, rather than for his own pleasure. This identification with the sentiments of Christ is obviously the work of the Holy Spirit, a Spirit "of power and love and self-control" (2 Tim. 1:7), whom we must invoke and to whom we must listen.

In the following section, we will first explore fortitude and then continue with the virtue to temperance. We will also take a closer look at other related virtues.

4.4.1. "Fortitude Out of Love"

Let us recall the classical definition of fortitude. It is "the moral virtue that in the face of hardships secures a firm and constant pursuit of the good.

517. Notes taken from preaching (AGP, P01 XII-1966, p. 12).

518. "There are two possible impediments to the human will submitting to the uprightness of reason. The first is that the attraction to something delightful turns it away from what right reason shows it: and this is avoided by temperance. The second is that the will separates it from what right reason indicates because it is difficult. To overcome this obstacle fortitude is necessary, the virtue by which one resists difficulties" (St. Thomas Aquinas, *S. Th.*, II-II, q. 123, a. 1, c.).

It reaffirms the resolve to resist temptation and overcome obstacles in the moral life."[519] In his preaching, St. Josemaría expresses the essence of this virtue in various ways:

> *The person with fortitude is one who perseveres in doing what his conscience tells him he ought to do. He does not measure the value of a task exclusively by the benefit he receives from it, but rather by the service he renders to others. The strong man will at times suffer, but he stands firm; he may be driven to tears, but he will brush them aside. When difficulties come thick and fast, he does not bend before them.*[520]

These are not theoretical affirmations. Behind them is a long experience of suffering and difficulties that St. Josemaría faced throughout his life and left the stamp of the cross on his soul. In passing, we note that both his biographers and eyewitnesses allude to this reality, at least in part. But more than on St. Josemaría's biography, let us focus on his doctrine.

The words quoted above can be applied both to the human virtue of fortitude as well as to the supernatural one. What is specific to the latter is that supernatural fortitude is placed at the service of God's love and is shaped by that love. Christian fortitude moves a person to face the obstacles to his holiness, whether external and internal (especially the inclination to evil, which is the ultimate cause of man's inner conflicts and his conflicts with others), with love for God and trusting in his grace.[521]

> Put up with your share of difficulties, like a good soldier of Jesus Christ (2 Tim. 2:3), *St. Paul tells us. A Christian's life is a fight, a beautiful war of peace, completely different from human warfare, which results from division and often hatred. The war of the children of God is a war against one's own selfishness. It is based on unity and love.* For though we live in the world, we are not carrying on a worldly war, for the weapons of our warfare are not worldly but have divine power to destroy strongholds. We destroy arguments and every proud obstacle to the knowledge of God (2 Cor.

---

519. *CCC*, no. 1808.

520. *Friends of God*, no. 77. See St. Thomas Aquinas, *S. Th.*, II-II, q. 123, a. 3, c.

521. See *Gaudium et Spes*, no. 14; *CCC*, no. 405.

> 10:3–5). *It is our relentless fight against pride, against our arrogance that predisposes us toward doing what is evil.*[522]

The majority of St. Josemaría's texts on fortitude are focused on the combat against evil that the Christian must wage. (We leave further discussion on this to chapter eight, where we will discuss sin and temptations as "the object" of the Christian struggle.) For the time being, let us focus only on the "subject," and how this virtue helps to shape Christ's image in the Christian, making his love "stronger" and keeping his charity from not slowing down in the face of the obstacles that interfere with the fulfillment of God's will.

In a homily appropriately entitled "The Strength of Love,"[523] St. Josemaría writes that *the only possible measure for the love of God is to love without measure.*[524] Precisely the virtue of fortitude strengthens the growth in love, overcoming difficulties that can hold people back from acting at all moments out of love. On another occasion he writes, *In every one of your actions, because you are relying on God's strength, you must behave as one motivated solely by Love.*[525]

By allowing God's love to rule his behavior through fortitude, the Christian not only remains with good intentions; fortitude actually ensures that his wishes become a reality. St. Josemaría vigorously expresses this idea in *The Way* by alluding to the example of the saints:

> *Willpower. Energy. Example. What must be done is done . . . without hesitation, without procrastination. Otherwise, Teresa of Ávila would not have been Saint Teresa . . . ; nor* Iñigo of Loyola, *Saint Ignatius.*
>
> *God and daring!* Regnare Christum volumus! *We want Christ to reign!*[526]

For a detailed explanation of this point, we refer the reader to the critical-historical edition of *The Way.*[527] The fortitude implicitly referenced in the text is considered as if existing within the virtue of charity. It is a fortitude filled with apostolic boldness for the expansion of the kingdom of God required by the ideal of taking the Gospel to all people.

---

522. *Christ Is Passing By*, no. 76.
523. See *Friends of God*, nos. 222–237.
524. Ibid., no. 232.
525. Ibid., no. 71.
526. *The Way*, no. 11.
527. See Rodríguez, "*The Way*" *Critical-Historical Edition, ad loc.*

This virtue is so necessary for holiness and apostolate that a "soft charity" that shuns sacrifice is simply not the one that loves with "all your strength" (Mark 12:30), as God requires. It would be unthinkable for a Christian to pretend to love without bringing into play all the energy that others employ for the sake of their good or not-so-good inclinations:

> *You tell me, yes, that you want to. Very good: but do you want to as a miser wants his gold, as a mother loves her child, as a wordling craves for honors, or as a sensual wretch seeks his pleasure? No? Then, you don't want to.*[528]

St. Josemaría reinforced this idea using graphic images and examples. *Recall that inscription often etched on ancient daggers:* place not your trust in me, if you lack heart.[529] This is a reference to the weapons made in Toledo that were famous for the quality of their steel. Of what use is a good weapon if the one who wields it lacks fortitude? A Christian needs fortitude because fulfilling the will of God, the supreme good that he loves, is a difficult good that calls for struggle (see Matt. 11:12), for an all-out battle. He must place his life on the line for our Lord Jesus Christ who "loved us and gave himself up for us, a fragrant offering and sacrifice to God" (Eph. 5:2; see also Gal. 1:4). Sacred Scripture says that "Love is strong as death" (Song 8:6), alluding thus to this necessity of fortitude[530] in the sense that just as death inevitably comes sooner or later, putting an end to everything in its path, so too, charity ought to overpower any obstacles and conquer, even if it means giving one's life.

> Love is strong as death (Song *8:6). This is one of the praises sung to our Lady, using words of Sacred Scripture. For Mary was strong in loving, strong in suffering, strong in teaching.*[531]

In order to allude to the vice contrary to fortitude by defect, St. Josemaría employs the colloquial Spanish word "*flojera*," which is an interior state of laziness. It is an apparently invincible condition used as an excuse for omitting certain obligations. He objects to such a justification. Aside from cases in which interior weakness arises from poor physical or psychological health, he points out that spiritual "laziness" is a moral defect, a voluntary

528. *The Way*, no. 316.

529. *Letter, January 9, 1959*, no. 59.

530. See, for example, *Christ Is Passing By*, no. 2.

531. Notes taken from preaching (AGP, P01 1973, p. 443).

capitulation to difficulties that leaves a person without the energy to follow Christ and to carry his cross daily. For St. Josemaría, this is a defect that can and should be confronted head on. The following point of *Furrow* indicates the tenor of his preaching on the subject:

> *You should not be surprised at feeling tired or at having sometimes to "go against the grain," without any spiritual or human consolation. See what someone wrote to me some time ago, and which I kept for those who naively consider that grace does away with nature: "Father, for a few days now I have been feeling tremendously lazy and lacking in enthusiasm for fulfilling the plan of life. I have to force myself to do everything, and I have very little taste for it. Pray for me so that this crisis may soon pass, for it makes me suffer a lot to think it could make me turn from my way."*
>
> *I answered only: Did you not know that Love demands sacrifice? Read the words of the Master slowly: "Whoever does not take up his Cross 'cotidie'—daily—is not worthy of Me." And further on: "I will not leave you orphans . . ." Our Lord allows that dryness of yours, which you find so hard, so that you may love him more, so that you may trust only in him, so that you may co-redeem with the Cross, so that you may meet him.*[532]

In face of the danger of this "laziness" [*flojera*], or however we want to label this temptation, human strength alone is insufficient. Love of God requires a kind of fortitude that conforms to the rule of faith and seeks divine help without relying exclusively on one's own qualities and energies. The psalmist exclaims, "for thou, O God, art my fortress" (Ps. 58[59]:9). "I can do all things in him who strengthens me" (Phil. 4:13; see 2 Cor. 12:10). St. Josemaría often repeated: "*Quia Tu es, Deus, fortitudo mea*"[533] (*Ps.* 42[43]:2), seeking his strength in God. When love for God informs courage, a person can carry out God's will, going against the grain, overcoming any lack of desire or enthusiasm. Then he overcomes the interior resistance against "complicating his life," even to the point of giving it up if necessary, as in the case of martyrdom. But there is no voluntaristic rigidness because he does not rely on his own strength. We humbly recognize that *all our fortitude is on loan*[534] and *we will come to sense deep in our hearts that when we are close to our Lord we are able to find joy in suffering, self-denial, and sorrow.*

---

532. *Furrow*, no. 149. See *The Way*, no. 994.

533. See *Furrow*, no. 66; *Christ Is Passing By*, no. 80; *Friends of God*, nos. 17, 131, 213; etc.

534. *The Way*, no. 728. See *Friends of God*, no. 218.

What a great source of strength it is for a son of God to know that he is so close to his Father! This is why, my Lord and Father, no matter what happens, I stand firm and secure with you, because you are my rock and my strength.[535]

Above all, St. Josemaría teaches people to practice Christian fortitude in the little things of ordinary life. Examples of the good exercise of this virtue would include following a schedule out of love of God, caring for details of material order, foregoing a whim, dealing calmly with an annoyance and resolving it, finishing work, not complaining when tired, and so on. In this way, with God's grace, a person acquires a strong will and "firmness of character" [*reciedumbre*],[536] which allows that person to respond more easily to the demands of charity in his sanctification and apostolate.[537]

St. Josemaría invites people to look at the Virgin Mary to learn how to follow Christ carrying the cross each day:

> *Marvel at Mary's steadfastness: at the foot of the Cross, with the greatest of human sorrows—there is no sorrow like her sorrow—filled with fortitude.*
>
> *And ask her for that same strength, so that you too can remain beside the Cross.*[538]

4.4.2. Patience and Serenity

Part of fortitude is having the patience to put up with trials, difficulties, temptations, and one's own miseries.[539] In describing this virtue, St. Josemaría echoes tradition on the whole, though he also highlights particular aspects. He explains that we need patience to struggle against our own miseries so that we do not act franticly in hope of obtaining quick results.[540] If a person did so, he would easily lose the right intention and forget that when fighting for love of God the battle is, in some sense, already won, even though the fruits may not be perceptible. With respect to others' defects, he holds that *patience moves us to be understanding with others, for we are convinced that souls, like good wine, improve with time.*[541] More generally, regarding

535. *Friends of God*, no. 246. Refer to 2 Kings 22:2.

536. This term is frequently found in St. Josemaría's preaching: see *The Way*, nos. 508, 610; *Furrow*, nos. 92, 137, 920; *The Forge*, nos. 527, 1055; etc.

537. See, for example, *The Way*, no. 19.

538. Ibid., no. 508.

539. *Letter, March 24, 1931*, no. 47. See St. Thomas Aquinas, *S. Th.*, II-II, q. 136, a. 4, c.

540. See *Friends of God*, no. 78.

541. Ibid.

the ideal of evangelizing others, he vividly states, *Foster your holy impatience . . . , but do not lose your patience.*[542]

"Love is patient" (1 Cor. 13:4). Shaped by charity, patience enables a person to face difficulties with the same serenity as the apostles, who were "rejoicing that they were counted worthy to suffer dishonor for the name [of Jesus Christ]" (Acts 5:41). In the Christian life, it is very important to *view things with patience. They aren't as we would wish, but as God's providence disposes: whatever they may be, we need to accept them with joy. If we see God behind each event, we will always be happy and serene. Thus we will show that our life is contemplative, and never become unnerved.*[543] If patience is not to become a stressful resistance, it needs the complement of serenity, a virtue that controls interior unrest when difficulties, excessive work, or various worries are prolonged. This virtue makes the soul a favorable setting for contemplation. Serenity is one of the virtues that appears with greater frequency in St. Josemaría's preaching.[544]

> [*Be*] *serene, but not with the serenity of the man who buys his own tranquility at the expense of ignoring his brothers or neglecting the great task* (*which falls to us all*) *of tirelessly spreading good throughout the world. We can keep calm because there is always forgiveness and because there is a solution for everything, except death; and for the children of God, death is life.*[545]

St. Josemaría speaks often of serenity as the virtue that curbs rash behavior and especially reactions of wrath.[546] In this sense, it seems that in his works "serenity" is the name frequently given to the classical virtue of meekness.[547] What is said about one can be applied to the other.

The self-giving [and] *meekness of the Christian, are born of love and lead to love.*[548] In order to love God and others, it is necessary to control anger and rage. Nonetheless, moderation does not always mean suppression. A meek person is not someone who is never upset, but rather someone who is upset when the love of God calls for it. In such cases, charity requires the aid of meekness. The Lord shows himself a model of this virtue: "Learn from me;

---

542. *Furrow*, no. 668.

543. Notes taken from preaching (AGP, P10, no. 227).

544. See *The Way*, no. 8; *Furrow*, nos. 112, 773, 860, 932; *The Forge*, nos. 115, 169, 343, 423, 467, 536, 642, 772, etc.

545. *Friends of God*, no. 79.

546. See *The Way*, no. 8; *The Forge*, no. 642.

547. See St. Thomas Aquinas, *S. Th.* II-II, q. 157, a. 1–2.

548. *Christ Is Passing By*, no. 136.

for I am gentle and lowly in heart" (Matt. 11:29). He gives us an example of how to live it not only when he meekly suffers the affronts of the Passion "like a lamb that is led to the slaughter" (Is. 53:7), but also when he expels the money changers from the temple (see John 2:15–17). In so doing, he teaches us how to react passionately in a holy manner up and against evil. Charity has a special need for this virtue in order to correct someone in an opportune way without giving up one's serenity. *Never correct anyone while you are still indignant about a fault committed. Wait until the next day, or even longer. And then, calmly, and with a purer intention, make your reprimand. You will gain more by one friendly word than by a three-hour quarrel. Control your temper.*[549]

The importance of this virtue for carrying out the apostolic mission of sanctifying the world from within derives from the Lord's words: "Blessed are the meek, for they shall inherit the earth" (Matt. 5:5). To imbue all human activities with a Christian spirit and to "inherit the earth," which is the inheritance of the children of God (see Ps. 2:8),[550] requires self-possession or self-mastery (see Luke 21:19). Self-possession involves meekness and not losing one's serenity when facing the opposition of those who reject the kingdom of Jesus Christ. St. Josemaría characterizes this opposition in the homily "Christ the King,"[551] when commenting on some verses of Psalm 2: "The kings of the earth set themselves, and the rulers take counsel together, against the Lord and his anointed [. . .]. He said to me, 'You are my son; today I have begotten you'" (Ps. 2:2, 7). The Christian's attitude in this situation is summed up by a subsection of this same homily: "Serene Children of God."[552]

4.4.3. Perseverance and Magnanimity

A part of fortitude is *perseverance that nothing can shake.*[553] This is naturally a reference to perseverance in our self-giving to God and others: *To persevere is to persist in love.*[554] Without this human virtue, our love for God would be relegated to particular times and circumstances; it would be a conditional love not determined to endure the difficulties, which is a necessary element for perfection according to the Lord's words: "he who endures to the end

549. *The Way*, no. 10. See *Friends of God*, no. 79.

550. On the meaning of "inherit" or "possess" the earth, in the New Testament, see Horst Balz et al., *Dizionario Esegetico del Nuovo Testamento* (Brescia: Paideia, 2004), vol. II, cols. 49–52.

551. See *Christ Is Passing By*, nos. 185–186.

552. Ibid., no. 185.

553. *The Way*, no. 934.

554. *Furrow*, no. 366.

will be saved" (Matt. 10:22; 24:13). A love for God that does not desire to last forever would not be true love at all.

Since love for God can and should manifest itself in every action, perseverance applies to all things: perseverance in prayer, in mortification, in the apostolate, in working, etc. In this sense, it means continuing in the pursuit of the good without giving in to discouragement. St. Josemaría refers multiple times to perseverance in the Christian vocation, and concretely in the vocation to Opus Dei. In this case, perseverance is practically synonymous to faithfulness,[555] because being faithful to lifelong commitments is the same as persevering in responding to the call that led to assume those commitments. On the other hand, perseverance is not simply about continuing to do something (*a blind consequence of the first impulse, the work of inertia*),[556] but about being exquisitely faithful at all times to those very commitments, observing them out of love with a renewed intentionality that the nature of those commitments requires.

Along with perseverance, the closely related virtue of magnanimity also forms part of the virtue of fortitude. St. Josemaría describes it as follows:

> *Magnanimity means greatness of spirit, a largeness of heart wherein many can find refuge. Magnanimity gives us the energy to break out of ourselves and be prepared to undertake generous tasks which will be of benefit to all. Small-mindedness has no home in the magnanimous heart, nor has meanness, nor egoistic calculation, nor self-interested trickery. The magnanimous person devotes all his strength, unstintingly, to what is worthwhile. As a result he is capable of giving himself. He is not content with merely giving. He gives his very self. He thus comes to understand that the greatest expression of magnanimity consists in giving oneself to God.*[557]

Charity needs magnanimity if we are to grow *to the measure of the love of the Heart of Christ.*[558] Jesús Ballesteros notes that in the thought of St. Josemaría "magnanimity appears intimately united to charity and implies the desire of doing things well for God and increasing 'care for the other' to the point of embracing the entire human family."[559]

555. See *The Way*, nos. 924, 983, 997.

556. Ibid., no. 983.

557. *Friends of God*, no. 80.

558. *Christ Is Passing By*, no. 167.

559. Jesús Ballesteros, "Toda persona es digna. No toda opinión es válida," in Antonio Malo (ed.), *La grandezza della vita quotidiana*, vol. III, p. 73.

In addition, love must manifest itself in good works. Magnanimity serves this dimension of charity. It leads us to lose the fear of undertaking great initiatives at the service of others. However, the works of charity that it fosters do not paradoxically have to be "spectacular" or "great," materially speaking. Thus, St. Josemaría prayed, *Jesus, may I be last in everything . . . and first in Love.*[560] It is possible to live an ordinary life magnanimously as Jesus did at Nazareth because, *"Great" holiness consists in carrying out the "little duties" of each moment.*[561]

This virtue moves a person to use the means to give abundant fruit according to God's will: "My Father is glorified by this, that you bear much fruit and become my disciples" (John 15:8). A magnanimous person seeks no less than *to gain the world and conquer it for God,*[562] and sets the ideal in motion in his concrete professional, social, or family environment.

If we carefully analyze St. Josemaría's life, we perceive the presence of magnanimity from the moment he receives a divine calling: *I was 14 or 15 when I began to feel the stirrings of Love, sensing that my heart was demanding something great and that it was love.*[563] That "something great" was not a human enterprise; it was a great love that would lead him to "become small" by allowing his Father God to lead him without being afraid of becoming an instrument for his magnificent plans of salvation.

4.5. Temperance, Chastity, and Poverty

Temperance is self-mastery.[564] In St. Josemaría's linguistic usage, the term "self-mastery" [*señorío*] occupies a noteworthy place. It implies dignity and integrity: "measure in demeanor or in actions, self-control and freedom in one's actions, subjecting the passions to reason."[565] When describing temperance as self-mastery (mastery over oneself and one's attraction to sensible goods), St. Josemaría makes the connection with the classical notion of this virtue that involves the interior harmony and control of one's impulses. The same can be said when he adds: *temperance makes the soul sober, modest,*

560. *The Way*, no. 430.

561. Ibid., no. 817.

562. *Furrow*, no. 526; see ibid., no. 858.

563. Notes taken from preaching, March 19, 1975 (AGP, P09, p. 216).

564. *Friends of God*, no. 84.

565. *Diccionario de la Real Academia Española de la Lengua.*

understanding. It fosters a natural sense of reserve which everyone finds attractive because it denotes intelligent self-control.[566]

Self-mastery, measure, rule over concupiscence (or, to use the language of the *Catechism of the Catholic Church*), "the rational use of the passions and appetites of our sensitive nature":[567] these are concepts that clash with contemporary culture as they imply the negative idea of "repressing human nature," or "impeding spontaneity." Perhaps this is the reason why St. Josemaría is concerned about clarifying that the effort required by temperance is the same one that is required to be free to love God and neighbor. He thus describes the temperate person as the one who:

> *knows how to do without those things that may harm his soul and he also comes to realize that his sacrifice is more apparent than real; for living this way, with a spirit of sacrifice, means freeing oneself from many kinds of slavery and savoring instead, in the depths of one's heart, the fullness of God's love. Life then takes on again shades and tones which intemperance had tended to blur. We find ourselves able to care for the needs of others, to share what is ours with everyone, to devote our energies to great causes.*[568]

A Christian needs temperance to be able to live out charity. At the same time, his temperance should be directed or "measured" by reason enlightened by faith, which makes the person aware of higher demands than those of reason. Let us now take a closer look at other virtues that are integral to temperance, such as chastity and poverty.

4.5.1. Chastity: Holy Purity

By revealing his image and likeness in man and woman, God has called them to reflect the communion of love among the divine Persons. All the gifts that he grants them have this same end. In particular, the sexual difference that he established by creating them male and female is *a divine gift,*

---

566. *Friends of God*, no. 84. Temperance "educates the soul" (in Spanish, literally: "*cría* el alma"). This is another way of referring to the Greek term "*sophrosyne,*" which means "good upbringing" [*buena crianza*]: the nobility and sober moderation that distinguish those who have received a good education. The term appears in 2 Tim. 1:7 and Tit. 2:2, but the Neo-Vulgate translates it in the first case as sobriety, and as prudence in the second, virtues which are undoubtedly implied in a different way in the "*sophrosyne*" but without identifying totally with it (see Pieper, *Zucht und Maß*, München 1949, pp. 10–12). In St. Josemaría, the notion is in full harmony with that of the *Catechism of the Catholic Church*: "Temperance is the moral virtue that moderates the attraction of pleasures and provides balance in the use of created goods" (*CCC*, no. 1809).

567. See *CCC*, no. 2341.

568. *Friends of God*, no. 84.

ordained to life, to love, to fruitfulness.[569] The object of the virtue of chastity or of purity (terms that are synonymous in St. Josemaría's preaching),[570] is to assign sexuality its proper place within the spiritual and corporal unity of the person so that it can accomplish its function in regard to the end of loving God and neighbor in each one's own state.[571]

St. Josemaría writes: *the sexual drive* [. . .] *is a noble human reality that can be sanctified. Note, therefore, that I never speak of impurity, but of purity.*[572] He affirms unambiguously the Christian doctrine defending the dignity of the body and the value of sexuality in the face of contrary gnostic and dualist notions: *sex is something noble and holy—a participation in God's creative power—which was made for marriage.*[573] Naturally a different matter is the degradation of this tendency brought about by sin. In the current situation, it is necessary to fight so as to put sexuality under the order of reason enlightened by faith. This is not a fight against sexuality but against its corruption.[574]

> *St. Thomas Aquinas comments that God has joined to the exercise of the different functions of human life a pleasure or satisfaction, which is, therefore, something good. But if man, inverting the proper order of things, seeks satisfaction as an aim in itself, in contempt of the good to which it is joined and which is its aim, he perverts its true nature and converts it into a sin, or an occasion of sin.*[575]

One could imagine that the notion of sexuality in the texts quoted above refers only to a capacity exercised in marriage. If this were the case, it would serve no purpose in the life of celibate persons for whom chastity would be a denial of sexuality. It would suffice to read the homily "For They

---

569. *Christ Is Passing By*, no. 24. See *CCC*, no. 2331.

570. Perhaps one could point out a slight nuance between the two terms. In speaking of chastity, one tends to think of the external manifestations of the virtue, while purity, rather, evokes the interior realm, the heart, which seems to be implied by the liturgical prayer that asks, "*ut tibi casto corpore serviamus, et mundo corde placeamus*" (Roman Missal, *Missae ad diversa*, *Collecta*: this prayer is also found among the texts suggested as preparation for Holy Mass; St. Josemaría recited it every day). The *Catechism of the Catholic Church* also points in this direction (see *CCC*, no. 2520 f.). Nevertheless, after examining the writings of St. Josemaría, it seems that he used them practically as synonymous.

571. See *Friends of God*, nos. 177–179, 184; *CCC*, no. 2337.

572. *Christ Is Passing By*, no. 5.

573. *Friends of God*, no. 185.

574. See ibid., nos. 184–185.

575. *Christ Is Passing By*, no. 25. The reference to St. Thomas Aquinas in the published text is quite ample: *S. Th.*, I-II, q. 31 y II-II, q. 141.

Shall See God"[576] to realize that St. Josemaría does not think that way. He considers sexuality to be a constitutive property of man and woman that affects the nucleus of their personality. He sums it up with the specific terms "manliness" [*virilidad*] and "femininity."[577] Chastity is not reduced to the habit that orders the procreative faculty; rather, it has a much broader object. It is the cleanliness of life that places its masculine or feminine traits, and especially its spiritual ones (the way of thinking, loving, feeling, and acting), at the service of the love of God and neighbor.

St. Josemaría seldom employs the terms "sex," "sexual," etc., not out of a negative vision of what he recognizes to be noble and sanctifiable, but rather because he distances himself from the pathological emphasis on this subject in a civilization marred by the pull of hedonism.[578] Against this ill, in fact, he reacts energetically, driven by the sense of his divine filiation:

> *In these times of violence and of brutal, savage sexuality, we have to be rebels: we refuse point blank to go with the tide, and become beasts. We want to behave like children of God, like men and women who are on intimate terms with their Father, who is in heaven and who wants to be very close to—inside!—each one of us.*[579]

He notes that those who are *obsessed by sex*[580] manifest an imbalance:

> *For normal people, sex comes in fourth or fifth place. First come spiritual ideals, with each person choosing his own. Next, a whole series of matters that concern ordinary men and women: their father and mother, home, children and so on. After that, one's job or profession. Only then, in fourth or fifth place, does the sexual impulse come in.*[581]

Nonetheless St. Josemaría points out, as we will discuss in chapter eight, that the effort to live holy purity *perhaps during certain periods moves to the first place.*[582] This can occur, for instance, due to pressure from an immoral

576. See *Friends of God*, nos. 175–189.

577. This is an idea that belongs to the common patrimony of Christian anthropology: see, for example, St. John Paul II, Apostolic Exhort. *Familiaris Consortio* (November 22, 1981), no. 11; *CCC*, nos. 2332 and 2361.

578. See *Friends of God*, no. 179.

579. *The Forge*, no. 15.

580. *Friends of God*, no. 179.

581. Ibid.

582. Notes taken from preaching, November 9, 1959 (AGP, P01 V-1978, pp. 20–21).

environment. But it can also occur that one may become disproportionately sensitive to sexual matters because interest in goods that should take precedence diminishes. The remedy then lies not only in combating temptations, but in fighting positively in other areas seeking to love God more intensely. The close link between purity and charity thus emerges as we will now explore.

Theological charity needs the virtue of chastity in order to display its vital power. St. Josemaría expresses this with the following image: *Charity is the seed that will grow and yield rich fruit under the fertile rain of purity.*[583] The fruits are the works of love for God and neighbor, and can be described as follows:

- Chastity is necessary to preserve and increase the love of God that the Holy Spirit pours into our hearts (see Rom. 5:5). St. Paul reminds the Corinthians: "Do you not know that your bodies are members of Christ? [. . .] Shun immorality. [. . .] Do you not know that your body is a temple of the Holy Spirit within you, which you have from God? You are not your own" (1 Cor. 6:15, 18, 19). Sins against chastity are opposed in particular to the indwelling of the Holy Spirit in the Christian because they introduce disorder where an intimate harmony between body and soul should reign. If the inclinations of the sensible appetite, which are part of being a man or a woman, are not subject to the spirit, the person will neither be subject to the action of the Holy Spirit. By contrast, the virtue of chastity enables the Christian to be a pure temple of the Spirit.

  For this reason, chastity bears a close relationship with contemplative life. Referring to Jesus' promise "Blessed are the pure in heart, for they shall see God" (Matt. 5:8), St. Josemaría notes that *the Church has always understood these words as an invitation to chastity.*[584] They not only constitute a proclamation of the beatific vision in the future life for those who have lived chastely out of love; they speak of purity also opening up the doors to a loving contemplation of God already here on earth. We can thus more easily fathom why St. Josemaría compares

583. *The Way*, no. 119.

584. *Friends of God*, no. 175. The following is a citation from a commentary of a Father of the Church in regard to that beatitude: "Those who have a completely clean conscience or who love chastity guard a healthy heart. No virtue is as necessary as this in order to see God." St. John Chrysostom, *In Matthaeum homiliae*, 15, 4.

chastity to the wings that enable a person to fly to the height of a life of prayer. Those who do not wish to love will view the wings as a heavy burden, where in fact, it is impurity that actually impedes contemplation by chaining the soul to sensual gratification.[585] For this reason, St. Josemaría suggests reciting the following prayer: *Remove, Jesus, that filthy crust of sensual corruption which covers my heart, so that I can feel and readily follow the touches of the Paraclete in my soul.*[586] There is an evident agreement with an ancient Christian author who writes, "to be chaste is to have a holy way of feeling."[587]

- Chastity is also indispensable for charity with one's neighbor. Since sexuality concerns in a particular way "the capacity to establish bonds of communion with another,"[588] a person who is unable to rule his sexual inclination has an impediment in giving himself to others. He may offer service to people, but his lack of interior purity will cloud his relations; he will have a deformed perception of the others that will lead him to perceive them in light of his own satisfaction. St. Josemaría focuses on an aspect central to Christians when he writes, *without holy purity one cannot persevere in the apostolate.*[589] By living chastity in a refined manner, a healthy friendship and trust can arise and grow, one that creates a good climate to draw souls closer to God. This virtue also engenders the spiritual sensitivity and strength to promote public morality in society, especially with reference to sexual matters.[590]
- A proper self-love and the pursuit of perfection for love of God also requires chastity. There is no doubt that for St. Josemaría, *among the chaste are found the finest men in every way.*[591] Personal fulfillment is only reached by one's self-giving to others; chastity opens the path to this self-giving, while impurity encloses a person within himself.

---

585. See *Friends of God*, no. 177. The image of wings has a long tradition behind it: see St. Augustine, *Sermo* 68,12.

586. *The Way*, no. 130.

587. Clement of Alexandria, *Stromata*, 55, 1.

588. *CCC*, no. 2332.

589. *The Way*, no. 129.

590. Certainly someone who does not live chastity can promote public morality, but he will do it "in spite of not living it." Here we are speaking of how chastity positively promotes a healthy moral atmosphere that facilitates the development of the human person. St. John Paul II speaks of promoting an authentic "human ecology." Encyclical *Centesimus Annus*, May 1, 1991, no. 38; see *CCC*, no. 2344.

591. *The Way*, no. 124.

Let us now consider the converse of the above: if charity needs chastity, chastity also "calls for" charity. *In order to be chaste (and not merely continent or decent) we must subject our passions to reason, but for a noble motive, namely, the promptings of Love.*[592] These "promptings of Love" elevate continence and honesty, give them supernatural life, and transform them into Christian chastity. As we know, charity presupposes faith and hope. In a Christian, chastity must be guided not only by right reason, but also by the light of a living faith; moreover, chastity must be sustained by the hope of blessedness in God.

Certainly all the human virtues "call for" charity in order for them to reach their fullness; however, purity (because of its close relation to love) calls for it in a special way. Its end is to protect human love from selfishness. St. Josemaría considers that chastity is *a virtue that keeps love young in any state in life.*[593] This is why he usually speaks of *holy purity*[594] to underline that it is purity for love of God. A point from *The Way* is very expressive: *How beautiful is holy purity! But it is not holy, nor pleasing to God, if we separate it from charity* [. . .]. *Without charity, purity is barren.*[595]

> These words refer to the Christian who separates purity from charity, practices it with his own strength, and fails to put it at the service of God and neighbor. They do not refer to someone who, though not having Christian faith, tries to live in a chaste way. St. Josemaría does not deny the value of chastity that all men who wish to live in accord with their dignity should practice, guided by right reason.

When charity gives life to chastity, it becomes clear that this virtue is *a joyful affirmation of love.*[596] It is not a denial or repression of sexuality; rather, it is a denial of its disorder. St. Peter writes, "I urge you as aliens and exiles to abstain from the desires of the flesh that wage war against the soul" (1 Pet. 2:11). This "denial of a denial" (of a disorder) becomes a "joyful affirmation" as it seeks to love and serve God by ordering sexuality to the true love.

There is another characteristic in St. Josemaría's teaching on this virtue that is worth emphasizing. For him, all the faithful should live "perfect chastity," each according to his or her own state in life. St. Josemaría does not

---

592. *Friends of God*, no. 177.
593. *Christ Is Passing By*, no. 25.
594. *The Way*, nos. 118, 119, 129 and 131.
595. Ibid., no. 119; see ibid., no. 280.
596. *Christ Is Passing By*, no. 25.

follow the usage found in classical treatises on the spiritual life that reserve the expression "perfect chastity" to refer to chastity for those who live in the state of the consecrated life. The reason is obvious: if it were impossible to live chastity perfectly in marriage, marriage would not be a path to holiness. In one of his homilies he thus emphasizes, *when I remind you now that Christians must keep perfect chastity, I am referring to everyone: to the unmarried, who must practice complete continence; and to those who are married, who practice chastity by fulfilling the duties of their state in life.*[597]

Justice imposes certain demands according to each person's profession, and fortitude calls for acting in one way or another depending on the difficulties that arise. In a similar way, holy purity too has different manifestations depending on the diversity of gifts that God grants. He states,

> *By divine vocation, some are called to live this purity in marriage. Others, foregoing all human love, are called to correspond solely and passionately to God's love. Far from being slaves to sensuality, both the married and the unmarried are to be masters of their body and heart in order to give themselves unstintingly to others.*[598]

Regarding chastity in marriage, St. Josemaría separates himself from the currents of thought that emphasize the danger for progress in the spiritual life derived from the attraction of the goods proper to married life:

> *The pure and noble love of spouses is a sacred reality which as a priest, I bless with both hands* [. . .]. *With regard to chastity in married life, I can assure all married couples that they should not be afraid of showing affection to one another, as this inclination is at the root of their family life. What our Lord expects from them is that they respect each other and be loyal to each other; that they act with refinement, with naturalness, with modesty. I will also tell them that their conjugal relations are honest when they are an expression of true love and therefore are open to fruitfulness, to children.*
>
> *To stop up the sources of life is a crime against the gifts that God has granted mankind and reveals that that person is moved by selfishness and not out of love. In that case, everything becomes clouded, because husband and wife begin to look at each other as accomplices, and the dissensions that are produced, if this state is allowed to continue, are almost always impossible to heal.*

597. *Friends of God*, no. 177.

598. *Christ Is Passing By*, no. 5.

When there is chastity in the love of married persons, their marital life is authentic; husband and wife are true to themselves, they understand each other and they feel united to each other. When the divine gift of sex is perverted, their intimacy is destroyed, and they can no longer look at each other honestly in the face.

Spouses should build their life together on the foundation of a sincere and pure affection for each other, and on the joy that comes from having brought into the world the children God has enabled them to have. They should be capable of renouncing their personal comfort if need be; and they should put their trust in the providence of God: having a large family—if such were the will of God—is a guarantee of happiness and of effectiveness, in spite of everything that the mistaken proponents of a life based on hedonism may say to the contrary.[599]

As far as chastity in celibacy is concerned, St. Josemaría's thinking is also completely positive. Far from focusing on the denial that celibacy entails, he underscores the goods attained from it. Thinking primarily on the apostolic celibacy of the laity and that of diocesan priests, he states

Charity [. . .] *presents chastity to us as a joyful affirmation, and apostolic celibacy as a greater commitment, which enables us to give our whole heart to God and which gives us full freedom for the apostolate.*[600]

Chastity in apostolic celibacy has the specific object (within the order of sexuality) to point out the best way to guide our thoughts, affections and actions, so that they be coherent with our commitment to God, and to protect it. Since the reason for celibacy is supernatural ("for the kingdom of God"), the chastity that keeps the heart undivided can only be a chastity shaped by charity.[601] This virtue permanently prolongs the act of

---

599. Ibid., nos. 24–25. The Pontifical Magisterium contemporary with St. Josemaría dedicated important documents to marriage and family in which it dealt at length with conjugal chastity, from the encyclical *Casti Connubii* of Pius XI (December 31, 1930) to *Humanae Vitae* of Paul VI (June 25, 1968), and passing through the constitution *Gaudium et Spes*, part II, ch. I, of Vatican II. St. Josemaría echoed this body of doctrine in his preaching from the perspective of the sanctification of family life, which situated him above any minimalistic viewpoints. Moral doctrine about what is licit and illicit in conjugal relations is clearly affirmed, but in a simple and elegant way. The accent is placed on the ideal of converting everything into prayer. We will see this in chapter seven, section 3.1.1.

600. *Letter, December 8, 1949*, no. 35. The traditional expression "undivided heart," applied to celibacy, is inspired by 1 Cor. 7:34. In regard to celibacy, see volume I, Preliminary Part, III.2.a.2.

601. See *The Way*, no. 164.

love that gave rise to one's commitment to God; it furthermore enables us to discover the *medium virtutis* ("golden mean") that goes beyond reason alone and reveals at all times what is virtuous behavior. It is *as far removed from sensuality as it is from insensitivity, and as far from sentimentality as it is from heartlessness or hard-heartedness.*[602] This "golden mean" does not consist in a cold or distant attitude toward others, nor in isolation from the environment in which the consequences of sin are perceived. On the contrary, precisely because of the apostolic meaning that it bears, celibacy calls for virtues that enable a noble and open friendship that does not fall into sentimentality. Chastity knows how to find the proper behavior that protects sincerity of heart;[603] discovers any disordered attachment of the heart promptly; and seeks to repair it so as to make decisions at all times in accord with the sentiments of Jesus Christ.[604]

In closing, let us recall what St. Josemaría considered to be common means to grow in this virtue: *keeping a watchful guard over our senses and our heart; the courage—the courage to be a "coward"—so as to flee from the occasions of sin; going to the sacraments frequently, particularly to the Sacrament of Confession; complete sincerity in our own spiritual direction; sorrow, contrition, and reparation after one's falls. And all this imbued with a tender devotion to our Lady.*[605]

4.5.2. Poverty and Detachment

The virtue of detachment can be understood in two ways: as detachment from oneself and as detachment from material goods. The first and more general sense refers to the attitude of the person who recognizes himself to be a beggar without anything of his own, and moreover as a sinner, but a sinner who trusts in God and depends on his mercy for everything. The second and more specific sense is that of poverty as temperance in the use of earthly goods that prompts us to consider them as gifts and to use them according to God's will.

Sacred Scripture speaks of the first sense when it refers to the "poor in spirit." The Lord calls them blessed "for theirs is the kingdom of heaven" (Matt. 5:3). In reality, this poverty is an aspect of humility. A church father

602. *Friends of God*, no. 183.

603. See *The Way*, no. 161.

604. See ibid., no. 134.

605. *Friends of God*, no. 185.

says that the poor in spirit "are the humble and contrite of heart."[606] St. Josemaría speaks of it when he invites us *to be thoroughly detached from ourselves, our intellectual talents, our health, our good name, our noble ambitions, our triumphs, our successes.*[607] Being poor in spirit is the foundation for poverty in the specific sense to which St. Josemaría refers when he declares: *poverty lies in being truly detached from earthly things.*[608] This is the sense in which we will speak of poverty shortly. We should keep in mind, however, that the expression "poor in spirit" is also used in the second sense of this virtue to distinguish it from "material poverty" (i.e., the simple privation of goods).[609]

Those who do not love and practice the virtue of poverty do not have Christ's spirit.[610] This is a universal principle for all Christians. Its practical application, however, depends on each one's vocation and mission, because *sometimes when people consider Christian poverty they take as their main point of reference the religious whose job it is to give, at all times and in all places, official and public witness of poverty. Such considerations run the risk of not recognizing the specific characteristics of a lay witness, lived interiorly, in the ordinary circumstances of everyday.*[611] For St. Josemaría, *a very important point, on which a correct understanding of the lay vocation depends [is that] poverty is not simply renunciation,* since lay people have to make use of *all created things to solve the problems of human life.*[612]

In the case of the lay faithful in the middle of the world, poverty with regard to earthly goods should intertwine two aspects: a complete interior detachment of those goods and the habitual disposition to use them to sanctify the world from within. *I advise you to make a very real effort to be detached from everything, and to do so without fear or hesitation. Then, when you go about your various duties, whether personal, family or otherwise, make honest use of upright human means with a view to serving God.*[613]

606. St. John Chrysostom, *In Matthaeum homiliae*, 15, 1.

607. *Friends of God*, no. 114. This is a common way of referring to the most radical meaning of this virtue. St. John Paul II, for example, speaks of poverty as "renunciation and consistent self-detachment." (Homily, "November 1, 2000," no. 3).

608. *Conversations*, no. 111.

609. See, for example, *The Way*, nos. 631, 632, 636.

610. *Conversations*, no. 110.

611. Ibid.

612. Ibid.

613. *Friends of God*, no. 118.

These two aspects (detachment and the right use of material goods) are not mutually exclusive. A person can be detached of the goods that he owns to the point of living as if he did not possess anything for himself (see 1 Cor. 7:30), and use them at the same time as a steward with the obligation of putting them to good use (see Matt. 25:14 ff.; Luke 12:42–44; 19;12 ff.).

> *The ordinary Christian has to reconcile two aspects in his life that may at first seem contradictory. There is, on the one hand,* real poverty (*in the sense that it can be seen and felt, and is made up of definite things*) *which should be an expression of faith in God and a sign that the heart is not satisfied with created goods, but rather that it aspires to the Creator; that it desires to be filled with the love of God and to be able to then give this same love to everyone. On the other hand, an ordinary Christian is and wants to be* one more amongst his fellow men, *sharing their way of life, their joys and happiness; working with them, loving the world and all the good things that exist in it; using all created things to solve the problems of human life, and to establish a spiritual and material environment which will foster personal and social development.*[614]

Having stated this principle of compatibility between both aspects of poverty in the case of laity, the question arises as to how this can be lived in practice. St. Josemaría proposes a path that is in accord with the principle of freedom, the true key for his doctrine on holiness in the middle of the world:

> *Achieving a synthesis between these two aspects is, to a great extent, a personal matter. It requires interior life, which will help us assess in every circumstance what God is asking of us. For this reason I do not want to give fixed rules, although I will give some general indications.*[615]

As with all human virtues, poverty has a "golden mean" and, aware of that, St. Josemaría offers some suggestions for reaching it. Though general, the following suggestions are, nevertheless, very useful:

> *Here you have some signs of true poverty: not having anything as one's own; not having anything superfluous; not complaining when one lacks even what*

614. *Conversations*, no. 110.

615. Ibid.

is necessary; when it is a question of choosing something for one's personal use, choosing what is poorest and least attractive.[616]

Let us take a closer look at each one of these practical guidelines:

(a) For St. Josemaría, "not having anything as one's own" is more than a generic interior disposition; it is a concrete sign of poverty recognizable in the way of using things, spending one's time, and of caring for one's health. *As far as I am concerned, one of the signs that we're aware of being lords of the earth and God's faithful administrators is the care we take of the things we use: keeping them in good condition, making them last and getting the best out of them, so that they serve their purpose for as long a time as possible and don't go to waste.*[617] He who is not accountable takes care of things differently than if he were. If someone sees himself as the owner of things, he disposes of his possessions as he pleases. Instead, if someone is aware of being a steward of those goods, he seeks to care for them and to make them last as much as possible, because he must render an account for them; the latter keeps account of expenses, uses instruments, tools and/or resources he needs for work wisely, etc. The same can be said about the use of one's time. Christian poverty entails not considering time as one's own "personal" good in the absolute sense of the term, but rather as a treasure to spend serving God and neighbor.[618] And lastly, something similar also holds for one's health: it is a gift in order to serve others and as such, the Christian should neither neglect it nor idolize it.

(b) "Not having anything superfluous" is another "sign" of poverty. Something is superfluous if it is not necessary to live according to one's vocation to holiness and to sanctify the activities in which one is involved, keeping in mind that what is "necessary" refers not only to the "absolutely necessary," but also to the "relatively necessary" for the good fulfillment of one's duties. The concrete distinction between "superfluous" and "necessary" will depend on each person's circumstances and will require a refined conscience. St. Josemaría invites people to not create *artificial needs* for themselves.[619]

---

616. *Instruction*, May 31, 1936, note 137. A clear precedent is found in St. Alphonsus Marie de Liguori, "Breve pratica per la perfezione raccolta dalle dottrine di S. Teresa," in *Opere di S. Alfonso Maria de' Liguori* (Turin: Marietti, 1845–1880), p. 462; "La vera sposa di Gesù Cristo, in *Opere Ascetiche di S. Alfonso M. de' Liguori* (Rome: Sant'Alfonso, 1933), vol. XIV, pp. 323–343.

617. *Friends of God*, no. 122.

618. See ibid., nos. 45–46, 50–52.

619. Ibid., no. 125.

> *Since poverty of the spirit does not consist in not having things but rather in being truly detached from what we have, we need to be vigilant so as not to be deceived by our imagination into thinking we can't survive unless we have certain things. As St. Augustine puts it:* Seek what suffices, seek what is enough, and don't desire more. Whatever goes beyond that, produces anxiety not relief: it will weigh you down, instead of lifting you up. (St. Augustine, *Sermo* 85,6)[620]

(c) "Not complaining when one lacks even what is necessary." It certainly is not contrary to poverty to seek to possess what is reasonable for the exercise of one's profession; to ensure the welfare of the family; to participate in a dignified manner in the various events of society, and so on. However, if a Christian lacks necessary things, he ought to discover in those circumstances God's fatherly providence. A spirit of poverty leads him "not to complain" because a complaint to which one consents would reveal (at least to a certain degree) that those goods are not desired for the sake of serving, and that there is a failure in completely trusting in God, who always grants everything that is truly necessary to those who ask and use the means at their disposal (see Matt. 6:26,31–32).

> *Let me assure you, it's something which I have touched with my own hands and seen with my own eyes: that, if you trust in God's Providence, if you abandon yourselves in his all-powerful arms, you will never lack the means to serve God, his Holy Church and the souls of men; and this without having to neglect any of your duties. You will then rejoice in the joy and peace which* mundus dare non potest (see John 14:27), *which possessing all the goods of the world cannot give.*[621]

Poverty of spirit is no less demanding or difficult than material poverty, and for this reason, he who loves and practices the first is not afraid of the second nor rebels if he suffers it. On the contrary, he receives it like one of *man's treasures on earth*,[622] just as a Christian accepts pain or illness. At times, he will dispose of goods to use them for love of God in the service of others; at others, the Lord will allow him to lack them and he will then joyfully offer this privation united to the Cross.

620. Ibid.

621. Ibid., no. 117.

622. *The Way*, no. 194.

In either case, he should be able to affirm with St. Paul, "I have learned, in whatever state I am, to be content. I know how to be abased, and I know how to abound; in any and all circumstances I have learned the secret of facing plenty and hunger, abundance and want. I can do all things in him who strengthens me" (Phil. 4:11–13).

(d) The last "sign" mentioned in the text above is "choosing what is poorest and least attractive" when choosing something for one's personal use. As with all the other of these "signs," this last one shines forth in the life of Jesus who "though he was rich, yet for your sake he became poor, so that by his poverty you might become rich" (2 Cor. 8:9). After abasing himself to the human condition, the Son of God chose the greatest poverty: to be born in a stable; to work as a craftsman; to not have a place to rest his head during his public ministry; to die on the Cross. "Choosing what is poorest and least attractive" is not to deny that the goods of the earth are goods, but rather to manifest that the first criterion for choosing a good is not personal satisfaction. To act in this way is a sign of detachment.[623]

In the end, all of these indications that St. Josemaría addresses to the lay faithful in order to help them practice the virtue of poverty in their ordinary lives can be summed up with an invitation to foster the outlook of a father or mother of a large and poor family. Thus, he states,

> *To my way of thinking, the best examples of poverty are those mothers and fathers of large and poor families who spend their lives for their children and who with their effort and constancy—often without complaining of their needs—bring up their family, creating a cheerful home in which everyone learns to love, to serve, and to work.*[624]

As we can gather from the preceeding discussion, the virtue of poverty in St. Josemaría's teaching is not the result of a negative outlook of the use of material goods, but rather a demand of love that seeks to place them at the service of God and of others. Charity needs poverty to express itself in acts having to do with the use of those goods; it calls for detachment. "You cannot serve God and mammon" (Luke 16:13), says the Lord. The young man was unable to follow Jesus "for he was very rich" (Luke 18:23). His failure indicates just how much detachment is needed in order to live a fully

---

623. See ibid., no. 636.

624. *Conversations*, no. 111.

Christian life.[625] The human virtue of poverty prepares a soul to listen to God's calls. It is *a sign that the heart is not satisfied with created things and aspires to the Creator; that it wants to be filled with love of God.*[626]

At the same time, poverty should be shaped by love of God. *Your heart should be in heaven. Only then will you be able to place it, in the right measure, in earthly realities.*[627] If charity cools, the heart tends to develop attachments to material goods and hence the "golden mean" of Christian poverty becomes blurry. It can then become difficult to distinguish between the "necessary" and the "superfluous," or to accept joyfully and without complaining the privation of that which would be practical, beneficial, or pleasant.

4.6. Virtuous Heroism in "Little Things"

In a market economy, a seller may offer his goods at lower than usual prices in hope of getting as many people to purchase them and thereby gain market share. The same cannot be said of the economy of grace, however. Holiness is offered to all and all can attain it, but heroism is always required. If it is at everyone's reach, it is not because it can be attained without effort, but because everyone is capable of the heroism it demands.

What exactly do we mean by heroism? In the ancient classical world, heroes were those figures who are remembered for the extraordinary feats they accomplished that were superior to common mortals, whether they were performed by real figures such as Alexander the Great or mythical ones such as Achilles. According to José Luis Illanes,[628] whereas the Greek ideal of heroicity did not reach its full vigor and scope since it was accessible only to the few, Christian revelation universalizes the concept. Every faithful, on account of being a child of God, is invested from the start with the greatness of Christ, and all the moments of that person's life are open to eternity. This means that at every moment the Christian can perform deeds

625. See *The Way*, no. 631. In this regard we can recall that St. John Paul II spoke of "a religious disinterest resulting from the consumer and secularist mentality" (Apostolic Letter *Novo millennio ineunte*, January 6, 2001, no. 46). The facility for consuming goods has led many to stop practicing the virtue of poverty, leading to a cooling off of charity.

626. *Conversations*, no. 110. This text has been cited more fully earlier.

627. Notes taken from preaching (AGP, P10, no. 180).

628. See Illanes, "La vida ordinaria entre la irrelevancia y el heroísmo," in Giorgio Faro (ed.), *La grandezza della vita quotidiana*, vol. IV, p. 36.

of incomparable value because he can love God and every person, thus bringing to fulfillment the greatest potential of his being. For ancient pagan heroism, achieving excellence in one virtue (whether it was valor, audacity, loyalty, etc.) was sufficient. But with Christianity, all the virtues are needed at the same time given that holiness consists in a heroism of love, and as such requires all the virtues.[629]

Many centuries had to go by for such understanding of Christian heroism. At first, the point of reference was the classical culture. For St. Augustine, the martyrs are the Christian heroes as it is they who faced extraordinary trials. He explains that they are the most worthy and illustrious citizens of the city of God because they fought with courage and shed their blood, and "if the ecclesiastical language would allow it, we would call them our heroes."[630] In a relatively short period of time, however, the Church accepted public veneration of saints who had not been martyrs, so that being an example was no longer tied to dying a martyr. The idea of heroism today, however, continues to be related with exceptional actions.

When Benedict XIV (1740–58) passed legislation on the causes of canonization, he declared that "heroic virtue is that which acts with ease, promptness, and pleasure above the common of men."[631] In such a way, heroism began to be associated with a manner of exercising the virtues (with ease, promptness, and pleasure) while still continuing to imply acting "above the common of men." Since this has been considered synonymous with "accomplishing extraordinary acts" materially speaking, the ancient notion of heroism had not yet been fully overcome, leaving heroism out of reach for the common faithful. This interpretation became obsolete with an explicit clarification by Benedict XV (1914–22) stating that heroism does not require exceptional feats.[632] He affirms that holiness "properly speaking consists only in conformity with the will of God expressed in a continuous and faithful fulfillment of the duties of one's state."[633] Neither holiness nor Christian heroism requires anything else.

---

629. See Benedict XIV, *De servorum Dei beatificatione et beatorum canonizatione*, Prati 1839–1842, III, 21, 7.

630. St. Augustine, *De civitate Dei*, lib. X, 21.

631. Benedict XIV, *De servorum Dei beatificatione et beatorum canonizatione*, III, 22, 1.

632. See Benedict XV, *Decree on the heroic virtues of the venerable Antonio M. Gianelli:* AAS 12 (1920): 172. See Pius XII, Homily, "April 5, 1948: AAS 40 (1948)": 149.

633. Benedict XV, *Decree on heroic virtues*, p. 173.

St. Josemaría's message presupposes all the development of these ideas. When preaching the universal call to holiness in ordinary life, he does not fail to note that *today, as yesterday, heroism is expected of the Christian,*[634] and that *sanctity is never something mediocre* [. . .]. *The goal is very high:* You must be perfect, as your heavenly Father is perfect" (Matt. 5:48).[635] Holiness is always heroic because it consists in the perfection of charity, in identifying oneself with Jesus Christ, and thus presupposes heroism because it entails fighting and overcoming the enemies of God's love within and without.[636] In its turn, heroic charity also requires the effort to exercise human virtues to the point of heroism.

> *Christ's invitation to sanctity, which he addresses to all men without exception, puts each one of us under an obligation to cultivate our interior life and to struggle daily to practice the Christian virtues; and not just in any way whatsoever, nor in a way which is above average or even excellent. No; we must strive to the point of heroism, in the strictest and most exacting sense of the word.*[637]

Notwithstanding the above, heroic charity does not necessarily call for earthshaking feats. St. Josemaría remarked with a sense of humor that, *They [people in general] have, unintentionally perhaps, done a disservice to Christian truth. They even said of some of them that as babies they did not cry, nor drink their mother's milk on Fridays, out of a spirit of penance. You and I came into this world crying our heads off, and we most assuredly drank our milk in total disregard for fasts and ember days.*[638] Sometimes there are extraordinary circumstances that call for putting one's life at risk or carrying out astounding feats to give witness to the Faith. But this is neither the only nor the principal way of being heroic. Just as a father calls his child "a hero" for making the effort to do well something that cost him a lot even though it was nothing special, the Christian can also achieve great deeds of love in ordinary life before the pleasing gaze of his Father God. Awareness of divine filiation helps us to understand this marvelous truth:

---

634. *Christ Is Passing By*, no. 82.

635. *Letter, March 24, 1930*, no. 19.

636. We will leave the theme of the Christian struggle for chapter eight. Here we mention it only because it is a requirement of the perfection of charity and it is what causes this perfection to be called "heroism."

637. *Friends of God*, no. 3.

638. *Christ Is Passing By*, no. 9.

> *Someone could perhaps imagine that in an ordinary life there is little to offer to God: insignificant things, things of little consequence. A small child, wishing to please his father, offers him what he has. They are all the valuables that he carries in his pocket, his* treasures*: a headless lead soldier, a spool without thread, some small stones, two buttons. And the father does not consider the childishness of the gift. He thanks the child and presses him to his heart with immense tenderness. Let us act that way with God, so that those childish things—those little things—become* big things, *because love is big. That is our way, making heroic out of Love the small things of each day, of each moment.*[639]

Living the virtues heroically does not consist, therefore, in carrying out unprecedented feats, but rather in fulfilling ordinary duties in a certain manner. Using an expression coined by St. Josemaría, we can say that it consists in *turning the prose of each day into hendecasyllables, into heroic verse.*[640] The term "heroic verse" (or also "epic verse") refers to what is considered adequate for poetry praising memorable accomplishments. In Greek and Latin, as well as in Spanish and in other languages, this kind of verse is typically written in hendecasyllabic form (i.e., where each line of the poem consists of eleven syllables according to a certain metrical pattern). St. Josemaría is convinced that ordinary duties, which could be expressed in "prose" because they are "commonplace," should be "sung" in "epic verse" when they are done out of love of God as one perseveres to practice the Christian virtues with the greatest perfection possible. The following is a concise description of this idea: *True heroism is found in commonplace and daily realities, done always with perseverance facing God and with an effort that nothing can undermine.*[641]

And to futher illustrate this idea, St. Josemaría refers to the role that mothers so often play:

> *How many mothers have you known who have been the heroines of some epic or extraordinary event? Few, very few. Yet, you and I know many mothers who are indeed heroic, truly heroic, who have never figured in anything spectacular, who will never hit the headlines, as they say. They lead lives of constant self-denial, happy to curtail their own likes and preferences, their time,*

639. *Letter, March 24, 1930*, no. 19.

640. *Christ Is Passing By*, no. 50. See *Furrow*, no. 500; *Conversations*, no. 116.

641. *Letter, August 8, 1956*, no. 40.

> *their opportunities for self-expression or success, so that they can carpet their children's lives with happiness.*[642]

St. Josemaría also employs some images that allow him to complete the characteristics of this heroism in ordinary life. One of these comes from the well-known character of a nineteenth-century French novel who imagined himself to be hunting lions within his own home. St. Josemaría uses this outlandish figure to express his teaching. The following text was addressed to homemakers but can be applied to any other profession:

> *You won't attain sanctity if you spend your whole life waiting for the big opportunity to be heroic. That's the story of Tartarin of Tarascon, which I've so often reminded you of. You won't find any lions in the hallways at home. In contrast, there are so many small things that require heroism: some, because of the constancy they demand; others, precisely because they have little human glamor.*[643]

Another image St. Josemaría uses is that of incense burning before an altar. The good aroma comes from the coals that without flames quietly burn the grains of incense. In the same way "the aroma of Christ" (2 Cor. 2:15) can be noted in a Christian *not in a sudden burst of flame, but in the constant redhot embers of virtues such as justice, loyalty, faithfulness, understanding, generosity and cheerfulness.*[644] Those virtuous acts in the ordinary life are, generally speaking, small acts, easy to carry out by themselves. The heroism consists in their number and their practice in a silent manner, without recognition. It is *the heroism of persevering in ordinary and everyday duties*[645] because *perseverance in little things for Love is heroism.*[646]

But might not this be a second-class, watered-down heroism, a substitute for the true heroism of great accomplishments? St. Josemaría's reply can be deduced from the following comment:

---

642. *Friends of God*, no. 134.

643. *Letter, July 29, 1965*, no. 55. At several occasions, St. Josemaría mentioned the figure of Tartarin de Tarascon in order to express this idea (see *Christ Is Passing By*, no. 36; *Friends of God*, no. 8; etc.). This was a character in the novels of Alphonse Daudet.

644. *Christ Is Passing By*, no. 36.

645. *Letter, March 24, 1930*, no. 19.

646. *The Way*, no. 813. See *The Forge*, no. 85.

> *Many who would willingly let themselves be nailed to a Cross before the astonished gaze of a thousand onlookers cannot bear with a Christian spirit the pinpricks of each day! Think, then, which is the more heroic.*[647]

This heroism in ordinary things is not of less significance because it is at everyone's reach. It is a "silent heroism" and its badge is naturalness. It consists of "embers" rather than "flames." It does what is difficult "as if it did not cost effort," without drawing attention to itself. "The universal call to holiness," comments José Orlandis, "does not entail any 'cheapening' of Christian life so that holiness is more or less degraded or the level of its heroic demands is lessened. On the contrary, it is precisely the case of reaching all the faithful and making the great demands of Christian heroism universal. It is, however, a heroism that is proper to each person, not that of others that would be unnatural; in sum, it is the heroism that God asks of each concrete individual as his or her own heroism, fulfilling the duties of one's state, and the specific circumstances of each person's life."[648]

The heroism of the Blessed Virgin Mary, *teacher of the sacrifice that is hidden and silent*[649] is a heroism in ordinary life. It is the heroism of Jesus' years in Nazareth, the highest example of virtue in everyday existence. Without doing anything out of the ordinary, Jesus acts heroically at every moment by surrendering himself completely to the Father's will, which ultimately leads him to giving his life on the Cross. On Calvary, Christ then reveals his love and perfect human virtues through his Passion and Death; but that love and those same virtues were present while living in Nazareth. Therefore, the Christian should look at Christ on the Cross to learn how to live the virtues while he takes up his daily cross.[650]

5. The Gifts and Fruits of the Holy Spirit

Before delving into the topic of this section, we would like to make a terminological clarification. The terms "gifts" and "fruits" should not be understood in a generic sense (given that every good is a gift and fruit of the Paraclete).

---

647. *The Way*, no. 204.

648. José Orlandis, *Mons. Josemaría Escrivá de Balaguer, Maestro de vida cristiana* (Pamplona: Eunsa, 1976), pp. 26–27.

649. *The Way*, no. 509. See *Christ Is Passing By*, no. 172.

650. See *The Way*, no. 277; *Christ Is Passing By*, no. 58; St. Thomas Aquinas, *Super Symbolum Apostolorum*, ch. 6 ("On the Cross we find an example of all of the virtues . . .").

Rather, these terms should be taken in a specific sense that designates the *seven gifts* mentioned in Is 11:2[651] and the *twelve fruits* referred to in Gal. 5:22–23.[652]

After this clarification, we should also mention that most typically, studies on the virtues are followed by a study of the "gifts and fruits of the Holy Spirit," because they lead the Christian and his acts to a perfection that is superior to that attained by the virtues. At the end of his homily "Human Virtues" and other texts, St. Josemaría invites us to follow the same sequence of subjects in this study:

> *When a Christian fights to acquire these virtues, his soul is preparing to receive the grace of the Holy Spirit fruitfully. In this way, his good human qualities are strengthened by the motions of the Paraclete in his soul. The Third Person of the Blessed Trinity,* the soul's sweet guest (Sequence *Veni, Sancte Spiritus*), *pours out his gifts: wisdom, understanding, counsel, fortitude, knowledge, piety, and fear of the Lord. Then, joy and peace can be perceived.* (see Gal. 5:22)[653]

As we can see, the effort to practice the virtues is the way the Holy Spirit uses to "pour out his gifts." When the gifts mature, they yield the fruits. In the above citation, St. Josemaría mentions two of them: joy and peace.

It would be of great interest to compare and contrast the theological notion underlying these ideas with the one held by the authors who debated

651. "And the Spirit of the Lord shall rest upon him, the spirit of wisdom and understanding, the spirit of counsel and might, the spirit of knowledge and piety, and the fear of the Lord (Is. 11:2, according to the Vulgate). Following the Masoretic text, the Neo-Vulgate gives us only six (piety is lacking). The Hebrew text of Is. 11:2 repeats, among the six gifts that it mentions, that of fear in verse 3, but the Greek version of the Septuagint translates this second reference to fear with a different term: "This is where the seven gifts of Catholic devotion derive from." Raymond Brown et al., *Nuovo Grande Commentario Biblico* (Brescia: Queriniana, 1997), p. 310. Faithful to a very ancient tradition which derives from the Fathers, the *Catechism of the Catholic Church* maintains the seven gifts (see *CCC*, nos. 1831 and 1845). In general, the Pontifical Magisterium following the publication of the Neo-Vulgate continues referring to the *sacrum septenarium*: see, for example, the seven addresses of St. John Paul II, from April 9 to June 11, 1989.

652. "The fruits of the Spirit are charity, joy, peace, patience, kindness, goodness, generosity, gentleness, faithfulness, modesty, self-control, chastity" (Gal. 5:22–23, according to the Vulgate). In this case also the Neo-Vulgate has a smaller number, following the Greek text: it only mentions nine (in place of "peace, patience" there is only "peace"; and in place of "modesty, self-control, and chastity," only "self-control." As is the case with the gifts, this difference between the two versions does not mean that the traditional number of the fruits is without foundation. The *Catechism of the Catholic Church* continues to mention the twelve and refers to the Vulgate (see *CCC*, no. 1832). Apart from this, the differences are not very notable, if one considers what St. Thomas says, after St. Augustine, in regard to the number of fruits: St. Paul did not make a complete listing (there are many others); he only pointed out some to show the kind of conduct of those who "live according to the Holy Spirit" (see St. Thomas Aquinas, *S. Th.*, I-II, q. 70, a. 3, ad 4).

653. *Friends of God*, no. 92.

the topic of the gifts of the Holy Spirit leading up to the Second Vatican Council.[654] Such study, however, would lead us far from the scope of our present work. We will limit our discussion to St. Josemaría's teaching on how the gifts and fruits of the Paraclete complete the spiritual life of a child of God in Christ.

5.1. The Gifts of the Holy Spirit and Contemplative Life in the Middle of the World

"The seven *gifts* of the Holy Spirit are wisdom, understanding, counsel, fortitude, knowledge, piety, and fear of the Lord."[655] Among these gifts, none is called "charity" or "love," even if it is the primary effect of the Paraclete in the Christian as well as the one that best corresponds to the action of the Spirit in the soul. However, this fact implies that the gifts themselves should be thought of as being at the service of charity. When the Holy Spirit is sent into the soul, he not only infuses charity in it but also moves the person to put charity into practice and govern all of his behavior by it. But a Christian may lack promptitude or ease in responding to the motions of the Paraclete. For this reason, in addition to charity which gives supernatural vitality to the human virtues, the Holy Spirit grants other permanent gifts that make the Christian docile to his inspirations at every moment.[656]

These gifts do not substitute charity or the other virtues but rather act conjointly. St. Josemaría reflects this in the homily "Toward Holiness" when he briefly describes what happens in the progress of the spiritual life: the soul *readily submits to the work of the life-giving Paraclete, who gives himself to us with no merit on our part: the gifts and the supernatural virtues!*[657]

---

654. An interesting summary of this debate can be seen in Cruz González Ayesta, *El don de sabiduría según Santo Tomás* (Pamplona: Eunsa, 1998), chapter 1, pp. 15–65 ("Discusiones sobre los dones del Espíritu Santo en la Teología del siglo XX"). St. Thomas Aquinas proposes his vision principally in *In III Sent.*, d. 34, q. 1, a. 2, c. (where he divides the gifts into two groups, corresponding to the "contemplative life" and the "active life"); see *S. Th.*, I-II, qq. 68 and 70 (on the gifts and the fruits in general); *S. Th.*, II-II, qq. 8, 9, 19, 45, 52, 121, 139 (on each of the gifts in correspondence to the seven principal virtues: the three theological and the four cardinal). Various studies show an evolution in the thought of Aquinas in regard to the relation between the virtues and the gifts (which evidently affected his understanding of the gifts themselves). We do not find this subject in St. Josemaría. We have taken the teaching of St. Thomas as the basic conceptual framework of our exposition, making use also of the study of Marie-Michel Philipon, *Los dones del Espíritu Santo* (Madrid: Palabra, 1983); orig.: *Les dons du Saint-Esprit* (Paris: Descale de Brouwer, 1964). As far as the Magisterium of the Church is concerned, it seems that the Encyclical of Leo XIII on the Holy Spirit, *Divinum illud munus* (May 9, 1897), is a clear point of reference for the teaching of St. Josemaría, who cites this document a number of times in his writings.

655. *CCC*, no. 1831.

656. See Leo XIII, Encyclical *Divinum illud munus* (May 9, 1897): *Acta Leonis XIII*, vol. XVII, 141.

657. *Friends of God*, no. 306.

> The distinction between "virtues" and "gifts" has been explained in various ways.[658] We recall that the virtues are habits that incline the Christian to move himself toward the good; the gifts, instead, are perfections that prepare or dispose him to respond with ease to the motions of the Holy Spirit. In both cases we are dealing with supernatural perfections that lead the Christian to act rightly, but they do it in different ways. Properly speaking, what is supernatural in the virtues of a Christian is the object and the end (for example, the object of faith is supernatural revelation and the end is the loving knowledge of the One and Triune God), but the *manner* of acting continues to be "according to the human condition."[659] Instead, under the action of the Holy Spirit who communicates his gifts and is present in the soul, the Christian acts in a *divine manner*: the criteria for action is "the Divinity itself participated by man."[660] According to Philipon, the gifts "allow the virtues to realize their acts with the greatest perfection possible. The cooperation of the virtues and the gifts points toward the same end by means of two different and complementary paths."[661]

Spiritual theology textbooks commonly consider the Christian life as a journey that goes from being governed by virtues to one where the gifts prevail, even though the virtues and the gifts are necessary at all times. Initially, the person advances primarily by means of the supernatural virtues, but the one who corresponds more generously to divine grace is led more and more by the Holy Spirit thanks to his gifts. For St. Josemaría it is clear that *the supernatural life that began in baptism* [. . .] *is strengthened with the growth of the gifts of the Holy Spirit.*[662] It is *a new mode of going about this earth, a mode that is divine, supernatural, marvelous.*[663]

---

658. See Ambroise Gardeil, "Dons du Saint-Esprit," in *Dictionnaire de Théologie Catholique*, 4 (1920): col. 1738 ff.; Michel-M. Labourdette, "Dons du Saint-Esprit," in *Dictionnaire de spiritualité ascétique et mystique*, 3 (1957): cols. 1616–1631.

659. St. Thomas Aquinas, *In III Sent.*, d. 34, q. 1, a. 3.

660. Ibid. See *S. Th.*, I-II, q. 68, a. 1.

661. Marie-Michel Philipon, *Los dones del Espíritu Santo*, p. 154. See St. Thomas Aquinas, *S. Th.*, I-II, q. 68, a. 4, c.; *CCC*, no. 1831. When Philipon says "the greatest perfection possible" we interpret it as a matter of a "divine perfection," or in other words, a divine way of acting, and not simply of "the greatest *human* perfection possible" as that would be proper of the virtues themselves.

662. Article "La Virgen del Pilar," in *Libro de Aragón*, Zaragoza 1976, p. 11.

663. *Friends of God*, no. 297.

It is commonly said that the gifts allow for a "divine manner" of acting, but in reality, it is about a "divine and human" way of acting, similar to that of Jesus Christ insofar as he is a man. In Christ, the divine person acts through his human nature, although not because he is a man elevated by grace but rather because he is God incarnate. The Christian, on the other hand, is a man elevated by grace, but he also enjoys a certain reflection of the Incarnation. To use St. Josemaría's words, *Christ wishes to become incarnate in our actions.*[664] Analogous to how the sacred Humanity of Christ allowed itself to be led by the Spirit (see Matt. 4:1; Luke 10:21), the gifts prepare a Christian for the Paraclete to govern him. His acts will no longer be only those of a man raised up by grace and the supernatural virtues; they will also be the works of Christ. Here, we stand before the mystery of the Christian's "divinization," of his "becoming God," and of his identification with the work of Christ that St. Josemaría proclaims.

There is no doubt that for St. Josemaría, this "divine way" of acting primarily led by the gifts of the Holy Spirit is the state of contemplation in ordinary life. He speaks of being *contemplatives, with the gifts of the Holy Spirit.*[665] Contemplation, which is the simple and profound loving knowledge of God, prayer which no longer requires words, can only take place thanks to the gifts of the Holy Spirit. The contemplation to which he refers is, however, a filial contemplation, the contemplation of the children of God in the middle of the world. And it is this that gives rise to a specific way of understanding the structure and unity of the gifts which we will describe in our following analysis.

First comes wisdom, which inclines a person toward contemplation or, that is, inclines him toward God as his ultimate end with the greatest perfection possible here on earth. Together with it comes the gift of piety, through which one becomes aware of one's divine filiation, the foundation of the contemplative life. Then, there ensue all the other gifts that predispose the person toward contemplation in the various aspects of daily existence and enable wisdom and piety to pervade the behavior of an ordinary Christian in his professional work, care for his family, participation in civic society, etc. Let us now take a closer look at this.

---

664. *Christ Is Passing By*, no. 174.

665. Notes taken from preaching, November 26, 1967 (AGP, P09, p. 87).

(1) For St. Josemaría, just as for a great part of the spiritual tradition, the first place among the gifts corresponds to *the gift of widsom*[666] that perfects *our loving knowledge of God and all that leads to and comes from him.*[667] It is a participation in the Wisdom of God who knows himself in the Word through which he has created the world, establishing the salvation of man and the renewal of the universe by means of the salvific Incarnation of the very "Word-Wisdom." Jesus Christ is the "wisdom of God" (see 1 Cor. 1:24) that reveals himself above all on the Cross. Christian wisdom is the "wisdom of the Cross" (see 1 Cor. 1:17–18).

Only the Holy Spirit, who "searches everything, even the depths of God" (1 Cor. 2:10) can bestow this wisdom on a Christian, but it is necessary that that Christian submit himself to the saving action of the Paraclete. In effect, wisdom is *a knowledge that is only attained with sanctity.*[668] It proceeds from love and makes a person *know God and rejoice in his presence*[669] to savor divine Love. It does this in a "practical" manner, throughout one's acting. The gift of wisdom helps us to see everything with the eyes of Christ, within God's plans; it allows us *to discover the* quid divinum [. . .] *present in each and every daily situation*[670] and *places us in a perspective from which we can judge accurately the situations and events of this life.*[671]

Strictly speaking, the act that derives from the gift of wisdom is none other than a loving knowledge of God, which we call contemplation. For St. Josemaría, it is a matter of contemplation in the normal tasks of secular life.[672] At the same time, he notes that contemplation increases wisdom[673] because the Holy Spirit multiplies his gifts in those who allow him to act.

In this context, it is appropriate to mention the invocation to the Virgin Mary as *Sedes Sapientiae* that St. Josemaría established to be recited

666. St. John Paul II reflects the tradition on the primacy of this gift when he affirms that it is "the first and greatest of the gifts" (Address, April 9, 1989, no. 1).

667. *Consecration to the Holy Spirit*, dated May 30, 1971, Solemnity of Pentecost, the day on which the founder consecrated Opus Dei to the Holy Spirit. See Vázquez de Prada, *The Founder of Opus Dei*, vol. III, pp. 427 ff.

668. Notes taken from preaching, June 1972 (AGP, P09, p. 176).

669. *Christ Is Passing By*, no. 133. See St. Thomas Aquinas, *S. Th.*, II-II, q. 45, a. 2, ad 1. "*Sapientia*" comes from "*sapere*": to savor, to taste. See the very ancient liturgical prayer: "*Deus, qui corda fidelium Sancti Spiritus illustratione docuisti, da nobis eodem spiritu recta sapere et de eius semper consolatione gaudere.*"

670. Notes taken from preaching, October 29, 1967 (AGP, P18, p. 330). See *Conversations*, nos. 116 and 121.

671. *Christ Is Passing By*, no. 133.

672. See ibid.

673. See *Friends of God*, no. 315.

at the end of any act of piety in Opus Dei. A point in *Furrow* explains the reason for his fondness for this short prayer: "*Sancta Maria, Sedes Sapientiae*"—*Holy Mary, Seat of Wisdom. Invoke Our Mother often in that way, so that she may fill her children, in their study, work and social relations, with the Truth that Christ has brought to us.*[674] He addresses the Virgin as "Seat of Wisdom" because she carries Christ, the "Wisdom" of God, in her womb. She is "seat" insofar as she is "mother." Wisdom never "gets up" from this seat because the mother continues to engender her Son's Mystical Body as she participates intimately in the economy of salvation. In her, we can observe the characteristics of the creative Wisdom described by the book of Proverbs, precisely in the fragment used by the liturgy of the Church for some Masses in honor of the Virgin Mary (see Prov. 8:22–31). The grandeur of her role as *Sedes Sapientiae* is revealed in particular by her contemplative life. St. Luke writes that "Mary kept all these things, pondering them in her heart" (Luke 2:19), and for this reason, St. Josemaría sees in her the *best teacher*[675] of contemplative life. As we have seen, he encourages us to implore her to fill her children with wisdom in "their studies, work, and social relations" so that they become *contemplatives in the middle of the world, amid the noise of the street.*[676]

(2) Together with the gift of wisdom, the *gift of piety* stands out in St. Josemaría's teaching. The former points to the contemplation of God, the last end of the spiritual life, while the latter, to its foundation, the awareness of being children of God. There is an order and unity between these two gifts.

To see how St. Josemaría understands the gift of piety, it is helpful to recall that on the human plane, *piety is the virtue of children*[677] that inclines Christians to honor their parents properly. When applied to God, it leads to treating him as Father with the veneration, trust, gratefulness, and dependence of a child. While this is the goal of the virtue of piety, the gift of piety offers a new principle of life. In effect, with the gift of piety the Holy Spirit bestows on us *the sense of our divine filiation, the joyful and supernatural awareness of being children of God and, in Jesus Christ, brothers and sisters of all mankind.*[678] *It helps us to become truly aware of our condition as children of*

674. *Furrow*, no. 607.

675. *Christ Is Passing By*, no. 174.

676. Ibid.

677. Ibid., no. 10. We refer to what was said about this in chapter four, section 3.1.

678. *Consecration to the Holy Spirit.*

God.[679] An example of the gift of piety stands out in a commentary of St. Josemaría to the verse of Psalm 2 that reads, "You are my son, today I have begotten you" (Ps. 2:7): *this is addressed to Christ—and to you and me if we decide to become* alter Christus, ipse Christus. *Words cannot go so far as the heart, which is moved by God's goodness. He says to us:* You are my son. *Not a stranger, not a well-treated servant, not a friend; that would be a lot already. A son! He gives us free access to treat him as sons, with a son's piety and I would even say with the boldness and daring of a son whose Father cannot deny him anything.*[680]

The gift of piety is seen as the foundation of the spiritual life and the basis of the other gifts. Thanks to piety, wisdom is the "wisdom of a son of God," which configures the entire Christian life. Likewise, the gift of understanding and the gift of science, as well as the other gifts, are the gifts of a child of God. This includes the gift of fear, which is a filial fear, as we will see.

Through the gift of piety, the Holy Spirit moves a Christian to feel he is a member of the family of the children of God, which is the Church. It starts him along the path of participating in the liturgy with a deep love and devotion without separating public worship from the interior worship offered up in the fulfillment of the duties of ordinary life. *Those who are pious, with a piety devoid of affectation, carry out their professional duty perfectly, since they know that their work is a prayer raised to God.*[681] *When devotion is sincere it leads one to work, to joyfully fulfill—even though it is hard—the duty of each day. Thus we are contemplatives, for there is a close tie between this interior supernatural reality and the external manifestations of human activity.*[682]

Fulfillment of the ordinary duties without piety would decrease the co-redeeming value that all good acts acquire in virtue of their union with the sacrifice of the Altar, the center and zenith of the life of the Church. The gift of piety shapes a "priestly soul" which, for a Christian who seeks holiness in the world, is united to a "lay mentality."[683]

---

679. *Friends of God*, no. 92. On the relation between the gift of piety and divine filiation, one might look at St. John Paul II, Address (May 28, 1989).

680. *Christ Is Passing By*, no. 185.

681. *The Forge*, no. 739. As can be seen, he used the term "beatería" [*sanctimoniousness*] to refer to the external manifestations of piety of a person who does not fulfill his professional duties, etc. That is a false piety, an appearance of intimacy with God, a deformation of a life which is blessed or happy [*beata*] in virtue of having true intimacy with God.

682. *Letter, May 6, 1945*, no. 25.

683. See chapter seven, section 1.5.1.

The gift of piety *leads us to believe in and savor God's fatherly love for us* (see 1 John 4:16), *and to realize that Christ our Lord, God and Man, is our firstborn brother.*[684] It predisposes us to see our neighbors as children of God and living members of the Mystical Body (or at least as persons called to be thus), and to seek the goods they need to live according to their dignity. The gift of piety, lastly, impels us to practice apostolate and all the works of mercy in a "divine way" of acting, superior to the virtues.

(3) The other gifts (*understanding, science, counsel, fortitude and fear of God*) contribute to the action of wisdom and piety, enabling for contemplation at all times and not only during the moments exclusively dedicated to prayer. They take on a special role because the need for them becomes more obvious in ordinary life.[685]

In order to explain this point, first, it is necessary to refer to the role of human virtues in contemplation, keeping in mind that the gifts enable one to carry out the acts of the virtues with a new perfection. In chapter one, we saw that for many authors who write about the spiritual life, the function of the human virtues in contemplation is reduced to moderating the soul's passions, thereby creating the necessary interior peace for contemplation. By thus limiting the function of the virtues, these authors are thinking of contemplation primarily in terms of times explicitly dedicated to prayer. The contemplation to which the lay faithful are called, however, also takes place in the fulfillment of a person's duties and therefore requires the moral Christian perfection of the very activity that is carried out given that it is no mere "prior condition" for contemplation, but rather its very "matter." And the perfection of the activities can only take place through the exercise of human virtues informed by charity. This is the reason why those virtues belong to the substance of contemplation in ordinary life just as the body belongs to the substance of human nature.[686] On the other hand, where Christian virtues exist, the gifts of the Holy Spirit are also present because they "extend to the entire field of both the intellectual and moral virtues,"[687]

684. *Letter, January, 25, 1961*, no. 54.

685. We say this only by way of hypothesis since it cannot be deduced immediately from the texts of St. Josemaría that we cite, but only by reading them within the setting of the spirit of sanctification in the middle of the world, which he transmitted.

686. See Javier López Díaz, "Virtudes humanas y contemplación cristiana," in Laurent Touze (dir.), *La contemplazione cristiana: esperienza e dottrina* (Rome: Libreria Editrice Vaticana, 2007), pp. 527 ff.

687. St. Thomas Aquinas, *S. Th.*, I-II, q. 68, a. 4, c.

thus making possible a perfection that is superior to virtuous acts. It hence remains clear that the gifts are necessary for contemplation in those actions requiring the practice of the virtues, especially in ordinary life. It is here that wisdom and piety receive a new contribution from the other gifts: a "divine way" of carrying out the acts of the intellectual and moral virtues that permit a person to experience in some sense the action of the Holy Spirit and to enter more deeply into the depths of God (see 1 Cor. 2:10).

The *gift of understanding* is given to us *to perfect our perception of the mysteries of faith.*[688] It helps us to assimilate Christian doctrine decisively and to nourish our prayer with it until we reach contemplative prayer. Particularly important for those who lead a life of contemplation in ordinary life is the contemplation of the hidden life of Christ in union with his sacrifice on the Cross, his resurrection, and ascension into heaven.

The *gift of science* (or knowledge) allows us to *understand properly what created things are, and what they ought to be according to the divine plan of creation and elevation to the supernatural order.*[689] Here, the importance of this gift for contemplation in ordinary life is also clear as it helps grasp the "divine" meaning of temporal realities. What St. Josemaría means by "understand[ing] properly what created things are" is that we should understand them from God's point of view; that is, we ought to grasp their deepest meaning and value, and realize easily and firmly how they are ordered to the glory of God. The gift of science sheds new light on earthly realities as a path to holiness and apostolate. For this reason it protects us from being deceived as our first parents were (i.e., by using created goods for the sake of "being like God").

The *gift of counsel* allows us to advise others *by correctly judging God's will at every moment and for each person.*[690] It gives us a supernatural ease in recognizing the divine plans in specific circumstances. Holiness, as we know, is reached within the Church, not in a solitary manner. The Holy Spirit guides persons to the heights of sanctity (contemplative life in the middle of the world) not only by acting in the soul directly, but also through members of the Church who help one another. The gift of counsel disposes a person to be very docile to that action of the Holy Spirit and to be his good instruments to guide others. *Even without talents, fame or fortune, we*

688. *Consecration to the Holy Spirit.* It is also called "the gift of intellect."

689. *Consecration to the Holy Spirit.*

690. Ibid.

can be effective instruments if we go to the Holy Spirit so that he may grant us his gifts.[691]

The *gift of fortitude* strengthens the faith in order to overcome obstacles in leading a contemplative life in the middle of the world, and to persevere in sustaining others along the path to holiness and apostolate. St. Josemaría thus prays, *Grant us the gift of fortitude, to make us steadfast in the faith, constant in struggle, and faithful in our perseverance.*[692] Even though the name of this gift is the same as that of the cardinal virtue, it is distinguished from it because it is not a human habit elevated by grace; instead, it is a new capability of the irascible appetite whereby it is disposed to be moved directly by the Holy Spirit. We then experience fortitude as if "on loan,"[693] that is, as something which completely exceeds capacity and, for that reason, it leads us to humility rather than pride. *Our fortitude is on loan: it is Christ's own fortitude, fortitude for the good of all souls.*[694]

Lastly, the *gift of fear of the Lord* is that gift which, in making us detest all sin, *impress*[*es*] *upon our hearts a spirit of adoration and a profound and sincere humility.*[695] As we can see, St. Josemaría points out that fear is ordered to a "spirit of adoration," a basic element for the contemplation of God. It is a filial adoration imbued by a deep humility that arises from the recognition of one's own lowliness, and at the same time from the simple familiarity of a child who wishes to please his father and desires others to do so as well. Fear of God is *the veneration of a son for his Father; never a servile fear, for your Father-God is not a tyrant.*[696] The fear that the Holy Spirit grants by means of this gift is not a "fear of God" that prompts us to flee from him. *St. John the Apostle wrote some words which really move me: "qui autem timet, non est perfectus in caritate." I like to translate them as follows, almost word for word—the fearful man doesn't know how to love.*[697] On the contrary, the gift of fear is an invitation to draw humbly to the divine majesty with utmost reverence, but also with absolute trust in his love and fatherly mercy.

In conclusion, we can say that for St. Josemaría, the gifts are perfections that complete the virtues, making contemplative life accessible to every

691. *Furrow*, no. 283.

692. *Consecration to the Holy Spirit.*

693. See *The Way*, no. 728.

694. *Letter, March 19, 1967*, no. 133.

695. *Consecration to the Holy Spirit.*

696. *The Way*, no. 435.

697. *The Forge*, no. 260.

Christian and, more specifically, making contemplative life in the middle of the world possible under the action of the Holy Spirit. Commenting on the preaching of St. Josemaría, Leo Scheffczyk states, "A spiritual fullness and supernatural richness open up from the conscience of the believer in living communion with the Divine Persons, which in some sense grasps the essence of grace from its highest peaks. This fullness converts his path in the world into a high road despite the experience of poor human weakness, and the misery and suffering that always accompany him. But the greatness of grace is such that it overcomes every smallness and earthly weakness and it lays the foundation for a vital attitude of trust, joy and optimism."[698]

These last words spill over into our next topic given that, when vivified by the gifts, the contemplative life manifests itself in its visible results, or that is, the fruits of the Holy Spirit.

5.2. The Fruits of the Paraclete and Apostolic Fruitfulness: "Sowers of Peace and Joy"

In his *Consecration to the Holy Spirit*, after imploring the Paraclete to bestow his gifts, St. Josemaría also asks him to grant us his fruits: *the fruits of your sovereign action in souls: charity, joy, peace, patience, kindness, goodness, longanimity, meekness, faith, modesty, continence, and chastity.*[699]

The distinction between gifts and fruits is suggested in some way in the text cited above at the start of this section when St. Josemaría says that the fruits *can be seen*[700] as the result of the virtues and gifts. "They can be seen" because they are the *acts* of a Christian that manifest the intensity of the supernatural life infused by the Holy Spirit, whereas the virtues and gifts are *habits.* The Lord says, "Thus you will know them by their fruits" (Matt. 7:20). The maturity of the fruits shows with an increasing clarity the life of Christ in the Christian.

In our following analysis, we will comment only on the first three (charity, joy and peace), because St. Josemaría refers to them more frequently than the other fruits, and because the number of fruits mentioned in Gal. 5:22–23 is not of primary importance. St. Paul does not provide a complete

698. Leo Scheffczyk, "Die Gnade in der Spiritualität von Josemaría Escrivá," pp. 75–76.

699. *Consecration to the Holy Spirit.* See Gal. 5:22–23 (according to the Vulgate, as we said above). See the twelve fruits themselves in *CCC*, no. 1832.

700. *Friends of God*, no. 92.

list; he only points out some fruits to describe the type of behavior of those "who live according to the Holy Spirit."[701]

(1) The first fruit is called "charity" (*caritas*). It is not the same as the virtue by the same name; rather, it consists in acts of love made perfectly divine by the action of the Paraclete. These acts are continuous, not sporadic or intermittent because when the virtues and gifts act, they imbue everything through and through. Insofar as it is a fruit, charity is like light and heat that a person in love with God "radiates." A point from *Furrow* depicts this with an attractive simplicity:

> *That friend of mine came up to me: "They tell me you are in love." I was very surprised and the only thing I could think to ask was where he got that news.*
> *He said that he could read it in my eyes, which shone with joy.*[702]

Without mentioning charity as a fruit, these words capture the essence of it as "being in love with God," a characteristic state of the interior life which in some way can be perceived from the outside. That someone is in love becomes obvious in his entire behavior, "because by loving God with his whole heart, directing everything toward him, all of his impulses are unified."[703] St. Josemaría calls this *unity of life*; all of a person's acts are unified when they are shaped by the virtue of charity. In some way, we can say that the fruit of the Holy Spirit called "charity" is the same as "unity of life."[704] St. Josemaría gives such importance to this subject that we will dedicate the epilogue of Part III to it after laying the necessary groundwork for its proper understanding.

(2) The second fruit is joy (*gaudium*). St. Thomas says that joy is "an act or effect of charity"[705] since "the virtue of charity inclines us to love and desire the beloved good and to rejoice in it."[706] Commenting on Galatians 5:22, Albert Vanhoye notes that "love carries joy with it because joy corresponds

701. See St. Thomas Aquinas, *S. Th.*, I-II, q. 70, a. 3, ad 4 (citing St. Augustine).

702. *Furrow*, no. 94.

703. St. Thomas Aquinas, *S. Th.*, II-II, q. 29, a. 3, c.

704. Referring specifically to priests, Vatican II associates unity of life to charity, pointing out that "they will find in the practice of pastoral charity itself the bond of priestly perfection which will reduce to unity their life and activity." Decree *Presbyterorum Ordinis*, no. 14. The same principle can be applied to all of the faithful.

705. St. Thomas Aquinas, *S. Th.*, II-II, q. 28, a. 4, c.

706. Ibid.

to the deepest desire of the heart and to the strongest aspiration of the human person that has been created to be loved and to love."[707]

St. Josemaría expresses this in his quintessential manner: *Cheerfulness is a necessary consequence of our divine filiation.*[708] Sometimes he adds that it is the consequence of the struggle to love as a child of God.[709] This affirmation is the same as saying that joy is an act and an effect of the virtue of charity because that is the essence of the life of a child of God. The Christian who knows himself to be a beloved child of the Father rejoices immensely from this dignity and love. Joy then becomes a proper characteristic of his life, the fruit of the action of the Paraclete. A point from *Furrow* describes it with the vividness of someone who experiences it: "*Happy?" The question made me think. Words have not yet been invented to express all that one feels—in the heart and in the will—when one knows oneself to be a son of God.*[710] Elsewhere, St. Josemaría comments: *let them be sad who are determined not to recognize that they are children of God.*[711]

To possess this fruit a person needs to cultivate it; above all, it is necessary to care for the quality of love. St. Josemaría urges people: *Servite Domino in laetitia, serve the Lord with joy* (*Ps 99:2*)[711] because "God loves a cheerful giver" (2 Cor 9:7). *Without cheerfulness it's impossible to serve. How would you like to be served by someone who was moaning and groaning?*[713]

When joy is lacking in Christian life, it is necessary to look for the reason and to examine why this fruit is absent. If there is sadness and it is not a "godly grief" (see 2 Cor. 7:9, more on this later), it may be due to a lack of love of God and the generosity of giving oneself in response to what God is asking. *You are unhappy?—Think: there must be an obstacle between God and me. You will seldom be wrong.*[714] This kind of sadness can also occur because we do not live charity with our neighbor. Often it is due to harboring resentments instead of forgiving right away: *What do we need to do in order to be happy? I'll give you my own personal experience: first, learn to forgive.*[715] It can also happen that the virtues that are

707. Albert Vanhoye, *Lettera ai Galati*, p. 138.

708. *The Forge*, no. 332.

709. See ibid., no. 105; *The Way*, no. 308.

710. *Furrow*, no. 61.

711. *Friends of God*, no. 108.

712. *Instruction*, May 1935/September 14, 1950, no. 69. Note that the RSV-CE translation "Serve the Lord with gladness" and is found at Psalm 100:2.

713. Ibid.

714. *The Way*, no. 662.

715. Notes taken from preaching, December 25, 1973 (AGP, P09, p. 206).

necessary for living charity are hardly developed. These virtues include fortitude, chastity, poverty, etc., or the set of virtues that are part of a "good character" and enable a person to face reality with a positive outlook and to make human relations agreeable. These virtues are wanting in *ill-humored and sour people, with a bitter zeal and brusque manners, who can never find anything good; who see everything as black; who fear the legitimate freedom of others; who don't know how to smile.*[716] In any event, when there is sadness the root cause is often a disordered self-love because just as joy is the effect of charity, *sadness is the end product of selfishness*[717] and *the cloak of your pride.*[718]

However, while "worldly grief produces death" (2 Cor. 7:10) there exists also a "godly grief" (2 Cor. 7:11) which is a consequence of love: it is caused by offenses against God and "produces a repentance that leads to salvation" (2 Cor. 7:10). A godly grief also refers to the sadness that derives from the natural resistance to suffer pain and death, even when it is accepted willingly for love of God in reparation for sin. It is the grief that Jesus as Redeemer experienced in the Garden of Olives (see Matt. 26:38; Mark 14:34) as well as those who wish to co-redeem with him.[719] This sadness expresses love; it is a source of merit and brings with it the hope of Jesus' promise: "Blessed are those who mourn, for they shall be comforted" (Matt. 5:4).

> We should not confuse sadness that comes from selfishness with the sadness we experience when we see others sin or lack love for God, or when we suffer when we are called to participate in the redemptive mission of Christ. We should also not confuse it with the fatigue caused by work or other hardships.

> *If we truly want to live for God, we will never lack cheerfulness, even when we discover our errors and wretchedness. Cheerfulness finds its way into our life of prayer, so much so that we cannot help singing for joy. For we are in love, and singing is a thing that lovers do.*[720]

(3) The third fruit is interior peace. As a point of reference for St. Josemaría's teaching, we can take St. Augustine's classic definition: peace is

---

716. *Letter, July 16, 1933*, no. 12.

717. *Friends of God*, no. 92. "Sadness is a vice caused by disordered love of oneself, which is not a special vice, but the general root of all of them" (St. Thomas Aquinas, *S. Th.* II-II, q. 28, a. 4, ad 1).

718. *The Way*, no. 260.

719. See *The Forge*, no. 252.

720. *Friends of God*, no. 92.

"*tranquillitas ordinis*,"[721] the tranquility or stability of order. Briefly we can say that in the spiritual life, a person has peace when the relations between him and God, him and others, and him and himself are "stably ordered."

Like joy, peace is considered a fruit of the Holy Spirit inasmuch as "it is an act proper to charity"[722] that the Paraclete bestows on souls together with his gifts (see Rom. 5:1–5). In effect, charity is a principle of interior harmony because it orders the will to God; and given that the will governs all the other faculties, these too are ordered to God. There is interior peace in the measure that there is "a good will" ordered to God by charity. In *The Way*, St. Josemaría expresses this idea as follows: *Peace, peace, you tell me. Peace is . . . for men of "good" will.*[723] In other words, peace of soul is primarily a consequence of the unconditional love of God above all things. A person loses his peace in the measure that he fails to commit himself to having a "good will" as an absolute principle. This occurs when that person consciously prefers created things to the Creator. Interior division and conflict thus ensue:

> *Your personal experience—those feelings of restlessness, despondency and bitterness—makes you realize the truth of those words of Jesus: no one can serve two masters!*[724]

One of two masters must give up his place. If mammon is preferred (see Matt. 6:24; Luke 16:13), peace is irrevocably lost and it cannot be replaced by appearances:

> *There is no peace in many hearts which vainly strive to make up for their intranquility of soul by continuous activity, by seeking a thin satisfaction in things which do not fill them but only leave a bitter aftertaste of sorrow.*[725]

Peace is also a consequence of charity inasmuch as charity desires the good that God wishes for others: that everyone be reconciled with him and that everyone love him. That is why "[Christ] is our peace" (Eph. 2:14), for he has reconciled us with God and one another. The sons and daughters of God participate in the mission of reconciling all human beings with God:

---

721. St. Augustine, *De civitate Dei*, XIX, 13, 1.

722. St. Thomas Aquinas, *S. Th.* II-II, q. 29, a. 4, c.

723. *The Way*, no. 759. See Lk. 2:14 [Vulgate].

724. *The Way*, no. 300. See Matt. 6:24.

725. *Christ Is Passing By*, no. 73.

"Blessed are the peacemakers [those who have peace and make peace], for they shall be called sons of God" (Matt. 5:9). To give peace to others is a characteristic proper to those who are aware of being children of God.

In this life, peace cannot be attained without struggling against sin, which separates us from God and others and which is the cause of interior division as we will see later on in chapter eight.

(4) "May the God of hope fill you with all joy and peace" (Rom. 15:13). Like the apostle Paul, St. Josemaría often refers to both of these fruits together.[726] This involves two acts of charity and two gifts, which, though different, are always present together. For this reason there is a common reference to joy "with peace" (*gaudium cum pace*), rather than just "joy" or just "peace." It is a *peaceful joy*[727] that maintains "tranquility in order" and vice versa, a joyful peace that delights because here it already possesses an anticipation of the definitive victory. *The* gaudium cum pace*—joy and peace—is the sweet and unfailing fruit of abandonment.*[728] It is a clear sign of being "aware of one's divine filiation" that leads a person to rest in God and to live his life in accord with that filiation. It is proof that a person is on his way to being identified with Christ.

Along these lines, St. Josemaría also preaches that *the children of God should always be sowers of peace and joy.*[729] *With charity, you will be sowers of peace and joy in the world.*[730] This meaningful expression indicates once again that holiness is inseparable from apostolate. Just as the fruits of a tree carry within them the seed of new fruit, the *gaudium cum pace*, fruit of the Holy Spirit, carries within it the capacity and the need to bear fruit in others. Whoever has it will necessarily be "a sower of peace and joy." The more a person possesses this fruit, the greater his apostolic zeal, the more effective his sowing of the Christian life. The fruits of the Holy Spirit (charity, joy, peace . . .) are neither "decorations" nor mere "manifestations" of a person's interior life; they are "apostolic fruits" in the sense that they contain the seed destined to be sown in other souls like the grain of wheat that falls into the ground and dies to yield new fruit (see John 12:24). Peace and joy are true fruits when they sprout in other souls. Scheffczyk correctly writes that the

---

726. See, for example, *The Way*, no. 758; *Furrow*, nos. 8, 78; *The Forge*, nos. 174, 900; *Christ Is Passing By*, no. 9; etc.

727. *The Forge*, no. 174.

728. *The Way*, no. 768.

729. *Furrow*, no. 59.

730. *Letter, July 16, 1933*, no. 3.

preaching of St. Josemaría manages "to open the Gospel and all of Christianity as a message of joy and as a religion of true spiritual happiness."[731]

In summary, we can remark that for St. Josemaría, the Christian life requires both the *gifts* and the *fruits* of the Holy Spirit: the gifts are demanded by the contemplative holiness he proposes and the fruits by the apostolic fruitfulness to which that holiness leads, which is the result of an exhuberance of charity, joy, and peace: the *love for God that overflows and communicates itself to others,*[732] and a *practical sowing of peace and joy.*[733] Contemplation in the middle of the world and apostolate are just as inseparable as the gifts of the Holy Spirit are from the fruits.

❂ ❂ ❂

Some Practical Applications

(1) *Intimacy with the Holy Spirit.* There is a basic truth that should be kept in mind in spiritual direction: *you are neither the model nor the molder. The model is Christ; the molder, the Holy Spirit, through grace.*[734] Certainly, there exist times when graces are especially available, such as given moments of a person's life, liturgical seasons such as Lent, a spiritual retreat, etc., but "the times or seasons which the Father has fixed by his own authority" (Acts 1:7) clearly do not depend on human design and strategic planning. The mysterious action of the Holy Spirit should be respected like the wind that "blows where it wills" (John 3:8), and spiritual direction should keep souls from placing obstacles to the motions of grace.

To this end, it is important to help others develop an intimate relationship with the Paraclete: *Get to know the Holy Spirit, the Great Unknown, the One Who has to sanctify you.*[735] We can foster this relationship by invoking the Holy Spirit and teaching others to do so, for example with prayers taken from the liturgy (such as *Veni, Sancte Spiritus . . .* ; *Veni, Creator Spiritus . . .* ; *Ure igne Sancti Spiritus . . .*). However, since the spiritual life is the radical initiative of the Holy Spirit in us, it is more a matter of listening and allowing him to guide us, rather than our speaking to him.

731. Leo Scheffczyk, "Die Gnade in der Spiritualität von Josemaría Escrivá," p. 77.

732. *Christ Is Passing By*, no. 122.

733. Ibid., no. 124.

734. *Letter, August 8, 1956*, no. 37.

735. *The Way*, no. 57.

Listening to the advice of his confessor, St. Josemaría soon discovered this truth: *I've been told: Make friends with the Holy Spirit. Don't speak; listen to him.*[736] He invites others to follow the same path:

> *I was praying calmly and received much light. I saw that the life of childhood, by making me aware that I am a son of God, brought me to love the Father. I saw that, before, I went through Mary to reach Jesus, whom I adore as friend, as brother, as his lover, for that is what I am. . . . Up to now, I knew the Holy Spirit was dwelling in my soul to sanctify it . . . , but I hadn't grasped the truth of his presence* [. . .]. *I feel Love within me, and I want to get to know him, to become his friend, his confidant . . . I want to facilitate his work of polishing, uprooting and enkindling . . . I won't know how to, but he will give me the strength. He will do everything, if I want it—and I do want it! Divine Guest, Master, Light, Guide, Love: may the poor donkey make you welcome and listen to your lessons, and be set aflame, and follow you and love you. A resolution: to "keep up," if possible without interruption, a loving and docile friendship and conversation with the Holy Spirit.* Veni Sancte Spiritus![737]

(2) *Learning to live charity.* The essence of Christian life is charity. It is a filial love for God that should be manifested especially in one's dealings with those who are closest:

> *A cheerful charity which is at once kindly and firm, human and at the same time supernatural. It should be an affectionate charity, knowing how to welcome everyone with a sincere and habitual smile, and how to understand the ideas and the feelings of others.*[738]
>
> *Put yourself always in your neighbor's shoes: you will then see the various issues or problems calmly; you will not get annoyed; you will be more understanding; you will be able to make allowances and will correct people however and whenever necessary; and you will fill the world with charity.*[739]

Love of oneself should also be true charity; otherwise it would be a disordered "self-love." If it is true charity (love of self out of love for God),

---

736. *Apuntes íntimos*, no. 864 (November 8, 1932), cited in Rodríguez, "*The Way," Critical-Historical Edition,* commentary on point 5).

737. Ibid. See *The Forge*, no. 430.

738. *The Forge*, no. 282.

739. Ibid., no. 958.

self-forgetfulness will be its hallmark. The paradox will only be apparent because whoever loves God knows that he is loved by him and abandons himself completely in his hands. *Don't place your ego in your health, in your reputation, in your career.*[740] It is necessary to learn how *to forget about oneself. For the love of God, and for the love of our fellow men, we have to burn before God like lamps flickering before the altar, consuming themselves until they are completely spent.*[741]

(3) *Guided by reason illumined by faith.* Charity presupposes faith. In order to help others grow in charity, often we need to begin with the head rather than the will. Thus, we have to strengthen faith and avoid voluntarism. This requires not only doctrinal knowledge but the "mental" outlook of trusting in God and in the means that he offers us in order to know what we ought to do. He has granted us the capacity to reason; he has spoken to us by means of Revelation safeguarded by the Magisterium, and he guides us through those who have the office of the Good Shepherd.

St. Josemaría says that his "pedagogy" *is made up of affirmations, not negations, and comes down to two things: to work with common sense and with supernatural sense. Among other manifestations of this pedagogy, there is one that can be expressed in this way: trusting a lot in God, trusting in others, and not trusting in ourselves.*[742] This attitude guarantees that faith will guide the spiritual life. In other words, reason fully trusts in God and in his ways, rather than trusting in its own light and strength. *Lord, put not your trust in me. But I, I put my trust in you.*[743]

(4) *Self-knowledge.* An important aspect of humility is realism in the spiritual life. In addition to knowing God, we need to know ourselves. St. Augustine would say: "*Noverim Te, noverim me*,"[744] "May I know you, may I know myself." It is not just about knowing that the human person is created, elevated, redeemed, etc.; instead, it is about knowing our unique and specific traits: our temperament, personality, virtues acquired by God's grace, dominant defects, etc. We acquire self-knowledge through prayer and spiritual direction, and require a spirit of self-examination.

---

740. Notes taken from preaching (AGP, P01 III-1970, pp. 7–8).

741. Ibid., p. 11.

742. *Letter, March 24, 1931*, no. 50.

743. *Friends of God*, no. 194.

744. St. Augustine, *Soliloquia* II, c. 1.

Besides knowing ourselves, we need to accept who we are without confusing this with self-complacency. We cannot ignore the reality of either our positive traits, limitations, or defects; in fact, we need to take all of them into account. A humble person, for example, is realistic; he knows his weaknesses and does not place himself in danger by dialoguing with temptation. He also knows how to be in his place and act with simplicity and without interior complications. *It can sometimes happen that even well-intentioned people create personal problems—really serious worries—which have no objective basis whatsoever. These problems arise in persons whose lack of self-knowledge leads to pride and a desire to be the center of attention, and to be favored by everyone. They want to appear always in a good light, to be personally secure. They are not content simply to do good and disappear. And so, many who could enjoy a wonderful peace of soul and great happiness become unhappy and unfruitful through pride and presumption.*[745]

(5) We have seen that the virtue of hope consists in the "hope of being saints" and the "hope of bearing apostolic fruit." St. Josemaría frequently refers to these "desires" because in the Christian life, hope is often manifested in holy desires that are not in fantasies. He sums this up in a point in *Furrow*: *Allow your soul to be consumed by desires—desires for loving, for forgetting about yourself, for sanctity, for heaven. Do not stop to consider whether the time will come to see them accomplished, as some overly shrewd adviser might suggest. Make them more fervent every day, for the Holy Spirit says that he is pleased with "men of desires." Let your desires be operative and put them into practice in your daily tasks.*[746]

(6) *The relationship between humility and self-giving to others.* St. Josemaría points out an effective path toward humility in the following point of *The Way*: *Giving oneself sincerely to others is so effective that God rewards it with a humility full of joy.*[747] These words teach us that charity excavates its own foundation of humility, because for a Christian, "giving oneself" is the exercise of charity that leads to growth in humility; this in turn allows the building of the Christian life to be higher and stonger.

745. *Christ Is Passing By*, no. 18.

746. *Furrow*, no. 628. By the expression "men of desires" he is alluding to Dan. 9:23: "*vir desideriorum es tu.*"

747. *The Forge*, no. 591.

(7) *The ideal of contemplation in the middle of the world.* The gifts of the Holy Spirit make contemplation possible in those times dedicated to prayer and in the occupations of ordinary life. The Paraclete grants them to those who do not place obstacles to them and to those who desire them, ask for them, and seek them. No one needs to possess special talents in order to do this: *There are souls who are hidden, unknown, deeply humble, self-sacrificing and holy, who have a wonderful supernatural outlook:* I thank you, Father, Lord of heaven and earth, that you did hide these things from the wise and understanding, and revealed them to babes (Matt. 11:25).[748]

748. Notes taken from preaching, June of 1972 (AGP, P09, p. 176).

APPENDIX

Filial Love and Spousal Love

When discussing divine filiation and charity (among other topics), we saw that St. Josemaría speaks of a Christian's love for God as "filial love." We refrained from using the term "spousal love" because, unlike other masters of the spiritual life, St. Josemaría hardly employs the term even though he was undoubtedly familiar with it. Here, we would like put forth some reflections on this noteworthy fact, but we would like to do so by way of an appendix to this volume because it is a subject that does not appear in St. Josemaría's writings.

Let us consider this issue in the following way: Throughout history many great spiritual masters such as St. Bernard, St. Teresa of Ávila, and St. John of the Cross have compared the Christian's union with God to a "spiritual marriage."[1] More generally, many spiritual authors speak of the love of God as "spousal" or "nuptial" love. After refining the terminology from what simply refers to what is earthly, these authors elevate it to a spiritual sense and apply the idea of the love between spouses on earth (which implies mutual self-giving, indissoluble commitment, openness to life, etc.) to speak of the love of God.

St. Josemaría often applies to the Virgin Mary the title of "spouse of the Holy Spirit" or "spouse of God," and according to Pauline doctrine (see Eph. 5:23–28), he refers also to the Church as the "spouse of Christ."[2] But when he deals with the relationship of a Christian with God, with Christ, or with the Church, St. Josemaría hardly ever uses the term "spousal." At first

1. A synthesis of this subject, in general, can be seen in Pierre Adnès, "Mariage spirituel," in *Dictionnaire de spiritualité ascétique et mystique*, 10 (1980): cols. 388–408 (with bibliography); Tomás Álvarez, "Matrimonio spirituale," Ermanno Ancilli (dir.), *Dizionario enciclopedico di spiritualità*, vol. II (Rome: Città Nuova, 1990), pp. 1542–1547.

2. See *The Way*, no. 496; *Furrow*, no. 801; *The Forge*, nos. 227, 461, 555, 584, 833; *Conversations*, no. 23; *Christ Is Passing By*, nos. 34, 73, 136, 145, 171, 176; *Friends of God*, nos. 274, 316; the homily "Loyalty to the Church" etc. We have discussed the Church as spouse of Christ in the teaching of St. Josemaría in chapter three, section 1.4. The Blessed Virgin is "spouse" in the same sense because she conceived the Son through the action of the Holy Spirit and because through her mediation we Christians are engendered to supernatural life (see chapter three, section 4).

sight, it may be surprising he does not. Since he calls the Christian "another Christ, Christ himself," one might think that the Christian could be called a "spouse" of the Church just as Christ is. And vice versa; given that the Christian is a member of the Church, the spouse of Christ, it appears reasonable to claim that he or she is a "spouse of Christ," and therefore also "spouse of God," as Jesus Christ is God.

Nevertheless, as we said above, St. Josemaría does not address God as "spouse," nor does he refer to the Christian's relationship with the Church in spousal terms. In the following text, for instance, he calls the Church "Spouse of Christ" but he calls her "Mother of the Christian" at the same time: *You have to love the Spouse of Christ, your Mother. She is, and always will be, pure and spotless.*[3]

In speaking of the union of the Christian with Christ, St. Josemaría still does not generally employ spousal terms. He does not say, for instance, that "the soul is a spouse of Christ," nor that the Christian should love Christ as a "spouse." He does this neither in his published works nor in the drafts of these works. He does it occasionally in his oral preaching on seven occasions from 1956 to 1959, the period immediately following Pius XII's encyclical *Sacra Virginitas* (March 25, 1954), where the Pope addresses lay women who have given themselves to the Lord, embracing apostolic celibacy. Choosing words of St. Ambrose, St. Athanasius, and other Fathers cited by Pius XII, St. Josemaría calls them *spouses*[4] of Christ. After these years, St. Josemaría does not use this metaphor except for two or three times in the 1970s[5] and always in short phrases without stopping to explain them.

The few texts we have just quoted indicate that he is familiar with the "spousal" terminology, something that is not surprising for an avid reader of the spiritual classics. At the same time, it is significant that he rarely employs this term in the almost 13,000 pages which comprise the sum of his writings

---

3. *The Forge*, no. 461. He habitually said "my mother the Church" or "our mother the Church" or other filial expressions: see *The Way*, nos. 518, 750; *Furrow*, nos. 49, 275, 354, 369, 409, 920; *The Forge*, nos. 461, 471, 583; etc.

4. Notes taken from preaching, November 12, 1956 (AGP, P02 XI-1956, p. 9); the same, for example, in AGP, P02 V-1957, p. 13, and in AGP, P02 XI-1957, p. 11. The encyclical *Sacra Virginitas*, no. 7, cites, for example, St. Athanasius: "Those who profess this virtue [virginity], the Catholic Church usually refers to as spouses of Christ" (*Apologia ad Constantium*, 33).

5. In the written texts taken from his oral preaching we have only found two instances in which he refers to the soul as spouse of Christ. It is possible that there are a few more in the complete recordings of his meetings with people.

and notes from his oral preaching.[6] Instead, he constantly addresses God as Father, following Jesus' words, "When you pray, say: Father, hallowed be thy name [. . .]" (Luke 11:2), and he speaks of God's love as a "filial love," a "love of God's sons or daughters," a love founded on the reality of adoptive divine filiation.[7] Undoubtedly, it is these "filial" expressions that dominate his preaching. As we did in chapter four, here we are referring obviously to the supernatural divine filiation of a Christian, not to the natural filiation to God every person enjoys by virtue of his or her created human condition.

How should we interpret these facts? What is St. Josemaría's reason for not describing more frequently the union between the Christian and Christ as a spousal union? Does this imply a rupture with previous spiritual teaching? Or, is there some relation between "filial love" and "spousal love"? And finally, what is the meaning of the few times he did employ the term "spousal" to describe the relation between the Christian and Christ?

In our opinion, it is useful to distinguish between two ways of speaking of a Christian's "spousal relation with God" and therefore of "spousal love for God." One way refers in general to the ordinary Christian (man or woman, married or celibate); the other refers specifically to the proper state of "consecrated virginity." To these two ways, we need to add a third, the "spousal" nature of the priesthood by virtue of the sacrament of Holy Orders. Traditionally, however, this is considered a spousal relation with the Church that derives from the fact that the priest (or bishop) is acting *in Persona Christi Capitis*, and therefore is acting like Christ, as the spouse of the Church. It is a "ministerial spousality" that originates in the sacrament of Orders, which is not applicable to the lay faithful, and therefore we will not discuss it in further detail here.[8]

As far as the first two ways are concerned, they differ in virtue of their foundation. In the case of ordinary Christians, the spousal relation derives only from baptism, while in the second, it derives specifically from the religious consecration, which, though different from that of baptism, presupposes it. This consecration takes place by the profession of the three vows of poverty, chastity, and obedience, and their formal acceptance by the Church.

---

6. See Flavio Capucci, *Josemaría Escrivá, santo. L'iter della causa di canonizzazione* (Milan: Ares, 2009), p. 20.

7. In chapter four we have cited numerous texts in this sense.

8. On this subject we refer to Laurent Touze, *L'avenir du célibat sacerdotal et sa logique sacramentelle* (Paris: Parole et Silence-Lethielleux, 2009).

Let us consider the first case. Upon being adopted as a child of God in the waters of baptism, every baptized person is committed to live in accord with that dignity by assuming the "baptismal commitments." These commitments unmistakenly represent a covenant with God. This covenant bears a certain resemblance to marriage because by its very nature, it is a pact of a love of friendship that incorporates a person to the Church as the body of which Christ is the Head. This covenant, moreover, requires indissolubility and is ordained toward fruitfulness, that is, to the transmission of supernatural life by means of the exercise of the common priesthood, a participation of Christ's priesthood. This is why we can confidently lean on a sound scriptural basis (see Song 4:8–12; Hos. 3:1 ff; Eph. 5:22–32; 2 Cor. 11:1–3; etc.) in speaking of a spousal relation with God through baptism. St. Thomas writes: "*in Baptismo fit quoddam spirituale connubium animae ad Deum*" [In Baptism, there is a certain spiritual marriage of the soul with God].[9] Every Christian can assume this spousal relation in his spiritual life precisely because it derives from baptism.

This spousal condition is in close relation to adoptive divine filiation. In reality, the term does not seem other than a different way of referring to the fact that filial union with God is established by an "adoption" that takes place in baptism itself because the one adopted as a child has a covenant with God. But the terms "filiation" and "spousal relation" are not on equal footing when it comes down to expressing the relation of a Christian with God. When we speak of a "spousal relation" to God, we use a metaphor to highlight a certain aspect implied by divine filiation; when we speak of "divine filiation," on the other hand, we do not use a metaphor, but rather proper language referred to God in an analogical sense. We can say that in baptism, the Christian is really made a "son or daughter of God" in an analogous way to how the Son is begotten in the Holy Trinity. However, saying that the Christian is made a "spouse of God" can only be said in a metaphorical way because there is no "spouse" in the Holy Trinity. In this latter case, we are not speaking by means of proper language, but rather metaphorically.[10]

Stated differently, when we say that a Christian is a son (or daughter) of God, we are using proper language in an analogical way, because there does exist a "subsistent Filiation" in the Trinity (i.e., the person of the Son), and the

9. St. Thomas Aquinas, *In IV Sent.*, d. 6, q. 1, a. 2, sc.

10. On the use of analogy and metaphor, see Rafael Díaz Dorronsoro, *Los nombres de Dios, de Jesucristo y de la Iglesia: el recurso a la metáfora y a la analogía* (Valencia: Edicep, 2009), pp. 17–66.

Christian indeed participates in it. (The Christian's filiation is called "adoptive" only to distinguish it from the natural filiation that exclusively belongs to the person of the Son.) When we say, however, that the Christian is a "spouse of God," we are speaking metaphorically because in the Trinity there is no "subsistent spousality" in which man can participate. "Spousality," or matrimony, is a created reality and when it is applied to God, it cannot be done by means of analogy with a subsistent reality in God, but only in a metaphorical way. Nevertheless, although adoptive filiation is also a created reality, it is a participation in the subsistent Filiation in God. For this reason, a Christian is a son (or daughter) of God in a proper sense, and not in a metaphorical one. St. John underscores this when he writes, "See what love the Father has given us, that we should be called children of God; and so we are." (1 John 3:1).

All throughout St. Josemaría's preaching, we find adoptive divine filiation with all its implications: filial love for God, identification with Christ, fraternal love, the apostolic mission, etc. Nevertheless, St. Josemaría also turns to human love to describe the love of the children of God. He often says, for example, *I like all the songs about pure holy love, for in them I find, interwoven, both human and divine love.*[11] He does not have any problem in applying what is said about the noble human love between a man and a woman in courtship or marriage to the love for God. This love for God, like that of those who are in love on earth, falls within the spirit of divine filiation that he preached because adoption as children leads all Christians (men and women, celibate, married or widowed) to a covenant of love with God.

> In St. Josemaría, love for God (charity) is a "filial" virtue. This filial quality includes a generic spousality that, as we have noted, corresponds to the "adoptive" character of filiation. In effect, adoption means assuming as a son or daughter someone who was previously not. Filial adoption is a sort of assumption like that of the Incarnation in which the Son assumes a human nature. The Incarnation is traditionally called the "marriage" of the divine Person [of the Word] with human nature and the basis for the "wedding" of Christ to the Church by which he joins her to himself as his mystical body (see Eph. 5:25; Rev. 19:7–9). In this sense, we could say metaphorically that whoever is adopted by God is "wedded" to him not in virtue of being a son (or daughter) but

11. *Conversations*, no. 92. Other examples are *The Way*, no. 824; *The Forge*, no. 435; *Christ Is Passing By*, no. 166; *Friends of God*, no. 184.

> in virtue of being "adopted." The only-begotten Son is not the "spouse" of the Father because he is not adopted; he is eternally engendered, and when he assumes a human nature and unites the Church to himself as his spouse, his "spousal love" is none other than an aspect of his filial love for the Father. So too in the Christian. Since his or her supernatural filiation is a participation in subsistent Filiation (i.e., in the Son), his or her love is, properly speaking, filial. Within this filial kind of love, the fact of being "adopted" (or "assumed as a child") carries with it a trait that, in metaphorical terms, can be called "spousal." We say "in metaphorical terms" because a term that is properly used to describe relations between creatures [i.e., the spousal relationship between a man and a woman] is being applied to describe an aspect of our relation to God (i.e., our filial adoption).
>
> Note that the position we have proposed regarding the relation between "adoption" and "spousality" is not held by those who reserve the former term for the moment when the Christian receives divine filiation (at baptism), and the latter term for the moment in which he commits himself freely to God. This manner of considering "spousality" as a further development of "adoptive filiation" is in the line of religious consecration that we will discuss later on. This position is not simply about referring to adoption metaphorically (lest the term "spousality" simply meant the discovery of the Christian vocation without any further commitment besides the one taken on at baptism). If the term "spousality" is understood, rather, as a commitment different from that which is proper to baptism, then we ought to state that St. Josemaría does not speak of it. He distinguishes between "being made adoptive children of God" in baptism, and "becoming aware of that filiation" and making a radical decision to live in accord with those baptismal commitments. The latter he calls "self-giving to God," not "marriage to God": it is the self-giving of the children of God who decide to love him with all their heart as well as with deeds.

But why does St. Josemaría hardly use the spousal metaphor? A conjecture that seems coherent with his biography and teaching is that, upon discovering the radical nature of the filial condition of the baptized, the spousal metaphor takes on a secondary role. Once God made him experience in a deep way his divine filiation as the foundation for the spiritual life, this gift led him to a profound contemplation of the Christian mystery in proper, filial terms, which can be expressed as follows: *each Christian is not simply* alter Christus: *another Christ, but* ipse Christus: *Christ himself!*[12] The understanding of the union with Christ implicit in these words transcends the metaphor of the spousal union *in the flesh* (see Matt. 19:5) even though it does not negate its worth for illustrating certain of its aspects.

St. Josemaría chooses to use proper (and not metaphorical) language more out of a spontaneous intuition than speculation; a choice that corresponds with a basic theological rule (especially in spiritual theology). Garrigou-Lagrange ennunciates it in the following way: "Metaphorical terms are necessary where proper terms do not exist, especially to express particular relations of God with souls of interior life. For this reason mystics speak metaphorically of the spiritual wedding and marriage to designate the rather transforming union of the soul with God."[13]

Our hypothesis is that the mystics to which Garrigou-Lagrange refers (especially St. John of the Cross, although before him were St. Bernard, Richard of St. Victor, and others) needed to turn to the spousal metaphor more than St. Josemaría after he experienced the supernatural reality of divine filiation by means of a gift from God. The Holy Spirit leads souls along different paths. He takes some to the divine depths by the beautiful spousal image and others through the more simple and direct path of our filial reality. In any event, filial adoption is also present in St. John of the Cross (even though he describes union with God in terms of a spiritual marriage), just as the metaphor of human love is present in St. Josemaría, even though he uses it exclusively to illustrate some aspects of the spiritual life founded on the sense of divine filiation.

To this we must add that for St. Josemaría, the metaphor of human love to refer to the divine life is not limited to the love of spouses. What he wishes to emphasize with this metaphor is, above all, that a Christian should love God with the same heart with which he loves people dear to him on earth. For this reason, St. Josemaría turns also to other forms of human love (between parents and children, or among siblings and friends), and he does so more than to spousal love. He states, for instance,

---

12. *Christ Is Passing By*, no. 104.

13. R. Garrigou-Lagrnge, *Three Ages of the Interior Life*, vol. II (Rockford, IL: Tan Books, 1989), part III, ch. 1, pp. 9–10 (within the section "The Theological Bases of the Terminology of Spiritual Writers"). The author presents this consideration after having distinguished between "analogy" (which he employs in saying God and creatures are good and wise) and "metaphor" (which he uses in saying that the Christian is a "spouse of God"). See St. Thomas Aquinas, *S. Th.*, I, q. 1, a. 9, ad 3.

> *We have to love God with the same heart with which we love our parents, our brothers and sisters, the other members of our family, our friends. It's the only heart we have.*[14]

Moreover, elsewhere, he writes,

> *Love our Lord passionately. Love him madly. Because if there is love, I would dare to say that not even resolutions are needed. My parents—think of yours—did not need to make any resolutions to love me: and what an effusion of tenderness they showed me, in little details every day. With that same human heart we can and should love God.*[15]

Now let us take a look at the second way of speaking of the spousal union with God: that which is proper and specific to the consecrated life.[16] Already in the second century we see formally appear in the Church the *Ordo virginum*, constituted by women who made a public profession of virginity for the kingdom of God and who were consecrated in a liturgical ceremony in which they received a distinguishing sign. Such a consecration was considered a "spiritual marriage" or "wedding" with God[17] and is considered to be the precedent for religious life, which tradition will consider as a sign of the "admirable wedding established by God in the Church."[18] The metaphor of the spousal union with God has thus remained for centuries closely tied to the religious vocation.[19]

St. Josemaría refers to this spousal union with God when he preaches to women religious. For example, in 1972 he addresses a Cistercian community, encouraging them to have *the great joy of knowing themselves to be*

---

14. *Christ Is Passing By*, no. 142.

15. *The Forge*, no. 503.

16. We use the expression "consecrated life" in the sense that it has in St. John Paul II's Apostolic Exhortation *Vita consecrata* (March 25, 1996), no. 10, to designate the state of life of those who cosecrate themselves to God by the profession of the vows of poverty, chastity, and obedience.

17. See Sacred Congregation for Divine Worship, *Ordo consecrationis virginum* (May 30, 1970); CIC, c. 604; *CCC*, nos. 923–924; St. Ambrose, *Exhort. virg.*, 31; *De virginibus* III, 3, 9; Pseudo Ambrose, *Laps. virg.*, 5, 20. A brief synthesis of the subject in the Fathers can be seen in Carlo Tibiletti, "Vergini - verginità - velatio," in *Dizionario patristico e di antichità cristiane* (Casale Monferrato: Marietti, 1983), col. 3560.

18. CIC, c. 607. The sources of this canon are: *Lumen gentium*, no. 44; Decree *Perfectae Caritatis*, nos. 1, 12 (see *Codex iuris canonici auctoritate Ioannis Pauli PP. II promulgatus: fontium annotationes*, Vatican City, 1989, *ad loc.*).

19. In recent times, St. John Paul II made wide use of this metaphor, extending it to all the faithful: see Apostolic Exhortation *Mulieris dignitatem* (August 15, 1998), no. 25. In this sense, it is founded on baptism alone, not on the specific post-baptismal religious consecration, and thus what we have said in the previous paragraphs is valid.

brides of Christ.[20] However, in general, he does not speak in this way to the common faithful. We believe he keeps the spousal metaphor for the religious state and does not apply it to the laity to avoid confusion between the lay vocation and the religious vocation, and between the specific characteristics of the spiritual life particular to each. We must reiterate that he teaches people to establish their spiritual life on the divine filiation received at baptism, cultivating at every moment an awareness of being children of God. In the religious life, the spiritual life is founded on a consecration made after baptism (i.e., the religious consecration by means of vows understood as a "spousal union" with God). This "spousal union" carries with it a certain "distancing" of oneself from the world, which means that a new relationship with temporal realities is established. This relationship has as its end to give witness of future goods: an eschatalogical witness, which is different from that of those whose mission is to sanctify the world from within.

In the final analysis, it is about two different ways to approach the spiritual life. Although they differ, they do not stand in opposition to one another as both originate in baptism and both look toward future glory. For this reason, the spousal metaphor is not entirely foreign to the laity; in fact, we have seen that there is a generic spousal relation founded on baptism. And even less is the spirit of divine filiation foreign to the religious:[21] it belongs to them by baptism, and their specific spousal consecration rests on it.

For the rest, we should not leave out that St. Josemaría recommended to the laity the reading of the great masters of the spiritual life, not only for them to admire their lofty expressions of love, but also for the laity to draw example and benefit from the substance of their spiritual doctrine which certainly possesses a universal value.

Before concluding, what should we say about the few occasions when St. Josemaría calls ordinary Christian women "spouses of Christ"? Throughout his life, St. Josemaría strove to recover a certain number of terms for the

---

20. Notes taken from preaching, October 1972 (AGP, P04 1972, vol. II, p. 830).

21. Think, for example, of the testimony of St. Theresa of Lisieux, who felt herself to be a small daughter of God. Despite this, after a historical review of what the mystery of filial adoption meant in the Patristic period, Jean Galot asked himself: "Has the filial perspective been sufficiently maintained and developed in the mystical tradition since then?" (a tradition, we should note, represented mostly by religious). His response was negative, on finding that "the figure of Father does not seem to have received all the attention that it merits; the paternal has not been recognized in all of its value. We hope that the experience of divine filiation will put more in evidence the face of That One whom Christ has taught us to call 'Father.'" Jean Galot, "Adozione divina," in Luigi Borriello (dir.), *Dizionario di mistica* (Vatican City: Libreria Editrice Vaticana, 2000), p. 55.

Christian faithful, which in practice were reserved to the religious vocation (even though in antiquity they belonged to all Christians). For example, the term "perfection" had become tied to the "state of perfection" proper of the religious in such a way that people did not think that life in the middle of the world (and particularly in marriage) could be a "path of perfection." For this, he sees the need to remind people: *Your duty is to sanctify yourself. Yes, even you. Who thinks that this task is only for priests and religious? To everyone, without exception, our Lord said, "Be ye perfect, as my heavenly Father is perfect."*[22]

In our opinion, the few "spousal" texts to which we have referred are an attempt to apply the spousal metaphor to the life of ordinary faithful by referring to the spousal relation based on baptism. It is a specific application of the metaphor that helps to illustrate some aspects of our filial adoption in baptism. But speaking in this way is ambiguous and could lead to misunderstanding if the term is not distinguished from the religious consecration. The same cannot be said of the term "perfection," given that it refers to everyone even though it is reached by means of different paths. There is a spousality specific to the religious, and it is necessary to recognize and protect its identity as a good for the entire Church. It is perhaps for this reason that St. Josemaría abandoned the term when addressing the laity.

It could happen that if the laity were introduced to the ideal of union with God tied to baptism in spousal terms, the concepts could be confused once again as had happened before in history, relegating divine filiation to a secondary plane. We must keep in mind that the metaphor of "marriage with God" awakens sentiments and interior attitudes that can replace divine filiation unless they are properly set under a "filial" framework.

In closing, we should note that this subject remains open for future reflection. Here, we have not examined the content of the (baptismal) spousal metaphor, since St. Josemaría does not do so. Neither have we tried to consider how it can add to an understanding of the reality of divine filiation. We have limited ourselves to showing the priority of the latter. If we were to carry out a future study, we would take as our starting point the analogy of divine filiation but attempt to explore the light that the metaphor of spousal love can shed on the mystery of the union between man and God.

---

22. *The Way*, no. 291.

INDEX

B

C

D

F

G

K

L

M

R

S

T

U

V